Research Methods in Linguistics

A comprehensive guide to conducting research projects in linguistics, this book provides a complete training in state-of-the-art data collection, processing, and analysis techniques. The book follows the structure of a research project, guiding the reader through the steps involved in collecting and processing data, and providing a solid foundation for linguistic analysis. All major research methods are covered, each by a leading expert. Rather than focusing on narrow specializations, the text fosters inter-disciplinarity, with many chapters focusing on shared methods such as sampling, experimental design, transcription, and constructing an argument. Highly practical, the book offers helpful tips on how and where to get started, depending on the nature of the research question. The only book that covers the full range of methods used across the field, this student-friendly text is also a helpful reference source for the more experienced researcher and current practitioner.

ROBERT J. PODESVA is an Assistant Professor in the Department of Linguistics at Stanford University.

DEVYANI SHARMA is a Senior Lecturer in Linguistics at Queen Mary University of London.

Research Methods in Linguistics

EDITED BY

ROBERT J. PODESVA

Stanford University

AND

DEVYANI SHARMA

Queen Mary University of London

CAMBRIDGE
UNIVERSITY PRESS

University Printing House, Cambridge CB2 8BS, United Kingdom

Published in the United States of America by Cambridge University Press, New York

Cambridge University Press is part of the University of Cambridge.

It furthers the University's mission by disseminating knowledge in the pursuit of education, learning, and research at the highest international levels of excellence.

www.cambridge.org
Information on this title: www.cambridge.org/9781107696358

© Cambridge University Press 2013

First published 2013

Printing in the United Kingdom by TJ International Ltd. Padstow Cornwall

A catalogue record for this publication is available from the British Library

ISBN 978-1-107-01433-6 Hardback
ISBN 978-1-107-69635-8 Paperback

Contents

Figures

Tables

Contributors

REBEKHA ABBUHL
California State University, Long Beach, US

R. HARALD BAAYEN
Eberhard Karls University, Tübingen, Germany, and University
of Alberta, Canada

JOHN BEAVERS
The University of Texas at Austin, US

HÉLÈNE BLONDEAU
University of Florida, US

PAUL BOERSMA
University of Amsterdam, Netherlands

ISABELLE BUCHSTALLER
Leipzig University, Germany

SHOBHANA CHELLIAH
University of North Texas, US

BART DE BOER
Vrije Universiteit Brussel, Belgium

PENELOPE ECKERT
Stanford University, US

SUSAN EHRLICH
York University, Canada

SUSAN GASS
Michigan State University, US

STEFAN TH. GRIES
University of California, Santa Barbara, US

DANIEL EZRA JOHNSON
Lancaster University, UK

ELSI KAISER
University of Southern California, US

GHADA KHATTAB
Newcastle University, UK

EREZ LEVON
Queen Mary University of London, UK

BETTELOU LOS
Radboud University, Netherlands

ALISON MACKEY
Georgetown University, US

NAOMI NAGY
University of Toronto, Canada

JOHN NEWMAN
University of Alberta, Canada

ROBERT J. PODESVA
Stanford University, US

TANYA ROMANIUK
Portland State University, US

NATALIE SCHILLING
Georgetown University, US

CARSON T. SCHÜTZE
University of California, Los Angeles, US

PETER SELLS
University of York, UK

DEVYANI SHARMA
Queen Mary University of London, UK

JON SPROUSE
University of Connecticut, US

ANS VAN KEMENADE
Radboud University, Netherlands

JAMES A. WALKER
York University, Canada

WILLEM ZUIDEMA
University of Amsterdam, Netherlands

ELIZABETH ZSIGA
Georgetown University, US

Acknowledgments

This book has been a truly collaborative enterprise. It could never have been produced without the expertise and dedication of our contributing authors, to whom we owe our greatest debt. In our effort to foster dialogue across the subdisciplines of our field, we have asked contributors to take a broad perspective, to reflect on issues beyond their areas of particular specialization, and to neatly package their ideas for a diverse readership. In rising to meet this challenge, authors have consulted scholars and readings that interface with their own areas of expertise, endured a lengthy external review and extensive revision process, and in all cases produced chapters that we think will be useful to wide swaths of researchers. We thank the authors for their significant contributions.

The initial impetus for this book came from our students, who ask all the right questions about data (who? when? how much?) and analysis (why? how?). We hope they find answers and new questions in these pages. We are also indebted to five anonymous reviewers who, at an early stage of this project, affirmed the usefulness of the proposed collection and made crucial recommendations regarding its scope, structure, and balance of coverage.

For their expert advice and truly generous contributions, we thank an army of reviewers and advisors, none of whom of course bears any responsibility for the choices ultimately made: David Adger, Paul Baker, Joan Beal, Claire Bowern, Kathryn Campbell-Kibler, Charles Clifton, Paul De Decker, Judith Degen, Susanne Gahl, Cynthia Gordon, Matthew Gordon, Tyler Kendall, Roger Levy, John Moore, Naomi Nagy, Jeanette Sakel, Rebecca Scarborough, Morgan Sonderegger, Naoko Taguchi, Marisa Tice, Anna Marie Trester, and Alan Yu.

We would also like to acknowledge our departments: the Department of Linguistics at Stanford University and the Department of Linguistics at Queen Mary University of London. The range of methods represented in the work of our closest colleagues continues to inspire us and push our field forward. Thanks also to the Department of Linguistics at Georgetown University and the Department of English at the National University of Singapore, where we spent significant time during the production of this volume.

Helena Dowson, Fleur Jones, Gnanadevi Rajasundaram, Christina Sarigiannidou, Alison Tickner and the team at Cambridge University Press provided efficient and very patient support throughout the production schedule. Finally, special thanks to Andrew Winnard at Cambridge University Press for his encouragement and support. Like us, he recognized the many challenges of developing such a project, but also shared our enthusiasm for its potential uses in a fast-developing field. We hope this book represents a proof of concept.

The editors and publisher acknowledge the following sources of copyright material reproduced in Chapter 8 and are grateful for the permissions granted:

Figure 8.1 Reprinted from *Journal of Memory and Language* 38, Allopenna, Magnuson, and Tanenhaus, Tracking the time course of spoken word recognition: evidence for continuous mapping models. Copyright 1998, with permission from Elsevier.

Figure 8.2 reprinted from:

(a) *Journal of Memory and Language* 38, Allopenna, Magnuson, and Tanenhaus, Tracking the time course of spoken word recognition: evidence for continuous mapping models. Copyright 1998, with permission from Elsevier.

(b) *Cognition* 73, Trueswell, Sekerina, Hill, and Logrip, The kindergarten-path effect: studying on-line sentence processing in young children, 89–134. Copyright 1999, with permission from Elsevier.

(c) *Cognition* 109, Brown-Schmidt and Konopka, Little houses and casas pequeñas: message formulation and syntactic form in unscripted speech with speakers of English and Spanish, 274–80. Copyright 2008, with permission from Elsevier.

(d) *Verb-Instrument Information During On-line Processing*, Rachel Sussmann, Copyright 2006, with permission from the author.

Figure 8.3 reprinted from:

(a) *Journal of Memory and Language* 49, Kamide, Altmann, and Haywood, Prediction and thematic information in incremental sentence processing: evidence from anticipatory eye movements, 133–56. Copyright 2003, with permission from Elsevier.

(b) *Cognition* 88, Weber, Grice, and Crocker, The role of prosody in the interpretation of structural ambiguities: a study of anticipatory eye movements, B63–B72. Copyright 2006, with permission from Elsevier.

(c) *Language and Cognitive Processes* 26, Kaiser, Consequences of subject-hood, pronominalisation, and contrastive focus, 1625–66. Copyright 2011, reprinted by permission of Taylor & Francis Ltd, www.tandf.co.uk/journals.

(d) *Cognition* 76, Arnold, Eisenband, Brown-Schmidt, and Trueswell, The rapid use of gender information: eyetracking evidence of the time-course of pronoun resolution, B13–B26. Copyright 2000, with permission from Elsevier.

Figure 8.4 Reprinted from *Cognitive Psychology* 49, Snedeker and Trueswell, The developing constraints on parsing decisions: the role of lexical-biases and referential scenes in child and adult sentence processing, 238–99. Copyright 2004, with permission from Elsevier.

1   Introduction

Devyani Sharma and Robert J. Podesva

> I would like to discuss an approach to the mind that considers language and similar phenomena to be elements of the natural world, to be studied by ordinary methods of empirical inquiry.
>
> Noam Chomsky 1995

> Linguists have forgotten, Mathesius argued, that the homogeneity of language is not an 'actual quality of the examined phenomena,' but 'a consequence of the employed method'.
>
> Uriel Weinreich, William Labov, and Marvin I. Herzog 1968

> Some have seen in modern linguistic methodology a model or harbinger of a general methodology for studying the structure of human behavior.
>
> Dell Hymes 1962

1   Overview

The three views expressed above remind us of the peculiar status of linguistics as a field. It represents a single discipline to the extent that it broadly shares a single object of analysis, but little else can be said to be uniform in terms of epistemology and method. Some linguists affiliate most closely with the social sciences, others with the natural sciences, and others with the humanities. Perhaps surprisingly, this diverse group has not (yet) splintered off into separate fields. Rather, the deep heterogeneity of the field has come to be seen by many as a strength, not a weakness. Recent years have witnessed a rise in creative synergies, with scholars drawing inspiration from the methods and data used by "neighboring" linguists in order to enrich and expand the scope of their own investigations.

This has occurred in part due to constant refinement of methodologies over time, leading to more clearly specified methodological norms within all subfields of linguistics, which in turn facilitate more targeted cross-fertilization and exchange. Sharing of methodological practices may take the form of bridge-building across subfields of linguistics, or exchanges of methods between linguistics and related fields. Bridge-building has taken many forms in recent work; a few examples include the adoption of corpora, experiments, and statistical measures in formal analysis (e.g., Bresnan and Ford 2010), the adoption of experimental methods in sociolinguistics (e.g., Campbell-Kibler 2009) and pragmatics (e.g., Breheny 2011), and the use of sociolinguistic sampling in laboratory phonology (Scobbie and Stuart-Smith 2012). Similarly, though less central to the present collection, methods have been exchanged profitably with neighboring fields as well, such as the borrowing into linguistics of genetic modeling (McMahon and McMahon 2005), clinical imaging (e.g., Gick 2002; Skipper and Small 2005; Martins et al. 2008), and sociological sampling principles (e.g., Milroy 1980; Eckert and McConnell-Ginet 1992).

In this climate of creative collaboration and innovation, particularly in methodology, the dearth of general reference texts on methods used in linguistics is striking. Almost all current overviews of methodology are specific to particular subdisciplines (one exception is Litosseliti 2010, a shorter volume than the present one). Specialization naturally permits greater depth and detail, and these texts are indispensable for research in specific fields. But at present, few of these texts are able to foreground insights and principles that should ideally be adopted across the field, nor foster interdisciplinary methods. It is still common in core areas of theoretical linguistics for courses to omit training in research methods at all, and for courses in other areas to only review methods in that field. New researchers in linguistics often complete their training without any exposure to entire methodological paradigms – for example, experimental methods, methods for elicitation, statistics, or ethnography – many of which could strengthen their research contributions. If students do expand their training, this often occurs much later and haphazardly. This collection aims to offer a wider overview and a more diverse toolbox at the outset of methods training.

Given the reality of greater cross-fertilization in linguistics today, a general reference text can also better reflect the exciting state of the field today, and can help promote recent trends and best practices in contemporary methods. The present collection has been developed with this goal in mind. It is intended for use in the training of advanced undergraduate and graduate students, while also serving as a reference text for experienced linguists embarking on research involving new domains, or researchers who simply wish to expand their repertoire or familiarity with methods used to solve general problems in research, such as eliciting language forms, sampling subjects, designing experimental tasks, or processing raw data.

2   Structure of the book

Given the extraordinary complexity of the field of linguistics, it is naturally impossible to provide a comprehensive introduction to all methodologies in a single volume. This collection is designed to be comprehensive in breadth, but not necessarily in depth. Each chapter incorporates suggestions for further reading, to enable readers with specific interests or questions to selectively extend their knowledge.

The volume follows a structure designed to encourage users – teachers, students, researchers – to take a wider view of questions of methodology and to aim for a more comprehensive set of methodological skills than simply those typically adopted for a particular subfield or question. While best practices tend to arise independently within each of the subfields of linguistics, many of the same issues surface from one subdiscipline to the next, and projects on seemingly unrelated topics often require attention to the same methodological concerns. For example, transcription is a concern for nearly all linguists, from those who focus on the details of speech articulation to those who analyze turn-taking in conversation. Similarly, any researcher who collects data from human subjects needs to devote attention to the composition of their sample. And all linguists who record speech, whether the recordings are intended for acoustic analysis, for survey materials, or simply as records of data elicitation sessions, need to grapple with many of the same issues. Finally, regardless of which statistical approaches dominate any given subdiscipline, the underlying theoretical assumptions are the same. For this reason, the volume is not strictly organized by subdiscipline, but rather follows the trajectory of any research project, highlighting general issues that arise in three core areas: data collection, data processing, and data analysis.

Part I (Data collection) focuses on types of data used in linguistics and best practices in the collection of each data type. The section starts, in Chapter 2, with Eckert's discussion of ethical issues that must be considered at the start (and for the duration) of any research project. The next two chapters cover methods of data collection that require working with relatively small numbers of informants. In Chapter 3, Schütze and Sprouse review recent methods used in the collection of grammaticality judgment data, and Chelliah guides the reader through the process of eliciting data for language description and documentation in Chapter 4. Researchers who work with larger numbers of participants must devote special consideration to sampling, discussed by Buchstaller and Khattab in Chapter 5. One special population that linguists frequently work with is children; we do not devote a specific chapter to children, but rather discuss issues pertaining to children as subjects where relevant (in Chapter 2, Chapter 5, and in the discussion of longitudinal data in Chapter 22, discussed below). Researchers might collect data from selected population samples using a wide array of instruments. While Chapters 3 and 4, described above, deal with close elicitation from fewer numbers of participants, other methods often use larger groups. These include surveys and interviews, discussed by Schilling in Chapter 6, experiments, as reviewed by Abbuhl, Gass, and Mackey in Chapter 7 and by Kaiser in Chapter 8, and ethnography, as discussed by Levon in Chapter 10. Levon's discussion of how to work with community members is an important concern not only for ethnographers, but for anyone who might need to make ties with community members for research purposes. The final three chapters of the section turn their attention to how to collect some of the most common media that linguists work with. Podesva and Zsiga cover methods for making sound and articulatory recordings in Chapter 9; Levon discusses concerns with working with video data in Chapter 10, and van Kemenade and Los discuss many of the challenges of working with textual data in Chapter 11.

Data often need considerable preliminary processing before analysis and interpretation. Part II (Data processing and statistical analysis) deals with some of the common challenges of processing data once they have been collected. Since transcription is involved in many subfields of linguistics, Nagy and Sharma provide common practices and recommendations in Chapter 12. Corpora are also increasingly used for a range of formal and variationist analyses, and Gries and Newman review how to construct and extract data from corpora in Chapter 13. The final three chapters of Part II focus on statistics, as linguists are now more than ever adopting a quantitative approach to linguistic analysis. Johnson describes the fundamentals of characterizing the basic distributional properties in a set of data in Chapter 14. Gries moves from descriptive statistics to the selection of appropriate statistical tests and how to execute them in Chapter 15. And Part II concludes with Chapter 16, in which Baayen covers the most widely used multivariate statistics, including multiple regression. Chapters 14–16 are cumulative; each is written under the assumption that readers will be familiar with concepts discussed in earlier statistics chapters.

Finally, Part III (Foundations for data analysis) is included because we believe that in many subfields of linguistics, such as theoretical argumentation or discourse analysis, the analytic process is itself a method that should be taught systematically. Furthermore, the intended analytic method directly informs data collection and processing stages, so these should be planned together. This third part is not intended as a comprehensive overview of theoretical approaches in linguistics, but rather a practical guide to analytic methods in major areas. In Chapter 17, Boersma reviews the fundamentals of speech acoustics and its most useful forms of representation for linguists. In Chapter 18, Beavers and Sells outline the incremental process of building a reasoned argument in theoretical linguistics. Computational models have increasingly become a key method for testing linguistic theories, and desiderata for a robust and reliable approach to developing such models are set out by de Boer and Zuidema in Chapter 19. The next two chapters cover analytical approaches in sociolinguistics, from the mostly quantitative approaches that dominate variation, reviewed by Walker in Chapter 20, to the mostly qualitative approaches that are prevalent in the study of discourse, discussed by Ehrlich and Romaniuk in Chapter 21. Part III concludes in Chapter 22 with Blondeau's comparison of synchronic and diachronic methods for analyzing language over time in different subfields of linguistics.

The volume will be supplemented with a companion website, so that links to more time-sensitive online resources can be made available to users of the book, and information on technological advances in software and equipment can be updated regularly.

As noted, the present collection is designed to enhance research in all subdisciplines of linguistics by sharing best practices relevant to shared challenges. We have aimed to facilitate this style of use with highlighted keywords within chapters, detailed cross-referencing across chapters, as well as a detailed index, and a few illustrations, described next, of how researchers might use the book.

3 Sample projects

In order to exemplify a few of the many ways this volume might be utilized, we briefly describe a few sample projects here, involving typical research questions in various subfields of linguistics. These examples highlight a few reasons why thinking about methodology strictly in terms of subdisciplines can be limiting, and demonstrate that a research project from any subdiscipline might make use of several different chapters spanning the three sections of the book.

3.1 Phonological analysis of an understudied language

Research on an understudied language requires finding language consultants (Chapter 5), attending to the ethical issues associated with working with human subjects (Chapter 2) and observing the community (Chapter 10). Upon entering the community, the student will focus primarily on language documentation (Chapter 4), which will likely draw on various forms of speaker introspection (Chapter 3). To facilitate note-taking, students may elect to record elicitation sessions (Chapters 9, 10), and resultant recordings can subsequently be used in acoustic analysis (Chapter 17). Depending on the phonological and phonetic phenomena under investigation, students may find it useful to collect articulatory data, such as static palatography, in order to ascertain the place of articulation of a sound (Chapter 9). Upon returning from the field, students could transcribe and construct a searchable corpus (Chapters 12, 13). Finally, students can refer to best practices in constructing a phonological analysis (Chapter 18), and phonological claims could be supported by identifying statistical trends in acoustic data or distributional facts gleaned from the corpus (Chapters 14–16).

3.2 Social analysis of variation or code-switching

An investigation of the social meaning of a linguistic feature or practice may take a qualitative and/or quantitative approach, any of which requires attention to ethical considerations (Chapter 2). Students focusing on patterns of production would likely need to establish contacts in a community (Chapter 10), decide which speakers to interview (Chapter 5), and audio-record interviews (Chapters 6, 9). In the context of ethnographic fieldwork (Chapter 10), students might find it helpful to ask speakers to introspect about their own and others' language use (Chapter 3) or to video-record naturally occurring interactions (Chapter 10). Students embarking on more quantitative investigations will likely need to sample a population appropriately (Chapter 5), transcribe data (Chapter 12), use basic scripting to extract and properly format data

(Chapter 13), and conduct statistical analyses (Chapters 14–16). Those who examine the strategic use of linguistic features may pay special attention to interactional factors – for example, considering how variables occur over the course of conversations or structure narratives (Chapter 21). Students examining social meaning from the perspective of perception may employ surveys and questionnaires (Chapter 6) and/or experiments (Chapters 7, 8), both of which require careful sampling (Chapter 5) and statistical analysis (Chapters 14–16). Finally, if the researcher is studying a phonological feature, the researcher will usually rely on basic principles of acoustic analysis (Chapter 17) and/or formal argumentation (Chapter 18) to establish the linguistic constraints on variation.

3.3   Analysis of a set of syntactic constructions

Currently, a student wishing to pursue a syntactic study rarely gets detailed input regarding research methods. However, this book may open up important methodological questions for such a project. First, the student would have to consider what combination of data would be appropriate for the given research question, including researcher or consultant intuition (Chapters 3, 4), corpus data (Chapters 11, 13), and experimental data (Chapters 7, 8) from an appropriate sample (Chapter 5). In building an analysis (Chapter 18), relevant glossing conventions might be used (Chapter 12) and quantitative measures requiring statistical analysis (Chapters 14–16) may be appropriate if several speakers have been consulted or if experimental methods were chosen.

3.4   Longitudinal study of second language acquisition

A study of change in an individual learning a second language could take a number of forms. The first consideration for the researcher would be what type(s) of learner to study (Chapters 5, 10) and the associated ethical implications (Chapter 2), whether to combine naturalistic and elicited data from that individual (Chapters 6, 7, 8, 10), and whether to use written or recorded responses (Chapters 6, 9, 10). The student should be advised to consider all aspects of longitudinal analysis (Chapter 22) before collecting any data. For instance, they may decide to favor data that can be replicated in a repeat run after a given period of time has elapsed. The subsequent analysis could rely on relevant chapters from Part III, depending on the nature of the linguistic phenomenon under investigation, and the student could refer to the chapters on statistics (Chapters 14–16) if they need to select appropriate quantitative measures for their analysis.

4   Concluding remarks

Every linguist would probably design a volume on linguistic methodology differently. Our focus in this collection has been on certain stages universally shared by any research project – data gathering, data processing, and data analysis. These shared concerns are prioritized over disciplinary divisions, but we have aimed to keep methodological norms within different fields of linguistics accessible and visible as well. We hope that the wide-ranging expertise shared by the contributing authors here will continue to support the creative new methodological practices we are already witnessing in the field.

References

Breheny, R. 2011. Experimentation-based pragmatics. In W. Bublitz and N. Norrick, eds. *Handbook of Pragmatics, Volume 1: Foundations of Pragmatics*. Berlin: Mouton de Gruyter, 561–86.

Bresnan, J. and M. Ford. 2010. Predicting syntax: processing dative constructions in American and Australian varieties of English. *Language* 86.1: 186–213.

Campbell-Kibler, K. 2009. The nature of sociolinguistic perception. *Language Variation and Change* 21.1: 135–56.

Chomsky, N. 1995. Language and nature. *Mind* 104.413: 1–61.

Eckert, P. and S. McConnell-Ginet. 1992. Think practically and look locally: language and gender as community-based practice. *Annual Review of Anthropology* 21: 461–90.

Gick, B. 2002. The use of ultrasound for linguistic phonetic fieldwork. *Journal of the International Phonetic Association* 32: 113–21.

Hymes, D. 1962. The ethnography of speaking. In T. Gladwin and W. C. Sturtevant, eds. *Anthropology and Human Behavior*. Washington, DC: Anthropology Society of Washington.

Litosseliti, L. 2010. *Research Methods in Linguistics*. London: Continuum.

Martins, P., I. Carbone, A. Pinto, and A. Teixeira. 2008. European Portuguese MRI based speech production studies. *Speech Communication* 50: 925–52.

McMahon, A. and R. McMahon. 2005. *Language Classification by Numbers*. Oxford University Press.

Milroy, L. 1980. *Language and Social Networks*. London: Basil Blackwell.

Scobbie, J. and J. Stuart-Smith. 2012. The utility of sociolinguistic sampling in laboratory-based phonological experimentation. In A. Cohn, C. Fougeron, and M. Huffman, eds. *The Oxford Handbook of Laboratory Phonology*. Oxford University Press, 607–21.

Skipper, J. I. and S. L. Small. 2005. fMRI studies of language. In K. Brown, ed. *The Encyclopedia of Language and Linguistics*, 2nd edn. Oxford: Elsevier Science.

Weinreich, U., W. Labov, and M. Herzog. 1968. Empirical foundations for a theory of language change. In W. Lehmann and Y. Malkiel, eds. *Directions for Historical Linguistics*. Austin: University of Texas Press, 95–188.

PART I

Data collection

2   Ethics in linguistic research

Penelope Eckert

1   Introduction

All one can hope to do in a chapter on research ethics is raise issues, for the burden of resolution falls to each of us in dialogue with those who stand to be affected by our work. Different kinds of linguistic research raise very different ethical issues. And inasmuch as linguists encounter an enormous variety of cultures, people, and situations in the course of their research, we need to recognize that our own system of ethics may not be the same as that of the people we are working with (see, e.g., Holton 2009). So no discussion of research ethics can be comprehensive and no formal set of guidelines can anticipate unique actions or circumstances. For this reason, I will not attempt to set out specific actions one should take while doing research, but I will discuss a number of areas that every researcher should consider carefully when embarking on work with human participants.

Most of the readers of this volume will be subject to government regulation and university ethics review, which can be both a help and a hindrance in fostering ethical practice. A central purpose of this chapter is to encourage researchers to step back from the bureaucratic process and examine their own practices more generally. They might then step back into the bureaucratic process and engage in it intelligently and actively. For researchers who do not have such institutional oversight, this chapter can be a starting point for reflection about their practices and their potential consequences. In some cases, particularly in communities that have been disenfranchised in other ways, communities may wish to control who does what with their language (see Bowern 2008 and Holtan 2009 for a thorough discussion of these issues). In some cases, particularly in communities that have had a history of exploitation (such as native communities in North America), there is formal community review of research proposals. But in other cases – and even once one has passed this review – the researcher must take into consideration the interests of others in the community. The common focus on the primary individual or individuals we work with often distracts us from a consideration of how linguistic work affects others in the community.

A discussion of research ethics in linguistics perhaps best begins with the 1992 book by Deborah Cameron et al. entitled *Researching Language*. This book puts power at the center of the discussion, challenging researchers to consider power relations not simply between themselves and their "subjects," but in the more general web of power relations that constitute the social, including the academic, world. The very decision about what to study and how to study it emerges in a web of power relations within academia and in society at large. Parties such as the media, government, and publishers have their own interests in language, which may be at odds with those of the research participants (or researchers), and can have a considerable effect on visibility, public attitudes, and funding. For a single and reasonably subtle case, see Simpson (2012). In keeping with this broader view, one might consider that research ethics comes into play not only in social relations, but in relation to regimes of knowledge. What kind of knowledge is linguistic competence? Is it intellectual property? And what kinds of knowledge are we generating when we study it?

2   Ownership, patrimony, and intellectual property

A thorny starting point is the basic question of the relation between language and those who use it. Linguists, particularly those working on endangered languages, generally feel a responsibility to the language itself, as a living, and all too often a dying, practice. This sense of responsibility is often shared with the communities who speak (or spoke) the language, opening possibilities for fruitful collaborations. But linguists' dependence on, and commitment to, linguistic diversity also leads us to a view of language and languages as the property not just of their speakers, but of humankind more generally. The analogy between linguistic and biological diversity intensifies this view, putting the linguist in the position of righteous activist. But closer to home, linguistic diversity is central to the health of the scientific endeavor. There is an awkward distinction between the interests of speakers and those of science, and it is one that linguists often ignore. And this can open the possibility for subtle and not-so-subtle abuse when linguists put the importance of the scientific record before the preferences of the speakers.

The United States regulations for research with "human subjects" defines human subjects as follows:

> (f) Human subject means a living individual about whom an investigator (whether professional or student) conducting research obtains (1) Data through intervention or interaction with the individual, or (2) Identifiable private information.   (Sec. 46.102)

The key phrase is "about whom." While this leaves gathering information about a language, hence much of the work that linguists do, potentially immune to federal regulation, it should not leave it immune to ethical review. The American and European ideology that a language is not part of a *whom* is simply wrong in some of the cultures that linguists work in. For most people in the world, language is inextricable from personal and community identity. Some cultures consider their language to be a cultural treasure, not to be shared with others.

3 Subjects, informants, participants, collaborators, consultants

Research on language always involves human agents – speakers, writers, readers, or hearers of the language in question. Researchers may work with these people in physical proximity, over phones and other media, or examine their texts intended for others. They may seek basic linguistic facts, judgments, recordings of unreflective speech, or automatic responses. The relationship between the researcher and the bearer of language can range from intimate to anonymous, from collaborator to manipulator, and from open to deceptive. Depending on the nature of the research, one might call this person by a variety of names – a *subject*, an *informant*, a *participant*, a *collaborator*, a *consultant*, and no doubt others. Considering the use of these terms could be one place to begin a discussion of the relationships between researchers and the speakers who provide them with data. It has become increasingly common to use the term *participant* for a variety of roles, and one might ask if this is not often a form of political correctness – like using *gender* when one is really thinking biologically rather than socially. It is important to recognize that different kinds of research call for very different relations between researcher and speaker, and very different ethical considerations come into play in different research situations.

Cameron et al. (1992) distinguish three kinds of ethical traditions based in distinct research relations which, in turn, emerge from different epistemological traditions. I will not go into these three kinds here because the issues behind them are more complex than a quick overview can do justice to. But underlying the distinctions are three elements:

1.   The researcher's ownership and control of the research ideas, hypotheses, procedures, results and interpretation
2.   The extent to which the researched are disinterested subjects of the researcher's activity
3.   The responsibility of the researcher to seek and use research knowledge for the benefit of the researched.

The three combine to describe a continuum from a model that is most suited to experimental work in which quite explicitly the researcher creates tasks for the researched to perform in relative ignorance of their purpose, and to work in which the researcher and researched collaborate to develop research that is in some way in the interests of the researched. Keren Rice (2006) argues that this last model is part of the ethical responsibility of people working on endangered languages. Indeed, quite early on, Ken Hale (1965, 1972) advocated working for the community in their revitalization activities, as they saw fit. He also advocated training speakers in linguistic analysis, which could be seen as simultaneously empowering the speakers and yielding superior research. He argued that by putting analysis in the hands of people with a direct interest in language documentation and revitalization, the resulting analysis would be better and the research would continue long after the initial researcher had left the community. There is a good deal of territory between these two models, and while greater agency on the part of the researched is in general desirable, each research question calls for its own methods and its own division of labor. Regardless of which of these is appropriate, all parties to the research need to be in agreement about what is happening.

4   Consent

The history of research abuse tells us that *consent* is the cornerstone of ethical research practices. While such abuse is more dramatic in medical research (e.g., the Tuskegee study by the United States Public Health Service that studied the course of syphilis without informing subjects that they had the disease, or offering available treatment), linguists have been known to resort to such things as surreptitious recording and publication of cultural secrets. People may be willing to run quite significant risks as research participants if they feel that the research is important enough; some may prefer not to participate out of suspicion or fear; and some may simply not be interested in participating in research activities. Undergraduates in research universities may be quite happy to be deceived for the sake of the success of psychological experiments, while people in non-academic contexts may not have a good basis for understanding this enterprise. Fundamental to ethical research is ensuring that research participants enter into the enterprise knowingly and willingly, and gaining their consent should be a process of establishing and maintaining trust. A serious difficulty arising from the elaborate consent procedures involved in institutional review is that they commonly distract the researcher from the fact that consent should not be a matter of getting a signature on paper, but the establishment of an informed working relationship. And there is no question that often the signed consent procedures required by some review bodies works against the interests of both the research and the researched.

Depending on the kind of research – for example, whether it involves a 15-minute experiment or long-term residence in the community of speakers – consent may be a one-time event or an ongoing process. The importance of consent depends on the potential effect the research may have on the participant or the participant's community. Completely anonymous observations of public behavior are arguably of no grave consequence to the people being observed. And one could say that by performing acts in public, an individual is giving implicit consent to having those actions observed and recorded. The actual anonymity, though, depends on the anonymity of the place, and the predictability of who would be engaging in activity in that place. The anonymity of the research setting itself can be important, since entire communities could suffer from observations that identify them even though they are anonymous with respect to individuals. This raises the issue of how we present our results, which I will return to below.

It is always important, though, to consider carefully how much detail about people and places is actually necessary to the presentation of research. We have a tendency to include detail for a variety of reasons, ranging from its potential for explaining the data to serving our vanity as field workers. It is up to each of us to limit ourselves to the former.

While language documentation usually involves very straightforward understandings between researcher and speaker about the nature of the work (see Chapter 4), other kinds of research involve a certain amount of vagueness or even deception. Sociolinguists prefer to downplay their interest in language in order to elicit as unselfconscious speech as possible (see Chapter 6). This means that they may prefer not to inform speakers of the kinds of analysis they will be doing of their recordings. In the case of survey interviews, if interviewees are randomly selected and do not know each other, full disclosure could follow the interview. But in cases where the researchers are creating a snowball sample (see Chapter 5) or remaining in the community doing ethnography (see Chapter 10), they may prefer to remain vague about their analysis. If we tell participants that we are interested in language, allowing them to think that our research needs are satisfied by the reading passages and word lists we have them read at the end of the interview, are we being sufficiently honest? Ultimately, every sociolinguist will have to answer this question for him or herself. In my own research in Detroit-area high schools in the early 1980s, I presented my research as an ethnographic study of high school social networks, with little mention of my interest in language. The ethnographic interest was indeed central to my work, and the first book I published based on that research was an ethnography, which many of my participants read and commented on in draft form. But did that fulfill my responsibility to the participants? Recently, I have had occasion to discuss this research with some of them, now in their forties, and told them about my linguistic interests and results. They were surprised but not bothered by that aspect of the work, but the question remains whether they would have been equally unbothered when they were in high school. There is little question that the issue of linguistic study of this sort is increasingly sensitive to the extent that the speakers feel that their language or dialect is stigmatized. And once again, this enters into a societal discourse of linguistic deficit that can make vulnerable speakers feel that interest in their language is stigmatizing. At the same time, the relationships that sociolinguists are able to establish with participants even to elicit spontaneous speech often establish them as champions of the local way of speaking, thus potentially helping to reduce the feeling of stigma more generally.

Psycholinguists often need to go beyond vagueness to deception, misleading speakers about the purpose of an experiment in order to manage the bias in responses (see Chapter 7). The extent to which these practices are ethical depends on the potential harm caused by the deception, and the approach taken to debriefing after the experiment. Experimental "subjects," particularly members of university subject pools, commonly go into the lab with the assumption that there can be deception, and accept this as part of the enterprise. There are cases in which the deception itself can carry some risk – for example, work on stereotype threat, in which participants' attention is drawn to their membership in some stereotyped group to see its effect on their performance in the experimental situation. In these cases, needless to say, complete debriefing is required afterwards. On the other hand, if the deception simply involves drawing a participant's attention to one part of the task in order to distract them from the part that is really of interest, the only point of debriefing might be to educate the participant. However, too much debriefing of this sort arguably offers no benefit to the participant and has the risk of biasing the participant pool, as participants may begin to enter experiments with the expectation of deception.

Getting informed consent involves not only telling people what you are going to do, but what you are not going to do. Ethnographers can be mistaken for spies, but also for social workers. In the latter case, participants might reasonably expect them to provide kinds of help they are unequipped and unqualified to provide. In field situations in which researchers are likely to hear personal information, they must establish in advance how to handle cases in which, for example, someone tells them about abuse. In other words, they must make it clear at the time they establish consent what kinds of things will and will not be kept confidential. The increasing frequency of fMRI studies in linguistics (see Chapter 8) presents an entirely new set of dilemmas, as it is not uncommon for MRI studies to reveal brain abnormalities (see Borra and Sorensen 2011). Participants might reasonably expect that the research MRI is a diagnostic procedure and that they will be told of any abnormalities, but linguists have neither the diagnostic expertise to deal with these incidental findings, nor the means to pay someone who does. Informed consent, then, must be clear about the limited nature of these experiments.

Consent should be not only informed, but voluntary. Researchers need to be alert to potential sources of coercion. Does the individual feel obligated or pressured, in some way, to agree to participate? If the researcher relies on a statusful insider to help recruit participants, such as a doctor, teacher, or official, will people feel an obligation to that person? In a community study, the knowledge that others are participating could create social pressure. And looking at it from the other perspective, if a researcher's presence creates the expectation of participation, is it the researcher's responsibility to include all comers whether he or she actually uses the resulting data or not? There are situations in which participation in research may carry some kind of status, and non-participation may create feelings of rejection or exclusion. The importance of these effects will vary tremendously from community to community, but researchers should be alert to the fact that there are cases in which the consequences can be important. This concern is of course magnified when payment is involved.

The researcher's responsibility is to make sure that participants understand what they are being asked to do, and what the implications of doing it will be. This may involve explaining to people who have never seen the internet what it means to have recordings of their speech made publicly available online. Informed consent assumes the ability to grasp the implications of participation in the research and to make decisions for oneself. People with undeveloped or diminished reasoning capacity (such as children or people with mental illness or dementia), or in socially vulnerable positions (such as prisoners, employees, or students), require special consideration. Institutional review boards (IRBs) dictate practice in many of these cases, but it is up to the researcher to consider the many sources of problems with informed consent. The fundamental issue in these situations is <u>whether the individual is sufficiently aware of the implications of participating in research, and sufficiently free to determine their level of participation.</u> An additional threat to consent is the fact that interviews tend to be not just about the interviewee, but about that person's acquaintances, friends, relatives, enemies. We need to ask ourselves at what point third parties become inadvertent research subjects, and when they do, we need to find a way to gain their consent.

Very small children are commonly inadvertent research subjects, particularly in early acquisition studies, with their parents or guardians providing consent on their behalf. As they mature and develop the capacity to understand the implications of participating in research, they are in a position to decide whether or not to participate. However, children are less likely to understand the research enterprise, to recognize potential risks, and to understand the roles and relations involved. They may, for example, confuse the researcher role with that of a teacher or social worker, or some other role that entails specific responsibilities. (Indeed, researchers should determine in advance what they will do if they learn that a child they are working with is abused or otherwise in danger.) For this reason, while minors must ultimately determine whether or not they participate in research, they can only give assent (verbal agreement to participate) and must also have the consent of the adults who are legally responsible for them. There are cases in which an IRB can waive the requirement of parental consent, but they do not generally apply in the case of linguistic research. The age of legal majority varies considerably across cultures, as do the conditions under which a person below that age can be emancipated. And it is up to researchers and review boards to determine whether the legal minors they are recruiting as participants have the maturity to give assent.

Documentation of consent is a sticky issue, and one of the magnets of hostility toward IRBs. Technically, in the United States, documentation of consent (signed consent) can be replaced by verbal consent in most cases of linguistic research. In many cases – for example, in research carried out in societies in which people are averse to signing official documents, or with populations with low literacy – a requirement of signed consent can stand in the way of recruiting participants and can threaten the peace of mind of those who do participate. Some IRBs recognize this and waive documentation in these cases, but if one's review board is overly conservative, it is the responsibility of the researcher to push back with explicit references to the governmental guidelines. Bowern (2010) provides information about some universities' IRB practices that could be useful in appealing to one's own IRB.

5   Institutional oversight

Institutional oversight of research involving human subjects is both a benefit and a problem. A major benefit is that human subjects review obliges us to think through the implications of our research procedures in advance, and can point out problem areas that we might not have anticipated. But while there is no question that institutional review has helped eliminate a number of abuses that have plagued research in the past, it has also attracted a certain amount of hostility on the part of the research community. Government-mandated human subjects review imposes a considerable bureaucratic burden on the university and, in turn, on the researcher. Any form of bureaucratic regulation is going to be unwieldy, and this is increased to the extent that human subjects protections are primarily designed for medical research. Even when universities have separate boards to review non-medical research, they often lack research experience in the areas they are reviewing. These are familiar problems, but perhaps the more serious consequence is that institutional oversight has also invited researchers to give over their ethical considerations to an external body that almost certainly knows less about the research and the conditions than they do. Rather than drawing back and openly or covertly refusing to comply with regulation, researchers might consider it part of their responsibility to become part of the solution by joining the review board and improving its practices from within, or providing the IRB with well-documented information about issues specific to their discipline.

It is smart practice for researchers to know the official regulations governing research, and to understand the intent behind those regulations. Federal regulations in the United States are administered by the Office for Human Research Protections, which is part of the Department of Health and Human Services of the federal government. These regulations were established with the intention that they should be flexible, giving local IRBs considerable discretionary authority. In the case of behavioral science research, the intention of flexibility is even greater, since it is recognized that these regulations were primarily developed with medical research in mind. Guidelines developed by professional organizations can be useful in negotiating with review boards, and should be drafted with this purpose in mind.

Not only are researchers responsible to their own IRB, they may be subject to review in the countries or communities in which they wish to pursue research. UNESCO keeps an international database on ethics in research,[1] and while many of the entries are restricted to biomedical research, a number cover research in the social sciences and humanities as well. The Harvard School of Public Health is also developing a database of human subjects protections around the world.[2] The number of review boards around the world is increasing, so before traveling

---

[1] UNESCO global ethics database. www.unesco.org/new/en/social-and-human-sciences/themes/global-ethics-observatory/access-geobs

[2] Harvard School of Public Health database. www.hsph.harvard.edu/ohra/hrpp-plan

abroad for research, linguists should familiarize themselves with the regulations in the countries they are going to work in. Below the national level, many communities, such as Native American tribes, also regulate research access. Others, such as minority communities near major universities, do not. The researcher should consider whether their presence and activities in these convenient locations constitute an undue burden on communities.

In an age of formal regulation of research, it is easy to become paternalistic in one's approach to research participants, particularly since human subjects review is done prior to beginning the research. Ethical decisions may be made in advance of familiarity with the actual research situation and the people and cultures involved. It is imperative that researchers rethink these decisions as they pursue the research and, where necessary, change their practices and their contract with their review board.

6   Research locales

6.1   Field research

The opportunity to do research in the field is a gift. People allow us to spend time in their space and to participate in their lives. In the process, we use resources, we cause a disturbance, and we gather information that benefits us, our field, and our careers. What is in it for them? Before we consider that, we might step back and ask, who is this *them*? When we do fieldwork, we are not simply working with one individual, but with an entire community. And if we are working with a single individual who is away from the community, we need to consider the community nonetheless. The issue of what constitutes the community is anything but simple. A linguist may gain entry into part of a split community, or may know the interests of some segment of the community they are working with, but be ignorant of other members' sentiments. There may be differences of opinion in the community about the value of the research, and about the proprietary status of language itself.

Communities, no matter how small, are always diverse. There are always differences in power and differences of opinion. And there are friendships, hatreds, alliances, and relations of all sorts that may affect people's perceptions of us and our role in the community. And inevitably, the relationships that the fieldworker develops will reverberate in some way through the community. Our ethical responsibility in the community – whether it is an isolated village in a very different culture to our own or a high school or neighborhood in our own community – extends to the community as a whole. Inevitably we will be associated more with some people than others, and that association can have an effect on relations in the community. From payment to small favors to simple friendship or attention, we will be providing commodities. And at the same time, we may be objects of suspicion and pose social liabilities for some. Allowing one's contacts to be limited to a subset of the community also poses the risk of findings that are not representative of all segments of the community, which affects not only the value of our work, but the equity of any measures based on that work.

Fieldwork done in the community brings together research and personal everyday interactions in a way that is often ambiguous – indeed, the personal and the professional are inseparable under these conditions. Particularly for the sociolinguist or linguistic anthropologist, every interaction may provide linguistic data or inform the social analysis. It is up to the researcher to make sure the members of the community recognize this, and to set up some kind of modus vivendi to accommodate it. In an ethnographic situation, participants should be able to say at any time that what they are doing or saying cannot be research material. In my own ethnographic work with elementary school kids, part of the consent process was to settle on, and practice, a special gesture that tells me that they want privacy. That said, anyone who has worked with children knows that they trust too easily, and the fact that after the first day nobody ever made that gesture in 3 years is an indication that children are not thinking about the potential consequences of allowing an ethnographer in their midst. In such cases, the ethnographer must take on the responsibility of picking and choosing what to record, and what to publish. Ethnographic research raises a variety of questions and dilemmas, but it also provides continuous opportunities for working out common understandings. It is important that the researcher establish with the community a shared set of principles.

Researchers are becoming increasingly familiar in communities around the world. There is still plenty of room for misunderstanding, though. It is not uncommon for linguists to be seen as spies or agents of external authorities. In a high school, the linguist runs the risk of being seen as a teacher's spy or an undercover narcotics officer. But it can work the other way as well, and create a kind of inappropriate trust. A linguist working with a vulnerable population may be seen as having powers or resources that he or she does not have (or does have but considers it inappropriate to provide). People might view the linguist as a social worker and may expect advocacy or protection of some sort. Fieldworkers must know from the start how they will create an unambiguous role, and how they will deal with unexpected problems if they should arise. Outside of the fieldworker's culture, there are many possible sources of misunderstanding about the fieldworker's nature, resources, capabilities, and responsibilities. Only some of these can be predicted, and it is up to the researcher to recognize at all times the possibilities for misunderstanding.

The researcher working with groups of children is likely to witness meanness, bullying, acts of racism. These are not just data, unaffected by the fieldworker's presence, for the presence of an adult introduces external moral authority, and a lack of response could be taken as approval. It is no longer considered that the researcher can maintain detachment, particularly in the eyes of research participants, so researchers need to establish in advance how they will respond to situations like this. In the case of children, it may be a good idea to establish this as part of the ground rules at the beginning of the research, but to remind them as situations arise. In the case of working in schools, the proper ethical thing to do can be judged within the fieldworker's own culture, but what if this takes place in a completely different culture? What if a fieldworker witnesses someone beating their child? These are dilemmas to which there is no single answer, but dilemmas that the individual fieldworker needs to work out as much as possible in advance.

6.2   Institutional locations

Doing research in institutional contexts raises an additional level of control. Research in prisons is highly restricted precisely because inmates are in a powerless position and unable to give completely voluntary consent. Federal regulations limit research in prisons to projects that are directly concerned with prisons or potentially of direct benefit to the inmates. In other words, prisoners can no longer serve as a convenient sample of the general population. This follows on years of abuse, in which prisoners served as subjects in medical research and drug trials. While prisons are a special case under US regulations, the dangers of captive research populations extends to a wide range of institutions. Schools, refugee camps, workplaces all require institutional permission, and the ethical pursuit of fieldwork in these settings begins with the understanding carved out with the gatekeepers.

The researcher needs to keep in mind that there are often conflicts of interest between those with authority over the institution and the people the researcher seeks to work with within. Administrators may want researchers to provide them with information about the populations under their control. They may, even inadvertently, impose in these populations a sense of obligation to participate. A school principal may inform teachers that they must let researchers into their classrooms, or teachers may inadvertently pressure students to participate by, for instance, offering to collect consent forms on the researcher's behalf. If they feel that a particular research project is in the company's interest, company executives may inform workers that they are to participate as part of their jobs. The research-er's first task in establishing a relationship with an institution is to come to a clear agreement guaranteeing that all participation is voluntary, and that an individual's participation or non-participation will have no effect on their status in the institution. This may often involve not letting those in charge know who actually participates. This extends to the university classroom and laboratory as well. It is difficult for employees to refuse to participate in a research activity when asked by their bosses, and for students to refuse when asked by their professors. As a result, using the classroom as a participant pool is highly problematic. Students can certainly be valuable resources when one is trying out ideas – polling students for intuitions can be useful both to the researcher and to the students. But instructors need to be sensitive to the fine line between trying ideas out with one's students and involving them involuntarily as research subjects. Laboratory experi-ments often use students from departmental subject pools set up specifically to add a layer of confidentiality between students, their professors, and experimenters. A properly run subject pool provides a non-experimental activity as an alternative for those who prefer not to participate, and maintains confidentiality about which option individual students choose.

6.3   Information media research

The explosion of information and communication technology in recent years has opened up all kinds of resources for linguistic research. And each of these brings with it new ethical dilemmas. The internet puts what might be considered private communication into a mass-available sphere. At the same time, it provides a platform for intentionally public communication. Determining, therefore, what kinds of internet communication are intentionally in the public domain is a complex problem. It is not always clear whether writers on the internet consider their texts to be private or not, and researchers should hold no illusions about their ability to provide anonymity for data culled from the internet. The internet is a goldmine for research on discourse, but such research commonly involves the publication of fairly large stretches of text. And while the internet provides access to apparently anonymous data, it also facilitates tracing those data and identifying their sources. As the threats that the internet poses to privacy increase, users are becoming increasingly aware of the dangers and hopefully are becoming more circumspect in their use. And, increasingly, internet sites are establishing explicit research guidelines. By the time we have come to the Twitter age, it is pretty clear to all users that their communications are not private. Nonetheless, if a person sends a message to a limited list, one can assume that they do not intend for it to go beyond, even if the sender recognizes that it might. In the end, it is up to researchers to be sure that they are not gathering and publishing data that the speakers intend to be private, or that can be traced to their origins if the data in any way pose a threat to the originators.

The ethical considerations in using any texts, of course, depend on the nature of the research. As Susan Herring (1996: 157) points out, "A speaker is unlikely to feel concern at being represented (anonymously and out of context) as having said, 'I was there for about uh six... six years...'" On the other hand, it is not uncommon for linguists to cite more personal or even incriminating stretches of speech. In such cases, if the speech shows up on an in-person recording, one would have to be in possession of the recording or a transcript to begin to identify the speaker. On the internet, on the other hand, the speaker's identity is far less secure.

7   Payment, ownership, advocacy, empowerment, and "giving back"

Many linguists emphasize the importance of "giving back," but what actually constitutes a contribution to the community is a complicated issue, and certainly not one that the researcher can resolve on his or her own. The understandings of research arrangements need to be built into the relationships that researchers enter into in the course of their work; otherwise there is potential for "giving back" to be paternalistic, and/or to serve the interests of some segments of the community at the possible expense of others.

The prototypical, and original, linguistic work involves a linguist working one-on-one with the speaker of the target language. In this case, the speaker-participant is not a research "subject," but a collaborator or consultant, and in some cases a co-author. The obligations of the researcher toward this speaker may vary considerably. In some cases, the researcher may be paying the speaker in exchange for their knowledge. The appropriateness of this depends on whether the community considers the language to be general knowledge that is anyone's to share. Paying consultants may involve a long-term financial arrangement or a one-time payment, and may involve payments in kind, such as locally valued commodities or help or expertise. Particularly in long-term fieldwork, this kind of compensation may blend seamlessly with the give-and-take of personal relationships – offering rides, helping with tasks, and so on. Since the line between the professional and the personal is often blurry in these situations, it is up to the fieldworker to consider the implications of each action carefully. Important ethical issues involve balancing fair payment against the potential for coercion, and adversely affecting relations within the community. In many cases, it may turn out that some kind of compensation to the larger community is more appropriate – to schools or other organizations. This should be established in cooperation with the participants and the community. Once again, this raises the question of what actually constitutes the community, which may better be determined on the basis of ethnographic work (see Chapter 10).

In some cases, people engage in research with the expectation that the results will be used in some way to benefit the community of speakers. This may involve documentation, preparation of pedagogical materials, and/or advocacy (see Rickford 1997). In all these cases, the form that this reciprocity takes is best determined by the speakers themselves rather than by the researcher's whim. In some cases, participants may not even want language-related support, but rather more general professional assistance (e.g., advice about resume-writing, job interviews, or other practical matters). Some communities are more concerned with "payback" than others. Most particularly, oppressed communities, and communities whose languages are disappearing, have a strong need and sense of need, and it is up to linguists to establish a clear understanding about their responsibility from the start. In his comparison of quite different situations, in Alaska and Indonesia, Holton (2009) points out that the issue of potential profit from the publication of language materials can create resentment in the community. There is also concern about communal profits as opposed to pay given to an individual consultant.

The issue of advocacy is quite explicit in the American Anthropological Association's ethical guidelines:

> Anthropologists may choose to move beyond disseminating research results to a position of advocacy. This is an individual decision, but not an ethical responsibility. This becomes an ethical issue if the conditions under which the research is given access to the language include an assumption of advocacy.

8   Data management

While our fieldwork may be fairly short-lived, we generally maintain the data from that fieldwork for a long time, if not for the rest of our lives. People who provide speech samples need to control the fate of those samples – to determine where their voices will go, who will have access to them, and for how long. When we collect large amounts of material, we may have data to work with for the rest of our careers. Do the speakers agree to us using their speech samples well into the future, and for differing purposes? The issue of future use of data has been particularly highlighted in recently publicized medical cases such as the successful Havasupai lawsuit against Arizona State University, and the best-selling story of Henrietta Lacks (Skloot 2010). In the case of the Havasupai, researchers at Arizona State University drew DNA samples for the purpose of finding the cause of widespread diabetes among tribe members – a project that was clearly in the interests of the tribe. This project yielded no beneficial results, and the samples were retained for use in research, without the donors' consent, that was not in their interests, most notably investigations of the tribe's origins. Henrietta Lacks was an African American woman whose cancer cells were used, without her knowledge or consent, to create an immortal cell line for cancer research.

From the outset, we need to establish with our speakers what will be the fate of data they provide us with, and this requires thinking well into the possible future. Some may want to pass their data on to others or contribute them (or a subset of them) to a widely available corpus. At the current historical juncture, a number of linguists are facing the ethical dilemmas associated with establishing corpora of recordings of people with whom they no longer have any means of contact. People differ in their feelings about this, and clearly each case must be decided on the basis of what the recordings are like and how possible it is to anonymize them. The reader is referred to Chapter 12 on anonymizing transcripts, and Chapter 13 on anonymizing corpora. Nowadays, it makes sense at the outset to establish levels of consent – whether speakers want their names associated with the data, whether they want the data to be available only to the researcher, the researcher's team, all researchers, or the general public, and whether they want the researcher to play samples of speech from these recordings at academic conferences.

Management of data may be far less of an issue for linguists than it is for other social scientists, since there is normally nothing risky about the potential disclosure of linguistic information. But this can lead linguists to be sloppy about the maintenance of personal information, from contact information to income data to pseudonym assignments. Whenever any researcher gathers personal information about speakers, that information needs to be protected. File encryption is a simple bottom line for data stored on computers. And of course many of the vehicles for speech that linguists elicit are intended to be private, such as interviews and personal narratives.

9   Regimes of knowledge

Finally, we should consider not just what happens to the speakers we work with, but what happens to the knowledge we generate. Individual linguists are not necessarily equipped to change society, or to "apply" their work. But it is a linguist's responsibility to understand the potential effect of research results and conclusions on wider regimes of knowledge. Am I making the best use of the data I have gathered? Can my study of the speech of underclass children feed a discourse of cultural deficit? Can my work on gender differences contribute to sexist discourses? If so, what can I do to usher this work into the world in a constructive manner? What do I need to do besides simply put the results out there? Whom should I be talking to about this research, and how? Ultimately, we are engaged in a meaning-making enterprise, and our ethical responsibility involves not just behaving well as we gather data, but doing what we can to make our participants' cooperation worthwhile.

References

Borra, R. J. H. and A. G. Sorensen. 2011. Incidental findings in brain MRI research: what do we owe our subjects? *Journal of the American College of Radiology* 8: 848–52.

Bowern, C. 2008. *Linguistic Fieldwork: A Practical Guide.* Houndmills, Basingstoke: Palgrave.

2010. Fieldwork and the IRB: A snapshot. *Language* 86: 897–905.

Cameron, D., E. Frazer, P. Harvey, M. B. H. Rampton, and K. Richardson.

1992. *Researching Language: Issues of Power and Method.* New York: Routledge.

Hale, K. 1965. On the use of informants in fieldwork. *Canadian Journal of Linguistics* 10: 108–19.

1972. Some questions about anthropological linguistics: the role of native knowledge. In Dell Hymes, ed. *Reinventing Anthropology.* New York: Random House, 382–97.

Herring, S. C. 1996. Linguistic and critical analysis of computer-mediated communication: some ethical and scholarly considerations. *The Information Society* 12.2: 153–68.

Holton, G. 2009. Relatively ethical: a comparison of linguistic research paradigms in Alaska and Indonesia. *Language Documentation and Conservation* 3: 161–75.

Rice, K. 2006. Ethical issues in linguistic fieldwork: an overview. *Journal of Academic Ethics* 4: 123–55.

Rickford, J. 1997. Unequal partnership: sociolinguistics and the African American community. *Language in Society* 26: 161–97.

Simpson, J. 2012. Yan Nhanu in the National Year of Reading. [Web log comment]. Retrieved from www.paradisec.org.au/blog/2012/01/yan-nhanu-in-the-national-year-of-reading

Skloot, R. 2010. *The Immortal Life of Henrietta Lacks*. New York: Crown.

3 Judgment data

Carson T. Schütze and Jon Sprouse

1 Preliminaries

This chapter covers what have traditionally been called grammaticality judgments in linguistics (which are more aptly referred to as acceptability judgments – see below). We examine such judgments from several angles, with the goal of assisting researchers in deciding whether and how to use this kind of data. Our goal in this chapter is to provide an introduction to the major themes that arise when using acceptability judgments as a data source for the construction of linguistic theories. Importantly, this chapter will not be a step-by-step guide for constructing a particular experiment, as the curious reader can find several fine introductions to the mechanics of experiment construction and analysis elsewhere (e.g., Chapters 7 and 8, and Cowart 1997). Instead, we intend this chapter to be an introduction to the theory underlying the methodology of acceptability judgment collection. Most of what follows will involve discussion of syntactic well-formedness judgments, because that is where the greatest amount of research about judgment data has been focused, but we believe that many of our remarks are also relevant for judgments at other levels of linguistic representation. Specific considerations regarding other sorts of judgments can be found elsewhere in this volume. For example, judgments about the lexicon and phonotactic well-formedness are generally gathered in the language documentation process (see Chapter 4); judgments about morphological processes might be gathered using the experimental methods that predominate in psycholinguistics (see Chapter 8); judgments about sociolinguistic variables might be gathered via a survey (see Chapter 6). For considerations specific to semantic judgments, see Matthewson (2004) and Chemla and Spector (2011).

This first section is comprised of issues that researchers should consider in deciding whether to use judgment data and how to collect them in general. The subsequent three sections look in more detail at issues of choice of task (Section 2), experimental design (Section 3), and data interpretation (Section 4). A brief conclusion completes the chapter.

1.1 The nature of judgment data

Speakers' reactions to sentences have traditionally been referred to as grammaticality judgments, but this term is misleading. Since a grammar is a mental construct not accessible to conscious awareness, speakers cannot have any impressions about the status of a sentence with respect to that grammar; rather, in Chomsky's (1965) terms, one should say their reactions concern *acceptability*, that is, the extent to which the sentence sounds "good" or "bad" to them. Acceptability judgments (as we refer to them henceforth) involve explicitly asking speakers to "judge" (i.e., report their spontaneous reaction concerning) whether a particular string of words is a possible utterance of their language, with an intended interpretation either implied or explicitly stated. The primary assumption underlying acceptability judgment experiments is that *acceptability* is a *percept* that arises (spontaneously) in response to linguistic stimuli that closely resemble sentences (i.e., strings of words). Acceptability is just like other percepts (e.g., brightness, loudness, temperature, pain) in that there are no methods for directly measuring the percept as it exists within a participant's mind. Instead, experimenters must rely on indirect measurement methods. One common method in the study of perception is to ask participants to *report* their perceptions along some sort of scale (e.g., Stevens 1956, 1957). In this way, an acceptability judgment is in fact a *reported perception of acceptability* (Chomsky 1965; Schütze 1996; Sprouse and Almeida 2013). As with all reported perceptions, acceptability judgments are a type of behavioral response that requires a (likely cognitive) explanation. Similarly, acceptability judgments can be used as evidence for making inferences about the cognitive systems that give rise to them, which syntacticians assume includes the grammatical system of the human language faculty (among other cognitive systems).

It has sometimes been suggested that claims made on the basis of acceptability judgment data do not necessarily bear on how the human language faculty is actually constructed unless their "psychological reality" has been tested via some experimental procedure using another dependent measure, such as time, error rate, electrophysiological response, and so on (Edelman and Christiansen 2003). This view belies a misunderstanding (Dresher 1995): acceptability judgments are themselves data about human behavior and cognition that need to be accounted for; they are not intrinsically less informative than, say, reaction time measures – in fact, many linguists would argue that they are more informative for the purposes of investigating the grammatical system. The use of the term "psychological reality" in this sense seems to be vacuous, as both acceptability judgments and other behavioral and electrophysiological responses are behaviors that can bear on the cognitive systems that subserve language.

Another objection to judgment data is that they demand awareness of language as an object of attention and evaluation – that is, metalinguistic awareness. This is claimed to make them artificial and undermine their external validity (e.g., Bresnan 2007). At one level, this is certainly true: reported perceptions require the participant to be aware of their perception and consciously report it using the responses made available to them. However, reported perceptions have long been considered a valid data type for the construction of cognitive theories because reported perceptions tend to be systematic in ways that can lead to the construction of falsifiable theories (e.g., Stevens 1957). This is no less true of acceptability judgments (reported perceptions of acceptability), which have led to the construction of grammatical theories that make falsifiable predictions about cross-linguistic variation, language acquisition, and even language processing.

Relatedly, though acceptability judgments are sometimes described as "introspections" or "intuitions," it should be clear that a reported perception is entirely distinct from both of these notions (Carr 1990; Schütze 1996). The terms intuition and introspection come from an early tradition of experimental psychological research pioneered by Wilhelm Wundt that assumed that individuals have (or can learn to have) direct access to cognitive systems. However, by the time of the cognitive revolution, few (if any) psychologists still believed that direct access to cognitive systems is possible. Modern linguistic theory, as a direct product of the cognitive revolution, has never assumed that speakers have direct access to the grammatical system, just the behavioral outputs of that system (see also Chomsky 1965; Schütze 1996).

1.2   The need for judgment data

Judgment data play a crucial role in linguistic investigation because they provide information not readily available from other kinds of data. Most importantly, they provide evidence (under certain assumptions) about the grammaticality of utterances that have never been naturally produced. (There are no known brain measures that are sensitive to all and only the ungrammatical sentences, and failure to appear in even a very large corpus [such as the Web] is not evidence for ungrammaticality; nor is appearance evidence for grammaticality – see Schütze 2009.) Acceptability judgments provide evidence about the status of phenomena that occur so rarely in spontaneous language use that we could not otherwise learn about them. And acceptability judgments sometimes demonstrate knowledge of language in speakers whose behavior on other tasks does not evince the same degree of knowledge: Linebarger, Schwartz, and Saffran (1983) showed this with respect to syntax for people with agrammatic aphasia, and Toribio (2001) showed that balanced bilinguals who (for ideological reasons) do not exhibit code-switching behavior nevertheless can provide judgments of the well-formedness of code-switched sentences. A further advantage of judgment data over spontaneous usage data is that the latter will include some proportion of production errors (slips of the tongue/pen/keyboard, etc.), the vast majority of which will be judged as ill-formed by the very speakers who produced them, and which therefore should not be generated by the grammar. Unlike analyzing corpora, collecting judgments allows the researcher to question speakers about what they have said. (See also the discussion of stimulated recall in Chapter 7.) And judgments can be collected in language communities where the use of expensive laboratory equipment is infeasible, and for which there are no corpora available. In light of all of these considerations, the increasingly common suggestion that acceptability judgments should be eliminated as a source of evidence for linguistics (e.g., Sampson 2007) would be not only counter-productive, but in fact lethal to the field's progress.

1.3   Formal and informal judgment collection

While the elicitation of acceptability judgments is itself a behavioral experiment – the speaker is asked for a voluntary response to a stimulus – the majority of judgment collection that has been carried out by linguists over the past 50 years has been quite informal by the standards of experimental cognitive science. Some have defended this practice on the grounds that it has worked sufficiently well in the past and has led to rapid development of the field (Phillips and Lasnik 2003; Phillips and Wagers 2007; Phillips 2009), while others have criticized linguistics for its informal approach (Keller 2000; Ferreira 2005; Wasow and Arnold 2005; Featherston 2007; Gibson and Fedorenko 2010, 2013), suggesting the field may be on shaky empirical ground as a result. The former group have sometimes suggested that following the recommendations of the latter group would entail wasted time and effort that would be better devoted to theoretical matters. We consider it an empirical question whether linguistics would arrive at different conclusions if it followed the more formal (and more time-consuming) experimental structure of nearby fields. We will therefore review recent experimental work that has sought to address the question directly, in the hopes of providing researchers with the information to decide for themselves how to go about collecting their data.

There are five major respects in which typical informal linguistic judgment gathering tends to differ from standard practice in psychology. It typically involves (i) relatively few speakers (fewer than ten), (ii) linguists themselves as the participants, (iii) relatively impoverished response options (such as just "acceptable," "unacceptable," and perhaps "marginal"), (iv) relatively few tokens of the structures of interest, and (v) relatively unsystematic data analysis. The first three issues – sample size, the naiveté of the participants, and response scales – have been explicitly studied; we discuss them in Sections 3.3, 3.4, and 2, respectively. (See also the discussion of sample size in Chapter 5.) As we shall see, it is not obvious what the "best" choice is in each case, because all methods appear to provide relatively reliable results. The latter two issues – number of tokens and statistical analysis – we take to be fairly uncontroversial; they are discussed in Sections 3.2.3 and 4.1, respectively. (See also Chapters 14–16 for more discussion of statistics.) For now, we look at some case studies that compare formally and informally collected judgment data.

Gibson and Fedorenko (2013) report such comparisons for seven sentence types taken from previous literature. The informally reported judgments for the relevant comparisons suggest that there are differences among the sentence types, but in their formal experiments Gibson and Fedorenko find no significant differences. (However, see Section 3.3 for more on two of the contrasts they tested.) This, they argue, proves that it is possible that the informal methods that have characterized data collection in syntactic theory have led to unsound theorizing. In contrast, Sprouse and Almeida (2012) adopted the following approach in an effort to determine how different the data underlying syntactic theory would be if formal experiments were used to establish a representative set of data points that form part of the foundation of generative syntactic theory. They tested 469 data points from an introductory syntax textbook (Adger 2003) in formal experiments using 440 naive participants, the magnitude estimation and yes-no tasks (see Section 2), and three different types of statistical analyses (traditional null hypothesis significance tests, linear mixed-effects models [Baayen, Davidson, and Bates 2008], and Bayes factor analyses [Rouder et al. 2009]). The results of that study suggest that the maximum replication failure rate between the informal and formal judgments for those 469 data points is 2 percent. When it comes to the data being used as the basis for ongoing research (i.e., examples in journal articles), Sprouse, Schütze, and Almeida (in press) randomly sampled 296 sentence types forming 148 two-sentence phenomena from *Linguistic Inquiry* published between 2001 and 2010. By re-testing this random sample in formal experiments, they were able to estimate a minimum replication rate for data points published in *Linguistic Inquiry* (2001–2010) with a margin of error of ±5 percent. They found that 95 percent of the phenomena replicated using formal experiments, suggesting a minimum replication rate for journal data of 95 percent ±5. Taken together, these studies suggest that replacing informal with formal judgment data would have very little impact on the shape or empirical coverage of syntactic theory (see also Featherston 2009 and Phillips 2009 for similar conclusions).

2   Judgment tasks

Judgment tasks can be divided into two categories: non-numerical (or qualitative) tasks and numerical (or quantitative) tasks. This distinction has direct implications for the types of research questions that they can be used to answer. As we will see, non-numerical tasks such as the forced-choice (Section 2.1) and yes-no tasks (Section 2.2) are designed to detect *qualitative* differences between conditions, but in the process they sacrifice some of the information about the *size of the difference*. In contrast, the numerical tasks such as Likert scaling (Section 2.3) and magnitude estimation (Section 2.4) are designed to provide information about the *size of the difference*, but in the process they may lose power to detect small differences between conditions.

2.1   Forced-choice task

In a forced-choice (FC) task, participants are presented with two (or more) sentences, and instructed to choose the sentence that is most (or least) acceptable (perhaps by filling in a corresponding circle or radio button), as in Figure 3.1. In this way, FC is explicitly designed to qualitatively compare two (or

What do you think that John bought?	O
What do you wonder whether John bought?	O

Figure 3.1. *An example of a two-alternative forced-choice task*

more) conditions, and directly answer the qualitative question, *Is there a difference between these conditions?* (The assumption is that if there is actually no difference, random answering should yield a roughly 50/50 split.)

There are two major benefits to FC tasks. First, FC tasks are relatively easy to deploy, since each trial in an FC task is an isolated experiment unto itself. In other words, participants do not need to see any sentences other than the two (or more) being directly compared in order to complete the trial accurately. (See Section 3.2.4 for the need to use fillers in quantitative tasks.) The second benefit of FC tasks is increased statistical power to detect differences between conditions (see Section 3.3). FC tasks are the only task explicitly designed for the comparison of two (or more) conditions; the other tasks compare conditions indirectly through a response scale (either yes-no, or a numerical scale).

There are two primary limitations of FC tasks. First, they can only indirectly provide information about the *size of the difference* between conditions, in the form of the proportion of responses (e.g., 80 percent choose condition 1 over condition 2, versus 65 percent choose condition 3 over condition 4 – see Myers 2009). Therefore, if the nature of the research question is simply to ascertain the existence of a predicted acceptability contrast, the FC task seems to be the optimal choice, but if the research question is quantitative in nature, it may be better to use one of the numerical tasks. Second, the task provides no information about where a given sentence stands on the overall scale of acceptability. For linguistic purposes, this is often important: a difference between two sentences, both of which are at the high or low end of the acceptability spectrum, may call for a different kind of explanation than a difference between two sentences in the middle of the spectrum.

2.2   Yes-no task

In the yes-no (YN) task, illustrated in Figure 3.2, participants are presented with one sentence at a time and instructed to judge the sentence as a member of one of two categories: acceptable/yes or unacceptable/no. The YN task is similar to the FC task in that it is primarily a qualitative task; however, there are also substantial differences. The YN task is designed to answer the question, *Does this sentence belong to the yes-category or the no-category?* In this way, the YN task probes the relationship between a single sentence and the two categories

What do you wonder whether John bought?	O Yes O No

Figure 3.2. *An example of the yes-no task*

presented to the participant (rather than the relationship between two sentences as in the FC task). However, it is not clear whether all speakers use the same category boundary between yes-no, nor whether the yes-no boundary in any given speaker maps to the theoretically relevant grammatical/ungrammatical boundary, assuming there is such a boundary.

The primary advantage of the YN task is that it is quick to deploy. Moreover, as with the FC task, several researchers have demonstrated that the YN task can be used to compare the relative difference between conditions, by computing the proportion of yes-responses for each condition (Myers 2009; Bader and Häussler 2010).

The primary disadvantage of the YN task is that it is likely less sensitive than the FC task at detecting qualitative differences between two conditions (because the difference is always relative to the category boundary) and likely less sensitive than the quantitative tasks at establishing numerical estimates of the difference between conditions (because the difference is indirectly computed through proportions).

2.3   Likert scale task

In a Likert scale (LS) task, participants are given a numerical scale, with the endpoints defined as acceptable or unacceptable, and asked to rate each sentence along the scale. The most commonly used scales, as in Figure 3.3, usually consist of an odd number of points (such as 1–5 or 1–7) because odd numbers contain a precise middle point; however, if the research goals require it, a preference can be forced by choosing an even number of points. One of the primary benefits of LS is that it is both numerical and intuitive. The former means that LS can be used to answer questions about the *size of a difference* between conditions by leveraging inferential statistical tests such as ANOVA and linear mixed-effects modeling.

The primary limitations of LS are all related to the use of the numerical scale. For example, the scale itself suggests that the intervals between points are uniform: the interval between 1 and 2 is one unit, the interval between 2 and 3 is one unit, and so on. However, because participants can only use the limited number of response points (i.e., there is no 3.5 on the scale), it is impossible to ensure that the intervals are truly uniform – that is, that subjects treat the difference between 1 and 2 the same as the difference between 4 and 5. This problem is compounded when aggregating across participants in a sample. In practice, this risk can be minimized by including anchoring examples at the beginning of the experiment to establish some of the points along the scale (see Section 3.2.1). Furthermore, participants'

Figure 3.3. *An example of a Likert scale task*

Standard:	Who thinks that my brother was kept tabs on by the FBI?
Acceptability:	100
Item:	What do you wonder whether John bought?
Acceptability:	____

Figure 3.4. *An example of the magnitude estimation task*

responses can be z-score transformed (see Section 4.1.1) prior to analysis to eliminate some additional forms of bias such as scale compression (e.g., using only points 3–5 on a 1–7 scale) or scale skew (e.g., using only the high end of the scale).

2.4   Magnitude estimation task

In the magnitude estimation (ME) task, participants are given a reference sentence and told that the acceptability of the reference sentence is a specific numerical value (e.g., 100). The reference sentence is called the *standard* and the value it is assigned is called the *modulus*. Participants are then asked to rate additional sentences as a proportion of the value of the standard, as in Figure 3.4. For example, a sentence that is twice as acceptable as the standard would be rated 200.

ME was developed by Stevens (1957) explicitly to overcome the problem of potentially non-uniform, and therefore non-meaningful, intervals in the LS task (in the domain of psychophysics). In the ME task, the standard is meant to act as a unit of measure for all of the other sentences in the experiment. In this way, the intervals between sentences can be expressed as proportions of the standard (the unit of measure). This offers the theoretical possibility of substantially more accurate ratings (Bard, Robertson, and Sorace 1996; Cowart 1997; Keller 2000; Featherston 2005a, 2005b) than the LS task. In addition, the response scale in ME is the entire positive number line, which means that participants can in principle report a potentially infinite number of levels of acceptability (Bard, Robertson, and Sorace 1996; Keller 2000), as opposed to the (typically small) finite number in the LS task. As a numerical task, an ME experiment requires the same design properties as an LS task (see Section 3). The choice of the standard can affect the amount of the number line that is available for ratings: a highly acceptable standard set at a modulus of 100 means that nearly all ratings will be between 0 and 100, whereas a relatively unacceptable standard means that nearly all ratings will be above 100. For this reason, and in order to prevent certain types of response strategies, it is normal practice to employ a standard that it is in the middle range of acceptability.

Unfortunately, a series of recent studies of the ME task have called into question many of its purported benefits. First, although the availability of any positive real number as a response would in theory allow participants to rate every stimulus differently, in practice this is not at all what they do. Rather, they use a small set of (typically whole) numbers repeatedly, and (many or all of) the members of that set often stand in a salient relationship to one another that does not seem to depend on the stimuli (e.g., multiples of five or ten). Second, one of the primary assumptions of the ME task is that participants truly use the reference sentence as a unit of measurement. In order for this to be true, participants must be able to make a ratio comparison of two sentences (e.g., the acceptability of sentence B is 1.5 times the acceptability of sentence A). Adapting a series of techniques developed in the psychophysics literature (Narens 1996; Luce 2002), Sprouse (2011) tested this assumption directly, and found that participants could not make ratio comparisons of the acceptability of two sentences. This failure of the primary assumption of the ME task suggests that participants may be treating the ME task as a type of LS task, only with an open and infinite response scale. Why this is true is still an open question, although one possibility is that the lack of a meaningful zero point for acceptability (i.e., the concept of absolutely no acceptability) prevents participants from making ratio judgments. This finding accords well with the results of a direct comparison between ME and LS tasks for several sentence types in German that was conducted by Weskott and Fanselow (2011): they found that there is no evidence of increased sensitivity of ME over LS, though there is increased variance, which is likely due to the increased number of response options in ME.

The burgeoning consensus among researchers is that the true value of ME lies in the increased number of levels of acceptability that participants can report – though this might come at the cost of higher variance and is not unique to ME (see Section 2.5) – and the sociological impact on the field of using a task that is perceived as more sophisticated than LS. Countervailing drawbacks include the fact that magnitude estimation is less intuitive for many participants than traditional scales (and hence more time-consuming and labor-intensive for experimenters), and some participants do not apply the task to sentence judgments in the intended way and their data must be discarded.

2.5   The thermometer task

Some researchers have proposed new tasks that are intended to combine the intuitive nature of point scales with the sensitivity of ME. For example, Featherston (2008) has proffered a "thermometer task" in which participants are given two reference sentences with associated acceptability values, such as 20 and 40 (analogous to freezing and boiling points). They can then choose values for target sentences along the real number line relative to those two points by treating it as a linear scale – for example, a target whose acceptability is halfway between the acceptability of the two reference sentences would be rated 30.

2.6   The fundamental similarity of acceptability judgment tasks

Before concluding this section, it is important to note that at a fundamental level, all of the acceptability judgment tasks are the same: the participants are asked to perform the same *cognitive task* – that is, to report their perceptions of acceptability. Because the cognitive task is the same, the data yielded by each task are likely to be very similar (modulo small differences in the response scale discussed above), especially when the criterion for comparison is the detection of differences between conditions. Indeed, this is exactly what has been found by several recent studies that have directly compared the various judgment tasks. For example, Bader and Haüssler (2010) compared ME and YN tasks for several sentence types in German, and found that both tasks detected differences between the conditions (at the chosen sample sizes). Similarly, Weskott and Fanselow (2011) compared the ME, LS, and YN tasks for several other sentence types in German, and found that all three tasks detected differences between the conditions (at the chosen sample sizes). Though there are likely to be differences between tasks with respect to statistical power (e.g., Sprouse and Almeida, "Power in acceptability judgment experiments," unpublished), when it comes to simply *detecting a difference* between conditions at relatively large sample sizes (e.g., twenty-five participants), the fact that the cognitive task is identical across these measures strongly suggests that choice of task is relatively inconsequential.

3   Designing judgment experiments

Chapters 7 and 8 of this volume provide general discussion of many issues in experimental design. There are also several excellent resources for interested readers to learn the mechanics of creating multiple lexicalizations, distributing items according to a Latin square, pseudorandomizing items, and so on (e.g., see Cowart 1997; L. A. Stowe and E. Kaan, "Developing an Experiment: Techniques and Design," unpublished). In this chapter we focus on methodological issues that are particularly germane to the design of judgment experiments.

3.1   Instructions

While there is no standard way of wording the instructions for a judgment experiment, there is general agreement that we want to convey to speakers that certain aspects of sentences are *not* of interest to us and should not factor into their responses. These include violations of prescriptive grammar rules, the likelihood that the sentence would actually be uttered in real life, and the truth or plausibility of its content. See Chapter 6 for more on these effects. We also want to avoid the question of the sentence being understandable, since uncontroversially ungrammatical sentences are often perfectly comprehensible (e.g., *What did he wanted?*). It is common to instruct participants to imagine that the sentences were being *spoken* by a friend, and ask whether the sentences would make them *sound* like a native speaker of their language. Crucially, this formulation invokes the spoken modality even with written surveys, and attempts to guide the participant toward a notion of acceptability that is tied to native-speaker ability rather than frequency or plausibility.

One question that is often asked by researchers who are new to acceptability judgments is to what extent the instructions of the experiment can influence the results. The consensus among experienced acceptability judgment experimentalists is that the exact nature of the instructions (modulo the issues discussed in the previous paragraph) matters relatively little. To put this another way, the experimenter has relatively little control over how participants choose to respond to the sentences presented to them. Cowart (1997) suggests that this means that experimenters should focus on controlling the experiment (materials, fillers, etc.) rather than controlling the behavior of the participant. Unfortunately, because most experienced experimenters do not believe that there is much effect of instructions on acceptability judgments, the formal data on this subject are relatively limited. Cowart (1997) compared what he calls "intuitive" instructions, like those described in the previous paragraph, with "prescriptive" instructions that explicitly asked participants to evaluate the well-formedness of sentences in the context of an undergraduate term paper, and found no substantive difference in the pattern of acceptability for several sentence types (though there was one significant absolute difference in the ratings of one of the sentence types).

3.2   Materials

3.2.1   Practice items

Acceptability judgment tasks are generally considered intuitively natural for participants. As such, explicit practice sessions are generally unnecessary to familiarize participants with the task. However, there are a few specific instances where certain types of practice items may be helpful.

In the LS task, it is common to provide *anchor* items for certain points on the scale, to help ensure that every participant uses the scale the same way (thus minimizing scale bias; see Section 4.1.1). An anchor item is a single sentence token that the researcher assigns to a single point on the rating scale. It is not necessary to provide an anchor for every point on the scale. Instead, it is common to provide an anchor for the lowest point (to establish a floor) and for the highest point (to establish a ceiling). Some researchers also provide an anchor for the midpoint of the scale. It is also common to include five to ten items at the very beginning of the survey whose sole purpose is to help the participants become familiar with using the scale. These items are not marked in any way, so the participant is unaware that they are distinct from the rest of the experiment. These items generally cover the full range of acceptability, so that by the end of the sequence the participant will have used every point along the scale at least once. These items are technically fillers in that they will not be analyzed in the service of an experimental hypothesis, but they may be more profitably thought of as *unannounced* practice items.

In the ME task, it is common to include an initial (announced) practice phase in which participants conduct a simple ME task comparing line lengths, to ensure that they understand the basic premise of the ME task. This practice phase is usually short, perhaps five to ten items. After the practice phase is concluded, participants are introduced to the idea of using ME to rate the acceptability of sentences. Given recent evidence that participants may not be making ratio judgments and instead may be treating ME tasks as a type of rating task similar to LS tasks (Sprouse 2011), it is probably also a good idea to include unannounced practice items with ME tasks as well.

3.2.2 Factorial designs

If you have chosen to conduct a formal experiment, it is likely that your hypothesis requires quantifying relative differences in acceptability, above and beyond simply establishing that two sentences are different (see Section 2 for more about the relationship between tasks and the types of information that they provide). In such cases, it is generally useful to consider using fully crossed factorial designs (see also Myers 2009 and Chapter 7). For example, imagine that you are interested in testing the effect of D-linking on Complex Noun Phrase Constraint (CNPC) violations. You would start by comparing the acceptability of a CNPC violation with non-D-linked wh-words (*what*) to the same configuration with D-linked wh-phrases (*which book*) as in (1):

(1)   a. What did you make the claim that John bought?
         b. Which book did you make the claim that John bought?

Imagine that you find that (1b) is more acceptable than (1a). Can you claim that D-linking improves the acceptability of CNPC violations? Not really. It may be that D-linking improves the acceptability of *all* sentences, even those that do not contain a CNPC violation. To test this, you need to compare two additional sentences:

(2)   a. What did you claim that John bought?
         b. Which book did you claim that John bought?

Now the question is whether the difference between (1a) and (1b) is smaller than, equal to, or larger than the difference between (2a) and (2b). This will tell us whether D-linking has a specific effect on CNPC violations, or whether it has the same effect on all extractions from embedded clauses. The four sentences in (1) and (2) form a *factorial design*, as there are two factors (embedded clause type and wh-phrase type), each with two levels (± island, ± D-linking), that give rise to the four conditions. Factorial designs are the best tool an experimenter has for isolating the factors that could give rise to relative differences in acceptability.

3.2.3 Multiple lexicalizations

Most hypotheses in linguistics are not about individual sentences but about types of sentences – that is, all sentences that have a particular structural property. This fact is sometimes obscured when reading linguistics articles, where often just one or two examples are presented. However, these are almost always intended to be representative exemplars. The assumption is that the author has considered a range of possible lexicalizations to verify the generality of their claim, and is simply saving space by not reporting all of them. The same procedure should apply in conducting formal experiments. Whenever possible, it is desirable to create multiple lexicalizations of each condition (ideally eight or more) and distribute them evenly among the participants, in an effort to minimize the contribution of particular lexical items, facts about real-world plausibility, and so on, to the results. In experiments with one sentence per trial rather than a pair of sentences to compare, we use a distribution procedure to ensure that no one participant sees the same lexicalization of related conditions. The most common distribution procedure is called a Latin square (for details of the mechanics, see Stowe and Kaan unpublished and Chapter 7).

3.2.4   Fillers

In most experiments it is beneficial to include filler items (i.e., sentences that are not related to the research question). These can serve at least three purposes. First, they can reduce the density of the critical comparisons across the whole experiment, reducing the chances that participants will become aware that a particular sentence type is being tested, which could trigger conscious response strategies. Second, they can be used to try to ensure that all the possible responses (yes and no, or points along a scale) are used about equally often. This helps to protect against scale bias, which occurs when one participant decides to use the response scale differently from other participants, such as only using one end of the scale (skew), or only using a limited range of responses (compression). (See also Section 4.1.1 for statistical approaches to mitigating the effect of scale bias.) Third, they can be used to investigate a separate research question.

3.3   Sample size and statistical power

Informal judgment experiments of the sort that linguists carry out every day tend to be conducted on relatively few participants (almost always fewer than ten),[1] whereas formal judgment experiments tend to use samples of twenty or more. Whether differences in sample size are relevant for the reliability of the results is an empirical question that can only be answered relative to the sentence types under investigation. Sprouse and Almeida (unpublished) analyzed the relationship between sample size and the probability of detecting a significant difference (also known as *statistical power*) for forty-seven two-sentence phenomena from *Linguistic Inquiry* 2001–2010 (Sprouse, Schütze, and Almeida in press) for all four judgment tasks: ME, LS, YN, and FC.

Sprouse and Almeida (unpublished) found that (i) the FC task is substantially more powerful than the other three tasks at detecting differences between

---

[1] Sometimes this is by necessity. In the case of languages spoken in remote locations and languages with few remaining speakers, collecting data from just one or two speakers may be all that a linguist can practically do (see Chapter 4). Nothing in what follows is meant to lessen the value of such linguistic fieldwork.

conditions, especially for small and medium-sized effects; (ii) the ME and LS tasks are approximately equally powered, albeit less powerful than the FC task; and (iii) the YN task is the least powerful of the four. Sprouse and Almeida provide several types of comparisons to illustrate these power differences, but perhaps the most striking is in terms of empirical coverage. Following the conventions of experimental psychology, Sprouse and Almeida assume that experimenters should strive for at least 80 percent power (i.e., an 80 percent chance of detecting a true difference when one exists) in their experiments. They then ran re-sampling simulations on their results to empirically estimate the number of phenomena in *Linguistic Inquiry* (2001–2010) that would be detected with 80 percent power for every possible sample size between five and one hundred participants. The results suggest that the FC task would be well-powered (i.e., reach 80 percent power) for the detection of 70 percent of the phenomena published in *Linguistic Inquiry* (2001–2010), with only ten participants each providing only one judgment per phenomenon (i.e., ten observations total). With only fifteen participants (each providing one judgment per phenomenon), the empirical coverage of the FC task rises to 80 percent of the phenomena in *Linguistic Inquiry*. In contrast, ten participants in the ME and LS tasks lead to less than 60 percent coverage of the phenomena in *Linguistic Inquiry*. The ME and LS tasks require thirty to thirty-five participants to reach the 80 percent coverage that the FC task achieves with only fifteen participants. Finally, the YN task only achieves 40 percent coverage with ten participants, and requires forty participants to reach 80 percent coverage. Of course, these power estimates are lower bounds, inasmuch as they assume that each participant provides only one judgment per condition. Increasing the number of judgments per condition will also increase statistical power, thereby decreasing the required sample sizes.

As a concrete example of the importance of understanding the relationship between sample size, task, and statistical power, let's take a closer look at two effects that have been reported in the linguistics literature using linguists' judgments, but have failed to replicate with larger, formal experiments. The first is the center embedding effect from Frazier (1985), attributed to Janet Fodor, where linguists' judgments suggested that doubly center-embedded sentences can be made more acceptable by deleting the second VP, as in (3b).

(3)   a. *The ancient manuscript that the graduate student who the new card catalog
            had confused a great deal was studying in the library was missing a page.
         b. ?The ancient manuscript that the graduate student who the new card
            catalog had confused a great deal was missing a page.

Formal experiments reported by Gibson and Thomas (1999) using an LS task failed to corroborate this difference. However, Sprouse and Almeida (2013) found that this is likely due to the relatively large sample sizes that are required to detect this difference in numerical rating tasks: they report that at least seventy-eight participants (giving one judgment each) are required to detect this difference with 80 percent power with the ME task. The fact that the FC task, which is likely the task used both by Fodor and by Frazier (1985) to detect the center-embedding effect, tends to be more powerful than numerical rating tasks at detecting differences (Sprouse and Almeida unpublished) is one possible explanation for the failure to replicate in Gibson and Thomas (1999).

A similar situation is reported by Gibson and Fedorenko (2013). They note that Gibson (1991) reported a contrast between doubly embedded object relative clauses in subject versus object position, as in (4), using informal judgments provided by himself and other linguists:

(4)   a. *The man that the woman that the dog bit likes eats fish.
            b. ?I saw the man that the woman that the dog bit likes.

However, Gibson and Fedorenko report that subsequent experiments using LS tasks have failed to replicate this result (unfortunately, they do not report the details of these experiments). Sprouse and Almeida (2013) tested this contrast in an FC task with ninety-nine naive participants, and then ran power analyses like those in Sprouse and Almeida (unpublished) to determine a target sample size. They found that a sample size of eleven is required to detect the difference in (4) with 80 percent power using the FC task. Although they do not have data for numerical tasks, based on the power analyses in Sprouse and Almeida (unpublished), phenomena that require eleven participants in the FC task tend to require thirty to thirty-five participants in the LS task. If the experiments reported by Gibson and Fedorenko (2013) used fewer than thirty to thirty-five participants, then the lack of replication of the Gibson (1991) informal results could simply be due to relative power differences between the FC and LS tasks.

There are two important lessons in these case studies. First, it is critical to understand the relationship between sample size, task, and statistical power when designing an experiment. Although it may seem impossible to estimate a required sample size *before* collecting the data, it is possible to use existing power studies, such as Sprouse and Almeida (unpublished), to estimate the sample size required for a given phenomenon by comparing your judgments of the size of the difference in your conditions to the phenomena that they tested. Second, it is important to realize that the failure to find an effect in a formal experiment does not mean that there is no effect to be found: the experiment may simply have been underpowered.

3.4   Naive versus expert participants

One of the most contentious aspects of judgment data is whether they should be collected from trained linguists versus naive speakers. It would not be especially surprising if it turned out that linguists do not have the same judgments as non-linguists (see below for empirical evidence on this point). Even if that is true, however, it does not follow that using linguists' judgments is bad for the field – that would depend on how and why linguists behave differently. This is a harder question to answer empirically, and in our opinion it remains an open one.

A priori, one can imagine at least two ways in which judgments from the two populations might diverge. One is that linguists as participants will likely be aware of the theoretical consequences of their judgments, and may be subconsciously biased to report judgments consonant with their theoretical viewpoints (Edelman and Christiansen 2003; Ferreira 2005; Wasow and Arnold 2005; Gibson and Fedorenko 2010, 2013). On the other hand, professional linguists may provide a sort of expert knowledge that increases the reliability, and possibly the sensitivity, of their judgments over non-linguists' judgments (see Newmeyer 1983, 2007, as well as Fanselow 2007, Grewendorf 2007, and Haider 2007, for possible examples in German; and Devitt 2006, 2010, Culbertson and Gross 2009, and Gross and Culbertson 2011, for a discussion of what could be meant by "expert knowledge"). Valian (1982) makes a case in favor of using such expert linguistic judgments, based on an analogy to wine tasting, which relies on the acquired ability to detect subtle distinctions that inexperienced wine drinkers simply cannot make. Linguists may have similarly heightened sensitivity, or they may be more practiced at factoring out aspects of sentences that are irrelevant to their grammatical status.

There are several examples of demonstrated differences between populations in the literature. For example, Spencer (1973), Gordon and Hendrick (1997), and Dąbrowska (2010) all report differences in ratings between linguists and non-linguists; Culbertson and Gross (2009) report differences between participants who have completed a formal experiment previously and participants who have not; and Dąbrowska (2010) reports differences between generative linguists and functional linguists in the ratings of CNPC violations. However, we know of no studies that have conclusively established the cause of the differences (which would require careful parametric manipulations of the relevant grouping factors over a series of experiments), and no studies that have demonstrated that these differences would lead to major differences in theoretical conclusions (indeed, many of the differences appear to be in absolute ratings, but not in the relative pattern of acceptability – the latter generally being the data upon which theories are built).

4   Interpreting judgment data

4.1   Statistical analysis

As in most of experimental psychology, the analysis of judgment data involves two steps: pre-processing, which covers operations performed prior to statistical tests, and the statistical tests themselves.

4.1.1   Data pre-processing

The pre-processing of numerical judgment data generally involves two steps. The first is common to all data in experimental psychology: the identification of participants who did not perform the task correctly, and the identification of extreme outliers in the responses. We will not discuss this basic step further as we assume that readers can consult general experimental textbooks for the logic and mechanics of participant and outlier removal (e.g., Stowe and Kaan unpublished), though it should be noted that there are as yet no generally agreed upon procedures for participant and outlier removal for acceptability judgments. The second step is common to many scale-based data types: each participant's responses are transformed using the *z-score transformation* to eliminate some of the potential scale bias that was mentioned above. The z-score transformation allows us to express each participant's responses on a *standardized* scale. It is calculated as follows: For a given participant P, calculate the mean and standard deviation of all of P's judgments. Next, subtract each of P's judgments from the mean. Finally, divide each of these differences by P's standard deviation. The resulting set of responses (z-scores) represents a *standardized* form of P's responses, as each response is expressed in standard deviation units from P's mean. The process is repeated for each participant so that every participant's responses are reported on a scale based on standard deviation units. The z-score transformation is a linear transformation, which means that it maintains all of the relationships that exist within the data (i.e., it adds no distortion).

Many researchers, including us, believe that the z-score transformation should be used routinely for both LS and ME judgment data. However, from time to time, some researchers disagree. The most common criticism of the z-score transformation for LS data is that LS data are not continuous, whereas the z-score transformation transforms these bounded responses into a continuous scale for each participant. However, if you plan to run parametric statistical tests on LS data (e.g., *t*-tests, ANOVAs, linear mixed-effects models), then you are already assuming that you can treat LS data as continuous for practical purposes. So there is no harm in applying the z-score transformation first, and there are many benefits. If you do not wish to treat LS data as continuous, then you should run non-parametric statistical tests. These tests convert each participant's data into ranks before analysis, which actually eliminates scale bias in the process, so there is no reason to run a z-score transformation prior to non-parametric tests. However, non-parametric tests are generally less sensitive than parametric tests (see Chapter 15), so this is less ideal than the use of z-score transformations and parametric tests.

The most common criticism of the use of z-score transformations for ME data is that ME data should be *log-transformed* instead. The purported rationale behind the log-transformation with ME data is that it will eliminate right-tail outliers that arise because the scale in ME tasks is open-ended to the right and bounded to the left. However, the log-transformation is a powerful transformation that is normally not recommended for simple outlier removal. It is a non-linear transformation, which means it distorts the relationships within the data; therefore it should only be used when absolutely necessary. The log-transformation is intended to be used when the distribution of the data is log-normal, which is a type of logarithmic distribution, as the log transformation (by definition) transforms a log-normal distribution into a normal distribution. Unfortunately, this means that if the log-transformation is applied to non-log-normal distributions, it will transform them into non-normal distributions. In our experience, judgments are never distributed log-normally (and are very often distributed normally), so the log-transformation is inappropriate.[2]

4.1.2   Statistical tests

The current best practice in the experimental syntax literature is to use *linear mixed-effects models* for the analysis of numerical judgment data (LS and ME), and to use *logistic mixed-effects models* for the analysis of non-numerical judgment data (FC and YN) (see Baayen 2007; Baayen, Davidson, and Bates 2008; and Chapter 16). However, as mentioned above, from time to time some researchers worry that parametric statistical tests should not be used to analyze judgment data, particularly LS data. The concern usually revolves around the response scale: many believe that LS tasks fail to meet the assumption of parametric tests that the responses are on an interval or ratio scale. While it is important to take the assumptions of statistical tests seriously, the actual situation is more complex. Parametric tests involve several assumptions (including random sampling from the parent population, normality of the parent populations of each condition, and homogeneity of the variances of the conditions) that are rarely met in psychological research. The question then is when it is tolerable to violate the assumptions and when it is not. A full discussion of this question is beyond the scope of this chapter (see Chapter 15; for interesting reviews of the use of null hypothesis significance testing in psychology, see Hunter and May 1993, Nickerson 2000, Gigerenzer, Krauss, and Vitouch 2004, and references therein). At a practical level, the nearly universal use of parametric tests in psychology suggests that the field has decided (consciously or not) that it is willing to tolerate the potential consequences of the violations of parametric tests. Hunter and May (1993) evaluate this decision in relation to the alternative – the adoption of non-parametric tests, which do not carry the same assumptions as parametric tests. They argue that the application of many standard parametric tests (e.g., *t*-tests and *F*-tests) in scenarios where the assumptions are not met (e.g., lack of random sampling) actually approximates the application of non-parametric tests (e.g., randomization tests).[3]

---

[2] We are not sure why many researchers assume that the log-transformation should be standard practice for ME experiments, but one possibility is that it has arisen due to the presence of log-transformations in early psychophysical studies, which were used for reasons not relevant to current judgment experiments.

[3] There are differences between the inferences licensed by parametric and non-parametric tests. For example, when all of the assumptions are met, parametric tests can be used to make inferences about population parameters from the samples in the experiment. Non-parametric tests, which do not assume random sampling, can only be used to make inferences about the sample(s) in the experiment itself. As Hunter and May point out (see also Nickerson 2000), it is relatively rare for experimental psychologists to be interested in population parameters; instead, they tend to be concerned with establishing a significant difference between two samples within a well-controlled experiment. So even this consequence of the parametric/non-parametric distinction may be relatively benign within experimental psychology.

4.2   Interpreting variation across participants

Finding a statistically significant effect for some set of participants does not mean that every participant demonstrated the effect. In practice, given sufficient statistical power, very few participants need to show the effect in order for the sample as a whole to show a significant effect. What should one make of such variability? What if 75 percent show the effect and 25 percent do not? What if only 25 percent show the effect, and 75 percent do not? (As Raaijmakers [2003] points out, statistical significance can still be achieved in such circumstances.) What if some of those who do not show the expected effect actually show the opposite effect? There seem to be three different approaches to this problem:

1.   Variation as noise: On this view, since all measurement involves noise, only the central tendency of the sample matters, and it is expected that not every participant or every item in the sample will show the difference. This interpretation is the default assumption in experimental psychology and much of the experimental syntax literature.

2.   Variation as dialect/idiolect: On this view, if a large enough proportion of participants do not show the predicted effect, this might be evidence for a different grammar for that subset of participants. In psychology, this is not usually a possible interpretation, because the population of interest is all humans; in linguistics, the population of interest is all speakers of a given language, so it is always a logical possibility that the participants who do not show an effect have a different grammar (or perhaps control additional lexical variants in the sense of Adger's (2006, 2007) combinatorial variability approach) from the speakers who do show the effect (den Dikken et al. 2007). Unfortunately, it is nearly impossible to establish the existence of a dialectal/idiolectal difference in a single experiment; conclusive evidence generally requires systematic parametric manipulations of potential dialectal/idiolectal grouping factors across several experiments. (See Chapter 5 for considerations in sampling participants, and Gervain (2003) for the potential use of cluster analysis for the detection of dialects/idiolects.)

3.   Variation as disconfirmation: On this view, given a strong hypothesis that ungrammatical sentences should be overwhelmingly judged to be unacceptable, a large enough proportion of participants that fail to show the predicted effect will be taken as evidence that the theoretical prediction is disconfirmed. If so, the difference (among those who do show it) is not due to the grammar. The assumption here is that a truly grammatical effect should not show a high degree of variability, whereas extra-grammatical effects may (Hoji 2010).

Some criticisms of informal experiments rest upon this assumption (Wasow and Arnold 2005; Gibson and Fedorenko 2010, 2013).

In the literature one can find instances of all three approaches – the field has evidently not reached a consensus on which one is appropriate, or indeed if the answer ought to vary as a function of the question being asked. One way to address the problem is to seek converging evidence from a wide array of types of data whenever possible. The assumption behind this is that random noise will not be consistent across tasks, while grammar-based variation should. Less obvious is the question of whether extra-grammatical sources of variation are expected to be consistent across tasks.

4.3   Interpreting gradience

The freedom provided by magnitude estimation and related tasks to distinguish a theoretically infinite number of levels of acceptability and to quantify the distances between those levels has been a catalyst for some researchers to replace a categorical model of grammar in which there are two distinct categories, grammatical and ungrammatical (possibly with distinctions among the latter), with a gradient model of grammar in which grammaticality is a continuous property. This possibility has recently been explored in several different ways, such as the Optimality Theory approach of Keller (2000), the Generative Grammar approach of Featherston (2005c), and the probabilistic approach of Bresnan (2007). While it is not surprising that judgment tasks yield continuous acceptability values, what is nontrivial is that respondents are consistent in their use of the intermediate levels of acceptability, suggesting that they are indeed tapping into a robust cognitive system that yields gradient results. The key question is whether those gradient results are a reflection of grammatical knowledge on its own, or grammatical knowledge in combination with factors that affect language processing, decision making, and so on, and are already known to display gradient behavior (working memory load, semantic plausibility, lexical and syntactic frequency, prototypicality, etc.).

It is not uncommon to encounter those who believe continuous acceptability necessitates a continuous (or gradient) syntactic system. However, there is no necessary link between the nature of acceptability and the nature of the syntactic system. For example, Armstrong, Gleitman, and Gleitman (1983) and Barsalou (1987) demonstrate that participants can give systematic gradient judgments about concepts that we know to be categorical, such as the concept of *even number*. This observation does not entail that our knowledge of mathematics fails to make a perfectly sharp distinction between even and odd numbers. Rather, our judgments can evidently be sensitive to factors other than our underlying competence. One possibility is that instead of rating the extent to which some number is even, participants may (not necessarily consciously) reinterpret the task as seeking a rating of how representative or typical the properties of a particular number are as compared to the set of even numbers as a whole. Putting it another way, when asked for gradient responses, participants will find some way to oblige the experimenter; if doing so is incompatible with the experimenter's actual question, they apparently infer that the experimenter must have intended to ask something slightly different. By the same logic, gradient acceptability judgments are perfectly compatible with a categorical model of competence. The (admittedly difficult) question facing the experimenter is whether gradient acceptability judgments are the result of the nature of the grammar, the result of gradient processing factors, or simply an artifact of asking participants to provide gradient responses.

5   Conclusion

In closing, we wish to emphasize two points. First, the correct interpretation of acceptability judgment data will ultimately require a theory of the judgment task itself (see Schütze 1996: 175). This will minimally include a theory of grammar, a theory of parsing, a theory of partial parsing in the case of ungrammatical sentences, a theory of rating tasks, and possibly other components. A priori we cannot know which of these components is the source of any given property of judgment data (e.g. gradience) – this is a classic "black-box" problem in cognitive science: several different unobservable systems contribute to the observable behavior. Second, the experimental and analytical techniques discussed in this chapter are no substitute for human thought. In particular, the fact that a carefully conducted experiment yields a significant result is not ipso facto important for any particular theories of grammar, processing, or what have you – it is up to the researcher to interpret it. Likewise, the fact that a carefully conducted experiment fails to yield a significant result does not mean that an effect does not exist – it could simply indicate a flaw in the design, including a lack of sufficient power. Determining what results mean is part of the art of doing science, not a task that the machinery of experimentation can do on its own.

References

Adger, D. 2003. *Core Syntax: A Minimalist Approach*. Oxford University Press.
    2006. Combinatorial variability. *Journal of Linguistics* 42: 503–30.
    2007. Variability and modularity: a response to Hudson. *Journal of Linguistics* 43: 695–700.
Armstrong, S. L., L. R. Gleitman, and H. Gleitman. 1983. What some concepts might not be. *Cognition* 13: 263–308.
Baayen, R. H. 2007. *Analyzing Linguistic Data: A Practical Introduction to Statistics using R*. Cambridge University Press.
Baayen, R. H., D. J. Davidson, and D. M. Bates. 2008. Mixed-effects modeling with crossed random effects for subjects and items. *Journal of Memory and Language* 59: 390–412.

Bader, M. and J. Häussler. 2010. Toward a model of grammaticality judgments. *Journal of Linguistics* 46: 273–330.

Bard, E. G., D. Robertson, and A. Sorace. 1996. Magnitude estimation of linguistic acceptability. *Language* 72: 32–68.

Barsalou, L. W. 1987. The instability of graded structure: implications for the nature of concepts. In U. Neisser, ed. *Concepts and Conceptual Development: Ecological and Intellectual Factors in Categorization*. Cambridge University Press, 101–40.

Bresnan, J. 2007. Is syntactic knowledge probabilistic? Experiments with the English dative alternation. In S. Featherston and W. Sternefeld, eds. *Roots: Linguistics in Search of Its Evidential Base*. Berlin: Mouton de Gruyter, 77–96.

Carr, P. 1990. *Linguistic Realities: An Autonomist Metatheory for the Generative Enterprise*. Cambridge University Press.

Chemla, E. and B. Spector. 2011. Experimental evidence for embedded scalar implicatures. *Journal of Semantics* 28: 359–400.

Chomsky, N. 1965. *Aspects of the Theory of Syntax*. Cambridge, MA: MIT Press.

Cowart, W. 1997. *Experimental Syntax: Applying Objective Methods to Sentence Judgments*. Thousand Oaks, CA: Sage.

Culbertson, J. and J. Gross. 2009. Are linguists better subjects? *British Journal of the Philosophy of Science* 60: 721–36.

Dąbrowska, E. 2010. Naive v. expert intuitions: an empirical study of acceptability judgments. *The Linguistic Review* 27: 1–23.

den Dikken, M., J. Bernstein, C. Tortora, and R. Zanuttini. 2007. Data and grammar: means and individuals. *Theoretical Linguistics* 33: 335–52.

Devitt, M. 2006. Intuitions in linguistics. *British Journal for the Philosophy of Science* 57: 481–513.

    2010. Linguistic intuitions revisited. *British Journal for the Philosophy of Science* 61: 833–65.

Dresher, E. 1995. There's no reality like psychological reality. *Glot International* 1.1: 7.

Edelman, S. and M. Christiansen. 2003. How seriously should we take Minimalist syntax? *Trends in Cognitive Sciences* 7: 60–1.

Fanselow, G. 2007. Carrots – perfect as vegetables, but please not as a main dish. *Theoretical Linguistics* 33: 353–67.

Featherston, S. 2005a. Magnitude estimation and what it can do for your syntax: some wh-constraints in German. *Lingua* 115: 1525–50.

    2005b. Universals and grammaticality: wh-constraints in German and English. *Linguistics* 43: 667–711.

    2005c. The Decathlon Model of empirical syntax. In M. Reis and S. Kepser, eds. *Linguistic Evidence: Empirical, Theoretical, and Computational Perspectives*. Berlin: Mouton de Gruyter, 187–208.

    2007. Data in generative grammar: the stick and the carrot. *Theoretical Linguistics* 33: 269–318.

    2008. Thermometer judgments as linguistic evidence. In C. M. Riehl and A. Rothe, eds. *Was ist linguistische Evidenz?* Aachen: Shaker Verlag, 69–89.

    2009. Relax, lean back, and be a linguist. *Zeitschrift für Sprachwissenschaft* 28: 127–32.

Ferreira, F. 2005. Psycholinguistics, formal grammars, and cognitive science. *The Linguistic Review* 22: 365–80.

Frazier, L. 1985. Syntactic complexity. In D. R. Dowty, L. Karttunen, and A. Zwicky, eds. *Natural Language Parsing: Psychological, Computational, and Theoretical Perspectives*. Cambridge University Press, 129–89.

Gervain, J. 2003. Syntactic microvariation and methodology: problems and perspectives. *Acta Linguistica Hungarica* 50: 405–34.

Gibson, E. 1991. A computational theory of human language processing: memory limitations and processing breakdown. Unpublished Ph.D. dissertation, Carnegie Mellon University.

Gibson, E. and J. Thomas. 1999. Memory limitations and structural forgetting: the perception of complex ungrammatical sentences as grammatical. *Language and Cognitive Processes* 14: 225–48.

Gibson, E. and E. Fedorenko. 2010. Weak quantitative standards in linguistics research. *Trends in Cognitive Sciences* 14: 233–4.

   2013. The need for quantitative methods in syntax and semantics research. *Language and Cognitive Processes* 28.1–2: 88–124.

Gigerenzer, G., S. Krauss, and O. Vitouch. 2004. The null ritual: what you always wanted to know about significance testing but were afraid to ask. In D. Kaplan, ed. *The Sage Handbook of Quantitative Methodology for the Social Sciences*. Thousand Oaks, CA: Sage, 391–408.

Gordon, P. C. and R. Hendrick. 1997. Intuitive knowledge of linguistic co-reference. *Cognition* 62: 325–70.

Grewendorf, G. 2007. Empirical evidence and theoretical reasoning in generative grammar. *Theoretical Linguistics* 33: 369–81.

Gross, S. and J. Culbertson. 2011. Revisited linguistic intuitions. *British Journal of the Philosophy of Science* 62: 639–56.

Haider, H. 2007. As a matter of facts – comments on Featherston's sticks and carrots. *Theoretical Linguistics* 33: 381–95.

Hoji, H. 2010. Hypothesis testing in generative grammar: evaluation of predicted schematic asymmetries. *Journal of Japanese Linguistics* 26: 25–52.

Hunter, M. A. and R. B. May. 1993. Some myths concerning parametric and nonparametric tests. *Canadian Psychology/Psychologie canadienne* 34: 384–9.

Keller, F. 2000. Gradience in grammar: experimental and computational aspects of degrees of grammaticality. Unpublished Ph.D. dissertation, University of Edinburgh.

Linebarger, M. C., M. F. Schwartz, and E. M. Saffran. 1983. Sensitivity to grammatical structure in so-called agrammatic aphasics. *Cognition* 13: 361–92.

Luce, R. D. 2002. A psychophysical theory of intensity proportions, joint presentations, and matches. *Psychological Review* 109: 520–32.

Matthewson, L. 2004. On the methodology of semantic fieldwork. *International Journal of American Linguistics* 70: 369–415.

Myers, J. 2009. The design and analysis of small-scale syntactic judgment experiments. *Lingua* 119: 425–44.

Narens, L. 1996. A theory of ratio magnitude estimation. *Journal of Mathematical Psychology* 40: 109–29.

Newmeyer, F. J. 1983. *Grammatical Theory: Its Limits and its Possibilities*. University of Chicago Press.

   2007. Commentary on Sam Featherston, 'Data in generative grammar: the stick and the carrot.' *Theoretical Linguistics* 33: 395–9.

Nickerson, R. 2000. Null hypothesis significance testing: a review of an old and continuing controversy. *Psychological Methods* 5: 241–301.

Phillips, C. 2009. Should we impeach armchair linguists? In S. Iwasaki, H. Hoji, P. Clancy, and S.-O. Sohn, eds. *Japanese/Korean Linguistics 17*. Stanford: CSLI Publications, 49–64.

Phillips, C. and Lasnik, H. 2003. Linguistics and empirical evidence: reply to Edelman and Christiansen. *Trends in Cognitive Sciences* 7: 61–2.

Phillips, C. and M. Wagers. 2007. Relating structure and time in linguistics and psycho-linguistics. In G. Gaskell, ed. *Oxford Handbook of Psycholinguistics*. Oxford University Press, 739–56.

Raaijmakers, J. G. W. 2003. A further look at the 'language-as-fixed-effect fallacy.' *Canadian Journal of Experimental Psychology* 57: 141–51.

Rouder, J. N., P. L. Speckman, D. Sun, R. D. Morey, and G. Iverson. 2009. Bayesian *t* tests for accepting and rejecting the null hypothesis. *Psychonomic Bulletin & Review* 16: 225–37.

Sampson, G. R. 2007. Grammar without grammaticality. *Corpus Linguistics and Linguistic Theory* 3: 1–32.

Schütze, C. T. 1996. *The Empirical Base of Linguistics: Grammaticality Judgments and Linguistic Methodology*. University of Chicago Press.

　2009. Web searches should supplement judgements, not supplant them. *Zeitschrift für Sprachwissenschaft* 28: 151–6.

Spencer, N. J. 1973. Differences between linguists and nonlinguists in intuitions of grammaticality-acceptability. *Journal of Psycholinguistic Research* 2: 83–98.

Sprouse, J. 2011. A test of the cognitive assumptions of magnitude estimation: commuta-tivity does not hold for acceptability judgments. *Language* 87: 274–88.

Sprouse, J. and D. Almeida. 2012. Assessing the reliability of textbook data in syntax: Adger's *Core Syntax*. *Journal of Linguistics* 48.3: 609–52.

　2013. The role of experimental syntax in an integrated cognitive science of language. In K. K. Grohmann and C. Boeckx, eds. *The Cambridge Handbook of Biolinguistics*. Cambridge University Press, 181–202.

Sprouse, J., C. T. Schütze, and D. Almeida. In press. A comparison of informal and formal acceptability judgments using a random sample from *Linguistic Inquiry* 2001–2010. *Lingua*.

Stevens, S. S. 1956. The direct estimation of sensory magnitudes: loudness. *American Journal of Psychology* 69: 1–25.

　1957. On the psychophysical law. *Psychological Review* 64: 153–81.

Toribio, A. J. 2001. Accessing Spanish-English code-switching competence. *International Journal of Bilingualism* 5: 403–36.

Valian, V. 1982. Psycholinguistic experiment and linguistic intuition. In T. W. Simon and R. J. Scholes, eds. *Language, Mind, and Brain*. Hillsdale, NJ: Lawrence Erlbaum, 179–88.

Wasow, T. and J. Arnold. 2005. Intuitions in linguistic argumentation. *Lingua* 115: 1481–96.

Weskott, T. and G. Fanselow. 2011. On the informativity of different measures of linguistic acceptability. *Language* 87: 249–73.

4   Fieldwork for language description

Shobhana Chelliah

1   Introduction

There are two exciting facets of language description: the fieldwork experience, which is necessary for data collection, and the process of discovery and analysis that leads to the description of the target language. In order for our record of language structures to be as accurate as possible, data collection is best conducted using rigorous methodology. The goal of language description is often not to capture just one speaker's internal grammar but to represent prevalent patterns for a community of speakers. In that sense, grammatical description is "fake" in that no one speaker will instantiate all the structures described in the grammar; at the same time, however, the grammar is "real" because the facts described therein are accepted by most speakers as accurately representing their language. The main product of descriptive fieldwork, whether a grammar or a targeted description of particular parts of a grammar, must therefore include data from a variety of speakers, favoring the most frequent patterns and noting common variations based on social or contextual factors.

2   Speakers and fieldworkers

A typical fieldwork project requires the participation of several speakers, in part due to differing talents and interests. The primary *consultants*, the speakers who participate on a regular basis in a project, will be those who are excited by language study. Some speakers show an amazing amount of linguistic sophistication even without linguistic training; for example, even if a speaker is unable to explain word class membership using terms such as "verb" and "noun," she might still identify the lexical category of a word by providing paradigms or synonyms (Dixon 1992). Some speakers show initiative by bringing their own analyses to field sessions or by asking community members for their opinions on constructions discussed with the field linguist. Some speakers may be good storytellers, others able to repeat things slowly and exactly to aid with transcription (a surprisingly difficult task; see Chapter 12). Some speakers may be ideal for recording conversations and narratives but may be too prescriptive to help with translation (they may be more interested in "correcting" data than commenting on it).

In practical terms, an ideal speaker on a field project is someone who is reliable and cooperative, and has the time to devote to regular sessions and to adhere to the work standards of the project. Where possible, it is very useful to have at least one speaker on the project who is fluent in both the target and contact language.[1] Fieldworkers conducting research in relatively conservative societies report that it is advisable to conform to community social norms – for example, by initially working with speakers of the same gender as the fieldworker (Chelliah and de Reuse 2011). In endangered language situations, all contributions of a "remem-berer" or "semi-speaker" (Evans 2001) will be invaluable.

Fieldwork for language description evokes images of remote locations, far from the researcher's base. Although remote fieldwork constitutes the focus of this chapter, language description may take place in almost any context. For instance, diasporic communities in large metropolitan centers may include a range of speakers (newly immigrated monolinguals to multilingual) of unusual languages. In such cases, language description can be pursued very close to the fieldworker's institution, with advantages such as lower travel costs and frequent returns to the consultants at different stages of analysis (see Vaux, Cooper, and Tucker 2007). However, since diasporic varieties can involve simplification or other types of change it is advisable to supplement such fieldwork with data from parallel non-contact groups.

Perhaps the most important advance we have made in our field, apart from the introduction of technologies in dealing with field data, is the increased role of speakers (see Chapter 2) who determine the record of their language by guiding linguists to culturally significant linguistic exchanges and performances (Mithun 2001; Rice 2012). We have come to recognize that the relationship between speaker and linguist is symbiotic since both can benefit from the outcomes. Products that may assist speakers in language maintenance and revitalization efforts include word lists, dictionaries, pedagogical grammars, annotated text collections, descriptive grammars, and oral histories. Speakers prefer such results to theoretically narrow treatments of a small set of grammatical facts (Cameron et al. 1992; Ameka 2006). Speakers can guide projects through group participatory research where community members, after basic training, can record, transcribe, and prepare dictionary entries and texts for publication in a standard orthography (Dwyer 2006: 55–6). Furthermore, linguists can assist language maintenance and revitalization efforts by getting involved in community-based projects that are not necessarily centered around language or designed and implemented by linguists. For example, Robert Henderson (University of California, Santa Cruz) has worked with a nongovernmental organization on a community-based health project where he was, in turn, able to record interviews with midwives; this work has yielded a corpus of question-answer pairs involving fine encoding of information status.

---

[1] Exceptions include monolingual fieldwork, where the onus of translation is on the fieldworker (Everett 2001).

3   Preparing for the field

Being prepared for linguistic fieldwork requires a degree of background knowledge in language typology specifically as it relates to the target language. In addition, the field linguist should be familiar with existing research on the target language in order to use, and in some cases evaluate, this material when preparing questions to ask in the field. The field linguist also needs to know about the culture and history of the field site and should be able to converse in a contact language unless conducting monolingual fieldwork or working through an interpreter.

A classic resource often consulted by fieldworkers is the three-volume collection *Language Typology and Syntactic Description* (Shopen 1985, 2007). A more recent resource geared specifically for fieldwork is the three-volume work by Dixon (2010a, 2010b, 2012). Kroeger (2005) and Payne (2006) provide useful reviews of morphosyntactic terminology. General sources of this type should be consulted alongside sources pertinent to the target language and genetically and typologically related languages. If general language description is intended, then the fieldworker should ideally be familiar with a number of topics (discussed in detail later):

- Phonetics and phonology. Useful phonetic and phonological terminology and concepts can be found in Ladefoged (2003) or Dixon (2010a). Research on the studied language might provide useful sources and items of particular interest in the chosen language (Gordon 2003). For transcription training before heading out to the field, fieldworkers can read about and listen to the sounds of genetically related or geographically adjacent languages. For example, recognizing the Southeast Asian sesquisyllable[2] helped my team transcribe initial syllables of Lamkang verbs (Northeast India, Tibeto-Burman), which were initially puzzling as they sometimes appeared to have a shortened vowel and sometimes no vowel at all.

- Lexical categories. To help with clause analysis, the fieldworker might review common morphological and syntactic criteria for determining lexical class membership. Of interest are category "cross-cutters" which may cause some confusion in description, e.g., nouns also used as locational adverbs, or stative verbs used for adjectival functions.

- Grammatical categories. For the description of common categories such as tense, aspect, mood, voice, valence-changing morphology, noun class, noun classifier, mirative, evidential, nominalizer, verbalizer, and

---

[2] A sesquisyllable is a sequence of a reduced syllable (characterized by reduced phonemic inventory, CV structure, and placement at the left edge of the prosodic word) and a fully formed syllable as in Lamkang [kᵊduul] 'I push'.

case marking, one might review common form and function correspondences, e.g., participant marking can occur as bound verbal
morphology and/or with nominal suffixes or adpositions.

- Morphology. It can be useful to review the terminology, definitions,
and criteria for classification of morphological categories (e.g., word,
morpheme, stem, root, theme, base) and morphological processes
(e.g., inflection, derivational nominalization or verbalization, valence-
changing processes). The fieldworker should be able to distinguish
between inherent (e.g., number) and relational (e.g., case) morphology
and how these are distributed within the different lexical categories. A
complication every descriptivist has to deal with is the place of
diachronic analysis in the description of a grammatical system. It
can be helpful to observe whether other researchers include or exclude
information on grammaticalization and lexicalization in analyses of
synchronic systems. For example, in Meithei the verb *thok-* 'be out'
also occurs with motion and activity verbs to mean 'to V outward' as in
cǝtthok- 'go out.' The researcher must decide if these are V+V compounds or V-derivational suffix sequences (see Chelliah 1997).
Merrifield et al. (2003) provide practice exercises for morphosyntactic
analysis; such exercises can be an enjoyable warm-up to field analysis.
- Syntax. For syntactic investigation, arguments or descriptions based
on purely theory-internal considerations are best avoided (Evans and
Dench 2006; see Chapter 18). There are integral relationships between
syntax and discourse phenomena of which the fieldworker should be
aware (Mushin and Baker 2008). Examples of typical properties
requiring careful characterization include word order, clause types,
relative clause structure, complement-taking predicates and complement types, non-verbal predication, and strategies of clause combination (e.g., coordination, subordination, parataxis, clause chaining, and
converbs).
- Semantics. Semantic investigation may cover a range of lexical and
formal semantic properties of a language. It is useful to be familiar
with basic lexical relations such as synonomy, homophony, antonymy,
polysemy, metonymy, or metaphor. Homophony and polysemy, for
instance, become important when glossing morphemes and compiling
word lists, as in the choice of an appropriate gloss for *run* in the
following sentences from Saeed (2009: 60): *I go for a run every
morning* vs *The tail-end batsmen added a single run before lunch.*
Careful lexical semantic description often involves the use of standard
syntactic tests, and truth-conditional description of sentence meaning
and interpretation requires familiarity with methodologies from formal semantics (see Matthewson 2004).
- Pragmatics. A review of standard descriptions of how languages link
speech acts to contextual and social information can help design

appropriate fieldwork materials. Further elements of interest might include rules of conversational implicature, inference, presupposition triggers (e.g., factive verbs such as *regret*, as in *Rani regrets that the wedding was called off*), and information packaging strategies (e.g., cleft constructions). Reviewing conversation analysis terminology (e.g., turn taking, overlaps, repair) – even though derived from our understanding of well-documented languages – can help train the analyst to attend to how morphology and syntax relate to particular points of conversational interaction.

A useful habit among fieldworkers who are writing either a *descriptive grammar* or a detailed description of a specific aspect of linguistic structure is to peruse other descriptive grammars. A common practice in the field is to create intermediary analyses called *sketch grammars* at regular intervals during the field trip, to take account of what is known and what still needs to be discovered (see Mosel 2006b). These interim descriptions can be enhanced by a familiarity with the elements of a good grammar; see Mosel (2006a) and Chelliah and de Reuse (2011) for lists and reviews of useful grammars.

Few languages have absolutely nothing written about them and for many now endangered languages it may even be possible to find old audio recordings of fluent speakers. So preparation for fieldwork also ideally includes a study of extant materials so that existing word lists, field notes, unpublished grammars, dictionaries, text collections, and religious materials are used to prepare the fieldworker for what to expect, even if in a very general sense.

It is also important to be familiar with the history and culture of the area and, if possible, social conventions and rules for social interaction in the region. This can provide a fieldworker with diverse types of preparation, including a background on language contact and the extent and reasons for bilingualism or multilingualism, familiarity with factors influencing language fluency or dialect variation, an understanding of the presence and status of contact languages, as well as speaker attitudes toward local languages, and basic familiarity with how to approach and interact with local residents.

Many fieldworkers learn a contact language to do fieldwork on a target language, but may put too much effort into learning the contact language with insufficient attention paid to the target language (Newman and Ratliff 2001: 5). The most comfortable, and arguably the most successful, field linguists are those who learn to speak the target language at the same time as making it an object of study. Everett (2001: 170) encourages doing linguistic fieldwork only in the target language, by what is known as the *monolingual method*, and states that if the fieldworker does not speak the target language, they are "working with a self-imposed handicap. Why should anyone want to turn down the clues, insights, intuitions, and constant grammar-learning and practice inherent in language learning if one is genuinely concerned with a deep professional understanding of (aspects of) the language in question?"

A number of common administrative and practical steps precede entering the field. The fieldworker may need to secure funding and obtain permission for fieldwork activities from the home institution (see Chapter 2) and from representatives at the field site (see Crowley 2007). Appropriate equipment and supplies for the field site must be assembled with care; this can be greatly helped with reference to checklists compiled by other fieldworkers. Specific recommendations on audio and video recording, and on brands and models of recording media, microphones, cables, plugs, jacks, tripods, and hardware and software for video recording are available via online as well as published sources (see Ladefoged 2003; Bowern 2008; Chelliah and de Reuse 2011; Sakel and Everett 2012). These sources also include important safety and back-up advice for ensuring careful collection and protection of audio material and notes, as well as advice for supplies in order to stay healthy, rested, and comfortable. In the past, homesickness, boredom, anxiety, culture shock, and feelings of inadequacy in conducting fieldwork or learning the target language were not often addressed, but today the implications of these experiences on fieldwork are widely addressed (see Newman and Ratliff 2001: 8). In addition, we know that there are very real dangers in many areas: civil unrest, fire, theft, injury, personal attack, physical or mental health issues, and poor weather conditions are all possibilities, and while it is not possible to prepare for every contingency, it is helpful to read about others' experiences and to think about how to deal with adverse conditions before getting to the field (see Research Center for Linguistic Typology 2009: 10).

4   Data collection for phonetic and phonological description

The heart of field investigation is the linguistic *field session* with a native speaker. This is where the speaker(s) and fieldworker sit in a relatively undisturbed spot for some length of time, with recorders and notebooks to gather data for language description. The field session can be an exciting time of discovery for all participants.

There are a number of special requirements for native-speaker consultants who participate in phonetic fieldwork (Maddieson 2001). While younger speakers may have clearer speech, older speakers can contribute more conservative pronunciations. Due to natural stochastic dispersion in phonetic articulation, a gender-balanced sample of several is preferable; nevertheless, even a couple of speakers can support extensive phonetic description.

Data collection often starts with a short period where the fieldworker gets accustomed to hearing and transcribing the target language by eliciting *word lists*. This task will be relatively easy for speakers, especially if the words elicited are common and prototypical (e.g., ask for the word for *bird* rather than *sparrow*).

One usually starts with a list of basic words from domains such as body parts, numerals, and kinship terms, and then supplements with word lists tailored for the language family being investigated. Some fieldworkers use pictures or point to items in the environment and observed activities to get nouns and verbs. References to culturally specific word lists for several language families can be found in Chelliah and de Reuse (2011). Narratives and other natural language data are good sources for activity-specific words (e.g., cooking, casting spells, or words used in religious ceremonies), register variants, and archaic words. Benefits of word elicitation are that they increase speaker confidence and build camaraderie between fieldworker and speaker.

In the initial stages of fieldwork a *narrow IPA transcription* is used, as the phonological system of the language is not yet established. A common error by first-time fieldworkers at this stage is to fatigue the consultant with repeated requests for repetition of the same word. Both the transcriber and the speaker tire with each repetition so that ultimately the words being produced are anything but natural. Alternative ways of dealing with difficult words include recording and transcribing the same words with another speaker, and examining the words with speech analysis software. As the list is compiled, it is useful to read back transcriptions to speakers and ask for corrections (though guarding against any prescriptive self-correction by speakers). With some speakers it is possible to develop a common terminology of articulation and this metalanguage can help with transcription.

Some fieldworkers are experienced enough to move quickly to *phonemic transcription*, eliminating subtleties of phonetic variation, but this transition must be made cautiously. Persistent variation in pronunciation between speakers may be a sign of dialectal variation, and transitioning to phonemic transcription or practical orthography (see Chapter 12) too soon will obscure this and other important distinctions, such as tone or vowel quality distinctions that might have grammatical meaning. To keep transcriptions consistent and transparent, it is common to avoid use of too many non-standard characters and diacritics.

To create audio recordings that allow for acoustic analysis, the recording environment needs to be carefully monitored (e.g., shutting off noisy appliances, closing windows and doors). A unidirectional microphone is typically used, and if recordings are made outdoors, a microphone windshield is advisable. Recordings are monitored using headphones, and the recorder and microphone are checked before each session for microphone placement and recorder-level settings. (See Chapter 9 for more details.)

To determine the phonemic system of the language, the fieldworker elicits and records words to establish minimal pairs if these are available (see Chelliah and de Reuse 2011 for procedures to follow when minimal pairs cannot be found). Since speakers will often not have explicit knowledge of phonetic and phonemic inventories of the target language, their answers to any direct questions about whether a particular sound exists in their language is not taken as analysis. Lists of common phonological processes and methods of phonological analysis may be useful reminders for the field analyst (see Bowern 2008; Chelliah and de Reuse 2011: 257–65).

A particularly difficult aspect of phonetic and phonological fieldwork is the transcription and the description of tone. In addition to the effect of the field-worker's own linguistic background – her L1 may not be a tone language or may use tone differently – there are challenges posed by the speaker's talents in consciously pronouncing words, pronouncing words with the same tone pattern consistently, and describing the tones produced. Since one speaker may speak the words with a clear tonal pattern, another repeat it, and yet another identify and name the tonal pattern, it is often useful to engage more than one speaker.

To record words and phrases for tonal analysis, the speaker can be presented with prepared lists of words in frames. A frame is a stable grammatical environ-ment in which to place the constituent under consideration and is used to understand segmental and suprasegmental features. A common frame for a verb-final language is: *She ____ said. ___ (by me) is liked*. "She said ____. I like the word ____." The frame guards against variable intonation or segmental effects on the studied constituent. A word list for tone research should contain a random sequence of tones (e.g., falling tones mixed with rising tones). The researcher should bear in mind that words later in the list will be affected by list final intonation; to control for this effect, earlier and later words in a list can be re-ordered and re-recorded. To check on tone transcription the fieldworker can sort words into like and unlike pitch patterns, with the help of a speaker, to see if the transcriptions are correct. At the next stage, speech analysis software can be used to compare pitch patterns with transcriptions (see Chapter 17). Careful listening comes before hypothesis-formulation, and hypotheses are developed before acoustic analysis.

Intonation has historically played a minor role in field studies. With easy access to software such as Praat, and the possibility of making high-quality digital recordings, we are now able to easily track pitch changes over constituents, so that we can, for instance, examine natural discourse for the encoding of speech acts.

Modern phonetic fieldwork requires knowledge of advanced technologies for recording and analysis, as well as an ability to interpret quantitative data and graphical representations such as spectrograms (see Chapter 17). Despite this, traditional methods, such as ear-training, elicitation and transcription techniques, and record keeping, remain important elements of phonetic and phonological fieldwork.

Finally, it is worth addressing the general issue of transcription and orthography (see Chapter 12), which arises as soon as fieldwork begins. When a speaker is literate, one practice is to give her a notebook where she can write down the words being elicited using whatever spelling conventions she is comfortable with. Where there is no tradition of writing in the community, it has become increasingly common for fieldworkers to assist in orthography development, since even a nascent writing system can serve several purposes: consultants learn to write down language examples from the community; elicitation tasks are enhanced, sometimes in basic ways (by consultants being able to read out lists for recording, for example); and predictable spelling patterns allow fieldworkers to identify common phonological processes. That being said, we should recognize that orthography design is dependent on a comprehensive understanding of a language's structure; aside from phonetic representation, this includes an understanding of phonological processes, word structure (e.g., to determine if morphemes are enclitics or suffixes), the implications of the system for reading (e.g., should words be written in shorter chunks for ease of reading in polysynthetic languages, and, if so, where should the breaks occur, how should they be indicated, and what are the preferences of the community?), and the implications of the system for writing (e.g., ease in typing and intuitive rules of diacritic use, correspondence between spelling and pronunciation). (See Grenoble and Whaley 2006, Hinton 2001, and Seifart 2006 for further discussion.) Speakers do not think of their writing system as just a method of representing speech on a page; it is a symbol of community identity, loaded with political and cultural value (Sebba 2007). The linguist's role is to facilitate community dialogue that will bring a consensus system or set of systems into use (Rice 1995).

5   Data collection for grammatical description

Two overlapping yet epistemologically distinct methods of elicitation are common in linguistic fieldwork. I will call these the *questionnaire-driven elicitation method* and the *text-driven elicitation method,* and will focus here on grammatical description.

In questionnaire-driven elicitation, the fieldworker systematically chases down data on specific constructions using a predetermined set of possible questions to be answered, constructions to be translated, or responses to linguistic or non-linguistic stimuli recorded. A series of questions, for example, might help the researcher discover how copular sentences work in a language, as in example (1):[3]

(1)   Copular sentences
         Copular sentences with nominal complement:
                  Is there an overt be copula? Is it optional or obligatory?
                  How is the predicate noun marked?
                  Give the order of the constituents.
         Copular sentences with adjectival complement:
                  Is there an overt be copula? Is it optional or obligatory?
                  How is the complement adjective marked?
                  Give the order of the constituents. . .

---

[3] These sentences are from the Lingua Descriptive Studies Questionnaire (Comrie and Smith 1977).

These questions may be prepared based on expected patterns for a particular language family or geographic area, or based on universal typological possibilities (see the extensive review of questionnaires in Chelliah and de Reuse 2011: 279–88).

The fieldworker cannot expect speakers to directly answer questions from a questionnaire, since in most cases the speaker will not be familiar with linguistic terminology. Instead, the fieldworker plans a set of tasks that will draw out the answers. Many different tasks can be used in data elicitation; the challenge is to find a good match between the grammatical construction being studied and the task. For example, to get at information on copular sentences the fieldworker might first elicit clauses describing the color and shape of items or the professions of the speaker's relatives. Or, to identify noun classes or classifiers, the fieldworker could present the speaker with a selection of culturally relevant objects of various sizes, shapes, colors, and number in various configurations. Non-linguistic stimulus-driven tasks may also use line drawings, photographs, and video-clips. Non-linguistic stimuli have several advantages: speakers do not require special training to understand the tasks; responses are clearly linked to stimuli and are therefore less ambiguous; and responses to the same stimulus by many speakers allows for easier contrasting between varieties (Majid 2012: 56). Majid cautions against presenting the speaker with too many stimuli, or stimuli that are too stylized or culturally foreign, as this can lead to speaker fatigue and confusion.

Another questionnaire-based way to elicit target language forms is to ask the speaker to create sentences using a lexical prompt. For example, the fieldworker may want to discover the case system of a target language. To do so, she could prepare a list of intransitive and transitive verbs and ask the speaker to use those verbs in sentences. While instructive, the resulting data will need to be checked against naturally occurring speech, as speakers tend to produce syntactically simple or pragmatically neutral constructions when responding to such tasks.

In other elicitation using linguistic stimuli, the fieldworker can manipulate examples in systematic ways and ask the speaker for her reaction. For example, the fieldworker may:

- construct a sentence in the target language and ask for a grammaticality judgment or other introspective statement. This is the classic "Can you say X?" or "Is X a possible sentence in your language?" method of elicitation, and it works well for very predictable and simple structures. Once the structures are even slightly unusual or pragmatically marked, judgments begin to vary across speakers. (See Chelliah 2001 and Chapter 3.)

- provide a sentence in the contact language and ask for a translation to the target language. This may seem like an obvious method of collecting reliable information, but since translation skills and proficiency in the contact language differ, the resulting data can be inaccurate, unidiomatic, or over-reliant on word-for-word translations. If this technique is used, the prompt itself should be easy to parse and should not contain contact-language idioms, e.g., *I don't mean to rain on your parade*.

- substitute a word or constituent in an existing construction with an alternative form. If I were trying to get at the meaning of English modals, for example, I might ask: "What is the difference in meaning between, *I should empty the trash*, and *I could empty the trash*?" The substitution method is often used when trying to define morphemes that speakers cannot easily translate, such as those that indicate modality, evidentiality, or mirativity.

- expand a few representative forms to collect a complete paradigm. Verb paradigms may be complex, indicating one or all of the following: tense, aspect, mood, person, number, gender, and participant marking. Noun and adjective paradigms are easier to build because the dimensions of variation are often fewer, e.g., number, gender or noun class, and case.

- add an adverb to a previously recorded construction to check for tense and aspect adjustments, e.g., *I rang the bell yesterday. *I ring the bell yesterday*; or move an adverb around to look for changes in meaning and scope, e.g., *Rajan rang the bell twice intentionally. Rajan rang the bell intentionally twice.*

- transform a construction (fieldworker-manipulated data) or ask the speaker to transform a construction (speaker-manipulated data). For example, a speaker could be asked to make a question of a statement or change a statement into an imperative.

- use linguistic terminology to elicit information from a linguistically sophisticated speaker. For example, once a fieldworker has determined that the speaker understands what is meant by "past tense," he might ask the speaker which morpheme is used to indicate this meaning.

A combination of tasks is usually used in a field session. It works best to balance difficult tasks with easier ones so as to minimize speaker fatigue. Task difficulty can be determined by considering the complexity of the question and the required knowledge of the target and contact language for task completion. In transcription tasks, conversations are more stressful because of overlaps and rate of speech. Narratives, which are more carefully enunciated and usually involve a single speaker, are easier to transcribe. Speaker fatigue is also a reason to keep fieldwork sessions relatively short (maximum two hours at a stretch) or include several breaks.

Questionnaires are often used when data must be collected quickly. They can be used reliably when the fieldworker already knows something about the target language and is able to evaluate the data produced through translation or interview tasks. We think of the question-and-answer format as fairly efficient in eliciting useful information, but there is much riding on how a question is asked, what the speaker perceives its intent to be, and how speakers frame their answers. For instance, direct questions can be interpreted as challenges (Milroy 1987: 41–51), while complicated questions with built-in hypothetical situations confuse some speakers. Others may resist reporting on the obvious, e.g., *Is grass green?* (Hopkins and Furbee 1991). So the fieldworker may ask a question, but the answer may not be a response to what was asked. There are plenty of other reasons why data from questionnaires must be vetted for undesirable research effects:

- Pragmatic vacuum. Grammaticality judgments requested without sufficient pragmatic information can lead to differing judgments between speakers if each speaker creates a slightly different pragmatic scenario and so interprets the construction differently (see Chapter 3).
- Speaker prescriptivism. Prescriptivism can prevent some speakers from accepting or offering constructions that they otherwise recognize and even use.
- Linguistic stimulus primes response. The fieldworker can also inadvertently prime the speaker to answer in a particular way, e.g., interlocutors will often copy the syntax of the prompt question.
- Research focus. The interviewer may also prompt production of a particular construction by revealing which form would be best for a favored analysis.
- Group dynamics. When data are elicited from a group of speakers, the opinion of the socially superior group member might win out.
- Pressure. A speaker's reactions may be unreliable because the fieldworker does not tolerate silence and presses him for an answer.
- Fatigue. The speaker may face repeated requests for the same type of data and this may lead to judgment fatigue.
- Orthographic influence. Although not as pertinent to grammatical description, spelling can skew speaker reports, e.g., a speaker might report fewer vowels because of a lack of different graphemes for vowel phonemes.

Questionnaire-driven elicitation has the advantage of potentially comprehensive coverage of a linguistic fact. However, one only gets the information asked for and there is therefore the danger of missing what Sapir has called the individual genius of a language (Sapir 1921: 120). For these reasons, the standard for the field currently is to balance data from questionnaires with data from other sources, such as natural discourse (for example, conversations, third and first person narratives, procedural texts, political or religious discourse).

Field investigation does not have to proceed in a linear fashion; all aspects of language inquiry can influence and inform each other, and these can be augmented simultaneously throughout the investigation to some extent (Dixon 2007, 2010a; Krishnamurti 2007: 58). When an elicitation method does not seem to be working, the experienced fieldworker knows to move on to something else. Flexibility and open-mindedness are generally appreciated by speakers (Newman and Ratliff 2001: 6–7; Everett 2001: 178–9), so the seasoned fieldworker is typically not nervous about dropping one task and starting another, or stopping one line of investigation and coming back to it later. In addition, speakers tend to respond well when they have a measure of control over the session rather than keeping to a strict elicitation schedule. Abbi (2001) provides an example of this: she elicited the word *chappati* 'Indian unleavened bread,' which then led to illustrations and examples in the target language of how the bread dough is prepared and cooked.

In text-driven elicitation, natural discourse is the starting point for grammatical investigation. This can be used to examine a single feature (subordinate clauses, for example) or for developing a comprehensive grammar. Importantly, text-driven elicitation is not just text collection and text annotation. One does not simply sift through annotated texts to find data for grammatical analysis. Rather, text anno-tation is interwoven with elicitation and supplemented by data from questionnaire-based elicitation. (See Dixon 2007, Chelliah 2001, Crowley 2007, Evans and Dench 2006, Mithun 2001, and Rice 2006 for more on this methodology.)

Text-driven elicitation can reduce some of the potential limitations of questionnaire-driven elicitation. Data gleaned from translated questionnaire sen-tences are generally limited to those that the fieldworker thinks to ask for and those that the speaker produces a direct response for; they can also sound awkward to other members of the community (Ameka 2006). By contrast, it is rare for speakers to reject textual data as strange or "not like our language." Following standard practice for scientific discovery, we should ideally require that judgments are broadly replicable, with wide agreement across community members. An annotated text corpus can help develop such data.

A variety of genres is necessary as each may utilize a different range of grammatical constructions. For example, a corpus with only traditional narratives will not include much data on future tense and modals, while a conversation would include these items but may not use remote past or story-world evidentials. There are also syntactic and morphological differences between traditional narra-tives and first-person narratives, since first-person narratives contain evaluative devices such as interjections, conditionals, and irrealis mood markers, many of which are typically absent in traditional narratives.

There are several ways of obtaining natural discourse. If the fieldworker wants information on specific grammatical constructions, she could provide stimuli that will necessitate the production of those constructions as part of natural discourse. She might have the speaker read a book and retell the story, describe or respond to pictures or photographs, watch a movie and narrate the events, translate a written story from the contact language into the target language, retell a traditional or contemporary story, or paraphrase a story written in the target language. The stimuli should be culturally relevant – dragons and princesses do not interest consultants in most areas of the world! An example of a controlled discourse task would be the retelling of the Pear Story (Chafe 1980), which can be used to study reference tracking and NP-marking choices. Less controlled activities would be to record a traditional folktale or personal narrative or monologue. Conversations yield a wealth of grammatical information, such as syntax and morphology that manipulate social distance and speaker stance and intention. Conversational exchanges can be prompted by, for example, initiating games or activities that require question-and-answer exchanges. Speakers may be requested to prepare scripted conversations to be used later as scripts for plays. Natural conversations can also be obtained by allowing speakers to record interactions that they deem important, with or without the presence of the fieldworker. (See Cukor-Avila 2006 and Enfield et al. 2007 for detailed methodology in fieldwork on conversations. See Edwards and Lampert 1993 and Chapter 12 for the transcription of conversation.)

Once texts are collected, their annotation becomes one of the main tasks in the field session. The researcher must prepare the sound files and/or text transcripts for review during the session. The creation of an annotated corpus of natural data thus involves a number of stages, almost all of which require the assistance of a native speaker, or different speakers at different stages of annotation.

- Record a narrative. To record a narrative, the fieldworker will need appropriate training in using high-quality digital and video recorders, taking into consideration microphone and camera placement, lighting, and synchronizing the beginning of video and audio recording. The researcher will need to document relevant *metadata*, such as the dates of collection, researcher and participant names or codes, genre of text, method and tools used in recording, location, the names of audio and other linked files, and the status of annotation. The researcher must obtain permissions for audio and video recording.

- Get a summary. The fieldworker often elicits a paraphrase or summary of the narrative directly after the "performance," to help with data translation and cataloging.

- Transcribe the narrative. The researcher transcribes the narrative by playing back segments to a native speaker, who repeats what she hears slowly. Playback may be facilitated by transcription software (see Chapter 12) that breaks the speech signal into smaller chunks, usually "phrases" delimited by pauses. The first few attempts at transcription are typically time-consuming, but phonetic and phonological observations can make the task enjoyable for the speaker. Literate native speakers can speed up the process by transcribing in a practical orthography first, and reviewing transcriptions with the field linguist later.

- Elicit word-for-word translations. The fieldworker elicits word-for-word annotations for the transcribed text. Translations do not need to be from the same person who provided the text; the fieldworker can get texts from monolingual speakers and translate with another speaker's assistance. Some prominent fieldworkers still manage this data in simple spreadsheets, but many use integrated databases that help to create a concordance, align sound to transcription, generate automatic lexica and dictionaries, and provide a variety of tools to keep annotations consistent through a corpus of texts. To create word-for-word annotations, the fieldworker imports segmented sound files and transcription into a database program such as Field Language Explorer (FLEx). Here, word-for-word translations can be directly inputted from the speaker.

- Create a morpheme gloss and a free translation. In addition to word glosses, the researcher will attempt to morphologically analyze words and gloss individual morphemes. Annotations might include such information as lexical category (e.g., noun, verb), function (e.g., nominalizer, adverbializer), and spelling or dialect variant. The richer the annotation, the more useful the data for later analysis.

Morphological analysis may take years to perfect, both in and away from the field. The quality and usefulness of annotation depends on the linguist's skill and her steadily increasing understanding of the target language. Using standardized terminology and abbreviations for morpheme analysis can allow other researchers to easily access the data and facilitate cross-linguistic comparison, e.g., the Leipzig Glossing Rules (Comrie, Haspelmath, and Bickel 2008; see also Section 5: Glossing, in Chapter 12).

The highest level of annotation is a sentence-by-sentence free translation, which, if included, requires constituent analysis. Speakers should not be expected to tell the fieldworker what the noun phrase or subject is, or even where the sentence begins and ends. For example, Meithei is a clause-chaining language where a series of non-finite clauses are strung together, ending with a finite verb indicating the end of the sentence. Speakers typically identify the subordinate clause as "the sentence" until they hear the non-finite clauses that immediately follow. At this point, speakers can be confused about how the Meithei (target language) construction corresponds to the contact language "sentence." Here, the analyst must decide where the sentence breaks are. This illustrates one of the many ways in which annotation *is* analysis.

The final product of a text collection is a set of annotated texts with the following levels of information that have been gradually developed over the duration of fieldwork and analysis: practical orthography, phonetic transcription, phonemic transcription, morpheme-by-morpheme breaks, morpheme gloss, word gloss, constituent gloss, free translation of clause, cultural notes, notes on gesture and gaze, and other commentary. A comprehensive discussion of possible annotation tiers is given in Schultze-Berndt (2006).

An important requirement of annotation software used by field linguists is that data outputs be importable by other programs and exportable to a variety of formats so that the results have long-term use and are universally accessible (Bird and Simons 2003). Also, it is preferable that fieldworkers use software that is free and easily accessible, so that interested community members can participate in annotation and/ or can download and use the text collections created through fieldworkers for their own purposes. For a review of software used in field linguistics, see Antworth and Valentine (1998). (See also Chapter 12 for further details on annotation software.)

The most useful annotated corpus will include samples from as many different speakers as possible, to take into account the possible effects of change-in-progress, age-grading, register modification, or dialect differences. In the case of endangered languages, younger speakers may not know traditional stories and ritual language, but may be able to carry on simple conversations. On the other hand, they may have memorized texts from elders, even if they are not fluent enough to converse in the language.

The native speaker and field linguist, who of course may herself be a native speaker, create a web of information resulting from discussions during text annotation. The linguist must also continually analyze in order to annotate. To help with analysis, he will often develop a questionnaire (also called an elicitation schedule) based on structures that come up during text annotation. Such targeted questioning can be guided by previously created analytic questionnaires, which help remind the field linguist of the possible breadth and range of the phenomena being investigated. For example, if the text in question includes negative constructions, the fieldworker might consult a standardized questionnaire on negation to see what information is usually of interest in relation to negation and construct an elicitation schedule with those questions in mind. In this way, annotation and grammatical analysis progress in tandem.

Text-based elicitation has been criticized for a few potential shortcomings: (1) a specific grammatical structure of interest to the researcher may never surface in a natural text corpus; (2) text-based elicitation is messy because information about particular parts of the grammar come at different times; and (3) it is time-consuming and not every fieldworker has months to devote to creating an annotated text corpus. The first criticism stems from a misunderstanding of this method. Text-driven elicitation does not mean that analysis will be based exclusively on the constructions found in the texts (unless this is a closed corpus with no fluent speakers); rather, these constructions form the basis of further elicitation, which occurs in tandem with text annotation. Text annotation can be suspended for a period while the researcher pursues a particular strand of analysis. The second criticism is accurate, although one redeeming feature of this messy way of gathering data is that the researcher's understanding of the language grows in a holistic fashion, and knowledge acquired can be continually cross-checked. The third criticism is also accurate, but proponents of text-based elicitation would suggest that, where possible, grammatical descriptions, be they grammars or other treatments of the data, are better served by data collected over a period of time for a deeper understanding of the grammar.

6   Data collection for semantic and pragmatic description

Methods for semantic fieldwork have developed rapidly in recent years, with creative innovation and collaboration across fields (see, e.g., Matthewson 2004).

To elicit word meaning, a researcher can simply point to an object and ask what it is named, or provide a name and ask what that refers to. A pitfall of this type of elicitation is what Evans and Sasse (2007) call the "level problem." Asking a speaker to identify an entity in a picture will probably elicit the name of that entity, but the researcher cannot be sure if the word provided refers to a specific type or a superordinate term, e.g., *python* versus *snake*. Also, pointing and naming will give us a name but not the sense or appropriateness of use of that name (Krifka 2011).

To elicit further information on the meaning and appropriateness of constructions (e.g., ambiguity, truth value, presupposition, felicity), a number of tasks can be borrowed from existing experimental methods used in first language acquisition, as described in Krifka (2011) and Matthewson (2004). For instance, to confirm the meanings of an ambiguous construction, one cannot simply ask if a sentence is ambiguous because, as Matthewson points out, speakers tend to believe that each sentence has a single meaning. Speakers will give you the preferred meaning and avoid the secondary reading. To get at the dispreferred reading, the fieldworker would have to set up a situation where the dispreferred reading is appropriate. The researcher would describe this with an unambiguous sentence. Once the speaker is primed in this way, the ambiguous construction would be introduced and a meaning elicited.

Truth value judgment (TVJ) tests used in first or second language acquisition studies can also be adapted for fieldwork. In a typical TVJ test, a subject is shown a situation (e.g., in a video, through play acting, or with puppets). Then a sentence is uttered related to the situation, and the subject has to judge whether the proposition is true or false, given the situation. One potential problem with TVJ tests is that items in the situation or picture can be misleading. Krifka gives the example of *Every farmer is feeding a donkey* where children may judge this as ungrammatical (rather than false) when, of all the donkeys viewed, there is one that is not being fed. TVJ tests designed with just visual stimuli are difficult or impossible with propositions that express habitual activity, generic expressions, interrogatives, exclamations, commands, and deictic expressions that make reference to speaker position (unless the speaker is in the picture). In these instances one could supplement with linguistic clues. For example, to get at appropriateness, felicity, falsity, or ambiguity, Matthewson uses metalanguage, such as asking consultants, "Does it sound like I am lying or mistaken about the facts, or just that I am saying something funny?"

A picture identification task is useful in studying presuppositions. Here the subject is shown a picture and then asked to pick the sentence that best describes the picture. A video or an enactment by the researcher can also be used. The subject will ideally select the sentence which describes the picture and also expresses the presuppositions the subject feels are necessary for correct interpretation of the picture. Krifka points out that the field researcher must be extremely careful in using sentences known to be grammatical and not only marginally so, as a sentence may be ruled out by the subject for grammaticality violations rather than an incorrect presupposition.

Acceptability tests are used to find out whether a proposition is felicitous in a given situation. In general, the method is to present the speaker with a situation, then present the proposition with and without some cueing item, such as focus intonation or adverbs. Krifka gives the following example: *JOHN went to Paris* versus *John went to PARIS* as replies to the question *Who went to Paris?* and *John went where?*

Any narrative produced through a carefully constructed prompt can contain constructions that trigger presuppositions. So controlled tasks involving natural speech production, such as the retelling of the Pear Story, can be useful in semantic and pragmatic fieldwork (Chelliah and de Reuse 2011).

7   Managing data

Data management is a crucial component of fieldwork. It includes skillful note-taking, detailed metadata collection, and safe storage and documentation of media (see Kendall 2008 for a discussion of some implications of data storage).

When using a questionnaire, field linguists may enter notes from field sessions directly on to a laptop or similar device, and save that data digitally. The majority of linguists we interviewed for our book on linguistic fieldwork (Chelliah and de Reuse 2011) still used traditional pen and bound notebooks, which tend to be more amenable to the types of multidimensional discussion that arises from text annotation. Useful organization of a field notebook page requires some practice: in addition to neatness and predictability of layout, one would want plenty of cross-referencing that creates a trail of related topics within and across notebooks (see Bowern 2008).

Several interrelated types of data are collected to complete even the simplest dataset. For example, when collecting and analyzing a word list the following possible "products" result:

- Field notes in notebooks where words were first written down in IPA
- Pictures of speakers who provided the data with other relevant metadata (e.g., age, gender, dialect, proficiency)
- Scans of field notes
- Audio and video recordings of that field session
- An elicitation schedule, with selected words for recording words in a controlled phonetic context
- Recordings of words in context
- Output of a speech analysis program on these data
- PowerPoint presentation on these data for a conference
- Related articles or data from related languages with cognates
- Digital backup files.

To access this related information efficiently, fieldworkers maintain a maximally informative naming system for each product; for example, names of digital files could include the following information: [Language Identifier]-[YearMonthDay of file creation]-[Initials of the file creator]-[Recording device/notebook#]-[Transcription/annotation software used in creating the file]-[Description of the file contents]. Each product is also recorded in a metadata database, which provides a way to standardize catalog information so that it is easily searched and included in a larger language archive. Archiving data in accessible repositories (not just the researcher's private computer) is necessary so that materials are backed up and accessible to the linguistic community, native speakers, and future generations.

A metadata database will include a selection of the following types of information for each piece of data generated from fieldwork: unique identifier (often the file name), language identifier (often the Ethnologue code), date of creation, creator (researcher's name), description, contributor (speaker's name or pseudonym/code), title of product (such as the name given to a conversation, e.g., *Raja talks about festivals*), format (e.g., .wav, .pdf), rights of access, length of file, genre of product, place recorded, related files, and location of product. It will also ideally include cross-references among files and materials, such as transcripts and matching audio or video files, to allow easy processing of complex field material.

All recordings and copies of notes should be saved in multiple locations, following what Austin (2006: 89) calls LOCKSS, i.e., "lots of copies keep stuff safe."

8   Endangered language documentation and language description

It is useful, in theory, to distinguish fieldwork that leads to language description, described above, from fieldwork that leads to language documentation (Himmelmann 2006). Fieldwork toward documentation is motivated by the need to preserve the unique and quickly disappearing linguistic practices of a speech community. The urgency of the task motivates certain distinct methodologies and practices in the field. For example, the Summer Institute of Linguistics uses Basic Oral Language Documentation (BOLD), which trains fieldworkers to quickly record as many language samples as possible in a short amount of time. Transcription time is reduced by having a speaker repeat recorded speech slowly into a recorder, with a first pass of morphological and syntactic annotation conducted away from the field. The collection process can be sped up even further by training speakers to record and then "orally" transcribe (record repetition in slow speech) what has been recorded (see Reiman 2010). In documentary linguistics, the important outcome is to create documentation that can be universally shared and accessed in perpetuity. To this end, the field has introduced useful standards in how digital technologies are used to record, annotate, and archive language data. These standards have been adopted by descriptive fieldworkers because descriptive field linguists often also work on endangered languages, and because they too need to build and annotate language corpora. The concerns and approaches of documentation and description also come together in that endangered language documentation often includes parallel work on language preservation and maintenance, which requires materials that can be mined for pedagogical purposes. Descriptive linguists may similarly produce materials such as reference grammars, annotated text collections, and dictionaries, which can be mined for pedagogical use. One can easily make an argument for documentation (recording the language) without description (analyzing the language with speaker input): consider what we have been able to learn from the Sumerian manuscripts without the assistance of Sumerian scribes. But documentation with description is ideal. (How much more could we have learned with the input of scribes!) To this end, we see more and more that descriptive and documentary projects involve teams of linguists and speakers who strive to document, describe, archive, and preserve with due urgency.

References

Abbi, A. 2001. *A Manual of Linguistic Field Work and Indian Language Structures*. Lincom Handbooks in Linguistics 17. Munich: Lincom Europa.

Ameka, F. K. 2006. Real descriptions: reflections on native speaker and non-native speaker descriptions of a language. In F. Ameka, A. Dench, and N. Evans, eds. *Catching Language: The Standing Challenge of Grammar Writing*. Trends in Linguistics. Studies and Monographs 167. Berlin: Mouton de Gruyter, 69–112.

Antworth, E. L. and J. R. Valentine. 1998. Software for doing field linguistics. In H. Dry and J. Lawler, eds. *Using Computers in Linguistics: A Practical Guide*. London and New York: Routledge, 170–98.

Austin, P. K. 2006. Data and language documentation. In J. Gippert, N. Himmelmann, and U. Mosel, eds. *Essentials of Language Documentation*. Berlin and New York: Mouton de Gruyter, 87–112.

Bird, S. and G. Simons. 2003. Seven dimensions of portability for language documentation and description. *Language* 79.3: 557–82.

Bowern, C. 2008. *Linguistic Fieldwork. A Practical Guide*. New York: Palgrave MacMillan.

Cameron, D., E. Frazer, P. Harvey, M. B. H. Rampton, and K. Richardson. 1992. Ethics, advocacy and empowerment: issues of method in researching language. *Language and Communication* 13.2: 81–94.

Chafe, W. L., ed. 1980. *The Pear Stories: Cognitive, Cultural, and Linguistic Aspects of Narrative Production*. Norwood, NJ: Ablex.

Chelliah, S. 1997. *A Grammar of Meithei*. Berlin: Mouton de Gruyter.

   2001. The role of text collection and elicitation in linguistic fieldwork. In P. Newman and M. Ratliff, eds. *Linguistic Fieldwork*. Cambridge University Press, 152–65.

Chelliah, S. and W. J. de Reuse. 2011. *Handbook of Descriptive Linguistic Fieldwork*. Dordrecht: Springer.

Comrie, B. and N. Smith. 1977. The Lingua Descriptive Studies Questionnaire. www.eva. mpg.de/lingua/tools-at-lingboard/questionnaire/linguaQ.php#syntax (accessed May 20, 2013). Department of Linguistics, Max Planck Institute for Evolutionary Anthropology.

Comrie, B., M. Haspelmath, and B. Bickel. 2008. The Leipzig Glossing Rules: conventions for interlinear morpheme-by-morpheme glosses. Leipzig: Department of Linguistics, Max Planck Institute for Evolutionary Anthropology and Department of Linguistics, University of Leipzig. Available at: www.eva.mpg.de/lingua/pdf/ LGR08.02.05.pdf (accessed July 8, 2013).

Crowley, T. 2007. *Field Linguistics. A Beginner's Guide*. Oxford University Press.

Cukor-Avila, P. 2006. Researching naturally occurring speech. *Encyclopedia of Languages and Linguistics*, 2nd edn. Oxford: Elsevier, 556–63.

Dixon, R. M. W. 1992. Naive linguistic explanation. *Language in Society* 21: 83–91.

2007. Field linguistics: a minor manual. *Sprachtypologie und Universalienforschung* (Focus on Linguistic Fieldwork, ed. A. Y. Aikhenvald) 60.1: 12–31.

2010a. *Basic Linguistic Theory. Volume 1: Methodology*. Oxford University Press.

2010b. *Basic Linguistic Theory. Volume 2: Grammatical Topics*. Oxford University Press.

2012. *Basic Linguistic Theory. Volume 3: Further Grammatical Topics*. Oxford University Press.

Dwyer, A. 2006. Ethics and practicalities of cooperative fieldwork and analysis. In J. Gippert, N. Himmelmann, and U. Mosel, eds. *Essentials of Language Documentation*. Berlin: Mouton de Gruyter, 31–66.

Edwards, J. A. and M. D. Lampert, eds. 1993. *Talking Data: Transcription and Coding in Discourse Research*. Hillsdale, NJ: Lawrence Erlbaum Associates.

Enfield, N. J., S. C. Levinson, J. P. de Ruiter, and T. Stivers. 2007. Building a corpus of multimodal interaction in your field site. In A. Majid, ed. *Field Manual Volume 10*. Leipzig: Max Planck Institute for Psycholinguistics, 96–9.

Evans, N. 2001. The last speaker is dead – long live the last speaker. In P. Newman and M. Ratliff, eds. *Linguistic Fieldwork*. Cambridge University Press, 250–81.

Evans, N. and A. Dench. 2006. Introduction: catching language. In F. Ameka, A. Dench, and N. Evans, eds. *Catching Language: The Standing Challenge of Grammar Writing*. (Trends in Linguistics. Studies and Monographs 167.) Berlin: Mouton de Gruyter, 1–39.

Evans, N. and H.-J. Sassex. 2007. Searching for meaning in the library of Babel: field semantics and problems of digital archiving. *Archives and Social Studies: A Journal of Interdisciplinary Research* 1.0: 260–320. http://socialstudies.cartagena.es/index. php?option+com_content&task=view&id=38&Itemid=33 (accessed May 20, 2013).

Everett, D. L. 2001. Monolingual field research. In P. Newman and M. Ratliff, eds. *Linguistic Fieldwork*. Cambridge University Press, 166–88.

Gordon, M. 2003. Collecting phonetic data on endangered languages. *15th International Congress of Phonetic Sciences*, 207–10.

Grenoble, L. A. and L. J. Whaley. 2006. Orthography. In *Saving Languages. An Introduction to Language Revitalization*. Cambridge University Press, 137–59.

Himmelmann, N. P. 2006. Language documentation: what is it and what is it good for? In J. Gippert, N. Himmelmann, and U. Mosel, eds. *Essentials of Language Documentation*. Berlin: Mouton de Gruyter, 1–30.

Hinton, L. 2001. New writing systems. In L. Hinton and K. Hale, eds. *The Green Book of Language Revitalization in Practice*. San Diego, CA: Academic Press, 239–50.

Hopkins, J. D. and L. Furbee. 1991. Indirectness in the interview. *Journal of Linguistic Anthropology* 1.1: 63–77.

Kendall, T. 2008. On the history and future of sociolinguistic data. *Language and Linguistic Compass* 2.2: 332–51.

Krifka, M. 2011. Varieties of semantic evidence. In C. Maienborn, K. Von Heusinger, and P. Portner, eds. *Semantics: An International Handbook of Natural Language Meaning*, 2 vols. Berlin: Mouton de Gruyter, Volume I, 242–67.

Krishnamurti, B. 2007. Fieldwork on Konda, a Dravidian language. *Sprachtypologie und Universalienforschung* (Focus on Linguistic Fieldwork, ed. Alexandra Aikhenvald) 60.1: 56–66.

Kroeger, P. R. 2005. *Analyzing Grammar. An Introduction*. Cambridge University Press.

Ladefoged, P. 2003. *Phonetic Data Analysis: An Introduction to Fieldwork and Instrumental Techniques*. Malden, MA: Blackwell.

Maddieson, I. 2001. Phonetic fieldwork. In P. Newman and M. Ratliff, eds. *Linguistic Fieldwork*. Cambridge University Press, 211–29.

Majid, A. 2012. A guide to stimulus-based elicitation for semantic categories. In N. Thieberger, ed. *The Oxford Handbook of Linguistic Fieldwork*. New York: Oxford University Press, 54–71.

Matthewson, L. 2004. On the methodology of semantic fieldwork. *International Journal of American Linguistics* 70.4: 369–415.

Merrifield, W., C. Naish, C. Rensch, and G. Story, eds. 2003. *Laboratory Manual for Morphology and Syntax*, 7th edn. Dallas, TX: SIL International.

Milroy, L. 1987. *Observing and Analyzing Natural Language. A Critical Account of Sociolinguistic method*. (Language in Society 12.) Oxford: Basil Blackwell.

Mithun, M. 2001. Who shapes the record: the speaker and the linguist. In P. Newman and M. Ratliff, eds. *Linguistic Fieldwork*. Cambridge University Press, 34–54.

Mosel, U. 2006a. Grammaticography: the art and craft of writing grammars. In F. Ameka, A. Dench, and N. Evans, eds. *Catching Language: The Standing Challenge of Grammar Writing*. (Trends in Linguistics. Studies and Monographs 167.) Berlin: Mouton de Gruyter, 41–68.

2006b. Sketch Grammar. In J. Gippert, N. Himmelmann, and U. Mosel, eds. *Essentials of Language Documentation*. Berlin: Mouton de Gruyter, 301–9.

Mushin, I. and B. Baker, eds. 2008. *Discourse and Grammar in Australian Languages*. (Studies in Language Companion Series 104.) Amsterdam and Philadelphia: John Benjamins.

Newman, P. and M. Ratliff. 2001. Introduction. In *Linguistic Fieldwork*. Cambridge University Press, 1–14.

Payne, T. E. 2006. *Exploring Language Structure. A Student's Guide*. Cambridge University Press.

Reiman, D. W. 2010. Basic oral language documentation. *Language Documentation and Conservation* 4: 254–68. http://nflrc.hawaii.edu/ldc/2010 (accessed May 20, 2013).

Research Center for Linguistic Typology. 2009. *Fieldwork Manual. Fieldwork and Your Wellbeing*. Bundoora, Australia: La Trobe University, Research Center for Linguistic Typology.

Rice, K. 1995. Developing orthographies: the Athapaskan languages of the Northwest Territories, Canada. In I. Taylor and D. R. Olson, eds. *Scripts and Literacy*. The Netherlands: Kluwer, 77–94.

2006. Let the language tell its story? The role of linguistic theory in writing grammars. In F. K. Ameka, A. Dench, and N. Evans, eds. *Catching Language: The Standing Challenge of Grammar Writing*. (Trends in Linguistics. Studies and Monographs 167.) Berlin: Mouton de Gruyter, 235–68.

2012. Ethical issues in linguistic fieldwork: an overview. In N. Thieberger, ed. *The Oxford Handbook of Linguistic Fieldwork*. Oxford University Press, 407–29.

Saeed, J. I. 2009. *Semantics*, 3rd edn. Malden, MA: Wiley-Blackwell.

Sakel, J. and D. Everett. 2012. *Linguistic Fieldwork : A Student Guide*. Cambridge University Press.

Sapir, E. 1921. *Language: An Introduction to the Study of Speech*. New York: Harcourt Brace.

Schultze-Berndt, E. 2006. Linguistic annotation. In J. Gippert, N. Himmelmann, and U. Mosel, eds. *Essentials of Language Documentation*. Berlin: Mouton de Gruyter, 213–51.

Sebba, M. 2007. *Spelling and Society: The Culture and Politics of Orthography around the World*. Cambridge University Press.

Seifart, F. 2006. Orthography development. In J. Gippert, N. Himmelmann, and U. Mosel, eds. *Essentials of Language Documentation*. Berlin: Mouton de Gruyter, 275–99.

Shopen, T., ed. 1985. *Language Typology and Syntactic Description. Vol. I: Clause Structure; Vol. II: Complex Constructions; Vol. III: Grammatical Categories and the Lexicon*. Cambridge University Press.

2007. *Language Typology and Syntactic Description. Vol. I: Clause Structure; Vol. II: Complex Constructions; Vol. III: Grammatical Categories and the Lexicon*, 2nd edn. Cambridge University Press.

Vaux, B., J. Cooper, and E. Tucker. 2007. *Linguistic Field Methods*. Eugene, OR: Wipf and Stock.

5   Population samples

Isabelle Buchstaller and Ghada Khattab

Data without generalisation is just gossip.
(Pirsig 1991: 55, in Chambers 2003: xix)

1   Introduction

So you want to investigate the language used by a group of people. One of the first questions you might ask yourself is: Who do I collect these data from? A crucial element of empirical linguistic work is to choose not only what type of data to collect (e.g., naturally occurring data, interview data, questionnaire data, experimental data; see Part I of this volume), but also which people to target for data collection. The most reliable method for finding out about the language use of a particular group of people would be to collect linguistic information from every single person in the *population*, which in the social sciences refers to all members of the community. Obviously, except for very small populations, this method is rather impractical, expensive, and time-consuming. Hence, most researchers only target "some people in the group in such a way that their responses and characteristics reflect those of the group from which they are drawn ... This is the principle of *sampling*" (De Vaus 2001: 60). The subgroup of people that reflects the population as a whole (in terms of their social and linguistic characteristics), and therefore lends itself to generalizations above and beyond the scope of the study, is called a *representative sample*. The question we need to ask as linguists is: To what extent are the findings reported on the basis of a subsample representative of the linguistic habits of a certain population or group?

Many social scientists would argue that representativeness can only be assumed if the characteristics of the sampled group match those of the population at large. This effectively means that our sample must not favor some sectors of the population over others (so that no sectors of the population are excluded or under- or over-represented). For example, in the past 50 years (except for 1981) the census of the United Kingdom was conducted at the end of April, which for many English universities fell during the Easter break. This meant that a large section of the student population were not at their regular place of study, but rather visiting their family back home (sometimes abroad) or on holiday. As a result, the census did not accurately reflect the populations that live in these areas; the data were *biased* toward non-student, non-foreign populations. This sampling bias was avoided in 2011, when the census was conducted during term time. Representativeness thus implies the avoidance of biases in the data that would make generalization impossible.[1]

Note, however, that in the field of linguistics, social representativeness is not easily achieved, since language varies across a wide range of social dimensions within a population, such as speakers' age, gender, sexuality, ethnic identity, regional background, educational level, and many others. Also to be taken into account are situational and conversational factors, such as the level of formality, the speaking style, accommodation to interlocutors, conversational topic, and ideological factors, among many others, each of which potentially introduces a bias into the sample. All of this leads to a considerable challenge for linguists: how do we sample in order to avoid biases in our data?

Sankoff (1974: 21) points out that every researcher must make a decision about their "sampling universe," namely, the groups or communities they want to investigate (e.g., the residents of a particular city or neighborhood, the members of a reading group or a garage band). Having made a decision about whom to investigate, "good data is [then] defined as language materials of sufficient type and quantity, as well as materials which take into account the social context in which the language data is gathered" (Sankoff 1974: 21–2; see also Milroy 1987: 18). As our initial sampling choices establish what type of population our data are representative of and about whom we can make generalizations, those sampling decisions fundamentally constrain the types of questions we can answer. For example, data from teenagers in an affluent suburb in the San Francisco Bay area (Buchstaller et al. 2010) cannot make any generalizations about people or of the state of California as a whole. If the study had intended to make more general claims it would have had to sample across a broader range of social groups (e.g., younger and older speakers, or a wide variety of social backgrounds across the whole state). Tagliamonte (2006) emphasizes the intimate connection between sampling method and research question: "At the outset, a (socio)linguistic project must have (at least) two parts 1) a (socio)linguistic problem and 2) appropriate data to address it."

Linguistic researchers have been using a wealth of different types of sampling methods – mostly adapted from sociology, developmental psychology, anthropology, or (economic) geography – which vary vastly with time and linguistic subdiscipline. Generally, these sampling methods fall into two basic groups: those that strive for representativeness, also known as probability methods, and those that do not, also called non-probability methods. "Non-probability methods cannot be used to make statistical inferences about the population from which

---

[1] A sample is hardly ever a perfect replication of the statistical distribution of all subgroups in the population; differences between sample and population are often due to biases called *sampling error*.

they are drawn. In choosing to adopt non-probability methods [such as single case studies] one must therefore accept that statistically rigorous representativeness is not a primary issue in the research design" (Rice 2010: 232). The main aim of this chapter is to describe the types of sampling that are commonly used in linguistic research, namely convenience sampling, random sampling, stratified sampling, ethnographic sampling, and network sampling. A secondary goal is to describe further issues that arise in specific linguistic subdisciplines.

2   Types of sampling

2.1   Convenience sampling

Some researchers recruit subjects bearing not only representativeness in mind, but also convenient accessibility. It is thus not surprising that the most frequent subject pool in convenience sampling is student volunteers. Obviously, convenience sampling excludes a great proportion of the total population, resulting in an unknown amount of systematic biases. This effectively means that there is a fair chance that a study based on convenience sampling reports skewed results, and we have to be careful about any inferences made. Research based on a convenience sampling is thus rather limited in its generalizability. Why do researchers rely on this sampling method? Primarily because it is quick and easy. Convenience sampling is often used in pilot studies since it allows the researcher to survey the field before setting up a more elaborate sample. It is also regularly used in experiments conducted in linguistic paradigms such as theoretical syntax/semantics/ phonology, which assume that there is little interpersonal variation (or that such variation is inconsequential for the theoretical model), due to a stable underlying representation across the population. Note that in some instances, convenience sampling is theory independent and therefore more justified – for example, when the speech community is so restricted that the researcher has to sample everyone they can get their hands on. This is particularly the case with fieldwork on endangered languages and/or very small speech communities.

2.2   Random sampling

De Vaus (2001: 60) argues that "the surest way of providing equal probability of selection is to use the principle of random selection. This involves listing all members of the population (this list is called a *sampling frame*) and then . . . 'pulling their names out of a hat.'" What this effectively means is that in a *random sample* of a group or community (i.e., a city such as London, a country such as Brazil), every member of that community has an equal chance of being chosen for participating in the research. Early sampling strategies used in linguistics included choosing people randomly out of telephone books or electoral registers. So in a population of a hundred people, for example, we might select twenty members based on a set of twenty randomly generated numbers between one and a hundred. The problem with this type of random sampling is that it "requires a good sampling frame. While these may be available in some populations (e.g. organisations such as schools, churches, unions), adequate lists are often not available for larger population surveys of a city, state or country" (De Vaus 2001: 64).

A more tractable way of sampling representatively is to construct a *systematic sample*. We do this by dividing the population size by the intended sample size and then sampling a representative fraction. For example, if the population is 10,000, but we only have time or money to sample 200, we interview one person out of every 50 (200/10,000) people (see Rice 2010). This can be more feasible than genuinely random selection, and can lead to a more even sample, but assumes a reliably homogeneous population.

The main asset of random sampling is that it can lay claim to representativeness in a statistical sense, which permits extrapolation from the sample studied to the larger population. It also allows the researcher to examine the full spectrum of the target population sampled. This is particularly the case when investigating a large complex community, "especially if it has a high degree of randomness, as in an urban setting in which the neighborhoods are not preselected, [which] requires some kind of indexing procedure in order to cluster the subjects into appropriate social groups" (Chambers 2003: 45).

But random sampling is not without its problems. As De Vaus (2001: 64) points out, the cost and effort involved are often "prohibitive. It would probably involve interviewers travelling long distances just for one interview … [Hence random sampling] is most appropriate when … the population is geographically concentrated or the data collection technique does not involve travelling." Furthermore, even supposedly random sampling methods tend to introduce biases into the sample, so that, for example, electoral registers are biased toward the adult native population and telephone books tend to be cut up by geographical areas such as wards, regions, or postal/telecommunication boundaries. Indeed, the random samples used in actual linguistic research hardly ever live up to the stringent exigencies of random sampling under a strict sociological definition: once chosen by the sampling frame, some people move away, refuse to participate, fall ill or die, turn out to be uncooperative, or simply cannot find the time. These individuals either leave gaps in the original survey design or have to be replaced by speakers that have the exact same social characteristics, reducing randomness in selection. Thus, in actual practice, random sampling is hardly ever completely random.

The uneven distribution of populations across space adds a further bias to the data: subgroups tend to be geographically or socially distributed in non-random ways, so the assumption of homogeneity that is necessary for random sampling is often invalid. Random sampling also virtually guarantees that interviewee and interviewer are complete strangers, which tends to result in rather formal speech styles. This is a problem for those linguistic subdisciplines that aim to investigate a range of different stylistic levels or tap into the interviewees' most casual speech behavior (see the Observer's Paradox, Chapter 6). Finally, in some linguistic subdisciplines, participants need to be recorded in labs, which is unfeasible if they are expected to travel from remote, randomly selected locations.

Despite all its shortcomings, however, in cases where the researcher does not know the area to be investigated or its salient social distinctions, random sampling might help to explore which social dimensions correlate with or indeed condition language use (see also Milroy and Gordon 2003).

2.3   Stratified random sampling (judgment or quota sampling) ▨

The difficulties associated with random sampling have led many linguists to weigh "the costs of achieving statistical representativeness against the limited additional benefits it might provide" (Milroy and Gordon 2003: 26). This is a particularly pertinent concern since "speech communities tend to consist of many varieties spoken by groups containing very different numbers of individuals, so that uniform sampling leads to redundancies for some groups and risks missing others entirely" (Sankoff 1988: 900). Contemporary linguistic research tends to rely instead on the principle that a sample needs to be representative for the purposes of the study. Linguists who use this reasoning decide "on the basis of prior experience" (Rice 2010: 240) which stratifying variable(s) matter in a population. They then identify in advance the types of speaker groups they want to investigate – those hypothesized to correlate with linguistic variability – and sample systematically from these groups. For example, a study that wants to investigate the language use of a certain area (such as a particular barrio of Buenos Aires) or of a certain ethnic group (such as Pakistani immigrants in Saudi Arabia) would divide the population into mutually exclusive subgroups, called *strata*, and sample within these subgroups, making sure that all the subgroups of the population are represented proportionately within the sampling frame. This technique, which has been widely adopted for sampling in linguistics, is called stratified random or judgment sampling.

Although the original conception of judgment sampling was based on sampling within each stratum (using, e.g., a fraction of 1/50th of every social grouping), later studies have suggested that the aim of a sample is not to be "a miniature version of the population but only that we have the possibility of making inferences about the population based on the sample" (Sankoff 1988: 900). For example, Gordon's (2001) study of phonological changes in two small towns in Michigan aimed at investigating the Northern Cities Vowel Shift. He collected data from sixteen speakers, equally stratified by age and gender in two towns, one relatively close to Detroit and another approximately halfway between Detroit and Chicago. Structuring his sample in such a way, Gordon was able to "examine the interactions of three important social variables [location, age and gender] . . . using a relatively small number of speakers . . . [Importantly], the choice of social variables to investigate was guided by the objectives of the study" (Milroy and Gordon 2003: 34).

Tagliamonte (2006) suggests that a stratified sample should be representative, at the minimum, with respect to age, sex, social class, and educational level. While these social categories have proven important for numerous large-scale studies, Chambers (2003) has pointed out that many artist and student communities tend not to be differentiated by factors such as gender or class. Furthermore, in many communities, particularly less well-studied, non-Western contexts, other factors – such as kinship, experience, urbanness, or religion – underlie the creation and perception of social divisions and linguistic usage. The very relativity of such criteria suggests that we need to consider the local context of the community when making decisions about our data collection strategy. Crucially, in the absence of prior experience with the people we aim to investigate, a sampling strategy that relies on predetermined categories might miss important local social contrasts, or might end up being governed by the prejudices or preconceptions of the researcher rather than orienting to local categories.

2.4   Ethnographic approaches

Ethnographic data collection is the antithesis of random sampling: notions such as randomness, representativeness, or indeed statistically generated generalizability of results are not relevant to this empirical methodology. Instead, ethnographic research aims at the discovery of *emic* categories, the social, cognitive, cultural, and linguistic contrasts that are salient in a particular community (as opposed to *etic* criteria, namely, extrinsic concepts and categories imposed by the researcher; see Chapter 10). Eckert (2000: 69) describes this approach succinctly: "while survey fieldwork focuses on filling the sample, ethnographic fieldwork focuses on finding out what is worth sampling."

Crucially, the local sociocultural distinctions acquired via ethnographic fieldwork expand the researcher's explanatory possibilities, allowing them to move beyond standardly assumed macrosocial categories, such as age, sex, and gender, and toward *participant-designed* categories. Indeed, the criteria for stratification that fall out of ethnographic research are generally not objective, global categories, but rather contrasts that reflect the procedures local participants employ in constructing and recognizing social worlds. This can result in groupings as unpredictable as, among the Wishram Chinook tribe (Hymes 1972), adults and children past babyhood as a first community, babies, dogs, coyotes, and guardian spirits as a second community, and those "whose guardian spirit experience had granted them the power of being able to interpret the language of the spirits" (p. 28) as a third.

Since a deep sense of the locally salient social groupings and values can only be achieved via sustained presence in the community, researchers doing ethnographic fieldwork typically "hang ... out" (Giddens 2006: 85) or live with the group whose practices are of interest, becoming a *participant observer* rather than merely an outsider/interviewer, and sampling data according to ethnographic relevance. Ethnographic research thus has the crucial advantage that it allows us not only to collect reports of the cultural context that might impinge on language use, but also to observe these practices first hand. The researcher's access goes beyond linguistic behavior to include other behavioral practices, attitudes, ideologies, and information on how the people understand their own and others' behavior, all of which can help us interpret linguistic practices. As such, the data produced by ethnographic fieldwork is, by its very nature, much *richer* than data resulting from other data collection techniques. It often documents informants' behavior in a variety of situations, and thus a range of speaking styles, including the vernacular sought after in variationist sociolinguistic research (see Chapter 6).

While unparalleled in terms of the depth and quality of the data produced, the ethnographic approach to sampling is also the most cost-intensive in terms of time and effort committed per researcher. As a rule of thumb, most researchers estimate an outcome ratio of at least 10:1 (ten hours spent in the field yield roughly one hour of recorded data). In addition, since the data are so highly specific to the local setting, the resulting findings are inherently difficult to compare, contrast, or collate with other datasets. Indeed, testing the reliability of findings culled from ethnographic data would mean spending an equal amount of time in the same community. Hence, ethnographic data is not representative in a statistical sense (see Eckert 2000; Tagliamonte 2006: 27); any generalized claims beyond the confines of this community have to be treated with care. Note, however, that the categorizations that emerge from ethnographic fieldwork are not merely subjective, but rather intersubjective since they (ideally) converge with the community's assessment.

2.5   Social network or snowball sampling

The technique known as the social network or snowball sampling technique also aims to investigate locally specific, participant-designed groups. Unlike ethnographic sampling, this approach does aim to examine quantitative variation across the group, but uses networks for the recruitment and sampling of participants. The term *friend-of-a-friend approach* in network sampling was coined by Lesley and James Milroy (1992), who contacted their participants by being referred from friend to friend, neighbor, or acquaintance in working-class neighborhoods in Belfast. In conjunction with this recruitment approach, they measured individuals' network status and found that linguistic variation did not necessarily correlate with the etic categories used in stratified sampling, but did correlate with certain types of networks.

While this approach shares some of the limitations of ethnographic fieldwork in terms of the time investment needed in order to enter the network, and the tact and emotional involvement required to operate within it, one of the inherent advantages of this technique is that informants are less likely to decline a request for an interview if the researcher has been referred to them by a friend. Another positive side effect of network sampling is that the researcher encounters a great amount of social information that flows in networks.

The Community of Practice approach is similarly concerned with the social practices of a subsection of the speech community, whereby membership is established by the participants themselves, rather than by the researcher (Holmes and Meyerhoff 1999: 175–6; Meyerhoff 2002: 527–8). A Community of Practice framework assumes that participants negotiate the meaning of linguistic variables and therefore may not always behave similarly with respect to their use of these resources (Eckert 1989, 2000). This sampling method can lead to more ethnographic analysis, with full immersion into a network, or it can be combined with random sampling, only using snowball sampling for recruitment purposes and to establish participant-designed categories, but aiming at a more stratified sample overall.

Social network sampling thus combines elements of random sampling and ethnography: whereas random and judgment sampling see the individual speaker as a representative of abstract, predefined social categories, such as age, gender, and class, social network sampling focuses on voluntary membership in participant-designed networks or social groupings. Unlike ethnographic methods, however, social network sampling usually does not entail the researcher's complete immersion into the local community.

The preceding subsections have shown that linguists draw on a wealth of strategies to collect samples from a given population or group of people. These sampling techniques can be, and often are, combined, so that, for example, networks might be recruited to fill in the sample cells for a judgment sample or, alternatively, an ethnographic project might attempt to contrast participant-designed categories against macro-social categories (see Labov et al.'s 1968 studies in South Harlem). Generally, though, the choices we make in terms of sampling strategies tend to be motivated by our theoretical persuasions about the fabric of social structure, our research questions, and, at times, our wider epistemological commitments. These choices have crucial consequences for the interpretation of data, since the type and amount of data we collect fundamentally determines the results we get, the statistical models we can use (see Chapters 14–16), and, ultimately, the questions we can answer.

2.6   Size matters

Once we have chosen our sampling method, the next question that arises is how much data is enough? Social scientists tend to believe in the mantra that big numbers are beautiful. This is because large samples allow us to draw more reliable inferences about the behavior of the whole population. Crucially, however, statisticians tell us that the choice of sample size essentially depends on the degree of accuracy we are aiming for: we need to choose the degree of error we are prepared to tolerate in our sample. Table 5.1 (from De Vaus 2001: 71) depicts the sample sizes needed in order to be 95 percent confident that the behavior of the sample chosen from the population is the same as the behavior of the population at large plus or minus the sampling error (for confidence limits, see also Moser and Kalton 1971; Woods, Fletcher, and Hughes 1986; also Chapter 15).

Table 5.1 *Relationship between sample size and sampling error. De Vaus 2001: 71*

Sampling error[a]	Sample size	Sampling error	Sample size
1.0	10000	5.5	330
1.5	4500	6.0	277
2.0	2500	6.5	237
2.5	1600	7.0	204
3.0	1100	7.5	178
3.5	816	8.0	156
4.0	625	8.5	138
4.5	494	9.0	123
5.0	400	9.5	110
		10	100

Notes: [a] This is in fact two standard errors.

Thus, for example, if we find that 34 percent in our sample of 816 people merge their low back vowels [ɒ] and [ɔ:], as is common in many American dialects, we can be 95 percent confident that between 37.5 and 30.5 percent (34 percent plus/minus 3.5 percent) of the population at large do indeed merge their vowels.[2] Table 5.1 reveals that increasing the sample size with smaller numbers has a disproportionately large effect on improving the sampling error. In fact, De Vaus points out that many survey companies restrict their samples to 2,000, because the extra cost involved in increasing the sample does not have enough payout in terms of increased accuracy. Giddens (2006: 88) suggests a similar figure for research in sociology, arguing that "studies of only two or three thousand voters, for instance, can give a very accurate indication of the attitudes and voting intentions of the entire population." These are obviously very large numbers that are unattainable for most linguistic research programs. We might want to ask what is the absolute minimum sample size that allows us to generalize from our data with reasonable confidence. Generally speaking, Neumann (2007: 222) gives as a rule of thumb for the social sciences that a small population (< 1,000) would be accurately represented by a sample of 300 (hence 3 percent), whereas a larger population (> 150,000) would require a sample size of at least 1,500.

Linguistic studies tend to be based on much smaller samples of informants than research in other areas in the social sciences (but see below). The reason for this is first and foremost a practical one: The lions' share of quantitative research in fields

---

[2] The numbers in Table 5.1 are given for very large populations. Indeed, De Vaus (2001: 71–2) points out that "the size of the population from which we draw the sample is largely irrelevant for the accuracy of the sample. It is the absolute size of the sample that is important. The only exception to this is when the sample size represents a sizable proportion of the population (e.g. 10 percent). In such cases a slightly smaller sample is equally accurate."

such as geography, demography, or political science is based on secondary data, which means that the cost of data collection and handling are borne by large agencies like the national census or commercial institutions. Also, those social scientists who do not work with pre-collected data tend to rely on surveys, questionnaires, GPS tracking, or notes from focus groups, none of which requires the time-intensive linguistic recording and transcription work which explodes data-handling time by a subdiscipline-dependent ratio (ten hours of word-for-word transcription per recorded hour; 1:100 for close phonetic transcription, and potentially even more when transcribing children's speech; see Chapter 12). Consequently, even linguistic projects that initially aimed for big numbers have not been able to process all the data gathered. For example, the Shuy, Wolfram, and Riley study (1967) randomly sampled and interviewed 254 families (702 subjects in total) in Detroit. Exigencies of time and data handling reduced the number of speech samples they could analyze to only sixty speakers, and the principal linguistic analysis was limited to thirty-six of those (Wolfram 1969). Thus, the great majority of linguistic studies tend to rely on a fraction of the sample size commonly used in other social sciences.

Note, however, that the ratio of observations to informant numbers in linguistics is in an inverse relationship to most other social science research. While, for example, a study on voting behavior or religious affiliation tends to collect one or very few observations from many informants, linguistic research typically relies on fewer informants, but collects many observations from every single one of them. For example, Khattab and Al-Tamimi (in press) collected longitudinal data from ten toddlers for a phonological acquisition study, but the token number in their statistical design was 5,697 words. Hence, linguistic research can attain a relatively large number of observations by relying on a smaller number of informants. What this effectively means is that in the field of linguistics, the notion of sample size needs to be further specified: Are we referring to the number of observations or the number of informants? Note that, ideally, linguistic research that relies on a large number of observations per speaker ought to treat speaker as a random variable in a mixed-effects model (see Roberts 2012; Johnson in press; also Chapter 16).

In fact, we might want to argue that large informant numbers are not even necessary for the purposes of language research. It is well known that "the larger the size and the lower the population heterogeneity, the more precise sample estimates will be" (Rice 2010: 230). Hence, the precision of a sample is a function not only of the number of observations, but also of the amount of variability within the population as regards the feature of interest. The fact that language is based on mutual intelligibility "places a limit on the extent of possible variation, and imposes a regularity (necessary for effective communication) not found to the same extent in other kinds of social behaviour" (Sankoff 1980: 51). Indeed, the kind of speech that tends to be investigated in most linguistic subdisciplines is more homogeneous than other types of variable behavior, since it is "not subject to the informants' control in the way that answers on voting choices [or other forms

Table 5.2 *The database for Spanish second language acquisition. Mitchell et al. 2008: 293*[3]

	TOTAL
Year 9 (13–14)	20
A2 students (17–18)	20
Undergraduate (19 plus)	20
TOTAL	60

of social behavior] would be" (Labov 1966: 180). Consequently, the recommendation in the literature is that "even for quite complex communities samples of more than about 150 individuals tend to be redundant, bringing increasing data-handling problems with diminishing analytical returns" (Sankoff 1980: 51–2).

In terms of minimum numbers, Meyerhoff and Schleef (2010) argue that five or six speakers per cell suffice in order to make statistically sound generalizations about the data collected. For example, the Spanish learner database created by Mitchell et al. (2008) consists of twenty learners of Spanish at each of three levels, illustrated in Table 5.2.

Making the sample more robust by adding just five speakers per cell would require fifteen more speakers overall. Including another factor, such as the speaker's motivation to learn Spanish (divided, say, into two levels, higher or lower), would require sixty more speakers overall, an increase of 100 percent. This example demonstrates the extent to which sampling design is fundamentally determined by practical considerations such as financial and temporal resources. Needless to say, if a researcher decides to exclude a factor, variation along this dimension must be controlled for rather than ignored in the sample, which effectively shrinks the size of the population under investigation.

2.7   Applications and developments

If we divide the data collection methods used across linguistic subfields into "armchair," "field," and "laboratory" (Clark and Bangerter 2004: 25), it is not surprising that the interest in sampling and stratification issues has primarily grown out of those subfields using empirical methods in which there is a perceived need to justify one's database. Since sociolinguistics, developmental linguistics, and cognitive linguistics place more weight on the representativeness of their data, these subdisciplines have historically contributed most to our knowledge base on sampling strategies. However, as linguists' thinking about the impact of social, cognitive, and idiolectal effects on language use and of the scientists' role in

---

[3] Age can be sliced up in a number of ways. In Table 5.2, it is treated as a categorical variable, but numerical age could also have been treated as a continuous variable. The decision about whether to treat age as continuous or categorical has important ramifications for the statistical model we choose for the analysis of our data (see Chapter 14).

defining and ratifying "social categories" has evolved, sampling methodology has become more precise throughout the field. In the remainder of this chapter, we provide a brief overview of how sampling has evolved in a selection of linguistic subdisciplines.

3   Sampling in subdisciplines of linguistics

3.1   Theoretical linguistics

Theoretical research in the generative tradition has often been associated with so-called "armchair" methods: "you imagine examples of language used in this or that situation and ask yourself whether they are grammatical or ungrammatical, natural or unnatural, appropriate or inappropriate" (Clark and Bangerter 2004: 25). This practice may have arisen out of (early) generativist claims that the intuitions of every native speaker fully represent linguistic competence (see Chomsky's 1965 concept of the "ideal speaker"). Indeed, if every native speaker has the same hard-wired language faculty – I-Language, bioprogram, or Universal Grammar, depending on the flavor of generative theory – consulting a range of speakers about the same phenomenon would only lead to replications of information and amount to a waste of time.

In recent years, theoretical linguistics has adopted increasingly sophisticated methods of sampling data, often continuing to rely on small numbers of respondents, but using more finely calibrated elicitation procedures (see Chapter 3). Usage-based theoretical research is also engaged in more robust empirical inquiry, often taking advantage of the ever-increasing number of pre-collected, pre-transcribed, even syntactically parsed corpora (see Chapters 11 and 13). Concerns with empirical methods, including questions of sampling, have consequently become more widespread in these subfields. Most recently, theoretical research, in particular situated at the interface with cognitive and/or sociolinguistics, has started to rely on very large samples (in terms of informants as well as observations). Wolk et al. (in press), for example, extracted 3,824 tokens of *'s*-genitive and *of*-dative constructions from the Archer Corpus (which spans the period 1650–1990), in order to demonstrate how short-term distributional fluctuations can trigger long-term changes in probabilistic grammars. A number of linguists have also used the World Wide Web to sample even larger numbers of tokens (e.g., Walter and Jaeger [2008], who extracted 260 million instances of *that is* and over 37 million instances of *this is*). Such large samples allow testing for a large amount of interacting effects. Research based on questionnaires, such as magnitude estimation, and collected via web-based platforms also tends to rely on larger numbers (see, e.g., Bard, Robertson, and Sorace 1996).

Note, however, that these large-scale projects are for the most part based on convenience samples and often give no information about the number or social profile of their informants. As such, they do not claim to sample randomly or to fill predetermined social strata, nor do they make any attempt at ascertaining the social homogeneity of their informants. While the social representativeness of these studies is not necessarily a given, the theoretical claim of most research in this field would be that the large numbers of observations allow for making generalizations in a statistical sense about the linguistic structure in their sample.

Sampling in theoretical fields that use experimental methods tends to follow standard social scientific practice most closely; elements of sampling and organization of participant pools are discussed further in Chapter 7.

3.2   Dialectology

The sampling strategy of early dialectological projects was driven by the perceived need to document a "genuine" or "pure" form of the language (see Milroy and Gordon 2003) before it disappeared, resulting in the practice of targeting conservative rural speakers who were assumed to portray the most traditional dialect features (non-mobile older rural males, or NORMs; see Chambers and Trudgill 1998). In the 1970s and 1980s, in line with the positivist epistemologies that pervaded the social sciences at the time, a range of sampling methods were adopted from economic geography. In particular, grid sampling, which involves superimposing a matrix of equivalently sized cells on the area to be sampled and selecting an equivalent number of participants from each, was adapted for quantitative dialectological projects. The rationale for this random spatial sampling was that it avoids the problem of missing small spatial structures, thus avoiding bias. Note, however, that grid sampling is the geographical equivalent to random sampling in a single speech community: it is a priori, static, and entirely independent of human activity (Romaine 1980; Milroy and Gordon 2003).

More recently, critical reflections on sampling in dialectology have problematized the operationalization of space as socially uniform carrier material over which linguistic variability can be superimposed (Britain 2004, 2010). Geographers as well as dialectologists have argued for socially sensitive projects relying on a greater amount of ethnographic fieldwork. As a consequence, sampling methods in contemporary dialectology have become increasingly cognizant of the fundamental role which human agency and social relations play in shaping and construing geography. This has resulted in the development of geo-demographically and socio-geographically sensitive sampling criteria (see, e.g., Cheshire, Edwards, and Whittle 1989, 1993; Buchstaller and Alvanides in press).

On the other hand, large-scale linguistic atlas projects sample vast numbers of informants across a geographical area, but the number of participants included in any one place tends to be relatively restricted. For example, the Linguistic Atlas of North America (Labov, Ash, and Boberg 2006) collected 417 speakers across the territory of English-speaking North America, but only two to six informants per locality. The Syntactic Atlas of the Netherlands Dialect is based on data in 250 cells of variable geographical size for the whole of the Netherlands (Barbiers, Cornips, and Kunst 2007), with two speakers per cell. Obviously, while these informants are assumed to represent the spatial location for which they stand, they tend not to be sampled on the basis of stratificational criteria, which means that their representativeness in the social scientific sense of the term is not necessarily a given. Indeed, many atlas-style projects (a notable exception is Kurath 1972) have focused on either urban (the Linguistic Atlas of North America) or rural (the Survey of English Dialects, the Syntactic Atlas of the Netherlands Dialect) speech, which reduces the demographic representativeness of the study to just this settlement type.

3.3   Variationist sociolinguistics

The quantitative paradigm established by William Labov in the 1960s and 1970s (Labov 1966) is the main framework within which sociolinguists investigate quantitative linguistic variability in its social setting. Naturally, sampling is inherently important to uncovering socially conditioned patterns of linguistic variation. Early sociolinguistic research drew heavily on random sampling, en vogue in other social sciences at the time (see Massey 1985).

Increasing awareness of and interest in stylistic and situational variability prompted the discipline to construct samples of various kinds to answer questions about the distribution of variability across social space and to acknowledge both inter- as well as intra-speaker variation. Judgment sampling seemed to alleviate many of the problems of random sampling and continues to be favored by many sociolinguistic research projects. Since the advent of network studies in the 1970s, a number of researchers have started to target smaller groups of self-defined communities, often drawing on the methods of participant observation, adapted from anthropological linguistics and ethnography (see Eckert 2000).

The wealth of sampling methodologies currently used in sociolinguistic research suggests that "researchers are now more relaxed than they once were about methodological issues such as whether or not their account ... [is] technically representative or whether strict random sampling procedures should be used. This shift in attitude ... enables researchers to select more freely from a range of methods those which, within a defensible theoretical framework, will best enable them to achieve their goals" (Milroy and Gordon 2003: 46–8). Tagliamonte (2006: 28) proposes that sociolinguistic research is now characterized by a certain mix-and-match attitude: "the critical component of this hybrid methodology for variationist analysis is that the researchers decide which type of representativeness is sufficient – or attainable – depending on the focus of the study."

3.4   Phonetics and sociophonetics

Traditional experimental phonetic/phonological research places stringent control over the technical methods used in data collection (Foulkes, Scobbie, and Watt 2010; Scobbie and Stuart-Smith 2012). A great deal of attention is paid to the physical environment in which recordings are made, favoring laboratory over naturalistic settings, and using high-quality recording equipment in order to capture the best sound quality for auditory, acoustic, perceptual, or articulatory analysis. Laboratory phonetic research also aims to control for as many of the potential linguistic confounds as possible when analyzing sounds, yielding elicitation techniques that result in rather stilted speech (e.g., words in isolation or embedded in the infamous carrier sentences which help control for speech rate, rhythm, and neighboring sounds). Due to this laborious and detailed methodology, small numbers of speaker and tokens are justified, and male speakers are often preferred over females due to the relative ease in analyzing their spectrographic outputs. Results regarding the phonetic pattern(s) of interest (e.g., consonants, vowels, or suprasegmental features) are normally taken to be characteristic of the language of the speaker, and not much information is collected about individual sociolinguistic backgrounds, although monolingual speakers who are thought to speak a standard representative variety are often recruited to avoid noise in the data.

More recently, however, advances in theory and technology have seen an unprecedented integration of the fields of phonetics and sociolinguistics, resulting in a revamping of methodologies used (Di Paolo and Yaeger-Dror 2010; Thomas 2011; Scobbie and Stuart-Smith 2012), with positive effects on sampling.

In terms of theoretical advances, a recognition of the place of speech variability and social variation in phonological theory and models of cognition (e.g., Pierrehumbert 2002; Hawkins 2003; Kristiansen 2006; Foulkes 2010) has necessitated the use of larger, socially stratified corpora to allow gradient listener- and speaker-induced sound change to be tracked either longitudinally or in apparent-time studies (e.g., Harrington 2006, 2010; Fromont and Hay 2008). In sociolinguistic research, interest in non-categorical fine-grained variation has risen due to the discovery of its role in subtle but regular and systematic changes in perception and/or production; these, in turn, have consequences for social uses of language and for language variation and change (e.g., Docherty and Foulkes 1999; Hay, Warren, and Drager 2006). This has necessitated the use of both stratified sampling, to recruit speakers from the varieties of interest, and snowball sampling, to recruit further speakers from the same networks (Milroy and Gordon 2003: 32; Scobbie and Stuart-Smith 2012: 611) Medium-sized annotated corpora (forty to sixty speakers) that have been designed for phonetic analysis using stratified sampling techniques include the Buckeye Corpus (Pitt et al. 2005), the Nationwide Speech Project (Clopper and Pisoni 2006), and the Kiel Corpus of Speech (Kohler 2001).

In terms of technological advances, more portable professional recording and improved sound transmission technology now allow researchers to combine higher-quality field recordings with more naturalistic conditions and larger participant pools, even for physiological investigations which were traditionally confined to the lab due to heavy articulatory equipment (Gick, Bird, and Wilson 2005; Scobbie, Wrench, and van der Linden 2008; Scobbie, Stuart-Smith, and

Lawson 2009). New automated measurement techniques, now available through popular software programs such as Praat (Boersma 2001) and EMU (Harrington 2010), have also made analyses of much larger datasets feasible. Further techno-logical development and guidance are still needed to enable researchers to process these datasets and normalize across speakers (Foulkes, Scobbie, and Watt 2010: 733).

At the other end of the spectrum, advances in sociophonetic theory have also highlighted the need to look at the individual and their identity in order to under-stand their phonetic behavior (Johnstone and Bean 1997; Wassink and Dyer 2004; Docherty 2007) and the subtle phonetic patterns they employ to signal group affiliation (e.g., Docherty and Foulkes 1999; Stuart-Smith 1999, 2007; Local 2003; McDougall 2004); this justifies the use of smaller numbers of participants in order to carry out more detailed analyses on each individual. Sampling in sociophonetics has also been concerned with the characteristics of the field-worker/interviewer, as these have been shown to influence the perception and production behavior of participants, and can actually be used as part of the experimental design/research question (e.g., Hawkins and Smith 2001; Clopper and Pisoni 2004; Hay, Warren, and Drager 2006; Delvaux and Socquet 2007; Foulkes, Scobbie, and Watt 2010).

3.5   Child language research

Sampling in child language research is inextricably linked to the age and stage of development of the child, the type of data that are possible to elicit, and the level of inference one is prepared to make about the verbal and non-verbal behavior that can be gathered.

Research with infants requires the use of indirect perceptual methodologies such as the High Amplitude Sucking, head-turn, and preferential looking techni-ques (e.g., Fernald and Kuhl 1987; Eilers, Wilson, and Moore 1977) to draw inferences about the children's "raw" perceptual abilities and their journey toward tuning in to their input languages (see Menn and Ratner 2000 for an overview of data collection methods in child language research). Sample sizes are normally between ten and twenty in this age group, but attrition is very high due to having to discard non-cooperating participants, so the number of infants initially recruited for the research can be much higher.

At the onset of speech (nine to twelve months), individual differences are key, and the rate at which children show comprehension and/or production of early words can vary widely, which makes studies of language development in the second year most suited to case studies, in order to thoroughly document the child's transition to language (e.g., Leopold 1939; Brown 1973). What also necessitates the use of small numbers is the relative difficulty in collecting, tran-scribing, and analyzing child speech compared with adult speech (Khattab and Roberts 2010). Young children's speech is often unintelligible and difficult to transcribe, and, for children who are making the transition from babbling to early words, a thorough analysis of word identification (e.g., Vihman and McCune 1994) is required to establish whether or not a given utterance is a real word. Children's smaller vocal tracts and mobile nature also offer challenges for acoustic analysis (Khattab and Roberts 2010).

The most common sampling methods for preschool children consist of cross-sectional designs using relatively large samples of children (a hundred or more), and capturing their production and/or perception abilities in order to derive norms for the development of various aspects of the grammar. Many such studies are carried out by speech and language therapists interested in early diagnosis of speech and language impairment (see Menn and Ratner 2000 for a summary). Since language development in this age range is very fast, researchers are careful to categorize children into narrow age bands, normally using six-month intervals. What tends to fall by the wayside in these studies, however, is a thorough discussion of individual differences or a detailed understanding of each child's overall (socio)linguistic abilities (Docherty and Khattab 2008).

At the other end of the spectrum are small group and single case studies of child language. What these studies lack in numbers, they more than make up for in meticulous analysis and attention to detail, particularly in longitudinal design (see Chapter 22). Understanding the process of language acquisition requires close attention to the input the child receives and the role of social context (home, day care center, neighborhood, etc.), and therefore also requires documentation and analysis of both adult (caregiver) and child language.

Finding children to participate in research can be more challenging than finding adults, due to the need to find willing parents first, followed by a strict ethical approval process in many countries. For recruiting young children, playgroups and early day care centers are often the first point of contact for the researcher, while schools and community centers can be targeted for older children. Demographic information about the institutions can provide the researcher with clues about various social characteristics of the target families, and recruiting from different institutions is a common way of tapping into different social categories. This sampling strategy can yield a representative sample for the subgroups that the researcher is interested in. However, a school choice based on the perceived social class, religious, or language background of its pupils according to official statistics can yield a population that is actually far from homogeneous in that respect, and the researcher needs to supplement this information with detailed language background questionnaires or interviews with the parents. Moreover, while categorization of the child's ethnicity, religion, social class, and so on, is normally derived from the caregiver's background, we need studies that capture children's individual expression of these social characteristics, in much the same way that children have been found to express gender that is above and beyond what is expected based on their biological development, based on socialization processes (Sachs, Lieberman, and Erickson 1973; Eckert 1997). This is possible with older children using ethnographic methods of data collection, but is much more challenging with younger children.

4 Conclusions

Any researcher in the field of linguistics has "specific social, [cognitive] or linguistic questions in mind when they start their research, and in order to ensure that their research adequately addresses those questions, they stratify their sample somewhat" (Meyerhoff and Schleef 2010: 7). Given that research in different linguistic subfields tends to ask very different questions, it is no surprise to find that the sampling strategies that have traditionally dominated these subdisciplines are vastly dissimilar too. More recently, however, <u>linguistics</u> as a discipline has witnessed a <u>readiness to leave behind methodological orthodoxy</u>, leading to a <u>relaxation of the concept of statistical representativeness</u> and a <u>convergence of sampling</u> methods across subdisciplines. In this chapter we have aimed not only to describe the most prevalent types of sampling tools used in linguistic research, but also to root these strategies in the questions and concerns they originated from and help to resolve.

References

Barbiers, S., L. Cornips and J. P. Kunst. 2007. The syntactic atlas of the Dutch dialects: a corpus of elicited speech and text as an on-line dynamic atlas. In J. C. Beal, K. P. Corrigan, and H. Moisl, eds. *Creating and Digitizing Language Corpora*. Hampshire: Palgrave Macmillan, Volume I, 54–90.

Bard, E. G., D. Robertson, and A. Sorace. 1996. Magnitude estimation of linguistic acceptability. *Language* 72: 32–68.

Boersma, P. 2001. Praat, a system for doing phonetics by computer. *Glot International* 5: 341–5.

Britain, D. 2004. Geolinguistics – diffusion of language. In U. Ammon, N. Dittmar, K. Mattheier, and P. Trudgill, eds. *Sociolinguistics: International Handbook of the Science of Language and Society*. Berlin: Mouton de Gruyter, 34–48.

2010. Conceptualisations of geographic space in linguistics. In A. Lameli, R. Kehrein, and S. Rabanus, eds. *Language and Space: An International Handbook of Linguistic Variation*. Berlin: Mouton de Gruyter, Volume II, 69–97.

Brown, R. 1973. *A First Language*. Cambridge, MA: Harvard University Press.

Buchstaller, I. and S. Alvanides. In press. Employing geographical principles for sampling in state of the art dialectological projects. *Journal of Dialect Geography*.

Buchstaller, I., J. Rickford, E. C. Traugott, T. Wasow, and A. Zwicky. 2010. The sociolinguistics of a short-lived innovation: tracing the development of quotative all across spoken and internet newsgroup data. *Language Variation and Change* 22: 191–219.

Chambers, J. K. 2003. *Sociolinguistic Theory*. 2nd edn. Malden, MA: Blackwell.

Chambers, J. K. and P. Trudgill. 1998. *Dialectology*. 2nd edn. Cambridge University Press.

Cheshire, J., V. Edwards, and P. Whittle. 1989. Urban British dialect grammar: the question of dialect leveling. *English World-Wide* 10: 185–225.

1993. Non-standard English and dialect leveling. In J. Milroy and L. Milroy, eds. *Real English. The Grammar of English Dialects in the British Isles*. London: Longman, 53–96.

Chomsky, N. 1965. *Aspects of the Theory of Syntax*. Cambridge, MA: MIT Press.

Clark, H. H. and A. Bangerter. 2004. Changing ideas about reference. In I. A. Noveck and D. Sperber eds. *Experimental Pragmatics*. Houndmills: Palgrave Macmillan, 25–49.

Clopper, C. G. and D. B. Pisoni. 2004. Effects of talker variability on perceptual learning of dialects. *Language and Speech* 47: 207–39.

2006. The nationwide speech project: a new corpus of American English dialects. *Speech Communication* 48: 633–44.

De Vaus, D. A. 2001. *Surveys in Social Research*. 4th edn. London and New York: Routledge.

Delvaux, V. and A. Soquet. 2007. The influence of ambient speech on adult speech productions through unintentional imitation. *Phonetica* 64: 145–73.

Di Paolo, M. and M. Yaeger-Dror. 2010. *Sociophonetics: A Student's Guide*. London: Routledge.

Docherty, G. J. 2007. Speech in its natural habitat: accounting for social factors in phonetic variability. In J. Ignacio Hualde and J. Cole, eds. *Laboratory Phonology*, 10 vols. Berlin: Mouton de Gruyter, Volume IX, 1–35.

Docherty, G. J. and P. Foulkes. 1999. Newcastle upon Tyne and Derby: instrumental phonetics and variationist studies. In P. Foulkes and G. J. Docherty, eds. *Urban Voices: Accent Studies in the British Isles*. London: Arnold, 47–71.

Docherty, G. J. and G. Khattab. 2008. Sociophonetics and clinical linguistics. In M. Ball M. Perkins, N. Müller, and S. Howard, eds. *The Handbook of Clinical Linguistics*. Oxford: Blackwell Publishing, 603–25.

Eckert, P. 1989. *Jocks and Burnouts: Social Categories and Identity in the High School*. New York: Teachers College Press.

1997. Gender and sociolinguistic variation. In J. Coates, ed. *Readings in Language and Gender*. Oxford: Blackwell, 64–75.

2000. *Linguistic Variation as a Social Practice. The Linguistic Construction of Identity in Belton High*. Malden, MA and Oxford: Blackwell.

Eilers, R. E., W. R. Wilson, and J. R. Moore. 1977. Developmental changes in speech discrimination in infants. *Journal of Speech & Hearing Research* 20: 766–80.

Fernald, A. and P. K. Kuhl. 1987. Acoustic determinants of infant preference for motherese speech. *Infant Behavior and Development* 10: 279–93.

Foulkes, P. 2010. Exploring social-indexical variation: a long past but a short history. *Laboratory Phonology* 1: 5–39.

Foulkes, P., J. M. Scobbie, and D. J. L. Watt. 2010. Sociophonetics. In W. Hardcastle, J. Laver, and F. Gibbon, eds. *Handbook of Phonetic Sciences*, 2nd edn. Oxford: Blackwell, 703–54.

Fromont, R. and J. Hay. 2008. ONZE Miner: the development of a browser-based research tool. *Corpora* 3: 173–93.

Gick, B., S. Bird, and I. Wilson. 2005. Techniques for field application of lingual ultrasound imaging. *Clinical Linguistics & Phonetics* 19: 503–14.

Giddens, A. 2006. *Sociology*. 5th edn. Cambridge: Polity Press.

Gordon, M. J. 2001. *Small-Town Values and Big-City Vowels: A Study of the Northern Cities Shift in Michigan*. Durham, NC: Duke University Press.

Harrington, J. 2006. An acoustic analysis of "happy-tensing" in the Queen's Christmas broadcasts. *Journal of Phonetics* 34: 439–57.

2010. *The Phonetic Analysis of Speech Corpora*. Malden, MA: Wiley-Blackwell.

Hawkins, S. 2003. Roles and representations of systematic fine phonetic detail in speech understanding. *Journal of Phonetics* 31: 373–405.

Hawkins, S. and R. Smith. 2001. Polysp: a polysystemic, phonetically-rich approach to speech understanding. *Italian Journal of Linguistics – Rivista di Linguistica* 13: 99–188.

Hay, J., P. Warren, and K. Drager. 2006. Factors influencing speech perception in the context of a merger-in-progress. *Journal of Phonetics* 34: 458–84.

Holmes, J. and M. Meyerhoff. 1999. The Community of Practice: theories and methodologies in language and gender research. *Language in Society* 28: 173–83.

Hymes, D. 1972. Models of the interaction of language and social life. In J. Gumperz and D. Hymes, eds. *Directions in Sociolinguistics: The Ethnography of Communication*. New York: Holt Rinehart and Winston, 35–71.

Johnson, D. E. In press. Progress in regression: why sociolinguistic data calls for mixed-effects models. *Language Variation and Change*.

Johnstone, B. and J. M. Bean. 1997. Self-expression and linguistic variation. *Language in Society* 26: 221–46.

Khattab, G. and J. Roberts. 2010. Working with children. In M. Di Paolo and M. Yaeger-Dror, eds. *Sociophonetics: A Student's Guide*. London and New York: Routledge, 163–78.

Khattab, G. and J. Al-Tamimi. In press. Early phonological patterns in Lebanese Arabic. In M. Vihman and T. Keren-Portnoy, eds. *The Emergence of Phonology: Whole-word Approaches and Cross-linguistic Evidence*. Cambridge University Press.

Kohler, K. J. 2001. Articulatory dynamics of vowels and consonants in speech communication. *Journal of the International Phonetic Association* 31: 1–16.

Kristiansen, G. 2006. Towards a usage-based cognitive phonology. *International Journal of English Studies, North America* 6: 107–40.

Kurath, H. 1972. *Studies in Area Linguistics*. Bloomington: Indiana University Press.

Labov, W. 1966. *The Social Stratification of English in New York City*. Philadelphia: University of Pennsylvania Press.

Labov, W., S. Ash, and C. Boberg. 2006. *Atlas of North American English: Phonology and Phonetics*. Berlin: Mouton de Gruyter.

Labov, W., P. Cohen, C. Robins, and J. Lewis. 1968. *A Study of the Non-Standard English of Negro and Puerto Rican Speakers in New York City*. Philadelphia: US Regional Survey.

Leopold, W. 1939. *Speech Development of a Bilingual Child: A Linguist's Record. Volume II: Sound Learning in the First Two Years*, 4 vols. Evanston, IL: Northwestern University Press.

Local, J. 2003. Variable domains and variable relevance: interpreting phonetic exponents. *Journal of Phonetics* 31: 321–39.

Massey, D. 1985. New directions in space. In D. Gregory and J. Urry, eds. *Spatial Relations and Spatial Structures*. London: Macmillan, 9–19.

McDougall, K. 2004. Speaker-specific formant dynamics: an experiment on Australian English /aɪ/. *International Journal of Speech, Language and the Law* 11: 103–30.

Menn, L. and N. Ratner, eds. 2000. *Methods for Studying Language Production*. Mahwah, NJ: Lawrence Erlbaum.

Meyerhoff, M. 2002. Communities of Practice. In J. K. Chambers, P. Trudgill, and N. Schilling-Estes, eds. *The Handbook of Language Variation and Change*. Oxford: Blackwell, 526–48.

Meyerhoff, M. and E. Schleef. 2010. Sociolinguistic methods for data collection and interpretation. In M. Meyerhoff and E. Schleef, eds. *The Routledge Sociolinguistics Reader*. London and New York: Routledge, 1–26.

Milroy, L. 1987. *Observing and Analysing Natural Language*. Oxford: Blackwell.

Milroy, L. and J. Milroy. 1992. Social networks and social class: toward an integrated sociolinguistic model. *Language in Society* 21: 1–26.

Milroy, L. and M. Gordon. 2003. *Sociolinguistics: Method and Interpretation*. Malden, MA: Blackwell.

Mitchell, R., L. Dominguez, M. J. Arche, F. Myles, and E. Marsden. 2008. SPLLOC: A new database for Spanish second language acquisition research. In L. Roberts, F. Myles, and A. David, eds. *EUROSLA Yearbook*. Amsterdam: John Benjamins, Volume VIII, 287–304.

Moser, C. and G. Kalton. 1971. *Survey Methods in Social Investigation*. 2nd edn. London: Heinemann.

Neuman, W. L. 2007. *Basics of Social Research: Quantitative and Qualitative Approaches*. 2nd edn. Boston: Allyn and Bacon.

Pierrehumbert, J. B. 2002. Word-specific phonetics. In C. Gussenhoven and N. Warner, eds. *Laboratory Phonology*, 10 vols. Berlin: Mouton de Gruyter, Volume VII, 101–39.

Pitt, M., E. H. Johnson, S. Kiesling, and W. Raymond. 2005. The Buckeye Corpus of Conversational Speech: labeling conventions and a test for transcriber reliability. *Speech Communication* 45: 90–5.

Rice, S. 2010. Sampling in geography. In N. Clifford and G. Valentine, eds. *Key Methods in Geography*. London: Sage, 230–52.

Roberts, N. 2012. Future temporal reference in Hexagonal French. *University of Pennsylvania Working Papers in Linguistics* 18.2: 97–106.

Romaine, S. 1980. A critical overview of the methodology of British urban sociolinguistics. *English World Wide* 1: 163–99.

Sachs, J., P. Lieberman, and D. Erickson. 1973. Anatomical and cultural determinants of male and female speech. In R. W. Shuy and R. W. Fasold, eds. *Language Attitudes: Current Trends and Prospects*. Washington, DC: Georgetown University Press, 74–84.

Sankoff, G. 1974. A quantitative paradigm for the study of communicative competence. In R. Bauman and J. Sherzer, eds. *Explorations in the Ethnography of Speaking*. Cambridge University Press, 18–49.

    1980. A quantitative paradigm for the study of communicative competence. In G. Sankoff, ed. *The Social Life of Language*. University of Philadelphia Press, 47–79.

    1988. Problems of representativeness. In U. Ammon, N. Dittman, and K. Mattheier, eds. *Sociolinguistics: An International Handbook of the Science of Language and Society*. Berlin: Mouton de Gruyter, 899–903.

Scobbie, J. and J. Stuart-Smith. 2012. The utility of sociolinguistic sampling in laboratory-based phonological experimentation. In A. Cohn, C. Fougeron, and M. Huffman, eds. *The Oxford Handbook of Laboratory Phonology*. Oxford University Press, 607–21.

Scobbie, J., J. Stuart-Smith, and E. Lawson. 2008. Looking variation and change in the mouth: developing the sociolinguistic potential of Ultrasound Tongue Imaging. Research Report for ESRC Project RES-000–22–2032.

Scobbie, J., A. A. Wrench, and M. van der Linden. 2009. Head-probe stabilisation in ultrasound tongue imaging using a headset to permit natural head movement. In R. Sock, S. Fuchs, and Y. Laprie, eds. *Proceedings of the 8th International Seminar on Speech Production*. Strasbourg: Institute de Phonetique, 373–6.

Shuy, R. W., W. Wolfram, and W. K. Riley. 1967. Linguistic correlates of social stratification in Detroit speech. Final Report, Project 6–1347. Washington, DC: US Office of Education.

Stuart-Smith, J. 1999. Voice quality in Glaswegian. In J. Ohala, Y. Hasegawa, M. Ohala, D. Granville, and A. Bailey, eds. *Proceedings of the XIVth International Congress of Phonetic Sciences*. Department of Linguistics, University of California, Berkeley, 2553–6.

2007. Empirical evidence for gendered speech production: /s/ in Glaswegian. In J. Cole and J. Hualde, eds. *Laboratory Phonology*, 10 vols. Berlin: Mouton de Gruyter, Volume IX, 65–86.

Tagliamonte, S. 2006. *Analysing Sociolinguistic Variation*. Cambridge University Press.

Thomas, E. R. 2011. *Sociophonetics: An Introduction*. Basingstoke and New York: Palgrave.

Vihman, M. and L. McCune. 1994. When is a word a word? *Journal of Child Language* 21: 517–42.

Walter, M. A. and T. F. Jaeger. 2008. Constraints on English that-drop: a strong lexical OCP Effect. In R. L. Edwards, P. J. Midtlyng, K. G. Stensrud, and C. L. Sprague, eds. *Proceedings of the Main Session of the 41st Meeting of the Chicago Linguistic Society*. Chicago Linguistic Society, 505–19.

Wassink, A. B. and J. Dyer. 2004. Language ideology and the transmission of phonological change. *Journal of English Linguistics* 32: 3–30.

Wolfram, W. 1969. *A Sociolinguistic Description of Detroit Negro Speech*. Washington, DC: Center for Applied Linguistics.

Wolk, C., J. Bresnan, A. Rosenbach, and B. Szmrecsányi. In press. Dative and genitive variability in Late Modern English: exploring cross-constructional variation and change. *Diachronica*.

Woods, A., P. Fletcher, and A. Hughes. 1986. *Statistics in Language Studies*. Cambridge University Press.

6   Surveys and interviews

Natalie Schilling

1   Introduction

> Intersubjective agreement is best reached by convergence of several kinds of
> data with complementary sources of error.   (Labov 1972b)

Early in the development of modern sociolinguistics, William Labov taught us
that there is no single best type of data or method for linguistic study, since all are
limited. Thus, our fullest understandings are reached only through approaching
our research questions from several angles, with each vantage point providing a
unique perspective that offsets its necessarily limited scope.

In this chapter, I examine two important and complementary methods for
collecting data on language in its social setting: *surveys* in which researchers
more or less directly elicit information on linguistic features, patterns, and interrelations; and *interviews* in which connected speech is elicited. In addition, I
consider methods designed specifically to elicit information on *language attitudes*,
though both surveys and interviews can provide valuable information on language
attitudes as well as language use. The chapter takes a largely variationist sociolinguistic approach, to complement the other chapters in Part I of this volume. Data
collection methods designed to glean information on language variation can usefully inform other types of linguistic study; at the same time, elicitations associated
with theoretical, anthropological, psycholinguistic, acquisitional, and other
approaches to language study can be invaluable for sociolinguistic research. For
example, data from a relatively relaxed, conversational interview might yield
information on stigmatized language features that are resistant to elicitation via
grammaticality judgment tasks; conversely, sociolinguists can use grammaticality
judgment tasks to distinguish accidental gaps from genuine ungrammaticality (see
Section 2.3).

I discuss both designing and implementing the various techniques, as well as
advantages, disadvantages, and purposes of each. At issue throughout is the
question of the "authenticity" of our data, and I consider whether it is possible
or even desirable to seek to remove researcher effects, in an effort to overcome
Labov's (1972b: 113) "Observer's Paradox": "To obtain the data most important
for linguistic theory, we have to observe how people speak when they are not
being observed."

2   Surveys and survey questionnaires

Since the late 1800s, linguists have been gathering data via survey questionnaires. The earliest surveys were designed to elicit a range of language forms – lexical, phonological, and grammatical – from across a wide geographic range, thereby obtaining a picture of language variation across space, with an eye toward how synchronic variation reflects historical connections and developments over time, in keeping with the then main current of linguistic study, historical/comparative linguistics. With the advent of structuralist linguistics, there came an interest in interrelations among elements in individual linguistic systems, so elicitation techniques for uncovering such relations were added to the empirical linguist's toolkit – for example, tasks designed to elicit judgments of "same" or "different" to determine minimal pairs, and sentence permutation tasks to determine the subject-verb forms constituting person-number paradigms. Generative linguistics brought in other types of elicitation – tasks designed to elicit grammaticality judgments (or, more properly, acceptability judgments; see Chapter 3 in this volume) and information on the structural limitations of forms – that is, which forms can and cannot be used, as well as in which environments they can grammatically occur.

In the sections that follow, we consider different modes of survey administration, as well as direct vs indirect means of eliciting lexical, phonological, and grammatical features. We also briefly examine how the elicitation of listener judgments has been usefully applied to sociolinguistic study, leaving full discussion of judgments of grammaticality and "same" vs "different" to Chapters 3 and 4. We devote special attention to a type of survey in which linguistic information is elicited completely indirectly – the rapid and anonymous survey – since this clever design mitigates observer effects on "naturalness" of data, while still ensuring that desired forms are produced.

2.1   Modes of administration: from long-distance to up-close to the World Wide Web

The first dialect geographic survey, Wenker's 1876 survey of German dialects (Mitzka 1952; cited in Chambers and Trudgill 1980: 15–36), was administered via postal questionnaire, since again, the aim of such early studies was to obtain information on language variation across wide geographic areas. However, researchers soon decided that it would be advantageous to send out trained fieldworkers to administer questionnaires in person; so starting with studies conducted in the late nineteenth century, most dialect geographic studies up until the past few decades have relied on face-to-face rather than long-distance methods. Among the earliest such studies are Gilliéron's 1896 linguistic survey of France (Gilliéron 1902–10; cited in Chambers and Trudgill 1980: 15–36) and Grierson's (1905) *Linguistic Survey of India,* conducted between 1894 and 1928, and resulting in the publication of an impressive eleven-volume description of hundreds of dialects of Indian languages, collected via elicitations and gramophone recordings. Important twentieth-century surveys conducted via in-person fieldwork include the various projects associated with the Linguistic Atlas of the United States and Canada, such as the *Linguistic Atlas of the Middle and South Atlantic States* (McDavid and O'Cain 1980), the *Linguistic Atlas of the Gulf States* (Pederson et al. 1986), the nationwide survey of US dialect regions conducted in connection with the *Dictionary of American Regional English* (DARE) project from 1965–70 (Cassidy 1985; Hall and Cassidy 1991, 1996; Hall 2002, 2012); and Orton et al.'s Survey of English Dialects (1950–1961; e.g., Orton, Sanderson, and Widdowson 1978).

Face-to-face surveys were long preferred over long-distance for a number of reasons. For example, they allow more control over who the respondents are, since they provide at least a degree of verification of participants' claimed demographic characteristics (e.g., age, sex, race). In addition, administering surveys in person allows researchers to record responses themselves (through on-the-spot phonetic transcription or audio recording), to record multiple responses indicative of variable usage, and to exchange clarifications. In addition, because in-person surveys are usually administered orally, respondents may be more relaxed than when filling out a written form, and so yield more naturalistic data.

However, long-distance surveys have their own advantages: they require much less time, effort, and money than in-person surveys, and so allow for broader population coverage in a shorter amount of time. In addition, one can argue that respondents may actually feel more rather than less comfortable with long-distance surveys, since the presence of a fieldworker who is either an advanced student or a professor may be intimidating. Some relatively recent sociolinguistic studies using written questionnaires include Chambers' (1994, 1998a, 1998b) study of lexical, phonological, and morphological variation in the "Golden Horseshoe" region of Canada (along the western tip of Lake Ontario, from Oshawa to Niagara Falls, and encompassing Toronto); Boberg, Roberts, and Nagy's McGill-New Hampshire-Vermont Dialect Survey (which investigates attitudes, lexical items, and pronunciations; see, e.g., Nagy 2001); and Gordon's investigation of the Northern Cities Vowel Shift in the American Midland (Gordon 2006).

In recent decades, technological advances have led researchers to long-distance survey methods that allow for both breadth of coverage and audio recording. Thus, for example, Labov, Ash, and Boberg's (2006) *Atlas of North American English* is based on a sweeping telephone survey (TELSUR) of larger population centers in the US. Interestingly, whereas traditional large-scale dialectological surveys were interested in obtaining information on historical forms and so focused on the most conservative speakers in the populations of study (i.e., non-mobile, older, rural males, or NORMs), TELSUR turns the tables on this traditional bias by purposely selecting young female respondents from urbanized areas, in order to record the usages of the most innovative speakers, and hence gain a current picture of ongoing language change. (See Chapter 5 for more on population sampling.)

Researchers increasingly have been turning to the convenience of internet-based surveys, which afford maximal geographic (and social) coverage with minimal time, effort, and expense. The latter also have the advantage of allowing for not only detailed audio recording of speech data, but also recording such measures as response time and eye movement. In addition, computer-based surveys enable one to relatively easily include computer-manipulated stimuli, in order to test subtle facets of linguistic perception. For example, Plichta, Preston, and Rakerd (2005) conducted an internet survey of people's perceptions of vowels associated with the Northern Cities Vowel Shift (currently taking place in much of the inland northern US), in which participants from both within and outside the Northern Cities region listened to computer-synthesized words with various degrees of vowel shift (e.g., words ranging along a continuum from *sod* to *sad*) in sentences offering no contextual clues (e.g., "Did you say, 'sod' or 'sad?'"), and then selected the word they thought they had heard.

Of course, with the return of long-distance surveys with no fieldworker presence during administration comes the return of the same disadvantages that plagued the earliest postal questionnaires, including inability to (at least partially) verify participants' self-characterizations and lack of immediate availability to either ask or answer clarification questions. A further caution in moving from the field to the World Wide Web is control over data access; while most internet surveys do not elicit specific identifying information (but only general information such as participant demographic characteristics), great care must be taken to guard potential identifying information from public access (e.g., audio responses to an internet survey that could be used to identify participants by voice).

2.2   Direct and indirect elicitation of linguistic features

Linguistic surveys can be composed of different types of elicitation frames, designed to yield different types of information. Almost all will elicit basic demographic information, often at the end of the survey, in order to reduce speaker self-consciousness, for example, about age or socioeconomic status. However, such placement is risky if the survey is long (as were traditional dialectological surveys, which sometimes could take an entire day to complete), since participants (and researchers) may tire and perhaps not finish the survey. Also often included in surveys are questions designed to elicit information on attitudes and orientations, to see if such matters correlate with patterns of language use – for example, use or non-use of local dialect forms, maintenance or attrition of an endangered language. (See Section 3 on surveys designed specifically to elicit language attitudes.) The bulk of the linguistic survey, however, involves eliciting information on linguistic features, structures, and systems.

In order to elicit particular linguistic features, researchers can use either direct elicitations (self-reports) or indirect ones. For example, the telephone portion of the Survey of Oklahoma Dialects (SOD-T), conducted in the mid 1990s (Bailey, Tillery, and Wikle 1997), included both types, including, for example, a number of direct elicitations of the type in example (1).

(1)   Have you ever heard the term "SNAP BEANS" used for the bean that you break in half to cook?

a. yes

{IF YES} How often would you use that term: all of the time, some of the time, not very often or never?

(1) all   2) some   3) not often   4) never

b. no

{IF NO} What term would you use?

Indirect elicitations can take several different forms (e.g., questions of the form, "What do you call . . .?" or fill in the blanks), and they may be used to elicit a full range of linguistic forms. For example, indirect elicitations of lexical items in SOD-T were formulated so that respondents could give more than one synonymous answer – for example, "What do you call those little bugs that get on you in the grass and make you itch?" (looking for *redbugs* or *chiggers*), and "What do you call the enclosed place where hogs are kept?" (looking for *pig pen* or *sty*). The Linguistic Atlas of the United States and Canada projects used questions that were a bit more indirect – for example, "Where did you keep your hogs and pigs?" "The thing you put in your mouth and work back and forth and blow on it. Do you remember any other names for it?" (looking for *harp, breath harp, mouth organ, harmonica,* etc.).

The Linguistic Atlas survey also included fill-in-the-blanks to elicit pronunciations and grammatical features. For example, variant pronunciations of the word *yolk* were elicited with the question, "What do you call the two parts of an egg? One is the white; the other is _____," while variants of the past tense of *drive* (e.g., *drove, druv, driv*) were elicited with "I wanted to hang something out in the barn, so I just took a nail and _____." To study Danish vowel mergers, Ejstrup and Hansen (2004) devised a task in which respondents spoke informally about a set of common objects, presented in picture form and selected to elicit target vowels.

Other elicitations can be even less direct: Thus, for example, Bailey, Tillery, and Wikle (1997) used the following frames to elicit phonological features, even though they seemed to be lexical elicitations: "When are you most likely to hear an owl hoot?" (looking for the pronunciation of /ay/ as either [aɪ] or [a:], not the lexical item *night*), and "Now what about those large birds that sit on telephone poles and swoop down to kill mice and other small animals, what do you call those?" (looking for the pronunciation of *hawk* as either [hɔk] or [hɑk] to elicit information on the /ɔ/-/ɑ/ merger taking place in much of the US in word pairs like *hawk/hock*).

Finally, researchers can use direct and indirect methods to elicit forms from entire semantic domains. For example, Teresa Labov (1992) elicited information on slang terms in various domains by having US students select terms from lists she provided (direct elicitations) of slang words for people, approval/disapproval, and being "under the influence," and by and by having them fill in blanks she left open in each category (indirect elicitations).

2.3   Direct and indirect elicitation of listener judgments

In addition to eliciting data on which linguistic features can be used in particular languages and language varieties, linguists need to know which forms and structures cannot be used. Further, if we are interested in language variation, we need to know which environments favor, disfavor and prohibit variable usages (see also Chapter 20). Because non-use in speech or straightforward elicitation may be due to accidental gaps rather than ungrammaticality, sociolinguistics can usefully apply sentence permutation and judgment tasks of the types discussed in Chapters 3 and 4.

As one example, in our study of ethnicity-based language variation in Robeson County, in Southeastern North Carolina, composed of residents of Lumbee Indian, African American and White ethnicity (Wolfram 1995; Wolfram and Dannenberg 1999), we observed in everyday conversation and in the sociolinguistic interviews from which we obtained the bulk of our data (see Section 4 below) that *I'm* could be used as a perfective, as in *I'm been there a long time* for "I've been there a long time," in Lumbee English. We also noted that the Lumbee seemed to be able to use the *I'm* form as part of simple past constructions, but we wanted to make sure. Hence, Wolfram (1995) devised a sentence permutation task designed to yield tense-marked auxiliaries that would provide more direct evidence of the tense-aspect status of *I'm* than we were able to obtain via observation or elicitation of conversational speech. The task involved having speakers make three types of changes to a number of stimulus sentences, some past tense (e.g., *I'm forgot to do it yesterday*) and some perfective (e.g., *I'm seen the toten* [i.e., presage of a fateful event]): (1) change positive to negative, (2) provide an elliptical version of the sentence via VP deletion, and (3) change declarative sentences to questions. Wolfram hypothesized that for the simple past sentences, *do* forms would surface (e.g., *I didn't forget to do it yesterday* rather than *I haven't forgot(ten) to do it yesterday*), while for the perfectives, we would get *have* (e.g., *I'm seen the toten, I know I have* rather than *I know I did*). For the most part, the results conformed to expectations, though we did get a few *have* forms with the past tense sentences and one or two isolated cases of *am* with perfectives (e.g., *Am I seen the toten?*). Hence, we were able to confirm that *I'm* could indeed be used to indicate both past and perfective meanings and that in such constructions the underlying verb is *do* or *have*, not *be*.

Sociolinguists also use judgment tasks to help determine structural limitations and linguistic systematicity. One important line of inquiry in variationist socio-linguistics has been the study of vowel mergers in progress, a task for which judgments of "same" or "different" can add invaluable information to that gleaned from conversational data. Some important mergers in progress that have been subject to sociolinguistic inquiry include the /ɔ/-/ɑ/ merger in US English (e.g., Herold 1990; Labov 1994: 316–19; Labov, Ash, and Boberg 2006), conditioned mergers such as /ɪ/-/i/ before /l/ in Southwestern US varieties (as in *filled/field*; e.g., Di Paolo 1988; Labov, Ash, and Boberg 2006), and /ir/-/ɛr/ (as in *beer/bear*) in Norwich, England (Trudgill 1988) and in New Zealand (Hay, Warren, and Drager 2006), and the seeming merger of /ay/ and /oy/ in Essex, England (as in *line/loin*; e.g., Labov 1994: 377–84).

The same/different task can take a number of forms, ranging from the very direct (e.g., playing the respondent a pre-recorded list of word pairs and having them state whether they are the same or different), to playing elements of the pairs interspersed with other items and asking for definitions, to constructing and reading (or playing) to respondents elaborate stories whose interpretation depends on the listener's understanding of one or more word pairs involved in ongoing merger (e.g., Labov 1994: 403–6).

2.4   Limitations of elicitation tasks

Despite the utility of surveys composed of linguistic elicitations for obtaining large-scale information on the use and patterning of particular features of interest, they do have their limitations. Even the best designed elicitation tasks are removed from how people use (and think about) language in everyday life, and people's reports of their linguistic usage may or may not match up with what they actually do. For example, direct elicitations such as "Have you ever heard the term 'snap beans?'" can induce respondents to claim knowledge and use of features they have never heard prior to the research situation, while less direct elicitations can be very difficult to devise and/or yield a wide range of responses falling far from the targeted item. Hence, for example, Bailey, Wikle, and Tillery (1997) report on their frustrating attempts to indirectly elicit double modal constructions from Southern US speakers, since there is virtually no single indirect frame that is guaranteed to yield a double vs a single modal. (Indeed, the elicitation frame for *might could* from the Linguistic Atlas of the Gulf States is cringingly unwieldy: "When you get something done that was hard work all by yourself and your friend was standing around without helping, you say _____.") In addition to inadvertently priming or failing to prime respondents to produce desired forms, elicitations can also induce people to purposely over- or under-report linguistic usages. In one well-known case, Trudgill (1972) noted both phenomena in a single city, Norwich, England, with women over-reporting their use of standard English features in direct elicitations compared with their actual usages in conversational interviews, and men under-reporting their use of standard variants. Most likely, these mismatches are due to the association, in many communities, of vernacularity with masculinity and what are often considered to be its component qualities, such as being tough or hardworking, and having "street smarts."

Issues regarding the social valuation of linguistic features also affect acceptability judgments and sentence permutation tasks, and studies must be designed quite carefully to steer respondents away from their tendency to confound linguistic grammaticality with social acceptability or "correctness," and corresponding rejection of well-formed constructions that do not correspond to standard forms. Further, non-linguists tend to focus on language content, not subtleties of linguistic form, and so base their responses on semantic sense, pragmatic felicity, and/or social appropriateness. For example, in our studies of Smith Island, Maryland, we were interested in learning about possible subject–verb agreement patterns with existential *it* (e.g., *It's a lot of crabs in the bay* for "There are a lot of crabs in the bay"; see, e.g., Parrott 2002), and so administered a series of judgment tasks to respondents selected for their interest in our dialect studies. However, even the most linguistically curious tended to focus on content rather than form, and stimuli such as "Can you say 'It's many politicians elected by Smith Islanders?'" were met with responses such as, "Actually, nobody would say that because it's not true." Further, when they did pay attention to form, they focused on prescriptive standards rather than grammatical dialectal usages, and so rejected forms because they were "illiterate" or "improper" rather than unnatural in the Smith Island dialect. (See Buchstaller and Corrigan 2011 on strategies for investigating non-standard linguistic grammatical usages; Chapters 3 and 4 in this volume also discuss the issue of subjective interpretations of judgment tasks.)

Finally, there are issues related more to the testing situation than the test items themselves – for example, ordering effects, participants' possible discomfort with the test-like nature of the elicitation task, and their resulting desire either to do "well" on the test by providing the answers the "teacher" (i.e., researcher) expects of them, or to get the test over with as quickly as possible, perhaps by giving the exact same response to every prompt. Such issues can be mitigated by including control frames and varying the order of frames, as well as framing elicitation tasks as "games" rather than test-like research tasks. For example, as part of his study of African American Vernacular English in Washington, DC, Fasold (1972) included a set of "Word Games" designed to uncover sources of non-conjugated *be* in African American Vernacular English – for example, distributive *be* vs *be* derived from deletion of *will* or *would*, as in "He be working" (regularly vs soon). However, we should always remain aware of possible mismatches between what people do and what they say they do; and ideally, elicitations will never form our sole source of data on language use. (See Chapters 3 and 7 for more on test effects and how to compensate for them.)

2.5   Rapid and anonymous surveys

One ingenious method of overcoming the unnaturalness of direct elicitations is the *rapid and anonymous survey*, in which linguistic elicitations are disguised as ordinary non-linguistic questions, and research participants respond exactly as they would in everyday life, in non-research contexts. The classic example is Labov's (1972a) study of *r*-pronunciation vs *r*-lessness in the speech of personnel in three New York City department stores, each catering to a different social class group. The elicitation frame was exceedingly clever in its simplicity: in each store, Labov asked workers the location of a particular item he had already determined to be on the *fourth floor*, thereby eliciting the desired variable in two word and phrase positions. Further, he obtained information on stylistic variation by asking each respondent to repeat the utterance in a more careful/emphatic style, by following his initial inquiry with "Excuse me?" Labov recorded each response immediately afterwards, by stepping out of view of the respondent and noting in writing whether each potential case of [r] was realized or not.

As predicted, the personnel in the store catering to the highest social class group, Saks, had the most *r*-pronunciation, in keeping with the fact that this variant was an incoming prestige form, and employees could be expected to accommodate to the speech of their prestigious clientele. The mid-level store, Macy's, had middle levels of /r/ usage and the greatest amount of "self-correction" in repetition, while workers in the bargain store, S. Klein, showed the lowest levels of *r*-pronunciation.

Clearly, a rapid and anonymous survey is advantageous in that it yields unself-conscious (and so presumably "natural") data on targeted features from a broad population in a short amount of time. At the same time, there are a number of limitations: the researcher can only obtain information on a very limited amount of linguistic data, since recording is done only in writing (since surreptitious audio recordings are widely considered to be unethical in linguistics; see Chapter 2), and social information is limited as well, since we can only guess at respondent demographics rather than directly elicit this information. Hence, Labov discusses the patterning of the (r) variable not only by department store (and specific occupation within each store), but also by gender, ethnicity, and age, but had to admit that his demographic categorizations could not be completely accurate, especially with regard to age. Finally, this method requires a very good ear, and its practitioners need to be very well trained in discerning phonetic detail without the computational aid to which so many linguists have become accustomed.

Because of the limitations of the rapid and anonymous survey, Labov stresses that they should only be used as preliminary or supplementary sources of data, never as the basis for an entire study. Nevertheless, they can be an invaluable complement to more direct elicitations and less pointed observations, since, as Labov says, "They represent a form of nonreactive experiment in which we avoid the bias of the experimental context and the irregular interference of prestige norms but still control the behavior of subjects" (Labov 1972a: 69).

3   Eliciting language attitudes

In addition to eliciting and observing information on language production, linguists are interested in obtaining information on listener perceptions, including their attitudes toward particular features, varieties, and variants, as well as those who use them. Whereas language attitudes can be directly elicited (e.g., in interviews or opinion surveys), typically they are investigated partially indirectly, via elicitation of attitudes toward speakers (not language per se), and sometimes elicitation of extralinguistic behaviors indicative of language attitudes.

Probably the most widely used method of eliciting language attitudes is the *Matched Guise Technique* devised by Lambert and his colleagues in the 1960s (Lambert et al. 1960). The classic version involves assembling a stimulus consisting of passages spoken (or read) in different languages or language varieties produced by a single speaker. In between-subjects designs, listeners are separated into randomized subgroups (see Chapter 7), each of which hears a subset of recordings. If listeners hear more than one recording, they are typically told that the different guises are produced by different individuals and are then asked to rate the speakers on various measures, usually along a so-called semantic differential scale, involving Likert scales for various semantic categories, often along status-stressing and solidarity-stressing scales (e.g., intelligent-unintelligent, friendly-unfriendly). The method is thus partially indirect, in that it involves direct elicitation of participants' attitudes toward speakers and only indirect elicitation of attitudes toward language.

Sometimes the adjectives chosen are based on previous studies, with the dimensions of status and solidarity again underpinning the choices. In such designs, several items (either semantic scales or attitudes questions) ideally measure the same underlying construct, such as status or solidarity, in order to counteract potentially unreliable effects caused by individual items. Each group of items for a single construct can be tested for internal reliability, and less reliable items can be removed from the analysis (Garrett 2010). The researcher may also choose to elicit potentially relevant dimensions via open-ended questions in a pilot study, perhaps with focus groups. For example, Williams' studies in the mid 1970s of language attitudes and education used semantic differential scales derived from pilot studies with small groups of teachers who evaluated children's speech using their own terms, which were then found to cluster along the dimensions of confidence-eagerness and ethnicity-nonstandardness (e.g., Williams 1974: 23; cited in Fasold 1984: 171–3).

The choice of speaker to produce the different guises is also a matter to be approached with care. Practically speaking, it is very difficult to find speakers who are fluent in the various languages or dialects the researcher wishes to study; hence the matched guise in its strictest sense is often replaced by the so-called verbal guise (Campbell-Kibler 2010: 378), which uses different speakers matched as closely as possible in terms of factors other than language or dialect per se that could influence listener judgments (e.g., voice quality, pitch and intonation, and speech rate). (Indeed, Williams' studies use different speakers, matched for ethnicity and social status, rather than a matched guise, per se.)

Further, whether one is using a matched guise or voice guise, one must also control for content. This can be done using reading passages rather than conversational speech; the trade-off, though, is that reading passages sound less natural than talk. Campbell-Kibler (2010: 380–1) suggests controlling for content without resorting to readings by using passages from spontaneous speech about similar topics (e.g., childhood games). If however, the exact same content must be used, then the unnaturalness can be alleviated by giving listeners a reason why the speakers are reading rather than talking – for example, perhaps they are allegedly auditioning for a job as a news anchor (Labov et al. 2006; cited in Campbell-Kibler 2010: 381) or for a radio commercial. A further method of circumventing the unnaturalness of having one group of speakers listen to the same passage as read by different speakers is to use a between-subjects design, in which the different guises are judgment by different, but rather large, groups of listeners (see Chapter 7).

The traditional method of eliciting language attitudes is plagued by the same problems as elicitations of speech production. The tasks are unnatural, and there is no guarantee that the results are reflective of listeners' genuine attitudes (which can be conceptualized as a mental "state of readiness; an intervening variable between a stimulus affecting a person and that person's response" [Fasold 1984: 147, citing Agheyisi and Fishman 1970: 138 and Cooper and Fishman 1974: 7]). This may be because listeners do not have free access to their attitudes or the ability to accurately convey them, or because they do not wish to express negative attitudes they might really hold. Thus, researchers have sought methods other than the matched guise/voice guise technique – for example, so-called "commitment measures," whereby language attitudes are assessed by observing behaviors (e.g., Fasold 1984: 153–8). For example, Bourhis and Giles (1976; described in Fasold 1984: 155–8) devised a task designed to measure people's attitudes toward four language varieties in Wales, by testing for correlations between the language variety in which an announcement was made to several audiences of theatregoers, and the extent to which each audience complied with the request to fill out a short questionnaire based on the content of the announcement. Among the findings were that Anglo-Welsh listeners were least responsive to broad Welsh-accented English, while Welsh listeners were most responsive to Welsh and least responsive to standard British English (RP). Clearly, designing a "commitment measure" in which actual non-linguistic behaviors are elicited is an extremely difficult task; it is also possible to indirectly measure language attitudes by gauging participants' purported behaviors. For example, Cooper and Fishman (1974: 16–17; cited in Fasold 1984: 179) devised a task to test the hypothesis that in Israel Hebrew is considered to be better suited for scientific arguments, while Arabic is considered better suited to traditional Islamic arguments. The task involved having Muslims who were bilingual in Hebrew and Arabic listen to four passages (two per group of participants): a scientific anti-tobacco argument in Hebrew and the same argument in Arabic, and a traditional anti-liquor argument in Arabic and the same thing in Hebrew. Language attitudes were indirectly assessed by having the participants indicate whether they would or would not support higher taxes on tobacco and liquor based on the arguments they heard; and results were conclusive indeed, with the anti-tobacco tax being far more highly favored among those who heard the scientific argument in Hebrew, and the anti-liquor tax far more favored among those who heard the traditional argument in Arabic.

In addition to considering how best to elicit attitudes and perceptions, there is also the question of exactly what listeners are attending to in making their judgments. As technology becomes more advanced, it is becoming easier to devise experiments designed to tease out the effects of minute aspects of the speech signal on attitudes and identifications. Hence, nowadays, researchers can use computer manipulations to construct a series of guises differing along only a single dimension, whether binary (e.g., -*in'* vs -*ing* endings) or scalar (e.g., the height of a particular vowel or length of a stop release burst). Similarly, the speech signal can be filtered to remove all segmental information leaving only intonational contour, or intonation can be flattened and segments can be scrambled, so that presumably all effects but evaluations/identifications of segments themselves, devoid of content or context, can be investigated (Thomas and Reaser 2004; Campbell-Kibler 2010: 381). This is not to suggest that digital manipulation of the speech signal is always easy, since some features lend themselves more readily to computer alteration than others. In addition, the quality of the stimuli may depend on the quality of the source recordings. If the source signal was recorded in a controlled environment, there will be fewer problems with manipulation, but it might sound artificial (since phonetics labs may constrain linguistic behavior). If the source signal is taken from spontaneous speech, it will sound more "natural" from an interactional perspective, but ambient noise may pose a challenge for digital manipulation (see Chapters 9 and 17).

As fascinating as studies attempting to get at perceptions of individual language components may be, the researcher would be wise to heed the caution of Auer, who points out that "the meaning of linguistic heterogeneity does not (usually) reside in individual linguistic features but rather in constellations of such features which are interpreted together ... [W]e do not interpret single variables but a gestalt-like stylistic expression" (2007: 12; cited in Soukup 2011: 350). Hence, it is not certain that ever more fine-grained analyses or syntheses of speech signals will yield ever-increasing gains in our understanding of language attitudes and speech perceptions, and experiments involving artificially manipulated speech should always be complemented with methods involving more naturalistic data, including elicitations based on listener judgments of excerpts from spontaneous speech, responses to questions about attitudes and perceptions, and, best, of all, observations of linguistic and extralinguistic behaviors reflective of language perceptions, attitudes, and ideologies, including, crucially, the quantitative patterning of variation according to social class and style that has been recognized as deeply rooted in linguistic evaluation since the inception of modern sociolinguistic study.

4   The sociolinguistic interview

One of the most important tools for collecting data on language in its social setting is the *sociolinguistic interview*. Like the rapid and anonymous survey, the sociolinguistic interview seeks to mitigate observer effects. However, in this case recordings are overt, but questions are much less pointed and are designed to steer interviewees away from focusing on specific linguistic forms, toward producing connected speech about topics of interest. Because recording and elicitation are overt, researchers do not have to confine themselves to a limited amount of linguistic and demographic/social information, but can ask for the linguistic and social information they need. In addition, researchers can set up recording equipment and the interview setting to ensure optimal audio quality. Further, since the typical sociolinguistic interview involves only two participants, and the interviewee is encouraged to talk as freely as possible, it also allows us to gather a maximal quantity of naturalistic speech data in a relatively short amount of time. Given these advantages, it is little wonder that the sociolinguistic interview has long been and continues to be the primary data-gathering tool of variationist sociolinguists as well as other linguists (e.g., in second language acquisition) who need to obtain in an efficient manner high-quality naturalistic conversational data for a range of research purposes.

4.1   Structuring the sociolinguistic interview

Basically, the sociolinguistic interview is a loosely structured interview designed to yield large quantities of speech from interviewees that is as casual and natural as possible, with the most "natural," "vernacular" speech held to occur when speakers focus their attention on what they are talking about rather than on speech itself. This focus on the vernacular, and the reasoning behind it, is captured in Labov's Vernacular Principle, which states that "the style which is most regular in its structure and in its relation to the evolution of language is the vernacular, in which the minimum attention is paid to speech" (Labov 1972b: 112).

Sociolinguistic interview questions are grouped into modules focused on particular topics, and the modules can be rearranged as the interview progresses to approximate the flow of natural conversation. Questions are focused on topics believed to be of fairly universal interest, as well as matters of particular interest to each community of study, and interviewees are encouraged to talk as long as they like on any topic that particularly interests them, to tell stories or narratives, and even to go off on tangents of their own. For example, Labov has long maintained that interviewees will tell particularly animated narratives and forget about the fact that they are being recorded (and so produce truly vernacular speech) if interviewers ask them his famous "danger of death" question: "Have you ever been in a situation where you were in serious danger of being killed, where you thought to yourself, *This is it . . .*" (Labov 1972b: 113).

In addition to questions designed to spark naturalistic conversation, the traditional sociolinguistic interview includes a series of tasks designed to yield increasingly self-conscious, careful, and hence standard speech: a reading passage, a word list, and a list of minimal pairs – that is, words that differ by only one phoneme in standard speech, but may or may not differ in pronunciation in vernacular varieties. For example, in Labov's (1966) foundational study of New York City's Lower East Side, the minimal pair task focused on *r*-lessness vs *r*-pronunciation in word pairs like *sauce/source*, *god/guard*, and so on. These tasks are administered after the conversational portion of the interview, to avoid calling attention to speech itself too soon.

In studies utilizing the full range of sociolinguistic interview tasks, the predicted patterns of stylistic variation were very often borne out, as for example in Labov's studies of New York City in the 1960s and of Philadelphia in the 1970s (e.g., Labov 2001), with interviewees showing higher usage levels of nonstandard, vernacular variants in casual speech, and increasingly elevated levels of standard forms as they move from casual to careful to reading passage to word list to minimal pair style.

4.2   Limitations of the sociolinguistic interview

Despite its seeming success in capturing and pinpointing vernacular speech as well as a range of other speech styles, the sociolinguistic interview has been subjected to a number of criticisms over the decades. For example, Wolfson (1976) famously contended that the sociolinguistic interview is actually quite *unnatural*, since interviewees expect interviews to be relatively formal, and they may become disconcerted or perhaps even angry when faced with an interviewer who does not have a highly structured questionnaire and so may seem unprepared for the interview.

In addition, even though sociolinguistic researchers are supposed to do their best to relinquish control to interviewees, it has still been argued that there are insurmountable power asymmetries in the sociolinguistic interview. The interviewer usually holds the more powerful conversational role of questioner and a more powerful social role as a researcher associated with a university rather than, for example, a member of a vernacular-speaking and/or minority community (e.g., Labov 1984; Milroy and Gordon 2003: 61–3).

Further, researchers have questioned whether the various contexts in the sociolinguistic interview (e.g., conversation, reading passage, word list) really are differentiated chiefly in terms of amount of attention to speech. For example, many (most) people have a specialized "reading register" that differs in a number of ways from spoken speech, not just in terms of a slightly increased degree of carefulness (e.g., Macaulay 1977; Romaine 1978, 1980; Milroy 1987: 173–8). The reading tasks associated with the traditional sociolinguistic interview can also add to interviewees' discomfort, thereby further increasing inherent power asymmetries, since many people are not accustomed to reading aloud; in addition, the "marginal" communities in which sociolinguists are so often interested may be characterized by low levels of literacy, rendering reading tasks even more awkward.

Finally, researchers have questioned the focus on vernacular, unselfconscious speech that underlies the Attention to Speech model, for several reasons.

Variationists increasingly are recognizing that people's everyday speech reper-toires include a variety of self-conscious as well as unselfconscious styles; and further, self-conscious, "stylized" linguistic usages are probably becoming more commonplace as people come into increasing contact with more languages, varieties, and variants (as well as their associated social meanings and norms for use) in the face of increasing mobility, globalization, and mediatization (Coupland 2007). In addition, self-conscious speech is more prevalent than we might like to think, even in sociolinguistic interviews, since interviewees can – and do – conceptualize them as occasions for dialect display, despite researchers' best efforts to relegate speech itself to the background (e.g., Trudgill 1972; Coupland 1980; Reah 1982; Schilling-Estes 1998). Further, no matter how seemingly unselfconscious a stretch of speech may be, we can question whether there really is any such thing as an individual's single "genuine" vernacular – a "default" style unaffected by any contextual factors – since people always shape their speech to fit the situation at hand and to suit their various purposes (e.g., Hindle 1979; Eckert 2000; Milroy and Gordon 2003: 49–51; Schilling-Estes 2008; see also Schilling 2013, Chapters 3–4, for extended discussions of the sociolinguistic interview and collecting data on stylistic variation).

4.3   Modifications of the sociolinguistic interview

Far from ignoring criticisms leveled against the sociolinguistic inter-view, variationists have long sought to address the seeming unnaturalness of the interview event, the power asymmetries the event entails, and the danger of interviewers exerting more control than they may realize. Thus, sociolinguists have modified the basic sociolinguistic interview technique in various ways, while still attempting to preserve its advantages in terms of amount of interviewee speech, efficiency, and sound quality.

Among the earliest modifications was moving from the one-on-one interview format to group interviews, with the idea that people being interviewed in peer groups would talk more with one another than the interviewer, and that the everyday interactional norms they have with peer group members would super-sede any artificiality brought on by attempts to conform to the interview event or the relatively standard speech of the interviewer. Hence, Labov et al. (1968) used peer group interviews in their early studies of African American children and teenagers in Harlem, and found that interviewer effects were minimized to such an extent that the interviewer often receded into the background while the teens talked among themselves. Other researchers have enjoyed similar success in recording teens in peer group interaction, as, for example, in Hewitt's (1982) study of London adolescents' use of Jamaican Creole and Cheshire's (1982) study of adolescents in Reading, England.

Another variant on the one-on-one interview was used by Wolfram and his research colleagues in their work in North Carolina beginning in the early 1990s (e.g., Wolfram, Hazen, and Schilling-Estes 1999). This involved pairs of researchers interviewing one or more interviewees. At first glance, such a tactic seems to swing the balance of power even farther toward the interviewer; however, it was found that breaking down the one-on-one dynamic by including an extra researcher was just as effective in reshaping the "interview" into a conversation as adding extra interviewees.

Of course, researchers also move beyond the interview format entirely – for example, by recording spontaneous conversations in which the researcher plays only a minor conversational role, if any, and by having participants make self-recordings as they go about their daily activities in a variety of settings, with a range of interlocutors. Such self-recordings can yield a wider range of speech styles than would be uncovered in sociolinguistic interview data; in addition, they might reveal that people have quite different patterns of language variation in everyday life than in the interview setting. For example, in a study of British Asian English in London, Sharma (2011) demonstrated that whereas interview data indicate that women in her study shift completely away from one highly salient Punjabi-derived phonetic trait, the use of retroflex /t/, self-recordings show quite robust use of this variant in other settings – for example, in the home domain.

Although moving away from one-on-one interviews may seem to be the direction to take in seeking to overcome the Observer's Paradox and obtaining truly "natural" data, we must remember that there are trade-offs in relinquishing the controls built into the one-on-one sociolinguistic interview. Multi-party interactions are noisier than individual interviews, and even if the researcher records each participant on a separate track or separate audio recorder, there will still be overlap between participants in the acoustic signal, rendering these parts unusable for acoustic analysis – even though they very likely constitute the most interactive portions of the interview. Further, talk may not always be the primary focus of peer group interactions. In addition, people may come and go, rendering it difficult to record necessary demographic and other social information on participants, as well as to ensure that all parties are aware that they are participating in a research study. (The reader is referred to Chapter 10 for full discussion of recording naturally occurring interactions not involving research interviews.)

Hence, despite the advantages of methods that break down the one-on-one interview structure, it really is difficult to devise a better instrument than the sociolinguistic interview in terms of efficiently obtaining large quantities of high-quality recorded speech that closely approximates everyday speech. In addition, although it can be argued that in theory the sociolinguistic interview is less than fully conducive to yielding "natural" speech due to asymmetries in social and conversational roles of interviewers and interviewees, in practice, most researchers have found that interviewer control readily falls away, as interviewees warm up to their topics and as interviewers realize that in the field they are no longer the "experts" they may be in the academy, but rather are "learners" who must cede power to their research participants, the ones who hold expert knowledge of the communities of study (see, e.g., Labov 1984: 40–1).

5   Concluding remarks: on overcoming the Observer's Paradox

In this chapter, we have explored several important data collection methods in linguistics – surveys designed to elicit linguistic features, patterns, and interrelations; experiments/surveys designed to yield information on language attitudes; and interviews designed to provide us with connected speech. We have also seen attempts to mitigate observer effects within each methodological perspective. For example, rapid and anonymous surveys allow researchers to elicit specific linguistic forms while keeping participants completely unaware of the research context. Conversely, participants in sociolinguistic interviews are at least initially aware that they are part of a study; however, the questions they are asked are designed to yield natural, connected speech, not isolated speech forms, and also to get them so interested in what they are talking about that the research context is at least backgrounded, if not completely forgotten. And finally, with respect to eliciting information on language attitudes, researchers employ not only matched guise techniques, whose test-like nature cannot be concealed, but also commitment measures in which language attitudes are assessed, not through self-reports, but through behaviors reflective of these attitudes – just as attitudes mediate between stimuli and behaviors in non-research contexts.

In closing, though, we should note that even if the research context can be made to fade into the background, we can never truly remove observer effects on speech – nor do we necessarily want to, since speech is always being observed by some listener, in both research and non-research contexts. It is, then, arguably better to attempt to identify and account for contextual effects, including observer effects, rather than seeking to abstract them away. In other words, it may be better to dispense with the Observer's Paradox rather than trying to overcome it, and to admit that there is no such thing as non-observed language data, and hence no such thing as one single "most important" type of language for linguistic theory – or any one "best" method for obtaining it.

References

Agheyisi, R. and J. Fishman. 1970. Language attitude studies: a brief survey of methodological approaches. *Anthropological Linguistics* 12.5: 137–57.

Auer, P. 2007. Introduction. In P. Auer, ed. *Style and Social Identities: Alternative Approaches to Linguistic Heterogeneity.* Berlin: Walter de Gruyter, 1–21.

Bailey, G., J. Tillery, and T. Wikle. 1997. Methodology of a survey of Oklahoma dialects. *SECOL Review* 21: 1–29.

Bailey, G., T. Wikle, and J. Tillery. 1997. The effects of methods on results in dialectology. *English World-Wide* 18.1: 35–63.

Bourhis, R. and H. Giles. 1976. The language of cooperation in Wales: a field study. *Language Sciences* 42: 13–16.

Buchstaller, I. and K. Corrigan. 2011. How to make intuitions succeed: testing methods for analyzing syntactic microvariation. In W. Maguire and A. McMahon, eds. *Analysing Variation in English*. Cambridge University Press, 30–48.

Campbell-Kibler, K. 2010. Sociolinguistics and perception. *Language and Linguistics Compass* 4.6: 377–89.

Cassidy, F., ed. 1985. *The Dictionary of American Regional English. Volume I: A–C*, 6 vols. Cambridge, MA: Harvard University Press.

Chambers, J. K. 1994. An introduction to dialect topography. *English World-Wide* 15: 35–53.

    1998a. Inferring dialect from a postal questionnaire. *Journal of English Linguistics* 26: 222–46.

    1998b. Social embedding of changes in progress. *Journal of English Linguistics* 26: 5–36.

Chambers, J. K. and P. Trudgill. 1980. *Dialectology*. Cambridge University Press.

Cheshire, J. 1982. *Variation in an English Dialect: A Sociolinguistic Study*. Cambridge University Press.

Cooper, R. and J. Fishman. 1974. The study of language attitudes. *International Journal of the Sociology of Language* 3: 5–19.

Coupland, N. 1980. Style-shifting in a Cardiff work setting. *Language in Society* 9: 1–12.

    2007. *Style: Language Variation and Identity*. Cambridge University Press.

Di Paolo, M. 1988. Pronunciation and categorization in sound change. In K. Ferrara, B. Brown, K. Walters, and J. Baugh, eds. *Linguistic Change and Contact: NWAV-XVI*. Austin: Department of Linguistics, University of Texas, 84–92.

Eckert, P. 2000. *Linguistic Variation as Social Practice*. Malden, MA and Oxford: Wiley-Blackwell.

Ejstrup, M. and G. F. Hansen. 2004. Vowels in regional variants of Danish. In P. Branderud and H. Traunmüller, eds. *Proceedings of FONETIK 2004*. Department of Linguistics, Stockholm University, 88–91.

Fasold, R. W. 1972. *Tense Marking in Black English: A Linguistic and Social Analysis*. Arlington, VA: Center for Applied Linguistics.

    1984. *The Sociolinguistics of Society*. Malden, MA and Oxford: Wiley-Blackwell.

Garrett, P. 2010. *Attitudes to Language*. Cambridge University Press.

Gilliéron, J. 1902–10. *Atlas Linguistique de la France*. 13 vols. Paris: Champion.

Gordon, M. J. 2006. Tracking the low back merger in Missouri. In T. Murray and B. L. Simon, eds. *Language Variation and Change in the American Midland: A New Look at "Heartland" English*. Philadelphia: John Benjamins, 57–68.

Grierson, G. 1905. *Linguistic Survey of India*. Calcutta: Office of the Superintendent, Government Printing.

Hall, J. H., ed. 2002. *The Dictionary of American Regional English. Volume IV: P–Sk*, 6 vols. Cambridge, MA: Harvard University Press.

    2012. *The Dictionary of American Regional English. Volume V: Sl–Z*, 6 vols. Cambridge, MA: Harvard University Press.

Hall, J. H. and F. Cassidy, eds. 1991. *The Dictionary of American Regional English. Volume II: D–H*, 6 vols. Cambridge, MA: Harvard University Press.

    eds. 1996. *The Dictionary of American Regional English. Volume III: I–O*, 6 vols. Cambridge, MA: Harvard University Press.

Hay, J., P. Warren, and K. Drager. 2006. Factors influencing speech perception in the context of a merger-in-progress. *Journal of Phonetics* 34.4: 458–84.

Herold, R. 1990. Mechanisms of merger: the implementation and distribution of the low back merger in Eastern Pennsylvania. Unpublished Ph.D. dissertation, University of Pennsylvania.

Hewitt, R. 1982. White adolescent creole users and the politics of friendship. *Journal of Multilingual and Multicultural Development* 3: 217–32.

Hindle, D. M. 1979. The social and situational conditioning of phonetic variation. Unpublished Ph.D. dissertation, University of Pennsylvania.

Labov, T. 1992. Social and language boundaries among adolescents. *American Speech* 67.4: 339–66.

Labov, W. 1966. *The Social Stratification of English in New York City.* Washington, DC: Center for Applied Linguistics.

1972a. The social stratification of (r) in New York City department stores. In *Sociolinguistic Patterns.* University of Pennsylvania Press, 43–69.

1972b. Some principles of linguistic methodology. *Language in Society* 1: 97–120.

1984. Field methods of the project on linguistic change and variation. In J. Baugh and J. Sherzer, eds. *Language in Use: Readings in Sociolinguistics.* Englewood Cliffs, NJ: Prentice Hall, 28–66.

1994. *Principles of Linguistic Change. Volume 1: Internal Factors*, 3 vols. Malden, MA and Oxford: Wiley-Blackwell.

2001. The anatomy of style-shifting. In P. Eckert and J. R. Rickford, eds. *Style and Sociolinguistic Variation.* Cambridge University Press, 85–108.

Labov, W., S. Ash, and C. Boberg. 2006. *The Atlas of North American English.* Berlin: Mouton de Gruyter.

Labov, W., P. Cohen, C. Robins, and J. Lewis. 1968. *A Study of the Non-Standard English of Negro and Puerto Rican Speakers in New York City*, 2 vols. Final Report, Cooperative Research Project 3288. Philadelphia: US Regional Survey, Volume I.

Labov, W., S. Ash, M. Baranowski, N. Nagy, M. Ravindranath, and T. Weldon. 2006. Listeners' sensitivity to the frequency of sociolinguistic variables. *University of Pennsylvania Working Papers in Linguistics: Selected papers from NWAV 34* 12.2: 105–29.

Lambert, W. E., R. C. Hodgson, R. C. Gardner, and S. Fillenbaum. 1960. Evaluational reactions to spoken languages. *Journal of Abnormal and Social Psychology* 60.1. 44–51.

Macaulay, R. K. S. 1977. *Language, Social Class, and Education: A Glasgow Study.* University of Edinburgh Press.

McDavid, R. I. Jr. and R. K. O'Cain, eds. 1980. *Linguistic Atlas of the Middle and South Atlantic States.* University of Chicago Press.

Milroy, L. 1987. *Observing and Analysing Natural Language.* Malden, MA and Oxford: Wiley-Blackwell.

Milroy, L. and M. Gordon. 2003. *Sociolinguistics: Method and Interpretation.* Malden, MA and Oxford: Blackwell.

Mitzka, W. 1952. *Handbook zum Deutschen Sprachatlas.* Marburg: Elwertsche Universitätsbuchhandlung.

Nagy, N. 2001. Live free or die as a linguistic principle. *American Speech* 76.1: 30–41.

Orton, H., S. Sanderson, and J. Widdowson, eds. 1978. *The Linguistic Atlas of England.* New York: Routledge.

Parrott, J. K. 2002. Dialect death and morpho-syntactic change: Smith Island weak exple-tive 'it'. *University of Pennsylvania Working Papers in Linguistics: Selected Papers from NWAV 30* 8.3: 175–89.

Pederson, L., ed., S. L. McDaniel, assoc. ed., G. Bailey, and M. Bassett, asst. eds. 1986. *Linguistic Atlas of the Gulf States.* Athens: University of Georgia Press.

Plichta, B., D. Preston, and B. Rakerd. 2005. 'Did you say "sod" or "sad"?' Speaker cues and hearer identity in vowel perception in an area of ongoing change. Paper presented at Methods XII: International Conference on Methods in Dialectology. Moncton, NB, August.

Reah, K. 1982. The Labovian interview: a reappraisal. *Lore and Language* 3.7: 1–13.

Romaine, S. 1978. Post-vocalic /r/ in Scottish English: sound change in progress. In P. Trudgill, ed. *Sociolinguistic Patterns in British English.* London: Edward Arnold, 144–57.

  1980. A critical overview of the methodology of urban British sociolinguistics. *English World-Wide* 1: 163–98.

Schilling, N. 2013. *Sociolinguistic Fieldwork.* Cambridge and New York: Cambridge University Press.

Schilling-Estes, N. 1998. Investigating 'self-conscious' speech: the performance register in Ocracoke English. *Language in Society* 27: 53–83.

  2008. Stylistic variation and the sociolinguistic interview: a reconsideration. In R. Monroy and A. Sánchez, eds. *25 Años de Lingüística Aplicada en España: Hitos y Retos* (Proceedings of AELSA 25). Murcia, Spain: Servicio de Publicaciones de la Universidad de Murcia, 971–86.

Sharma, D. 2011. Style repertoire and social change in British Asian English. *Journal of Sociolinguistics* 15.4: 464–92.

Soukup, B. 2011. Austrian listeners' perceptions of standard-dialect style-shifting: an empirical approach. *Journal of Sociolinguistics* 15.3: 347–65.

Thomas, E. R. and J. Reaser. 2004. Delimiting perceptual cues used for the ethnic labeling of African American and European American voices. *Journal of Sociolinguistics* 8.1: 54–87.

Trudgill, P. 1972. Sex, covert prestige, and linguistic change in the urban British English of Norwich. *Language in Society* 1: 179–95.

  1988. Norwich revisited: recent linguistic changes in an English urban dialect. *English World-Wide* 9: 33–49.

Williams, F. 1974. The identification of linguistic attitudes. *International Journal of the Sociology of Language* 3: 21–32.

Wolfram, W. 1995. Delineation and description in dialectology: the case of perfective I'm in Lumbee English. *American Speech* 71: 5–26.

Wolfram, W. and C. J. Dannenberg. 1999. Dialect identity in a tri-ethnic context: the case of Lumbee American Indian English. *English World-Wide* 20: 179–216.

Wolfram, W., K. Hazen, and N. Schilling-Estes. 1999. *Dialect Change and Maintenance on the Outer Banks.* (Publications of the American Dialect Society 81.) Tuscaloosa, University of Alabama Press.

Wolfson, N. 1976. Speech events and natural speech: some implications for sociolinguistic methodology. *Language in Society* 5: 189–209.

7   Experimental research design

Rebekha Abbuhl, Susan Gass, and Alison Mackey

Researchers in the field of linguistics have a wide range of methodologies at their disposal. One approach that has seen a marked increase in recent decades is experimental research, which in the wider social sciences is open to a large number of possible designs (Kirk 2003, for example, lists forty for quantitative research alone; see also Lavrakas 2008). In this chapter, we provide an overview of experimental design options available to linguistics researchers, as well as a brief overview of mixed methods, an increasingly common option for investigating complex research questions. The discussion reviews general principles in experimental design, with examples from a selection of subfields. (For further details of experimental methods in theoretical linguistics and psycholinguistics in particular, see Chapters 3 and 8.) The chapter concludes with a discussion of common data collection techniques relevant to experimental designs that are used in a variety of subfields in linguistics.

1   Fundamentals

Researchers adopting a quantitative approach seek to investigate phenomena by collecting numerical data and analyzing those data statistically. To facilitate this statistical analysis and to control for extraneous variables, quantitative researchers typically recruit a large number of participants and carefully design all aspects of the study before collecting data. In this design process, the quantitative researcher faces a number of questions, including: Do I need more than one group? If so, how many groups are needed to address the research question(s)? How should participants be placed into groups? How will data be collected from the participants, and how often? If an *experimental* approach is adopted – for example, observations or measurements to be collected under relatively controlled conditions – what will the treatment consist of (e.g., stimuli, timed response, feedback)? How will extraneous variables be addressed?

Asking and answering these questions is important for ensuring three general desiderata of quantitative research in any discipline: *validity*, *reliability*, and *replicability*. A study possessing internal validity is one where the researcher can, with some degree of confidence, conclude that it was the stimulus or treatment that was responsible for observed effects and not chance or some other factor, such as practice, maturation, or measurement problems. In addition, the results of an externally valid study can be generalized beyond the immediate sample. That is, if a study possesses external validity, the results should hold true not only for the participants in the study, but for a larger population as well. Reliability refers to the consistency of measurement, both by different raters (inter-rater reliability) and by different instruments (instrument reliability) (Abbuhl and Mackey 2008). The final component, replicability, is also an essential component of quantitative research. A replicable study refers to one whose results can be repeated with other subject populations and in other contexts. As Porte (2012) notes, a study that cannot be replicated should be treated cautiously by the field.

No research design in and of itself will guarantee that a study is valid, reliable, and replicable. However, if researchers are familiar with the advantages and disadvantages of the many available designs, they will be able to make more informed decisions on how to structure their studies and minimize potential problems.

2   Variables and participants

One way of classifying experimental research designs is by the number of *independent* and *dependent* variables present in the experiment. An independent variable is the variable manipulated by the researcher; the dependent variable is the variable that is measured. For example, in a hypothetical study about grammaticality judgments, the independent variable could be whether the participant is a native or non-native speaker, and a possible dependent variable could be scores on the grammaticality judgment test. Here, since there is only one independent variable, the experiment is characterized as *single-factor*, and since this independent variable consists of two groups, it is said to have two levels. Finally, since there is only one dependent variable (scores), it would be considered a *univariate* design. Ultimately, experimental design is inextricably linked to both data collection and the choice of statistics used later (see Chapters 15 and 16).

Another way that research designs can be classified is whether they are *between-subjects* or *within-subjects.* In the former, each level of the independent variable is comprised of different participants. For example, if a researcher is investigating the effect of using time limits when administering a grammaticality judgment test, one group would have a time limit and the other would not. Different individuals would be in the two groups. In the within-subjects designs, the same individuals are assigned to all levels of the independent variable. In our experiment here about grammaticality judgment tests, all individuals would be assessed under two conditions: once with a time limit and once without.

In one of the simplest of between-subjects designs (a single-factor, univariate, between-subjects design), there is one independent variable and one dependent variable. For example, Ribbert and Kuiken (2010) compared two different groups of participants – native speakers of German who were long-term residents of the Netherlands and a group of native speakers of German who lived in Germany – with respect to their judgments of German sentences with infinitive clauses. The researchers found that the Germans living in the Netherlands made significantly more mistakes on the grammaticality judgment test than did the Germans in Germany, leading them to conclude that first language (L1) attrition can occur even if the speakers use the L1 on a consistent basis, and even if they emigrated after puberty.

This basic design can be made more complex by increasing the number of dependent variables, resulting in a *multivariate* design. An example of a single-factor, multivariate, between-subjects study is Fine et al.'s (2011) comparison of individuals with and without Parkinson's disease with respect to their performance on two different verbal fluency tasks. The first task involved the production of common nouns (names of animals) and the second involved proper nouns (boys' names). There were thus two dependent variables. The researchers found that although the two groups performed similarly on the common noun verbal fluency task, the group with Parkinson's disease performed significantly worse than the otherwise healthy individuals on the proper name verbal fluency task, providing evidence that the retrieval of the two types of words may not depend on the same neural pathways.

In both Ribbert and Kuiken (2010) and Fine et al. (2011), the researchers employed a comparison group – a group that is equivalent to the main group under investigation (the emigrants in the first study and the patients with Parkinson's disease in the second) in all respects save for the independent variable (emigrant status in the first study and disease status in the second). The presence of such a comparison group allows researchers to isolate more carefully the effects of the independent variable. The term "control" group is also used to refer to the comparison group, especially in studies where a specific treatment (e.g., stimuli, instruction, or feedback) is provided to the main group under investigation (i.e., the "treatment" group). The presence of a comparison/control group is one of the essential characteristics of experimental research designs.

3   Dealing with extraneous variables

Once the dependent and independent variables have been established, it is standard to aim to control or otherwise minimize the effect of other extraneous sources of variability in the data or in the population. In any given experiment, there are likely to be *extraneous* (or *confounding* or *nuisance*) variables that affect the results of the experiment but are not part of the research design. These factors can skew measurements and cause results to be invalid or unreliable. For instance, in a study in which gender is the sole independent variable, failing to control for age may lead to a higher average age in one or the other group, with an age effect ultimately being interpreted as a gender effect.

Despite a researcher's best efforts, some unknown factors will always be at play in any given participant group. For this reason, another essential characteristic of experimental designs is random assignment of participants to groups, excluding, of course, the independent variables that are the focus of the research. In *simple random assignment*, every participant has an equal chance of being assigned to every level of the independent variable. This is one way that researchers employing between-groups designs can address error variance, or "the statistical variability of scores caused by the influence of variables other than your independent variables" (Bordens and Abbot 2008: 283). Returning to our example of grammaticality judgment tests, whether or not the participants receive a time limit is unlikely to be the only difference between groups (other differences may include factors such as test anxiety, literacy levels, and educational background, not all of which can be controlled by the researcher). If individuals are randomly placed into groups, then it is unlikely that all the participants with "high test anxiety," for example, will cluster into one group and therefore the effect of that extraneous variable may be minimized. Simple random assignment may be accomplished by assigning each individual in the sample a number and then using a software program or random number table to randomly select as many numbers as are needed.

One alternative to simple random assignment is to employ a *block design*. In this design, subjects are matched on one or more characteristics that may influence the dependent variable. Salkind (2010) provides an example of a hypothetical experiment on two different techniques for memorizing Spanish vocabulary items. The independent variable was thus "technique" (two levels) and the dependent variables in his example were the number of trials required to learn the vocabulary list. As Salkind explains, a researcher investigating this issue may suspect that an extraneous variable (e.g., general intelligence) may influence the results. To control for this individual difference so that the treatment effects are not obscured, the researcher could pair individuals with similar IQs and then randomly assign one of the pair to the control group and the other to the experimental group (Cohen, Manion, and Morrison 2007). In this way, the researcher could help to ensure that the same number of individuals from each IQ level experience each level of the independent variable (Clark-Carter 2010). If the independent variable has three or more levels, then the researcher must find a set of individuals (e.g., three individuals with the same IQ) and randomly distribute them across the levels of the independent variable. This may become logistically problematic as the number of levels of the independent variable increases (finding three or more individuals with the same IQ, for example, is more difficult than finding only two) or if the number of extraneous variables to be matched increases. In this case, it is typically recommended that error variance be reduced not through blocking, but by employing a within-subjects design – especially if a large subject pool is not available to the researcher (e.g., Bordens and Abbot 2008).

As mentioned earlier, the within-subjects design (also referred to as a repeated measures design) involves using the same participants for all levels of the independent variable. As every group in the experiment is comprised of the same individuals, inter-individual differences can be better controlled. Essentially, each person is acting as her or his own control in a within-subjects design, as each person is a member of every group (Salkind 2010). In a simple, single-factor, univariate, within-subjects design, there would be one independent variable and the participants would be assessed at least twice, once under each condition. This design can be made more complex, of course, by adding additional dependent variables. In one example of a single-factor, multivariate, within-subjects design, Knoch and Elder (2010) compared the writing produced by non-native speakers of English under two different time conditions (30 minutes and 55 minutes), with respect to the fluency, content, and form of writing. No significant differences were uncovered between the two conditions with respect to those particular dependent variables.

One potential limitation of the within-subjects design concerns order effects, also known as *carryover effects*. A carryover effect is when a previous treatment influences the participants' behavior in a subsequent treatment (Myers, Well, and Lorch 2010). This includes practice effects (participants becoming more skilled at a particular activity by virtue of having completed it more than once) and fatigue effects (participants' performance decreasing due to tiredness or boredom). To address this problem, researchers commonly make use of *counterbalancing*, in which different, randomly assigned participants complete the different levels of the independent variable in different orders. Returning to Knoch and Elder's (2010) study, for example, the researchers used a counterbalanced design, with half of the participants writing under the 30-minute condition first and the other half writing under the 55-minute condition first.

Knoch and Elder's (2010) study made use of *complete counterbalancing*, in which every possible ordering of participants is addressed. When there are two levels to the independent variable, complete counterbalancing is relatively simple; however, when the number of levels of the independent variable increases, complete counterbalancing becomes notably more complex. For example, let us say (hypothetically) that Knoch and Elder (2010) decided to add a third time condition to their study, so now they are investigating students' writing under three time conditions (30, 55, and 90 minutes). With complete counterbalancing, there would be six possible orders; if the researchers decided to add a fourth time condition (e.g., 120 minutes), there would be twenty-four possible orders. In the event that the researchers chose to compare five conditions, they would be faced with 120 possible orders. As at least one participant needs to be assigned to each order, and ideally more than one, a completely counterbalanced design involving an independent variable with more than two levels could require a larger number of participants than the researcher has access to. In such situations, researchers commonly employ *partial counterbalancing*. In this type of counterbalancing, a subset of possible orders from the total set of possible orders is chosen, often through the use of a *Latin squares design* (Goodwin 2009; Myers, Well, and Lorch 2010).

A	B	C	D
D	A	B	C
C	D	A	B
B	C	D	A

Figure 7.1. *4×4 Latin squares design*

A Latin squares design is a grid of numbers or letters, with each number/letter representing a different condition in the study. The grid has as many rows and columns as there are conditions in the study. For example, in our hypothetical study comparing essays written under four time conditions (30, 55, 90, and 120 minutes), we would have a 4×4 Latin squares design, as depicted in Figure 7.1. "A" represents the first time condition (30 minutes), "B" the second time condition (55 minutes), and so on. As can be seen in Figure 7.1, the "A" condition, along with all the other conditions, occurs once in each row and once in each column. The benefit of this design is that each condition appears in each of the four possible positions without requiring complete counterbalancing.

The minimum number of participants for this particular Latin square design would be four – one participant for every row/ordering. Ideally, of course, a researcher would employ more than one participant per row/ordering; even so, this strategy greatly reduces the number of participants that are required. If a researcher investigating the four time conditions decided to use a completely counterbalanced design and used ten participants per condition, the required number of participants would be 240. With the Latin squares design and ten participants per ordering, the number of participants required would be only forty.

4   Factorial designs

All of the above designs are considered single-factor designs as there is only one independent variable. However, it is also possible to have more than one independent variable; such a design is called a *multi-factor* or, more commonly, *factorial* design. This type of design allows the researcher to examine the effect of each independent variable separately (these are called main effects) and to look at possible interactions between the independent variables (these are known as interaction effects). Examining multiple variables at once is more parsimonious and cost-effective than conducting multiple separate experiments on each independent variable; in addition, factorial designs allow the researcher to determine whether the effect of one independent variable depends on the value of another independent variable (e.g., if the effect of instruction depends on the age or proficiency of the learner). In one of the simplest of factorial designs, a 2×2 between-subjects factorial design, there are two independent variables, with each independent variable having two levels and each participant being randomly assigned to only one of the four treatment combinations. Similarly, in a 2×2 within-subjects factorial design, there are two independent variables and each independent variable has two levels. Unlike the between-subjects design, however, participants in the within-subjects design experience each of the four conditions. In an example of the latter, Phillips, Kazanina, and Abada's (2005) first experiment employed a 2×2 within-subjects factorial design to investigate the effects of wh-dependency (present or absent) and dependency length (one clause or two clauses) on the perceived processing difficulty of English sentences by native speakers of English. The researchers found significant main effects for presence of wh-dependency and wh-dependency length, as well as a significant interaction between the two, with sentences containing a wh-dependency of two clauses in length being rated as significantly more difficult to understand than sentences containing a one-clause wh-dependency or no wh-dependencies.

This basic design can be made more complex by adding additional levels to the independent variables. For example, in a 2×3 factorial design, there are two independent variables, with the first independent variable having two levels and the second three. In Fernald and Morikawa (1993), the researchers used a 2×3 between-subjects factorial design to examine the main effects of the mother's native language (Japanese or English) and infant age (6, 12 or 19 months) to examine inter alia the amount of speech directed toward infants. One of their findings was that Japanese mothers spoke significantly more to their infants than did American mothers, with no significant interaction effects between age and language. Factorial designs can also be expanded to include more than two independent variables; in a $2\times2\times2$ factorial design, for example, there are three independent variables, each with two levels. Designs employing three independent variables are fairly common in linguistics; however, factorial designs employing four or more independent variables are rare, due in part to the difficulty of interpreting interaction effects among four variables. In this case, researchers typically recommend using other designs, such as regression (Salkind 2010; see Chapter 16 for more information on regression analysis).

In studies where there are multiple independent variables, it is common for one or more of these variables to be within-subjects and one or more of the variables to be between-subjects, resulting in a *mixed design*. The advantage of this design is that it allows researchers to examine different types of effects simultaneously in one experiment. For example, in Kavitskaya et al. (2011), the researchers investigated the repetition of pseudo-words by Russian-speaking children with specific language impairment (SLI) and by typically developing (TD) controls. The researchers had one between-subjects independent variable with two-levels (group: SLI or TD) and two within-subjects factors. The first within-subjects factor was the number of syllables in the word (one, two, or three) and the second was the syllable structure of the word (CV, CVC, VC, CCV, CCVC, CVCC, VCC, CCVCC). Using this $2\times3\times8$ mixed design, the researchers found that there was a significant main effect for group, as well as for syllable number and syllable structure. There was a number of significant interaction effects as well, including one between group and syllable number. These results led the researchers to conclude that the number of syllables in the pseudo-word was a significant determinant of the children's performance on the repetition task, and that children with SLI made significantly more errors than the TD children with words at every length.

Often, such experimental designs will involve mixed-effects modeling in the statistical analysis (see Chapter 16). In experimental sociolinguistics, an emerging field, mixed-effects models have been advocated, as they allow variables such as word and speaker to be treated as random effects, while other independent variables (e.g., age, gender, class) are treated as fixed effects (Johnson 2009).

5   Pretest-posttest designs

Pretest-posttest designs, if they employ a control group and random assignment of participants to groups, are also examples of experimental designs. One example of an experimental pretest-posttest design is the two-group, pretest-posttest design, also known as the *controlled pretest-posttest design*. Both groups are assessed prior to the treatment, one group forgoes the treatment, and both groups are assessed after the treatment. If the researcher finds that the treatment group's scores are different (e.g., statistically higher) than those of the control group, then, all other things being equal, the researcher can cautiously conclude that the treatment was responsible. Variations of this basic design include employing multiple posttests (to assess the long-term effect of the treatment) and using multiple control groups, as in the Solomon four-squares design. In this latter type of design, there are two control groups and two experimental or treatment groups. A pretest and posttest are administered to one treatment group and one control group, with the remaining groups only taking the posttest. The purpose of having two groups forgo the pretest is to determine whether the pretest sensitized the participants to the research topic and thus affected their posttest scores (Cohen, Manion, and Morrison 2007). While the Solomon four-group design is not common in the field of linguistics, one example can be found in Özkan and Kesen's (2009) study on the effect of different types of grammar instruction on students' grammatical accuracy.

An additional example of a controlled pretest-posttest design is known as the *switching replications design*. In this two-group design, both groups receive a pretest. One group then receives the treatment, and both groups are then assessed again. The second group then receives the treatment, and finally, both groups are assessed for a third time. Although this type of design is useful when denying the treatment to one group is not feasible or desirable, it is rare in the field of linguistics. In one of the few studies to employ this design, Huemer et al. (2010) investigated the effect of repeated reading on the reading speed of Finnish children in their first language.

If the pretest-posttest design does not employ a control or random assignment, it is said to be *quasi-experimental.* Although this design lacks strong internal validity, it can be useful when random assignment of participants to groups or the use of a control group is not possible. An example of a quasi-experimental design is the one-group, pretest-posttest design. This design is not common in the field of linguistics due to the fact that the absence of a control group makes it difficult to determine whether any observed changes from pretest to posttest were due to the treatment or whether they were the result of other extraneous variables (e.g., maturation). One suggested improvement to this design is to use a double pretest. If the difference between the first pretest and second pretest is smaller than the difference between the second pretest and the posttest (assuming equal time intervals between tests), then the researcher can more confidently conclude that the participants' performance on the posttest was due to the treatment, not maturation (Salkind 2010).

More commonly, researchers employ quasi-experimental designs that do involve control groups, including the non-equivalent groups posttest-only design and the non-equivalent groups pretest-posttest design. In both of these designs, there is a control and a treatment group, but the participants are non-randomly assigned to both (e.g., if the researcher is dealing with intact groups or classes, randomly assigning participants to the various levels of the independent variable may not be logistically possible). The non-random assignment makes it difficult to determine whether any observed changes are due to the independent variable. Possible methods for strengthening these designs include using the Solomon four-squares or switching replications design discussed above, as they can help the researcher more confidently rule out the effects of maturation and other extraneous variables.

Another type of quasi-experimental design is the *time-series design* (see Chapter 22 for details). Here, a (typically small) group of participants is measured repeatedly both prior to and after the treatment. These multiple measures enhance the internal validity of the design and allow the researcher to establish the participants' performance or level of knowledge prior to the treatment and to determine whether there are changes after the treatment and over time (Abbuhl and Mackey 2008). Jones and Ryan (2001), for example, used this procedure to investigate the relationship between speaking and stuttering rates.

6   Mixed-method approaches

Many different variations of the research designs discussed above are possible, including factorial designs that make use of partial counterbalancing, and within-subjects approaches that employ pretests and posttests, among many others. It is also possible to combine these various experimental designs with qualitative approaches to yield a mixed-methods design. As researchers have long acknowledged, quantitative and qualitative approaches are not incompatible, and employing both approaches in a principled manner in a single study can facilitate a deeper understanding of complex phenomena (e.g., Angouri 2010; Salkind 2010; Hashemi 2012).

This section will briefly cover some of the more common research designs available to quantitative researchers interested in adding a qualitative phase (or "strand") to their research. It should be kept in mind that the options discussed below are neither rigid nor exhaustive (see, e.g., Creswell and Plano Clark 2011, and Tashakkori and Teddlie 2010 for more detailed overviews, as well as Angouri 2010 and Hashemi 2012 for discussions of mixed methods as they apply to the field of linguistics). As Creswell and Plano Clark (2011) note, although it is useful for researchers new to mixed-methods research to become acquainted with the various typologies for framing mixed-methods designs, there is also merit to adopting a more dynamic approach, in which researchers "focus on a design process that considers and interrelates multiple components of research design rather than placing emphasis on selecting an appropriate design from an existing typology" (p. 59).

The most common approach to mixed-methods design is generally referred to as the *convergent parallel design* (Creswell and Plano Clark 2011). In this design, the quantitative data collection and qualitative data collection occur independently and concurrently (e.g., administering a large-scale survey and simultaneously conducting focus group interviews). The results of the two strands of research are merged at the interpretation stage, and both strands receive equal emphasis. This approach can allow for triangulation of methods and can be useful for gathering complementary sets of data. Kim (2009), for example, used this approach to investigate native and non-native English-speaking teachers and their assessments of students' oral English performance. The quantitative strand focused on the internal consistency and severity of the teachers; the qualitative strand focused on the specific evaluation criteria the teachers used to evaluate their students.

Concurrent timing is also used in the *embedded design*. Here, in the overall framework of a quantitative study, the researcher may add a qualitative strand. The quantitative strand, however, would receive focal emphasis. (The reverse is also possible: in an overall framework of a qualitative study, the researcher may add a secondary quantitative strand.)

Options that employ sequential timing are also possible. In the explanatory sequential design, the researcher begins with a quantitative strand. This strand receives the greatest emphasis in the study, and the results of this strand are followed up with a qualitative phase, which help the researcher explain the initial quantitative results. Nakata (2011), for example, conducted a study on Japanese EFL high school teachers and their views of learner autonomy using a question-naire (the quantitative strand); the results of this phase of the research informed the follow-up qualitative focus group interviews. Beginning with a qualitative phase is also possible: in an exploratory sequential design, the researcher begins with a qualitative phase, which, in turn, informs a quantitative phase used to test or generalize the findings from the first phase.

7   Eliciting data for experimental designs

Just as researchers must make principled decisions concerning research design, so must researchers give careful thought to the design of data collection techniques they employ in relation to those designs, as these will impact the study's validity, reliability, and replicability. Consideration must be given to the goals of the study and the characteristics of the participants, as well as to the advantages and disadvantages of the various data collection techniques that are available. In the section that follows, we will provide a brief, non-exhaustive overview of some of the more common data collection techniques available in different subfields of linguistics for experimental methodologies. Further details on data collection can be found in various chapters in Part I of this volume.

In theoretical linguistics, data collection typically involves the linguist mining her or his own intuition or, alternatively, investigating large-scale spoken and written corpora. Debates continue on the value of introspective data collection methods in theoretical linguistics (see, e.g., Featherston 2007; den Dikken et al. 2007). Some have argued that corpus-based studies possess some advantages over relying on intuition; for instance, examples of particular constructions that did not occur to the linguist might be found in a corpus, and using corpora can limit the amount of influence that the researcher has on the language collected (Miller and Cann 2001; see McEnery and Hardie 2011 and Chapter 13 for more information on corpus-based studies in linguistics). Conversely, certain syntactic constructions (or other linguistic phenomena of interest) may be infrequent in existing corpora, and for this reason, combining corpus-based data with experimental data may be of use to researchers. Chapter 3 contains a full discussion of data elicitation techniques for theoretical linguistics.

Combining corpus and experimental data is also common in the field of psycholinguistics (Gilquin and Gries 2009). For example, a researcher may investigate the frequency of a particular syntactic construction in a corpus and then collect experimental data using one or more of the many procedures available to psycholinguists, including lexical decision tasks, eye-tracking, priming, sentence completion, moving window experiments, and acceptability judgment tasks (see Fernández and Cairns 2011 for a recent overview of these techniques). Psycholinguists also make use of a variety of neuroimaging techniques to determine which areas of the brain are active during different types of language processing, including electroencephalography (EEG), which measures electrical activity in the brain, and functional magnetic resonance imaging (fMRI), which measures blood flow levels in the brain (Fernández and Cairns 2011). Chapter 8 offers a more detailed review of such techniques in psycholinguistics.

Neuroimaging techniques are also being employed in other areas of linguistics, including first language acquisition. For example, researchers have employed fMRIs, positron emission tomography (PET), and functional near infrared spectroscopy (fNIRS) to study infants' brain activity when listening to language – techniques that are particularly useful when studying infants who are not yet actively producing speech. Other techniques that do not require the child to produce language include habituation techniques to study infants' discrimination of sounds, and the preferential looking procedure for measuring infants' early language comprehension (see Hoff 2012 for a detailed overview). For young children who have reached the stage of speech production, there are a number of techniques for assessing phonology (e.g., collecting spontaneous speech examples or using elicited productions, such as naming objects and repeating words or non-words), vocabulary (e.g., standardized tests such as the Peabody Picture Vocabulary Test, and parental reports such as the MacArthur-Bates Communicative Developmental Inventories), and syntax (e.g., elicited imitation, act-out tasks, and elicited production), among many others. Corpora are also used alongside experiments in studies of first language acquisition, the most well-known child language corpus being the Child Language Data Exchange System (CHILDES). (See Hoff 2012 and Menn and Ratner 2000 on data collection procedures in first language acquisition.)

With respect to phonetics, researchers also have available to them a range of methods, ranging from the more naturalistic approach of having fieldworkers phonetically transcribe responses to questionnaire items (an approach that is widely used to investigate language variation; see Chapter 6), to the more controlled approaches involving the acoustic analysis of speech (see Thomas 2011 for a recent review; see also Chapters 4, 9, and 17). In experimental elicitation, participants may be asked to read words in isolation or in connected prose, with the goal of conducting an acoustic analysis of intonation, word stress, tone, and various features of consonants and vowels (Ladefoged 2003). There is also a range of imaging techniques to investigate the vocal tract during the production of speech, such as X-rays, computed tomography, MRIs, and ultrasound (see Stone 2010 for an overview of these and other laboratory techniques). In addition to informing debates on phonology and phonetics, these analyses may be used in sociolinguistic studies on language variation, first language studies on the development of pronunciation, and second language studies on the phonological development of non-native speakers.

In the field of pragmatics, researchers have traditionally relied on various forms of written questionnaires, including discourse completion tasks (an off-line paper-and-pencil task, where participants are asked to write down how they would respond to particular situations) and multiple-choice questionnaires (where respondents choose how they would respond from a set of possible responses), to gather information about language use and behavior (Kasper 2008). Although this form of data collection is still well-represented in the literature, Kasper (2008) also notes that there is a growing emphasis on employing more dynamic data collection techniques that allow researchers to investigate talk in context. This may take the form of audio and/or video recordings of authentic talk, as well as various forms of elicited conversation, including conversation tasks, where participants are requested to discuss a particular topic, and sociolinguistic interviews, during which the interviewee is asked about her or his life history and attitudes as a means of gathering examples of vernacular speech. Pragmatics researchers may also employ role plays to elicit specific speech events, a technique which may be particularly useful for speech acts that are infrequent in naturally occurring speech (see Chapters 10 and 21 for more information). Recently, more narrowly experimental designs and elicitation methods have been implemented in the emerging field of experimental pragmatics, with participants responding to verbal and non-verbal stimuli much as in psycholinguistic experiment designs (see Noveck and Sperber 2004).

A similar range of approaches has been employed in studies investigating code-switching and attitudes toward bilingualism (see Nortier 2008 for a recent review). Off-line questionnaires can be used to gather information on participants' language history (e.g., what languages are known and when they were learned), language dominance (which language the participant is more proficient in), and, to some extent, attitudes toward code-switching, different languages, and bilingualism in general. Questionnaires can also be combined with naturalistic observations (which are useful for gathering information on participants' language behavior in context) and/or more controlled data collection procedures, such as the matched-guide technique. In this experimental technique, a single individual is recorded producing different varieties of speech; respondents then rate the perceived qualities of each "speaker" (e.g., trustworthiness, intelligence), thereby indirectly providing evidence of their attitudes toward the different varieties of speech (see Chapter 6 for further discussion of the elicitation of language attitudes). Sentence repetition tasks, during which participants repeat sentences with instances of "natural" or "unnatural" code-switching, can also be used to gather information on constraints in code-switching.

Second language (L2) researchers also use many of these data collection techniques to investigate how older learners acquire a non-native language. Psycholinguistic techniques, such as priming experiments, are well represented in the literature (see McDonough and Trofimovich 2009 for an overview); neuro-imaging techniques are gaining traction (see, e.g., Sabourin 2009); and the techniques discussed above with respect to phonology, pragmatics, and syntax have been used extensively since the field's inception (see Chaudron 2005; Dörnyei 2007; Gass and Mackey 2007; Mackey and Gass 2012 for overviews, as well as IRIS (Instruments for Research into Second Languages), a digital repository of data collection techniques for L2 researchers). Additional techniques include the use of interactive tasks to assess, for example, the effect of feedback on learners' developing interlanguage grammars (see Ellis 2003 for an overview), and stimulated recalls and think-aloud protocols to tap into learners' on-line thought processes as they complete a task (see Gass and Mackey 2000; Bowles 2010 for more information). There are also a variety of techniques for investigating learners' developing reading (Koda 2012) and writing skills (Polio 2012).

The data collection techniques outlined above differ along a number of dimensions, including the degree of contextualization, presence of time constraints, and types of demands placed on the participants. Data collected in controlled contexts are more amenable to experimental designs, but a point often made in the literature is that there is a trade-off between control and generalizability (data gathered in a controlled context may not be generalizable to more "authentic" contexts). Triangulation of methods – including the use of mixed-methods research – is thus often recommended. Researchers also need to consider the demands the technique places on the participants themselves. To illustrate this point, we will next briefly consider the use of children in linguistics research, and in particular, second language acquisition research.

8   Designing experiments involving children

First language acquisition researchers working with children have long tailored their data collection procedures to the physical and cognitive capabilities of their participants. For example, as discussed above, for infants who do not yet produce speech, techniques such as the preferential head-turn procedure and the conditioned head turn are useful (for those infants who have sufficient muscle control for head turning). For young children who do produce speech, there is a range of techniques (e.g., truth value judgment tasks and act-outs) that allow the researcher to tap into the children's linguistic knowledge.

In addition to considering children's speech and physical abilities, researchers also need to consider their maturity levels. As discussed in detail in Chapter 5, children pass through a variety of maturational stages as they get older. In early childhood, children are learning to think symbolically and have difficulties with abstractness, logic, and taking others' viewpoints. Their presuppositional skills (the ability to make assumptions about a listener's knowledge) are relatively undeveloped as well, leading to difficulties with providing sufficient (and relevant) information to interlocutors. This is commonly referred to as the "egocentric" stage. During middle childhood, children develop their logical abilities, as well as their abilities to take others' perspectives. Conversationally, their turn-taking abilities increase and they have the ability to make a wide range of speech acts (e.g., requests, invitations). They also have greater metalinguistic awareness at this stage. However, they still experience difficulties with abstract thought. These difficulties largely disappear by early adolescence. At this time, children's conversational abilities progress as well, and they are able to maintain topics and respond to feedback and requests for clarification (Philp, Mackey, and Oliver 2008).

These maturational stages must be kept in mind when deciding on tasks or activities for participants. For example, a young child in the egocentric stage may not understand that the contents of her or his mind are not public knowledge and thus may not be able to grasp the purpose of an interactional task. For example, if two young children are separated by a divider and are engaged in a one-way task where one child has to describe a sequence of blocks to a second child, who in turn has to listen and then rearrange her own blocks in the correct order, the first child may rely on egocentric descriptions (e.g., "pick up the block that looks like my toy"). If the second child is not familiar with the first child's toys, this description will be of little use.

Similarly, young participants may not be able to successfully complete tasks that require complex reasoning, logic, or high levels of metalinguistic awareness. For this reason, traditional grammaticality judgment tests (which ask participants to determine whether a given string of words is grammatical or not) may prove to be too abstract for children. Bialystok (1987) offers a child-friendly alternative, which involves having a puppet present various sentences to children, some of which are (un)grammatical and of some of which are (non)sensical. The children are told that it is "fun to be silly" and to just tell the puppet when he says something wrong but not silly – for example, "Why is the cat barking so loudly?" would be silly, and "Why the dog is barking so loudly?" would be wrong. Truth value judgment tests can also be used to gather information on children's knowledge of grammar. In this procedure, a short skit is acted out in front of children and, at the end, a puppet comments on what happened in the skit. The children must tell the puppet whether the statement is true or false. This procedure has been used to gather information on children's interpretation of backwards anaphora among other aspects of grammar (e.g., Crain and Lillo-Martin 1999).

The elicited imitation approach can also be used with children, potentially as a game. Elicited imitation involves aurally presenting sentences of varying complexities and investigating the degree to which the child is able to repeat the sentence. The underlying assumption is that if the child does not have full control over the grammatical structures contained within the sentence, the sentence will be difficult to repeat. A variation of this basic technique is to present both grammatical and ungrammatical sentences and to have the participants repeat the sentences back in correct English (Erlam 2006). Gerken (2000), for example, suggests that the experimenter can place a small speaker inside a puppet, and then pretend that she or he cannot understand that puppet. The researcher can ask the child to "translate," by repeating what the animal said. Puppets can also be used in elicited production techniques with children. For example, in order to elicit complex constructions from children that may be rare in spontaneous speech (such as object wh-extraction), researchers can have the child interact with a puppet as in example (1), from Crain (1991):

(1)   RESEARCHER: The rat looks hungry. I bet he wants to eat something.
            Ask Ratty what he wants.
        CHILD: What do you wanna eat?
        RAT: Some cheese would be good.

There are also behavioral considerations that may impact the ability of the children to successfully complete given tasks. For example, it has been said that young children are less bound by social and task constraints (Philp, Oliver, and Mackey 2006; Philp, Mackey, and Oliver 2008). To minimize the chances that off-task behavior will occur, it is once again important to employ "child-friendly" tasks (ones that they will find interesting, not too cognitively challenging, and appropriate to their maturational level). In addition, it is important to provide clear instructions, so the child participants can understand what is expected of them. If the child participants are second language learners, the researcher may also consider providing those instructions in the first language, in order to minimize misunderstandings and potential conflicts.

Ethical matters come into play immediately when conducting research with children. One of the essential components of obtaining informed consent is making sure that participants are competent enough to make an informed decision regarding their participation in the study. Children are no exception to this, but present specific challenges (see Fine and Sandstrom 1998; Alderson 2000). Ethical issues related to working with children are discussed further in Chapter 2.

In summary, pursuing an experimental research paradigm involves making a series of decisions on the dimensions of language structure or language variation being studied, the range of potential influences being considered, and the number, grouping, assessment, and treatment of the chosen participants. Addressing these issues adequately and carefully before starting the research can help in the creation of studies that are valid, replicable, and reliable, helping researchers come closer to answering questions of general interest to the field.

References

Abbuhl, R. and A. Mackey. 2008. Second language acquisition research methods. In K. King and N. H. Hornberger, eds. *Encyclopedia of Language and Education. Volume X: Research Methods in Language and Education*, 2nd edn. Dordrecht: Springer, 1–13.

Alderson, P. 2000. Children as researchers: the effects of participation rights on research methodology. In P. Christensen and A. James, eds. *Research with Children: Perspectives and Practices*. London: Falmer Press, 241–57.

Angouri, J. 2010. Quantitative, qualitative or both? Combining methods in linguistic research. In L. Litosseliti, ed. *Research Methods in Linguistics*. London: Continuum, 29–45.

Bialystok, E. 1987. Influences of bilingualism on metalinguistic development. *Second Language Research* 3: 154–66.

Bordens, K. and B. Abbott. 2008. *Research Design and Methods: A Process Approach*. Boston: McGraw Hill.

Bowles, M. 2010. *The Think-Aloud Controversy in Second Language Research*. New York: Routledge.

Chadron, C. 2005. Data collection in SLA research. In C. Doughty and M. Long, eds. *The Handbook of Second Language Acquisition*. Oxford: Blackwell, 762–828.

Clark-Carter, D. 2010. *Quantitative Psychological Research: The Complete Student's Companion*. New York: Psychology Press.

Cohen, L., L. Manion, and K. Morrison. 2007. *Research Methods in Education*. London: Routledge.

Crain, S. 1991. Language acquisition in the absence of experience. *Behavioral and Brain Sciences* 14: 597–650.

Crain, S. and D. Lillo-Martin. 1999. *An Introduction to Linguistic Theory and Language Acquisition*. Malden, MA: Blackwell.

Creswell, J. and V. Plano Clark. 2011. *Designing and Conducting Mixed Methods Research*. Thousand Oaks, CA: Sage.

den Dikken, M., J. Bernstein, C. Tortora, and R. Zanuttini. 2007. Data and grammar: means and individuals. *Theoretical Linguistics* 33: 335–52.

Dörnyei, Z. 2007. *Research Methods in Applied Linguistics*. Oxford University Press.

Ellis, R. 2003. *Task-Based Language Learning and Teaching*. Oxford University Press.

Erlam, R. 2006. Elicited imitation as a measure of L2 implicit knowledge: an empirical validation study. *Applied Linguistics* 27: 464–91.

Featherston, S. 2007. Data in generative grammar: the stick and the carrot. *Theoretical Linguistics* 33: 269–318.

Fernald, A. and H. Morikawa. 1993. Common themes and cultural variations in Japanese and American mothers' speech to infants. *Child Development* 64: 637–56.

Fernández, E. and H. Cairns. 2011. *Fundamentals of Psycholinguistics*. Malden, MA: Wiley-Blackwell.

Fine, E., D. Delis, B. Paul, and J. Filoteo. 2011. Reduced verbal fluency for proper names in nondemented patients with Parkinson's disease: a quantitative and qualitative analysis. *Journal of Clinical and Experimental Neuropsychology* 33: 226–33.

Fine, G. and Sandstrom, K. 1998. *Knowing Children: Participant Observation with Minors*. Beverly Hills, CA: Sage.

Gass, S. and A. Mackey. 2000. *Stimulated Recall Methodology in Second Language Research*. Mahwah, NJ: Lawrence Erlbaum.

2007. *Data Elicitation for Second and Foreign Language Research*. Mahwah, NJ: Lawrence Erlbaum.

Gerken, L. 2000. Examining young children's morphosyntactic development through elicited production. In L. Menn and N. Ratner, eds. *Methods for Studying Language Production*. Mahwah, NJ: Lawrence Erlbaum, 45–52.

Gilquin, G. and S. Gries. 2009. Corpora and experimental methods: a state-of-the-art review. *Corpus Linguistics and Linguistic Theory* 5: 1–26.

Goodwin, C. 2009. *Research in Psychology: Methods and Design*. New York: Wiley.

Hashemi, M. 2012. Reflections on mixing methods in applied linguistics research. *Applied Linguistics* 33: 206–12.

Hoff, E. 2012. *Research Methods in Child Language: A Practical Guide*. Malden, MA: Wiley-Blackwell.

Huemer, S., M. Aro, K. Landeri, and H. Lyytinen. 2010. Repeated reading of syllables among Finnish-speaking children with poor reading skills. *Scientific Studies of Reading* 14: 317–40.

Johnson, D. 2009. Getting off the GoldVarb standard: introducing Rbrul for mixed-effects variable rule analysis. *Language and Linguistics Compass* 3: 359–83.

Jones, P. and B. Ryan. 2001. Experimental analysis of the relationship between speaking rate and stuttering during mother–child conversation. *Journal of Developmental and Physical Disabilities* 13: 279–305.

Kasper, G. 2008. Data collection in pragmatics research. In H. Spencer-Oatey, ed. *Culturally Speaking: Culture, Communication and Politeness Theory.* London: Continuum, 279–303.

Kavitskaya, D., M. Babyonyshev, T. Walls, and E. Grigorenko. 2011. Investigating the effects of syllable complexity in Russian-speaking children with SLI. *Journal of Child Language* 38: 979–98.

Kim, Y.-H. 2009. An investigation into native and non-native teachers' judgments of oral English performance: a mixed methods approach. *Language Testing* 26: 187–217.

Kirk, R. 2003. Experimental design. In J. Schinka and W. Velicer, eds. *Handbook of Psychology. Volume II: Research Methods in Psychology.* Hoboken, NJ: John Wiley & Sons, 3–32.

Knoch, U. and C. Elder. 2010. Validity and fairness implications of varying time conditions on a diagnostic test of academic English writing proficiency. *System* 38: 63–74.

Koda, K. 2012. How to do research on second language reading. In A. Mackey and S. Gass, eds. *Research Methods in Second Language Acquisition: A Practical Guide.* Malden, MA: Blackwell, 158–79.

Ladefoged, P. 2003. *Phonetic Data Analysis: An Introduction to Fieldwork and Instrumental Techniques.* Oxford: Wiley-Blackwell.

Lavrakas, P., ed. 2008. *Encyclopedia of Survey Research Methods.* Thousand Oaks, CA: Sage.

Mackey, A. and M. Gass. 2012. *Research Methods in Second Language Acquisition: A Practical Guide.* Malden, MA: Wiley-Blackwell.

McDonough, K. and P. Trofimovich. 2009. *Using Priming Methods in Second Language Research.* New York: Routledge.

McEnery, T. and A. Hardie. 2011. *Corpus Linguistics: Method, Theory and Practice.* Cambridge University Press.

Menn, L. and N. Ratner, eds. 2000. *Methods for Studying Language Production.* Mahwah, NJ: Lawrence Erlbaum.

Miller, J. and R. Cann. 2001. Data collection in linguistics. In R. Mesthrie, ed. *Concise Encyclopedia of Sociolinguistics.* Oxford: Elsevier, 769–71.

Myers, J., A. Well, and R. Lorch. 2010. *Research Design and Statistical Analysis.* New York: Routledge.

Nakata, Y. 2011. Teachers' readiness for promoting learner autonomy: a study of Japanese EFL high school teachers. *Teaching and Teacher Education* 27: 900–10.

Nortier, J. 2008. Types and sources in bilingual data. In L. Wei and M. Moyer, eds. *The Blackwell Guide to Research Methods in Bilingualism and Multilingualism.* Malden, MA: Blackwell, 35–52.

Noveck, I. and D. Sperber. 2004. *Experimental Pragmatics.* London: Palgrave.

Özkan, Y. and A. Kesen. 2009. The third way in grammar instruction. *Procedia – Social and Behavioral Sciences* 1: 1931–5.

Phillips, C., N. Kazanina, and S. Abada. 2005. ERP effects of the processing of syntactic long-distance dependencies. *Cognitive Brain Research* 22: 407–28.

Philp, J., A. Mackey, and R. Oliver. 2008. *Second Language Acquisition and the Younger Learner.* Amsterdam: John Benjamins.

Philp, J., R. Oliver, and A. Mackey. 2006. The impact of planning on children's task-based interactions. *System* 34: 547–65.

Polio, C. 2012. How to research second language writing. In A. Mackey and S. Gass, eds. *Research Methods in Second Language Acquisition: A Practical Guide*. Malden, MA: Blackwell, 139–57.

Porte, G., ed. 2012. *Replication Research in Applied Linguistics*. Cambridge University Press.

Ribbert, A. and F. Kuiken. 2010. L2-induced changes in the L1 of Germans living in the Netherlands. *Bilingualism: Language and Cognition* 13: 41–8.

Sabourin, L. 2009. Neuroimaging and research into second language acquisition. *Second Language Research* 25: 5–11.

Salkind, N., ed. 2010. *Encyclopedia of Research Design*. Thousand Oaks, CA: Sage Publications.

Stone, M. 2010. Laboratory techniques for investigating speech articulation. In W. Hardcastle and J. Laver, eds. *The Handbook of Phonetic Sciences*. Oxford: Blackwell, 11–32.

Tashakkori, A. and C. Teddlie, eds. 2010. *SAGE Handbook of Mixed Methods in Social and Behavioral Research*. Thousand Oaks, CA: Sage.

Thomas, E. 2011. *Sociophonetics: An Introduction*. Basingstoke, UK: Palgrave.

8   Experimental paradigms in psycholinguistics

Elsi Kaiser

1   Introduction

This chapter provides an introduction to some of the key methods commonly used in psycholinguistic research. We will focus on three main types of methods: reaction-time-based methods, visual-attention-based methods, and brain-based methods, and also briefly mention other kinds of approaches. As will become clear over the course of this chapter, each of these categories consists of multiple experimental paradigms, and choosing the "right" one often comes down to which method is most appropriate for a particular research question. It would be inaccurate to characterize one method as better than the others, since each has its own strengths and weaknesses. In what follows, we will consider each method in some depth, and comment on the ease of implementation and data analysis.

For the most part, the discussion in this chapter will focus on language comprehension, but some discussion of production methods is also included (see also Bock 1996 for an in-depth review of production methods). This asymmetry is a reflection of the greater body of prior work that exists on language comprehension. In the past, production has received considerably less attention, mostly due to methodological challenges.

This chapter focuses largely on so-called *on-line methods* – that is, methods that tap into real-time aspects of language processing. On-line methods play an important role in psycholinguistic research, because many of the processes underlying human language processing are very rapid (on the order of milliseconds), transient, and not accessible to introspection. For example, data from eye-tracking has shown that during auditory language processing, listeners briefly activate a set of words that overlap acoustically with the word they are hearing (e.g., hearing "beaker" will result in "beetle" and "speaker" also being briefly activated due to the word-initial and word-final overlap respectively, Allopenna, Magnuson, and Tanenhaus 1998). These activations are very short-lived and we are not consciously aware of them, though they can be reliably detected by time-sensitive methods such as eye-tracking. In a different linguistic domain, research looking at Binding Theory using self-paced reading suggests that when people read reflexive pronouns ("himself," "herself"), they not only activate the syntactically licensed antecedent (e.g., the local subject "John" in a sentence such as "Bill thought that John owed himself another chance to solve the problem"), but also briefly consider gender-matching entities that are not syntactically licensed as the antecedents (e.g., the matrix subject "Bill") (Badecker and Straub 2002; but see Sturt 2003 for a different view). Similar intrusion effects have also been obtained for negative polarity items (e.g., expressions like "any," "ever," as in Vasishth et al. 2008). Similar to the transient activation of multiple lexical items, these effects are below the threshold of our conscious perception, but can be detected with the right kinds of experimental paradigms. Because information about these kinds of phenomena often plays a key role in the formulation and testing of theories and models of language processing, on-line methods can provide critical insights.

Another area where on-line methods have made important contributions has to do with the way in which the human language processing system accesses and makes use of different kinds of linguistic information, such as syntactic vs semantic information. A sentence like "The witness examined by the lawyer turned out to be unreliable" is syntactically temporarily ambiguous, because when only the first few words are available ("The witness examined ..."), a comprehender might be tempted to interpret "the witness" as the agentive subject of the verb "examined" – an interpretation that is subsequently shown to be false. This kind of situation, where the parser builds a syntactic structure that is later shown to be incorrect, is called garden-pathing. However, if the comprehension system makes immediate use of semantic animacy cues, a sentence like "The evidence examined by the lawyer turned out to be unreliable" should not result in a garden path: since "the evidence" is inanimate, it cannot be the subject of "examine." This brings up the question of modularity, a key theme in psycholinguistics: does the language processing system use both syntactic and semantic cues (as well as other cues) when parsing a sentence (an interactive system), or is the system modular – in particular, do early stages of processing only make use of syntactic information? A range of on-line methods have been used to investigate this question (e.g., Ferreira and Clifton 1986; Trueswell, Tanenhaus, and Garnsey 1994; Clifton et al. 2003), which has significant implications for our understanding of the architecture of the language processing system.

On-line methods have also made crucial contributions to our understanding of language production. For example, Griffin and Bock (2000) and Gleitman et al. (2007) recorded speakers' eye-movement patterns in scene-description experiments, to explore the temporal relationship between scene apprehension and linguistic formulation: Do speakers first process the "gist" of the scene before starting to build a linguistic representation of the event shown in the scene, or can these processes overlap in time? If they are separate processes, then there is no reason to expect people's eye movements upon first perceiving the scene to correlate with their subsequent linguistic choices. However, Gleitman et al. (2007) found that people's eye-movement patterns during the first 200 ms of observing the scene predict what they end up saying moments later – in contrast to the findings of Griffin and Bock (2000), who found no such correlation. Research in this area is still ongoing (see, e.g., Kuchinsky 2009; Myachykov et al. 2011; Hwang 2012).

In sum, on-line methods allow us to gain insights into transient effects that are often not explicitly "noticed" by language users, and also make it possible to learn about the time-course of both language production and comprehension. Because many psycholinguistic theories make explicit claims about the relative timing and relations between different aspects of language processing, on-line methods often play a crucial role in allowing us to compare competing theories.

However, it is important not to disregard off-line methods. Off-line approaches, such as questionnaires and surveys, are widely used, and provide crucial information about final interpretations (i.e., the final outcome of language processing). In addition, because people engage in real-time (on-line) processing before reaching their final (off-line) interpretation, these final interpretations can yield insights into the nature of on-line processing as well. Experimental paradigms often combine both off-line and on-line measures to yield insights that would not be available from either method on its own (e.g., response-contingent analyses in eye-tracking studies, such as McMurray, Tanenhaus, and Aslin 2002; Runner, Sussman, and Tanenhaus 2003). Off-line methods are discussed elsewhere in this volume (Chapters 3 and 6).

It is worth emphasizing that there are many components to a successful experiment: in addition to selecting an appropriate method, the researcher also needs to keep in mind other key issues, such as research ethics and human subjects approval, experimental design, the construction of critical items and filler items, well-worded instructions and the appropriate methods of data analysis. These topics are addressed in other chapters in this volume (Chapter 7 on experimental design, Chapter 3 on collecting judgments, and Chapter 2 on research ethics). It is also worth mentioning the benefits of combining insights gained from experimental work with other means of data collection, such as frequency patterns (and other kinds of information) computed from corpus analyses (Chapter 13), which has become increasingly common in recent years (e.g., Trueswell 1996; Gibson 2006; Levy 2008; Jaeger 2010).

2   Reaction-time methods

One of the most widely used approaches for investigating real-time language processing involves measuring *reaction times* – that is, how rapidly people perform different kinds of linguistic tasks. For example, researchers have measured how quickly people read sentences, how quickly people start to produce sentences, and how quickly people recognize strings of letters (or strings of phonemes) as being real words or nonsense words. Intuitively, the idea is that reaction times provide an indication of processing complexity. It is often assumed that longer reaction times are associated with increased processing load and processing difficulty. For example, in a task where participants are shown words and asked to indicate whether they are real words or non-words (a lexical decision task), reaction times are sensitive to a range of word-level properties, including word frequency: high-frequency words are recognized faster than low-frequency words (Whaley 1978), suggesting that retrieving lower-frequency words from memory carries a greater processing load. In the domain of production, when participants are shown a picture and asked to name the object, similar frequency effects arise: participants name pictures faster and more accurately when the name of the picture is a high-frequency word than when it is a low-frequency word (Oldfield and Wingfield 1965). On the syntactic level, it has been found that structurally more complex sentences – like sentences with relatively long syntactic dependencies – are read more slowly than sentences with a simpler structure (e.g., Grodner and Gibson 2005).

There are a range of different methods that focus on measuring reaction times and the speed/duration of different processes, including lexical decision, self-paced reading, recording people's eye movements during reading and, on the production side, production tasks that measure speech-onset latencies. We discuss these below.

In *lexical decision tasks*, participants see or hear words and are asked to indicate whether they are real words of English (or whichever language is being tested), often by pressing one key/button to indicate "yes" and another one to indicate "no." Normally, all critical words are real words (i.e., should trigger "yes" responses), but the experiment as a whole also contains a number of nonsense words (usually on fillers trials), to prevent participants from developing a strategy of always responding "yes." A wide range of linguistic issues have been investigated using lexical decision tasks, including lexical access and syntactic processing (see Goldinger 1996 for an overview on word-level research; Love and Swinney 1996 and Shapiro et al. 2003 for syntactic investigations of issues such as ellipsis and relative clauses). Many of these experiments use a method called *cross-modal lexical decision*, where the target words are shown in writing on the computer screen at the same time as participants hear words or sentences (hence the term "cross-modal": both written and auditory modalities are used). Alternatively, some experiments use a "unimodal" approach, where only one modality is involved (e.g., all stimuli are written; Gernsbacher 1990). These kinds of studies normally make use of the phenomenon of semantic priming (i.e., the fact that a target word is recognized faster if the comprehender has previously encountered a semantically associated word; Meyer and Schvaneveldt 1971). Thus, if a person has recently seen the word "nurse," recognition of the semantically associated word "doctor" will be facilitated, relative to a situation where presentation of "doctor" is preceded by an unrelated word (e.g., "juice"). The underlying assumption is that presentation of a word activates the word's representation and this results in activation spreading to related concepts/words, which in turn facilitates the subsequent recognition of those words.

Some of the best-known examples of cross-modal tasks come from the early work of Swinney (1979) and Onifer and Swinney (1981) on the processing of homophones (words that sound the same but that have two different meanings, e.g., "ring," "crane," "coach"). In Swinney and Onifer's experiment, participants listened to sentences like "The housewife's face literally lit up as the plumber extracted her lost wedding ring from the sink trap," which biased one meaning of the ambiguous word "ring." As participants heard the sentence, they were asked to do a lexical decision task with target words shown in the screen. The targets included words like "bell" (related to the meaning of "ring" that is not supported by the contextual bias of the sentence), "finger" (related to the meaning of "ring" that is contextually appropriate), as well as control words, unrelated to the meaning of the sentence but matched in frequency to "bell" and "finger" respectively. Swinney and Onifer manipulated whether the target word (e.g., "bell") was shown on the screen right at the offset of the homophone in the auditorily presented sentence ("ring"), or 1.5 seconds after the offset of the homophone. Interestingly, their results show that, when probing right at the offset of the homophone, both meanings of the ambiguous word "ring" are initially activated (i.e., recognition of both "bell" and "finger" is facilitated), relative to the control words. Thus, even if the context biases one meaning, both meanings are briefly activated. (Swinney and Onifer show that this occurs even if the two meanings of the ambiguous words differ in frequency/dominance.) However, when the target word was shown 1.5 seconds later, only the contextually appropriate meaning was still activated. These early findings suggest that initial lexical access is relatively unconstrained, but that the contextual biases kick in rapidly and suppress the irrelevant meaning. By using the cross-modal paradigm, Swinney and Onifer were able to tap into an ephemeral, unconscious effect that would not have been detectable by off-line methods.

The lexical decision methodology has a number of advantages. Experiments are inexpensive to implement, there are a number of software options available, data analysis is fairly straightforward, and the methodology is technologically very portable – all that is needed is a computer and headphones/speakers. In addition, in the case of cross-modal lexical decision, the auditory nature of the stimuli means that this method can be used to investigate issues related to prosody and phonetics. However, although this method has generated important insights regarding language processing, it also comes with some challenges. First, the task is arguably different from natural language processing: normally, when listening to sentences, we are not asked to simultaneously perform lexical decision tasks on words. Thus, the ecological validity of this method is not very high, and one could ask whether this could distort language processing. Second, one inherent limitation of this method is that on any one trial, only one point in time can be probed – for example, the target word can be presented 1,000 ms after the auditory presentation of the word of interest, or right at the offset of the word, but not both, at least not on the same trial. Thus, this methodology yields a "snapshot" of what is happening at a particular point in time (e.g., which meanings are activated at that point, and to what level), but it does not provide continuous information about how things change over time.

Another widely used method that relies on reaction time measurements is the *self-paced reading* paradigm. In essence, this method measures how much time people spend reading words or phrases. There are a number of variants of self-paced reading, especially in terms of how fine-grained the temporal measurements are. In one variant, participants read entire sentences and press a button when they are done, which allows for the measurement of whole-sentence reading times. In other variants, sentences are presented clause-by-clause or word-by-word, which allows for increasingly fine-grained measurements of how much time readers spend on each part of the sentence. The majority of current self-paced studies use a word-by-word moving window set-up, which means that words are displayed one by one, and each button press results in the previous word being covered by (e.g., by dashes or Xs) and the next word being revealed (e.g., changing from dashes to a word: `--- --- ------ => The --- ------ => --- cat ------ => --- --- meowed`). This allows researchers to record how much time a person spends on one word before moving on to the next word, which can help shed light on what points in a sentence are associated with increased processing load/processing difficulty.

For example, Stowe's (1986) seminal work used self-paced reading to investigate whether encountering a wh-expression will create an expectation for an upcoming gap (trace) where that element would have originated. She tested sentences like those in example (1). In (1a), the verb "bring" is immediately followed by the gap, whereas in (1b), the gap occurs later in the sentence. In the control condition (1c), there is no wh-expression (i.e., no reason to posit a gap). Self-paced reading showed that readers did indeed expect a gap at the earliest possible location: "us" in (1b) is read more slowly than "us" in (1c) – that is, it causes processing difficulty ("filled-gap effect"). This suggests that this is an active/forward-looking process (Frazier and Clifton 1989). When the processing system sees a "filler" (e.g., a wh-element that originated elsewhere in the sentence), it starts searching for a gap right away. The competing view, that gaps are posited only when there is no other possible parse available (Fodor 1978) is not supported by these results.

(1)   My brother wanted to know. . .
      a.   . . . who Ruth will bring __ home to Mom at Christmas.
      b.   . . . who Ruth will bring us home to __ at Christmas.
      c.   . . . if Ruth will bring us home to Mom at Christmas.

This example illustrates how self-paced reading can be used to assess the validity of different theories of language processing, and also highlights a key property of this method: When it comes to the interpretation of reading times, everything is relative. To know whether a word causes a slowdown in reading time, it needs to be compared to another word (e.g., "us" in (1b) and (1c)). When designing self-paced reading studies, researchers need to ensure that they have the right kind of base-line/control conditions to compare with the experimental conditions.

Interestingly, recent findings suggest that equating slower reading times with processing difficulty is not as straightforward as has often been assumed. According to Hale (2003), a sudden drop in parsing uncertainty leads to a processing slowdown because the system has further work to do to specify the representation. Thus, one might observe a reading time slowdown not because the comprehender is struggling with a particularly syntactically difficult construction, but because the current word reduces uncertainty about the syntactic structure at hand (see also Levy 2008 on how existing results can be reanalyzed in terms of surprisal, i.e., how (un)predictable – and thus how informative – a particular word is in a given context). Many of the insights related to notions such as uncertainty, ambiguity, and information density – which have implications not only for ease of processing but also for patterns in language production – are closely tied to or generated from insights from corpus-based work (e.g., Aylett and Turk 2004; Jaeger 2010; Piantadosi, Tily, and Gibson 2012).

Self-paced reading has been used to investigate a range of issues, especially in the syntactic domain, such as the processing of temporally ambiguous sentences (e.g., Garnsey et al. 1997), non-canonical word orders/scrambling (e.g., Kaan 2001; Kaiser and Trueswell 2004), and unambiguous but structurally complex sentences (e.g., Gibson 1998; Grodner and Gibson 2005). Researchers have also used self-paced reading to probe the interpretation of pronouns and reflexives (e.g., Badecker and Straub 2002; Dillon et al. 2009; He and Kaiser 2012), as well as effects of syntactic priming (e.g., Traxler and Tooley 2008). The widespread use of this method is at least partly due to the fact that, compared to various eye-tracking methods, self-paced reading is very inexpensive, and relatively easy to implement and analyze (see Baayen and Milin 2010 for a discussion of new data-analysis approaches). Self-paced reading is also highly portable – all one needs is a computer and a keyboard or, for more accurate timing, a button box. A button box is a special device – essentially a "box" with buttons/keys on it – that allows for more accurate timing than keyboards or computer mice (Li et al. 2010). Furthermore, while self-paced reading is not as fine-grained as eye-tracking during reading, it has nevertheless proven to be a very useful method, capable of detecting even subtle aspects of processing (see Mitchell 2004).

However, self-paced reading has been criticized for lacking ecological validity: normally, we do not see words one by one, and during natural reading we are able to backtrack and jump forward if needed, something that self-paced reading does not allow. Thus, one might wonder whether making people read in a relatively unnatural and slow fashion might create artifacts that are not present in normal reading. This concern is exacerbated if experimenters decide to segment a sentence in a particular way (e.g., to present the subject and the verb together, and the object separately from them). In addition, the fact that in self-paced reading, participants have to consciously decide to press a button to advance to the next word sets it apart from normal reading, where we proceed through text using highly practiced, relatively automatic eye movements (see Staub and Rayner 2007 for discussion). Another challenge of self-paced reading is the existence of spill-over effects. It is often the case that the impact of a particular word on processing time does not show up until a word or two later. However, these complications can be circumvented by not placing a critical word in sentence-final position and by designing target sentences so that they include carefully controlled spill-over regions that follow the word(s) of interest. These regions provide a buffer for the results to show up in the reading times. In sum, despite some limitations, self-paced reading has proven to be a very fruitful method, and has generated a large number of insightful findings.

Self-paced reading is often regarded as the "lower-tech" cousin of *eye-tracking of written text*. In eye-tracking paradigms, participants read text on a computer screen as their eye movements are recorded. The text can be displayed in a holistic manner (i.e., does not need to be displayed word by word), which allows for a more natural reading experience. However, the eye-tracking devices used in reading experiments need to be highly accurate in order to be able to record, with letter-by-letter accuracy, where people are looking. Different technologies have been developed over the years to allow for maximum accuracy (see Duchowski 2007 for a technical discussion). In early research, bite bars were sometimes used to stabilize participants' heads to improve the accuracy of the tracking, but fortunately current systems no longer require this.

Even before the advent of modern technology, in 1879 a French ophthalmologist, Louis Émile Javal, noticed that when people read, their eyes do not move smoothly over the text, but rather proceed in stops and starts. In fact, in order to read a line of text, we need to move our eyes from one point to the next, because it is not possible to see the entire line with equal clarity. This is because there is only a small region of the retina (the light sensitive layer at the back of the eye), called the fovea, that allows for high-acuity vision. If you extend your arm directly in front of you, the area of your thumb nail corresponds roughly to the area of the fovea on the retina. We can also see things in the parafoveal region (area around the fovea) and the peripheral region to some extent, just not very well. In essence, we move our eyes in order to bring visual input (e.g., words) into the foveal region, so that we can perceive them clearly.

The nature of eye movements to objects and images is discussed below, in the section on visual-world eye-tracking. Here, I focus on the nature of eye movements during reading. Thanks to decades of intensive research, today we know a great deal about the nature of fixations (when the eyes pause and fixate on a particular region) and saccades (rapid movements) during reading. In reading English, saccades last an average of 20–50 ms and normally move over six to nine characters. Most saccades move forward through text, but around 10–15 percent are regressions (i.e., the person looks back toward earlier text). Fixations last much longer than saccades, 200–250 ms on average. Because visual input is largely suppressed during saccades, the duration of fixations provides an indication of the time during which information is being obtained from text (see Rayner 1998; Rayner and Juhasz 2006 for overviews of eye movements during reading). There is variation in fixation duration, saccade length and the frequency of regressive eye movements, which vary from person to person and text to text, and are also influenced by lexical properties (e.g., frequency and word length). Less skilled readers and harder passages are associated with shorter saccades, longer fixations and more regressions.[1] Thus, these measures can be used as a measure of processing load during reading.

There are many different ways of analyzing eye-movement patterns, and some of the standard measurements for individual words include first fixation duration (how long the initial fixation on a word lasts), single fixation duration (if only one fixation is made on a word, how long that fixation is), and gaze duration (the sum of all fixations on a word or region before the eyes move on to another word). In addition to focusing on individual words, researchers are often also interested in eye movements on a particular region/chunk of words (e.g., the region where a temporarily ambiguous sentence is disambiguated). Some of the standard measurements for analyzing eye-movement patterns in regions include first-pass reading time (the total duration of all fixations in a region, from when a reader first enters a region to when they first leave it) and total reading time (the total duration of all fixations in a region, including regressive movements back to that region from later points in the text). For a detailed introduction to the different measurements, see Clifton, Staub, and Rayner (2007).

Different measurements can shed light on different points in the comprehension process – for example, if a particular experimental manipulation influences first-pass reading times, the effect is often regarded as an "early" effect, but if an experimental manipulation only has an effect on total reading time, it can be regarded as a "later" effect. This distinction between early and late can be crucial when assessing competing theories of language processing (e.g., the question of when different kinds of information – including semantic cues, syntactic factors, and discourse context – guide readers' parsing decisions). Thus, in contrast to self-paced reading, which only provides one measure (how long a person looked at a word or region before pressing a button to move on), eye-tracking during reading offers a considerably more nuanced and detailed view of reaction-time patterns during reading.

With both self-paced reading and eye-tracking during reading, comprehension questions are often interspersed into the experiment, to ensure that participants are paying attention to the experimental stimuli. Existing work by Stewart, Holler, and Kidd (2007), using self-paced reading, showed that the frequency and type of comprehension questions that readers are asked can have a significant effect on the manner of processing. In their study, some readers received "shallow" questions that were easy to answer, and other received "deep" questions that required more careful attention to the sentences in the experiment. Their results suggest that when all questions are "shallow," readers only construct underspecified representations of the sentences that they are reading. Thus, if we are interested in using reaction time measures to investigate specific aspects of sentence processing, it is important to make sure that the participants are indeed processing the sentences at the level that we think they are.

---

[1] These patterns are also sensitive to differences in writing systems (see Rayner and Juhasz 2006 for an overview).

In addition to experimental approaches, there is also recent corpus-based work using eye movements recorded during the reading of naturally occurring, longer stretches of text. For example, the Dundee Corpus (Kennedy and Pynte 2005) was collected by having ten people read a number of newspaper texts as their eye movements were recorded. Thanks to recent advances in statistical analysis, such as mixed-effects models (Baayen 2008), it is possible to use these eye movements to test a range of hypotheses and to assess how well existing theories of sentence processing fare when applied to natural texts (Demberg and Keller 2008). These are very promising developments, as they allow us to take steps toward increasing the ecological validity of psycholinguistic research. For a related discussion, see Chapter 13.

The reaction-time methods discussed so far have been centered on language comprehension. However, many approaches used in language *production* research also measure reaction time – for example, in the form of *speech onset latencies* (i.e., how quickly people start to utter a word or sentence). One classic method involving speech onset latencies is the *picture-word interference paradigm,* where people see pictures with written words superimposed on them (or sometimes see the words shortly before the images, near the images, or hear them over headphones), and are asked to name the picture. In general, researchers have found that naming latencies are slower when the interfering word is semantically related to the picture, and faster when the printed word is phonologically related – though the precise nature of these effects depends on the relative timing of when the picture and the word appear (see Griffin and Ferreira 2006). These findings suggest that speech production involves at least partly distinct processes of conceptual/semantic activation on the one hand, and phonological encoding on the other. (For an example of speech onset latencies being used to investigate aspects of sentence-level production, see Ferreira 1996.)

The measurement of speech onset latencies can be greatly facilitated by the use of a voice key. Today, many experimental software packages include a voice-key function, which monitors the input from the microphone and is triggered when it exceeds a certain amplitude threshold: when the participant's speech is loud enough (above the amplitude threshold), the voice key will record the time when this happens. The threshold at which the voice key triggers/responds to the input can be adjusted. However, one challenge with voice keys has to do with the fact that different sounds differ in their amplitude (loudness). For example, a word starting with the fricative "s" will normally take longer to trigger the voice key than a word starting with "m" or a vowel, due to acoustic differences between these sounds (Kessler, Treiman, and Mullennix 2002; Duyck et al. 2008). An alternative approach is to measure speech onset in the actual recorded waveforms. This approach can be very precise, but it can also be very time-consuming, depending on the number of trials. An automated approach is proposed by Duyck et al. (2008), who have developed a voice key which uses more sophisticated methods of signal detection.

3   Visual attention

In recent years there has also been a large number of studies using visual-world eye-tracking (for recent overviews, see Tanenhaus and Trueswell 2006; Huettig, Rommers, and Meyer 2011). In contrast to reading eye-tracking, which uses written stimuli, in a visual-world study a participant is normally presented with auditory linguistic stimuli (in a comprehension study), or produces spoken language (in a production study). In comprehension studies, the auditory stimuli are coupled with objects or a visual display – for example, in Allopenna, Magnuson, and Tanenhaus's (1998) study on spoken word recognition, people heard instructions like "Click on the beaker" and saw a computer screen showing a picture of a beaker, a speaker, a beetle, and a baby carriage (see Figures 8.1 and 8.2a). The fact that visual-world eye-tracking allows for the linguistic stimuli to be presented auditorily means that it is suitable for investigating issues linked to the acoustic aspects of speech, including the processing of different kinds of prosodic cues (e.g., contrastive focus in Ito and Speer 2008; Watson, Gunlogson, and Tanenhaus 2008), as well as phonetic information such as voice onset time (McMurray, Tanenhaus, and Aslin 2002).

Visual-world eye-tracking is well-suited for psycholinguistic work because, as initially discovered by Cooper (1974) and subsequently demonstrated by Allopenna, Magnuson, and Tanenhaus (1998), Dahan et al. (2001), and others, people's eye movements are very closely time-locked to the speech stream. In other words, we tend to automatically look at what we think is being talked about.

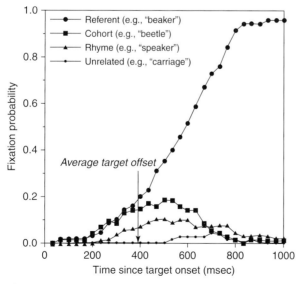

Figure 8.1. *Visual-world eye-tracking graph showing the probability of fixating objects on the screen (0 ms = onset of the critical word, e.g.,* beaker*) Allopenna et al. 1998*

"The essential finding is that as a word unfolds in the acoustic input, so the eyes move toward whatever in the visual scene that unfolding word *could* refer to" (Altmann and Mirković 2009: 587–8). Thus, eye-movement patterns can provide a real-time indication of how people interpret auditory input. Eye movements can also shed light on aspects of language production (e.g., Griffin and Bock 2000; Gleitman et al. 2007; Hwang 2012).

In their seminal 1995 paper, Tanenhaus et al. (see also Eberhard et al. 1995) report a comprehension study where participants carried out instructions like "Put

(a)

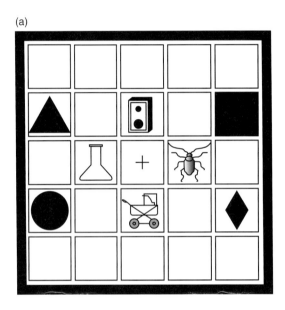

(b)

Figure 8.2. *Examples of object-array displays*
(a) *Allopenna et al. 1998;* (b) *Trueswell et al. 1999;* (c) *Brown-Schmidt and Konopka 2008;* (d) *Sussman 2006*

(c)

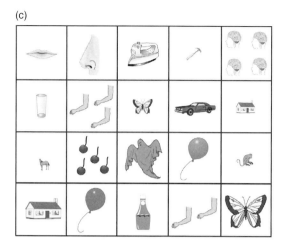

(d)

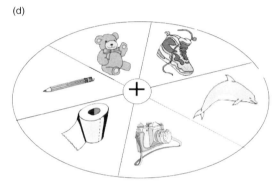

Figure 8.2. *(cont.)*

the apple on the towel in the box" with real objects (see Trueswell et al. 1999 for an extension of this work to children). In one condition, participants saw an apple on a towel, an apple on a napkin, an empty towel, and a box (two-referent context; see Figure 8.2b for a similar display). In another condition participants saw an apple on a towel, a pencil, an empty towel, and a box (just one apple: one-referent context). The question was, are participants garden-pathed by the modifier "on the towel," which is temporarily ambiguous between a modifier interpretation (the apple that is on the towel . . .) and a destination interpretation (the apple is to be moved to the towel). Participants' eye movements show that in the one-referent context, they were indeed temporarily garden-pathed: hearing "on the towel" triggered looks to the empty towel, the potential but incorrect destination. In the two-referent contexts, the proportion of looks to the empty towel did not differ from the unambiguous control condition (i.e., no garden-pathing). This shows how visual-world eye-tracking can be used to gain insights into the kinds of syntactic structures that people build in real time as speech unfolds, and also to show the crucial effects of contextual factors: in a two-referent context where modification is pragmatically necessary, participants were able to use the contextual information to avoid being garden-pathed.

Importantly, visual-world eye-tracking studies can be set up so that they do not require participants to engage in any meta-linguistic or unusual tasks, and do not require the use of written materials. This means that pre-literate children or non-literate adults can also participate in visual-world eye-tracking studies, which sets them apart from many other psycholinguistic methods (see Trueswell et al. 1999; Arnold, Brown-Schmidt, and Trueswell 2007 on children's language-processing abilities; and Mishra et al. 2012 for research comparing low- and high-literacy participants).

Due to its rich temporal and spatial nature, visual-world eye-tracking data can be visualized and analyzed in a range of different ways. In contrast to eye-tracking during reading, where the focus is mostly on temporal measures (e.g., duration of fixations), visual-world eye-tracking analyses focus on the location of the fixations (i.e., where people are looking). One of the most common approaches for visualizing the data is to compute the proportion of fixations to particular objects or regions over time. For example, at 250 ms after the onset of the critical word, 65 percent of all recorded fixations (from all participants) are to object X, whereas 10 percent of fixations are to object Y. Once this information is plotted with time on the x-axis and proportion of fixations on the y-axis, what emerges is the widely used eye-tracking graph showing how fixation patterns change over time. The proportion of fixations to different objects can be calculated over different time-windows, resulting in more or less fine-grained information (e.g., what proportion of fixations are to object X in the time segment 250–255 ms after the onset of the critical word vs what proportion of fixations are to X in the first 500 ms after the onset of the critical word). When considering the timing of eye movements, it is important to keep in mind that, currently, 200 ms is usually regarded as a good estimate of the time needed to program and execute an eye movement (see Hallett 1986), and thus, the earliest point at which one can expect stimulus-driven eye movements is about 200 ms after the start of the critical word. (However, for a shorter estimate of 100 ms, see Altmann 2010. Further research is needed to examine the details of this process.)

An example graph showing fixation probabilities plotted over time is shown in Figure 8.1, from the Allopenna, Magnuson, and Tanenhaus (1998) study mentioned earlier. Participants saw displays with four objects (see Figure 8.2a for an example), and were given instructions like "Pick up the beaker" (using the computer mouse). However, before hearing the instruction, participants were told to look at the cross in the middle of the display; see Figure 8.2a). The fixation probabilities shown in Figure 8.1 were computed in 33-ms increments (due to the sampling rate of the video tape). As can be seen in Figure 8.1, there is not much happening during the first 200 ms: fixation probabilities to the four objects are around 0, as participants are probably still fixating on the central cross. Then, fixations to the target (e.g., "beaker") and its cohort competitor (e.g., "beetle") start at around 200 ms after the onset of the target word, and looks to the rhyme competitor (e.g., "speaker") start at around 300 ms (see Allopenna, Magnuson, and Tanenhaus 1998 for further discussion).

In addition to fixation proportions over time, visual-world eye movements can also be plotted/visualized in other ways, including the proportion of trials on which a particular object was fixated during a particular time interval, the cumulative proportion of trials on which a particular object was fixated, and the timing/latency of the first fixation to a particular object after the critical word has been auditorily presented. The reader is referred to Altmann and Kamide 2004 for detailed discussion. In addition, response-contingent analyses can also be very revealing: these are analyses where the eye-movement data are grouped, based on what the person's final response was (e.g., did they click on object Y or object Z?), or what kind of sentence they chose to produce (e.g., did they mention the agent or the patient of the depicted event first?), to see how and whether the eye-movement patterns differ, depending on the final outcome of the task (comprehension: Runner, Sussman, and Tanenhaus 2003; Kaiser et al. 2009; production: Griffin and Bock 2000; Gleitman et al. 2007; Hwang 2012).

The question of how to analyze visual-world eye movements statistically has been hotly debated in recent years. One of the key challenges is that eye movements are state-dependent. In other words, the current state affects future states: if a participant is already fixating a particular object, she cannot make a saccade to what she is already looking at. This can complicate data analysis, especially if there are baseline differences: consider a situation where participants are already looking more at object X than at object Y, even before they hear the noun referring to object X. This baseline preference for X means that on all those trials where X is already being fixated, the linguistic input cannot trigger saccades to it, simply because a person cannot saccade to what they are already looking at. In essence, baseline differences can distort the effects that the experiments are interested in testing. In order to tackle these kinds of issues, new methods are being developed (e.g., Barr 2008; Mirman, Dixon, and Magnuson 2008; Tanenhaus et al. 2008; Barr, Gann, and Pierce 2011).

Because the visual-world eye-tracking method involves both visual and linguistic stimuli, researchers need to pay careful attention to the properties of their visual displays, to avoid creating confounds in the experimental design. Some of the issues to keep in mind include recognizability of the images, the visual salience of the images, and their positions on the screen. If a particular image is hard to recognize or visually highly salient (e.g., much bigger or brighter than other images), it may attract a high proportion of fixations for these reasons, thereby distorting the data. Thus, it is best to minimize size differences whenever possible and to ensure that all images are recognizable. Many researchers use pre-normed picture sets whenever possible (e.g., line drawings in Snodgrass and Vanderwart 1980). Another important consideration in comprehension studies has to do with the position of the eyes as the critical word or sentence is presented.

Ideally, participants should be looking at a neutral location that is equidistant from the objects of interest, in order to avoid creating biases and to minimize complications due to base-line differences (see discussion of statistical analyses above). In many experiments, each trial begins with a fixation cross that draws the participants' eyes to a central/neutral location. In other experiments, where the displays are scenes accompanied by narratives, the narrative might mention a "look-away" object that is in a neutral location. For example, the image in Figure 8.3c from Kaiser (2011a) is from a study on pronoun interpretation, and the objects on the table are mentioned before the critical pronoun "he" occurs, in order to draw participants' eyes to a neutral location that is equidistant from both of the potential antecedents for the pronoun (namely, the two men standing on the sides of the display).

(a)

(b)

Figure 8.3. *Examples of clip-art displays*
(a) *Kamide at al. 2003;* (b) *Weber et al 2006;* (c) *Kaiser 2011a;* (d) *Arnold et al. 2000*

(c)

(d)

Figure 8.3. *(cont.)*

There are a number of different display types that have been used in visual-world eye-tracking studies. In some experiments, participants interact with real objects – for example, while carrying out commands such as "Put the frog on the napkin in the box" (Tanenhaus et al. 1995; see Figure 8.2b for a similar set-up), or "Tickle the frog with the feather" (Snedeker and Trueswell 2004). In many other studies, the visual stimuli are shown on the computer screen. Many of these studies use a grid-type set-up – for example, with four images positioned in four quadrants on the screen (Allopenna, Magnuson, and Tanenhaus 1998; see Figure 8.2a). Some studies have used a circular arrangement of objects (Sussman 2006; see Figure 8.2d), and others have used larger grids (Brown-Schmidt and Konopka 2008; see Figure 8.2c). In some cases, experiments have used pseudo-realistic clip-art scenes (comprehension: Arnold et al. 2000; Kamide, Altmann, and Haywood 2003; Weber, Grice, and Crocker 2006; Kaiser 2011a;

production: Griffin and Bock 2000; Gleitman et al. 2007), in which the entities mentioned in the linguistic stimuli are incorporated into a scene. In general, it is very important to balance the locations of the critical objects. In languages like English that are read from left to right, people have a bias to look first to the top-left corner of the screen, and in general tend to look from left to right. Thus, if the display is divided into four quadrants, ideally, the target object (and other critical objects) should occur an equal number of times in each of the four quadrants.

As an intriguing complement to the experiments conducted with these visual displays, Altmann (2004) has conducted comprehension studies using a blank-screen paradigm, where people's eye movements are tracked after the display has been shown and then removed. In other words, the eye movements that are recorded and analyzed occur in front of *a blank screen*. Results from this paradigm show that eye movements are not dependent on a visual scene being present at the same time, and allow us to gain new insights into the mental representations that people build based on visual information. (See also Spivey et al.'s [2000] work on eye movements in the absence of visual input.)

In contrast to reading eye-tracking, where the participant's task is straightforward (namely, to read the text), in visual-world eye-tracking, a range of different tasks have been used. In light of the classic findings of Yarbus (1967) that different kinds of tasks result in strikingly different eye-movement patterns, many researchers agree that having a clearly specified task is an important component of visual-world studies. In work on language comprehension, some experimenters use a passive-listening paradigm, where participants are instructed to listen to sentences as they see pictures (Kamide, Altmann, and Haywood 2003). These kinds of listening tasks are often combined with an error-detection task, such as asking participants to indicate whether the sentence matches the scene by responding "yes" or "no," and in some cases correcting the mismatch on the "no" trials (Altmann and Kamide 1999; Arnold et al. 2000; Kaiser and Trueswell 2004). There is also a large body of experiments using tasks with explicit physical goals – for example, studies where participants are asked to carry out instructions such as "Tickle the frog with the feather," "Put the frog on the napkin in the box," or "Click on the beaker", either using their hands or the mouse. On the production side, task effects have also been observed. For example, Griffin and Bock (2000) observed different eye movements when participants were looking at a picture of an event in an "extemporaneous speech" setting (they could see the picture while they described it) compared to a "prepared speech" setting, where participants first observed the event and prepared an utterance for subsequent production.

Another kind of task involves more or less unscripted interaction between two participants, one of which is usually eye-tracked (e.g., Brown-Schmidt and Tanenhaus 2008; see also Ito and Speer 2008). These kinds of interactive tasks are often highly engaging for the participants, and arguably much more natural than "solo" experiments. An interactive paradigm can be especially well-suited for investigating phenomena related to dialogue, such as the intonational properties associated with given vs new, the referential terms that conversational partners converge on, and restriction of referential domains (Brown-Schmidt and Tanenhaus 2008; Watson 2010).

Although the majority of comprehension studies using visual-world eye-tracking use acoustic input combined with scenes or objects on the computer screen, researchers have also explored the use of words on the screen (e.g., McQueen and Viebahn 2007; Holsinger 2013). For example, in McQueen and Viebahn's (2007) study on effects of different kinds of phonological competitors on spoken-word recognition, each screen showed four words, one in each quadrant of the screen. The advantage of using words rather than pictures allows researchers to side-step the challenge of having to find clear pictures for all concepts. For example, in Holsinger's work on idiom processing, it would have been very difficult to find images of some of the target items ("kick the bucket," meaning to die, or "to pull someone's leg," meaning to joke with someone or to trick someone), and even if one could find images, there was a risk of introducing a confound by some pictures being more complex than others. Use of printed words allows these difficulties to be circumvented.

In recent years, researchers have also developed alternatives to "proper" eye-tracking systems, including video-based approaches and webcam systems. Building on the preferential-looking paradigm used in acquisition research, Snedeker and Trueswell (2004) conducted a series of experiments where they used video-cameras to record people's eye movements as they interacted with objects (see sample display in Figure 8.4). In this set-up, the camera is inside the platform, with the lens in the center. In related work, Kaiser (2011b) displayed scenes on a computer monitor and used a video-camera above the monitor to record people's eye movements. More recently, researchers have also started to use webcams to record people's eye movements (Chung, Borja, and Wagers 2012). Crucially, if one wants to investigate the time-course of people's responses to auditory stimuli, the cameras need to have accurate audio-video time-lock, in order to allow for accurate coding of eye movements relative to the spoken stimuli. The poor-man's eye-tracking system has a number of advantages: it costs much less than an actual eye-tracker, and it is highly portable and can be used with both adults and children. However, data analysis is rather time-intensive, as it is done by hand, and the resolution of this method is more limited: Whereas a visual-world eye-tracking system can distinguish a large number of positions on the screen, poor-man's eye-tracking is probably best used for a maximum of four or five regions of interest (e.g., the four corners and the center of the display). Nevertheless, Snedeker and Trueswell (2004) showed that for four-object displays, the accuracy of poor-man's eye-tracking is comparable to a visual-world eye-tracking system.

There are also other, less well-known methods related to visual-world eye-tracking that have been used in psycholinguistic research, including pupillometry and mouse-tracking. In *pupillometry*, people's pupil diameters are measured as

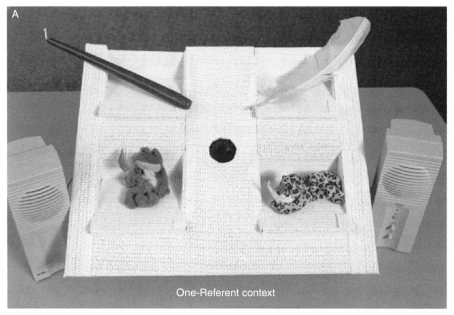

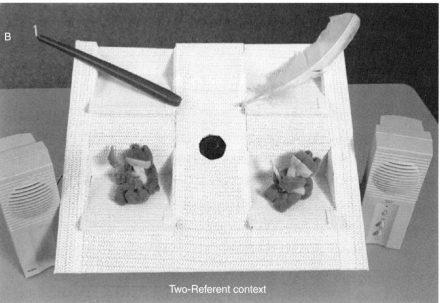

Figure 8.4. *Poor man's eye-tracking,* "Tickle the frog with the feather."
Snedeker and Trueswell 2004

they engage in tasks. Most modern eye-trackers have pupil-measurement capabilities. Pupillometry hinges on the observation that pupil diameter is sensitive not only to external factors such as brightness, but also to internal factors such as emotion, attention, and cognitive load (Beatty and Kahnemann 1966). In the domain of language, Just and Carpenter (1993) showed that the processing of object-extracted relative clauses (harder to process than subject-extracted relative clauses) was also associated with larger pupil size. More recently, Engelhardt, Ferreira, and Patsenko (2010) looked at garden-path sentences like "While the woman cleaned the dog that was big and brown stood in the yard," where "the dog" is temporarily ambiguous between an ultimately incorrect direct object interpretation (*the woman cleaned the dog*) and a matrix subject interpretation (... *the woman cleaned, the dog stood in the yard*). They found that when prosodic cues and syntactic structure conflict (e.g., no prosodic break between "cleaned" and "dog"), there was a reliable increase in pupil diameter, compared to conditions where prosodic cues and syntactic structure were aligned (prosodic break after "cleaned"). Pupillometry taps into processing load, and in this respect it resembles reaction-time methods – but has the advantage of allowing researchers to use spoken language. However, some methodological questions remain open (for example, what parameters to use in analyses, e.g., average diameter, maximum diameter/dilation, or time to reach maximum dilation).

Another gradient method that has emerged from the visual-world eye-tracking literature is *mouse-tracking* (i.e., where the screen coordinates of the computer mouse are recorded as participants move it to click on a picture or location on the screen). Spivey, Grosjean, and Knoblich (2005) showed participants screens with two objects in the top-left and top-right corners, and instructed participants to click on one of them. They manipulated whether the other pictured object was a phonological cohort of the target word (e.g., "candle" and "candy" vs "candle" and "jacket," on trials where participants are instructed to "Click on the candle"). They found that in the presence of a phonological competitor object, the average mouse-movement trajectory is deflected toward the competitor (although participants eventually click on the target object): the path of the mouse reflects the temporary competition between two lexical items triggered by the matching onsets. This is reminiscent of visual-world eye-tracking studies like Allopenna, Magnuson, and Tanenhaus (1998). Although mouse-tracking has not been used very much in psycholinguistic research, it is gradually becoming better known (Morett and MacWhinney 2013).

4   Other methods for researching language production

In the domain of language production, there are also other methods that have been used, in addition to the ones mentioned above. A detailed overview is provided by Bock (1996), including discussion of both observational and experimental methods, addressing different levels of language processing (e.g., phonological, lexical, and syntactic).

For example, analyses of the types of *errors* and their frequency have been very fruitful, in both naturalistic and experimentally elicited data, shedding light on phenomena such as lexical access and phonological encoding, subject–verb agreement and syntactic structure-building (see Bock 1996 for details). On the syntactic level, Ferreira (1996) explored whether sentence production is facilitated or hindered by the availability of syntactic choices. Participants were asked to produce sentences with verbs like "give," which allow two kinds of double-object constructions (to-datives like "I gave the toys to the children," and double-object constructions like "I gave the children the toys"), or verbs like "donate," which only allow one kind of structure (the to-dative construction "I donated the toys to the children"). Participants saw a prompt like "I gave," followed by two or three more words (e.g., "toys"/"children"/"to," which would necessitate production of a to-dative structure, or just "toys"/"children," which allowed production of either structure), and were asked to produce a sentence. Data from error rates showed facilitatory effects in the presence of syntactic flexibility: participants made fewer errors (e.g., word substitutions, omissions of function words) when they could choose between two syntactic structures – suggesting that syntactic flexibility has a facilitatory effect.

Priming paradigms have also made important contributions to our understanding of language production. Lexical decision tasks (mentioned above) often make crucial use of the phenomenon of semantic priming. In addition, other priming studies focus on the syntactic level, in particular the observation that hearing or producing a particular syntactic structure can facilitate subsequent comprehension or production of that structure (e.g., Bock 1986 and many others). In one common format for syntactic priming, participants first hear a prime sentence and are asked to repeat it aloud (e.g., an active or passive sentence), and are then asked to indicate if they have encountered it already in the course of the experiment. Then participants see a thematically unrelated picture, which can be described with either the active or the passive voice. After participants produce a spoken sentence describing the pictured event, they again indicate if they have already seen the picture in the course of the experiment. The recall tasks, as well as a large number of filler/distractor trials (some of which do involve repetition), are included in order to mask the priming manipulation. The key question, of course, is whether the syntactic properties of the prime sentence influence participants' syntactic choices in the picture-description task (or in a fragment completion task, which is also frequently used). A large body of research shows that this is indeed the case, both within and across languages (e.g., Bock 1986; Desmet and Declercq 2006). When exploring effects of syntactic priming on speakers' syntactic choices, it is also important to take into account (or control for) other factors that might influence those choices (e.g., productive active or passive, a double-object sentence or a to-dative, and so on). Corpus-based studies have led to important insights in this domain (e.g., Bresnan et al. 2007 on double-object verbs).

Recent work on syntactic priming has started to explore the relationship between linguistic and non-linguistic representations (e.g., Scheepers et al. 2011 on the relation between arithmetic and syntactic structure).

Other methods for investigating sentence-level aspects of production include *recall tasks,* which hinge on the fact that although we are very good at remembering the gist of what we heard, we are much less skilled at recalling the actual linguistic structure. As a result, people tend not to simply "reproduce" what they heard, but to "reconstruct" it, and change it in different ways which offer insights into the nature of language production (see Bock 1996).

5   Brain-based measures

In recent years, research on language processing has benefited greatly from the development of non-invasive neurolinguistic techniques such as event-related brain potentials (ERPs), functional magnetic resonance imaging (fMRI) and magnetoencephalography (MEG). In this section, for reasons of space, I focus on language comprehension. (One recent review of language production research using brain-based measures is Indefrey 2007.)

This section focuses mostly on ERPs and fMRI, as they have been used for longer than MEG. However, in recent years MEG has emerged as a highly promising – albeit technologically rather demanding – approach, due to the fact that it has excellent temporal and spatial resolution (see the work of Pylkkänen and McElree 2007). Compared to the methods discussed earlier in this chapter, brain-based methods are generally more technologically challenging to set up and to analyze, with fMRI and MEG arguably being the most demanding and most expensive. However, these methods offer a means of gaining insights into neuro-linguistic processing in a non-invasive way, with normal populations, and thus offer a new window into how language is processed.

5.1   Event-related brain potentials

In contrast to reaction-time measures and eye-tracking, event-related brain potentials (ERPs) tap into a neurological, rather than a behavioral, response. ERPs are computed by measuring electrical activity at the scalp, by means of electrodes that are part of an electroencephalogram (EEG). Each electrode records the brain activity at its location at fixed intervals (e.g., every 2 ms). The term "event-related" refers to the fact that these measures of brain activity are time-locked to a particular event/point of interest, such as the start of a word, the appearance of an image, or the onset of a particular phoneme. Thus, participants are presented with a particular stimulus (visual or auditory) and the electrical activity ("brain waves") triggered by this stimulus are measured. Crucially, a large number of stimuli are presented to a number of participants and then averaged. This averaging process is what permits the ERP pattern to emerge, since it allows the relevant signal to emerge from the noise (the other brain activity that is always taking place).

ERP methodology has been used to investigate a wide range of linguistic issues, including speech perception (e.g., Näätänen et al. 1997), the process of semantic integration (e.g., Kutas and Hillyard 1980), syntactic issues (e.g., Hagoort,

Brown, and Groothusen 1993; Friederici 2002), and discourse-level representations (e.g., Burkhardt 2006; Kaan et al. 2007).

To understand the usefulness of ERP, it is important to consider the brain responses triggered by different linguistic stimuli. Unlike a method such as self-paced reading, which simply indicates how quickly someone is progressing through the text, ERPs can offer more specific information about *how* the brain reacts to different kinds of stimuli. Brain waves can be characterized in terms of their timing (how soon after the onset of the stimulus do they emerge? when do they peak?), their polarity (are they positive or negative deflections from a base-line condition?), how long they last (duration), and how they are distributed on the scalp. (Modern ERP systems can have as many as 128 electrodes, so it is possible to obtain detailed information about the scalp distribution of participants' responses. However, the question of how the scalp distribution patterns relate to the underlying source of the brain response is not a straightforward matter; see Luck 2005 and Kaan 2007 for discussion.)

So far, several ERP components related to language processing have been identified, though the question of how different components map onto different aspects of linguistic processing is still under debate. It has traditionally been claimed that syntactic processing difficulties – like syntactic re-analysis or syntactic anomalies/violations – result in a *P600,* a positive-going wave that peaks around 500–600 ms after the onset of the critical word/stimulus (Osterhout and Holcomb 1992; Hagoort, Brown, and Groothusen 1993; Friederici, Hahne, and von Cramon 1998). For example, Hagoort, Brown, and Groothusen (1993) found that ungrammatical words like "throw" in a sentence such as "The spoiled child throw the toys on the floor" resulted in a P600. On the semantic side, it is traditionally claimed that semantic anomalies or difficulties with semantic integration result in a negative-going wave, the *N400*, which peaks around 400 ms after the onset of the relevant word/stimulus. For example, in their classic paper, Kutas and Hillyard (1980) found semantically anomalous words like "socks" in "He spread the warm bread with socks" resulted in an N400. (It is important to keep in mind that the notions of positive vs negative are *relative* to a control condition; a wave that is described as a negative-going wave may in fact be positive, but less positive than the control condition, i.e., it is a negative deflection from the control condition.)

However, recent work suggests that the mapping between P600 and syntax and N400 and semantics is not as straightforward as one might have thought. For example, recent work has shown that semantic violations (e.g., "For breakfast the eggs would only eat toast and ham") can also trigger P600 (e.g., Kim and Osterhout 2005; see also Kuperberg 2007), suggesting that this component should not be regarded as a straightforward marker of syntactic anomaly.

In addition to the P600 and N400, a third type of component has also attracted attention in recent years, namely the *LAN* (left-anterior negativity). It has been suggested that there are two subtypes of LAN: the (regular) LAN, which peaks at around 400 ms after stimulus onset, and the *ELAN* (early left-anterior negativity), which peaks a mere 100–200 ms after stimulus onset. The precise nature of the linguistic processes that trigger (E)LANs is still under debate, but it has been suggested that the ELAN is associated with very rapid, automatic processing of structural information (Friederici, Pfeifer, and Hahne 1993), whereas the LAN can be triggered by morpho-syntactic difficulties (Friederici 2002). In sum, the precise cognitive processes associated with these different components are still under investigation, but many important insights have been obtained in the process of researching the nature of these brain responses.

Another intriguing ERP component is the *mismatch negativity* (*MMN*), which has been shown to arise when listeners perceive an "oddball" sound in a stream of otherwise expected sounds. For example, one could manipulate fine-grained properties of sounds (such as voice-onset time, manner, or place of articulation, duration, etc.), and then test if listeners notice "oddball" sounds whose properties differ from the "standard" sounds. In this way, the MMN response can be used as a tool to see what distinctions listeners are able to perceive. The MMN shows up as a negative-going waveform around 100–200 ms after the start of the deviance, and tends to be frontally distributed. Strikingly, the MMN has been shown to occur even when people are not attending to the stimulus, and even when they are asleep, which has been used to argue that it taps into pre-attentional auditory discrimination (Näätänen 2001). This particular ERP component has been successfully used to explore whether adults and children are able to perceive phonetic contrasts that do not exist in their native languages (Näätänen et al. 1997; Cheour et al. 1998 on Finnish and Estonian adults and children listening to Estonian vowels).

Like all methods, ERPs have their advantages and disadvantages (see Kaan 2007 for a detailed discussion). On the plus side, ERPs provide a continuous signal of brain responses with high temporal resolution, and do not require participants to engage in additional artificial tasks, such as button-pressing or lexical decision. Furthermore, ERPs can be used to investigate both written and spoken language, and can thus be utilized for a broad range of research questions. The fine temporal resolution of ERPs means that they can be used for phonetic investigations (e.g., discrimination of voice onset time), even in young infants – since no secondary task is needed.

However, ERPs also have some drawbacks. The number of trials needed to obtain interpretable data is often much greater than in many behavioral paradigms. Whereas a visual-world eye-tracking study with four conditions might have twenty-four or thirty-two target items (six or eight per condition), an ERP study with four conditions might have 160 target items in total (see Kaan 2007 for discussion). This is necessary in order to make sure that the signal is sufficiently clearly perceptible among the noise (signal-to-noise ratio). The large number of stimuli has consequences on experiment length, and care must be taken to ensure that participants do not get tired or develop strategies due to extended exposure to the stimuli. Another complication comes from physiological phenomena such as eye movements and blinks, which can influence the brain response and thus may mask or confound the ERP components being investigated. Whenever possible, participants are instructed to sit very still and to avoid blinking during certain times. To avoid eye movements, in studies with written presentation of stimuli, the words are often presented at the center of the screen (word-by-word or phrase-by-phrase), and the presentation speed is controlled by the experimental software (not by the participant). This makes it possible to align participants' brain responses to the crucial points of interest, but the presentation rate may be perceived as artificial or too slow – which could impact processing. (However, as Kaan 2007 notes, studies using slow visual presentation have led to results that largely parallel outcomes of studies using natural speech, which can help alleviate potential concerns regarding this aspect of the method.)

5.2   Functional magnetic resonance imaging

Functional magnetic resonance imaging (fMRI) has better spatial accuracy than ERPs, but lower temporal accuracy. The use of fMRI technology represents a significant improvement over older blood-measurement-based methods, such as positron emission tomography (PET), which required the injection of a radioactive contrast agent into the participant's bloodstream. The fMRI methodology investigates blood flow in different brain regions during linguistic and cognitive tasks using magnetic resonance imaging (MRI). In essence, neural activity consumes oxygen, and to compensate for increased oxygen use, oxygenated blood is pumped into the region of the brain that is currently active. Oxygenated and deoxygenated blood have different magnetic properties (since the iron in blood is magnetic), and it is this oxygenation level that is detected by fMRI. However, blood flow responses are rather slow (often on the order of several seconds), and thus the temporal resolution of fMRI is quite low, despite its excellent spatial resolution. Another challenge posed by fMRI is the fact that the system, when running, is very noisy. Participants must wear powerful headphones that provide protection from the noise, and make it possible for them to hear auditory input. However, conducting production studies can be challenging, as the recordings of the participant's speech also capture the noise of the magnet; special analyses must be done to extract the relevant speech information from the recordings. In sum, like other methods, fMRI has both strengths and weaknesses.

A key property of fMRI experiments is that their designs need to be subtractive. The brain's blood oxygenation levels in one condition are compared to the blood oxygenation levels in another condition, to see which regions are more active in one condition than in the other (e.g., one condition is subtracted from the other). Thus, the notion of activation, in the fMRI literature, is inherently relative. This means that choosing the right kind of control/baseline condition is crucial. Using a "resting" baseline, where participants are given no task, is not necessarily the best choice, as participants may still be engaging in processing related to the experiment (e.g., thinking more about the tasks in the experiment). If the experimenter decides to use a control task as a baseline, it is important to think very carefully about how and whether the activation patterns caused by that task can impact the outcomes of the subtractive comparisons that are used to establish activation levels (see Skipper and Small 2006 for further discussion and references).

One of the central questions regarding fMRI research concerns localization of function. Many researchers have used fMRI to investigate whether distinct cortical regions are engaged in different kinds of linguistic processing. The traditional, historical view – derived from research on patients with brain damage – hinges on the distinction between Broca's and Wernicke's areas, historically regarded as associated with production and comprehension processes, respectively. However, more recent findings have shown it to be a great oversimplification (see Fedorenko and Kanwisher 2009 for an overview). Nevertheless, Fedorenko and Kanwisher suggest that we should not give up on the idea of functional specialization. They note that current research relies on group analyses, which they suggest is problematic given the extent of individual anatomical variation, and argue that conducting functional localization analyses for individual subjects provides a means of sidestepping this problem.

6 Conclusions

This chapter has presented an overview of some of the key methods used in psycholinguistic research. As we have seen, different methods have different strengths and weaknesses, and a crucial task that all psycholinguists face is choosing the correct method for the particular theoretical question that they are interested in investigating. However, it is important not to become fixated on one single method, and to keep in mind that the various methodological tools are best regarded as complementary to each other. It is crucial to ensure that the channels of communication between researchers working in different methodologies remain open. Obtaining complementary and convergent data from different methods is what will ultimately help to further our understanding of language processing.

References

Allopenna, P. D., J. S. Magnuson, and M. K. Tanenhaus. 1998. Tracking the time course of spoken word recognition: evidence for continuous mapping models. *Journal of Memory and Language* 38: 419–39.

Altmann, G. T. M. 2004. Language mediated eye-movements in the absence of a visual world: the blank screen paradigm. *Cognition* 93.3: 79–87.

2010. Language can mediate eye movement control within 100 milliseconds, regardless of whether there is anything to move the eyes to. *Acta Psychologica. Special Issue: Visual Search and Visual World: Bridging Language, Memory and Attention* 137.2: 190–200.

Altmann, G. T. M. and Y. Kamide. 1999. Incremental interpretation at verbs: restricting the domain of subsequent reference. *Cognition* 73: 247–64.

2004. Now you see it, now you don't: mediating the mapping between language and visual world. In J. Henderson and F. Ferreira, eds. *The Interface of Language, Vision, and Action: Eye Movements and the Visual World*. New York: Psychology Press, 347–86.

Altmann, G. T. M. and J. Mirković. 2009. Incrementality and prediction in human sentence processing. *Cognitive Science* 33.4: 583–609.

Arnold, J. E., S. Brown-Schmidt, and J. C. Trueswell. 2007. Children's use of gender and order-of-mention during pronoun comprehension. *Language and Cognitive Processes* 22.4: 527–65.

Arnold, J. E., J. G. Eisenband, S. Brown-Schmidt, and J. C. Trueswell. 2000. The immediate use of gender information: eyetracking evidence of the time-course of pronoun resolution. *Cognition* 76: B13–B26.

Aylett, M. and A. Turk. 2004. The smooth signal redundancy hypothesis: a functional explanation for relationships between redundancy, prosodic prominence, and duration in spontaneous speech. *Language and Speech* 47.1: 31–56.

Baayen, R. H. 2008. *Analyzing Linguistic Data. A Practical Introduction to Statistics Using R*. Cambridge University Press.

Baayen, R. H. and P. Milin. 2010. Analyzing reaction times. *International Journal of Psychological Research* 3.2: 12–28.

Badecker, W. and K. Straub. 2002. The processing role of structural constraints on the interpretation of pronouns and anaphors. *Journal of Experimental Psychology: Learning, Memory and Cognition* 28: 748–69.

Barr, D. J. 2008. Analyzing 'visual world' eyetracking data using multilevel logistic regression. *Journal of Memory and Language. Special Issue: Emerging Data Analysis* 59: 457–74.

Barr, D. J., T. M. Gann, and R. S. Pierce. 2011. Anticipatory baseline effects and information integration in visual world studies. *Acta Psychologica* 137: 201–7.

Beatty, J. and D. Kahneman. 1966. Pupillary changes in two memory tasks. *Psychonomic Science* 5: 371–2.

Bock, K. 1986. Syntactic persistence in language production. *Cognitive Psychology* 18: 355–87.

1996. Language production: methods and methodologies. *Psychonomic Bulletin and Review* 3.4: 395–421. doi:10.3758/BF03214545

Bresnan, J., A. Cueni, T. Nikitina, and H. Baayen. 2007. Predicting the dative alternation. In G. Boume, I. Kraemer, and J. Zwarts, eds. *Cognitive Foundations of Interpretation*. Amsterdam: Royal Netherlands Academy of Science, 1–33.

Brown-Schmidt, S. and A. E. Konopka. 2008. Little houses and casas pequeñas: message formulation and syntactic form in unscripted speech with speakers of English and Spanish. *Cognition* 109: 274–80.

Brown-Schmidt, S. and M. K. Tanenhaus. 2008. Real-time investigation of referential domains in unscripted conversation: a targeted language game approach. *Cognitive Science* 32.4: 643–84.

Burkhardt, P. 2006. Inferential bridging relations reveal distinct neural mechanisms: evidence from event-related brain potentials. *Brain and Language* 98: 159–68.

Cheour, M., R. Ceponiene, A. Lehtokoski, A. Luuk, J. Allik, K. Alho, and R. Näätänen. 1998. Development of language-specific phoneme representations in the infant brain. *Nature Neuroscience* 1: 351–3.

Chung, S., M. F. Borja, and M. Wagers. 2012. Bridging methodologies: experimental syntax in the Pacific. *Linguistic Society of America 86th Annual Meeting*, Portland, OR.

Clifton, C. Jr., A. Staub, and K. Rayner. 2007. Eye movements in reading words and sentences. In R. van Gompel, ed. *Eye Movements: A Window on Mind and Brain*. Amsterdam: Elsevier, 341–72.

Clifton, C. Jr., M. J. Traxler, M. T. Mohamed, R. S. Williams, R. K. Morris, and K. Rayner. 2003. The use of thematic role information in parsing: syntactic processing autonomy revisited. *Journal of Memory and Language* 49: 317–34.

Cooper, R. 1974. The control of eye fixation by the meaning of spoken language: a new methodology for the real-time investigation of speech perception, memory and language processing. *Cognitive Psychology* 6: 84–107.

Dahan, D., J. S. Magnuson, M. K. Tanenhaus, and E. M. Hogan. 2001. Subcategorical mismatches and the time course of lexical access: evidence for lexical competition. *Language and Cognitive Processes* 16: 507–34.

Demberg, V. and F. Keller. 2008. Data from eye-tracking corpora as evidence for theories of syntactic processing complexity. *Cognition* 109: 193–210.

Desmet, T. and M. Declercq. 2006. Cross-linguistic priming of syntactic hierarchical configuration information. *Journal of Memory and Language* 54: 610–32.

Dillon, B., M. Xiang, W.-Y. Chow, and C. Phillips. 2009. The processing of long-distance and local anaphora in Mandarin Chinese. Poster presented at the 22nd Annual Meeting of the CUNY conference on Human Sentence Processing. March, Davis, CA.

Duchowski, A. T. 2007. *Eye Tracking Methodology: Theory and Practice*, 2nd edn. London: Springer-Verlag.

Duyck, W., F. Anseel, A. Szmalec, P. Mestdagh, A. Tavernier, and R. Hartsuiker. 2008. Improving accuracy in detecting acoustic onsets. *Journal of Experimental Psychology. Human Perception and Performance* 34.5: 1317–26.

Eberhard, K. M., M. J. Spivey-Knowlton, J. C. Sedivy, and M. K. Tanenhaus. 1995. Eye-movements as a window into spoken language comprehension in natural contexts. *Journal of Psycholinguistic Research* 24: 409–36.

Engelhardt, P. E., F. Ferreira, and E. G. Patsenko. 2010. Pupillometry reveals processing load during spoken language comprehension. *Quarterly Journal of Experimental Psychology* 63: 639–45.

Fedorenko, E. and N. Kanwisher. 2009. Neuroimaging of language: why hasn't a clearer picture emerged? *Language and Linguistics Compass* 3: 839–65.

Ferreira, F. and C. Clifton. 1986. The independence of syntactic processing. *Journal of Memory and Language* 25: 348–68.

Ferreira, V. S. 1996. Is it better to give than to donate? Syntactic flexibility in language production. *Journal of Memory and Language* 35: 724–55.

Fodor, J. D. 1978. Parsing strategies and constraints on transformations. *Linguistic Inquiry* 9: 427–74.

Frazier, L. and C. Clifton, Jr. 1989 Successive cyclicity in the grammar and the parser. *Language and Cognitive Processes* 4.2: 93–126.

Friederici, A. 2002. Towards a neural basis of auditory sentence processing. *Trends in Cognitive Sciences* 6: 78–84.

Friederici, A. D., E. Pfeifer, and A. Hahne. 1993. Event-related brain potentials during natural speech processing: effects of semantic, morphological and syntactic violations. *Cognitive Brain Research* 1: 183–92.

Friederici, A. D., A. Hahne, and D. Y. von Cramon. 1998. First-pass versus second-pass parsing processes in a Wernicke's and a Broca's aphasic: electrophysiological evidence for a double dissociation. *Brain and Language* 62: 311–41.

Garnsey, S. M, N. J. Pearlmutter, E. Myers, and M. A. Lotocky. 1997. The contributions of verb bias and plausibility to the comprehension of temporarily ambiguous sentences. *Journal of Memory and Language* 37: 58–93.

Gernsbacher, M. A. 1990. *Language Comprehension as Structure Building*. Hillsdale, NJ: Erlbaum.

Gibson, E. 1998. Linguistic complexity: locality of syntactic dependencies. *Cognition* 68: 1–76.

2006. The interaction of top-down and bottom-up statistics in the resolution of syntactic category ambiguity. *Journal of Memory and Language* 54: 363–88.

Gleitman, L., D. January, R. Nappa, and J. Trueswell. 2007. On the give and take between event apprehension and utterance formulation. *Journal of Memory and Language* 57: 544–69.

Goldinger, S. D. 1996. Auditory lexical decision. *Language and Cognitive Processes* 11: 559–67.

Griffin, Z. M. and J. K. Bock. 2000. What the eyes say about speaking. *Psychological Science* 11: 274–9.

Griffin, Z. M. and V. S. Ferreira. 2006. Properties of spoken language production. In M. J. Traxler and M. A. Gernsbacher, eds. *Handbook of Psycholinguistics*, 2nd edn. London: Elsevier, 21–59.

Grodner, D. and E. Gibson. 2005. Consequences of the serial nature of linguistic input. *Cognitive Science* 29: 261–91.

Hagoort, P., C. Brown, and J. Groothusen. 1993. The syntactic positive shift (SPS) as an ERP measure of syntactic processing. *Language and Cognitive Processes* 8: 439–83.

Hale, J. 2003. The information conveyed by words in sentences. *Journal of Psycholinguistic Research* 32.2: 101–23.

Hallett, P. E. 1986. Eye movements. In K. R. Boff, L. Kaufman, and J. P. Thomas, eds. *Handbook of Perception and Human Performance*, 2 vols. New York: Wiley, Volume I, Chapter 10, 1–112.

He, X. and E. Kaiser. 2012. Is there a difference between 'You' and 'I'? A psycholinguistic investigation of the Chinese reflexive *ziji*. *University of Pennsylvania Working Papers in Linguistics* 18.1, *Proceedings of the 35th Annual Penn Linguistics Colloquium*. Available at http://repository.upenn.edu/pwpl/vol18/iss1/ (accessed June 12, 2013).

Holsinger, E. 2013. Representing idioms: syntactic and contextual effects on idiom processing. *Language and Speech* 56.3: 373–94.

Huettig, F., J. Rommers, and A. S. Meyer. 2011. Using the visual world paradigm to study language processing: a review and critical evaluation. *Acta Psychologica* 137: 151–71.

Hwang, H. 2012. Investigating coordination of lexical and structural information cross-linguistically. Unpublished Ph.D. dissertation, University of Southern California.

Indefrey, P. 2007. Brain imaging studies of language production. In G. Gaskell, ed. *Oxford Handbook of Psycholinguistics*. Oxford University Press, 547–64.

Ito, K. and S. R. Speer. 2008. Anticipatory effect of intonation: eye movements during instructed visual search. *Journal of Memory and Language* 58: 541–73.

Jaeger, T. F. 2010. Redundancy and reduction: speakers manage syntactic information density. *Cognitive Psychology* 61.1: 23–62.

Just, M. and P. A. Carpenter. 1993. The intensity dimension of thought: pupillometric indices of sentence processing. *Canadian Journal of Psychology* 47: 310–39.

Kaan, E. 2001. Effects of NP-type on the resolution of word order ambiguities. *Journal of Psycholinguistic Research* 30.5: 527–45.

2007. Event-related potentials and language processing. A brief introduction. *Language and Linguistics Compass* 1.6: 571–91.

Kaan, E., A. Dallas, and C. M. Barkley. 2007. Processing bare quantifiers in discourse. *Brain Research* 1146: 199–209.

Kaiser, E. 2011a. Focusing on pronouns: consequences of subjecthood, pronominalisation, and contrastive focus. *Language and Cognitive Processes* 26: 1625–66.

2011b. Salience and contrast effects in reference resolution: the interpretation of Dutch pronouns and demonstratives. *Language and Cognitive Processes* 26: 1587–624.

Kaiser, E. and J. C. Trueswell. 2004. The role of discourse context in the processing of a flexible word-order language. *Cognition* 94.2: 113–47.

Kaiser, E., J. T. Runner, R. S. Sussman, and M. K. Tanenhaus. 2009. Structural and semantic constraints on the resolution of pronouns and reflexives. *Cognition* 112: 55–80.

Kamide, Y., G. T. M. Altmann, and S. L. Haywood. 2003. Prediction and thematic information in incremental sentence processing: evidence from anticipatory eye movements. *Journal of Memory and Language* 49: 133–56.

Kennedy, J. and A. Pynte. 2005. Parafoveal-on-foveal effects in normal reading. *Vision Research* 45: 153–8.

Kessler, B., R. Treiman, and J. Mullennix. 2002. Phonetic biases in voice key response time measurements. *Journal of Memory and Language* 47: 145–71.

Kim, A., and L. Osterhout. 2005. The independence of combinatory semantic processing: evidence from event-related potentials. *Journal of Memory and Language* 52: 205–25.

Kuchinsky, S. 2009. From seeing to saying: perceiving, planning, producing. Unpublished Ph.D. dissertation, University of Illinois at Urbana-Champaign.

Kuperberg, G. 2007. Neural mechanisms of language comprehension: challenges to syntax. *Brain Research* 1146: 23–49.

Kutas, M. and S. A. Hillyard. 1980. Reading senseless sentences: brain potentials reflect semantic incongruity. *Science* 207: 203–5.

Levy, R. 2008. Expectation-based syntactic comprehension. *Cognition* 106.3: 1126–77.

Li, X., Z. Liang, M. Kleiner, and Z.-L. Lu. 2010. RTbox: a device for highly accurate response time measurements. *Behavioral Research Methods* 42: 212–25.

Love, T. and D. Swinney. 1996. Co-reference processing and levels of analysis in object-relative constructions: demonstration of antecedent reactivation with the cross modal priming paradigm. *Journal of Psycholinguistic Research* 25.1: 5–24.

Luck, S. 2005. *An Introduction to the Event-Related Potential Technique*. Cambridge, MA: MIT Press.

McMurray, B., M. Tanenhaus, and R. Aslin. 2002. Gradient effects of within-category phonetic variation on lexical access. *Cognition* 86.2: B33–B42.

McQueen, J. M. and M. C. Viebahn. 2007. Tracking recognition of spoken words by tracking looks to printed words. *Quarterly Journal of Experimental Psychology* 60.5: 661–71.

Meyer, D. E. and R. W. Schvaneveldt. 1971. Facilitation in recognizing pairs of words: evidence of a dependence between retrieval operations. *Journal of Experimental Psychology: General* 90: 227–34.

Mirman, D., J. A. Dixon, and J. S. Magnuson. 2008. Statistical and computational models of the visual world paradigm: growth curves and individual differences. *Journal of Memory and Language* 59.4: 475–94.

Mishra, R. K., N. Singh, A. Pandey, and F. Huettig. 2012. Spoken language-mediated anticipatory eye movements are modulated by reading ability: evidence from Indian low and high literates. *Journal of Eye Movement Research* 5.1: 1–10.

Mitchell, D. C. 2004. On-line methods in language processing: introduction and historical review. In M. Carreiras and C. E. Clifton, eds. *The On-line Study of Sentence Comprehension: Eyetracking, ERP and Beyond*. New York: Psychology Press, 15–32.

Morett, L. M. and B. MacWhinney. 2013. Syntactic transfer in English-speaking Spanish learners. *Bilingualism: Language and Cognition* 16.1: 132–51.

Myachykov, A., D. Thompson, C. Scheepers, and S. Garrod. 2011. Visual attention and structural choice in sentence production across languages. *Language and Linguistics Compass* 5: 95–107.

Näätänen, R. 2001. The perception of speech sounds by the human brain as reflected by the mismatch negativity (MMN) and its magnetic equivalent (MMNm). *Psychophysiology* 38: 1–21.

Näätänen, R., A. Lehtokoski, M. Lennes, M. Cheour, M. Huotilainen, A. Iivonen, M. Vainio, P. Alku, R. Iimoniemi, A. Luuk, J. Allik, J. Sinkkonen, and K. Alho. 1997. Language-specific phoneme representations revealed by electric and magnetic brain responses. *Nature* 385: 432–4.

Oldfield, R. C. and A. Wingfield. 1965. Response latencies in naming objects. *The Quarterly Journal of Experimental Psychology* 17: 273–81.

Onifer, W. and D. Swinney. 1981. Accessing lexical ambiguities during sentence comprehension: effects of frequency-of-meaning and contextual bias. *Memory and Cognition* 9.3: 225–36.

Osterhout, L. and P. J. Holcomb. 1992. Event-related brain potentials elicited by syntactic anomaly. *Journal of Memory and Language* 31: 785–806.

Piantadosi, S. T., H. Tily, and E. Gibson. 2012. The communicative function of ambiguity in language. *Cognition* 122: 280–91.

Pylkkänen, L. and B. McElree. 2007. An MEG study of silent meaning. *Journal of Cognitive Neuroscience* 19: 1905–21.

Rayner, K. 1998. Eye movements in reading and information processing: 20 years of research. *Psychological Bulletin* 124: 372–422.

Rayner, R. and B. Juhasz. 2006. Reading processes in adults. In K. Brown, ed. *The Encyclopedia of Language and Linguistics*, 2nd edn, 14 vols. Oxford: Elsevier Science, Volume X, 373–8.

Runner, J. T., R. S. Sussman, and M. K. Tanenhaus. 2003. Assignment of reference to reflexives and pronouns in picture noun phrases: evidence from eye movements. *Cognition* 89.1: B1–B13.

Scheepers, C., P. Sturt, C. J. Martin, A. Myachykov, K. Teevan, and I. Viskupova. 2011. Structural priming across cognitive domains: from simple arithmetic to relative clause attachment. *Psychological Science* 22.10: 1319–26.

Shapiro, L. P., A. Hestvik, L. A. Lesan, and A. R. Garcia. 2003. Charting the time course of VP-ellipsis sentence comprehension: evidence for an initial and independent structural analysis. *Journal of Memory and Language* 49: 1–19.

Skipper, J. I. and S. L. Small. 2006. fMRI studies of language. In K. Brown, ed. *The Encyclopedia of Language and Linguistics*, 2nd edn. Oxford: Elsevier Science.

Snedeker, J. and J. C. Trueswell. 2004. The developing constraints on parsing decisions: the role of lexical-biases and referential scenes in child and adult sentence processing. *Cognitive Psychology* 49.3: 238–99.

Snodgrass, J. G. and M. Vanderwart. 1980. A standardized set of 260 pictures: norms for name agreement, image agreement, familiarity, and visual complexity. *Journal of Experimental Psychology: Human Learning and Memory* 6: 174–215.

Spivey, M., M. Grosjean, and G. Knoblich. 2005. Continuous attraction toward phonological competitors. *Proceedings of the National Academy of Sciences* 102.29: 10393–8.

Spivey, M. J., M. J. Tyler, D. C. Richardson, and E. E. Young. 2000. Eye movements during comprehension of spoken scene descriptions. *The Proceedings of the 22nd Annual Cognitive Science Society Meeting*, 487–92.

Staub, A. and K. Rayner. 2007. Eye movements and on-line comprehension processes. In G. Gaskell, ed. *The Oxford Handbook of Psycholinguistics*. Oxford University Press, 327–42.

Stewart, A. J., J. Holler, and E. Kidd. 2007. Shallow processing of ambiguous pronouns: evidence for delay. *Quarterly Journal of Experimental Psychology* 60: 1680–96.

Stowe, L. A. 1986. Parsing WH-constructions: evidence for on-line gap location. *Language and Cognitive Processes* 1: 227–45.

Sturt, P. 2003. The time-course of the application of binding constraints in reference resolution. *Journal of Memory and Language* 48: 542–62.

Sussman, R. 2006. Verb-instrument information during on-line processing. Unpublished Ph.D. dissertation, University of Rochester, NY.

Swinney, D. 1979. Lexical access during sentence comprehension: (re)consideration of context effects. *Journal of Verbal Learning and Verbal Behavior* 18: 645–60.

Tanenhaus, M. K. and J. C. Trueswell. 2006. Eye movements and spoken language comprehension. In M. J. Traxler and M. A. Gernsbacher, eds. *Handbook of Psycholinguistics*, 2nd edn. Elsevier Press, 863–900.

Tanenhaus, M. K., M. J. Spivey-Knowlton, K. M. Eberhard, and J. E. Sedivy. 1995. Integration of visual and linguistic information in spoken language comprehension. *Science* 268: 1632–4.

Tanenhaus, M. K., A. Frank, T. F. Jaeger, M. Masharov, and A. P. Salverda. 2008. The art of the state: mixed effect regression modeling in the visual world. Presentation at the 21st CUNY Sentence Processing Conference. Chapel Hill, NC.

Traxler, M. J. and K. M. Tooley. 2008. Priming in sentence comprehension: strategic or syntactic? *Language and Cognitive Processes* 23.5: 609–45.

Trueswell, J. C. 1996. The role of lexical frequency in syntactic ambiguity resolution. *Journal of Memory and Language* 35: 566–85.

Trueswell, J. C., M. K. Tanenhaus, and S. M. Garnsey. 1994. Semantic influences on parsing: use of thematic role information in syntactic disambiguation. *Journal of Memory and Language* 33: 285–318.

Trueswell, J. C., I. Sekerina, N. M. Hill, and M. L. Logrip. 1999. The kindergartenpath effect: studying on-line sentence processing in young children. *Cognition* 73: 89–134.

Vasishth, S., S. Bruessow, R. L. Lewis, and H. Drenhaus. 2008. Processing polarity: how the ungrammatical intrudes on the grammatical. *Cognitive Science* 32.4: 685–712.

Watson, D. G. 2010. The many roads to prominence: understanding emphasis in conversation. In B. Ross, ed. *The Psychology of Learning and Motivation*. Burlington, MA: Elsevier Science: Volume 52, 163–83.

Watson, D. G., C. Gunlogson, and M. Tanenhaus. 2008. Interpreting pitch accents in on-line comprehension: H* vs L+H*. *Cognitive Science* 32: 1232–44.

Weber, A., M. Grice, and M. W. Crocker. 2006. The role of prosody in the interpretation of structural ambiguities: a study of anticipatory eye movements. *Cognition* 99: B63–B72.

Whaley, C. 1978. Word–nonword classification time. *Journal of Verbal Learning and Verbal Behaviour* 17: 143–54.

Yarbus, A. L. 1967. *Eye Movements and Vision*. New York: Plenum. (Originally published in Russian 1962.)

9   Sound recordings: acoustic and articulatory data

Robert J. Podesva and Elizabeth Zsiga

1   Introduction

Linguists, across the subdisciplines of the field, use sound recordings for a great many purposes – as data, stimuli, and a medium for recording notes. For example, phoneticians often record speech under controlled laboratory conditions to infer information about the production and comprehension of speech in subsequent acoustic and perception studies, respectively. In addition to analyzing acoustic data, phoneticians may employ articulatory methods to observe more directly how speech is produced. By contrast, sociolinguists often record unscripted speech outside of a university environment, such as a speaker's home. Sometimes these recordings themselves constitute the data (e.g., for sociophonetic analysis), while other times they may be transcribed at varying levels of detail (see Chapter 12), with the resultant text serving as the data (e.g., for the analysis of lexical or morphosyntactic variation and discourse analysis). In a similar vein, some language acquisitionists capture naturally occurring conversation in adult–child interactions. The research purposes of these recordings may not be determined until some time after the recordings are made, after a longitudinal corpus for a given child has been collected. It is likewise common for language documentarians to make extensive speech recordings in the field. Some field recordings simply serve as a record of elicitation sessions (e.g., when the researcher is ascertaining phrase structure), while others may be used for acoustic analysis (e.g., if phonetic elements of the language are the object of study). In the latter case, articulatory methods can be employed to more accurately describe phonetic properties of speech, such as a sound's place of articulation or details of the airstream mechanism. As discussed in Chapter 8, sound recordings can also be used as stimuli in perception studies, where listeners may be asked first to listen to a brief audio recording and then to identify whether a particular string of sounds is a real word (Chapter 8); to evaluate how educated the speaker of a brief utterance sounds (Chapter 6); or to rate how accented an L2 speaker sounds (Chapter 7). Linguists may also make use of archival recordings to investigate questions of language change. Proficiency in making sound recordings is thus an increasingly useful skill for linguists of most persuasions.

This chapter provides an overview of how to make sound recordings and collect articulatory data. As the output of speech production and the input to speech comprehension, the acoustic signal occupies the central position in the speech stream. And since capturing the acoustic signal is important for studies concerned with speech production and comprehension alike, we focus primarily on recording acoustic data in this chapter (Section 2). In Section 3, we describe the most common methods for visualizing, recording, and analyzing the mechanics of speech articulation. We do not cover the design of perception studies here, as the relevant considerations are discussed in Chapters 6, 7, and 8. We conclude in Section 4.

2   Acoustic data

When recording audio data, one needs to decide who to record, what to record them saying, how to display recording materials, what equipment to use, and how to instruct speakers to sit and comport themselves in the recording environment. Because making a decision about each of these issues depends largely on the research questions posed, we describe three of the most common scenarios in detail in this section: making recordings in the laboratory, making recordings in the field for sociolinguistics, and making recordings in the field for language documentation. Although we discuss these scenarios separately, and while individual researchers may find one of these scenarios more closely related to the kind of work they do than others, the reader is encouraged to read through all three scenarios. Methods are increasingly borrowed across the subdisciplines, and researchers may find it useful to adopt hybrid methodologies. Before we discuss the particulars of each scenario, we review some considerations that pertain to all recording situations.

2.1   General considerations

First, it is important (and perhaps also trivial) to point out that we live in the digital age. Computers cannot represent truly continuous data, so analogue signals are instead encoded as a finite but extremely large number of sequentially ordered discrete bits that, when pieced together, sound continuous (see Ladefoged 1996 and Johnson 2012 for more detailed discussions of *digital signal processing*). While technologies that can capture a sound signal in analogue still exist, few of us still own devices that can play analogue recordings. More importantly, recordings need to be in digital format to do any of the things a linguist might want to do with them – analyze them acoustically (see Chapter 17), manipulate them for use in a perception study (see Chapter 6), upload them to a database, and so on. If recordings ultimately need to be converted to digital form, it is most efficient to record them digitally from the start.

When creating a digital recording, you first need to decide how many times an amplitude value should be recorded over the course of a second. This value is known as the *sampling rate*, which determines the frequency range that can be captured reliably by the digital signal. Only those frequencies up to half of the sampling rate (a value known as the *Nyquist frequency*) are faithfully captured. So a recording sampled at 44 kHz (CD-quality) can faithfully represent frequencies up to 22 kHz, which represents the upper limit of the frequency range that humans can reliably hear. In practice, this is much higher than is necessary for speech. The highest linguistically meaningful frequencies in the speech signal (e.g., front cavity resonances of fricatives) appear at less than 11 kHz (e.g., Stevens 1998, Ladefoged 2003) – so a sampling rate of 22 kHz is generally sufficient for capturing whatever frequencies a linguist might be interested in. As digital technology progresses, however, recording systems can sample the signal at increasingly higher rates. In fact, some applications do not allow sampling at a rate lower than 44 kHz – which, at present, is the de facto standard sampling rate.

One thing to bear in mind is that the higher the sampling rate, the larger the file size. As disk space is relatively cheap, we recommend against trying to save space by using lower sampling rates. Using a higher sampling rate will also maximize the range of future uses for recordings. For example, data collected for vowel analysis (which only requires a sampling rate of about 10 kHz) can be repurposed for fricative analysis, but only if they were recorded at a sufficiently high sampling rate (22 kHz or more). It is better to sample at a high rate and downsample (or decrease the sample rate by low pass filtering) at a later date, if there is reason to think that a lower sampling rate may improve accuracy (Ladefoged 2003: 26).

A second consideration when creating a digital recording is the *sample size*. The sample size, measured in bits, specifies the number of units the amplitude is divided into. Not all recorders allow you to choose a bit rate, but high-fidelity audio systems typically have a bit rate of at a least 16 bits (which represents $2^{16} = 32,000$ gradations in the amplitude domain). Some allow 20- and 24-bit sample sizes (Cieri 2010), though the standard appears to be 16 bits. It is also worth pointing out that not all acoustic analysis software can handle sample sizes larger than 16 bits.

Many recorders allow you to specify the format of the audio data they produce. It is imperative that you choose an *uncompressed* format, what is known as linear pulse code modulated (PCM) format. PCM data can be saved in a number of file formats, such as .wav (waveform audio file format, the main format used on Windows systems) – the most common audio file format used by linguists – and .aiff (audio interchange file format, the main format used on Mac systems). Other formats will be compressed in one way or another, to save disk space. Although most compression algorithms are designed to minimize the *perceptible* distortion of the acoustic signal, they all distort the signal, which calls into question how faithfully the compressed audio signal represents what was actually uttered. Although some research has shown that certain forms of acoustic analysis are still possible with compressed audio, we strongly recommend avoiding compressed formats if at all possible. When using a new recorder, keep an eye out for the default data format – in many cases, it will be MP3! Also bear in mind that much of the data available on the internet is compressed, which limits the kinds of acoustic features that can be reliably analyzed.

An important goal when recording the acoustic signal is to maximize the robustness of the linguistic signal, by achieving as high a *signal-to-noise ratio* as possible. This can be accomplished in several ways. First, the microphone should be close to the speaker's mouth. According to the *Law of Inverse Squares*, as the source of sound (i.e., a speaker's mouth) moves away from a microphone, the intensity of the sound will decrease at a rate of the square of the distance. Thus, a microphone located 2 feet from a speaker's mouth will be four times less intense than one located only a foot from the speaker's mouth. Second, the recording level should be set as high as possible without clipping (or overloading the signal), through the gain button. The precise level will depend on the recorder being used and how loudly the speaker is talking. Sometimes, the gain is represented as a strip of lights built into the recorder's hardware, arranged as a meter bar (usually green and yellow lights are fine, while red lights indicate clipping), while for other recorders, the gain is represented through the software interface (in the recorder's display window). Either option will suffice, as long as the recorder enables you to adjust the gain as the recording unfolds. As speakers will modulate their volume over the course of a recording, it is important to keep an eye on the recording level, and to adjust the gain as necessary. A final strategy for maximizing the signal-to-noise ratio is to minimize the ambient noise. As the potential sources of noise vary as a function of the recording scenario, I will postpone the discussion of ambient noise until Section 2.2.

Perhaps the most important step in preparing to make a recording is getting well acquainted with the recording equipment. The recording equipment should be tested several times prior to the recording session with the speaker; and even after the speaker has arrived, you should make and listen to a brief test recording to ensure that the data you are about to collect will meet your standards. Once you are sure your recording set-up is functional, and you have obtained whatever permissions are needed (see Chapter 2), begin all recordings with an announcement of the date, time, speaker (or some identifier, if speaker confidentiality is being maintained), the researcher(s) present, and the purpose of the recording. It would be a good idea also to include this information in a text file of metadata that is stored along with the recording, and/or to encode some of this information in the recording's file name, but recording the metadata in the audio record itself ensures that this information will be retained, even if the text file is deleted or the file name changed.

2.2   Common recording scenarios

While the issues discussed up to now are relevant to making audio recordings for any purpose, the remaining considerations (e.g., which kinds of recorders and microphones to use, what materials to record, and how to position equipment) depend on specific recording scenarios.

2.2.1   Recording in the laboratory

One of the most common sites for capturing audio data is the phonetics laboratory, specifically in a sound-proof recording booth. The most common types of data collected in this context are recordings intended for subsequent acoustic analysis (see Chapter 17) and recordings intended for subsequent use as stimuli in perception studies (see Chapters 6 and 8).

There are considerable advantages associated with making audio recordings in a laboratory setting. First, the acoustic specifications are as close to ideal as possible, with ambient noise all but eliminated. Second, the equipment set-up in a phonetics lab is more or less stable, so recording a speaker will generally not require extensive reconfiguration of equipment or testing. Finally, laboratory equipment (e.g., recorders, microphones) is typically of very high quality, which further ensures high-quality recordings.

The current standard for digital recording in a lab is to record directly onto a computer's hard drive. In the recent past, labs have used other technologies, such as analogue and DAT (digital analogue tape) recorders, but these technologies have waned as direct-to-computer techniques have become dominant. (Analogue recorders required digitization before recordings could be analyzed acoustically, and DAT recorders required transferring the digital file recorded on the cassette tape to a computer hard drive.) It should be noted that computers are a potential source of noise, as the spinning hard drive and occasional whirring fan can compromise the signal-to-noise ratio, so computers are generally located outside of the recording booth (most booths allow the relevant cables to pass in and out of the booth through a conduit). Another popular technology is the *solid state recorder*, where audio data are stored on flash media instead of a spinning disk. While recording on a solid state recorder will likely produce pristine audio in this environment, when paired with the right microphone, the extra step of transferring audio recordings from the solid state recorder to the computer can be avoided by recording directly to the computer. Data can also be uploaded to a server more easily in the latter case.

Selecting the right microphone is one of the keys to a good audio recording. Most high-quality microphones are *condenser microphones* (i.e., they have their own power supplies). These power supplies can take one of several forms, with the microphone powered by a battery residing in the same unit as the microphone itself; a battery residing in a separate power pack; or phantom power supplied by the recording device or sound mixer.

In addition to the issue of whether a microphone requires a dedicated power source, microphones also differ in terms of directionality. In general, it is preferable to use a *directional microphone* (also known as cardioid or unidirectional), which generally captures the audio coming from a single direction (i.e., the direction the microphone is pointing in). The microphone can therefore be pointed in the direction of the speech signal, which will be picked up more robustly than ambient noise outside of this direct path. In contrast to directional microphones, *omnidirectional microphones* capture noise emanating from all directions (as the name implies); see Section 2.2.3 for an example of how omnidirectional microphones can be useful in the field.

A final consideration relates to how the microphone is held up or *mounted*. Laboratories typically make use of stand-mounted microphones, though other options include head-mounted microphones, lavalier (or tie-clip) microphones, and hand-held microphones. See Figure 9.1 for an example of common microphone mounts. Head-mounted microphones are preferable for obtaining reliable data on intensity, as the distance between the source of speech and the microphone is held constant; on the other hand, speakers are unlikely to move considerably from one moment to the next when seated in front of a table-mounted microphone. See Section 2.2.2 for a discussion of using lavalier microphones in the field. Hand-held microphones are generally not used in linguistics research.

Microphones can attach to recorders in a variety of ways, most often, if not exclusively, through XLR, mini-stereo, and USB jacks, all illustrated in Figure 9.2. While most high-quality recorders and microphones use XLR connections, XLR jacks can be converted to stereo and vice versa via rather inexpensive adapters. Microphones with USB connections are another attractive option, particularly when recordings are made directly to a computer hard drive. At present, the quality of USB microphones is highly variable, though low-noise options are available.

Once the researcher has settled on a recorder and microphone, the speaker needs to be positioned with respect to the equipment. In lab recordings, speakers typically sit in front of a table on which the microphone (usually stand-mounted) is resting. The microphone should never be placed directly in front of the airstream,

Figure 9.1. *Common microphone mounts: stand-mounted (left), head-mounted (middle), and lavalier (right)*

Figure 9.2. *Microphone jacks: XLR (left), mini-stereo (middle), and USB (right)*

but rather at a 45-degree angle from the corner of the speaker's mouth, approximately one open palm's width away. Positioning the microphone in front of the airstream can lead to *clipping* and/or transients in the acoustic signal that correspond not to properties of the airstream in the vocal tract (e.g., stop release bursts, which are of interest to linguists), but rather external properties of the airstream (e.g., the airstream hitting the surface of the microphone, which is of little interest to linguists).

The only remaining consideration at this point is how to display recording materials, which will depend on the nature of the data. Many researchers working on segmental phonetics will ask speakers to read a *word list* that exemplifies the contrasts under analysis (see Chapters 4 and 18). In such cases, all words should be checked in advance with each speaker, to make sure that all the words exist in their lexicon. During the recording, words are typically embedded in a *carrier phrase* like "Please say __ for me" – an utterance that makes sense regardless of what word fills the blank. The target word is usually phrase-medial to avoid the effects of phrase-final lengthening. The researcher should pay special attention to the sounds immediately preceding and following the target word, to facilitate the identification of segment boundaries. If vowel-initial words are under investigation, for example, the word just before the blank should not end in a vowel – since it would then be difficult to isolate the border between two adjacent vowel sounds (see Chapter 17 for more on the acoustic properties of different classes of sounds). Words are most often represented in the language's orthography, though words can also be elicited by having speakers provide translations for English words spoken by the researcher, which may be necessary when working with an illiterate speaker or a language without a standardized orthography. Words can be displayed as a list on a sheet of paper, in which case the paper should be placed on a stand (not held by the speaker, since the rustling of paper will compromise the quality of the recording); individually on cards, though the speaker will need to be instructed not to speak while the cards are being moved; as a list on a computer screen; or individually on a computer screen, perhaps even through a timed PowerPoint presentation (standardizing how long each word is displayed can have the added advantage of standardizing speech rate). In any case, words should be randomized, and it is common for multiple repetitions for each word to be collected. Displaying words individually militates to some extent against speakers producing a list intonation, which can have significant consequences for the phonetic realization of target words.

Researchers interested in connected speech, post-lexical phonological processes, or suprasegmentals may find it useful to record *reading passages*. Passages are sometimes written specifically for fulfilling the needs of a specific study (e.g., when certain words are needed in particular prosodic contexts), but often standard reading passages are used, such as Fairbanks' (1960: 127) Rainbow Passage, which is designed to exemplify a wide range of the sounds of English in a diverse array of phonological contexts. Speakers should be allowed to familiarize themselves with reading passages before beginning the recording.

In spite of all its advantages, one disadvantage of making recordings in a laboratory setting is that it constrains the range of linguistic styles that speakers produce, which tend toward more careful, citation-style speech. For many research questions, this limited range of styles does not pose a significant problem. However, linguists interested in more vernacular speech styles may find it more fruitful to analyze data produced in the field.

2.2.2   Recording in the field: sociolinguistics

Sociolinguists most often record unscripted dialogue outside of institutional contexts, usually in the form of *sociolinguistic interviews*, which are generally informal conversations between one or two interviewees and one or two interviewers, intended to elicit unguarded speech (see Chapters 6 and 10 for extended discussions about sociolinguistic interviews and recording social interaction).

While conversational speech is much more likely to exhibit linguistic features of sociolinguistic interest than speech recorded in laboratory contexts, it also makes it more difficult to draw comparisons across speakers (since everyone is saying something different, the features of interest are being produced in different phonological, grammatical, and discourse contexts), though see Chapters 16 and 20 for statistical techniques for dealing with this variability.

Another challenge of recording in the field is reducing the ambient noise captured in the recording. This issue can be addressed in part by choosing the right microphone (see the discussion below), but also by finding the right environment for making recordings. In general, rooms with many hard surfaces should be avoided, as they reflect sound and thus compromise the clarity of the speech signal. Indoor sources of noise include televisions, radios, refrigerators, lighting, air conditioning and heating units, computers, clocks, and phones (Cieri 2010: 27). Noises from outside, such as wind, rain, and traffic, can also disrupt recordings, even when recordings are made indoors. In some environments, like speakers' homes, it is possible to minimize noise by turning off the noisiest of appliances. At the same time, researchers must bear in mind that they are guests and should respect speaker's comfort levels, even if it means that recording quality is compromised. Once, we made a recording in nearly 100 degrees heat and asked the interviewee if we could turn off the air conditioner. She did so willingly, but proceeded to (very audibly) fan herself with a nearby piece of paper (the consent form, incidentally) from time to time. While those segments of the interview were not usable for acoustic analysis, we felt it was more important for her to be comfortable (and safely cool) than for us to have pristine data.

The last 10 years have witnessed tremendous advancements in the development of portable digital recorder technology. Many options – solid state recorders of varying sizes, CD recorders, minidisk recorders, cell phones, and laptop computers, to name just a few – have all been successfully employed in sociolinguistic research. We do not recommend using minidisks (an obsolete technology) or CD recorders (due to the inconvenience associated with waiting for the CD to be burned, and because of the possibility of scratching CDs), but we would like to comment on the other three options.

In a recent study, De Decker and Nycz (2011) report that recordings made on an iPhone (through the Voice Memo app) are of sufficient quality for reliably extracting the first and second vowel formant (though measurements for the third formant were more variable). Subsequently, applications designed specifically for sociolinguistic use in the field have been developed, with some even allowing for files to be automatically uploaded to a cloud. De Decker and Nycz also report that recordings made with a Macbook Pro were sufficient for the analysis of vowel formants. An obvious advantage to recording with laptops and iPhones is that many speakers have grown rather accustomed to the ubiquity of cell phones and computers; they may be less likely to categorize these devices as recording instruments, and accordingly may be more inclined to produce unselfconscious speech. However, given the difficulty associated with faithfully capturing higher frequencies, it may be preferable to use recorders that can better handle frequencies above 3,000 Hz.

We recommend using solid state digital recorders, two examples of which are shown in Figure 9.3, simply to maximize the kinds of analyses that can be conducted. Most solid state recorders can be configured to record uncompressed data onto a flash memory card.

With portable equipment comes the need for portable power; do not rely on the availability of an electrical outlet. Bring batteries, and because you will go through many, it is a good idea to buy rechargeable batteries, which of course necessitates the purchase of a charger. Bring twice as many batteries as you think you might need to each recording session, and get in the habit of charging your batteries every night. Although batteries hold their charge better, over time, if they are completely discharged between chargings, what is gained in battery life is lost in data quality – as it can be extremely disruptive to have to change batteries during the middle of a conversation or story.

As far as microphones are concerned, we recommend using directional *lavalier* (tie-clip, lapel) *microphones* with their own power packs. Using a directional microphone will maximize the likelihood that the speech of the interviewee will

Figure 9.3. *Solid state recorders: Marantz PMD660 (left) and Zoom H2n (right)*

be isolated, and that ambient noise will be minimized (though certainly not eliminated). We recommend lavalier microphones because they are small and can be immobilized by clipping them onto speakers' shirts (ask speakers to clip microphones on for themselves). Higher-end recorders may have two input jacks, for a left and right microphone signal. You may find it beneficial to record the speech of the interviewer with a separate directional microphone or, if there is more than one interviewer, with an omnidirectional microphone. Provided that you feed two separate microphones into the left and right microphone jacks, the recorder will keep the two channels distinct from one another. Separating the left (interviewee) channel from the right (interviewer) channel is trivial with most acoustic analysis software applications. We strongly caution against using built-in microphones, even though most recorders have them, since such microphones are usually unable to isolate the speech signal and over-represent ambient noise.

Compared to laboratory recordings, keeping the signal-to-noise ratio high for field recordings is a significant challenge. It should be noted that the signal-to-noise ratio will be lower for recordings collected in the field than for lab recordings. This is due to the fact that there is more ambient noise outside of controlled laboratory conditions and because people use a much wider dynamic range in conversational speech than they do in the lab, where speakers will produce relatively more consistent loudness levels throughout the recording – so the appropriate gain for one part of the conversation might not be appropriate for other parts.

2.2.3   Recording in the field: language documentation

What constitutes "the field" can vary considerably from one project to another. While "the field" will, for some, conjure images of rainforests, deserts, and tundra, a great many more researchers conduct field research work much closer to home, in collaboration with a language consultant, often in the consultant's home or workplace. Whatever the research locale, it is essential – as it was for sociolinguistic recordings – for equipment to be highly portable. In spite of this similarity, recording for the purposes of language documentation differs significantly from recording for sociolinguistic purposes in one main respect: recording equipment need not be made inconspicuous. Language consultants are well aware that their language is under investigation – indeed, they are explicitly asked to reflect on the structure of their language – so seeing a microphone or a recorder in plain sight should have negligible effects on the kind of data collected in this scenario.

For this reason, *head-mounted microphones* are preferred. These directional microphones, located at a constant distance from the speaker's mouth, zero in on the speaker's voice while minimizing other noise. Directional microphones aimed toward speakers' mouths will usually pick up the speech of the researcher as well, though certainly not nearly as robustly. If knowing precisely what the researcher is saying is important, as is typically the case in the elicitation of unfamiliar languages, we recommend capturing the researcher's voice on a separate channel, with a separate microphone. In cases where there is more than one researcher, as in the case of a field methods class, the researchers can be collectively recorded using an omnidirectional microphone.

It is similarly not very important to make recording devices inconspicuous in this particular recording scenario. So while small portable recorders like those discussed in the previous section are all viable options when making recordings for language documentation purposes, so too are laptop computers.

We have recommended recording strategies that most faithfully and robustly capture the speech signal, even though obtaining high-quality audio recordings is not an important concern for many domains of language description (e.g., research on the structure of relative clauses). Given that disk space is relatively cheap, and because one never knows what research questions might arise in the future, we recommend erring on the side of collecting needlessly clean recordings. This is especially important in the case of an endangered language, where elicitation sessions on clausal syntax may unfortunately come to double as records of the language's sound system. For more issues relating to language description, see Chapter 4.

2.2.4   Other recording scenarios

Although we have just presented three rather different scenarios for collecting acoustic data, we do not mean to suggest that the methods that are common in one cannot be imported fruitfully into others. For example, phoneticians may be interested in connected speech processes that are better represented in spontaneous speech than read speech. In these cases, spontaneous speech data can be elicited in the lab, resulting in recordings that, though less controlled in terms of linguistic form, nonetheless still exhibit high signal-to-noise ratios. Similarly, socio-linguists who are primarily interested in conversational interview data, may addi-tionally collect word list data to expand the stylistic range of data collected for each speaker. While recording word lists is a common practice in sociolinguistics, words are often not elicited in the same way as they would be in a phonetic study (e.g., with respect to the issues of randomization and collecting multiple repetitions).

In Figure 9.4, we present a range of alternative techniques for collecting sound recording data. All are worthwhile, but some are better suited to answering particular questions than others. As we move from left to right, we proceed from the least spontaneous speech to the most spontaneous speech. We also go from elicitation tasks that do not closely approximate the speaking situations we most often encounter to tasks that very closely correspond to real-life speaking situations. We also go from methodologies for which it is very easy to compare across speakers, since they are saying the same things in the same linguistic contexts, to methodologies for which it is more difficult to compare across speak-ers. Finally, the data collection techniques on the left represent approaches that often make use of very visible, and often expensive laboratory equipment, while those on the right represent approaches making use of smaller, yet still relatively expensive equipment. Space constraints prevent us from discussing each techni-que in detail, though we list the alternatives to provide a sense of what can be done besides word lists and interviews.

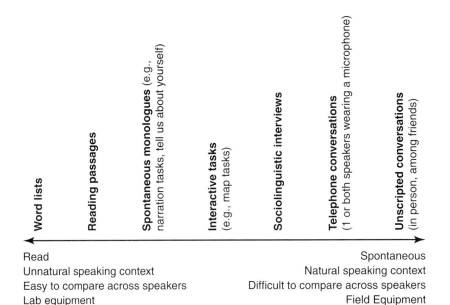

Figure 9.4. *Range of data collection scenarios*

Although Figure 9.4 implies a trade-off between audio quality and the naturalness of speaking situations, this need not be the case. A number of interactional phonetics laboratories (e.g., Tyler Kendall's at the University of Oregon; Norma Mendoza-Denton's at the University of Arizona; Rob Podesva's at Stanford University) are comfortable interactive spaces that have been built with acoustical specifications that approach or equal those of sound-proof and sound-attenuated booths. The goal in such spaces is to collect highly interactive audio (and video) interactions that are also characterized, unlike many field recordings, by a high signal-to-noise ratio.

2.3   Managing recordings

After recordings are made, it is imperative that data are backed up immediately. We recommend backing up the data once on a computer hard drive, again on a portable external hard drive (USB drives that do not require a power supply are preferred), and, if an internet connection is available, to a server or cloud. Audio files should be labeled in a systematic way (so develop a file-naming convention that works for your purposes), and metadata should be stored in accompanying text files and ideally also in a database or spreadsheet for your records. As it can be difficult to work with large audio files, you may find it helpful to divide long recordings into more manageable pieces, the size of which will depend on the kind of research being performed. Some researchers may find it useful to take notes on the content of recordings right away, which can be entered into field notes (see Chapter 10), a sound file annotation (see Chapter 17), or transcription software (see Chapter 12).

3   Articulatory data

A researcher using acoustic analysis must infer the shape or movement of articulators in the vocal tract by working backwards from the output, using formulas that relate specific acoustic signatures to particular vocal tract states. It is also possible, however, to directly visualize the vocal tract. In this section, we review a number of commonly used devices for directly measuring articulator shape, position, or movement. The discussion is organized around the difficulty and expense of the technique. "Easy" techniques involve equipment you may already have or that is inexpensive to obtain, that requires little or no specialist training, and that can be used anywhere. These include video and static palatography. "Medium" techniques involve equipment that may cost several thousand dollars to obtain, but that any linguist can learn to use and that can be used in a typical departmental linguistics lab or carried into the field. Such equipment includes electropalatography (EPG), sonography, electroglottography (EGG), and masks for aerodynamic measures. To use the "Difficult" techniques, you probably need access to someone with specialized medical training, a medical school, and/or a really large lab budget. While such techniques might be beyond what the readers of this chapter would use themselves, it is likely that they will encounter the results in published research, so it is worth learning how such techniques work. Difficult techniques include endoscopy, magnetic resonance imaging (MRI), the electromagnetic mid-sagittal articulometer (EMMA), and electromyography (EMG).

The set of devices that can be used for articulatory investigations is in principle limited only by ingenuity, and we can cover only the most commonly used methods here. Other more obscure devices (such as the velotrace, plethysmograph, and strain gauges) are described in Horiguchi and Bell-Berti (1987), Ohala (1993), and McGlone and Proffit (1972), respectively. Also, even though X-rays have been important tools for imaging the vocal tract, present-day studies typically avoid the methodology, given the health risks associated with extended exposure. X-ray databases are nonetheless still available (Munhall, Vatikiotis-Bateson, and Tohkura 1995). Finally, we do not discuss methodologies that capture brain function or attention during speech production; for a discussion of these techniques, including eye-tracking, fMRI, PET scans, and ERP, see Chapter 8. For a comprehensive introduction to articulatory phonetics, see Gick, Wilson, and Derrick (2013).

For each technique, we briefly describe the kind of data that can be collected (and why a linguist might care about such data), what is involved in setting up and running an experiment, an example of what data collected with this technique looks like, and a few pros and cons. No matter what technique you decide to use, you should consult someone with experience who can give you more detailed guidance. Here, we aim to give you an idea of what is available, as well as aid you in understanding and interpreting the results of others.

3.1   Easy techniques

3.1.1   Video

While most of what goes on in the act of speaking happens inside the mouth and thus requires more sophisticated imaging tools, a *video camera* can capture any visible aspects of speech communication. Such aspects might include interpersonal interactions, facial expression, gaze, and gestures with the hands and other parts of the body. This is of course useful for the investigation of signed languages, but studies of the integration of speech with other body movements have turned up interesting data on both interpersonal interaction and general temporal coordination (see Chapter 10 for more on recording interaction). In terms of articulation per se, the linguist might be interested in investigating lip position, to document bilabial vs labiodental place of articulation, for example. In Figure 9.5, two stills extracted from a video clip document two different kinds of bilabial constriction in the Sengwato dialect of Setswana: compression for [ɸ] (left) vs rounding in secondary articulations such as [sʷ] (right).

For a linguistic video study, you will need only a camera, which should be set up on a tripod for stability. A mirror held at a 45-degree angle to the side of the subject's face can capture a simultaneous side view. Numerous video editing programs are commercially available; one video annotation and editing tool popular with linguists is ELAN, available as a free download from Language Archiving Technology (www.lat-mpi.eu/tools/elan). One thing to be careful of in video studies is subject privacy: you may choose to capture only the lips, as in Figure 9.5, or obscure the eyes, or obtain permission to use the full face image (see Chapter 2 on research ethics).

An obvious drawback to using video to analyze speech production is that video cameras can capture only what can be seen external to the speaker, and only under the proper lighting conditions.

3.1.2   Static palatography

Static palatography offers a quick and (literally) dirty way to investigate patterns of tongue contact against the palate. It can be used to compare place

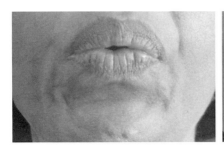

Figure 9.5. *Lip position for [ɸ] (left) and [sʷ] (right) in Sengwato*

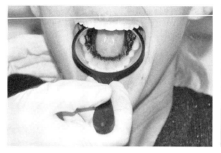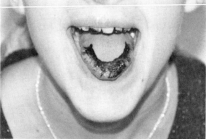

Figure 9.6. *Palatogram (left) and linguogram (right) of American English /t/*

of articulation among coronal articulations – for example, to document whether a particular articulation is dental or alveolar, apical or laminal.

Static palatography involves painting the tongue or palate of a subject with a mixture of oil and charcoal. Activated charcoal can be ordered from any pharmacy, without a prescription: its pharmacological use is as a poison antidote, so ingesting a small amount is not harmful. Mix a teaspoon of charcoal with a teaspoon of vegetable oil, and stir until it is the consistency of black paint. A drop of mint extract will make the mixture taste like toothpaste. In addition to your charcoal paint and a small paintbrush, you will also need a small mirror, a few inches square, and a camera to record your results.

To image the pattern of tongue contact on the palate, have your subject stick out his tongue, and paint the tongue with the charcoal and oil mixture, being careful to cover the tip and sides. Go back as far as you can without triggering a gag reflex. You have to work quickly, as the subject cannot close his mouth or swallow. After the tongue is covered, have the subject articulate one consonant – for example, [ata]. The paint will rub off where the tongue touches the palate, leaving the pattern of tongue contact. To get an image of the pattern, hold the mirror at a 45-degree degree angle inside the subject's mouth, and snap a picture of the image in the mirror (as shown in Figure 9.6, left). Afterwards, allow the subject to rinse and spit.

To obtain an image of the part of the tongue that contacts the palate (technically a *linguogram*), paint the palate instead, and have your subject articulate the same consonant. The paint will rub off the palate onto the tongue. Have your subject stick out his tongue, and photograph (Figure 9.6, right).

Static palatography is fun and easy, and gives a good sense of contact in three dimensions, not just the mid-sagittal plane. Drawbacks are that it is messy, and not all subjects are willing to have their tongues painted and photographed. Additionally, the technique only works for coronal consonants in isolation. Because of the gag reflex, and the difficulty of getting a picture, back consonants cannot be investigated. Only a single consonant in isolation can be produced, or the paint will just smear. Finally, the technique does not lend itself to quantification.

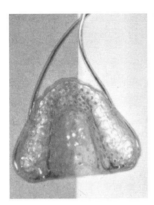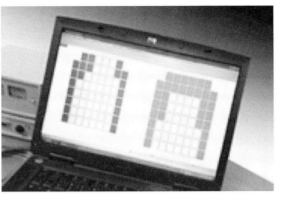

Figure 9.7. *Artificial palate with embedded electrodes (left); sample patterns for /s/ and /t/ (right)*
http://speech.umaryland.edu/epg.html (left)
http://www.rds-sw.nihr.ac.uk/succcess_stories_lucy_ellis.htm (right)

3.2   Medium techniques

3.2.1   Electropalatography

Electropalatography (EPG) works on the same principle as static palatography, but instead of paint, an artificial palate embedded with electrodes and attached to a computer records the pattern of tongue contact (Figure 9.7, left). When the tongue contacts an electrode, a signal is sent to the computer, which can then compute the pattern (Figure 9.7, right).

EPG is an improvement over the paint-and-charcoal technique, in that it can image tongue contact in running speech (the electrodes do not smear). The researcher can see patterns of contact changing as the constriction is formed and then released, not just maximum constriction (frame rates are typically 100–200 Hz). EPG also allows quantification, as the number of electrodes and specific pattern activated can be compared across different articulations.

The drawbacks of EPG include cost: the system itself will cost several thousand dollars, and the artificial palates must be custom-made from a dental cast, at significant additional cost for each subject. For subjects, the palates may take some getting used to (they feel like an orthodontic retainer), so speech may not be entirely natural. Finally, the technique can measure where the contact is made on the palate, but not which part of the tongue is making it.

3.2.2   Sonography

Sonography is in some ways the opposite of electropalatography: with this technique, you can see tongue position, but not palate contact (at least not directly). Like EPG, sonography involves an initial expense to acquire the equipment, in the order of $25,000 at the time of writing. Once acquired, however, it costs very little more to use. Portable sonographs, not much bigger than a laptop, are available for use in fieldwork.

In linguistic sonography, a transducer is held under the subject's chin (Figure 9.8, left). Gel spread on the skin facilitates unbroken contact. The transducer emits a series of sound waves that travel up from the transducer through the skin and tongue muscle, and then bounce back when they reach the border

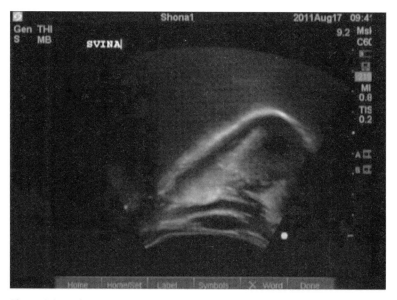

Figure 9.8. *Subject holding a sonograph transducer (top); sonograph image for the vowel /i/ (bottom)*
Gick 2002

between the tongue surface and the air inside the vocal tract. The equipment measures the time delay between transmission and reception, and converts that measure to a distance between transducer and tongue surface. Repeated measurements produce an outline of the surface of the tongue, as shown in Figure 9.8 (right).

The pros of sonography are that it is direct and non-invasive, and can record changes in tongue shape over time, in real time (although the acquisition rate, typically 40 ms per frame, may not be fast enough to capture fast-moving articulations such as taps). Subjects enjoy watching the moving images of their own tongues (though they should be allowed to do this before and after the experiment, not during, so that they do not get distracted.) Programs for tracing and quantitatively comparing different tongue shapes are widely available.

Because of its non-invasiveness, sonography has grown in popularity, not only in the field of phonetics, but also sociolinguistics, to investigate questions of language variation and change. Recent studies have demonstrated that articulatory variation can surface in the absence of significant variation in the acoustical signal (Lawson, Stuart-Smith, and Scobbie 2008; Mielke, Baker, and Archangeli 2010; De Decker and Nycz 2012). For example, De Decker and Nycz (2012) draw on ultrasound data to show that some speakers achieve tense variants of /æ/ with a raising/fronting tongue gesture, while others exhibit no evidence of such a gesture.

One disadvantage of sonography is that is not always possible to image the tongue tip, if there is not a direct line, through muscle only, from transducer to tongue tip. An air space under the tongue tip, or interference from the hyoid bone, may prevent the sound waves from reaching the very front of the tongue. Additionally, the tongue and palate cannot be imaged at the same time, so that patterns of tongue-to-palate contact or constriction cannot be measured directly. In order for an image of the palate to be obtained, the subject can be asked to hold a swallow of liquid in the mouth, eliminating the air border at the top of the tongue, so sound waves travel through the tongue and through the liquid, bouncing back when they hit the palate, allowing an outline of palate shape to be imaged. Then, in order to discover tongue position in relation to the palate, as would be necessary to investigate place of articulation, the two separate images of tongue and palate must be overlaid. In order for this overlay to work, it is crucial that neither the subject's head nor the transducer move at all during the imaging session, so as not to change the alignment. Finding an effective head-stabilization technique that does not compromise the comfort of the subject is probably the most challenging aspect of using sonography. Some approaches involve immobilizing the subject's head and the transducer (see Davidson and De Decker 2005 for an inexpensive and portable method); other approaches allow head movement, but measure the movement and compensate for it (see Whalen et al. 2005 for a description of HOCUS, the Haskins optically corrected ultrasound system).

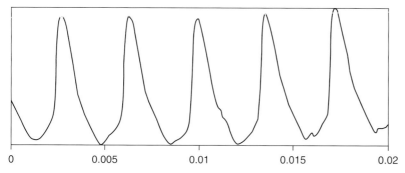

Figure 9.9. *Example of an EGG waveform during modal voicing*

3.2.3   Electroglottography

Electroglottography (EGG) uses electrical impedance to measure opening and closing of the glottis. It is often used for studies of voice quality. In EGG, electrodes are held against the skin of the neck, on either side of the larynx. Typically, a Velcro strap holds them in place. Then, a very weak current is passed between the electrodes – the current is so weak it cannot be felt at all by the subject, but the strength of the current can be detected by the technology. Electrical impedance between the two electrodes is greater when the vocal folds are open than when they are closed, so that a graph of the measured impedance shows the relative opening and closing of the glottis (Figure 9.9).

EGG is non-invasive, and involves no discomfort other than a snug Velcro collar. It allows direct measurement of glottal state, bypassing the vocal tract filter. Initial cost is again several thousand dollars, but there is no additional cost per use. Placing the electrodes properly, directly on either side of the vocal folds, can be tricky, depending on the subject's body type. Because of differences in laryngeal anatomy, EGG may work better on male subjects, where the location of the larynx is often more readily apparent, than on female subjects.

3.2.4   Aerodynamic measures

Aerodynamic measures record oral and/or nasal airflow. For certain sounds, it matters a lot how much air is flowing where. A linguist might want to measure the degree of vowel nasalization, for example, or the pressure differential in front of and behind the constriction in a fricative.

The technique involves a mask, similar to an oxygen mask, that is held over the face while the subject is speaking (Figure 9.10, left). The mask may be split, to have separate chambers for the nose and mouth. Screens in the mask allow air to move in and out, so that the subject can continue to breath and speak, while transducers in the mask measure air flow and air pressure. To measure pressure behind a constriction, the end of a small plastic tube can be placed just behind the lips (or, with slightly more care, just behind the tongue front). Figure 9.10 (right) shows pressure build-up behind the lips during a bilabial fricative.

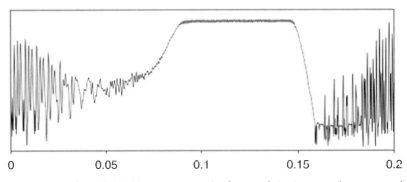

| 0 | 0.05 | 0.1 | 0.15 | 0.2 |

Figure 9.10. *Using a pressure/airflow mask (top); trace of pressure at the lips during [aɸa] (bottom)*

A direct measure of airflow can be very useful, because airflow and intraoral pressure are very hard to infer from the acoustic record, if it can be done at all. A drawback is that airflow measures from the transducers are hard to calibrate. Further, while muffled speech can be heard through the mask, one cannot collect a clear acoustic record while the mask is being used.

3.3   Difficult techniques

3.3.1   Endoscopy

For linguistic research, an *endoscope* is used to take video or still images of the larynx, and thus can be used to investigate states of the vocal folds

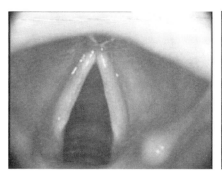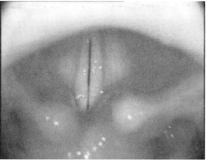

Figure 9.11. *Pictures of abducted (left) and adducted (right) vocal folds, taken via*
flexible endoscope
http://www.voicedoctor.net/media/normal-vocal-cord

during different types of phonation or articulation (Figure 9.11). The technique
involves positioning a camera in the vocal tract. With a rigid endoscope, the camera
is at the end of a rigid tube that is held toward the back of the mouth, with the camera
pointing downward to image the larynx. With a flexible endoscope, the tube is
inserted through the nasal passages, until it passes through the velar port and hangs
down in the back of the throat. The flexible endoscope thus allows direct visualization of the larynx without interfering with articulation: the subject can speak
normally while images are being captured. If a numbing agent is sprayed into the
nose prior to insertion, any discomfort is more psychological than physical.

This technique is probably between medium and difficult. The technology is
not any more expensive than other "medium" techniques, it is pretty easily
portable, and technically one does not need medical training to insert a tube up
a subject's nose. It is, however, a lot more invasive than holding a transducer under
a subject's chin, and is not a technique that every subject or every linguist would
be comfortable with.

3.3.2   Magnetic resonance imaging

Magnetic resonance imaging (MRI) can provide the linguist with
beautiful, clear pictures of the whole vocal tract. In MRI imaging, the subject is
placed in a magnetic field – a large plastic tube surrounded by a huge magnet.
When the magnet is turned on, all hydrogen atoms in the subject's body align to
the field. A radio pulse sent to a specific depth and location is used to disrupt the
field and knock the atoms out of alignment. After the pulse passes, the atoms
return to alignment, but in doing so they give off energy, which is detected by the
technology. The amount of energy is correlated with the amount of hydrogen,
which is correlated with type of tissue and tissue density, so boundaries between
different types of tissue show up crisply.

The ability to image the whole vocal tract simultaneously is especially useful.
MRI can be used to create a series of images over time, although acquisition rate is

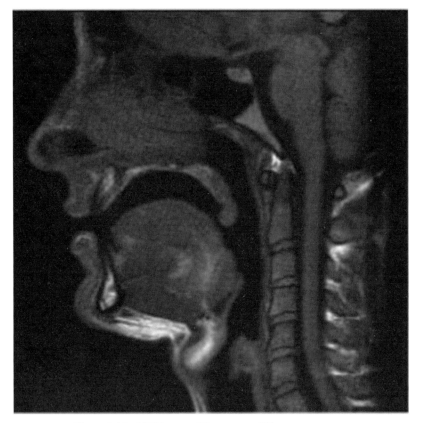

Figure 9.12. *MRI image of Portuguese [ã]*
Martins et al. 2008

somewhat slow as of this writing: while MRI movies are possible, the technology is mostly used to capture steady-state images. The technology also allows the linguist to visualize a slice in any dimension, showing, for example, grooving of the tongue during fricatives, or a cross-section of pharyngeal width.

The main drawback of MRI imaging is that it is very expensive – a machine is more expensive than a linguistics department could afford (even if it had the space). Linguists generally work in collaboration with a hospital or medical school, which will negotiate charges by the hour. The equipment is definitely not portable – you must bring your subjects to the lab, and not everyone is comfortable in the small tube. Also, the magnets make a lot of noise, so you cannot get good acoustics at the same time as the image.

3.3.3   Electromagnetic mid-sagittal articulometry

A substitute for MRI can be *electromagnetic mid-sagittal articulom-etry* (EMMA). This technique shows how articulator position changes over time, and can be used to determine velocity as well. In EMMA, small pellets are affixed (with non-toxic adhesive) to surfaces in the vocal tract: along the surface of the tongue to measure tongue movement, on the lips to measure their movement, on the lower teeth to track the jaw, and on the upper teeth as a landmark. Due to the gag reflex, the back of the tongue and velum cannot be imaged.

The articulometer consists of a plastic frame that the subject sits inside (Figure 9.13, left). The frame holds three magnetic coils. As the subject speaks, the pellets move through the magnetic fields created by these coils, and pellet movement, in either two or three dimensions, can be tracked. An example movement track is shown in Figure 9.13 (right).

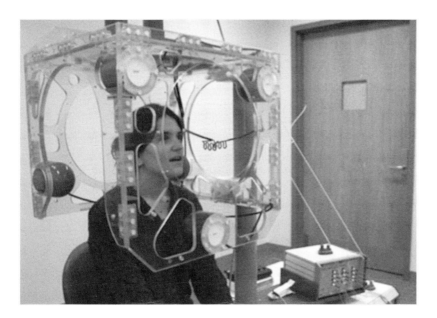

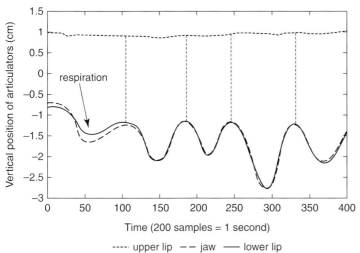

Figure 9.13. *EMMA apparatus (top); ample movement trace (bottom) http:// beckman.illinois.edu/news/2007/10/100307 (top); Fagel and Clemens 2004 (bottom)*

Like MRI, EMMA can provide data from more than one articulator at a time. Unlike MRI or sonography, EMMA tracks movement of a set of specific points, rather than overall articulator shape (which can be either a plus or a minus). As with sonography, EMMA cannot directly measure contact, although contact can be inferred from changes in velocity. The technique is also somewhat invasive, similar to EPG, in that sensors must be placed inside the mouth. Additionally, the pellets sometimes fall off, and data are lost.

3.3.4   Electromyography

The final technique to be covered is *electromyography* (EMG). This technique directly measures electrical activity in a muscle. EMG involves inserting tiny wire probes ("hooked wire electrodes") into the muscle under examination. When the muscle contracts, the electrode picks up the electrical signal given off by the firing muscle cells, and sends the signal to a connected computer. By coordinating the EMG signal with the speech signal, a researcher can determine which muscles are contracting for which speech sounds.

This technique has been used to study laryngeal muscles and tongue muscles, and can be the only way to get information on their specific activity. What laryngeal muscles are activated during glottal opening, or pitch lowering? What tongue muscles are active during fronting? Figure 9.14 shows some sample EMG data from Thai.

Unfortunately, EMG is not pain-free for the subject. Generally, linguists only use EMG on themselves or willing colleagues, and it must be performed by a medical doctor. Even so, it can be difficult to get accurate readings. Laryngeal

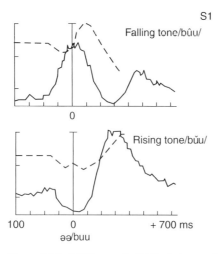

Figure 9.14. *EMG trace (solid line) shows a burst of activity in the cricothyroid muscle during pitch raising (dotted line) in Thai falling and rising tone Erickson 1976*

muscles are small and relatively inaccessible, tongue muscles are intertwined, so it can be hard to be sure that the electrode is in the right place.

Some of these more difficult techniques notwithstanding, articulatory measurements are not beyond the reach of the typical linguist or linguistics lab. And all linguists can benefit, if only by reading articulatory studies, from the information that such studies provide. For more detail about the techniques discussed here, see Gick (2002), Ladefoged (2003), and Stone (2010).

4   Concluding remarks

Whenever a researcher makes a sound (acoustic or articulatory) recording for the purposes of linguistic research, there are many considerations to bear in mind, and many things can go wrong. We cannot emphasize strongly enough the importance of extensive practice with the recording procedure. When recording acoustic data, the researcher should always think about how to reduce ambient noise and ensure that the microphone is sufficiently close to the speaker's mouth. Similarly, when recording articulatory data, the researcher should make sure that speakers are properly positioned with respect to the equipment. In both cases, pay special attention to ensure that speakers are comfortable (see Chapter 2).

Although sound recordings fall squarely under the purview of research methods in phonetics, their utility across the subdisciplines of our field is becoming increasingly evident. While all kinds of linguists can likely identify some useful purpose for acoustic recordings, we would like to encourage further thinking about how recording speech articulation might shed light on issues outside of phonetics proper. The fact that multiple articulatory configurations can result in similar acoustic outputs (e.g., Mielke, Baker, and Archangeli 2010; De Decker and Nycz 2012) raises questions about the nature of contrast (phonology), how children acquire such patterns (language acquisition), the role that articulatory variation might play in language change (historical linguistics), and whether such variation is socially meaningful (sociolinguistics). As the field of linguistics becomes more interdisciplinary, we hope that the methods we have discussed here will be used to address an ever expanding set of questions.

References

Cieri, C. 2010. Making a field recording. In M. Di Paolo and M. Yaeger-Dror, eds. *Sociophonetics: A Student's Guide*. London: Routledge, 24–35.

Davidson, L. and P. De Decker. 2005. Stabilization techniques for ultrasound imaging of speech articulations. *Journal of the Acoustical Society of America* 117: 2544.

De Decker, P. and J. Nycz. 2011. For the record: which digital media can be used for sociophonetic analysis? *University of Pennsylvania Working Papers in Linguistics* 17: 51–9.

2012. Are tense [æ]s really tense? The mapping between articulation and acoustics. *Lingua* 122: 810–21.

Erickson, D. M. 1976. A physiological analysis of the tones of Thai. Unpublished Ph.D. dissertation, University of Connecticut.

Fagel, S. and C. Clemens. 2004. An articulation model for audiovisual speech synthesis: determination, adjustment, evaluation. *Speech Communication* 44: 141–54.

Fairbanks, G. 1960. *Voice and Articulation Drill Book*, 2nd edn. New York: Harper and Row.

Gick, B. 2002. The use of ultrasound for linguistic phonetic fieldwork. *Journal of the International Phonetic Association* 32: 113–21.

Gick, B., I. Wilson, and D. Derrick. 2013. *Articulatory Phonetics*. Malden, MA: Wiley-Blackwell.

Horiguchi, S. and F. Bell-Berti. 1987. The Velotrace: a device for monitoring velar position. *Cleft-Palate Journal* 24: 104–11.

Johnson, K. 2012. *Acoustic and Auditory Phonetics*, 3rd edn. Malden, MA: Wiley-Blackwell.

Ladefoged, P. 1996. *Elements of Acoustic Phonetics*, 2nd edn. University of Chicago Press.

2003. *Phonetic Data Analysis: An Introduction to Fieldwork and Instrumental Techniques*. Malden, MA: Blackwell.

Lawson, E., J. Stuart-Smith, and J. Scobbie. 2008. Articulatory insights into language variation and change: preliminary findings from an ultrasound study of derhoticization in Scottish English. *University of Pennsylvania Working Papers in Linguistics* 14: 102–10.

Martins, P., I. Carbone, A. Pinto, and A. Teixeira. 2008. European Portuguese MRI based speech production studies. *Speech Communication* 50: 925–52.

McGlone, R. E. and W. R. Proffit. 1972. Correlation between functional lingual pressure and oral cavity size. *Cleft Palate Journal* 9: 229–35.

Mielke, J., A. Baker, and D. Archangeli. 2010. Variability and homogeneity in American English /ɹ/ allophony and /s/ retraction. In C. Fougeron, B. Kuehnert, M. Imperio, and N. Vallee, eds. *Laboratory Phonology*, 10 vols. Berlin: Mouton de Gruyter, Volume X, 699–719.

Munhall, K. G., E. Vatikiotis-Bateson, and Y. Tohkura. 1995. X-ray film database for speech research. *Journal of the Acoustical Society of America* 98: 1222–4.

Ohala, J. J. 1993. The whole body plethysmograph in speech research. *Journal of the Acoustical Society of America* 93: 2416.

Stevens, K. N. 1998. *Acoustic Phonetics*. Cambridge, MA: MIT Press.

Stone, M. 2010. Laboratory techniques for investigating speech articulation. In W. Hardcastle, J. Laver, and F. E. Gibbon, eds. *Handbook of the Phonetic Sciences*, 2nd edn. Malden, MA: Wiley-Blackwell, 9–38.

Whalen, D., K. Iskarous, M. K. Tiede, D. J. Ostry, H. Lehnert-Lehouiller, E. Bateson-Vatikiotis, and D. S. Hailey. 2005. *Journal of Speech, Language, and Hearing Research* 48: 543–53.

10   Ethnography and recording interaction

Erez Levon

1   Introduction

Shortly after I arrived in Israel to begin fieldwork on language among Israeli lesbian and gay activists, I went out for a drink with three of my male informants. As we waited for the bartender to bring us our beers, Roee, one of the men I was with, leaned over to me and, indicating the bartender with his head, said *wai, eize birz hu, naxon?* ('Wow, he's a *birz*, isn't he?'). Though I could tell that he was commenting on the bartender, I had to admit that I did not understand the word *birz*, and I asked Roee to translate it for me. Roee began to laugh, and then explained that the word *birz* meant 'handsome man' in an Israeli gay slang variety called *oxtchit*. My interest was immediately piqued. I had never heard of an Israeli gay slang variety before, and I was eager to know where the variety came from and how it was used. The men I was with that evening explained to me that *oxtchit* was a variety predominantly used by a specific kind of effeminate gay man in Israel, called *oxtchot*, though it was also sometimes used by other gay men as a "secret" variety.

Taking this explanation at face value, I spent the next few weeks finding out all that I could about *oxtchit*. Yet the more I looked into it, the more my understanding of *oxtchit* contradicted what I had originally been told. For example, I never saw *oxtchit* being used as a "secret" variety, a way to hide what one says from prying ears. Instead, I only ever heard it being used in a joking manner between friends. In addition, I noticed that only some of my male informants ever used *oxtchit* at all – and that the ones that did were the polar opposite of the effeminate gay men I had been told were the variety's primary users. As I spent more time in the field and got to know my informants' worldview better, I came to realize that the reality of *oxtchit* was very different from what had been described to me previously. *Oxtchit* was not spoken by *oxtchot*, nor was it a secret or "identity-affirming" variety. Rather, I came to understand that *oxtchit* was an enregistered voice (e.g., Agha 2005), a linguistic materialization of gendered alterity that is used exclusively as a form of mockery (Goffman 1974) by certain gender-normative gay men in Israel (see Levon 2012).

I describe my experience with *oxtchit* in Israel in order to demonstrate how my analysis of the variety – both in terms of its function and its distribution – was only possible because I was able to develop an understanding of the variety's meaning *within* the community in which it was used. In other words, successfully analyzing *oxtchit* required the kind of insight that only ethnographic fieldwork could provide. In this chapter, I describe how we go about achieving this kind of insight in linguistic research. I go through the various steps involved in conducting ethnographic fieldwork, including planning an ethnographic project, accessing a community of speakers, collecting both audio- and video-recorded data, and processing and writing up findings. My goal is to describe ethnographic methods in a way that is both useful and relevant to as wide a linguistics readership as possible, and, as a result, to demonstrate that the underlying precepts of ethnography form the foundation of "best practices" in linguistic field research more broadly.

Ethnography is a term that is very often used, but not always clearly defined. Its origins lie in research by sociocultural anthropologists in the first decades of the twentieth century, and particularly in the "participatory observation" method advocated by Malinowski (1922). For Malinowski, the goal of social science research was to understand how the behavior observed within a community is linked to the beliefs and interpretive practices characteristic of that group. In order to achieve this, Malinowski claimed that researchers must work to develop an insider's perspective, which would allow them to interpret the behaviors they observe in light of the social context in which those behaviors are located. Yet at the same time, Malinowski argued that the scientific analysis of behavior requires more than simply seeing the world through an informant's eyes. It necessarily also relies on a researcher's ability to keep one foot outside of the goings-on of a community so that she can extrapolate the larger social forces that are in play and so come to refutable generalizations about social structure. In other words, according to Malinowski ethnography is about generating a theory of social behavior that is based on both an insider and a more outsider perspective (sometimes also called *emic* and *etic* views, respectively; see Pike 1967). The difficulty in ethnographic research often lies in finding the right balance between the two. This point is succinctly summarized by Geertz (1983: 57, cited in Duranti 1997: 86):

> The real question . . . is what roles the two concepts [insider and outsider] play in [ethnographic] analysis. Or, more exactly, how, in each case, ought one to deploy them so as to produce an interpretation of the way a people lives which is neither imprisoned within their mental horizons, an ethnography of witchcraft as written by a witch, nor systematically deaf to the tonalities of their existence, an ethnography of witchcraft as written by a geometer.

A belief in the importance of an ethnographic approach to the study of language also has a long history in linguistics. Sakel and Everett (2012: 156), for example, cite Boas' (1917) critique of the then available documentation on Native American languages as "one-sided and incomplete . . . because we hardly have any records of daily occurrences, everyday conversation, descriptions of industries, customs and the like." For Boas, it was impossible to fully describe the form of a language without taking into account the cultural viewpoint of those who spoke it. In making this point, Boas echoes Malinowski's view, essentially arguing for the centrality of ethnographic knowledge to linguistic theory. And while our conceptualization of language as an object of study has certainly changed since Boas' time (particularly with the advent of both the generativist and the variationist paradigms), many linguists would nevertheless still agree with the basic premise of Boas' claim: that rigorous theorizing is not possible without adequate description, and that, in turn, adequate description often requires knowledge about how speakers themselves understand the phenomenon in question. This suggests that ethnographic methods are not restricted to sociolinguistics. Everett (1985, 2005), for example, argues that understanding Pirahã phonology requires intricate knowledge of culturally specific discourse "channels" (or registers), knowledge that it is only possible to obtain through prolonged ethnographic observation. Even in less "exotic" linguistic locations, ethnographic observation often provides highly useful information regarding variation in optionality and/or gradient grammaticality that speaks directly to the interest of all linguists (e.g., Vaux and Cooper 1999; Newman and Ratliff 2001). Finally, it has always been a central tenet of sociolinguistic research that understanding patterns of language variation and language change is impossible without also understanding the social matrix within which those patterns are embedded (e.g., Labov 1963). The point here then is that the foundational argument of ethnography – that speakers' own interpretations of their behavior also matter – is relevant across the discipline of linguistics, even for those researchers who may not normally think of ethnography as a part of what they do.

2   Planning your project

All research requires advance planning, and ethnography is certainly no exception. In fact, there are a variety of additional things to consider when preparing an ethnographic field project that go above and beyond the standard concerns for linguistics research.

As in all projects, the first thing a researcher needs to consider is what the focus of the project is. While in other research traditions initial planning is often formulated as a series of research questions to be resolved, ethnography tends to adopt a more inductive, data-driven, bottom-up approach in which relevant social and linguistic phenomena emerge over the course of ethnographic observation. According to Blommaert and Jie (2010: 12), "this is what makes ethnography a demanding approach: it is not enough (not by a very long shot) to follow a clear, pre-set line of inquiry and the researcher cannot come thundering in with preestablished truths." That being said, it is nevertheless important to have at least a preliminary idea of a social phenomenon in mind. As you proceed through your fieldwork, this idea will become refined, and it is entirely possible that your focus will shift over time. A key principle of ethnography is that while you may plan for any eventuality before you begin your fieldwork, the real trick is to be prepared for the fact that your need to adapt in the field will be ever-present. Nevertheless, it is often helpful to begin planning your project by delineating a series of workable questions that your research will potentially address.

The "workability" of ethnographic research questions is judged primarily on the same grounds as for any other kind of project. In particular, you want to ensure that your questions are:

- **Relevant** – Would your research go beyond being simply a description of a case study and (i) fill an empirical gap and/or (ii) contribute to the development of relevant (social and linguistic) theory?
- **Original** – Does your research represent a new contribution to knowledge? How does your research build on and improve previous work in this area?
- **Methodologically sound** – Is your study practically and ethically feasible (i.e., can you actually do what you set out to do)? Will you be able to answer the question that you set? Is the scope of your research too large or too small?

Determining the extent to which an ethnographic project is methodologically sound requires some careful consideration. One of the biggest challenges in this regard is determining whether you will actually be able to answer the questions that you set. Put another way, are your research questions operationalized such that you can state what kinds of evidence you would need to collect in order to provide an answer for the question? Again, even though much ethnographic work is focused on broader social forces and how those forces may be reflected and/or constructed through language, it is important to ensure that the questions you ask have empirical answers. For example, say you are interested in examining issues of gender and power in mixed-sex interactions. A question like "Do men have power over women in conversation?" is going to be a very difficult one to provide any sort of answer for since it depends on what is meant by "power" and how one determines who is more powerful in a conversational interaction. You can, however, rephrase this question in a more empirically focused way: "In mixed-sex interaction, what function do men's uses of simultaneous speech (e.g., interruptions and overlaps) serve, and to what extent does this use allow men to achieve conversational dominance over women?" This second question is a more "operationalized" one in that you can immediately determine what will be investigated (i.e., simultaneous speech in mixed-sex interaction) and what conclusions that investigation will lead to (i.e., that men do or do not achieve conversational dominance). In a real ethnographic project, even finalized research questions will most likely not be as specific as this example, but it is nevertheless important to bear the question of operationalizability in mind.

Very closely linked to this is the issue of whether you can practically and ethically investigate the topic (for a detailed discussion of ethical issues in linguistics research, see Chapter 2). One of the first things to consider in this regard is whether you can identify an appropriate and accessible population of speakers that allows you to address the question. In certain instances there may be practical impediments to your achieving this goal (e.g., you want to study mono-lingual speakers of Amharic, for example, and are unable to be in contact with them) or there may be ethical impediments (e.g., you want to study language-in-interaction during parent–child arguments). You should also consider whether the population you have in mind is adequate for addressing your question. If you want to study language and gay men, for example, do you need to compare gay men's practice to that of other speakers in order to obtain a valid result? In this case, research has demonstrated that such a comparison is not always necessary (e.g., Podesva 2007), but it is nevertheless a question worth asking. Related to this is the issue of how you plan to assess community membership to begin with. Membership criteria for certain communities (e.g., work colleagues) are more clearly delineated than others (e.g., friendship groups), and it is important that you know in advance what you take being a community member to entail and how you plan on determining that on a case-by-case basis. (Note that certain theoretical perspectives have well-defined criteria for inclusion. For example, the Communities of Practice approach [Eckert and McConnell-Ginet 1992] defines membership in terms of joint engagement in a mutual endeavor. For those working within a Communities of Practice approach, devising your own inclusion criteria is therefore less of an issue.)

Another common concern with respect to the practicality of your research has to do with the scope of your project. There is often a temptation for researchers to make projects too big (e.g., "I'm going to study young British men"), as a way of trying to ensure their work is relevant. The problem with this is that if a research question is too large in scope it becomes unanswerable. Recall that ethnographic research entails spending large amounts of time interacting with your informants and getting to know them on a relatively personal level. It would be impossible to do so for a population as large as "young British men." It is also not clear that such a population actually represents the kind of "community" for which ethnography is designed, since ethnography tends to focus on smaller, more locally meaningful groups, rather than those based on large, demographic categories (e.g., Hymes 1974; Eckert and McConnell-Ginet 1992). When planning an ethnographic proj-ect, it is therefore important to identify a bounded and internally cohesive group of speakers that you would be able to interact with on a regular basis and whose observed behavior would allow you to fully address your research goals (see Chapter 5).

A final, yet very important, point to consider when selecting a community is whether you would be able to gain access to it in the first place. This is different than the actual mechanics of gaining access to a community, which I discuss in Section 3. What I have in mind here is a more preliminary question regarding whether access is even possible and, if so, the quality of access that could be achieved. In all interaction-based research projects, it is crucial to be mindful of cultural and other sensitivities – even those that you may not necessarily be aware of (see Chapter 2). Whether you are planning on conducting elicitations with a single informant, doing a series of one-off interviews, or spending a prolonged period of ethnographic observation within a community, you need to bear in mind that how your informants relate to you and your social positioning (in terms of your race, sex, sexuality, social class, nationality, etc.) could have an impact on the kinds of information they provide you with (and whether they grant you access in the first place). Could I, for example, as a white man, gain access to conduct an ethnography of language as it is used in an African American women's beauty parlor? Perhaps. Though even if I did there would be a very real question regarding the extent to which I would be able to achieve genuine "insider" status. In saying this, I do not mean to imply that research can only ever be conducted in communities of which you are already a member. But this question of positioning deserves careful attention throughout the life of any ethnographic project, including in the initial planning stages. (There is extensive discussion in the anthropological literature of this issue; see, e.g., Kulick and Wilson 1995; Murphy and Dingwall 2001.)

Once you have a suitable community in mind, the next steps in planning your project include enhancing your background knowledge of the community in question and preparing any preliminary data collection materials. In terms of background knowledge, you obviously want to read as much as you can about the community and the topic you will soon begin studying. Primarily, this will include academic research on the subject, though it is also important to seek out popular sources, such as news stories, films, and other media products. In addition, you want to ensure that you review relevant academic outputs in related disciplines if they exist (psychology, sociology, anthropology, cultural studies, etc.) and that you collect whatever specialist technical information (e.g., census results and other statistics) that is available. It is also always a good idea to get in contact with other researchers who have worked on your or a related topic. They are normally happy to help and will be able to provide you with valuable insight and practical tips for your work. Finally, if it is possible it can also be a good idea to talk informally with people in the community and to spend some time there. All of these activities will help to prepare you before you embark on your own research. At the same time, however, collecting this kind of background information can cause you to develop certain preconceived notions about the community you study. As an ethnographer, you need to train yourself to leave these kinds of assumptions behind and to be open to developing your own, sometimes incompatible, interpretations of community dynamics.

Finally, the advance preparation of any data collection materials will help relieve the amount of work you have to do once in the field. These could include things like recruitment materials (e.g., flyers, texts of emails) and preliminary schedules of questions for interviews (both of these are also normally required for IRB review). In addition, you want to make sure that you have acquired, learned how to use, and tested all recording devices, and that you have all the necessary peripherals (e.g., microphones, batteries, cables; see Chapter 9 for details of sound recording in linguistics research; see also Chapter 1 for a discussion of preparing research instruments). Some projects also require acquiring specialist linguistic knowledge (up to and including learning a new language). While it is certainly possible to learn a language while in the field, it will vastly reduce your future workload to at least begin the process beforehand.

3   Accessing a community

Gaining access to a community is both the first and one of the most crucial components of ethnographic research. This is because the way you gain access will often shape your positioning within that community, and hence the direction that your research is able to take. There are a variety of different ways in which ethnographers gain access, and it is important to consider which of the options available is right for you and your project (see Chapter 5 on different population sampling techniques in linguistics research).

Perhaps the most common method for gaining access in ethnographic research today is the *friend-of-a-friend technique* (e.g., Milroy and Gordon 2003), where the researcher is brought into a community by a mutual friend or acquaintance. This mutual friend is already a member of the community herself, and so introduces the researcher to other community members. The benefit of the friend-of-a-friend method is that it allows you to enter a community as something other than a stranger. This normally means that other community members will be less wary of you than they might have been, and may even feel encouraged to participate in your research and help you to establish a more personal connection. At the same time, entering a community with the status of "friend" can also carry with it certain obligations. As Schilling-Estes (2007: 180) notes, "if one capitalizes on one's friendships, it is typically expected to give something back in return." Being known in a community as a friend can also make it somewhat awkward to begin data collection in earnest, especially if you are not immediately forthright about your reasons for being there (more on this last issue below).

Another way of avoiding entering a community as a complete stranger is to make use of a *broker* (Schilling-Estes 2007), or a recognized and semi-official gatekeeper of a group. Brokers include people like local teachers, government or religious officials, or even former researchers who have worked with the community in question. These people normally have a certain degree of authority in a community, and are thus able to encourage community members to participate. In certain cases, working with a broker may be required because of the structure of a given community (it may be a closed community that is suspicious of outsiders) or because of certain ethical regulations that are in place (working in schools or with minors normally requires the use of brokers, as does working with certain sensitive populations that have been subject to ethical abuses in the past; see Chapter 2). The benefits of working with a broker are largely the same as for the friend-of-a-friend method, though it is important to realize that the aura of officialdom that comes with brokers may impact upon the relationships you establish with community members. Because brokers carry a certain amount of power and authority within the community, researchers who are introduced by brokers can also be perceived as being in positions of power, which can in turn affect your ability to establish personal connections with informants. Finally, as guardians of their community's image, brokers often want to portray their community in the best possible light. This may mean that they will only introduce you to some community members and not to others. As a researcher working with a broker, it is therefore important not to let your fieldwork be governed by a broker's idea about the community (while remaining grateful of the access you have been granted and respecting your broker's wishes).

In certain cases, gaining entry to a community is not an issue because you are studying a group of which you are already a member. In these instances, you will normally already have a personal relationship with community members and require no additional introductions. The difficulty in this type of research, however, is making the transition from "regular community member" to "researcher" as smooth as possible. This involves careful consideration of how you plan on establishing an adequate analytical distance from the community, and how you intend to explain to other members the new identity of "participant observer" you will be assuming. We discuss the issue of explaining your project to community members below.

Finally, you may find that you have no choice but to enter a community as a stranger. You could, for example, have no acquaintances who are themselves community members and know of no official gatekeepers (or wish to avoid gatekeepers) to the community you want to study. This is perhaps the most difficult way to gain access to a community, but it is sometimes necessary. If you are in this situation, the best way to proceed is to somehow make a "friend" within the community, who will then be able to introduce you to other community members. In other words, create a "friend-of-a-friend" situation from scratch. You can do this by trying to attend any organized meetings or activities the community may have (if they are open to the public) or simply to frequent places where you know that community members will be, in the hope of striking up a conversation with one of them. In his work on the *'yan daudu* in Nigeria, for example, Gaudio (2009) describes how he began to attend various public *'yan daudu* events on his own. After having seen him at a number of such events, some community members came over and began to chat with him, which eventually led to Gaudio gaining access to the group. You can also try adopting a particular role within the community that will grant you access to community members. Mendoza-Denton (2008), for example, worked as a teaching assistant in a Northern California high school in order to gain access to the Latina gang girls she eventually studied. Similarly, Josey (2004) worked as a babysitter in Martha's Vineyard so as to gain access to families in the local community. An advantage of this kind of approach – essentially creating a position for yourself within the community – is that you can potentially have multiple access points to different parts of the community in question.

No matter which of the mechanisms for gaining access you use, it is always important in ethnographic research to think about your eventual positioning within a community. As mentioned above, different access techniques have different implications for how researchers may be viewed in the community being studied and, relatedly, for the kind of data and participants you are going to get. The important thing is to be aware of these issues, and to try to mitigate any concerns that your positioning may create. Sometimes there is very little that you are able to do. Informants may react to things about you that you have no control over (your ethnic identity, for instance, or your sex). The effects of these reactions can be both positive and negative. Kulick (1998), for example, discusses how when he first began studying transgendered prostitutes, or *travesti*, in Brazil, the fact that he is not himself Brazilian made it much easier for his *travesti* informants to feel comfortable with him, since they assumed that he was not aware of the negative stereotypes regarding *travesti* that circulate in Brazilian society. In other cases, it may be to your advantage to cultivate a certain amount of distance between yourself and your informants, even if your informants do not perceive there to be one at the start. In my own work in Israel (Levon 2010), I found that strategically insisting on my "American-ness" was at times very helpful and allowed me to gain access to a wider variety of informants (including lesbians, Palestinians, and gay Orthodox Jews) than would have been possible otherwise. Both because my name is recognizably Israeli and because I was able to interact with all of my informants in Hebrew, I was initially "read" by many of my future informants as an Israeli gay man, with all of the ideological baggage that such a perception implied. Gaining access to a diverse population therefore required me to try to downplay my "Israeliness" to certain informants, and I did so by presenting myself as an American academic. The point is that the issue of finding the right balance between insider and outsider status is ever present in ethnographic research, and sometimes the factors that determine whether you are viewed as an insider or an outsider may be beyond your control.

One of the key ways in which you can attempt to manage your informants' perceptions of you is in how you introduce and explain your project (and your presence in the community) in the first place. Again, the kind of access mechanism you employ could have consequences for how you end up explaining your work. Brokers, for example, tend to want a more formal explanation of your project, complete with verification of your institutional backing. Research in your own community, in contrast, often entails a more informal and prolonged process of explanation until your informants actually understand that your position within the group has shifted from simply being a member to also being an analyst (though even here unobtrusive reference to institutional backing – on an information sheet or a consent form, for example – can also be useful at times). In all cases, the thing to remember is that people are not normally used to being observed in their everyday interactions, and this may make some people uncomfortable. For example, I had certain informants who, particularly at the beginning of my fieldwork, told me that they felt like rats in a maze with someone (i.e., me) watching their every move. How you mitigate these kinds of concerns will depend very much on the kind of relationship you have with your informants and how comfortable you feel talking to them about the details of your project. On the whole, informants are normally much more willing to accept a situation, even a somewhat uncomfortable one, if they know what they are getting themselves into, and can at times react very negatively if they are only later made aware of what your research is actually about. Obviously, it is important to balance the needs of your project with your responsibility to your informants (see Chapter 2), but a researcher should never forget that ultimately it is the informants who are being generous with their time and granting you privileged access to their lives. It is a researcher's obligation to respect this.

A key point in all of the preceding discussion is that your own self-awareness as an ethnographer in a community cannot be emphasized enough. Any ethnography is always the product of that particular researcher. It is precisely because you are who you are that you are interested in what you are interested in. This means that the things that you will notice over the course of your ethnography are also a product of who you are, how you have been trained and how you relate to the community you are studying. Your job as an ethnographic researcher is to articulate precisely how you and your positioning affect the environment you are studying. To borrow Duranti's (1997) terminology, your task is to integrate three voices in your analysis – your voice as a researcher, the voice of the community you are studying, and the voice of your disciplinary tradition. While this often means that ethnography can be difficult, slow, and personally disorienting, it is precisely this messiness that allows you to develop a nuanced understanding of your community.

4   Data collection

There are a variety of ways of collecting linguistic and social information once you have gained access to a community. In ethnography, these include:

- participant observation
- ethnographic interviews
- self-recordings
- collection of community artifacts.

This section discusses each of these data collection methods in turn, focusing primarily on those that are not discussed elsewhere in this volume.

4.1   Participant observation

Participant observation is the primary data collection method of ethnographic research, and serves to distinguish it from other kinds of interaction-based linguistic field methods. In participant observation, your goal is to become both an active member of the goings-on of a community and to observe those activities as they unfold. It is by achieving this dual status of active member and external observer that ethnography is able to achieve the kinds of analytical insights into the workings of a community that are described at the beginning of this chapter.

In practical terms, this means that as a researcher you need to participate in as many of the group's activities as you can. What activities there are will depend largely on the unique properties of the group you are studying, but could include a mixture of both more "formal" events (e.g., meetings, parties, lectures, work activities) and more informal encounters (e.g., lunch breaks, coffee among friends, bumping into people on the street). In all types of group activities, you want to focus on a set list of properties or characteristics that will inform your future analyses of the community. According to Richards (2003), ethnographic observation of social interactions should focus on the following areas:

- the physical settings of events
- the systems and procedures that are followed at these events
- the people who take part in the events
- the practices (including language) that are observed at these events.

As in all kinds of research, your goal in paying attention to these components of interaction is to identify systematic patterns of behavior that are socially meaningful within the community. Eckert (1989), for example, details how the salient divisions among social groupings in the high school she studied were evident in the places students chose to eat their lunch. In other words, the physical setting of eating lunch was not without social meaning, and helped to structure the other social practices in which her informants engaged. In participant observation, it is important to be sensitive to details such as these, and to cast your analytical gaze as widely as possible, since you never know what may end up being meaningful.

Geertz (1973) describes the process of ethnography as "thick description," or a description that is sensitive to the potentially meaningful nature of different activities and events. Geertz's classic example, which he borrows from Ryle (1971), is of two boys rapidly contracting the eyelids of their right eyes. For one of these boys, the movement is an involuntary twitch. For the other boy, however, the movement is a wink, an action that carries social meaning. According to Geertz, the goal of ethnography is to distinguish between the twitches and the winks, and to come to understand the social function of the winking. Doing this, however, can be very challenging. Agar (1996) suggests that a good place to start is by staying alert to what he calls "rich points," or the gaps in understanding that inevitably occur when you observe a community other than your own. For Agar, unexpected events – events that you do not understand and that may even conflict with your own assumptions about the world – are the primary unit of data for ethnographic analysis, since they force you to step outside of your own worldview and try to understand the perspective of others. In other words, an ethnographer's job after encountering a rich point is to develop an understanding of the system of beliefs within which the rich point makes sense. This will then help you to distinguish between events that are socially meaningful and those that are not.

4.2   Field notes

Because ethnography is essentially a process of stepping outside of your own perspective and coming to understand the perspective of others, it is a highly reflexive practice. In other words, ethnography requires you to be thinking constantly about your own awareness of events and activities in the field as you progress from confusion to understanding. Keeping detailed *field notes* is the principal method used by ethnographers to document this voyage. Part personal diary, part record of rich points encountered in the field, your field notes are the place for you to reflect on the process of conducting your research and to record your misapprehensions, your feelings of vulnerability, and your moments of insight and breakthrough. In addition to the various data points you collect, your own personal story of your ethnography as chronicled in your field notes will comprise a major part of the ethnographic analysis you eventually write. For this reason, it is important to develop the habit of writing field notes on a very regular basis (i.e., at least daily) throughout your time in the field. Even if you have nothing concrete to report, the act of writing about your ongoing experiences will force you to reflect on the process of your research and to question ideas, beliefs, and interpretations that you might otherwise take for granted.

In addition, field notes serve a very practical purpose of providing you with a single space for recording all of your impressions and observations. Since you will also be participating in community events, it may not always be possible to take notes during interactions. You should then jot down your memories as soon as possible afterwards, since details tend to be the first thing we forget. In order to help you make sure that you have captured all of the potentially relevant pieces of information, it is a good idea to structure your notes according to a template that you use (with minor modifications) for all events you observe (that will also aid in the analysis of your observations further down the line). Sakel and Everett (2012: 102) provide a list of "meta-data" that should be collected for language elicitation projects, which I have adapted here to suit ethnographic studies:

- type of event observed (formal/informal, meeting/conversation, etc.)
- file names/numbers of any recordings of the event (see discussion of recording below)
- date and time of the event (both in absolute terms, e.g., July 18, and also in relative ones, e.g., in the afternoon immediately following a group meeting)
- community members involved in the event and their degree of participation in the event (e.g., Mary and Jane having a conversation, with Jack sitting nearby and eavesdropping)
- location of the event, including a physical description of the built environment
- languages used (if you are studying a multilingual community)

- notable linguistic characteristics of the event (e.g., topics, perceived use of particular linguistic forms)
- notable social characteristics of the event (e.g., clothing, behavior, emotional responses).

Keeping track of a set list of characteristics like this will help you to compare and cross-reference your observations in the future. In order to do so, you also need to make sure that you write your notes as clearly and transparently as possible, to ensure that you can access the relevant information in the future (while you may know who "Mr. A" is at the time of observation, for example, you may have completely forgotten by the time you get around to doing your analysis). Also, be sure to create back-ups of all your notes (e.g., handwritten notes and electronic files) that you save in multiple locations.

4.3   Making recordings

Because of the difficulties of noticing everything while also parti-cipating, it is often a good idea to record interactions (in audio and, if possible, video formats) where you can. If you plan on analyzing patterns of language use in interaction, recording becomes essential. Recording unstructured inter-actions is somewhat different than recording more structured tasks (such as interviews). To begin, while informants will generally accept the idea that events like interviews are normally recorded, they may show a bit more reticence in having their daily (and seemingly uneventful) interactions recorded. If this is the case, you need to be able to calm your informants' concerns and ensure that interactions take place with as little disturbance as possible. A good tactic is to tell your informants that the recordings are really for you, to help you remember what occurs. You can also try to get blanket consent for recordings at the start of your fieldwork (i.e., that your informants agree to be recorded whenever you are present) and that way you do not need to indicate that you have begun recording each time you do. It is nevertheless crucial that your informants are aware that any recordings you make could end up being used as part of your data for analysis, and that they have consented to this beforehand (see Chapter 2).

As in sociolinguistic interviews (see Chapter 6; Labov 1984), when recording interactions you should try to minimize any overt observer effects. You do this by trying to make the recording equipment as inconspicuous as possible and ensuring that the act of recording impedes the progression of whatever event or activity you are observing as little as possible. These two concerns (inconspicuousness and versatility) will inform the kinds of recording equipment you use (and hence the types of recording you ultimately make). Before turning to some detailed consid-erations of things to think about when planning recordings, it is important to note that recording equipment will normally comprise a substantial part of your research budget. While it is of course possible to record both audio and video on a variety of widely available consumer electronics (e.g., mobile phones, Dictaphones), in some cases recordings made with this type of equipment may not be of a sufficiently high quality for linguistic analysis. It is always a good idea to use state-of-the-art commercial-grade equipment when conducting academic research, if at all possible.

When thinking about audio equipment (see also Chapters 4 and 9), you probably want to use a device that is small and relatively portable. This will allow you to move the equipment out of open view, which may help to alleviate unwanted observer effects.

If it is possible, video-recording is also an excellent idea in ethnographic fieldwork. In addition to the information you can capture in audio, video recordings of interaction provide you with a rich record of the myriad social practices your informants are engaged in and can provide insight into the ways in which attitudes and social ideologies can become physically embodied (Grimshaw 1982; Bourdieu 1991). Moreover, video is often instrumental in helping you to determine who precisely is speaking (and to whom), and can provide valuable clues as to the intended and perceived meanings of particular statements or actions (by giving you information about people's facial expressions when speaking, for example). Finally, video also provides you with an array of non-linguistic information (including things like gaze, bodily disposition, and gesture) that can be very useful to your research (Goodwin 2007). Goodwin (2000), for example, analyzes a dispute between two young girls, Carla and Diana, during a game of hopscotch. Carla accuses Diana of cheating in the game, and uses a range of semiotic tools to express her displeasure. In addition to certain conventionalized linguistic forms (including a lexico-syntactic frame and a particular prosodic contour), Carla also makes uses of certain hand gestures and a specific bodily disposition. More than simply reinforcing the semiotic message carried in language, Goodwin argues that these gestural and bodily practices serve as a tool for engaging Diana's attention and ensuring that Carla's objection cannot be overlooked. For Goodwin, an analysis of this interaction that only considered the linguistic channel would be incomplete, since crucial social action is also being performed via what he calls "embodied stances."

Video recording has many of the same technical requirements as successful audio recording does. You should ensure that any recording equipment is as inconspicuous and/or unobtrusive as possible, and it should be portable enough for you as the researcher to transport on your own. As with audio recordings, you should also plan to use external microphones when recording video, as the microphones built into most video equipment are not suitable for linguistic analysis. Unlike audio, in video you have additional factors to take into account. One of these is where the video camera will be positioned, and thus who will be in the camera's field of vision. It is normally considered best practice to have the camera on a tripod to reduce unnecessary movement in the image, so you have to decide whether you want the camera to capture the entire scene of whatever action you are observing, or some more limited frame (you can also consider using multiple cameras to capture different angles). There are both strengths and weaknesses to both of these options, and this topic is discussed in great detail in the literature on visual anthropology (e.g., Pink 2007). It would be a good idea to familiarize yourself with the issues discussed there if you plan on doing video recordings for your project. You may also need to acquire and familiarize yourself with basic video-editing software in order to make the most of the material you collect.

Another thing to consider when making video recordings is the issue of confidentiality of your informants. While it is fairly easy to guarantee confidentiality when you are recording audio only, recording images of people raises a host of additional ethical concerns (this is by virtue of the fact that it may be easier to identify someone from a video image than from an audio recording). While a full discussion of the ethics of video recording is beyond the scope of this chapter (though see Chapter 2), the same basic principles of ethical research apply. Most importantly, you must ensure that your informants are aware of the risks of video recording and that they provide informed consent to being recorded in this way. As a way of managing confidentiality issues, it may be appropriate to offer your informants the option of providing staged consent whereby they consent to certain activities (e.g., audio recordings), but not others (video recordings), or even consent to being audio- and video-recorded, but not to having those recordings played in public (e.g., at conferences).

For both audio and video recordings, it is imperative that you label all of your recordings immediately after making them. It is also a good idea to cross-reference the file names of recordings in your field notes, and to make multiple copies of recordings that you store in different locations (e.g., laptops, external drives, portable media). Finally, be sure to organize your recordings in such a way that you will be able to access your raw data easily in the future.

A final point in relation to participant observation more generally is the amount of data you can expect to collect. There are two things that can help in this regard. The first, already mentioned above, is to structure the empirical materials you collect in a simple and transparent way. This includes keeping detailed lists of your informants (complete with all relevant social information), as well as continually annotating and cross-referencing field notes and transcribing recordings. There are a number of software packages available to help you to do all this. The second way in which you can try to reduce the information overload of ethnography is to begin analyzing your findings along the way. Unlike some other data collection methods, ethnography is an explicitly reflective endeavor and researchers are encouraged to think about the implications of the data they are gathering throughout their time in the field. Doing so will help you to identify the direction that your research is taking, and allow you to focus more closely on a subset of the data you collect. At the same time, it is crucial not to narrow your analytical focus too early and to remain alert to "rich points" (see Section 2; Agar 1996), where your assumptions about the community, its language, or its speakers may be shown to be under-informed.

4.4   Ethnographic interviews

Interviews done as part of an ethnography are similar in format to semi-structured sociolinguistic interviews, though they often do not have the requirement of strict comparability and elicitation of a style range (see Chapter 6). The only issue I would like to highlight here is deciding when during your field research to hold interviews. It is normally not common practice to conduct interviews right away, since you will presumably not have had enough time to acquire sufficient information about the community, nor will you yet have established a personal rapport with your informants. At the same time, holding interviews after having spent a great deal of time in the field can be somewhat awkward, and could mean that you have to adapt any standardized interview schedule you may have developed beforehand to suit the level of intimacy you will have developed with the interviewee (this awkwardness is similar to the one experienced if you try to conduct a formal interview with your best friend, for example). One way around this issue of how to time interviews is to commit from the start to holding multiple interviews with the same informants throughout your time in the field. Doing so would allow you to collect a large and diverse body of both social and linguistic information, and may help to establish the interview setting as one of the "genres" in which you interact with your informants. Of course, your ability to conduct multiple interviews may be constrained by the amount of time you have and your progress in other types of data collection. Nevertheless, the question of when to conduct an interview is always a pertinent one.

4.5   Self-recordings

In addition to recordings and observations when you as the researcher are present, the use of *self-recordings* (or "non-participant observation") is becoming more and more common in sociolinguistic ethnography. Self-recordings allow you to obtain data from a wider variety of social contexts than is normally possible, and have the added benefit of engaging your informants more concretely in the research process (by self-recording, informants in a certain sense become research assistants, which can provide them with an empowering sense of ownership of the project). At the same time, using self-recordings can also mean that you may not be able to understand the dynamics of a particular interaction as well as you would have if you had been present. There is a trade-off, then, in using self-recordings, between obtaining a broader and more diverse sample of speech contexts and the potential loss of insider knowledge that such diversity can imply.

The mechanics of self-recordings are fairly straightforward, and normally just involve providing (some subset of) informants with recorders and microphones and asking them to record a certain number of interactions, potentially in certain specified contexts. What is difficult about using self-recordings is that you as the researcher relinquish control over this portion of your data collection. For this reason, it may be helpful to provide informants with detailed instructions about what to do and when to do it. These instructions could include such seemingly obvious details as "make sure the recorder is turned on" and "plug the microphone in." It could also be a good idea to be as specific as possible about what information you would like to obtain. If you are interested, for example, in determining how a particular informant speaks while at work, while at home with her partner, and while out with friends in a bar, you could ask that informant to try and make recordings in those specific locations. The point is that your informant cannot read your mind and will never be as invested in the details of your project as you are. While it may be possible to provide your informants with nothing more than a general request to record themselves in as many different contexts as possible, in doing so you may not get the results that you need. In some situations, you may need to reveal more detail regarding your research interests than is usually shared, in order to clearly guide your collaborating informant. Fieldworkers in sociolinguistics tend not to specify the detailed linguistic focus of their studies to participants, as this can introduce unwanted distortions in the form of hypercorrection or hypocorrection. Fortunately, the use of self-recording with semi-informed collaborators does not necessarily lead to significant performative shifts, possibly because the exigencies of the actual interaction tend to dominate (e.g. Sharma 2011). In addition, you should always agree on a time period in which self-recordings will be completed (with the knowledge that informants may not necessarily stick to your agreement). Finally, while it is important to trust that your informants will take good care of your equipment, you should be prepared for any eventuality, including possible damage and/or loss of the equipment you loan out.

4.6   Community artifacts

The final type of data usually collected in ethnography is a record of any artifacts of the community's cultural life that you encounter. By artifacts, I mean the physical materials, images, broadcasts, and other media products that are relevant to your informants' lives. Which community artifacts surface as important will become clear over the course of your ethnography, but could include things like the films and other media that your informants like to watch, the music that they listen to and the websites they frequent. It could also include the cars they drive and the food they eat. Finally, it is also a good idea to collect any news broadcasts or other popular stories that may mention the community, as a way of developing a better understanding of the broader context in which the community is situated. These artifacts, very much like the remnants of ancient civilizations we find in museums today, will help you to paint a broader picture of the social life of the community you study, including the ideologies about that community that circulate, and could help support your interpretations of observed linguistic practice in the future.

4.7   Leaving the field

A common question in ethnography is how to know when you are ready to stop observing your community – that is, when you have enough data to be able to conduct your analysis. While it is difficult to provide precise guidelines for this (and while there may also be practical constraints that come into play), many ethnographic researchers talk about what gets called a "saturation point," or the point at which you no longer seem to be collecting any new information. Anthropologist Don Kulick once described this to me as "knowing what your informants will say before you ask them the question." While I was at first skeptical that I would ever reach such a moment in my own research, it did eventually come, and it was at that moment that I knew I was ready to leave the field. That said, it is important to remember that leaving the field does not mean that your ethnography is complete; your interpretations of what you observed will continue to change and develop over time.

5   Follow-up and writing

Although the write-up of an ethnography is an individual process that goes beyond the scope of this chapter, two points related to the analysis and presentation of ethnographic data are worth mentioning.

The first has to do with how to go about organizing and processing your data. I mentioned in Section 4.3 that it might be helpful to use qualitative data analysis software to help you to structure and organize your data. Whether you use software to help you or not, the first step in preparing for analysis is always to read through all of your data carefully and repeatedly. During this initial reading phase, it may be a good idea to write yourself analytical memos (Hesse-Biber and Leavy 2006), or sketches of the potentially meaningful patterns that you think are emerging. After familiarizing yourself with your data in this way, you should then proceed to code it. The process of coding ethnographic data is very similar to the one used for coding quantitative data (which you may also do), and essentially entails assigning "codes" or categories to small chunks of your data (e.g., portions of transcripts, discourse events) to allow for future comparison. Throughout this reviewing and coding process, you may find it helpful to work with one or more consultants from within the community. This can be done more formally, such as in playback sessions (e.g., Rampton 1995) or by hiring a consultant, or it can be done through more informal follow-up with community members. In both cases, continued contact with community members means that you have people with intimate knowledge of your research context that you can bounce your ideas and interpretations off of. For researchers working in languages other than their own or in multilingual environments, native consultants are often an invaluable analytic resource.

The second point relates to writing up the findings of an ethnography. Unlike many other forms of social science inquiry, ethnographic analyses are often presented as a kind of narrative of the people and experiences you encountered. The goal of this narrative is to tell the story of the community in question, and to describe your observations and interpretations in such a way that a reader comes to understand the inner workings of a potentially unfamiliar culture or community. Certain techniques, such as producing vignettes of important events or portraits of emblematic people, are commonly used to give life to ethnographic descriptions, and to provide the necessary empirical support for analytical claims. What this means is that during the analysis process, you should be thinking about how you ultimately plan to present your findings and ensure that you have the materials necessary (e.g., the right quotations, the good anecdotes) to do so.

6 Conclusion

Through this chapter, I have attempted to provide a brief overview of the basic precepts and methods of ethnographic research. While ethnography may not be appropriate for all linguistics projects, the principles which underlie ethnographic approaches, including a sustained respect for research participants and a detailed attention to the social context of speech, ultimately apply to all forms of linguistics field research.

References

Agar, M. 1996. *The Professional Stranger: An Informal Introduction to Ethnography.* New York: Academic Press.

Agha, A. 2005. Voice, footing, enregisterment. *Journal of Linguistic Anthropology* 15: 38–59.

Blommaert, J. and D. Jie. 2010. *Ethnographic Fieldwork: A Beginner's Guide.* Clevedon: Multilingual Matters.

Boas, F. 1917. Introduction. *International Journal of American Linguistics* 1: 1–18.

Bourdieu, P. 1991. *Language and Symbolic Power.* Cambridge, MA: Harvard University Press.

Duranti, A. 1997. *Linguistic Anthropology.* Cambridge University Press.

Eckert, P. 1989. *Jocks and Burnouts: Social Categories and Identity in the High School.* New York: Teachers College Press.

Eckert, P. and S. McConnell-Ginet. 1992. Think practically and look locally: language and gender as community-based practice. *Annual Review of Anthropology* 21: 461–90.

Everett, D. 1985. Syllable weight, sloppy phonemes and channels in Pirahã discourse. *Proceedings of the Berkeley Linguistics Society* 11: 408–16.

    2005. Cultural constraints on grammar and cognition in Pirahã. *Current Anthropology* 46: 621–46.

Gaudio, R. 2009. *Allah Made Us: Sexual Outlaws in an Islamic African City.* Oxford: Blackwell.

Geertz, C. 1973. Thick description: toward an interpretive theory of culture. In *The Interpretation of Cultures: Selected Essays*. New York: Basic Books, 3–30.

    1983. *Local Knowledge: Further Essays in Interpretive Anthropology*. New York: Basic Books.

Goffman, E. 1974. *Frame Analysis: An Essay on the Organization of Experience*. Cambridge, MA: Harvard University Press.

Goodwin, C. 2000. Action and embodiment within situated human interaction. *Journal of Pragmatics* 32: 1489–522.

    2007. Participation, stance and affect in the organization of activities. *Discourse & Society* 18: 53–73.

Grimshaw, A. 1982. Sound-image data records for research on social interaction: some questions and answers. *Sociological Methods and Research* 11: 121–44.

Hesse-Biber, S. and P. Leavy. 2006. *The Practice of Qualitative Research*. London: Sage Publications.

Hymes, D. 1974. *Foundations in Sociolinguistics: An Ethnographic Approach*. Philadelphia: University of Pennsylvania Press.

Josey, M. 2004. A sociolinguistic study of phonetic variation and change on the island of Martha's Vineyard. Unpublished Ph.D. dissertation, Stanford University.

Kulick, D. 1998. *Travesti: Sex, Gender and Culture Among Brazilian Transgendered Prostitutes*. University of Chicago Press.

Kulick, D. and M. Wilson, eds. 1995. *Taboo: Sex, Identity and Erotic Subjectivity in Anthropological Fieldwork*. London: Routledge.

Labov, W. 1963. The social motivation of a sound change. *Word* 19: 273–309.

    1984. Field methods on the project of linguistic variation and change. In J. Baugh and J. Scherzer, eds. *Language in Use: Readings in Sociolinguistics*. Englewood Cliffs, NJ: Prentice Hall, 28–53.

Levon, E. 2010. *Language and the Politics of Sexuality: Lesbians and Gays in Israel*. Basingstoke: Palgrave Macmillan.

    2012. The voice of others: identity, alterity and gender normativity among gay men in Israel. *Language in Society* 41: 187–211.

Malinowski, B. 1922. *Argonauts of the Western Pacific*. London: Routledge and Kegan Paul.

Mendoza-Denton, N. 2008. *Homegirls: Language and Cultural Practice Among Latina Youth Gangs*. Oxford: Blackwell.

Milroy, L. and M. Gordon. 2003. *Sociolinguistics: Method and Interpretation*. Oxford: Blackwell.

Murphy, E. and R. Dingwall. 2001. The ethics of ethnography. In P. Atkinson, A. Coffey, S. Delamont, J. Lofland, and L. Lofland, eds. *The Handbook of Ethnography*. London: Sage Publications, 239–51.

Newman, P. and M. Ratliff, eds. 2001. *Linguistic Fieldwork*. Cambridge University Press.

Pike, K. 1967. *Language in Relation to a Unified Theory of Structure of Human Behaviour*. The Hague: Mouton.

Pink, S. 2007. *Doing Visual Anthropology*. London: Sage Publications.

Podesva, R. 2007. Phonation type as a stylistic variable: the use of falsetto in constructing a persona. *Journal of Sociolinguistics* 11: 478–504.

Rampton, B. 1995. *Crossing: Language and Ethnicity Among Adolescents*. London: Longman.

Richards, K. 2003. *Qualitative Inquiry in TESOL*. Basingstoke: Palgrave Macmillan.

Ryle, G. 1971. *Collected Papers. Volume II: Collected Essays, 1929–1968*, 2 vols. London: Hutchinson.

Sakel, J. and D. Everett. 2012. *Linguistic Fieldwork*. Cambridge University Press.

Schilling-Estes, N. 2007. Sociolinguistic fieldwork. In R. Bayley and C. Lucas, eds. *Sociolinguistic Variation*. Cambridge University Press, 165–89.

Sharma, D. 2011. Style repertoire and social change in British Asian English. *Journal of Sociolinguistics* 15.4: 464–92.

Vaux, B. and J. Cooper. 1999. *Introduction to Linguistic Field Methods*. Munich: Lincom Europa.

11   Using historical texts

Ans van Kemenade and Bettelou Los

1   Introduction

> The fact is, Phaedrus, that writing involves a similar disadvantage to painting. The productions of painting look like living beings, but if you ask them a question, they maintain a solemn silence.   Plato 1975: 96

This chapter is on how we can bring the evidence from textual data to bear on linguistic analysis, primarily in historical linguistics. Linguistic analysis comes in many varieties, however, and before we discuss the value of textual data, we should briefly consider what the object of study of linguistics is. Much depends here on theoretical perspective: to mention some examples, linguists concerned primarily with language use may be interested in spoken language use, variation in register, interactive modes, language use as a marker of social status, including prestige-driven norms, and so on. Linguists working from a formal perspective will be interested in speakers' language competence – the internalized grammar that is assumed to be the core of a speaker's knowledge of language.

These various types of linguists have very different objects of study, but with respect to the use of textual data, they have an important thing in common: written language is a derivative, situated at some remove from the chosen object of linguistic investigation. This position has long been recognized: Delbrück states in his *Introduction to the Study of Language*, a Neogrammarian "manifesto," that "The guiding principles for linguistic research should accordingly be deduced not from obsolete written languages of antiquity, but chiefly from the living popular dialects of the present day" (Delbrück 1882: 61). De Saussure, too, notes that "writing is foreign to the internal system of the language. Writing obscures our view of the language, writing is not a garment, but a disguise" (de Saussure 1983: 24). Linguistic research, however, often has to rely on written texts; the linguist interested in the syntax or lexicon in language use, unlike phonology, for instance, requires a very large database in order to ensure that there is a reasonable chance that it contains a more or less full range of constructions or lexical items, and the collection (recording and transcription) of spontaneous speech is more costly than the collection of written texts. Another motivation for studying written texts is to study the effect of written conventions on the spoken language: in languages that are highly standardized, the prescriptive norms of the standard language are likely to influence the spoken language use of speakers, either consciously or unconsciously. Linguists may, of course, also be interested in the language of texts in its own right, for the study of genres and writing conventions, for stylistic purposes, for the analysis of language ideologies (see Chapter 21), or for the study of narrative and other literary techniques (see Traugott and Pratt 1980).

This chapter is aimed at readers who plan to use texts for the purpose of linguistic analysis. Many of the methodological points made in this chapter are likely to be equally valid for other types of textual research, as these must base themselves on an interpretation of the language evidence as well. The chapter will focus on the use of textual data in historical linguistics, a field that cannot employ data collection methods typically used with native speakers, such as introspection (Chapter 3), elicitation (Chapter 4), questionnaires (see Chapter 6), or experiments (Chapter 7). While for the study of present-day language use, linguists have access to sources for spoken and written language use, historical linguistic research must by its very nature base itself on written texts. We will discuss some pitfalls and caveats that follow from this in Section 2. Section 3 will discuss the use of textual material for the sociolinguistic study of language change. Section 4 will focus on electronic text corpora, which has made data gathering much quicker, and allows us to resolve some of the pitfalls discussed in Sections 2 and 3.

Other caveats and pitfalls have to do with misinterpretations or misrepresentations of the data, particularly when investigators rely on databases that were created by others in order to answer a specific research question, which may mean that crucial context is missing. Most of these problems boil down to a failure to compare like with like: drawing conclusions from samples that not only differ in historical period but also in dialect, or in genre or register, or in data type. These caveats will be discussed in Section 5. There are ways of creatively making "the best use of bad data" (Labov 1994: 11); we will discuss some examples of circumventing data gaps in Section 6.

Throughout the chapter, our examples will be drawn primarily, though not exclusively, from historical English. They will, however, be framed in such a way as to bring out their general relevance.

2   Studying language change through written texts

Linguists using texts to study language structure must infer properties of historical stages of spoken language from written evidence. However, oral and written language can diverge in a number of ways. Authors of written texts, unlike speakers in natural conversational settings, cannot rely on immediate hearer feedback to repair hitches in communication, but have to anticipate such hitches by being more explicit and expressive than they would have been as speakers. When speakers become authors and hearers become readers, they cannot rely on cues from prosody and intonation, but have to find different ways of getting their message across. Written styles differ from oral styles accordingly, by their use of compensatory strategies to help the reader through the text. Such styles do not develop overnight, but require a literary culture, which in turn depends for its development on rates of literacy and the availability of texts. Studies of oral versus literate strategies suggest that in literate traditions "the meaning is in the text," in the actual written words, while in oral situations "the meaning is in the context" and in the implications of communicative acts (Fleischman 1990: 22, quoting Goody and Watt 1968; see also Olson 1977; Bauman 1986). Texts from earlier periods often reflect oral speech styles more closely: they use parataxis (strings of loosely connected main clauses) rather than hypotaxis (subclauses embedded in main clauses), and discourse particles whose functions are difficult to identify, repetitions, unexpected resumptive pronouns, left dislocations, and inconsistent use of tenses (Fleischman 1990: 23).

Literate traditions develop stylistic conventions in writing (Perret 1988). Other conventions develop as the result of explicitly formulated views. Lenker's (2010) study charts the development of new written styles once English, in the course of the late Middle English (ME) and Early Modern English (EModE) period, had re-established itself as a language that was also suited to more elevated modes of discourse. Writers expressed explicit views on style, leading to an emerging consensus over the EModE period about the conventions of various genres, and ideas about appropriate registers for certain discourse domains. Lenker also shows how these developments were reflected in syntactic change, with adverbial connectors and logical linkers shifting from clause-initial to clause-medial position (Lenker 2010: 233ff.).

One of the hallmarks of oral versus written styles is the way clauses are connected. The development of a written style tends to involve a tighter syntactic organization: instead of the loosely organized string of main clauses ("parataxis") characteristic of oral styles, written styles tend to have complex sentences, with embedding ("hypotaxis") of subclauses that function as subjects, objects, or adverbials of a higher clause.[1]

Example (1) shows a left-dislocation in present day English (PDE), a sentence beginning with an NP (*The people who earn millions and pay next to no tax*) that is connected to the following clause (*those are our targets*) by the demonstrative *those*, which refers back to the NP. This configuration is paratactically rather than hypotactically organized: the NP has no syntactic function in the actual clause.

(1)   The people who earn millions and pay next to no tax, those are our targets.

(Birner and Ward 2002: 1413)

Such paratactic constructions are very frequent in Old English (OE). An example is (2), where the clauses and phrases are connected by time adverbs (*Siððan* 'afterwards, then,' *þa* 'then'), in bold; note that the punctuation, which influences our interpretation of what is a subclause and what a main clause, may not reflect that of the manuscript and is very likely to have been added or interpreted by the editor:

---

[1] For the general problem of defining the subclause/main clause distinction on the basis of morpho-syntactic criteria that are cross-linguistically valid, see Cristofaro (2003).

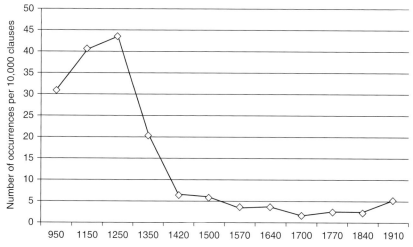

Figure 11.1. *Demonstrative elements in dislocates*
Los and Komen (2012)

(2) **Siððan** wæs Se III dæg faraones gebyrtyd;
     Then   was The third day Farao's birthday;
     þa   worhte he mycelne gebyrscipe his cnihtum;
     then   prepared he great feastACC his servantsDAT
     þa   amang þam **þa** geþohte he þara
     then   among those then remembered he theGEN
     byrla   ealdor;   & ðæra bæcestra.
     cup-bearersGEN head   and theGEN bakersGEN
     'Then on the third day it was Farao's birthday; he then had a great feast
     prepared for his servants; it was then, among his servants, that he
     remembered the head of the cup-bearers and the head of the bakers'
     <Gen (Ker) 44.10>[2]

Comparing the various stages of OE, ME, and EModE, the relative numbers of
such paratactic constructions can be seen to go down (Figure 11.1).

The question is whether such figures reflect genuine language change or whether
they are the result of the development of written conventions. They probably reflect
both. Written conventions tend to have tighter restrictions on what elements can be
elided, and on co-reference relations between elements, and tend to rely to a larger
extent on explicit syntactic constructions like clefts to meet information-structural
needs that may be met by prosodic means in oral styles (see Pérez-Guerra in press).
A comparison of oral and written PDE shows that left-dislocations are a feature of
spoken rather than written styles (Gregory and Michaelis 2001), and the fact that
such written conventions developed in the course of ME and EModE underlies
some of the decline in the graph. However, as the construction in (1) is now only

---

[2] The reference to an OE text enclosed in < > follows the system of short titles as employed in Healey
     and Venezky (1985 [1980]), in turn based on the system of Mitchell, Ball, and Cameron (1975,
     1979).

possible with subjects, marginally with objects, but not with adverbials such as *then* as in (2) or with adverbial clauses, we can assume that the decrease in numbers shown in Figure 11.1 also reflects language change.

It is not only emerging conventions for written styles that may obscure investigations into language change, but also the rise of pro- and prescriptivism as a consequence of higher levels of literacy and education. The eighteenth century was a time of increased social mobility in England: with education becoming more widely available, there was a growing need for normative grammars to help speakers acquire the socially prestigious variety. The existence of socially prestigious varieties has interesting consequences for language change, because speakers who are trying to acquire a language or lect after childhood find it harder to acquire its more subtle phonological, morphological, or syntactic aspects, and may hypercorrect, overshoot their mark. An example is the hypercorrect phrase *between you and I*, which is the side effect of speakers trying to avoid the non-prestigious *and me* as the second conjoin of a subject (*Peter and me went to the cinema*), or hypercorrect *whom* in *Whom shall I say is calling*? (Lasnik and Sobin 2000).

For the study of language change on the basis of historical texts, this means that investigators should be aware of the existence of *pro-* and *prescriptive norms*. If there are periods in which the relativizer *which* is felt to be more correct in formal written styles than *that*, or in which pied-piping (*the hotel in which I stayed*) is felt to be more correct than preposition stranding (*the hotel which I stayed in*), it is quite likely that a comparison of the various sub-periods in a diachronic corpus will show frequent preposition stranding in ME, more pied-piping in EModE, and, perhaps, an increase in stranding in PDE. Such fluctuations should be interpreted correctly – that is, not necessarily as linguistic change, but as the waxing and waning of the influence of a prescriptive rule. The rule against stranding is well known, as is the ban on split infinitives, double negation, *who* for *whom*, and so on, many of which can be identified in metalinguistic commentaries of the time. However, there are also rules that do not have such high profiles, and are not taught in school, so that the general public and linguists alike are not aware of their existence. Some Dutch publishing houses, for instance, stipulate that in sub-clauses, the so-called "red" order of past participle and perfect auxiliary (the Dutch parallel of English *has done*) is the only one allowed, not the "green" order (*done has*), because the latter is supposed to be a German word order. The results of any investigation based on texts that are affected by more subtle prescriptive pressures may easily lead to conclusions about language change that are not in fact correct. This is why diachronic investigations always need to pay attention to any variation or exceptional cases in the data that might turn out to be correlated with certain registers or genres – they might be a sign of pro- or prescription rather than a reliable guide to actual language change. We will come back to this in Section 3.

This emphasis on the differences between oral and written styles does not mean that data that show an apparent linguistic change rather than a genuine change are worthless: investigations into change in the spoken or the written language are equally of interest to various research agendas. The point is that data need to be interpreted correctly, and should be embedded in an informed scenario of change.

3   The use of texts for historical sociolinguistics

The previous section addressed the problem of inferring potential differences between written and spoken language on the basis of (historical) texts. Such problems are further compounded when analyzing the nature of language variation on the basis of historical texts, with the question of dialectal or sociolinguistic variation in mind. This type of research question requires a social analysis of any particular text: From what dialect area is the author of the text, or the characters featured in the text? How accurate are literary representations of dialect likely to be? What is the author's social status and education? What is the purpose of the text and what is its intended audience/readership? What is the genre and the register of the text within its particular historical context?[3]

The researcher needs to be able to compare texts from different regions, genres, and social backgrounds to arrive at a comprehensive picture of the nature of the variation in the corpus. For the problem of recognizing *dialect variation* in texts, we can appeal to a long-standing philological tradition of textual study, in which an inventory of the dialectal characteristics of particular texts has been a central concern. That it is possible to analyze sociolinguistic variation on the basis of texts was suggested early on by Romaine (1982), and there is now a considerable literature on historical sociolinguistics. (See, for example, Nevalainen and Raumolin-Brunberg [2003] for English; Ayres-Bennett [2004] for French; Vandenbussche [2007] for Flemish.) These works provide extensive methodological pointers for the sociolinguistic study of historical texts. One of the most important of these is to come to a *representative corpus* of text samples, with appropriate *metadata* representing the socially relevant characteristics of the texts. Nevalainen and Raumolin-Brunberg (2003) present many quantitative case studies on the basis of their *Corpus of Early English Correspondences*, tracking the social factors underlying language change in sixteenth- and seventeenth-century English. Ayres-Bennett (2004) focuses on a qualitative analysis of social distinctions in language use in seventeenth-century France, basing her observations on the relation between the representation of language in texts and a corpus of metalinguistic commentaries, including observations on the French language, dictionaries, grammars and commentaries, didactic works, treatises on pronunciation, orthography, and versification. Vandenbussche has compiled many studies on the characteristics of texts produced by lower-class writers in nineteenth-century Flanders (e.g., Vandenbussche 2007).

---

[3] The terms "genre" and "register" require some clarification here. In general, genre refers to text types such as fiction, essays, letters, drama. Register is generally reserved for the degree of formality of texts. The two are closely interwoven, of course.

Corpus-based research into *register variation* has provided ways in which written and spoken texts can be compared in linguistic terms across time (see, e.g., Biber and Finegan 1992, 1994). Biber and Finegan identify three dimensions of textual characteristics, correlating with the oral/literate character of texts: informational vs involved production, elaborated vs situation-dependent reference, and abstract vs non-abstract style, where in each case there is a scale from formal written (e.g., essays) to informal spoken text (e.g., dialogue in drama). These correlate with a range of linguistic features, allowing an index for each text. The reader may note that these can be matched with a social analysis of the texts involved. On this basis, it has been established in historical sociolinguistics research that, for instance, personal letters pattern more like conversation and drama than other written genres, such as fiction, essays, and medical and legal prose. Thus, comparing register/genre differences with what is known about such differences in synchronic states (i.e., in PDE) can be highly instructive, as they set a potential benchmark for differences between genres in historical texts (which of course cannot be taken as absolute; for instance, in English, personal letters as a genre have been treated as close to literary or public writing by some writers at some points in history, and as close to casual conversation by others at other times).These methods are also helpful for an analysis of texts for which the social analysis is absent. Warner (2006) is an example of this: to mine an existing database that was not structured according to genre variation, he uses the criteria of average word length and type-token ratio in order to arrive at a characterization of the stylistic level of sixteenth- and seventeenth-century texts that plausibly corresponds with the oral-literate contrast.

These new approaches to extrapolating historical social contexts can feed into other related areas of study. Establishing sociolinguistic subtleties in a historical corpus can feed back into more formal analysis by helping identify those genres and registers most likely to resemble spoken language. The analysis of text genre and register also draws on traditions in literary studies, and in turn provides a linguistically grounded methodological basis for them.

4   Electronic text corpora

It is probably not an exaggeration to say that the study of textual data was revolutionized in the computer age, as a result of massive *digitization* of written texts: even basic concordance software now allows the researcher to comprehensively search for particular lexical strings, including spelling variants, dialect features, lexical collocations, and with a direct link to the context in which they occur, in a size and type of corpus of the researcher's own choosing, as long as it is digitized text. This alone allows us to study data in a less error-prone way and with a comprehensiveness that was hitherto unimaginable. The previous section makes it clear that, in order to do quantitative sociolinguistic work in particular, a systematic corpus of texts is indispensable.

Many digitized corpora have been morphologically and syntactically *annotated*, allowing more focused explorations into the language of earlier historical stages, in tandem with advances in linguistic theory. Corpora that are syntactically parsed and cover various historical stages exist for English, Faroese, French, Icelandic, and Portuguese, with several more in the making for Dutch, German, and Chinese, among others. The availability of such large databases has inevitably changed working practices: the historical linguist no longer has to trawl laboriously through editions, making human errors along the way; the data that took months or even years to collect can now be called up in an afternoon, by the judicious use of search software and the formulation of search queries. The new method poses its own challenges: Are the queries correct? Do they find what they are supposed to find? If the query refers to morphological and/or syntactic tags, has the researcher made sure that those tags cover exactly what they intend to investigate? Researchers cannot rely on the bare numbers thrown up by the queries, but need to check the search files in order to make sure that no data are included that should be excluded, or excluded that should be included (see Chapter 13 for more detail on the use of corpora). Researchers need to be aware that electronic corpora are only as good as the texts on which they are based. Text corpora tend to be based on editions, but do not typically offer the benefit of the editor's footnotes or introduction, which may provide the facts of dating (important if an early manuscript is only available in late copies) and indicate where the text stops and the editor's interpretation takes over. Case-endings may have been tacitly expanded from flourishes and diacritics in the manuscripts; passages may have been expanded by fragments from other poems where the editor has added a beginning to the poem from some other source. Earlier (nineteenth- and early twentieth-century) editorial practices went so far as to deliberately "archaize" the text. Punctuation is usually inserted in editions to help the reader, but they may also wrong-foot the reader; see Mitchell (1980) for examples. (For a history of punctuation, see Parkes 1992.)

Researchers need to be aware of such limitations of electronic corpora. However, electronic corpora simultaneously offer many advances in text analysis. One such advantage is the ease of identifying statistical outliers. In Los' (1999) investigation into which verbs could take a *to*-infinitival complement in OE, the example in (3), one such statistical outlier, occurred: it was the only example in the data collection of Callaway (1913) of the verb *cunnian* 'try' being followed by a bare rather than a *to*-infinitival complement (*cunnian* and its bare-infinitival complement in bold):

(3)　　　uton **cunnian**,　gif we magon,　þone　reþan wiðersacan　on his geancyrre
　　　　　let-us try　　　if we may　　the　　cruel enemyACC　　on his return
　　　　　gegladian <ÆCHom I 30 450.18>
　　　　　appeaseINF
　　　　　'let us try, if we can, to appease the cruel enemy on his return'

Callaway followed the punctuation of the edition (Thorpe 1844–46), which, judging by the commas in (3), took *gif we magon* as a complete clause with "comment" status, an embedded interruption distinct from the syntax of the main clause. This interpretation would imply that the bare infinitive *gegladian* is the complement of *cunnian*. However, the original manuscript has no punctuation at all in this sentence (Clemoes 1955–6, cited in Healey and Venezky 1985). The availability of the electronic Toronto Corpus, not tagged or parsed, but containing almost all the surviving OE texts) made it easy to call up all instances of the verb *cunnian* to see whether they would shed light on the interpretation of (3). About 75 percent of all occurrences of *cunnian* in the Toronto Corpus are followed by an indirect question with *gif* 'if' or *hwæper* 'whether.' In the absence of any other attestations with a bare infinitival complement, (3) is in fact best interpreted as yet another such indirect question, with the reading 'let us try/test whether we can appease the cruel enemy on his return,' where *gegladian* is not in fact a complement of *cunnian*. The unexplained outlier in the *to*-infinitival data is thus accounted for with the help of new electronic corpus data.

An important side effect of the use of corpora is that standards set by peer review have become more demanding. As data gathering can now be done quickly, thanks to corpora and search software, the value of a paper is determined by the quality of the analysis and interpretation of the data rather than by presentation of the data alone. Peer reviewers usually have access to the same corpora, and are able to check the results claimed in a paper, again resulting in higher standards.

5   Caveats and pitfalls

One of the most important messages in studying language in texts, especially over time, is that we must establish standards of *comparability*. This caveat holds for genre and register, as discussed in Section 2, but it also applies to comparing texts of the same dialectal provenance, or to distinguishing between competence and performance data. We discuss some examples of this below.

5.1   Comparing like with like: dialect, register, genre

With respect to register and genre, the text material available for various historical stages is often quite diverse (including, e.g., for English, various kinds of poetry, legal documents, homilies, saints' lives, prescriptive grammars, inscriptions, translations from Latin) and it is difficult to find texts suitable for comparison across historical periods. For instance, OE texts are mostly formal, written in the OE literary language, and are influenced to varying degrees by Latin, directly in the case of glosses and translations, or indirectly as in homilies and saints' lives. In the case of poetry, they may also be influenced by the ancient habits and constraints of the Old Germanic alliterative four-stress line. The language adopted in these genres is different and sometimes hard to compare with that of the ME texts, which comprise, for instance, a rich array of colloquial poetry and other religious texts beside homilies. The dialect in which most OE texts are written, the West-Saxon *Schriftsprache* (Southern), is only sparsely represented in the extant texts of the early ME corpus, because few texts from the South in that period have survived. Most ME texts are from the Midlands or the North. There is therefore no dialect continuity, and any change we see in a comparison between Old and Middle English texts (e.g., any comparison of the last OE sub-period and the first ME sub-period) may not have been as drastic or as quick as the data suggest. The syntax of the southern dialects appears to be more conservative than that of the Midlands or the North, which means that the rate of loss of Object-Verb order, or the Particle-Verb order, tends to be assessed as fairly steep, suggesting that the change was quicker than was in fact the case. This problem is practically universal in historical linguistics: the balance of wealth and power in the Middle Ages tended to shift from region to region, so most texts were produced in region A in one period and in region B in the next. Furthermore, the survival of manuscripts is subject to the vagaries of history, rendering a degree of arbitrariness. The best a researcher can do is be explicit about data gaps or genre mismatches in their work.

5.2   Comparing like with like: competence and performance

Diachronic investigations have to work with what is known as *performance data*, actual written language use rather than *competence*, the native speaker's internalized grammatical system that allows him or her to construct sentences and judge them on their acceptability (see Chapter 3). The relation between performance (whether written or spoken) and competence has been the object of systematic study to some degree only in sociolinguistics, so we have to be very careful in drawing conclusions about the extent to which the historical texts reflect the grammars of the native speakers who produced them. The most obvious issue here is the question of *negative evidence*. If a construction is not attested in texts of an earlier period, does this mean it was structurally impossible? Again, the situation boils down to comparing like with like: if the relevant structures cannot be found in a synchronic (PDE) "performance" corpus either, even if PDE speakers have no problem constructing them by introspection, the chances are that we are not comparing like with like (i.e., we are comparing performance data from earlier periods to present-day competence data). We present some case studies as examples.

The OE text corpus is sufficiently large to allow at times categorical statements of the type *only NPs with accusative case can passivize* (see Russom 1982) or *"to" is part of the infinitival phrase and cannot be moved* (see Fischer 1996), especially if these phenomena are further confirmed by cross-linguistic evidence from related, living languages. The subsequent rise of passivization of dative NPs, or the splitting of *to*-infinitives, represent ME innovations and have come to be considered as evidence of language change. But unattested structures cannot always be taken as evidence of absence or of diachronic change. Mittwoch

(1990: 107–8) discusses the difficulties of assessing the status of negation in accusative-and-infinitive constructions – for instance, in examples from introspection such as the sentence in (4) (Mittwoch's example (33), slightly adapted):

(4)   John saw Mary/her not leave

Constructions such as (4) combine an object NP (*Mary/her*) and a bare infinitive (*leave*), and occur after verbs of perception (like *see*) and certain verbs of causation (like *let* or *make* in PDE). Mittwoch makes the point that negated accusative-and-infinitive constructions in PDE are at best "borderline, denizens of some limbo region between the grammatical and the deviant," and adds that, in 5 years of looking out for real-life utterances, she never encountered a single example, "not even one meant ironically" (Mittwoch 1990: 108). This illustrates the gap between performance data and those constructed by introspection. Both have their own valuable contribution to make: the corpus will yield information about usage that might not surface in the laboratory, whereas the laboratory will yield information about structure that might not surface in a corpus study (whether they complement each other completely is a different matter; the extra information produced by each probably does not fully compensate for the other's blind spot). A similar point could be made about the accusative-and-infinitive construction with *to*-infinitives after verbs of thinking and declaring, where scholars construct grammatical examples like *I believe them to have a dog* (e.g., Miller 2002: 149), but also need to account in some way for the fact that such sentences tend not to show up in performance corpora where the construction occurs overwhelmingly in the passive, and is restricted to quite formal registers (e.g., Mair 1990).

The nature of the surviving text material often makes it difficult to find data of the subtlety required for many kinds of analyses. For example, van Kemenade (1987) and Koopman (1990) show that we can get some interesting insights into OE word order if we analyze sequences of verbs in embedded clauses as verb clusters, essentially morphological units. Two examples are given in (5):

(5)   a. þæt hie   gemong   him   mid sibbe *sittan mosten* <Or 8.52.33>
              that they among themselves in   peace settle must
              'that they must settle in peace among themselves'

           b. ðæt he   Saul   ne *dorste ofslean*   <CP 28.199.2>
              that he   Saul   not dared   murder
              'that he didn't dare murder Saul'

This analysis is modeled on analyses for similar verbal clusters in modern German and Dutch, as exemplified in (6a) and (6b) respectively:

(6)   a. dass   der   Johann das   Büchlein   *haben*   *wollte*
              that   John   the   booklet   have   wanted

           b. dat   Jan   het   boekje   *wilde*   *hebben*
              that   John   the   booklet   wanted   have
              'that John wanted to have the booklet'

If such an analysis in terms of verb clusters is appropriate, we expect to find further parallelisms. For instance, German and Dutch have long verbal clusters, as in (9a) and (9b) respectively.

(9) a. weil er die Kinder *singen hören* *können* *hat*
     because he the children sing hear can has

    b. omdat hij de kinderen *heeft* *kunnen* *horen* *zingen*
     because he the children has can hear sing
    'because he could have heard the children sing'

Such long verb clusters do not appear in the OE texts. Their absence might reflect their ungrammaticality in OE, in parallel with German and Dutch. However, the absence may be due to rarity in the naturalistic use of this construction. Once again, the availability of corpora now makes it possible to check how frequent these clusters are in the written present-day languages. Coupé and van Kemenade (2009) show that they are generally absent in the full Old West Germanic and Gothic textual record, even though they develop in the Dutch language area from the thirteenth century onward, which would seem to indicate on comparative grounds that they do not form clusters in OE in the way that they do in present-day German or Dutch. But the simple fact is that we have no direct evidence as to the grammatical status of verb clusters in OE.

These and other cases show that we must always be aware of the strengths as well as the limitations of a corpus of performance data.

5.3 Using data from the secondary literature

When investigating any set of facts, it is useful and necessary to turn to handbooks and other existing literature first. There is a massive amount of literature based on a substantial body of text research, even predating the corpus revolution. One example of this is Visser's (1963–73) monumental *An Historical Syntax of the English Language*, which includes much of his database. This database needs to be mined with caution (see also Denison 1993: 5). For instance, Lieber (1979) and Lightfoot (1981) claim that OE has indirect passives on the basis of Visser's faulty examples (which crucially leave out dative case markers on the relevant NP, as pointed out by Russom 1982 and Mitchell 1979). Visser's strength lies particularly in the periods after OE; his OE examples are best checked separately, as they include evidence from interlinear glosses, which are completely unreliable as a guide to syntactic practice.

There are many excellent late nineteenth- and early twentieth-century studies about various syntactic phenomena which include the primary database. A problem that may arise here is that the database may have been set up originally to answer a particular research question, with unfortunate consequences if it is later used to answer different questions altogether. One database that has been extensively mined throughout the twentieth century is Callaway's *The Infinitive in Anglo-Saxon* (1913). Brinton (1988) consults it to find out whether the OE verb *onginnan* 'begin' is showing signs of grammaticalization, in view of the fact that its Middle English reflex *gan* has grammaticalized into an auxiliary, its meaning bleached from 'begin' to something akin to the meaning of the PDE auxiliary *do*.

(7)   Witodlice...ongann se hiredes   ealdor to agyldenne þonc pcning
        truly began the   householdGEN elder to pay   the penny
        <ÆCHom II, 5 46,137>
        'Certainly repaid (*began to repay) the elder of the house the penny'

                                                        (Brinton 1988: 160)

She concludes that *onginnan* cannot mean 'begin' in this OE example either, because the situation is punctual. The sentence in its entirety, however, is (8):

(8)   Witodlice   fram ðam   endenextan ongann se hiredes   ealdor
        truly   from the   last-ones began the houseGEN   elder
        to agyldenne þone pening. <ÆCHom II, 5 46,137>
        to pay   the   penny
        'Truly, from the last ones began the lord of the household to pay the penny.'

The problem is that Callaway, for reasons of space, omitted an indirect object, *fram ðam endenextan* 'from the last ones,' whose plurality would crucially have demonstrated that the event described by the infinitive is iterative, and therefore durative rather than punctual.

6   Making the best of data gaps

Linguists working with texts (e.g., for the study of language change, genre comparison, or dialect comparison) have to make do with those texts that have survived the vicissitudes of time. The record may not always yield what we want: texts from crucial areas and from crucial periods may be missing. The texts we do have lack several dimensions of the spoken word, and, of course, any direct access to native speaker competence. We end this chapter with two examples of creative solutions to these problems.

OE has a rule of verb placement similar to that in Modern Dutch and German, but with an important difference: with specific types of first constituent, the finite verb (in bold in (9)) will always follow immediately in second position, as in Modern Dutch or German, whether the subject, in third position, is nominal or pronominal (as *he* in (9)) (see van Kemenade 1987):

(9)   Þa   **gemette** he ðær ænne   þearfan nacodne <ÆLS (Martin) 61–2>
        then Met   he there a   beggar naked
        'Then he met a poor man, naked'

However, with other types of first constituent, like *Æfter þysum wordum* 'after these words' in (10), subject nominals are still in third position, but pronouns are not: they precede the finite verb, which now looks to be in third place (in bold):

(10)   Æfter þysum wordum he **gewende** to þam ærendracan <ÆLS (Edmund) 83>
            After these words he turned to the messenger
            'After these words he turned to the messenger'

Kroch, Taylor, and Ringe (2000) make a case that Northern Middle English, due to language contact with the Scandinavian invaders in the late OE period, only had constructions of the type in (10). Kroch, Taylor, and Ringe use tenth-century Northern glosses (i.e., interlinear translations, which are generally assumed to be unreliable as evidence) as indirect evidence: where the Latin original does not spell out pronominal subjects, the OE gloss must add them, and this is done in the word order as in (9) rather than (10). They argue on the basis of this fact that in the North, the contact situation with Old Norse (which, like Dutch and German, has V2 as in (9)) may have affected the verb-second rule directly. This creative use of an atypical data source helps to address a particular problem arising out of gaps in the OE record.

The problem of not having access to spoken data is circumvented in Getty (2000). The grammaticalization of (pre)modals, from lexical verbs into auxiliaries, can be expected to have been accompanied by the usual grammaticalization phenomena: bleaching of semantic content, loss of stress, phonetic reduction. Poetry, as a rule, is not used in syntactic investigations for a number of reasons: archaic structures tend to persist in poetry beyond their shelf life in the spoken language, and the requirements of rhyme and meter may also skew the results. However, Getty argues on the basis of the metrical nature of OE poetry that premodals grammaticalize to some extent between early and late OE: they are significantly less likely to occur in stressed positions in the late OE *Battle of Maldon* than in other, undatable but presumably older, poetry.

7   Conclusion

We have seen in this chapter that working with texts, in particular historical texts, raises a number of specialized issues that require specialized treatment. These may be summed up generally in one question: how and to what extent does the text (or collection of texts) yield the answers to the research question, or, perhaps, how can we make it yield the best possible answer to the research question? We have addressed a range of issues that bear on this question, boiling down to the representativeness of the textual evidence for the type of information that we may wish to draw from the texts.

References

Ayres-Bennett, W. 2004. *Sociolinguistic Variation in Seventeenth-Century France: Methodology and Case Studies*. Cambridge University Press.

Bauman, R. 1986. *Story, Performance, Event: Contextual Studies of Oral Narrative*. Cambridge University Press.

Biber, D. and E. Finegan. 1992. The linguistic evolution of five written and speech-based English genres. In M. Rissanen, O. Ihalainen, T. Nevalainen, and I. Taavitsainen, eds. *History of Englishes: New Methods and Interpretations in Historical Linguistics*. Berlin: Mouton de Gruyter, 688–704.

   1994. Introduction: situating register in sociolinguistics. In D. Biber and E. Finegan, eds. *Sociolinguistic Perspectives on Register*. New York and Oxford: Oxford University Press, 3–12.

Birner, B. and G. Ward. 2002. *Information packaging*. In R. Huddleston and G. K. Pullum, eds. *The Cambridge Grammar of the English Language*. Cambridge University Press, 1363–427.

Brinton, L. J. 1988. *The Development of English Aspectual Systems: Aspectualizers and Post-verbal Particles*. Cambridge University Press.

Callaway, M. 1913. *The Infinitive in Anglo-Saxon*. Washington D.C.: Carnegie Institution of Washington.

Coupé, G. and A. van Kemenade. 2009. Grammaticalization of modals in English and Dutch: uncontingent change. In P. Crisma and G. Longobardi, eds. *Historical Syntax and Linguistic Theory*. Oxford University Press, 250–70.

Cristofaro, S. 2003. *Subordination*. Oxford Studies in Typology and Linguistic Theory. Oxford University Press.

de Saussure, F. 1983.*Course in General Linguistics*. Trans. Roy Harris of *Cours de Linguistique Générale*, reconstructed from students' notes after Saussure's death. London: Duckworth.

Delbrück, B. 1882. *Introduction to the Study of Language: A Critical Survey of the History and Methods of Comparative Philology of Indo-European Languages*. Breitkopf und Härtel: Leipzig. (Translation of *Einleitung in das Sprachstudium* (Bibliothek indo-germanischer Grammatiken, Bd. 4.)

Denison, D. 1993. *English Historical Syntax*. London: Longman.

Fischer, O. C. M. 1996. The status of to in Old English to-infinitives: a reply to Kageyama. *Lingua* 99: 107–33.

Fleischman, S. 1990. *Tense and Narrativity: From Medieval Performance to Modern Fiction*. London: Routledge.

Getty, M. 2000. Differences in the metrical behavior of Old English finite verbs: evidence for grammaticalization. *English Language and Linguistics* 4: 37–67.

Goody, J. and I. Watt. 1968. The consequences of literacy. In Jack Goody, ed. *Literacy in Traditional Societies*. Cambridge University Press, 27–68.

Gregory, M. L. and L. A. Michaelis. 2001. Topicalization and left dislocation: a functional opposition revisited. *Journal of Pragmatics* 33: 1665–706.

Healey, A. D. and R. L. Venezky. 1980 [1985]. *A Microfiche Concordance to Old English*. Toronto: The Pontifical Institute of Mediaeval Studies.

Koopman, W. 1990. Word order in Old English. Unpublished Ph.D. dissertation, University of Amsterdam.

Kroch, A., A. Taylor, and D. Ringe. 2000. The Middle English verb-second constraint: a case study in language contact and language change. In S. C. Herring, P. van Reenen, and L. Schøsler, eds. *Textual Parameters in Older Languages*. Amsterdam and Philadelphia: John Benjamins, 353–91.

Labov, W. 1994. *Principles of Linguistic Change. Volume 1: Internal Factors*. Oxford: Blackwell.

Lasnik, H. and N. Sobin. 2000. The who/whom-puzzle: on the preservation of an archaic feature. *Natural Language & Linguistic Theory* 18: 343–71.

Lenker, U. 2010. *Argument and Rhetoric: Adverbial Connectors in the History of English* (Topics in English Linguistics 64). Berlin and New York: Mouton de Gruyter.

Lieber, R. 1979. The English passive: an argument for historical rule stability. *Linguistic Inquiry* 10: 667–88.

Lightfoot, D. 1981. The history of noun phrase movement. In C. L. Baker and J. McCarthy, eds. *The Logical Problem of Language Acquisition* Cambridge, MA: MIT Press, 86–119.

Los, B. 1999. *Infinitival Complementation in Old and Middle English* (LOT Dissertation Series 31). The Hague: Thesus.

Los, B. and E. Komen. 2012. Clefts as resolution strategies after the loss of a multifunctional first position. In T. Nevalainen and E. C. Traugott, eds. *Rethinking Approaches to the History of English*. New York: Oxford University Press, 884–98.

Mair, C. 1990. *Infinitival Complement Clauses in English: A Study of Syntax in Discourse*. Cambridge University Press.

Miller, D. G. 2002. *Nonfinite Structures in Theory and Change*. Oxford University Press.

Mitchell, B. 1979. F. Th. Visser, an historical syntax of the English language: some caveats concerning Old English. *English Studies* 60: 537–42.

1980. The dangers of disguise: Old English texts in modern punctuation. *Review of English Studies* n.s. 31: 385–413.

Mitchell, B., C. Ball, and A. Cameron. 1975. Short titles of Old English texts. *Anglo-Saxon England* 4: 207–21.

1979. Addenda and corrigenda. *Anglo-Saxon England* 8: 331–3.

Mittwoch, A. 1990. On the distribution of bare infinitive complements in English. *Journal of Linguistics* 26: 103–31.

Nevalainen, T. and H. Raumolin-Brunberg. 2003. *Historical Sociolinguistics: Language Change in Tudor and Stuart England*. London: Longman.

Olson, D. R. 1977. From utterance to text: the bias of language in speech and writing. *Harvard Educational Review* 47: 257–81.

Parkes, M. B. 1992. *Pause and Effect: An Introduction of the History of Punctuation in the West*. Aldershot: Scolar Press.

Pérez-Guerra, J. In press. Discourse status and syntax in the history of English: some explorations in topicalisation, left-dislocation and there-constructions. In A. Meurman-Solin, M.-J. López-Couso and B. Los, eds. *Information Structure and Syntactic Change*. Oxford University Press.

Perret, M. 1988. *Le Signe et la Mention: Adverbes Embrayeurs "Ci," "Ça," "La," "Iluec" En Moyen Français (XIVe–XVe Siècles)*. Geneva: Droz.

Plato. 1975. *Phaedrus and Letters VII and VIII*. Trans. Walter Hamilton. Harmondsworth: Penguin.

Romaine, S. 1982. *Socio-Historical Linguistics: Its Status and Methodology*. Cambridge University Press.

Russom, J. H. 1982. An examination of the evidence for OE indirect passives. *Linguistic Inquiry* 13: 677–80.

Traugott, E. C. and M. L. Pratt. 1980. *Linguistics for Students of Literature*. New York: Harcourt Brace Jovanovich.

van Kemenade, A. 1987. *Syntactic Case and Morphological Case in the History of English*. Dordrecht: Foris.

Vandenbussche, W. 2007. Lower class language in 19th century Flanders. *Multilingua* 26.2–3: 279–90.

Visser, F. Th. 1963–73. *An Historical Syntax of the English Language*, 4 vols. Leiden: E. J. Brill.

Warner, A. 2006. Variation and the interpretation of change in periphrastic DO. In A. van Kemenade and B. Los, eds. *The Handbook of the History of English*. Maldon: Blackwell, 45–67.

PART II

Data processing and statistical analysis

12 Transcription

Naomi Nagy and Devyani Sharma

To write Faetar, you have to use the Italian spelling system, because it's the only system the speakers know.

When you write Faetar, you should use French orthography because that will indicate the Gallic roots of the language.

Of course, the only option is to use the International Phonetic Alphabet to write Faetar, so that linguists around the world are able to understand the details of our unique language.

1 Introduction

The reconstructed vignette above, based on actual conversations with speakers of Faetar, an endangered language spoken in two small villages in southern Italy (Nagy 2000, 2011a), illustrates some of the many uses that transcription has. Researchers (and the transcribers they hire) may not even be aware of all the potential downstream uses of their transcriptions. The most common understanding of the purpose of transcription in linguistics is contained in the third statement. However, a linguist's decision to transcribe in a standardized orthography or in the International Phonetic Alphabet (IPA) can influence later uses of the text. Deviations from the traditions of one's field can even be perceived as ideologically charged. As Kendall (2008: 337) puts it,

> the act of transcription [. . .] is often undertaken as a purely methodological activity, as if it were theory neutral. Each decision that is made while transcribing influences and constrains the resulting possible readings and analyses (Ochs 1979; Mishler 1991; Bucholtz 2000; Edwards 2001). Decisions as seemingly straightforward as how to lay out the text, to those more nuanced – like how much non-verbal information to include and how to encode minutiae such as pause length and utterance overlap – have far-reaching effects on the utility of a transcript and the directions in which the transcript may lead analysts.

Acknowledgments: We are very grateful to the following people who shared their transcribing experiences, expertise, and protocols: Julie Auger, Jenny Cheshire, Ashwini Deo, Nathalie Dion, John Du Bois, Sue Fox, Alexandra Georgakopoulou, Kirk Hazen, Dagmar Jung, Tyler Kendall, Shana Poplack, Ben Rampton, Rena Torres Cacoullos, Albert Valdman, Anne-José Villeneuve, and Walt Wolfram. All personal communications cited in the text are from July 2011.

Transcription can serve a wide range of functions, as a single transcript may eventually be used for multiple analyses. Within linguistic research, a transcript may be used, for instance, for quantitative analysis of morphosyntactic or discourse variables, as a guide for auditory phonetic analysis, for qualitative analysis of conversation, discourse, or interaction, and for theoretical linguistic analysis. In addition to serving linguistic research, the transcriptions may become a legacy, providing documentation of a particular point in a language variety's development, as well as recording information about the culture of the society who used the variety. Often, only transcripts (not accompanied by the recordings they represent) are shared with the public and other researchers, making their accuracy critical, as they must represent everything deemed important from the original recording. Transcripts might even be used by the community long after research is completed: Transcripts from Walt Wolfram's research (pers. comm.) have been used by members of the community to compile oral history CDs (e.g., *Ocracoke Speaks 2001*), and communities have even asked the researchers on that project to transcribe tapes for them. These many different needs and uses set different requirements for transcription practices and protocols.

In this chapter, we discuss various dimensions of two broad questions: what to transcribe and how to transcribe it, what Bucholtz (2000) terms "interpretive" and "representational" decisions respectively. The chapter breaks these two dimensions down to cover a range of issues: aspects of form and content when transcribing, transcribing across languages, the advantages of different types of software in transcription, transcriber effects, transcription protocols, and practicalities of planning transcription.

2   How much to transcribe

Although we may think of transcription as a more or less mechanical "translation" from an oral medium to a text medium, there are in fact many decisions that must be made regarding what parts of a recording to include and what level of detail to indicate for those segments.

The very first decision is whether the voice recording needs to be transcribed at all. Some researchers find it more efficient to proceed directly to extracting the relevant materials or examples from the audio stream, and either transcribe only the relevant passage or code directly without transcribing (Labov's course on sociolinguistic fieldwork methodology in Philadelphia has used this approach). Other linguists prefer to transcribe first so that all material is available in text form. This minimizes the likelihood of missing certain examples and, in the long run, may save time if the recording will be used for a variety of purposes; the Ottawa-Hull Corpus (Poplack 1989), Sankoff and Thibault's Montreal Anglophone project (Sankoff et al. 1997), and the Montreal Francophone Corpora (Sankoff and Sankoff 1973) use this approach. In some such cases, particularly in sociolinguistics, standard practices are employed for the selection of segments to be transcribed – for instance, omission of the first 10 minutes of a sociolinguistic interview (to avoid speech produced during the less comfortable initial stages of a recording session), or selection of more and less formal speech segments from certain interview topics for stylistic analysis (Labov 2001).

At times, researchers may try to optimize how much can be transcribed by "farming out" the work to professional transcribers. Here, it is worth bearing in mind that linguists are never as close to their object of study as when they are transcribing. The very act of transcription helps the researcher find and understand patterns in the data, seeing elements that may be elusive and fleeting in the original oral form. For this reason, many linguists feel that it is crucial to transcribe as much of their own data as possible.

It is common for researchers simply not to have the funding or time to transcribe a portion of the data collected, particularly with time-consuming bilingual transcription. In some such cases, alternative analyses that permit very limited transcription or auditory processing of data are pursued. In others, only a portion is transcribed. For instance, funding restrictions in Sharma's Dialect Development and Style project meant that recordings from only forty-two of seventy-five individuals could initially be transcribed and analyzed (Sharma and Sankaran 2011); in this case, care had to be taken to select a balanced subsample from each demographic group to avoid skewing in the transcribed portion. In yet other cases, some of the original oral data may not be transcribed simply because more was collected than necessary. For example, the Heritage Language Variation and Change (HLVC) project (Nagy 2009, 2011b) compares speech across forty speakers in each of six languages, and has targeted one hour of transcribed conversational speech as sufficient to represent each speaker. In these cases, decisions must be made about which portions of an interview that exceeds one hour should be included. In the case of the HLVC project, the analysis of sociolinguistic variables focuses on data from 15 minutes into the interview onward, but demographic information about speakers is extracted from any portion of the recording. Therefore, transcription begins at the beginning of the recording, but after the first hour is transcribed, transcribers select only the portions they expect to be useful for demographic description for partial transcription.

Finally, it can happen that portions are not transcribed because they cannot be understood. This is more often the case if the researcher is not a native speaker of the language being studied, as is often the case in endangered language documentation. Sometimes, elements of the context that made understanding possible at the time of the utterance (e.g., gestures or off-microphone interactions) are not recoverable when transcribing. Ambient noise may also make it impossible to determine exactly what was said. In Nagy's experience documenting Faetar, she first transcribed and translated a first draft herself, and then went over any unclear sections with a native speaker. Because speakers, upon seeing a transcript of their own speech, often wish to improve upon what they are recorded as saying, assistants were sought who were not the original speaker.

The question of how much to transcribe extends to elements of content as well. Researchers must make ethical decisions regarding how much personal information to transcribe and how to respect the anonymity often promised to research participants (see Chapter 1). Names of speakers and individuals mentioned are often excluded (or pseudonyms substituted), but further identifying information may also need to be eliminated or altered. Fox and Cheshire (2011) distinguish between *allowable* and *anonymized* references in their Multicultural London English project; examples of both are provided in (1).

(1)   Allowable vs anonymized references

Allowable

> Havering (a borough where their research was conducted)
> I buy my jeans in Mare Street. (general sense of street name)
> I used to work in a bar down near Liverpool Street. (general sense of street name)
> I'm from E8. (postcode area)

Anonymized

> My name's (name of speaker) and I live in Hackney.
> I live in (name of street).
> I go to (name of school).
> if you play football with us yeh over (name of park). (specific places when describing an event)
> some white girl from your area. she goes (name of school) she knows (name of girl). (references to schools that could lead to the identity of an individual)
> I hated Miss (name of teacher).
> Any private information e.g., phone numbers, addresses, specific clubs attended

They also suggest that we carefully consider whether to include references to sexual orientation, date of birth, and "public" individuals such as locally known musicians. It is not always possible to know what information may identify the speaker, depending on the audience, and researchers differ in their views of their obligation to protect the anonymity of speakers who have agreed to be recorded for research purposes. This issue is discussed thoughtfully in Childs, Van Herk, and Thorburn (2011: 176).

Once the relevant segments to be transcribed have been identified, the researcher faces the immediate question of how closely and faithfully to represent the linguistic forms contained in these segments. The sections that follow explore the principles underlying some of these choices.

3   Orthographic choices

Transcription serves as a tool, a "handle" for the original oral recordings, both during primary analysis and for later uses of the data, which may be years later and not necessarily by the original researcher. Therefore, a well-documented, transparent, and reflexive *orthographic system* is crucial.

The most precise system for transcription is the *International Phonetic Alphabet (IPA)*; see Ladefoged and Disner (2012) for details. This system, usually described as *phonetic transcription* as opposed to other *orthographic transcription*, can potentially render almost all phonetic details of recorded speech faithfully, which may be of crucial importance if the aim of transcription is, for instance, language description or documentation (see Chapter 4). Selective use of IPA may be employed in a transcript if specific dialect variation or contextualization cues are being tracked in a stretch of recorded speech. However, at some point, the time and labor costs of transcribing in IPA must be balanced against the quantity of data to be transcribed and the goals of the research.

In a seminal sociolinguistic research report, Poplack (1989: 430) summarized this orthography issue as follows:

> In planning the transcription of a computer corpus, there is a major trade-off between size of the data base and level of detail of the transcription. For syntactic and lexical work especially, the larger the corpus the better, with the point of diminishing returns nowhere in sight, since a large number of interesting constructions and forms (e.g., most loan-words) are exceedingly rare in natural speech. However, massive corpus size renders fine phonetic transcription unfeasible. Too much detail tends to sharply diminish the utility of automated treatment of the corpus since conventional alphabetical order is lost, and lexically identical forms may be ordered in many different positions.

Given these concerns, the Ottawa-Hull French Project adopted an orthographic approach, rather than phonetic (ibid., p. 431). Pronunciation of particular phonemes was not specified, though omission of entire morphemes was represented by Ø, and English borrowings are spelled in English, even when incorporated into French morphology, such as *feeler* and *meaner* (ibid. pp. 432–3).

It is worth noting here that even if phonetic orthography is technically dispensed with – in cases where the transcript is to be used for syntactic analysis, for instance – the transcriber must be alert to phonetic distinctions in order to make orthographic judgments. In Bresnan, Deo, and Sharma (2007), the phonetically "faithful" transcription of verb forms in the *Survey of English Dialects* (Orton et al. 1962–71) were converted to a smaller set of lexical classes that formed the basis of the syntactic analysis of variation in *be*, but fine phonetic distinctions were important in determining the lexical classification of forms. Similarly, in the analysis of syntactic features such as copula omission (e.g., Labov 1969), phonetic reduction of *are* to either 'r or Ø must be extremely carefully coded during transcription, as any phonetic trace of the form is crucial for the outcome of the quantitative syntactic analysis.

The field is now moving toward greater use of *time-aligned transcription* (i.e., textual representations that match stretches of recorded media). Such transcription (currently produced by software discussed later) has multiple advantages: researchers can easily access the original audio(-visual) segment associated with a particular stretch of text; the software usually allows for customized tiers for further interlinear glossing and tagging of the extract; and data can easily be converted to useful and integrated display formats for presentation (see Thieberger and Berez 2012).

In time-aligned transcription, more "standard" orthography, as opposed to phonetic transcription, is increasingly useful, as phonetic detail may be visualized or easily coded where relevant in later passes through the data. This use of standard orthography also makes computer-assisted analysis easier as different transcribers are less likely to transcribe things differently. As Edwards (2001: 324) observes, "(f)or purposes of computer manipulation (e.g. search, data exchange, or flexible reformatting), the single most important design principle is that *similar instances be encoded in predictably similar ways*" (original emphasis). No matter what specific decisions are made, they should be recorded in a *transcription protocol* that is shared with all researchers using a particular corpus (details are discussed in Section 7).

In the case of morphosyntax, a small set of variants can optionally be agreed upon, noted in the transcription protocol, and used in the transcription (e.g., *ain't*). In the case of phonetic variation and the rendering of connected speech, this is much less common. Researchers generally avoid the use of *eye dialect* (i.e., the use of folk orthographic representations to indicate non-standard pronunciations or simply casual style – e.g., *iz* for *is*). This is primarily for reasons of consistency and later searchability of the transcript, but also to avoid unwarranted stereotyping of the speaker in question (see Preston 1982 and Bucholtz 2000 for discussions of this point). Where non-standard phonetic forms are relevant to the analysis, they can either be coded using IPA or added in later where relevant.

However, standard orthography is not entirely feasible in unstandardized languages. Auger (pers. comm.) notes that, for her work with Picard, a variety spoken in northern France, the orthography she uses has been developed by the Ch'Lanchron group, who publish books and a quarterly magazine in Picard. It is an analogical orthography, in that it maintains parallels with the orthography of French, a language closely related to Picard and in which all Picard speakers are fluent. However, this orthography is flexible: geographical variants can be spelled differently. For instance, *he was* can be written *il étouot, il étoait, il étot*, depending on how it is pronounced.

Since even in languages as standardized as English, speech often includes "words" that do not have standardized spellings, it is useful to prepare a list of such forms that anyone working on a particular corpus can follow. An example from the Sociolinguistic Archive and Analysis Project (SLAAP) is given in (2):

(2)   SLAAP spelling conventions, examples (Kendall 2009)

Uh-huh	Uh-uh	Gonna
Uh-hum	Okay	I'm'a
Mm-mm	Mkay	Wanna
Mm-hm	Nyah	Kinda

Hazen (2010), for a project in which transcriptions are created in a word processor, takes a slightly different approach:[1]

(3)   West Virginia Dialect Project (WVDP) spelling conventions (Hazen 2010)[2]

Use the underlying items in the transcript and standard orthography. Do not try to mimic the speaker's speech (i.e. He ain't going to do it. Not – 'e en't gonna do et) . . .

- Type out 'gonna' as 'going to,' 'wanna' as 'want to,' etc. Contractions do not need to be altered.
- Spell numbers (i.e., two thousand and one)
- Don't use abbreviations (i.e. WV) unless the speaker actually says them.
- Do not use ellipsis marks (. . .) because they show up as one character in Word.
- Time Stamps: place every few minutes, or enough that one is visible on the screen at any point of scrolling through the document. More is better! Ex- [12:03]
- Spacing: Single-space the interview but double-space when speakers change.
- Quote marks: insert when needed, including internal dialogue (thoughts).
- Comments: add to the margins using Word's comment feature – not the typescript.
- Transcribe everything that both the interviewer and interviewee say. Never write 'Kirk rambling,' etc.

Examples such as *gonna* and *wanna* indicate how transcription can slip into functioning as coding. Orthographic choices of this type directly affect the use of a transcript for morphosyntactic analysis, as they affect automatic searches. If a corpus is tagged (see Chapter 13), then a formal and explicit level of notation mediates between the representation of speech and the searchable representation of syntactic structures. However, if it is not tagged, the choice of orthographic form is crucial, and systematic notation of any deviation from a standard form (e.g., infinitival *to*) must be noted in the transcription protocol. The only exception, as noted in Section 4, may be when a short transcript is subjected to a one-time analysis, with a focus on qualitative interpretation and no need for searchability or computational tractability.

Linguists differ in decisions regarding the inclusion of non-linguistic sounds (e.g., coughs, laughs, burps), false starts and hesitations, fillers (e.g., *er, um, y'know*), incomplete (and therefore often uninterpretable) words, and code-switches to a language that is not the focus of investigation. Many of these choices

---

[1] Samples of transcription and coding protocols mentioned in this chapter are available on the companion website that accompanies this volume (in particular, Valdman 2007; Hazen 2010; Nagy 2011c; Torres Cacoullos 2011).

[2] We note that this excerpt represents a work in progress. The WVDP is now archived in SLAAP. In that version, sixty-seven interview transcripts are time-aligned at the utterance-level (Hazen, pers. comm., October 20, 2012).

are directly determined by the intended use of the transcript and the analytic approach favored by the researcher, discussed next.

A final detail of orthographic representation that the researcher must decide on concerns the imposition of *segmentation* or *punctuation* on spoken language. Speech may be a more or less continuous stream of sound, but it is helpful for readers of a transcript (and possibly for the transcriber as well) to break the stream into segments. Some researchers (e.g., Hazen 2010) work with large chunks, making textual divisions between speaker turns and punctuating sentences. By contrast, Julie Auger uses punctuation insofar as it reflects prosodic organization. She marks pauses, intonational breaks, and interruptions (pers. comm.). Similarly, Rena Torres Cacoullos (pers. comm.) segments transcription into intonation units to provide boundaries that seem more relevant to spoken language.

One danger in the use of punctuation in transcription is different interpretations by users of the transcribed data: a comma may indicate an intonational unit for the transcriber, but may be perceived as marking a pause by a research assistant engaged in coding, and the following phonetic environment may be incorrectly coded as a pause rather than a phonetic segment. For this reason, a detailed and explicit transcription protocol of coding conventions must be used; this is dis-cussed in the final section.

Once again, the particular use of a transcript can determine punctuation choices. When punctuation is used with conventionalized meanings (e.g. upper-case letters for loudness or question marks for rising intonation in conversation analysis), the common preference is to minimize punctuation of any kind other than those transcription conventions. To ease reading of a transcript in such cases, line breaks may be introduced at various natural discourse boundaries. These cases are discussed in the next section. In the case of language documentation, transcribing and linguistic analysis go hand in hand, and it is necessary to revise the form of the transcription repeatedly as the linguist's understanding of the structure of the language develops (see Chapter 4; Jung and Himmelmann 2011: 204).

4   Representing dialogue

Transcripts vary enormously in how faithfully they preserve details of the delivery of talk (i.e., the manner in which speech was produced and the dynamics of the interaction). There is no "correct" level of detail. Indeed, Mishler (1991) has shown how the same interaction has been transcribed differ-ently in research for different analytic purposes. One can argue, however, that there is a correct level of detail for a given research question. As Edwards (2001) notes, the choice of conventions is generally driven by the nature of the interaction and the analytic goal or framework.

As noted earlier, an inevitable trade-off exists between detail in transcription and the amount that can be transcribed. However, feasibility is not the only consideration. The manner in which an utterance was produced may not be relevant to certain kinds of theoretical analysis, so the goal in transcription is by no means to include as much detail as is feasible. In transcription used for quantitative sociolinguistic analysis, details such as hesitations, overlapping speech, loudness, and other production phenomena are often omitted or simplified. In any kind of analysis, however, the transcriber must always be alert to the potential importance of even these elements. For example, Sharma (2005) noticed that self-repairs in interviewee's echoic usage (structures that paralleled the interviewer's speech) corresponded with certain language ideologies expressed in interviews. This incidental evidence would have been obscured by inexact transcription or omission of either interviewer speech or self-repairs, both of which were initially deemed irrelevant to the core focus of the study.

As we move toward qualitative sociolinguistic modes of analysis, analysis tends to require more faithful documentation of fine details of speech production, interactional structure, and non-verbal activity. Because of the increased attention to these features, transcription for discourse analysis (used broadly here to include discourse, narrative, interaction, and conversation analysis) tends to eliminate the use of any punctuation other than those conventions explicitly listed. To retain readability and to reconstruct the rhythm of the interaction, discourse analytic transcripts use frequent line breaks at boundaries such as turn constructional units (TCUs), intonational phrases, breath groups, or informational phrases (syntactic constituents with a unified intonational contour, often marked by pauses; Gumperz and Berenz 1993). Line numbering is crucial in such transcripts, as are speaker codes.

As part of a wider debate over the principles and practices of conversation analysis and other forms of discourse analysis (see Chapter 21), a fair amount of discussion has taken place over degrees of detail in transcription, with both greater and less detail being critiqued as potentially impeding analysis.

Conversation analysis has developed a particularly detailed set of notation conventions. One common notation system is the Jefferson Notation System (Atkinson and Heritage 1984; Hutchby and Wooffitt 1998; Jefferson 2004). These systems aim to track linguistic and contextual cues in conversation and to model the sequence and timing of an interaction by using notation of the kind illustrated in example (4) (see also Appendix 21.1 in Chapter 21).

(4)	(.)	barely noticeable pause, usually less then 0.2 seconds
	(.3), (2.6)	timed pauses
	↑word, ↓word	onset of noticeable rise or fall in pitch
	A: word [word	
	B: [word	start of overlapping talk
		(closed brackets ']' are sometimes used to mark the end of overlap)
	.hh, hh	in-breath and out-breath respectively
	wo(h)rd	laughter or related style of utterance of word
	wor-	sharp termination

wo:rd	lengthening of sound preceding colon(s)
(words)	transcriber uncertain of transcribed words
( )	unclear talk (sometimes each syllable is represented with a dash)
A: word=	
B: =word	no discernible pause between turns
word, WORD	two degrees of increased loudness
°word°	start and end of quieter speech
>word word<	faster speech
<word word>	slower speech
((sniff))	transcriber's notation of non-verbal details

Marginally less detailed conventions that are also widely used include those developed by Gumperz and Berenz (1993), du Bois et al. (1992), and Potter and Hepburn (2005). In many cases, an initial "rough" transcription is used, employing a subset of conventions, and this can subsequently be worked into a much "finer" documentation of talk as action as the researcher's understanding becomes refined through multiple listenings.

In (5)–(7), we illustrate different degrees of detail in the marking of conversational speech. The researcher must decide which of numerous aspects of speech should be represented in a transcript.

In (5), the coding of the transcript reflects much more detail, with particular attention to timing, silence, and breathing. Notice how intuitive characterizations of speech production (e.g., 'lo in line 3 or haveta in line 18) are more acceptable in this context as the data are not being subjected to computerized searches, and are favored to add vivid accuracy to the rhythm of dialogue.

(5)   (from Schegloff 2001: 235)

```
01                 1+ rings
02      Marcia:    Hello?
03      Donny:     'lo Marcia,=
04      Marcia:    Yea[:h      ]
05      Donny:        =[ ('t's) D]onny.
06      Marcia:    Hi Donny.
07      Donny:     Guess what.hh
08      Marcia:    What.
09      Donny:     hh My ca:r is sta::lled.
10                 (0.2)
11      Donny:     ('n) I'm up here in the Glen?
12      Marcia:    Oh::.
13                 {(0.4)}
14      Donny:     { hhh }
15      Donny:     A:nd.hh
16                 (0.2)
17      Donny:     I don' know if it's possible, but {hhh}/(0.2) } see
18                 I haveta open up the ba:nk.hh
19                 (0.3)
```

20	Donny:	a:t uh: (.) in Brentwood?hh=
21	Marcia:	=Yeah:- en I know you want- (.) en I whoa- (.) en I
22		would, but- except I've gotta leave in aybout five
23		min(h)utes. [(hheh)
24	Donny:	[Okay then I gotta call somebody else.
25		right away.
26		(.)
27	Donny:	Okay?=
28	Marcia:	=Okay [Don]
29	Donny:	[Thanks] a lot.=Bye-
30	Marcia:	Bye:.

Schegloff (2001: 236) points out that rendering the above exchange in the approximate format in (6) below would appear to omit little – just silences, breathing, volume, timing – but it is this material, within its sequential context, that indicates the underlying actions being attempted, achieved, and avoided. Note, of course, that the level of detail in the transcript in (6) might be adequate if the focus of the analysis simply dealt with the syntactic structure of requests.

(6)   (from Schegloff 2001: 236)
      My car is stalled (and I'm up here in the Glen?), and I don't know if it's possible, but, see, I have to open up the bank at uh, in Brentwood?

However, even the detailed transcript in (5) is selective, and by no means exhaustive in terms of transcription detail. If an analysis focuses more on how meaning is conveyed through prosody – specifically, negative evaluation through mimicry in the next example – then the transcriber might choose to include shifts in pitch, as in (7). Even more detail in the transcription of prosodic structure can be achieved by notation systems such as ToBI notation (Tones and Break Indices; Silverman et al. 1992) or interlinear tonetic notation (Cruttenden 1997).

(7)   (from Couper-Kuhlen 2001: 24)
      The extract is from a phone-in program; M is the moderator of the show and C is a caller

M:	then we go to Hardwick. (.)
	and there we get –
	(.) h sexy Sharon.
	↓hi!
C:	(0.4) °hello° –
M:	{1} °hello° –
	how are you Sharon –
C:	°all right [thanks°
M:	[oh: ↑cheer up dear,
C:	he hh
M:	cheer up;
	for goodness sake;
	don't – don't put me in a bad mood;
	at (.) one o'clock;

Transcripts that are time-aligned with video recording can add further crucial detail of facial or body gesture, direction of gaze, intended addressee, or other contextually disambiguating information, some of which might ultimately be included in the finer transcript presented as part of an analysis (see Chapter 10 for the potential importance of these elements in ethnographic data collection).

In practice, analysts select among available transcription codes of speech production as suits their needs in a particular analysis, and develop new ones for specialized notation (always providing a full list of conventions used). This practice can, consciously or unconsciously, render alternative readings of the data inaccessible to a reader. As in the area of language documentation, therefore, transcription has not been seen as a neutral or mechanical activity in discourse analysis (Ochs 1979; Bucholtz 2000). Indeed, transcription is very much part of analysis in qualitative sociolinguistic research (see Chapter 21 for further examples). In terms of what she calls the *interpretive* dimension (i.e., selecting what material to include in a transcript), Bucholtz (2000) offers an example from a police interrogation that shows how the selective omission of parts of a dialogue as "incomprehensible" produces a very different picture of the motivations of the participants involved. Similarly, in terms of what she terms the *representational* dimension (i.e., orthographic choices), Bucholtz offers an example of how the speech of an African American man is subtly, possibly unconsciously, reshaped in a radio transcript, both standardizing his speech, thereby removing elements of coherence and continuity, as well as retaining random elements for colloquial character. Bucholtz observes that academic transcription is as politically fraught as these instances of "lay" transcripts: whether colloquial detail is retained or omitted, a transcript is always bound to be a representation of an individual's speech that has been heavily mediated by the transcriber/researcher. Ochs (1979) notes that even the choice of column-format transcription (in which each speaker has a different column) or vertical format (in which each speaker follows the previous speaker vertically) might influence the analyst's or the reader's sense of who dominates the interaction. Sensitivity, reflexivity, and transparency in these choices is therefore vital. (See Edwards 2001 for further details on transcribing discourse.)

5   Glossing in multilingual transcription

Variationist sociolinguistic analysis often presents speech data with little markup, highlighting the element under study fairly informally, as in (8).

(8)   Sample transcription from a variationist analysis:
        I think Ø he thought Ø it was really cool that I spoke French and that I was bilingual. (Liz; Blondeau and Nagy 2008)

This is only possible when the language being studied and the working language are the same, or if the language being studied is well known to the intended audience. Speech transcribed in a language other than that of the analyst or the published work necessarily involves added layers of *interlinear glossing* and *translation*. As with "monolingual" transcription, speech transcribed in a different language may be used to perform phonological, morphological, syntactic, socio-linguistic, or some other form of analysis; in each case the information that must be included in interlinear notation differs. Even when the language being studied is the same as the working language, interlinear markup can be useful for tracking formal properties of the transcript (this is done extensively in corpus linguistics; see Chapter 13 for details). In this section, we discuss bilingual transcription and in section 6 we briefly review current transcription software that allows bilingual or other types of inter-linear markup.

When transcribing an extract from one language for study in another, formal linguists generally use separate rows to indicate morpheme-by-morpheme gloss-ing and idiomatic translation. In the commonly used Leipzig Glossing Rules (Comrie, Haspelmath, and Bickel 2008), the original language is transcribed on the first row using a regular script or IPA, usually with each word tab-separated. The second row includes translation glosses that align vertically with the relevant word in the first row. These can either consist of whole-word translations, as in (9), or finer standardized abbreviations for morphological detail, as in (10). The final row provides a smooth or idiomatic translation into the working language.

(9)   Interlinear glossing using IPA (Faetar)

phonetic (IPA):	u	tʃin	i	awardá	dəvan	də	la	portə
gloss:		the	dog	he	waited	in-front	of	the	door

translation: 'The dog waited in front of the door.' (Speaker F11B; Nagy 2000: 112)

(10)   Interlinear glossing using standardized orthography (Beaver Athabaskan)

orthographic:	dáwótt'yedye	aadi
gloss:	what.kind.of.place	3.said

translation: 'She said what kind of place.'
(yaamaadzuyaaze transcr001; Jung and Himmelmann 2011: 209)

Example (10) differs from (9) in using an orthography specific to the language, rather than IPA, and a richer system of morphological description in the gloss. This type of transcription must be accompanied by a glossary of abbreviations, as shown in (11).

(11)   Sample of morphological categories used in glosses (Jung and Himmelmann 2011: 209)
Abbreviations: 1,2,3 = first, second, third person (usually indexing the subject argument if not otherwise specified), ANIMO = animated object, ARE = areal, ASP = aspectual, CNJ = conjugation, DIM = diminutive, DU = dual, ELOO = elongated object, HAB = habitual, LOC = locative, FOC = focus, O = object, PFV = perfective, PL = plural, POSS = possessive, PRT = particle, SG = singular, V = valency.

The researcher may choose to make finer distinctions in morphological detail. For instance, the example in (12) distinguishes between cliticization (marked with "="), suffixation (marked with "–"), and monomorphemic information (marked with "."). Like example (10), this example uses a standardized Romanization rather than IPA in the first line.

(12)   Interlinear glossing with morphological detail (Hindi)
        radhaa ne hii   bacchon ko   kahaanii   sunaayii
        radhaa=ERG=FOC   child–PL=ACC   story.F   hear–CAUS–PERF.F.SG
        'It was Radha who told the children a story.' (based on Sharma 2003: 61)

For longer extracts, a reference key of grammatical morphemes can allow the transcriber to focus on simpler lexical glossing and only fill in grammatical detail later, if needed. One concern when developing interlinear glosses for bilingual transcription is the difficulty of dealing with expressions whose semantic value changes across dialects or across different diachronic stages (Ashwini Deo, pers. comm.). In such cases, either a selected semantic variant with variable forms or a selected form with variant meanings must be tracked in the transcripts, possibly with a notation for shifted semantic values across the dataset.

When speakers use more than one language within a single conversation, additional complications exist. As noted above, segments in the "wrong" language may simply not be transcribed. However, when linguists are interested in the full repertoire of speakers, rather than just one of the languages produced, additional markup may be required. Several options are described in Nagy (2012).

6   Transcription software

Current transcription software allows the transcriber to include glossing in a separate *tier*, whereby each entry on the transcript tier is linked to its matching entry on the glossing tier. In such software, translations or glosses are often just one of several tiers of annotation that might be applied to a transcript, whether bilingual or not.

Early (socio)linguistic transcripts were handwritten or typed, and later word-processed, with the end result being a paper document that could be read and marked up. Digital versions have become increasingly searchable and have slowly moved away from traditional text formats. The major shift is to separate content from form in the transcript and to facilitate links between different elements of markup. In this section we describe a few capabilities currently available in transcription software for the basic transcription of data, its coding and annotation, display options, and potential for data sharing.

When selecting software for transcription, it is advisable to consult colleagues and software manuals in order to select the most appropriate and powerful software for the intended use and analysis of the data. We first briefly outline the advantages of various commonly used transcription software (all open-source and available for download at no cost at the time of writing). In general, files can be converted among these different tools.

Transcriber is a graphical user interface tool for speech segmentation and speech transcription. It is used in research involving close phonetic analysis, as its functionalities include spectrograms and energy plots, segmentation of the speech signal and fine manipulation of segment boundaries, and audio playback capabilities. Transcriber specializes in annotation of the speech signal, and allows labeling of speech turns and topic changes; it is not designed for multi-tier morphosyntactic or other annotation, or for fine conversational detail such as overlapping speech. Transcriber is widely used for simple transcription with time codes, rather than for any form of analysis. By contrast, the software packages that we describe next permit transcription as part of diverse linguistic analysis capabilities.

Praat (Boersma and Weenink 2007) is used for transcription with fine-grained time alignment and is also specialized for use by phoneticians (see Chapter 9 for other uses of the software). Advantages for transcription and analysis include automatic annotation, multi-tier phonetic and speaker information, integration with a powerful graphical interface for phonetic analysis, and a scripting facility for specialized automated coding or analysis. Aside from extensive use in phonetics, Praat has also been used in the Sociolinguistic Archive and Analysis Project (SLAAP; detailed instructions and information are available online; see also Kendall 2008, 2009).

CLAN (MacWhinney 2000) is a set of interlinked programs originally developed as part of the CHILDES database for the study of child language acquisition, but now widely used in other fields, such as second language acquisition and sociolinguistics. It currently serves as the standard tool for transcription, coding, and analysis of TalkBank Corpus databases. A transcript can be created and edited in either CHAT (used more in acquisition studies) or CA (used more in conversation analysis) format; these formats can import from and export to other software, such as Praat and ELAN. As is common in such software, standardized formatting for *metadata* encoding is used (i.e., information about the participants and the recording, including any analyst-designated codes; also see discussion in Chapters 4 and 13). CLAN is favored by conversation analysts for several reasons: keyboard shortcuts for classic CA symbols, direct continuous or segmented playback of linked audio/video with highlighting of active segments, and automatic overlap alignment. In addition to these functionalities for transcription, CLAN permits multi-tier annotation of the transcript for specific linguistic analysis (e.g., word class, grammatical information, phonetic features, prosody, or language choice; further details of electronic annotation and markup are covered in Chapter 13). Other advantages of CLAN include compatibility with non-Roman fonts and built-in analysis programs.

ELAN (Wittenburg et al. 2006), produced by the Max Planck Institute of Psycholinguistics, can also be used to annotate audio and video files on multiple linked tiers with time-aligned annotations. ELAN offers more fine-grained, multiple parallelism in annotation than CLAN (e.g., partiture or "musical score" style presentation of multiple speakers), so is well-suited to transcription involving gestural, postural, and proxemic detail. It has been widely used in the documentation of endangered languages, sign languages, and in sociolinguistics. It includes sophisticated search functions, basic concordance functions, and some statistics regarding frequency of occurrence of different annotated items. Because it is easy to import to and export from, ELAN is compatible with numerous other transcription systems and applications, including Transcriber, CLAN, and Praat. Text is in Unicode (in many different scripts, including IPA) and annotation and transcription files are stored as XML.

This is a small sample of software currently used for transcription. Other software often includes more specialized capabilities. For instance, **TypeCraft**, a web-based system, has the added advantage of permitting multi-party collaboration via a MediaWiki shell, with options for complex tagging, morphological word-level annotation, and an automatic parser. **Fieldworks Language Explorer** (FLEx), produced by SIL, is designed specifically for language documentation and allows for grammatical markup, XML output, morphological analysis and bulk editing, and complex non-Roman script use (see Chapter 4); however, it does not currently have multi-platform or multi-user capabilities. Software is in a constant state of ongoing development and refinement, and we are likely to see advances soon in automated transcription and coding.

Once a transcript is completed, it can be displayed in a number of ways. Kendall (2008: 342) illustrates four different ways of visually presenting transcripts generated from transcription software, including a format much like the traditional text approach, but including time-stamps indicating when each utterance occurs in the recording, and a "graphicalized" version that illustrates the time flow of the conversation but not the text itself. ELAN transcriptions can be exported as traditional text files, but may also be used via ELAN's graphic interface, in which (overlapping) turns of different speakers, the waveform and/or video recording, and tiers for transcription and different types of markup are all simultaneously visible and time-linked. Both ELAN and SLAAP permit links to Praat so that spectrograms or other visual acoustic representations can be displayed and edited, and both also permit playback of any segment of the recording from the same display. These advances allow representation of pauses, overlaps, latching, and other such details, without explicit transcription (though these must still be coded if relevant to analysis). Edwards (2001) illustrates a number of options for displays that arrange speaker turns relative to data codes and/or researcher commentary, including a vertical multi-tier format (the most common choice), column format, or a nested or interspersed format.

A basic text in one file with markup or other annotation in a separate file or separate tiers makes it easier to use the same base transcript for a variety of purposes down the road. Given that the transcription will be marked up and made messy for linguistic analysis, but must be clean and clear for other users, separate files, or separate tiers which can be exported as separate files, are recommended. Creating separate tiers (or separate files) requires distinguishing between the *basic text* and *annotation*, or additional information. In the HLVC project, we transcribe the speech of the main research participant on one tier and all other speakers, including the interviewer, on other tiers. A new tier, referred to as a *token tier*, is created in which to mark tokens of each dependent variable being examined. This *daughter tier* is linked (time-aligned) to the tier on which the main participant's speech is transcribed. Independent internal (linguistic) variables are coded as daughter tiers to the token tier in which the dependent variable is coded. External (social, stylistic) variables, often spanning longer time segments, may be coded as well. All tokens and codes may then be exported to a spreadsheet or statistical analysis program for quantitative analysis.

Each new version of the transcript – for example, when proofread by a second researcher, or when a new variable is coded – should be stored as a separate file or tier, with a formalized naming convention described in the protocol. This makes it possible to retrace back to the original file if errors or omissions are discovered, or if different practices are applied at different stages of the research project.

Due to space limitations, we do not discuss the *storage* of transcripts in detail here, save to note that the digitization of transcription has led to significant innovations and improvements in this area as well; Kendall (2008) offers a useful discussion of linguistic data storage.

7   Planning transcription: time, transcribers, and accuracy

A common practical question in planning transcription is how much time it is likely to require. The response depends on how much information is to be included in the transcription, whether the transcript is time-aligned with audio/ video files, and the level of experience of the transcriber with writing in the language/orthography being used and with transcribing in general. Estimates for native speakers transcribing English orthographically range from $4\times$ (4 hours to transcribe 1 hour of speech) to $10\times$. In the HLVC project, transcribing rates for different languages being transcribed by research assistants who rarely write their native languages range from $12\times$ to $28\times$. In this project, Italian, Korean and Ukrainian are transcribed in standard orthography (fastest). Russian is transcribed in standard orthography by keying in Roman characters (transliteration), which are then convertible to Cyrillic via a web-based application. Cantonese and Faetar are transcribed using IPA (slowest).

In Poplack's (1989) Ottawa-Hull French Project, the goal was to maximize the initial rate of transcription, with a follow-up *correction phase*. Two researchers, working with tape recorders and foot pedals (now often replaced by keystrokes to control a digital recording on the same computer as is used for transcribing), after a year of transcription practice, "reached an average transcription rate of a half hour of speech per day" (Poplack 1989: 431) (i.e., a rate of approximately $16\times$). (We assume these were native speakers of French.) A range of factors are noted that contribute to the range of rates from $7\times$ to $18\times$ (ibid.): congestion of the time-sharing facility or lab, the number of persons participating in the interview, the rapidity and articulation of their speech, background noise, volume of the recording, and position of the microphone. In a more recent study (Poplack, Walker, and Malcolmson 2006: 194), this time of English, transcription rates are reported in terms of word counts rather than chronological length of the interview, making comparisons difficult. The overall calculation is that the team transcribed 2.8 million words in 2,471 person-hours.

Time-aligned transcription is initially more time-consuming than text-only transcription, but economies are gained in the long term because it is easier to check transcriptions and the broader context via the direct links between the transcription and the recording. Also, broader transcription is feasible as the first pass, with phonetic details being measured or coded later only for relevant segments.

Finally, transcription for qualitative sociolinguistic analysis is naturally far more time-consuming and is therefore frequently limited to carefully selected extracts. In these cases, transcription is an integral part of the analytic process, so requires direct and constant involvement of the primary researcher(s).

This leads to a second common question in planning transcription, namely who should do the transcribing. Once again, this depends on the level of detail to be included, the relative experience of different project participants, and, in many cases, the (non-)availability of funds. As indicated throughout this chapter, there are significant advantages to the researcher doing some or all of the transcription needed, as crucial coding decisions and analytic insights emerge throughout the process. Students and research assistants can certainly be trained and used for some transcription, with both training and financial benefits.

In the HLVC project, both transcription and proofreading are carried out by students who are community members and heritage speakers when possible, otherwise native speakers of a similar variety of the language. Transcribers are generally paid because the work is very slow. However, a number of HLVC transcribers work as volunteers, finding that working with the data is interesting and of potential benefit to their community.

Jung and Himmelmann (2011) highlight the fact that in language documentation work, or indeed any work where the transcriber is not as familiar with the language as the speakers, transcription needs to be conducted in close contact with native speakers, and therefore often in the field (see Chapter 4), with potentially important outcomes:

> working on transcription may lead to the emergence of a new linguistic variety, as it involves the creation of a new written language. This is particularly true in those instances where recorded texts are carefully edited for publication in a local (e.g. educational) context, a process documented, perhaps for the first time, in a rigorous way in Mosel's work on Teop (see Mosel 2004, 2008). But it actually also occurs in similar, though less systematic ways in transcription ... (Jung and Himmelmann 2011: 202)

Jung and Himmelmann (2011: 205) also note what an unnatural activity transcription is, especially for languages which are not (frequently) written, and make the valuable recommendation that a researcher transcribe a recording in their own language before engaging in work on another language or in training native speakers to transcribe.

A third central issue in organizing the transcription phase of a project effectively is accommodating the need for corrections and inter-rater reliability checks. Transcriber effects are unavoidable. Anyone who has transcribed recorded data has experienced surprise at discovering that chunks of audio material have been entirely overlooked in the transcript, frequently due to the natural human facility of attending to the salient constituents of a message and tuning out material perceived to be irrelevant to the message. Even for experienced researchers, repeated listening and editing of transcripts is a basic component of producing an accurate transcript. More specific transcriber effects can also arise. Jung and Himmelmann (2011: 208–9) point out that transcribers who are community members may resist transcribing, or transcribing verbatim, certain elements of a recording because of lack of comprehension (possibly due to dialect differences), taboo, disbelief, a desire to tell less or more than is in the recording, and a general (and very natural) concern more for the message than the form of utterances. Sometimes elements are omitted because there is no straightforward translation for them in the linguist's language, as is the case for Beaver evidentials when being translated to English as part of the transcription process (ibid.: 212).

Despite these transcriber effects, some universal and some culture-specific, certain practices can facilitate the accuracy of transcription. Especially in more selective transcription and transcription that is accompanied by coding of the data, it is important that the transcription protocol be well documented. This is vital for replicability by later researchers and also because linguists seem nowhere close to adopting universal standards for transcription, even as they approach it for metadata. Protocols should record decisions such as orthography, punctuation, identification, text formatting, glossing, and tier codes if relevant, and anonymization of speakers and others mentioned. Dated versions should be archived as updates are made so that later researchers can retrieve information accurate to the versions of the transcriptions they use.

Poplack (1989: 433) describes a number of decisions that need to be made regarding ambiguous and non-standard gender and number marking, forms with multiple attested spellings, neologisms, analogical extensions, omissions, additions, and loanwords. She notes that transcribers were encouraged to consult the protocol regularly to ensure consistency in decision-making, at all stages of transcription and correction, and that a simplified version of this protocol would be made available to users of the corpus.

Even with a scrupulous protocol, it remains vital that transcripts be checked several times, by the transcriber as well as, ideally, by another researcher, a stage that can be time-consuming. Poplack (1989: 435–6) calculated that it takes 15–20 hours for a first pass to correct a 2,000-line transcript that had already been passed through an automatic "clean-up" program that fixes recurrent typos, and an additional 10 hours for a second pass. An estimate of one error per 520 words remains after this careful process, which Poplack suggests is good enough to use the transcription for research without recourse to the recordings. In the Quebec English project, correction is reported to take 2.5–33 hours per interview, for a total of 1,536 hours for three passes over the 2.8 million-word corpus (Poplack, Walker, and Malcolmson 2006: 194–5).

Given the investment of resources for transcription, it is ideal if arrangements can be made for multiple uses of the transcription. The increasing mutual compatibility among transcription and analysis software is allowing linguistics as a discipline to overcome subdisciplinary divides and to share data easily with richer, more robust, and more interdisciplinary results.

References

Atkinson, J. M. and J. Heritage. 1984. *The Structure of Social Action*. Cambridge University Press.

Blondeau, H. and N. Nagy. 2008. Subordinate clause marking in Montreal Anglophone French and English. In M. Meyerhoff and N. Nagy, eds. *Social Lives in Language: Sociolinguistics and Multilingual Speech Communities*. John Benjamins: Amsterdam, 273–314.

Boersma, P. and D. Weenink. 2007. Praat: Doing phonetics by computer. Available at www.praat.org (accessed June 20, 2013).

Bresnan, J., A. Deo, and D. Sharma. 2007. Typology in variation: a probabilistic approach to be and n't in the Survey of English Dialects. *English Language and Linguistics* 11.2: 301–46.

Bucholtz, M. 2000. The politics of transcription. *Journal of Pragmatics* 32: 1439–65.

Childs, B., G. Van Herk, and J. Thorburn. 2011. Safe harbour: ethics and accessibility in sociolinguistic corpus building. *Corpus Linguistics and Linguistic Theory* 7.1: 163–80.

Comrie, B., M. Haspelmath, and B. Bickel. 2008. The Leipzig Glossing Rules: conventions for interlinear morpheme-by-morpheme glosses. Leipzig: Max Planck Institute for Evolutionary Anthropology and University of Leipzig. Available at: www.eva. mpg.de/lingua/pdf/LGR08.02.05.pdf (accessed July 8, 2013).

Couper-Kuhlen, E. 2001. Intonation and discourse: current views from within. In D. Schiffrin, D. Tannen, and H. E. Hamilton, eds. *The Handbook of Discourse Analysis*. Oxford: Blackwell, 13–34.

Cruttenden, A. 1997. *Intonation*, 2nd edn. Cambridge University Press.

Du Bois, J. W., S. Cumming, S. Schuetze-Coburn, and D. Paolino, eds. 1992. Discourse transcription. *Santa Barbara Papers in Linguistics 4*. Department of Linguistics, University of California, Santa Barbara.

Edwards, J. 2001. The transcription of discourse. In D. Tannen, D. Schiffrin, and H. Hamilton, eds. *Handbook of Discourse Analysis*. Oxford: Blackwell, 321–48.

Fox, S. and J. Cheshire. 2011. From sociolinguistic research to English language teaching. *Methods in Dialectology 14*, University of Western Ontario, August 2–6.

Gumperz, J. J. and N. B. Berenz. 1993. Transcribing conversational exchanges. In J. A. Edwards and M. D. Lampert, eds. *Talking Data: Transcription and Coding in Discourse Research*. Hillsdale, NJ: Lawrence Erlbaum, 91–121.

Hazen, K. 2010. Step one, step two . . . The big picture of the West Virginia Dialect Project. University of West Virginia ms. (See the companion website for this volume.)

Hutchby, I. and R. Wooffitt. 1998. *Conversation Analysis*. Cambridge: Polity Press.

Jefferson, G. 2004. Glossary of transcript symbols with an introduction. In G. H. Lerner, ed. *Conversation Analysis: Studies from the First Generation*. Amsterdam: John Benjamins, 13–31.

Jung, D. and N. P. Himmelmann. 2011. Retelling data: working on transcription. In G. Haig, N. Nau, S. Schnell, and C. Wegener, eds. *Documenting Languages: Achievements and Perspectives*. Berlin: Mouton De Gruyter, 201–20.

Kendall, T. 2008. On the history and future of sociolinguistic data. *Language and Linguistic Compass* 2.2: 332–51.

  2009. *The Sociolinguistic Archive and Analysis Project User Guide. Version 0.96 (second DRAFT–June 2009)*. http://ncslaap.lib.ncsu.edu/pdfs/SLAAP_UserGuide_v096.pdf (accessed July 8, 2013).

Labov, W. 1969. Contraction, deletion, and inherent variability of the English copula. *Language* 45: 715–62.

  2001. *The anatomy of style-shifting*. In P. Eckert and J. Rickford, eds. *Style and Sociolinguistic Variation*, 85–108.

Ladefoged, P. and S. Disner. 2012. *Vowels and Consonants*, 3rd edn. Malden and Oxford: Blackwell.

MacWhinney, B. 2000. *The CHILDES Project: Tools for Analyzing Talk. Volume I: Transcription Format and Programs. Volume II: The Database*. Mahwah, NJ: Lawrence Erlbaum. Available at: http://psyling.psy.cmu.edu/papers/guides/talkbank. html (accessed July 8, 2013).

Mishler, E. G. 1991. Representing discourse: the rhetoric of transcription. *Journal of Narrative and Life History* 1: 255–80.

Nagy, N. 2000. *Faetar*. Munich: Lincom Europa.

  2009. *Heritage Language Variation and Change*. Available at: http://projects.chass. utoronto.ca/ngn/HLVC (accessed 25 June 2013).

  2011a. Lexical change and language contact: Faetar in Italy and Canada. *Journal of Sociolinguistics* 15: 366–82.

  2011b. A multilingual corpus to explore geographic variation. *Rassegna Italiana di Linguistica Applicata* XLIII.1–2: 65–84.

  2011c. Faetar transcribing guide. University of Toronto ms. (See the companion website for this volume.)

  2012. Heritage Language Documentation Corpus (HerLD). Workshop sur l'annotation des corpus multilingues, Paris. Available at: http://projects.chass.utoronto.ca/ngn/ pdf/HLVC/Transcribing_multilingual_speech.pdf (accessed 25 June 2013).

Ochs, E. 1979. Transcription as theory. In E. Ochs and B. Schieffelin, eds. *Developmental Pragmatics*. New York: Academic Press, 43–72.

Orton, H., W. J. Halliday, M. V. Barry, P. M. Tilling, and M. F. Wakelin. 1962–71. *Survey of English Dialects: The Basic Material*, 4 vols. Leeds: E. J. Arnold for the University of Leeds.

Poplack, S. 1989. The care and handling of a megacorpus. In R. Fasold and D. Schiffrin, eds. *Language Change and Variation*. Amsterdam: Benjamins, 411–51.

  2007. Foreword. In J. Beal, K. Corrigan, and H. Moisl, eds. *Creating and Digitizing Language Corpora*. Houndmills: Palgrave-Macmillan, ix–xiii.

Poplack, S., J. A. Walker, and R. Malcolmson. 2006. An English "like no other"?: language contact and change in Quebec. *Canadian Journal of Linguistics* 51.2/3: 185–213.

Potter, J. and A. Hepburn. 2005. Qualitative interviews in psychology: problems and possibilities. *Qualitative Research in Psychology* 2: 38–55.

Preston, D. 1982. Ritin' fowklower daun 'rong: Folklorists' failures in phonology. *Journal of American Folklore* 95: 304–26.

Sankoff, D. and G. Sankoff. 1973. Sample survey methods and computer-assisted analysis in the study of grammatical variation. In R. Darnell, ed. *Canadian Languages in their Social Context*. Edmonton: Linguistic Research Inc., 7–63.

Sankoff, G., P. Thibault, N. Nagy, H. Blondeau, M.-O. Fonollosa, and L. Gagnon. 1997. Variation and the use of discourse markers in a language contact situation. *Language Variation and Change* 9: 191–218.

Schegloff, E. A. 2001. Discourse as interactional achievement III: the omnirelevance of action. In D. Schiffrin, D. Tannen, and H. E. Hamilton, eds. *The Handbook of Discourse Analysis*. Oxford: Blackwell, 229–49.

Sharma, D. 2003. Discourse clitics and constructive morphology in Hindi. In M. Butt and T. Holloway King, eds. *Nominals: Inside and Out*. Stanford: CSLI Publications.

2005. Dialect stabilization and speaker awareness in non-native varieties of English. *Journal of Sociolinguistics* 9.2: 194–225.

Sharma, D. and L. Sankaran. 2011. Cognitive and social forces in dialect shift: gradual change in London Asian speech. *Language Variation and Change* 23: 1–30.

Silverman, K., M. Beckman, J. Pitrelli, M. Ostendorf, C. Wightman, P. Price, J. Pierrehumbert, and J. Hirschberg. 1992. ToBI: a standard for labeling English prosody. In *Proceedings of the 1992 International Conference on Spoken Language Processing*, October 12–16, Banff, Canada, pp. 867–70.

Thieberger, N. and A. Berez. 2012. Linguistic data management. In N. Thieberger, ed. *The Oxford Handbook of Linguistic Fieldwork*. Oxford University Press.

Torres Cacoullos, R. 2011. Transcription notes. Pennsylvania State University ms. (See the companion website for this volume.)

Valdman, A. 2007. NSF Behavioral and Cognitive Sciences grant #0639482.

Wittenburg, P., H. Brugman, A. Russel, A. Klassmann, and H. Sloetjes. 2006. ELAN: a professional framework for multimodality research. In *Proceedings of LREC 2006, Fifth International Conference on Language Resources and Evaluation*, May 22–28, Genoa, Italy.

Appendix 12.1 Tools and software discussed in this chapter

CLAN	http://childes.talkbank.org/clan
ELAN	Max Planck Institute for Psycholinguistics, The Language Archive, Nijmegen, The Netherlands. http://tla.mpi.nl/tools/tla-tools/elan
FLEx	http://fieldworks.sil.org/flex
Leipzig Glossing Rules	www.eva.mpg.de/lingua/resources/glossing-rules.php
Praat	www.fon.hum.uva.nl/praat
Transcriber	http://trans.sourceforge.net
TYPECRAFT	The Natural Language Database. http://typecraft.org (All websites accessed July 8, 2013.)

13   Creating and using corpora

Stefan Th. Gries and John Newman

1   Introduction

Over the last few decades, corpus-linguistic methods have established themselves as among the most powerful and versatile tools to study language acquisition, processing, variation, and change. This development has been driven in particular by the following considerations:

a.   technological progress (e.g., processor speeds as well as hard drive and RAM sizes);
b.   methodological progress (e.g., the development of software tools, programming languages, and statistical methods);
c.   a growing desire by many linguists for (more) objective, quantifiable, and replicable findings as an alternative to, or at least as an addition to, intuitive acceptability judgments (see Chapter 3);
d.   theoretical developments such as the growing interest in cognitively and psycholinguistically motivated approaches to language in which frequency of (co-)occurrence plays an important role for language acquisition, processing, use, and change.

In this chapter, we will discuss a necessarily small selection of issues regarding (i) the creation, or compilation, of new corpora and (ii) the use of corpora once they have been compiled. Although this chapter encompasses both the creation and use of corpora, there is no expectation that any individual researcher would be engaged in both these kinds of activities. Different skills are called for when it comes to creating and using corpora, a point noted by Sinclair (2005: 1), who draws attention to the potential pitfalls of a corpus analyst building a corpus, specifically, the danger that the corpus will be constructed in a way that can only serve to confirm the analyst's pre-existing expectations. Some of the issues addressed in this chapter are also dealt with in Wynne (2005), McEnery, Xiao, and Tono (2006), and McEnery and Hardie (2012) in a fairly succinct way, and more thoroughly in Lüdeling and Kytö (2008a, 2008b) and Beal, Corrigan, and Moisl (2007a, 2007b).[1]

---

[1] Details of corpora and software mentioned in this chapter are provided in Appendices 1 and 2 (URLs accessed June 26, 2013). These are rapidly developing domains and information provided here is naturally only current as at the time of writing. Updated lists are available on the companion website for this volume.

2   Creating corpora

2.1   The notion of a "corpus": a prototype and dimensions of variation

The notion of a *corpus* can best be defined as a category organized around a prototype. Most generally, a corpus can be described as "a body of naturally occurring language" (McEnery, Xiao, and Tono 2006: 4), thereby distinguishing a corpus from word lists, dictionaries, databases, and so on. These days, the prototypical corpus is a *machine-readable* collection of language used in authentic settings/contexts: one that is intended to be *representative* for a particular language, variety, or register (in the sense of reflecting all the possible parts of the intended language/variety/register), and that is intended to be *balanced* such that the sizes of the parts of the corpus correspond to the proportion these parts make up in the language/variety/register (see McEnery, Xiao, and Tono 2006: 5; Hunston 2008: 160–6; Gries 2009: Chapter 1). However, many corpora differ from an ideal design along these (and other) parameters; in fact, there is disagreement as to whether just *any* body of naturally occurring language can be called a corpus. Kilgarriff and Grefenstette (2006: 334), by way of introducing and advocating the study of data from the World Wide Web, adopt a definition of a corpus as "a collection of texts when considered as an object of language or literary study." On the other hand, Sinclair (2005: 15) explicitly excludes a number of categories from linguistic corpora (e.g., a single text, an archive, and, in particular, the World Wide Web). Beyond being a body of naturally occurring language, then, it is difficult to agree on any more particular definition of what a corpus is or is not. Note, too, that some collections of language can diverge from the prototypical property of being "naturally occurring language," and yet are still happily referred to as corpora by their creators. As an example, consider the TIMIT Acoustic-Phonetic Continuous Speech Corpus, made up of audio recordings of 630 speakers of eight major dialects of American English. For these recordings, each speaker read ten "phonetically rich" sentences – a uniquely valuable resource for the study of acoustic properties of American English, but not what one would consider naturally occurring language.

A detailed overview of corpora, illustrating the range of types of corpora that are being studied within linguistics, can be found in the chapters of Lüdeling and Kytö (2008a: 154–483). Apart from the above criteria defining prototypical corpora, one can distinguish corpus types by the media that hold the data: written text (web, text documents, historical manuscripts; see Chapter 11 for details on the use of diachronic corpora); audio; video and audio; audio and transcribed spoken texts based on the audio, and so on. There is often an assumption that a corpus will include written language or transcriptions of spoken language (which arguably represents the prototypical kind of language use), but it is important to appreciate that collections of naturally occurring speech in the form of audio files ("speech corpora," as opposed to transcriptions of spoken language) are valid corpora.

Ostler (2008: 459) remarks on the artificiality of distinctions between speech-based and text-based corpora in light of the increasing use of multi-tiered annotations of audio and video data (see Chapter 12 for details on transcription and multi-tier annotation). One may also choose to distinguish corpus types by content or source: synchronic vs historical, national corpora, learner corpora, academic discourse, children's language, interviews, static vs monitor corpora, multilingual, web-based, and so on. Corpora, as used in linguistics, are created with particular purposes of study in mind and the variety of corpus types should not be surprising – it is no more than a reflection of the richness and multi-facetedness of language use and the many perspectives one can bring to the study of language. One cannot therefore speak of a "standard" in corpus construction or design in the sense of a set of protocols that must be adhered to in order for the corpus to be admissible in corpus linguistics; the conception of "corpus" as a category around a prototype is more appropriate (see Gilquin and Gries 2009: Section 2). Further information on selected corpora can be found in Appendix 13.1.

There are now many large corpora of high quality available, where "large" means, say, 100 million words or more. We emphasize, though, that smaller corpora also have their place alongside the larger corpora. The key consideration is to have an appropriate match of research goal and corpus type/size, and, for some research goals, even quite a small corpus constructed by a researcher can yield insightful results. Berkenfield (2001), using a corpus of just 10,640 words, was able to carry out research on phonetic reduction of *that* in spoken English; Thompson and Hopper (2001) successfully explored transitivity in a corpus of multi-party conversations consisting of just 446 clauses; Fiorentino (2009) studied ordering of adverbial and main clauses in an Italian corpus consisting of 26,000 words for the written part of the corpus and 32,000 for the spoken part. Smaller corpora such as these can suffice when the focus of the study is a relatively frequent phenomenon, but would not be advisable if the focus is a relatively rare phenomenon. Granath (2007), reflecting on the different results obtained from searching for an English inversion structure like *Thus ended his dreams*, found reason to appreciate both the 1 million-word corpora and the 50 million-word corpora used in the study: "in the end, combining evidence from large and small corpora can give us information that neither type of corpus could provide on its own" (Granath 2007: 183).

2.2   Collecting the corpus data

In this and the following section, we describe the main steps involved in preparing and annotating a new corpus, before reviewing readily available corpora in Section 2.4. It is fair to say that most corpora are created with the expectation that they are, in some sense, representative of something larger than themselves – what we referred to as the prototypical corpus in Section 2.1 – rather than the ultra-pragmatic view of a corpus held by Kilgarriff and Grefenstette. Consequently, an initial and profound decision relates to exactly what the corpus

Table 13.1 *A subset of the Uppsala Learner English Corpus. Adapted from Table 1 in Johansson and Geisler 2011: 140*

Level	School year	Boys		Girls	
		Mean essay length in words	Number of essays	Mean essay length in words	Number of essays
Junior high	Year 7	228.0	5	217.0	5
	Year 9	221.8	5	234.0	5
Senior high	Year 1	220.8	5	190.0	5
	Year 3	277.8	5	245.0	5
Total		237.1	20	221.5	20

is supposed to be representative of and what sampling technique is to be used (see Chapter 5 for a more general discussion of sampling). One very basic kind of decision guiding the collection of language data concerns the categories that form the basis of the sampling: categories of language users (e.g., gender, age, socioeconomic class, geographical location), categories of the language products (e.g., spoken language, written language, register of language use, text type, formality of the language), or a combination of both of these. A noteworthy example of how categories of language users can figure prominently in corpus data is the sub-corpus of the Uppsala Learner English Corpus used in Johansson and Geisler (2011). For the purposes of their study of the syntax of Swedish learners of English, the authors carefully chose learners' essays to balance the numbers of boys and girls and the levels of the school year, as summarized in Table 13.1.

Typically, it is categories such as register (i.e., categories relating to properties of the product rather than the user) that are the preferred basis for structuring the more common corpora in use (see the examples of widely used corpora in Section 2.4). This is due in part to the unavailability of sociodemographic data on speakers and writers in the case of many texts (as retrieved, for example, from the World Wide Web), but it may also be due to the view that the variation between, say, spoken and written modalities is far more significant than variation between male and female speech or writing. The approach adopted in creating the Canadian component of the International Corpus of English (ICE-CAN) offers a practical way of proceeding: data are basically sampled on the basis of categories of register (broadly understood), such as spoken vs written, spoken dialogue vs spoken monologue, spoken dialogue private vs spoken dialogue public, written printed vs non-printed, but some attempt is made to balance the numbers of male and female speakers in the data collection. The *metadata* on speakers contributing to the spoken part of ICE-CAN and available as part of the distribution of the corpus, summarized below, is in fact extensive enough for a sociolinguistically oriented use of the corpus:

a.   date of recording
b.   place of recording
c.   gender
d.   age
e.   mother tongue
f.   other languages spoken
g.   self-reported ethnicity
h.   occupation
i.   educational profile
j.   professional training
k.   overseas experience

The decision as to what the corpus should be representative of will always have a huge impact on how the corpus data will be collected: recordings of natural conversation, recorded interviews, conversation from TV programs, fictional texts or journalese (from the web or processed by optical character recognition [OCR] software), blogs and chat-room data, general content crawled/collected from the web are but a few possible data sources, and careful decisions as to what can and must be included are required, and, realistically, will often have to be balanced with what is possible within the restrictions of particular research agendas and goals. Sometimes there can be hidden biases in making decisions about representativeness, skewing the data collected in unintended ways. A typical bias may favor a "standard" or better known variety of language over less prestigious (dialectal, colloquial) varieties, or favor the collection of data from more educated speakers. Newman and Columbus (2009), for example, found an (unintended) over-representation of vocabulary relating to the education domain in a number of the conversational corpora in the International Corpus of English project, most likely a consequence of the easy availability of speakers from the education sector as contributors of data. Of course, the researcher may quite consciously opt for data specifically restricted to a standard variety, educated speakers, or other factors, but it should not be thought that a corpus must be restricted in this way. In addition, there is a variety of further restrictions on the collection of data which often have to do with what speakers/writers allow to be done with their speech/texts. For example, for reasons of copyright or the traditions of speech communities, not everything that can be found on the Web can be added to a corpus that is intended for use by others.

    These days, the World Wide Web offers a useful starting point for obtaining text which can be utilized for the construction of corpora. Collections of published materials (out of the range of current copyright) such as Project Gutenberg provide a wealth of literary texts in many languages that can be exploited for the creation of customized digital corpora. But, as already indicated above, there is an abundance of material available for downloading apart from literary texts: newspaper collections, Wikipedia entries, university lectures, film scripts, translations of the Bible, blogs, and so on. Oral history projects provide opportunities for the creation of spoken corpora. Consider, as just one example, the Southern Oral History Program, which began in 1973 with the aim of documenting the life of the American South in tapes, videos, and transcripts. According to the website, this project will ultimately make 500 oral history interviews available over the internet (400 are already available), selected from the 4,000 or so oral history interviews carried out over 30 years. The interviews cover a variety of topics in recent North Carolina history, particularly civil rights, politics, and women's issues. As of writing, the index contains a list of 496 topics. Interviews can be read as text transcript, listened to (or downloaded) with a media player, or both simultaneously. Note, also, that applications such as HTTrack (for Windows/Unix) or Sitesucker (for Mac) can currently be used with many sites, enabling an automated mirroring of whole websites.

Our emphasis in this chapter is on creating and using corpora as written or transcribed texts, but some comments on collecting spoken data are in order (see Chapters 9 and 11 for many observations directly relevant here). One issue immediately confronting a researcher collecting data directly from a speaker is how to minimize observer effects. Inconspicuousness and versatility are two key goals in managing the collection of speech data (intended to reflect natural, non-self-conscious use of language), as discussed in Chapters 6 and 9. The CallHome American English Speech Corpus, for example, follows a procedure which is likely to reduce any observer effect. The corpus is based on recorded telephone conversations lasting up to 30 minutes, where the participants are fully aware that they are being recorded. The transcripts which derive from these recordings, however, are based only on 10 contiguous minutes from within those 30 minutes. While this strategy does not exclude some self-consciousness on the part of the speakers, it does serve to lessen any such effect, since the speakers cannot know in advance which 10 minutes are being utilized for the transcript. A second issue surrounding the collection of spoken data concerns the quality of the audio/video recording. Needless to say, one aims for the best quality possible (WAV rather than MP3 format for audio files, for example), though sometimes a lesser quality may suffice. The corpora in the International Corpus of English project, for example, are designed primarily for distribution as corpora in the form of text files where the spoken data have been transcribed into regular English orthography. In such cases, the quality of the recording must be good enough for reliable transcription, even if it falls short of what a researcher carrying out a fine acoustic analysis requires. Finally, creating a speech corpus in which the acoustic characteristics are of importance leads naturally to additional kinds of metadata compared with those listed above. Below is a summary of the metadata available in the CallHome American English Speech Corpus.

Metadata for a conversation recording:
a.   total number of speakers
b.   number of females and males
d.   number of speakers per channel and number of males/females per channel

e.   difficulty (overall quality of the channel in terms of number of speakers, background noise, channel noise, speed, accent, articulation)
f.   background noise (amount of sound not made by the speakers, e.g., baby crying, television, radio)
g.   distortion (echo and other types of recording problems)
h.   crosstalk (audibility of the channel A speaker on channel B, and vice versa)

Metadata for the caller:

i.   gender
j.   age
k.   years of education
l.   where the caller grew up
m.   telephone number called

Once first versions of video/sound/text files have been obtained, typically one or more follow-up steps are necessary, which are discussed in the following section.

2.3   Preparing the corpus data

The first versions of files obtained in the first collection step hardly ever correspond to the desired final versions. Rather, such files typically require two additional steps before they can be used and made available as corpus files: they virtually always need to be cleaned up and standardized, and they often need to be marked up and annotated. In today's age of increased data sharing, it is important to standardize corpus files to facilitate later use by other researchers with different goals.

2.3.1   Cleaning up and standardizing

The first versions of files typically need to be cleaned of any undesired information they may contain. Files which include information that is protected for privacy reasons need to have such information edited in some way (see Chapters 2 and 12). For example, if one gathers recordings of authentic conversation, it is often necessary to protect the speakers' privacy as well as the privacy of those whom a speaker talks about in their absence. (Imagine a case where, during a recording, a speaker mentions that her neighbor cheated on last year's tax report or that her brother's visa has expired.) Data like these require careful consideration of how much one can and must anonymize the data. In ICE-CAN, for example, names other than those of public figures were anonymized through the use of pseudonyms.

Files obtained from the internet or other sources can be in one of any number of formats (.txt, .html, .xml, .pdf, .doc, etc.) and will almost invariably require some editing for them to be used most effectively. In using files from the Web as a convenient example, editing *may* include, but is not limited to the tasks listed below:

a.   converting all files into one and the same interoperable file format and language encoding (e.g., converting data into Unicode text files);

b.   removing and/or standardizing unwanted elements (e.g., deleting unwanted HTML tags such as image references, title, body, table, and other tags, links, scripts, etc.);

c.   standardizing different spellings and character representations (e.g., standardizing ü and ü into ü, etc.);

d.   identifying files downloaded more than once and deleting copies.

This kind of editing typically requires ready-made tools with particular features, or, better still, the use of a programming language. An example of a ready-made application at the time of writing is the free cross-platform Java-based text editor jEdit. While jEdit has many attractive features, it includes three key features relevant to formatting texts for corpus-based research: (i) it accepts a wide range of *language encodings*, including UTF-8 and UTF-16; (ii) it allows for search and replace over multiple files; (iii) it features search and replacement operations using *regular expressions*, which are a method to describe simple or very complicated sequences of characters in files (see Table 13.11). Software like jEdit and other text editors intended for programmers force the user to be more attuned to properties of files which become important in working with corpus tools, such as language encodings and (Unix- vs Windows- vs Mac-style) line breaks. Regular expressions increase the power of editing considerably, allowing options such as finding and deleting all annotation contained within angular brackets, adding an annotation at the beginning of each line, removing some variable number of lines of text at the beginning of a file, such as all text within <teiHeader>...</teiHeader>, features that are not necessarily available in typical word-processing software.

2.3.2   Marking up and annotating

Once one has files that are cleaned up and standardized as desired, a second preparatory step usually involves enriching these with desired information they do not yet contain. Such information serves to facilitate the retrieval of linguistic patterns and their co-occurrence with other (linguistic or extra-linguistic) data. Usually, one distinguishes markup and annotation.

In the case of written or transcribed data, the *markup* section of a file refers to metadata about the file and might include information such as when the data in the file were collected, a description of the source of the data, when the file was prepared, basic social information about participants if relevant, and other such details. Figure 13.1 shows an example of markup from the beginning of the Extensible Markup Language (XML) version of the Brown Corpus, distributed as part of Baby BNC v.2. The elements of markup conform to the specifications laid down by the Text Encoding Initiative (TEI), a consortium of interested parties, which are concerned with establishing standards for sharing documents. Angled brackets < and > demarcate the tags which enclose metadata; / indicates a

```
<teiHeader>
      <fileDesc>
            <titleStmt>
                   <title>Sample A01 from The Atlanta Constitution</title>
                   <title type="sub"> November 4, 1961, p.1 "Atlanta Primary &"
                   "Hartsfield Files"
                   August 17, 1961, "Urged strongly &"
                   "Sam Caldwell Joins"
                   March 6,1961, p.1 "Legislators Are Moving" by Reg Murphy
                   "Legislator to fight" by Richard Ashworth
                   "House Due Bid&"
                   p.18 "Harry Miller Wins&"
                   </title>
            </titleStmt>
            <editionStmt>
                   <edition>A part of the XML version of the Brown Corpus</edition>
            </editionStmt>
            <extent>1,988 words 431 (21.7%) quotes 2 symbols</extent>
            <publicationStmt>
                   <idno>A01</idno>
                   <availability><p>Used by permission of The Atlanta Constitution
                   State News
                   Service (H), and Reg Murphy (E).</p></availability>
            </publicationStmt>
            <sourceDesc>
                   <bibl> The Atlanta Constitution</bibl>
            </sourceDesc>
      </fileDesc>
      <encodingDesc>
            <p>Arbitrary Hyphen: multi-million [0520]</p>
      </encodingDesc>
      <revisionDesc>
            <change when="2008-04-27">Header auto-generated for TEI version</change>
      </revisionDesc>
</teiHeader>
```

Figure 13.1. *Markup in the TEI Header of file A01 in the XML Brown Corpus*

closing tag. All the information in the TEI header, for example, is found between the opening tag <teiHeader> and the closing tag </teiHeader>; the header, in turn, consists of a file description within the <fileDesc> tags, a title statement within the <titleStmt> tags, an edition statement within the <editionStmt> tags, and so on, as seen in Figure 13.1. The TEI guidelines for markup of texts are intended to apply to all kinds of texts and are not designed specifically for the files of a linguistic corpus. An extension of the TEI guidelines specifically intended for corpus markup (and annotation) is the Corpus Encoding Standard (CES) and the more recent version of these standards designed for XML, namely Extensible Corpus Encoding Standard (ECES).

The *annotation* part of a file refers to elements added to provide specifically linguistic information (e.g., part of speech, semantic information, and pragmatic information). Most commonly, annotation takes the form of part-of-speech tagging of words. The first sentence of the Brown Corpus is shown in a parts-of-speech annotated form in (1a). The tags used in this sentence are explained in (1b) – full details can be found in the Brown Corpus Manual (khnt.aksis.uib.no/icame/manuals/brown/INDEX.HTM). Other tagsets are the various versions of

```
<p>
    <s n="1">
            <w type="AT">The</w>
            <w type="NP" subtype="TL">Fulton</w>
            <w type="NN" subtype="TL">County</w>
            <w type="JJ" subtype="TL">Grand</w>
            <w type="NN" subtype="TL">Jury</w>
            <w type="VBD">said</w>
            <w type="NR">Friday</w>
            <w type="AT">an</w>
            <w type="NN">investigation</w>
            <w type="IN">of</w>
            <w type="NP">Atlanta's</w>
            <w type="JJ">recent</w>
            <w type="NN">primary</w>
            <w type="NN">election</w>
            <w type="VBD">produced</w>
            <c type="pct">``</c>
            <w type="AT">no</w>
            <w type="NN">evidence</w>
            <c type="pct">''</c>
            <w type="CS">that</w>
            <w type="DTI">any</w>
            <w type="NNS">irregularities</w>
            <w type="VBD">took</w>
            <w type="NN">place</w>
            <c type="pct">.</c>
    </s>
</p>
```

Figure 13.2. *The first sentence (and paragraph) in the text body of file A01 in the XML Brown Corpus (the tags beginning with p, s, and w mark the paragraph, sentence, and each word respectively)*

Constituent Likelihood Automatic Word-tagging System (CLAWS) and the University of Pennsylvania (Penn) Treebank Tagset. Figure 13.2 shows the same annotated sentence in an XML format.

(1)   a. The/at Fulton/np-tl County/nn-tl Grand/jj-tl Jury/nn-tl said/vbd Friday/nr an/at investigation/nn of/in Atlanta's/np$ recent/jj primary/nn election/nn produced/vbd ``/`` no/at evidence/nn "/" that/cs any/dti irregularities/nns took/vbd place/nn ./.

       b. at = article; np-tl = proper noun, also appearing in the title (of the newspaper article, in this case); nn-tl = singular common noun, also appearing in the title; jj-tl = adjective, also appearing in the title; vbd = past tense of verb; nr = adverbial noun; nn = singular common noun; in = preposition; np$ = possessive proper noun; jj = adjective; cs = subordinating conjunction; dti = singular or plural determiner/quantifier; nns = plural common noun; . = sentence closer; "= punctuation

Sometimes, a tagging system allows for multiple tags to be associated with one and the same word. In general, the CLAWS tagger assigns to each word in a text one or more tags (regardless of the context in which it occurs) and then tries to identify the one best tag based on the frequency of word-tag combinations in the immediate context. However, sometimes the algorithm is unable to clearly identify one and only one tag and uses a hyphenated tag, such as VVG-NN1 instead (as

Table 13.2 *Four tagging solutions for English* rid

	I am now completely rid of such things.	*You are well rid of him.*	*I got rid of the rubbish.*
CLAWS tagger	past participle	past participle	past participle
Infogistics	verb base	verb base	past participle
FreeLing	adjective	verb base	past participle
(Brill-based) GoTagger	adjective	adjective	adjective

```
<mw c5="PRP">
        <w c5="PRP" hw="in" pos="PREP">in </w>
        <w c5="NN2" hw="term" pos="SUBST">terms </w>
        <w c5="PRF" hw="of" pos="PREP">of </w>
</mw>
```

Figure 13.3. *The annotation of* in terms of *as a multi-word unit in the BNC XML*

when *singing* in the sentence *She says she couldn't stop singing* is tagged VVG-NN1). The hyphenated tag in this case, as used in the British National Corpus (BNC), indicates that the algorithm was unable to decide between the VVG (the -*ing* form of a verb) and NN1 (the singular of a common noun), but the preference is for the VVG tag.

Hyphenated tags are employed by Meurman-Solin (2007) as a way of indicating the range of different functions that can be expressed by the word in a diachronic corpus of English, creating, in effect, tags which embody grammaticalization facts. Certainly, there should be no expectation that part-of-speech tagging algorithms will produce identical results. Consider the tags assigned to *rid* in the three sentences in Table 13.2, based on four automatic tagging programs, where it can be seen that there is no uniform assignment of the part of speech of *rid* in any of the three sentences given. Here we see indications of a re-grammaticalization of a past participle as an adjective, just one example of how any part-of-speech system needs to be critically assessed.

Another way in which multiple tags can refer to one word involves multi-word units. For instance, the complex preposition *in terms of* is tagged in the BNC XML, as shown in Figure 13.3 (for expository reasons, we have added line breaks to highlight the annotation's structure).

Transcription of spoken language presents considerable challenges, at least if one wishes to highlight faithfully features of spoken language (see Newman 2008; see also Chapter 12). The annotated transcription in (2), a sample of transcribed spoken language taken from ICE-CAN, illustrates some of this complexity. Overlapping strings are indicated by <[>...</[>, with the complete set of overlapping strings contained within <{>...</{>, stretching across both speaker A and speaker B. The tags <{}>...</{}> indicate a "normative replacement," where a repetition of *they* (in casual, face-to-face conversation) is indicated. This annotation allows for searching on the raw data (containing the original two instances of *they*) or on the normalized version (containing one instance of *they* within <=...></=>). The example in (2) illustrates only a tiny fraction of the challenges presented by spoken language. The Great Britain component of the International Corpus of English (ICE-GB) contains syntactic parses for all the data, which make the annotation even more complex.

(2)   <$A> <ICE-CAN:S1A-001#34:1:A> I think some of the trippers actually do
           a bit of the portaging by themselves <}> <-> they> </-> <=> they </=>
           </}> bring it to the other end and they come back to help the kids with
           <{> <[> their packs </[>
           <$B> <ICE-CAN:S1A-001#35:1:B> <[> I see </[> </{>

The advent of extremely large multimodal corpora such as the corpus created through the Human Speechome Project (90,000 hours of video and 140,000 hours of audio recordings) takes the problems of dealing with audio and video to another level altogether, requiring the development of new kinds of tools to manage the extraordinary amount of data involved (Roy 2009).

Just as with cleaning up and standardizing data, the processes of marking up and annotating typically require more sophisticated tools than mere word-processing tools. For some tasks (e.g., straightforward replacement operations), general-purpose applications such as sophisticated text editors may be sufficient. For some more specialized tasks, ready-made applications with a graphical user interface are available. For example, language-encoding converters (Encoding Master for Windows/Mac, iconv for Unix/Linux, at the time of writing) and annotation software such as ELAN, Transcriber, and Soundscriber (Windows) are available (see Chapter 12 on transcription). Some larger and more automatic processes such as part-of-speech tagging, however, would normally be carried out by running scripts in a programming environment, though some graphical user interface (GUI) applications are also available (e.g., GoTagger for English and the Windows interface to TreeTagger for English and other languages).

To exemplify at least one application here, TreeTagger is a suite of scripts (currently available for Linux, Windows, and Mac) that would suit the needs of most researchers wanting to tag a corpus for part of speech. Some basic knowledge of programming environments is required to run these scripts, though running them is not a daunting task. To illustrate what is involved, (3) shows the one-line command needed to tag an English sentence, with the output directed to the screen as three columns (each word in the input, a tag, and a lemmatized form of the word). The tags are based on the Penn Treebank tagset. In this example, DT = determiner, VBP = non-[3rd person singular present] of a verb, NNS = plural common noun, WDT = Wh-determiner, NN = singular common noun, SENT = sentence closer. It is equally straightforward to tag a whole file or a directory of files. The tagging requires language-specific parameter files which are available for a dozen or so languages (including English, German, Italian, Dutch, Spanish, Bulgarian, Russian, French, Mandarin). TreeTagger includes a training module which allows one to create a new parameter file for any language, trained on a lexicon and a training corpus. A "chunker" script outputs the tagged words plus some grouping into syntactic constituents. When run on the sentence in (3), for example, the chunker script would insert noun cluster (NC) tags around *some words* and *a sentence*, and verb cluster (VC) tags around the one-word verb clusters *are* and *make*. As reported by Schmid (1994), using TreeTagger to tag for parts of speech in an English corpus achieved over 95 percent accuracy.

```
(3)  $    echo 'These are some words which make a sentence.'  |
          cmd/tree-tagger-english
          reading parameters ...
          tagging ...
          finished.
           These      DT     these
           are        VBP    be
           some       DT     some
           words      NNS    word
           which      WDT    which
           make       VBP    make
           a          DT     a
           sentence   NN     sentence
           .          SENT   .
```

2.4   Several widely used corpora

Before turning to how corpora are used, we briefly present here a few widely used corpora with an eye to showcasing different kinds of data and annotation (see Appendix 13.1 for more information on access to these corpora). Readers should be aware that the Linguistic Data Consortium (LDC, www.ldc.upenn.edu) makes available many high-quality corpora, some free to non-members and others available through an annual subscription. It is also worth mentioning the Child Language Data Exchange System (CHILDES) database and associated tools, the child language component of the TalkBank project. Between them, CHILDES and TalkBank offer a great variety of freely available adult and child language corpora in various media, with an option of playing streaming audio and video through the internet. TalkBank, for example, includes corpora designed for the study of aphasia, dementia, second language acquisition, conversation analysis, and sociolinguistics. The CHILDES system of transcription and coding has in turn given rise to the Language Interaction Data Exchange System (LIDES), which aims to standardize transcription and coding for spoken multilingual data (LIPPS 2000; Gardner-Chloros, Moyer, and Sebba 2007).

The Brown Corpus (Kučera and Francis 1967) holds a unique place in the history of corpus linguistics. It represents the first systematic and, at the time, large-scale attempt to sample written American English containing material which

Table 13.3 *Sub-corpora of the Brown written corpus*

Genre	Words	% of total
News	88,000	8.8
Editorials	54,000	5.4
Reviews	34,000	3.4
Religion	34,000	3.4
Skills and Hobbies	72,000	7.2
Lore	96,000	9.6
Belles lettres	150,000	15
Miscellaneous	60,000	6
Learned	160,000	16
General fiction	58,000	5.8
Mystery	48,000	4.8
Science fiction	12,000	1.2
Adventure	58,000	5.8
Romance	58,000	5.8
Humor	18,000	1.8
Total	1,000,000	

first appeared in print in the year 1961. The corpus, described by the authors as a "Standard Corpus of Present-Day American English," has become known as the Brown Corpus since it was created at Brown University. The corpus contains approximately 1 million words in 500 samples of 2,000+ words each, divided into fifteen sub-categories, shown in Table 13.3. There is quite a spread of writing styles represented in the corpus, with written language being the clear guiding principle in the collection of data. Drama writing, for example, was excluded on the basis of belonging more to the realm of spoken discourse. Fiction writing was included, as long as there was no more than 50 percent dialogue. The design of the Brown Corpus has been adopted in the creation of a number of other 1-million-word English corpora: the Lancaster-Oslo-Bergen Corpus (LOB), the Freiburg Brown Corpus (FROWN), the Freiburg LOB Corpus (FLOB), among others. The corpora mentioned here enable corpus-based comparative studies of American and British written English in 1961 (Brown, LOB), American English in 1961 and 1991 (Brown, FROWN), and British English in 1961 and 1991 (LOB, FLOB).

The International Corpus of English (ICE) has been mentioned already: it is a global project whereby English language materials from many national varieties of English are being collected and marked up according to common guidelines. The primary aim of ICE is to collect material for comparative studies of English worldwide, based on the adoption of a common corpus size (approximately 1 million words) and design. As of April 2012, there were twenty-four varieties of English represented in the project, according to the ICE website. These varieties include better-known ones such as Great Britain and the US, as well as

Table 13.4 *Sub-corpora of the ICE corpora*

Mode	Genre	Words	% of total
Spoken (60%)	Private	200,000	20
	Public	160,000	16
	Unscripted	140,000	14
	Scripted	100,000	10
Written (40%)	Student Writing	40,000	4
	Letters	60,000	6
	Academic Writing	80,000	8
	Popular Writing	80,000	8
	Reportage	40,000	4
	Instructional Writing	40,000	4
	Persuasive Writing	20,000	2
	Creative Writing	40,000	4
	Total	1,000,000	

lesser-known ones such as Malta, Philippines, and Sri Lanka. A full description of the project, as originally conceived, is given in Greenbaum (1996) and Greenbaum and Nelson (1996). A breakdown of the sub-parts of an ICE corpus can be seen in Table 13.4.

The Michigan Corpus of Academic Spoken English (MICASE) is a corpus of spoken academic English as recorded at the University of Michigan (Simpson et al. 2002) between 1997 and 2002. It consists of transcriptions of almost 200 hours of recordings, amounting to about 1.8 million words (according to the MICASE website). Individual speech events range in length from 19 to 178 minutes, with word counts ranging from 2,805 words to 30,328 words. Table 13.5 provides word counts for an untagged version of MICASE in which hyphenated parts of a word and parts of a word separated by apostrophes count as one word.

The BNC contains a collection of written and transcribed spoken samples of British English reflecting a wide range of language use and totaling about 100 million words. The corpus has been published in various editions: the two most widely used (containing the same samples) being the BNC World Edition (2001), marked up in the Standard Generalized Markup Language (SGML), and the BNC XML Edition (2007). Most of the language samples date from the years 1985–93, but some written language samples were taken from the years 1960–84. For the "context-governed" part of the spoken component, data were collected based on particular domains of language usage; for the "spoken demographic" part, conversations were collected by 124 volunteers recruited by the British Market Research Bureau, with equal numbers of men and women, approximately equal numbers from each age group, and equal numbers from each social grouping. Table 13.6 provides a breakdown of the sub-parts of the BNC, with size in terms of

Table 13.5 *Sub-corpora of the MICASE spoken corpus*

Genre	Words	% of total
Small Lectures	333,338	19.7
Large Lectures	251,632	14.8
Discussion Sections	74,904	4.4
Lab Sections	73,815	4.4
Seminars	138,626	8.2
Student Presentations	143,369	8.2
Advising Sessions	35,275	2.1
Dissertation Defenses	56,837	3.4
Interviews	13,015	0.8
Meetings	70,038	4.1
Office Hours	171,188	10.1
Service Encounters	24,691	1.5
Study Groups	129,725	7.7
Tours	21,768	1.3
Colloquia	157,333	9.3
Total	1,695,554	

Table 13.6 *Sub-corpora of the BNC*

Mode	Genre	"w-units"	% of total "w-units"
Written (87.9%)	Imaginative	16,496,420	16.8
	Informative: natural and pure science	3,821,902	3.9
	Informative: applied science	7,174,152	7.3
	Informative: social science	14,025,537	14.3
	Informative: world affairs	17,244,534	17.5
	Informative: commerce and finance	7,341,163	7.5
	Informative: arts	6,574,857	6.7
	Informative: belief and thought	3,037,533	3.1
	Informative: leisure	12,237,834	12.4
Spoken: context-governed (6.1%)	Educational/Informative	1,646,380	1.7
	Business	1,282,416	1.3
	Public/Institutional	1,672,658	1.7
	Leisure	1,574,442	1.6
Spoken: spoken demographic (4.2%)	Respondent Age 0–14	267,005	0.3
	Respondent Age 15–24	665,358	0.7
	Respondent Age 25–34	853,832	0.9
	Respondent Age 35–44	845,153	0.9
	Respondent Age 45–59	963,483	1.0
	Respondent Age 60+	639,124	0.6
	Total	98,363,783	

Table 13.7 *Sub-corpora of the written component of COCA, as of April 2011*

Genre	Sub-genre	Words	% of total
Spoken (20%)	Spoken	90,065,764	20.6
	Fiction	84,965,507	19.4
Written (80%)	Magazine	90,292,046	20.6
	Newspaper	86,670,481	19.8
	Academic	85,791,918	19.6
	Total	437,785,716	100

"w-units," where a "w-unit" is similar to an orthographic word of English, but may also include some multi-word units (i.e., sequences of orthographic words, such as *a priori, of course, all of a sudden*).

The Corpus of Contemporary American English (COCA) is a corpus of contemporary American English sampled from the years 1990 onward (see Davies 2008–; Davies 2011), which is only available via a Web interface. The corpus is being added to each year (i.e., it is a "monitor corpus"). At the time of writing it contains more than 437 million words of text, equally divided among spoken, fiction, popular magazines, newspapers, and academic texts, as shown in Table 13.7. The spoken samples are taken from transcripts of unscripted conversation from more than 150 different TV and radio programs. The Corpus of Historical American English (COHA) is an equally impressive historical corpus of American English sampled from the period 1810–2009, consisting of more than 400 million words, with the same kind of interface as COCA.

The Buckeye Corpus of Conversational Speech was created primarily to support the study of phonological variation in American English speech (Pitt et al. 2005, 2007). The corpus consists of forty "talkers" from Columbus, Ohio, who were each interviewed at Ohio State University in 1999–2000. The interviewees were told prior to the interview that the purpose of the interview was "to learn how people express 'everyday' opinions in conversation, and that the actual topic was not important" (Pitt et al. 2005: 91). Debriefing on the true purpose of the interview and obtaining further consent of the interviewee were carried out after the interview had taken place. The target length of each interview was 60 minutes. The corpus includes high-fidelity WAV files, consists of a total of 305,652 words, and comes with phonemic labeling and orthographic transcription.

The six corpora singled out for discussion here give some sense of the kind of material that linguists work with as corpora. Clearly, there is considerable variation along many parameters as one compares these corpora: specialized (English as spoken in an academic context, informal interview speech, historical data) vs general (spoken and written language in a variety of contexts); written language vs speech; relative balance in the size of the main sub-parts of a corpus, as in COCA, vs skewing in the size of the main sub-parts, as in the BNC; single medium such as electronic texts vs multimedia. This variability in design also points to a need for caution when making direct comparison across the corpora or when a researcher relies solely upon a particular corpus with its own idiosyncratic design to establish "baseline" frequencies of occurrence of words or patterns.

Obviously, many more corpora than those mentioned above are available. For instance, Xiao (2008) refers, by our count, to more than 130. Even the category of "national" corpora alone (i.e., corpora designed to be representative of a range of usage of a national language by native-speakers) includes more than twenty (three just for Polish), and that number has likely increased in the years since Xiao's overview was published. One particularly important desideratum for the future of corpus linguistics and the neighboring field of natural language processing is to recognize resources in languages other than English and to appreciate the need to develop tools and software applicable to all the languages of the world.

3   Using corpora

The previous section discussed a variety of topics concerned with how to create corpora. In this section, we will turn to how to study corpora. In Section 3.1, we will briefly introduce the three main corpus-linguistic methods, and in Section 3.2, we will discuss the kinds of applications and tools that corpus linguists use in their research.

3.1   Analytical tools of corpus linguistics

Corpus linguistics is inherently a distributional discipline because, essentially, corpora only offer answers to the following questions regarding the distributions of linguistic items:

a.   How often and where does something occur in a corpus?
b.   How often do linguistic expressions occur in close proximity to other linguistic expressions?
c.   How are linguistic elements used in their actual contexts?

The following three sections will discuss each of these methods in turn.

3.1.1   Frequency lists and dispersion

Frequency lists are the most basic corpus-linguistic tool. They usually indicate how frequent each word or each *n*-gram (a chain of *n* adjacent words) is in a (part of a) corpus. Examples are shown in the three panels of Table 13.8.

Crucially, this method assumes a working definition of what a word is, which is less straightforward than one may think and less straightforward than many corpus programs' default settings reveal: how many words are *John's book* and *John's at home*, or *isn't it*?

There are a variety of ways in which frequency lists are used and/or modified. First, one has to decide whether one needs the frequency lists of word forms or

Table 13.8 *Frequency lists: words sorted according to frequency (left panel); reversed words sorted alphabetically (center panel); 2-grams sorted according to frequency (right panel)*

Words	Frequency	Words	Frequency	Words	Frequency
the	62,580	yllufdaerd	80	of the	4,892
of	35,958	yllufecaep	1	in the	3,006
and	27,789	yllufecarg	5	to the	1,751
to	25,600	yllufecruoser	8	on the	1,228
a	21,843	yllufeelg	1	and the	1,114
in	19,446	yllufeow	1	for the	906
that	10,296	ylluf	2	at the	832
is	9,938	yllufepoh	8	to be	799
was	9,740	ylluferac	87	with the	783
for	8,799	yllufesoprup	1	from the	720

lemmas: should *run*, *runs*, *running*, and *ran* all be grouped together under the lemma RUN or not? Second, in order to be able to compare frequencies of words from corpora of different sizes, frequencies are often normalized as a ratio of occurrences per million words. Third, comparisons of frequency lists can give rise to interesting data, as when a frequency list of a (usually smaller) specialized corpus is compared to one of a (usually larger) general reference corpus. For example, one can compute for each word in a corpus w the percentage p_1 that it makes up of a corpus c_1 and divide it by the percentage p_2 that *it* makes up in a different corpus c_2, and when you order the resulting relative frequency ratios by their size, the top and the bottom will reveal the words most strongly associated with c_1 and c_2.

It is important to realize how such lists decontextualize each use: one only sees how often, say, *and*, *gracefully*, and *in the* appear, but not where in the file or in which context(s). One way to obtain some information about where in a (part of a) corpus a word occurs is by exploring the *dispersion* of a word. In the left panel of Figure 13.4, the x-axis represents the distribution of the word *perl* in the Wikipedia entry for "Perl," and each occurrence of the word *perl* is indicated by a vertical line. It is very obvious that the highest density of occurrence occurs at the end of the file (where the reference section is located). In the right panel, the corpus has been divided into ten equally sized parts, and a barplot represents the frequencies of *perl* in the ten bins. Again, *perl* is particularly clustered in the final 10 percent of the file. Also, the dispersion of a word in a corpus can be quantified, and the right panel provides two such measures of dispersion, Juilland's D and chi-square. Such measures are particularly useful because two words may have (about) the same frequency of occurrence, but one of them may be evenly spread out through the corpus (reflecting its status as a common word), while the other may be much more unevenly distributed (reflecting its status as a more specialized

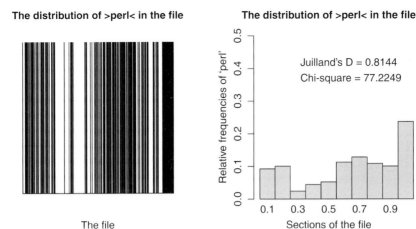

Figure 13.4. *Two ways of representing the dispersion of a word (*perl*) in a file*

word that is just very frequent in particular registers or topics). An example would be the words *having* and *government*, which occur roughly equally frequently in the BNC Baby, but the former is much more evenly spread out throughout the corpus. Similarly, words may be very unequal in frequency but still equally dispersed; for instance, *any* and *the* have very different frequencies in the BNC Baby corpus (4,563 and 201,940 respectively), but dispersion measures reflect that both of them are function words; see Gries 2008 for more discussion.

3.1.2   Collocations

Just like dispersion plots, the second most basic corpus-linguistic tool focuses on a particular linguistic element *w* (typically a word) and provides some information on where *w* is used. However, unlike dispersion plots, the information about where *w* occurs does not use the location in the file/corpus as a reference, but lists which words are most frequently found around *w*. The standard format in which collocations are displayed is exemplified in Table 13.9. Such tables are read vertically – not horizontally – such that the frequencies listed reveal how often a word occurs in a particular position around the node word, here *general* or *generally*. You can immediately see how words are used and which larger expression it enters into: meaningful collocations such as *General Motors* (found thirty-one times), *Attorney General* (twenty-three), *Secretary General* (sixteen), *General Assembly* (fifteen), and others immediately stand out.

In a small table like Table 13.9, these few interesting collocations can be identified immediately, but it is also obvious that many collocations involve function words (*the*, *and*, *in*, *to*, *a*, …) that are so widely dispersed that they will show up in every word's vicinity. Corpus linguists have therefore developed a variety of so-called association measures, most of which essentially quantify how much more frequent a collocate is around a word of interest *w* than one would expect given *w*'s and that collocate's overall frequency in a corpus. In such an

Table 13.9 *Excerpt of a collocate display of* general/generally

Left 2	Freq L2	Left 1	Freq L1	Node	Right 1	Freq R1	Right 2	Freq R2
the	53	the	121		motors	31	of	52
of	28	in	54		and	15	the	30
and	20	a	40		assembly	15	and	25
to	20	of	31		the	14	in	12
in	15	attorney	23		of	12	to	12
a	13	and	19		public	12	that	11
it	12	secretary	16		business	10	as	11
by	9	is	12		s	10	with	8
is	8	more	10		ized	9	for	8
be	7	was	10		izations	7	a	8

approach, collocates are then ranked by their association strength rather than their overall frequency; widely used measures are Mutual Information *MI*, *t*, the log-likelihood ratio, and the Fisher-Yates exact test. Space does not permit us to discuss this in more detail, but see Wiechmann (2008) for a comprehensive discussion.

3.1.3   Concordances

Probably, the most common corpus-linguistic tool currently used is the KWIC (key word in context) concordance – that is, a display of the word of interest in its immediate context. Consider Table 13.10 for part of a KWIC concordance of *alphabetic* and *alphabetical*.

This is the most comprehensive display, showing exactly how the two adjectives are used, but the large amount of information comes at the cost that this display usually needs a human analyst for interpretation, whereas frequencies and collocate displays can often be processed further automatically. This type of table would normally be saved into a tab-delimited text file, which can then be opened with a spreadsheet software (e.g., LibreOffice Calc) so that every match (i.e., every row) can be annotated for linguistic variables of interest. The resulting file would exhibit the case-by-variable format discussed in Chapter 15 and could then be loaded into statistics software and analyzed as discussed there.

With increasingly complex use of concordancing, it quickly becomes necessary to learn about regular expressions, mentioned earlier. This is because while one can search for the two forms of *alphabetic* and *alphabetical* separately, the manual spelling-out of search patterns becomes cumbersome if many thousands of verb lemmas are being retrieved. Even worse, there are many applications where the desired result cannot even be spelt out *a priori*: if you want to find all words ending in -*ic* or -*ical*, then you cannot always predict which forms might exist in usage in a given corpus; the same holds if you want to find all verbs ending in *ing* or *in'*. Regular expressions, a technique for describing (sets of) character

Table 13.10 *Excerpt of a concordance display of* alphabetic *and* alphabetical

File	Line	Preceding context	Match	Subsequent context
A6S	687	and the invention of	alphabetic	writing.
BN9	81	and seven first-class counties taken in	alphabetical	order of rotation.
H99	1583	seeks to negotiate the problems of the	alphabetical	subject approach as outlined in
EES	788	a word is a contiguous sequence of	alphabetic	characters.
B2M	196	provided the basis for an	alphabetical	sort within each functional category.
CHA	3656	and then put them into	alphabetical	order.
EA3	516	to isolate the cultural consequences of	alphabetic	literacy.
F7G	656	But you would put it in	alphabetical	order
CLH	1422	most languages with writing systems	alphabetic	fingerspelling has been available for over
KCY	2439	again I can put the type in	alphabetical	ascending order

Table 13.11 *Examples of regular expressions*

Regular expression	"Translation"
colou?r	finds both *color* and *colour* because the u is made optional by the ?
smokin[g']	finds both *smoking* and *smokin'* because either g or' are allowed after the n
\bg[eo]t(s|t(ing|en))?\b	finds at least *get*, *gets*, *getting*, *got*, and *gotten* as individual words
[-\w]+ly\b	sequences of word characters and hyphens ending in *ly*
<w (dtq|pnq).*?<w prp [^<]*?<c pun\?	wh-words followed by other words until a preposition before a question mark (to find cases of preposition stranding, such as *What are you talking about?*)

sequences, can handle such cases. Table 13.11 lists a few simple examples that showcase the potential of regular expressions (examples are based on SGML/XML annotation of the BNC).

3.2   Tools for analysis in corpus linguistics

We have come to expect a range of basic features relevant to a corpus-based analysis, as listed below, and consequently there is an expectation that software tools will incorporate some selection of these.

a. open multiple files
b. accept a variety of language encodings, especially Unicode
c. calculate frequency of words, parts of words, sequences of words, and so on
d. calculate frequency of parts of speech in a part-of-speech tagged corpus
e. calculate frequency of patterns allowing for wild card searches
f. return concordance lines for a search pattern (word, phrase, part of speech)
g. return concordance lines with variable length of lines
h. return collocates of a search pattern (word, phrase)
i. calculate measures of strength of association between words
j. return a list of n-grams
k. save and export results

Four different kinds of approaches are available to corpus linguists, only the fourth of which covers all the functionality mentioned in the list above and more.

The most restricted of these approaches arises when a corpus is only available via a Web interface, as is currently the case with BNCWeb, MICASE, COCA, and many others. Here, the user is completely dependent on the functionality made available in the interface and the correctness of what is made available. While the search facilities of many online corpora are far-reaching, studies that require extensive frequency information or large amounts of contexts usually cannot be undertaken with such corpora.

Second, a situation often more useful to the analyst arises when a corpus can be installed on one's own hard drive and comes with a specific software to explore that corpus. For example, the ICE-GB comes with a tool designed specifically for it (ICECUP III; see Nelson, Wallis, and Aarts 2002) and which allows inspection of many features of the corpus. As another example, the BNC XML edition currently comes with Xaira searching software (Xiao 2006). In such cases, the advantages are that the linguist has the whole corpus available for more individual queries and that the corpus software is tailored to the precise format of the corpus. However, this type of corpus software is sometimes not as user-friendly as it could be, users are still restricted to the functionality of the program, and the ability to work with one corpus software does not transfer to other corpora.

Third, and perhaps most widely used, the corpus linguist has the corpus on his/her hard drive and uses a ready-made general corpus program for retrieval and other operations. Apart from some commercial applications that are restricted to the Microsoft Windows operating system (e.g., Wordsmith), several free alternatives are available, the most useful of which is perhaps AntConc, because it is the only tool we are aware of that runs on the three major operating systems, is good at handling different encodings, and possesses powerful regular expressions that, unlike nearly all other currently available tools (including the commercial ones), allow it to handle many kinds of annotations flexibly. AntConc has a built-in

Keywords feature which identifies words overused in one corpus by reference to another corpus. While corpus tools like AntConc allow parallel analysis of disparate corpora, users are still dependent on the functionality that is included in the programs. This also means, for example, that hardly any of the widely used ready-made programs can read CHAT files well, an annotation format widely used in language acquisition research and the CHILDES database mentioned above.

The fourth and final scenario, one that is becoming increasingly common, involves researchers having corpora on their hard drive and using general purpose programming languages to process, manipulate, and search files. We devote the next section to this topic.

3.3   Programming tools for corpus linguistics

The huge advantage of programming languages is that they are immensely more versatile and powerful than any ready-made software. This allows researchers to pursue research more efficiently, creatively, and within one environment (as opposed to having to learn and use different applications for, say, web-crawling, cleaning up files, standardizing them, retrieving concordances, annotating them, analyzing them statistically, and plotting some graphs). There is a well-known downside to using programming languages and that is the learning curve for the novice user. However, the potential benefits to be gained from persevering and achieving a basic and comfortable literacy in a programming language far outweigh, in our opinion, any learning pains. And there are two additional considerations to bear in mind when thinking about the pros and cons of investing time in learning programming languages: (1) there is a vast number of ways in which programming knowledge can be put to good use in dealing with digital information quite apart from corpus linguistics; (2) once you have learned one programming language, like R, then you generally have some advantage when it comes to learning another one.

Typically, programming languages can be installed on any modern desktop computer or laptop; they may have to be installed as stand-alone applications or they may be already included as part of the computer's installed software (e.g., Perl and Python are bundled with the Mac OS). Examples of well-known programming languages are Perl, C#, Java, PHP, Python, and Ruby. While Perl was probably the most widely used programming language for many years, an increasing number of researchers are now using Python and R, which therefore deserve brief exemplification here. Both Python and R are freely downloadable and available as cross-platform installations (Linux/Unix, Mac OS, Windows). A researcher can choose one or more GUIs for each of these languages to create a more friendly or helpful interface (e.g., color coding in the script, help or documentation available through pull-down menus).

For the purposes of corpus linguistics, the comprehensive package of Python tools known as the Natural Language Toolkit (NLTK) has many attractive features. The best introduction to NLTK is Bird, Klein, and Loper (2009), also currently available as a free online eBook at the NLTK website; Perkins (2010) is a useful additional text. Figure 13.5 shows a log of a session working with

```
 1. >>> import nltk
 2. >>> from nltk.corpus import PlaintextCorpusReader
 3. >>> corpus_root = '/Users/Myname/Desktop/MyFiles/'
 4. >>> MyFiles = PlaintextCorpusReader(corpus_root, '.*.txt')
 5. >>> MyFiles.fileids()
    ['Emma.txt', 'Pride_and_Prejudice.txt']
 6. >>> words = MyFiles.words()
 7. >>> words[:10]
    ['The', 'Project', 'Gutenberg', 'EBook', 'of', 'Emma', ',', 'by', 'Jane', 'Austen']
 8. >>> sents = MyFiles.sents()
 9. >>> sents[:3]
    [['The', 'Project', 'Gutenberg', 'EBook', 'of', 'Emma', ',', 'by', 'Jane', 'Austen'],
    ['This', 'eBook', 'is', 'for', 'the', 'use', 'of', 'anyone', 'anywhere', 'at', 'no',
    'cost', 'and', 'with', 'almost', 'no', 'restrictions', 'whatsoever', '.'], ['You',
    'may', 'copy', 'it', ',', 'give', 'it', 'away', 'or', 're', '-', 'use', 'it', 'under',
    'the', 'terms', 'of', 'the', 'Project', 'Gutenberg', 'License', 'included', 'with',
    'this', 'eBook', 'or', 'online', 'at', 'www', '.', 'gutenberg', '.', 'org']]
10. >>> paras = MyFiles.paras()
11. >>> paras[:3]
    (results omitted here)
12. >>> words1 = nltk.Text(words)
13. >>> words1.concordance("friend", lines = 10)
        Building index&
        Displaying 10 of 289 matches:
        family , less as a governess than a  friend , very fond of both daughters , but
        , they had been living together as   friend and friend very mutually attached ,
        been living together as friend and  friend very mutually attached , and Emma d
        n the wedding – day of this beloved  friend that Emma first sat in mournful tho
        every promise of happiness for her  friend . Mr . Weston was a man of unexcept
        derer recollection . She had been a  friend and companion such as few possessed
        the change ?– It was true that her   friend was going only half a mile from the
        as not only a very old and intimate  friend of the family , but particularly co
        el so much pain as pleasure . Every  friend of Miss Taylor must be glad to have
        t Smith ' s being exactly the young  friend she wanted – exactly the something
14. >>> words1.similar('friend')
        Building word-context index&
        father sister mother own family daughter letter mind time brother aunt
        wife life and heart way side cousin eyes feelings
15. >>> words1.collocations()
        Building collocations list
        Frank Churchill; Lady Catherine; Miss Woodhouse; Project Gutenberg;
        young man; Miss Bates; Miss Fairfax; every thing; Jane Fairfax; great
        deal; dare say; every body; Sir William; Miss Bingley; John Knightley;
        Maple Grove; Miss Smith; Miss Taylor; Robert Martin; Colonel
        Fitzwilliam
16. >>> MyFiles_tag=[nltk.pos_tag(sent) for sent in sents]
17. >>> MyFiles_tag[13][:10]
        [('Emma', 'NNP'), ('Woodhouse', 'NNP'), (',', ','), ('handsome', 'NN'),
        (',', ','), ('clever', 'RB'), (',', ','), ('and', 'CC'), ('rich', 'JJ'),
        (',', ',')]
```

Figure 13.5. *Python session illustrating some functions in NLTK*

NLTK and illustrates just a sample of the functions that are available in this module. In this session, a directory of two English .txt files (downloaded from Project Gutenberg and pre-processed using jEdit) is loaded as a corpus with the name "MyFiles" (lines 3–4). One can obtain a list of all the files that make up the corpus (line 5). In this case, there are just two files: one being the Project Gutenberg file for the novel *Emma* and another for the novel *Pride and*

Prejudice, both by Jane Austen. The corpus consisting of these two files is broken down into a list of words (line 6) and then a list of the first ten words can be displayed (line 7). As can be seen from the display of the first ten words, the files have not been pre-processed and some metadata about Project Gutenberg appears as the first ten words. Similarly, one can break the corpus into sentences (line 8) and view the first three sentences (line 9), or paragraphs (line 10) and view the first three paragraphs (line 11). Further commands can produce a set of the first ten concordance lines based on the search term *friend* (line 13), words which occur in similar contexts as *friend* (line 14), and significant bigrams (line 15). It is possible to add part-of-speech tags (not always accurate) to create a tagged corpus MyFiles_tag (line 16) and print out the first ten words and punctuation marks of the first tagged sentence (= sentence 13 of the corpus) of Jane Austen's *Emma*.

R is an open-source programming language and environment originally designed for statistical computing and graphics, but with all the functionality of "normal" multipurpose programming languages, including loops, conditional expressions, text processing with and without regular expressions, and so on. Figure 13.6 exemplifies how very easily a rough frequency list can be created in

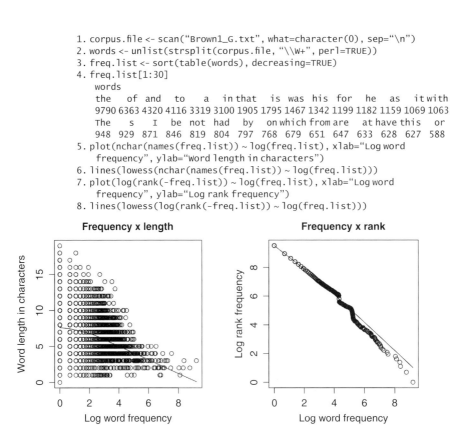

Figure 13.6. *R session to create a frequency list of a file from the Brown Corpus and the resulting plots*

just four lines of code in a short R session: first, a corpus file is loaded (line 1), then it is split up into words (in a somewhat simplistic way, line 2), then R computes a sorted frequency list of the whole file (line 3) and prints out the thirty most frequent words and frequencies (line 4). Then, two of Zipf's laws are tested by (i) plotting words' lengths against their frequencies (line 5; note that the frequencies are logged in order to better represent the distribution of frequencies in a corpus) and adding a summary line (line 6), and by (ii) plotting words' frequency ranks against their (logged) frequencies (line 7) and adding a summary line (line 8).

Given that corpora continuously increase in size and diversity, it is becoming increasingly important that corpus linguists use tools that are not restricted to particular formats, encodings, sizes, or other design factors, and recent changes show that the field is making great strides to this end. If this trend continues, the field will transform into an even more exciting discipline and contribute more than its share to insightful studies of all aspects of language.

Appendix 13.1 Corpora referred to in this chapter

Baby BNC Details of this collection of corpora, with XAIRA, can be found at www.natcorp.ox.ac.uk/corpus/babyinfo.html. Payment required.

BNC The British National Corpus can be accessed online at no cost through two interfaces: Mark Davies' website at corpus.byu.edu/bnc and William Fletcher's Phrases in English site at phrasesinenglish.org. Information on purchasing the corpus (and other releases of samples of the BNC) may be found at www. natcorp.ox.ac.uk. Online access to the BNC is also provided for BNC licensees. A full description of the BNC can be found in the Reference Guide for the British National Corpus (XML Edition) at www.natcorp.ox.ac.uk/docs/URG.

Brown The Brown Corpus may be downloaded at no cost through the "language commons" collection at www.archive.org/details/BrownCorpus and the NLTK package of Python at www.nltk.org. It can be searched online through the LDC at online.ldc.upenn.edu/login.html and the Corpus Concordance English at www.lextutor.ca/concordancers/concord_e.html. The corpus is included in the ICAME Corpus Collection available on CD-ROM through ICAME at icame.uib.no/cd. Different versions of the corpus may segment the corpus differently. The language commons version contains the 500 x 2,000 word samples as separate files; the ICAME version contains fifteen files reflecting the sub-categories in Table 13.3. Both tagged and untagged versions of the corpus are included in the ICAME Corpus Collection; an XML tagged version of the Brown is included as part of BabyBNC v.2 which is available at www.natcorp. ox.ac.uk.

Buckeye The Buckeye Corpus, together with a manual, may be obtained at no cost by following instructions on the homepage of the project at buckeyecorpus.osu.edu.

CallHome The CallHome American English Speech corpus is available at cost through the Linguistic Data Consortium at www.ldc.upenn.edu.

CHILDES The Child Language Data Exchange System, developed by Brian MacWhinney, is accessed freely at childes.psy.cmu.edu.

COCA The Corpus of Contemporary American English is freely accessible online at www.americancorpus.org, but not distributed as a corpus. A full description of the corpus can be found at this website.

COHA The Corpus of Historical American English is freely accessible online at corpus.byu.edu/coha, but not distributed as a corpus. A full description of the corpus can be found at this website.

FLOB The Freiburg LOB corpus is included in the ICAME Corpus Collection and is described in the accompanying manual. Available for purchase from icame.uib.no/cd.

FROWN The Freiburg Brown Corpus is included in the ICAME Corpus Collection and is described in the accompanying manual. Available for purchase from icame.uib.no/cd.

ICAME The International Computer Archive of Modern and Medieval English Collection is available for purchase on CD-ROM at icame.uib.no/cd.

ICE Information on obtaining corpora of the International Corpus of English is available through the ICE website at ice-corpora.net/ice/index.htm. At the time of writing, ICE corpora for Canada, Jamaica, Hong Kong, East Africa, India, Singapore, and Philippines are available at no cost and can be downloaded from the ICE website; ICE corpora for Great Britain, New Zealand, and Ireland are available on CD-ROM at relatively low cost.

ICE-CAN The Canadian component of the International Corpus of English is freely available at ice-corpora.net/ice/index.htm and is described more fully in Newman and Columbus (2010).

LOB The Lancaster-Bergen-Oslo Corpus (written) corpus is included in the ICAME Corpus Collection and is described in the accompanying manual. Available for purchase from icame.uib.no/cd.

MICASE The Michigan Corpus of Academic Spoken English is freely accessed online at quod.lib.umich.edu/m/micase. A full description of the MICASE project and the corpus can be found in the MICASE manual available at micase.elicorpora.info. Individual XML transcripts of the files can be downloaded at no cost. A version of the whole corpus can also be purchased through the MICASE website.

TalkBank This collection of corpora and transcripts is accessed freely at talkbank.org.

TIMIT The Acoustic-Phonetic Continuous Speech Corpus is available for purchase through the Linguistic Data Consortium.

Uppsala Learner English Corpus This corpus is described in Johansson and Geisler (2009, 2011).

(All websites accessed July 8, 2013.)

Appendix 13.2 Tools and software referred to in this chapter

AntConc Concordancer. www.antlab.sci.waseda.ac.jp/software.html

CES. Corpus Encoding Standard. www.cs.vassar.edu/CES

CLAWS. The Constituent Likelihood Automatic Word-tagging System tagset(s). ucrel.lancs.ac.uk/claws

ELAN. EUDICO Linguistic Annotator software. www.lat-mpi.eu/tools/elan

FreeLing. nlp.lsi.upc.edu/freeling

GoTagger. web4u.setsunan.ac.jp/Website/GoTagger.htm (for notes in English on this Windows-only tagger:

hi.baidu.com/seanxpq/blog/item/7aa9db03f8bffc0f738da50e.html)

HTTrack. www.httrack.com

Infogistics. www.infogistics.com

jEdit. www.jedit.org

LibreOffice Calc. www.libreoffice.org

NLTK. Natural Language Toolkit. www.nltk.org. An electronic version of the accompanying book (Bird, Klein, and Loper 2009) is also available at this site.

Penn Treebank Tagset. www.comp.leeds.ac.uk/ccalas/tagsets/upenn.html

Project Gutenberg. www.gutenberg.org

R. www.R-project.org

Sitesucker. http://sitesucker.us/home.html

Southern Oral History Program. docsouth.unc.edu/sohp

Transcriber. trans.sourceforge.net

TreeTagger. www.ims.uni-stuttgart.de/projekte/corplex/TreeTagger/DecisionTree Tagger.html (for the Windows interface to TreeTagger: www.smo.uhi.ac.uk/ ~oduibhin/oideasra/interfaces/winttinterface.htm)

Wordsmith. Corpus linguistic software available for purchase at www.lexically. net/wordsmith

XCES. Corpus Encoding Standard in XML format. www.xces.org

(All websites accessed July 8, 2013.)

References

Beal, J. C., K. P. Corrigan, and H. L. Moisl, eds. 2007a. *Creating and Digitizing Language Corpora. Volume I: Synchronic Databases*. Basingstoke and New York: Palgrave Macmillan.

2007b. *Creating and Digitizing Language Corpora. Volume II: Diachronic Databases*. Basingstoke and New York: Palgrave Macmillan.

Berkenfield, C. 2001. The role of frequency in the realization of English *that*. In J. L. Bybee and P. J. Hopper, eds. *Frequency and the Emergence of Linguistic Structure*. Philadelphia: John Benjamins, 281–307.

Bird, S., E. Klein, and E. Loper. 2009. *Natural Language Processing with Python: Analyzing Text with the Natural Language Toolkit*. Sebastopol, CA: O'Reilly Media.

Davies, M. 2008–. *The Corpus of Contemporary American English (COCA)*. Available at www.americancorpus.org (accessed June 26, 2013).

　　2011. The Corpus of Contemporary American English as the first reliable monitor corpus of English. *Literary and Linguistic Computing* 25.4: 447–65.

Fiorentino, G. 2009. The ordering of adverbial and main clauses in spoken and written Italian. In B. Lewandowska-Tomaszczyk and K. Dziwirek, eds. *Studies in Cognitive Corpus Linguistics*. Frankfurt am Main: Peter Lang, 207–22.

Gardner-Chloros, P., M. Moyer, and M. Sebba. 2007. *Coding and analyzing multilingual data: the LIDES project*. In Beal, Corrigan, and Moisl. Volume I: 91–120.

Gilquin, G. and S. Th. Gries. 2009. Corpora and experimental methods: a state-of-the-art review. *Corpus Linguistics and Linguistic Theory* 5.1: 1–26.

Granath, S. 2007. Size matters–or thus can meaningful structures be revealed in large corpora. In R. Facchinetti, ed. *Corpus Linguistics 25 Years On*. Amsterdam and New York: Rodopi, 169–85.

Greenbaum, S., ed. 1996. *Comparing English Worldwide: The International Corpus of English*. Oxford: Clarendon Press.

Greenbaum, S. and G. Nelson. 1996. The International Corpus of English (ICE) project. *World Englishes* 15.1: 3–15.

Gries, S. Th. 2008. Dispersions and adjusted frequencies in corpora. *International Journal of Corpus Linguistics* 13.4: 403–37.

　　2009. *Quantitative Corpus Linguistics with R: A Practical Introduction*. London and New York: Routledge.

Hunston, S. 2008. *Collection strategies and design decisions*. In Lüdeling and Kytö, eds. Volume I, 154–68.

Johansson, C. and C. Geisler. 2009. The Uppsala Learner English Corpus: a new corpus of Swedish high school students' writing. In A. Saxena and Å. Viberg, eds. *Multilingualism: Proceedings of the 23rd Scandinavian Conference of Linguistics*. Uppsala: Acta Universitatis Upsaliensis, 181–90.

　　2011. Syntactic aspects of the writing of Swedish L2 learners of English. In J. Newman, H. Baayen, and S. Rice, eds. *Corpus-based Studies in Language Use, Language Learning, and Language Documentation*. Amsterdam: Rodopi Press, 139–73.

Kilgarriff, A. and G. Grefenstette. 2006. Introduction to the special issue on the web as corpus. *Computational Linguistics* 29.3: 333–47.

Kučera, H. and W. N. Francis. 1967. *Computational Analysis of Present-day English*. Providence, RI: Brown University Press.

LIPPS–Language Interaction in Plurilingual and Plurilectal Speakers Group. 2000. A Document for Preparing and Analysing Language Interaction Data. Special issue of the *International Journal of Bilingualism* 4.2.

Lüdeling, A. and M. Kytö. eds. 2008a. *Corpus Linguistics: An International Handbook. Volume I*. Berlin and New York: Mouton de Gruyter.

　　2008b. *Corpus Linguistics: An International Handbook. Volume II*. Berlin and New York: Mouton de Gruyter.

McEnery, T. and A. Hardie. 2012. *Corpus Linguistics: Method, Theory, and Practice*. Cambridge University Press.

McEnery, T., R. Xiao, and Y. Tono. 2006. *Corpus-based Language Studies: An Advanced Resource Book*. London: Routledge.

Meurman-Solin, A. 2007. The manuscript-based diachronic corpus of Scottish correspondence. In Beal, Corrigan, and Moisl. Volume II, 127–47.

Nelson, G., S. Wallis, and B. Aarts. 2002. *Exploring Natural Language: Working with the British Component of the International Corpus of English*. Amsterdam and Philadelphia: John Benjamins.

Newman, J. 2008. Spoken corpora: rationale and application. *Taiwan Journal of Linguistics* 6.2: 27–58.

Newman, J. and G. Columbus. 2009. Education as an over-represented topic in the ICE corpora [Part II]? Presentation for the 15th International Conference of the International Association for World Englishes (IAWE), October 22–24, Cebu City, Philippines.

  2010. *The ICE-Canada Corpus. Version 1*. Available at: http://ice-corpora.net/ice/download.htm (accessed June 26, 2013).

Ostler, N. 2008. Corpora of less studied languages. In Lüdeling and Kytö, eds. Volume I, 457–83.

Perkins, J. 2010. *Python Text Processing with NLTK 2.0 Cookbook*. Birmingham, UK: Packt Publishing.

Pitt, M. A., K. Johnson, E. Hume, S. Kiesling, and W. Raymond. 2005. The Buckeye Corpus of Conversational Speech: labeling conventions and a test of transcriber reliability. *Speech Communication* 45.1: 89–95.

Pitt, M., L. Dilley, K. Johnson, S. Kiesling, W. Raymond, E. Hume, and E. Fosler-Lussier. 2007. *Buckeye Corpus of Conversational Speech* (2nd release) [www.buckeyecorpus.osu.edu]. Columbus, OH: Department of Psychology, Ohio State University (Distributor).

Roy, D. 2009. New horizons in the study of child language acquisition. *Proceedings of Interspeech 2009*. September 6–10, Brighton, England. Available at: www.media.mit.edu/cogmac/publications/Roy_interspeech_keynote.pdf (accessed June 26, 2013).

Schmid, H. 1994. Probabilistic part-of-speech tagging using decision trees. *Proceedings of International Conference on New Methods in Language Processing*, September, Manchester, UK.

Simpson, R. C., S. L. Briggs, J. Ovens, and J. M. Swales. 2002. *The Michigan Corpus of Academic Spoken English*. Ann Arbor, MI: The Regents of the University of Michigan.

Sinclair, J. 2005. Corpus and text – basic principles. In Wynne, 1–16.

Thompson, S. A. and P. J. Hopper. 2001. Transitivity, clause structure and argument structure. In J. L. Bybee and P. J. Hopper, eds. *Frequency and the Emergence of Linguistic Structure*. Philadelphia: John Benjamins, 27–60.

Wiechmann, D. 2008. On the computation of collostruction strength: testing measures of association as expressions of lexical bias. *Corpus Linguistics and Linguistic Theory* 4.2: 253–90.

Wynne, M., ed. 2005. *Developing Linguistic Corpora: A Guide to Good Practice*. Oxford: Oxbow Books. Available at: www.ahds.ac.uk/creating/guides/linguistic-corpora/index.htm (accessed June 26, 2013).

Xiao, R. 2006. Xaira–an XML-aware indexing and retrieval architecture. *Corpora* 1.1: 99–103.

  2008. Well-known and influential corpora. In Lüdeling and Kytö, eds. Volume I, 383–457.

14   Descriptive statistics

Daniel Ezra Johnson

1   Introduction

When we have a small amount of data, we can avoid statistics completely. In such cases, we can inspect and discuss each and every *observation* or data point. For example, if we measured the fundamental frequencies (F0) of three siblings' speech, we might observe that Betty's voice was 25 Hz lower than Sue's, but 100 Hz higher than Frank's. It would probably be uninteresting to report a statistic like the average pitch of the family. With a larger dataset, like F0 measurements taken from 1,000 men and 1,000 women, the situation is reversed. It is no longer possible to discuss each data point individually, and while it can still be useful to make graphs that display every observation, we will usually be less interested in individual points and more interested in the patterns or trends formed by groups of points.

This is where *descriptive statistics* come in. Descriptive statistics generally constitute the second step in a quantitative analysis. The first step is to display the data in a tabular or graphical format, using a histogram, bar chart, scatterplot, cross-tabulation, or other method. This will reveal any peculiarities of the data that will shape further analysis. For example, a severely skewed dataset may motivate a transformation, or the use of non-parametric statistics. The second step is the descriptive statistics themselves, which distill the complexities of the data down to a small, manageable set of numbers, abstracting away from details (and noise) in order to describe the basic overall properties of the data. This process can suggest the answers to existing questions or inspire new hypotheses to be tested.

So if we take a single variable like voice pitch, we can talk about its distribution (are all pitches equally common or are there one or more "peaks" at certain frequencies?), its central tendency (what is the most typical pitch for a woman's voice?), its dispersion (how much do men's voices vary in pitch?), as well as higher-order properties like skewness and kurtosis. If we take two variables at once, we can report on their association or correlation (e.g., what is the relationship between voice pitch and the age of the speaker?).

Descriptive statistics describe samples of data, but they do not attempt to answer questions (make inferences) about the larger populations from which the samples are drawn. So if we measured the pitch of twenty English speakers and twenty German speakers, descriptive statistics might tell us that the English sample had an average F0 that was 10 Hz higher than the German sample. If we wanted to know what to make of this result – in particular, whether the difference could be due to mere chance (sampling error) – we could perform a statistical test called a *t-test*. But in doing so, we would be leaving the domain of descriptive statistics and entering the realm of inferential statistics (Chapter 15).

Different types of variables often call for distinct statistical methods; these are discussed in Section 2. Data distributions are covered in Section 3, and the following three sections discuss how to describe distributions: beginning with measures of central tendency or "averages" in Section 4, continuing with measures of dispersion or "spread" in Section 5, and concluding in Section 6 with higher-order descriptive statistics. In Section 7, we discuss how to quantify the extent to which variables relate to one another: association and correlation. Since the chapter will have been concerned primarily with continuous, numeric variables up to this point, Section 8 turns its attention to descriptive statistics for categorical variables. The chapter concludes with Section 9.

2   Types of variables

The most basic descriptive statistic of all refers to the type of variable under consideration. Until we identify the type of variable, we do not know which other statistics are appropriate to apply. Linguistic variables, collected through acoustic analysis, impressionistic judgment, experimental measurement, questionnaire categories, counting within corpora, and more, run the gamut of variable types.

The most fundamental division here is between continuous and categorical variables. *Continuous variables* are numeric measurements that can theoretically take on any value, or at least any value within a certain range. F0 is an example of a continuous variable; in principle it can take on any positive value, even though in practice no one has a mean F0 of 5 Hz or 500 Hz. Formant measurements, reaction times, and lexical frequencies are other examples of continuous variables. For truly continuous variables, no two observations are ever identical. However, we can sometimes treat more granular numeric variables, like frequency counts, ratings on a scale, or values that have been rounded, as if they were continuous. Continuous variables are the input to linear regression (see Chapter 16).

It is sometimes important to distinguish between *interval-scale* and *ratio-scale* continuous variables. Interval-scale variables do not have a natural zero point, so it is meaningless to perform multiplication, division, and certain other mathematical and statistical operations. For example, on the Fahrenheit scale, it is not meaningful to take a ratio of temperatures, and say that 80 degrees is twice as hot as 40 degrees. However, we can compare intervals, and say that an increase of

20 degrees is twice as large as an increase of 10 degrees. On the Kelvin scale, though, where absolute zero is defined meaningfully, not only can we compare intervals, but we can also take ratios. For example, we can indeed say that 400 K is twice as hot as 200 K. Here and throughout this chapter, we will sometimes employ non-linguistic examples in order to make concepts or arguments clearer. Here, we have shown how interval-scale and ratio-scale variables can measure temperature, with the difference lying in the choice of a relatively non-meaningful (Fahrenheit) vs meaningful (Kelvin) zero point. A related issue arises when we use a subject's date of birth as an independent variable. We could use "1900," "1925," "1950," "1975," or "0," "25," "50," "75" for the same four speakers, and while the means will be interconvertible and the standard deviations will not change, the second approach gives more useful coefficients in regression, since we will not be making any predictions about 0 A.D.

Unlike continuous variables, *categorical variables* have values that fall into two or more distinct categories, rather than having a range of intermediate possibilities. If there are more than two categories, we can make a distinction between ordinal and nominal variables. For ordinal variables, the categories have a natural order; the categories of nominal variables have no natural order. Classic examples of ordinal sociolinguistic variables are the contraction and deletion of the African-American English copula (*he is tall*, *he's tall*, *he tall*) and the lenition of coda /s/ in Spanish, first to [h] and then to zero (*los libros*, *loh libroh*, *lo libro*). Examples of nominal variables are the alternation among *that*, *which*, and zero in introducing a relative clause (*the cake that I prefer*, *the cake which I prefer*, *the cake I prefer*), or whether a quotation is introduced with *say*, *go*, *be like*, or some other variant. In these cases, there is no obvious ordering of the possibilities.

If there are only two categories, then we are dealing with a *binary* (or dichotomous) variable. This type of variable is very common in linguistics, in both phonology and syntax. Binary variables can involve the presence vs absence of some element (e.g., the word-final coronal stop in *last chance* or the negative *ne* in French). More generally, binary variables can capture any alternation between two possibilities, as in the (ing) variable (*gone fishing* vs *gone fishin'*), the dative alternation (*he gave John the book* vs *he gave the book to John*), or the particle alternation (*she took out the trash* vs *she took the trash out*). Binary variables are the usual input to logistic regression (Chapter 16).

In this chapter, we will mainly discuss descriptive statistics as applied to continuous variables. We will cover descriptive statistics for categorical variables, including binary variables, in Section 8.

3   Distributions

When we have a variable, especially a continuous one, one of the first things we should do is examine its *distribution*. The temptation is to skip

```
2 | 2599
3 | 0000222344444444455555555556666666677777888888888889999999
4 | 0000000000001111112222222222222222223333333334444444444555555555555556666666777777788889999
5 | 0000011122222333444455555566677888888999999
6 | 000001112222223333333334444555555555666666677778999
7 | 00000111111222222222222333333333333334444444444445555555555555556666666666667777777778888888888 9999999
8 | 00000001111122222223333334444445677
```

Figure 14.1. *Stem-and-leaf plot of daily temperatures for Albuquerque in 2010*

ahead to summary statistics like the mean and standard deviation. These do describe the distribution in an overall way, but as always, a picture is worth a handful of numbers. A distribution refers to the frequency of the values of a variable. It asks how often the variable took on particular values as opposed to others.

This question applies to linguistic variables of whatever sort. Sometimes, the distribution is expected (or hoped) to fit a particular shape called *normal* (see below), enabling the use of more powerful parametric statistics instead of having to rely on less powerful but equally useful non-parametric statistics.

Suppose our variable is the average daily temperature in Albuquerque in 2010 (ADTA 2011). Naturally, the data consist of 365 measurements. We can display it in raw form as follows: 30, 35, 36, 33, 34, . . ., 39, 40, 35, 37, 22 (this only shows the first five and the last five days of the year). This format is not very useful. If we were interested in 2010 for its own sake, we might want to make a plot of temperature against time, showing how the temperature changed over the course of the year (very roughly speaking, it went up and then down!). This would be one version of a *bivariate* (two-variable) distribution. But if we are more interested in how 2010 measures up against other years, then we want to describe the *univariate* distribution of the 2010 data. For example, we might want to know how many days were below 30 degrees. (Four.) And how many days were above 90 degrees. (None.)

The *stem-and-leaf plot*, popularized by Tukey (1977), is one way of showing a univariate distribution. For the 2010 Albuquerque temperatures, if we divide the data into 10-degree ranges, we obtain the stem-and-leaf plot in Figure 14.1.

Each temperature is split up into a "stem" and a "leaf" – for example, 29 is split into 2 (shown on the left) and 9 (shown on the right). The plot shows that there were 4 days in the 20s (22, 25, 29, 29), and that there were more days in the 40s and 70s than in the 50s and 60s, and so on. Once you know how to read it, a stem-and-leaf plot is more immediately revealing than a conventional table of frequencies, such as Table 14.1. The table shows absolute frequency (number of days in each temperature range) and relative frequency, the latter expressed as a percentage (number of days in each range divided by the total number of days, 365, multiplied by 100). Annual temperature data have a fixed denominator of 365 (or 366), but if we were going to compare distributions with different N (the total number in a distribution is usually called N) then the relative frequency is much more useful.

Table 14.1 *Frequency table of daily temperatures for Albuquerque in 2010*

Temperature range	Absolute freq. (days)	Relative freq. (100 * days/365)
20–29	4	1%
30–39	54	15%
40–49	82	22%
50–59	45	12%
60–69	50	14%
70–79	96	26%
80–89	34	9%

The most common way to display a univariate distribution of a continuous variable is neither a stem-and-leaf plot nor a frequency table. It is the type of graph that Pearson (1895) called a *histogram*. A histogram is a kind of bar chart (sometimes called a column chart, since the bars are vertical), with the value of the variable shown on the x-axis and its frequency shown on the y-axis. We must break the continuous x-axis into categories called bins, as we have already been doing. The bins can be of any width, although the histogram gives less useful information if they are too wide or too narrow. Figure 14.2 is a histogram of the Albuquerque temperature data. Note that the histogram is essentially an upright stem-and-leaf plot, minus the detailed information about the exact temperatures. The height of each bar is equal to the number of days where the average temperature fell into that bin. We see that the distribution has peaks in the 40s and 70s, as noted earlier. Distributions with two peaks are called *bimodal* (a frequency peak is called a *mode*; see Section 3). We also see that there are no *outliers*, that is to say, no days where the temperature was noticeably higher or lower than any other day. This distribution is not noticeably *skewed* to the left or to the right. If there had been a few days with temperatures in the 10s, a few in the 0s, and 1 or 2 days below zero, that would be a left-skewed distribution: a distribution with a long left tail. Similarly, if there were a long right tail, that would be called a right-skewed distribution (see Section 6).

In reporting linguistic research, distributional plots should be used more often than they are. They can be used in two main ways: at the outset of analysis, to reveal the shape of the data (and at the same time, revealing what simplifications or distortions are involved with taking means, standard deviations, etc.); or applied at the end, to the *residuals* (or *error terms*) of a linguistic model, to verify that the variation not accounted for by the model is not strongly correlated with any of the variables in the model, which would indicate a lack of fit of the model.

In Section 1, we discussed vocal pitch of men and women in a hypothetical way. A real dataset with F0 information is the classic Peterson and Barney (1952) study of American English vowels. Peterson and Barney recorded thirty-three men, twenty-eight women, and fifteen children reading a set of ten words, twice each. The words contained a range of vowels, all in the same consonantal environment: *heed*, *hid*,

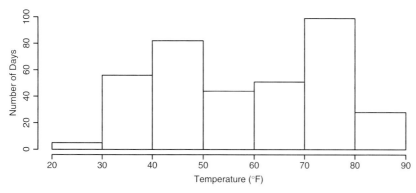

Figure 14.2. *Histogram of 2010 Albuquerque temperatures*

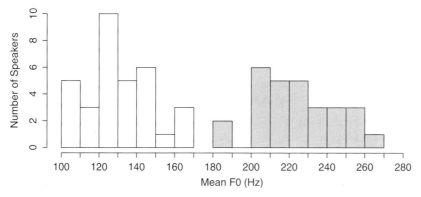

Figure 14.3. *Histogram of men's and women's mean F0.*
Johnson, based on Peterson and Barney 1952

head, and so on. Taking the mean F0 for each adult speaker leads to the histogram of Figure 14.3, which shows the men in white and the women in grey. As we might expect, the distribution of F0 in Figure 14.3 is strongly bimodal, with a peak around 125 Hz representing the most typical men and one around 205 Hz representing the most typical women. It also looks like both men and women, especially women, have right-skewed distributions (with longer right tails).

We can reduce the skew of this data by performing a logarithmic *transformation* (usually using the natural logarithm, but it does not matter). This makes a great deal of sense for F0 data, because pitch is perceived logarithmically: doubling the frequency makes the pitch go up one octave; quadrupling it makes it go up two octaves. It is therefore natural to log-transform F0 (and arguably higher formant frequencies as well). We see the result of this transformation in Figure 14.4, where the male and female distributions are still somewhat right-skewed, but less so.

Besides its natural applicability to pitch data, the log transformation is often employed to change the distribution of other skewed datasets so that they are closer to a *normal distribution*. Normal (or Gaussian) distributions are a particular family of bell-shaped curves, as illustrated in Figure 14.5. They are defined by two

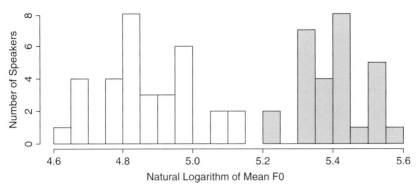

Figure 14.4. *Histogram of men's and women's natural-log-transformed F0.*
Johnson, based on Peterson and Barney 1952

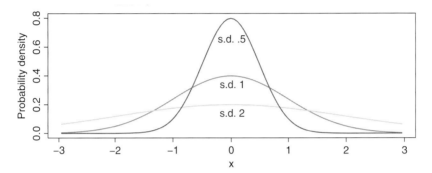

Figure 14.5. *Three normal distributions: mean = 0, standard deviations = {0.5, 1, 2}*

parameters, the mean and the standard deviation (see Sections 3 and 4 below). Figure 14.5 shows the standard normal distribution (standard deviation 1) as well as a narrower normal distribution (standard deviation 0.5) and a wider one (standard deviation 2). The y-axis is probability density; the total area under each curve is 1. A property of normal distributions is that 95 percent of the values fall between –1.96 and +1.96 standard deviations from the mean, regardless of what the standard deviation is. Continuous variables often follow normal distributions quite naturally, because a large number of factors cause them to vary, and the sum of a large number of random variables always follows a normal distribution (this is called the Central Limit Theorem). Other continuous variables – reaction time measurements being one example – are usually log-transformed to make them more normal.

Real data will never be precisely normal, and besides inspecting the data with a histogram, there are several other ways to estimate how close to normal a dataset is, including other graphical methods like the quantile-quantile (or Q-Q) plot, and formal tests like the Shapiro-Wilk test, as discussed in Chapter 15. *Parametric* statistics, which require that data be distributed normally or according to some other probability density function (see Chapter 15), make assumptions about the distribution of the data. However, data do not have to be precisely normal in order to perform most statistical analyses. Methods are called *robust* to the extent they can tolerate deviations from assumptions like normality. *Non-parametric* methods are a class of robust statistics that make no assumptions about data distribution, so they can be used with highly skewed data. Non-parametric methods are also often the most appropriate choice for analyzing ordinal and nominal data.

4   Central tendency

If we needed to describe a variable and could only use a single number, we would surely report a measure of *central tendency.* The central tendency is a "best estimate" of the value of the variable; different definitions of "best" result in different measures, such as the mean, median, and mode. It is almost always essential to calculate central tendency, as it is the principal number that gets reported for a distribution, or compared between groups.

By far the most commonly used measure of central tendency with continuous variables is the *arithmetic mean*, or simply the *mean*. The arithmetic mean is the sum of all the values of the variable, divided by N, the number of observations. The mean is informally called the average, but this term can be ambiguous and should be avoided. When it is appropriate, the calculation of a mean (and the comparison of means) is the powerhouse of descriptive and parametric statistics. There is also a *geometric mean* – the Nth root of the product of all the values – best used when (a) the quantities being compared are on different scales, or (b) when a logarithmic/exponential relationship exists. For example, the geometric mean of 1, 10, and 100 is 10, which depending on the details of the situation may be a more sensible mid-point than the arithmetic mean of 37. A third type of mean, the *harmonic mean* – the reciprocal of the arithmetic mean of the reciprocals of the values – is often used when the quantities are ratios or rates. So if one travels from point A to point B at 50 miles per hour, and returns at 100 miles per hour, the average speed (total distance / total time) is the harmonic mean of 50 and 100, or 66.6 miles per hour (not the arithmetic mean, 75, or the geometric mean, 70.7). While there are few clear applications of the harmonic mean in linguistic research, note that in the field of pattern recognition, the F1 score is defined as the harmonic mean of precision and recall.

The *median* is defined quite differently. If the values of the variable are placed in order from smallest to largest, the median is the value in the middle. (If N is even, we take the mean of the two middle values.) Outliers – unusually small or large values – will affect the mean, but will have little or no effect on the median, so the median is preferred when large numbers of (valid) outliers exist. Also, if the distribution is very skewed (see Section 6), the mean can be misleading. In the million-word Brown Corpus of English, there are 45,215 word types, which occur between 1 and 69,836 times each. The *mean* word frequency is 22, which would point to words like *refund*, *sphere*, and *Florida* as typical in frequency. But in reality only 10 percent of word types are this frequent or more so. On the other hand, the *median* word frequency is 2, exemplified by rarer words like *kelp*, *starchy*, and *Tchaikovsky*. Some 58 percent of word types are this frequent or more so, showing that the median, not the mean, successfully represents something like the mid-point of word frequency. In the case of an ordinal variable, such as the five-point survey's popular "strongly agree, agree, neither agree nor disagree, disagree, strongly disagree," there is no possibility of calculating a mean response, because we only have information on ordering, not distance, between the categories. Ordinal variables therefore call for medians and median-based statistics, including non-parametric methods.

The third measure of central tendency is the *mode*, the most common value in a distribution. In the Brown Corpus example, the modal frequency for word type would be 1, since more word types have a frequency of 1 (19,130) than any other value. A variable always has a single mean and a single median, but it can have more than one mode, if more than one value is equally frequent. A variable with two modes is bimodal, but as we saw above, the term bimodal can be applied more broadly whenever the frequency distribution has two peaks, even if they are not equally frequent. For a nominal variable, with unordered categories (e.g., noun, verb, adjective, preposition), we cannot establish a mean or a median; the mode is the only central tendency that is defined.

Household income is more tangible than most linguistic variables, and is a classic way to explore the differences between the mean, median, and mode. We will look at household incomes under $200,000 in the United States in 2009 (US Census Bureau 2011a). The histogram in Figure 14.6 reveals a right-skewed distribution of income (with a longer right tail), and the mean, median, and mode are labeled. The mean, $57,990, is equal to the total income of all the households, divided by the number of households. This answers the question, "If all the income were redistributed equally among the households, how much would each household make?" This is an interesting question, but we are usually more interested in reporting the actual income of a typical household. We can do this

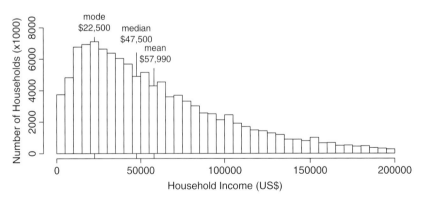

Figure 14.6. *Histogram of 2009 household income, with central tendencies labeled*

with the median or the mode. The median, $47,500, would be the midpoint of all the households, if they were sorted by income. In other words, half the households made less than $47,500 and half made more than $47,500 (besides those that made $47,500). This answers the question, "What is the income of the middle household?" The mean is the most commonly used measure of central tendency, but it is often the median that tells us what we are more interested in knowing. The relative position of the mean and median is related to skewness (see Section 5). In a right-skewed distribution, like this one, the mean is usually greater than the median. In a left-skewed distribution the mean is usually less than the median. The mode is the income bin with the most households in it; this is $22,500. The mode answers the question, "If we choose a household at random, what is its income most likely to be?" More households made $22,500 than any other amount. Despite the appeal of the mode, it is rarely reported as a measure of central tendency (and the mode is not necessarily a central value, just the most common value). For household income, it is most common to report the median.

In linguistics, a common right-tailed distribution is the *Zipf's Law* relationship, where, in a corpus for example, token frequency is inversely proportional to type rank: the most common word occurs twice as often as the second-most-common word, and so on. These distributions follow a *power law* function of the general form $y = 1/x$, where the mean, median, and mode are far apart, a distribution much more skewed than any set of acoustic or articulatory measurements are likely to be. As a general rule, we expect repeated measurements to approximate an unskewed *normal distribution*, where the mean, median, and mode are quite close together.

Returning to the Albuquerque temperature data, the mean temperature is 58.2 degrees (we can imagine dividing all the degrees equally among all the days). The median temperature is 58.9 degrees (182 days were colder, 182 were warmer). And there are two modes: 5 days were 44.8 degrees and 5 days were 74.6 degrees.

For the Peterson and Barney pitch data, the mean of the speaker F0 values (each of which is itself a mean of 20 individual observations) is 173 Hz overall, 131 Hz for men and 223 Hz for women. The median values are 163 Hz overall, 126 Hz for men and 223 Hz for women. The generally higher values for the means reflect the right-skewed distribution of the untransformed F0 data. The male data had two modes, as three men had F0s of 122 Hz and three more were at 126 Hz. The female data had four modes, with two women each at 201, 207, 231, and 252 Hz. Recall that for continuous variables, no two values are underlyingly identical, so the result for the mode will always depend somewhat on how the values are binned (the F0 measurements were rounded to the nearest Hz, the temperatures to the closest 1/10 of a degree; the household incomes were placed in $5,000-wide bins).

The median (like the mode) is relatively immune to the presence of outliers and other extreme values, while the mean is more affected by them. A few unusually high values will pull the mean up noticeably, and a few extremely low values will pull it down. Since such outliers may represent measurement errors or other "bad data," we may prefer to use the median, or a more robust version of the mean such as the truncated or Winsorized mean (see Erceg-Hurn and Mirosevich 2008).

Above, we have graphically displayed the distribution of variables by using histograms. When comparing two or more distributions, the box plot (or box-and-whiskers plot; Tukey 1977) is especially useful. See Chapter 15 for more details.

5   Dispersion

A measure of central tendency describes the average, middle, or most typical value of a variable. A measure of *dispersion* tells us how much the values vary on either side of the central tendency. For example, a variable where all the values are clustered near the mean would exhibit low dispersion, while a widely ranging variable would show high dispersion. Dispersion is an essential part of the description of any variable's distribution. Furthermore, a given difference in central tendency means more in the context of low dispersion than high dispersion. For example, words that are twice as long as the mean might be fairly common in English and even more so in German – but people with twice the average number of toes are an extreme rarity.

A common application of dispersion in sociophonetics is to help determine if two vowel clouds represent merged or distinct categories. One can carry out separate *t*-tests for each formant, or calculate the position of each data point along a single (diagonal) axis and perform one *t*-test, or use more complex methods (e.g., *Hotelling's T-squared, Pillai's trace*). In all cases, the greater the dispersion, the greater a difference in mean position is required to support the hypothesis of distinct categories. Another use of dispersion is in normalizing vowel formants across speakers (e.g., the Lobanov method). Speakers differ in their mean formant frequencies, but also in their dispersion, so both must be equalized.

For a continuous variable, the easiest dispersion statistic to calculate is the *range*, which is simply the maximum value minus the minimum value. This measurement is obviously very sensitive to outlying values. When there are no real outliers, it can be useful. Our daily temperatures in Albuquerque stretched from 22 to 87, so the range is 65 degrees. We usually report the range alongside the median, which is 59 degrees (rounded to the nearest degree).

The concept of *quantiles* helps us to define a more robust and more frequently used measure of dispersion called the *interquartile range*. Quantiles are the dividing points obtained when you divide the data values into equally sized subsets or bins. Here, the number of observations is equal across bins, not the width of the bins. For example, *percentiles* result from dividing the data into 100 equal bins. The 50th percentile is the same as the median. The 25th, 50th, and 75th percentiles are otherwise known as the 1st, 2nd, and 3rd *quartiles* (the break points from dividing the data into four equal bins). The difference between the 1st and 3rd quartiles is the interquartile range (IQR), a good measure of dispersion. The values within the IQR comprise the middle half of the data. The IQR also forms the "box" part of a box-and-whiskers plot (see Chapter 15). The "whiskers" of a standard box plot stretch at most +/– 1.5 IQR out from the ends of the box; any data point further away is considered to be an outlier. For the Albuquerque temperatures (median 59 degrees), the IQR is 31 degrees. For Peterson and Barney's male speakers' F0 (median 126 Hz), the IQR is 22 Hz. For the female speakers' F0 (median 223 Hz), the IQR is 25 Hz.

By far the most commonly used measure of dispersion is the *standard deviation*, a quantity derived from the *variance*. The variance is the sum of the squared distances between each data point and the mean, divided by the number of observations, N. So for the dataset (1, 3, 4, 5, 6, 7, 9), the mean is 5, the distances from the mean are (–4, –2, –1, 0, 1, 2, 4), and the squared distances are (16, 4, 1, 0, 1, 4, 16). N is 7, making the variance $(16 + 4 + 1 + 0 + 1 + 4 + 16) / 7 = 42 / 7 = 6$. (By showing formulas and calculations, this chapter sometimes goes over math that in practice is done by a computer running a statistics package. However, it is useful to understand what is going on inside statistical operations and tests, which can otherwise become "black boxes.") The standard deviation is the square root of the variance, or in this case, $\sqrt{6} = 2.45$. Taking the square root ensures that the units of the standard deviation are the same as the units of the original data. This makes the standard deviation easier to interpret than the variance, which will often be expressed in unnatural units such as square degrees, square dollars, or square Hz.

When the data are a sample drawn from a larger population – like the Peterson and Barney F0 data, but not the Albuquerque temperature data or the US household income data – we must replace N with N – 1 in the variance and standard deviation formulas. The sample variance above would be $42 / 6 = 7$, and the sample standard deviation would be $\sqrt{7} = 2.65$. (The reason we use N – 1 instead of N in the divisor, called *Bessel's correction*, is because we would otherwise be underestimating the variance and standard deviation by using the distances of each point from the sample mean instead of the population mean.)

Two distributions can have similar means but very different standard deviations (and vice versa). We recall that the mean of the 2010 Albuquerque temperature distribution was 58.2 degrees. The standard deviation of these 365 temperatures is 16.5 degrees. In San Francisco during the same year, the mean daily temperature was 57.5, almost the same as in Albuquerque. But in San Francisco, the standard deviation was only 6.0 degrees, reflecting the much smaller seasonal temperature variation in that city.

The standard deviation for the F0 of the Peterson and Barney male speakers is 17.0 Hz, and for the female speakers it is 20.5 Hz. We can see that for these data, whether we use IQR (22 vs 25) or standard deviation (17 vs 20.5) as a measure of dispersion, we find the value for the women is slightly higher than for the men. Figure 14.7 illustrates the dispersion of the Peterson and Barney F0 measurements, separated between men and women. For each group, the figure shows a box plot, which identifies the median and the IQR, and a histogram labeled with the mean and +/– 1 and +/– 2 standard deviations from the mean.

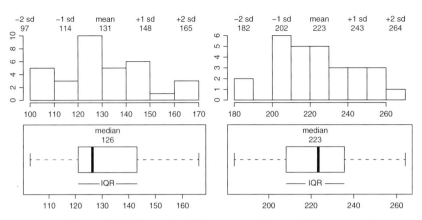

Figure 14.7. *Dispersion of Peterson and Barney F0 for men and women*

In analyzing a continuous variable, we usually choose between reporting the mean and standard deviation, on the one hand, or the median and interquartile range, on the other. If there are significant outliers, or if the data are quite skewed, the median is preferred. Median-based statistics are also preferred if the variable is ordinal. If the variable is nominal, only the mode is well defined.

Although this chapter does not cover tests for statistical significance (see Chapters 15 and 16), such tests make use of the kinds of descriptive statistics discussed thus far. Non-parametric tests, for example, refer to medians (e.g., *Mood's median test*) or ranks (e.g., the *Mann-Whitney test*), while parametric statistical tests (e.g., the *t*-test) employ means and standard deviations. In inferential statistics, much use is made of the fact that 95 percent of the values of any normally distributed dataset will fall between −1.96 and +1.96 standard deviations from the mean.

The measures of dispersion discussed above are all expressed in the same units as the variable itself. There are also *dimensionless* measures of dispersion, which are useful for comparing dissimilar datasets. A parametric example is the *coefficient of variation*, the absolute value of the standard deviation divided by the mean. A non-parametric example is the *quartile coefficient of dispersion*, the IQR (difference between first and third quartiles) divided by the sum of the first and third quartiles. Using these measures, we could demonstrate that the US household incomes are more dispersed than the Albuquerque temperatures.

6   Higher-order descriptive statistics

In this section, we will discuss *skewness* and *kurtosis*. These properties of a distribution are not as basic as central tendency and dispersion, but they are important nonetheless. Two distributions could match exactly in central tendency and dispersion, but be quite different according to these higher-order measures.

We have already referred to the skewness of a distribution in informal terms. Left-skewed distributions have a longer left tail, while right-skewed distributions have a longer right tail. Calculating skewness is a formal way of describing where a distribution lies along this dimension. Recall that the variance is the average squared difference from the mean of a variable's values. To calculate skewness, we take the average *cubed* difference from the mean, and divide this by the cube of the standard deviation. If the distribution has many values well above the mean, when these are cubed it will create large positive terms in the skewness formula. If the distribution has many values well below the mean, there will be large negative terms in the skewness formula. All in all, positive skewness means a distribution is right-skewed, and negative skewness means it is left-skewed.

Unlike the mean and standard deviation, skewness is a dimensionless quantity, without units. Any symmetric distribution has a skewness of zero, because the left and right tails are mirror images of one another. Symmetric distributions include – though of course are not limited to – normal distributions. For this reason, skewness is one measure of non-normality, while the absence of skewness is no guarantee of normality.

Above, we observed that the distribution of American incomes is noticeably skewed to the right, with a long tail of higher values. The calculated skewness for 2009 United States household incomes is 0.99. We can make an interesting contrast between the United States and Canada in this respect, if we compare 2009 personal incomes between $5,000 and $100,000 (Statistics Canada 2011; US Census Bureau 2011b). The means (US: $33,008; Can.: $35,045) and standard deviations (US: $22,027; Can.: $22,519) are quite similar between the two countries. However, the skewness figures are more noticeably different (US: 0.92; Can.: 0.84). This reflects a greater inequality of wealth in the United States, a difference which would show up even more strongly if we included higher incomes.

In Section 2, we observed informally that the Peterson and Barney pitch distributions were skewed to the right for both men and women. We can now quantify this skew: the men's data have skewness of 0.46, the women's have skewness of 0.16. As noted, one way to reduce this skewness is the log transformation, which reduces it to 0.22 for men and –0.02 for women. (The base of the logarithm used does not affect the change in skewness.)

Any distribution following Zipf's Law is inherently skewed to the right. Zipf's Law says that the frequency of a word is inversely proportional to the frequency rank of the word. So, for example, the second most common word should be half as frequent as the most common word, and the third most common word should be one-third as frequent as the most common word. We can see a pattern like this in the Brown Corpus of American English (Francis and Kucera 1964), where the 10th most common word occurs 9,801 times, the 100th most common word occurs 904 times, and the 1,000th most common word occurs 104 times. For the distribution as a whole, the skewness is a whopping 95.6. Log-transforming the frequencies reduces the skewness to 1.45, although the transformed distribution is still one big right tail, certainly far from normal.

Kurtosis measures the extent to which a distribution has a pointy peak (leptokurtic) or a rounded peak (platykurtic). We can graphically assess kurtosis by comparing our variable to a normal distribution with the same standard deviation. (In fact, all normal distributions have the same kurtosis.) The formula for kurtosis is the same as for skewness, except we substitute the fourth power for the cube in both the numerator and denominator. To calculate the *excess kurtosis* (usually just called kurtosis), we subtract 3 to account for the kurtosis of a normal distribution. After this correction, leptokurtic distributions have positive kurtosis, platykurtic ones have negative kurtosis.

Normally distributed data has zero (excess) kurtosis, although the converse is not true: zero kurtosis does not guarantee normality. Like skewness, kurtosis is a dimensionless quantity, making it easy to compare across different variables.

Our temperature distribution is platykurtic, with a rounded "peak" (actually two peaks). Its (excess) kurtosis is −1.37. Our pitch data, with men and women combined, has a similarly wide double peak; its kurtosis is −1.25. On the other hand, our household income distribution has a pointier peak; it is slightly leptokurtic, with a kurtosis of 0.41. Our word frequencies are extremely leptokurtic, having a very sharp peak at 69,836 (representing the word "the"), while most of the values are less than 10. The kurtosis for this dataset is 11,877!

Skewness and kurtosis are underused in the linguistics literature, but it is better to calculate and report them than to compare the shapes of distributions informally. The analysis of vowel formant clouds usually relies on means, with standard deviations employed for difference-of-means testing and normalization, but the acoustic analysis of some consonantal features like fricatives has found spectral skewness and kurtosis to correlate with key perceptual distinctions.

7   Association

The previous sections mostly dealt with one variable at a time. They described various properties of distributions, like central tendency and dispersion. They also compared variables taken from different datasets (e.g., showing that a particular income distribution is more skewed than a particular F0 distribution). This section will compare variables taken from the same dataset. So if we were talking about the physical traits of a certain set of people, we might discuss the relationships among their heights, weights, and eye colors.

In linguistics, a great deal of research involves identifying the associations between variables. For example, in sociolinguistics we might want to know which of a set of social and linguistic variables might affect the phonetics of a sound, the rate of occurrence of a phonological rule, or a choice between morphological or syntactic structures. In experimental research the purpose is very often similar: to establish the existence and strength of the relationship between an independent and a dependent variable. For example, in a lexical decision experiment, we might measure the effect on reaction time between various types of potential primes. The accurate assessment of an association can be complex, especially when there are many other variables to be controlled for, and/or repeated measurements from subjects and from items. One flexible approach is *mixed-effects regression* (see Chapter 16). This section will cover only much simpler statistics.

If knowing the value of variable X does not help you predict the value of variable Y, then the two variables are *independent*. If the values are related in any way, then the variables are *dependent* or *associated*. Associations can take many forms, but to the extent that an association is linear – "if X goes up by a certain amount, then Y goes up or down by a certain amount" – we can measure it with a statistic called the Pearson *correlation*.

If we compared the heights and weights of a large group of people, we would find a strong positive correlation. Knowing someone's height helps you to predict their weight (not precisely, of course, but to a large extent). Taller height goes along with heavier weight, which makes the correlation positive. On the other hand, eye color is independent of both height and weight. Knowing someone's eye color does not help you predict their height or weight.

The relationship of association or independence between two variables is always a two-way street. If height can help us predict weight (association), then weight can help us predict height. And if eye color does not predict height (independence), then height does not predict eye color. Famously, correlation (two-way) does not imply *causation* (usually one-way, if it exists at all).

Figure 14.8 is a plot showing a non-linear association, between the 2010 Albuquerque temperature data (on the y-axis), and the day of the year (on the x-axis). Of course, we know that temperature is highly dependent on the time of year, but we have an up-and-down trend, not a straight-line trend. If we plot the data over 5 years, as in Figure 14.9, we see a cyclical trend. We might try to model this relationship with a sine wave or similar function, but certainly not with a straight line.

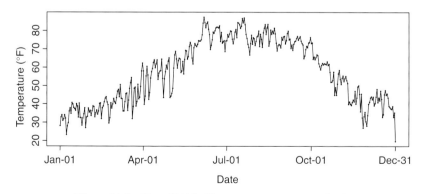

Figure 14.8. *Plot of 2010 Albuquerque temperatures by date*

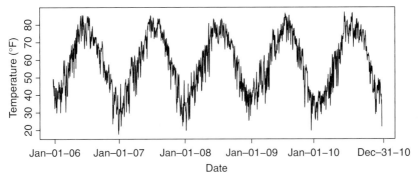

Figure 14.9. *Plot of 2006–2010 Albuquerque temperatures by date*

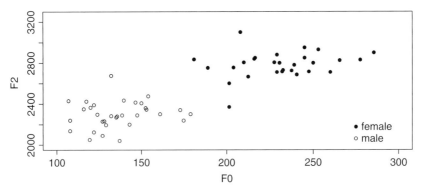

Figure 14.10. *F2 vs. F0 for* heed *in Peterson and Barney data*

As with any statistic, it is important to graph data before attempting to calculate a Pearson correlation. If the relationship between two variables is not basically linear, then the Pearson correlation coefficient can be very misleading. For example, the correlation between date and temperature for the 2006–10 Albuquerque data is only 0.04, even though we know – and can see – that temperature is highly dependent on time. The association is simply not linear.

To illustrate a more appropriate use of the Pearson correlation, suppose we want to know if there is a relationship between the fundamental frequency of a speaker's voice (otherwise known as F0 or pitch) and the higher formant frequencies observed in vowel production. As a quick test using the Peterson and Barney data, we can plot F2 against F0 for the word *heed*, averaging the two observations of the word made for each speaker, and shading the points according to sex, as in Figure 14.10. The figure shows almost no overlap between the men's and women's points. Women clearly have higher F0 and higher F2 than men; therefore the variables are associated. The points lie roughly on a line, so we can go ahead and calculate a Pearson correlation. (The upward-sloping relationship seems to be less strong if we look at the men's or women's data separately; see below.)

Correlations always range between −1 and +1. For the Pearson correlation, −1 means that all the points fall exactly on a downward-sloping line, and +1 means that they all fall exactly on an upward-sloping line. We expect to see a positive correlation between F0 and F2 here, since the points fall close to − but not right on − an upward-sloping line.

The Pearson correlation is defined as the *covariance* of the two variables divided by the product of their standard deviations. To understand covariance, let us consider the first five male speakers. Their F0 values are (173, 148, 108, 153, 134), with a mean of 143. Their F2 values are (2340, 2290, 2240, 2345, 2280), with a mean of 2299. For each speaker, we take the difference between their F0 and the F0 mean and multiply it by the difference between their F2 and the F2 mean. This gives us (30 * 41, 5 * −9, −35 * −59, 10 * 46, −9 * −19) * = (1230, −45, 2065, 460, 171). The covariance is the mean of these products. For these five speakers it is 776, but for the whole dataset it is 12,287 (the unit is squared Hz). The standard deviation for F0 is 52.5 Hz, and for F2 it is 277.4 Hz, making the Pearson correlation coefficient (12,287 / (52.5 * 277.4)) = 0.844. The symbol for the Pearson correlation, a dimensionless quantity with no units, is r.

If we square r = 0.844, we get *r-squared* = 0.712. The value of r-squared, which always falls between 0 and 1, has a very useful interpretation. It is the proportion of the variance in F2 that is accounted for by F0. That is, knowing F0 decreases our error in predicting F2 by 71 percent. R-squared is most often used this way, to summarize the fit of a *model*: how much of the variance in the dependent variable is accounted for by the independent variable(s). On the other hand, r is more often used to measure the correlation between two variables when we are not thinking of one as the predictor and the other as the predicted variable.

A related number is the slope of the *regression line*, the best-fitting straight line drawn through the points (see Chapter 16). The *regression slope* is the correlation multiplied by the standard deviation of the y-axis variable, and divided by the standard deviation of the x-axis variable. Here we have 0.844 * (277.4 / 52.5) = 4.46. This means that F2 increases 4.46 Hz for each 1-Hz increase in F0. Looked at the other way round, the Pearson correlation r is a standardized version of the regression slope. It says that F2 increases by 0.844 standard deviations for every 1-standard-deviation increase in F0.

Although there is a high correlation (0.844) between F0 and F2 for the men and women combined, the correlations for men alone (0.160) and for women alone (0.245) are much lower. Although it is a general principle that correlations are smaller when variables are observed over a restricted range, the decrease here is extreme. We conclude that F2 is associated with sex more than it is with F0. This is why we see greater F2 variability between the sex groups and fairly little within them. (A regression analysis, of the sort covered in Chapter 16, would tell us that F0 is no longer a significant predictor of F2 once sex is included in the model.)

As a parametric statistic, the Pearson correlation works best when both variables are roughly normally distributed. The Pearson method is also sensitive to outliers. If our data deviate greatly from normality, and especially if there is a nonlinear relationship between the variables, it is better to use a non-parametric measure of correlation such as *Spearman's rho* or *Kendall's tau*.

Spearman's rho is calculated using the same method as *r* (covariance divided by product of standard deviations), but the data are transformed into ranks first. Ranks just look at the ordering of the numbers, not their values, so (10, 3, 6, 1, 100) and (8, 0, 7, –100, 1,000) would both become (4, 2, 3, 1, 5). Non-parametric methods often involve using ranks, which convert continuous data to an ordinal scale. This makes the methods less powerful – more data are often required to observe an effect – but more robust against outliers and skewed or multimodal distributions. While Pearson's *r* quantifies the linearity of a relationship, Spearman's rho assesses its monotonicity. In a perfectly *monotonic* relationship, as one variable increases, the other consistently increases or decreases (but not both). If both variables consistently move in the same direction, we have rho = 1, and if they consistently move in opposite directions, rho = –1.

For example, suppose that x = (1, 2, 3, 4, 5). If y = x, Pearson's *r* is 1, because the points fall exactly on a straight line. If y = x² = (1, 4, 9, 16, 25), Pearson's *r* is 0.98; the points are close to a straight line, but not quite. If y = x³ = (1, 8, 27, 64, 125), r = 0.94. If y = 10ˣ = (1, 10, 100, 1,000, 10,000), r = 0.76. Whenever the data follow a curve rather than a straight line, the Pearson correlation will depart from 1. However, in all four cases, Spearman's rho is still 1, because the relationship is perfectly monotonic; in each case, as x goes up, y always goes up. This relationship is demonstrated in Figure 14.11.

Kendall's tau is another non-parametric correlation coefficient, which has a fairly simple geometric interpretation (Noether 1980). If we make a scatterplot of our variables, pick any two points at random, and join them with a line, then Kendall's tau is the probability that this line will have a positive (upward) slope, minus the probability that it will have a negative (downward) slope. We can see that this quantity will fall in the familiar range between –1 and +1, and that a perfect monotonic relationship between x and y will again result in a coefficient of

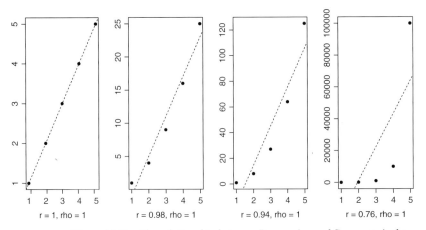

Figure 14.11. *The relationship between Pearson's* r *and Spearman's rho*

+/– 1. Kendall's tau tends to be smaller than Spearman's rho, but the two are similar.

Since both Spearman's rho and Kendall's tau disregard the numerical distance between the values in determining a correlation coefficient, both methods are also appropriate for use with ordinal data, where the concept of distance between values does not exist. We will discuss descriptive statistics for ordinal and nominal data in the next section.

8   Descriptive statistics for categorical data

In the sections above, we have discussed descriptive statistics for continuous variables, defined broadly as numeric measurements made to some reasonable level of precision. We may have rounded our temperatures to the nearest degree and recorded our pitch measurements as the closest Hz, but it did not stop us from treating them as continuous variables.

This section will discuss descriptive statistics appropriate for the three main types of categorical variable: ordinal, nominal, and binary. The categories of ordinal variables have a natural order (e.g., a *Likert scale*: strongly disagree, disagree, neither agree nor disagree, agree, strongly agree). The categories of nominal variables have no natural order (e.g., type of tree: elm, ginkgo, maple, oak, pine). Binary variables, with only two categories, can behave in some ways like continuous variables. For example, we can take the mean of a binary variable, but this is not possible for ordinal or nominal variables.

Linguistic investigations often employ categories as independent variables, while the dependent variables are continuous; our analysis of voice pitch by sex was an example of this. It is also common for dependent variables to be categorical. Responses to experimental scales, such as acceptability judgments, identity reports, and ratings of speech samples (guises) along personality dimensions are ordinal variables, though they can sometimes be treated as continuous. Articulatory judgments can be ordinal – front, central, back; raised, canonical, lowered – or nominal, as in rating /r/ as a trill, tap, approximant, or uvular sound. Binary linguistic dependent variables include many morphological and syntactic alternations, and some phonological ones. The VARBRUL/GoldVarb method (a type of logistic regression) was developed for binary alternations (see Chapter 20). The methods given here are simpler ways of describing and quantifying distribution and association.

To assess the distribution of an ordinal or nominal variable, we typically use a *bar chart* (the term "histogram" should be reserved for continuous variables). Figure 14.12 is a bar chart showing the distribution of quotative variants taken from a corpus collected in York (UK) in 2006 (Durham et al. 2012). We see that over 60 percent of the tokens are *be like*, with *say* coming in a distant second place, under 20 percent, and *go* and zero each comprising about 10 percent of the data.

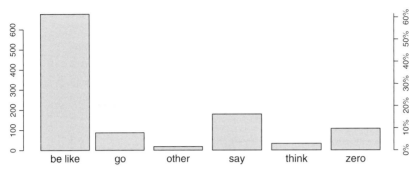

Figure 14.12. *Counts and proportions of quotative variants in 2006 York corpus*

For nominal data like these, the order of the bars is arbitrary (in Figure 14.12, it is alphabetical) and the concept of the distance between bars is undefined. This means that we cannot calculate a mean or a median for a nominal variable with three or more categories. The mode or most frequent value, however, is well-defined: here it is *be like*. The standard deviation is also meaningless in this context. To report the dispersion of a nominal variable, we can use the *index of dispersion*, which is close to 0 if most of the data fall in a single category, and is equal to 1 if the data are equally distributed among all the categories. If N is the total count, k is the number of categories, and f is a vector of the counts for each category, then the index of dispersion = $(k * (N^2 - sum(f^2))) / (N^2 * (k-1))$. For the quotative data overall, the index of dispersion is 0.69. For the female speakers, the index is 0.65, while for the males it is 0.76. This is a concise way of saying that the males used a more diverse array of quotative forms, although *be like* is in the majority for both groups (females 65 percent, males 56 percent).

With ordinal variables, a greater range of descriptive statistics can be used. The values of an ordinal variable have a meaningful order, so concepts like "more," "less," "highest," and "lowest" are well defined. This allows us to use the median and some of the measures related to it, like the interquartile range. However, unless a variable has a large number of categories, this is not always very useful. Variables measured on a discrete scale are often best treated as ordinal, although treating them as continuous is a common practice. With some types of scales, an ordinal analysis is necessary because the spacing may not be even (slightly agree, agree, strongly agree). We will now examine data from an experiment where subjects rated sentences on an eleven-point scale.

The first experimental item is the syntactically questionable sentence, "Mary has had more drinks than she should have done so." This was rated by 335 subjects. The bar chart in Figure 14.13 displays the range of rating categories on the x-axis, from 0 to 10. The number of responses in each category is measured on the y-axis. A chart like this is a good way to visualize and begin to interpret the results of acceptability judgment tasks (Chapter 3), as well as responses from questionnaires (Chapter 6) or experiments (Chapter 7). We can see from Figure 14.13 that the distribution skews toward the right, and the mode is the lowest possible rating (0 = completely

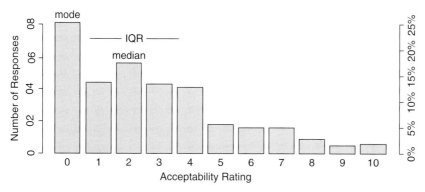

Figure 14.13. *Distribution of 335 ratings for* "Mary has had more drinks than she should have done so" *(0 = completely impossible, 10 = perfectly natural)*

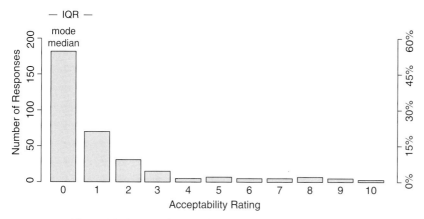

Figure 14.14. *Distribution of 335 ratings for* "Who did John see George and?" *(0 = completely impossible, 10 = perfectly natural)*

impossible). A few responses are up toward the high end of the scale (10 = perfectly natural). The range of the variable is 10 – 0 = 10. The median rating – the 50th percentile, or middle value – is 2. As far as dispersion, the 25th percentile is 1, and the 75th percentile is 4, making the interquartile range 4 –1 = 3. The index of dispersion is 0.94.

Figure 14.14 shows the distribution of a more clearly unacceptable sentence, "Who did John see George and?" This distribution is much more skewed. The total range is still 10, and the mode is still 0, but now the median value is 0 as well. The interquartile range is 1 – 0 = 1, reflecting a less widely dispersed set of scores. Accordingly, the index of dispersion is considerably less: 0.71.

When a variable is binary (also called *dichotomous*), we can report a kind of mean. For example, if the variable is "yes" or "no" votes, we would count each "yes" as 1, each "no" as 0, and calculate an ordinary mean using these numbers. So 30 "yes" votes and 20 "no" votes would be reported as 30 / 50 = 0.60 = 60 percent yes. This measure of central tendency is called the *mean of a proportion*, or *p*. (We would be unlikely to talk about the median or mode of a proportion.) To measure dispersion for a binary variable, we can take these 1s and 0s and calculate a standard deviation, but the result is not independent from the mean. If the mean of a proportion is *p*, the standard deviation is $\sqrt{(p * (1 - p))}$. For this reason, the standard deviation of a proportion is not very useful as a statistic.

We now turn to measures of association for categorical data. In discussing association above, we introduced several correlation coefficients for continuous variables. Of these, the Spearman and Kendall coefficients are most appropriate for ordinal variables (or if we have one ordinal and one continuous variable).

Suppose we want to check a possible correlation in the sentence rating task. We want to know if the same subjects who gave high ratings to the Mary sentence were also more lenient in judging the John/George sentence. We find a Kendall tau of 0.27, indicating that there is indeed a small degree of correlation. This value of tau means that if we pick two of the 335 subjects at random, the probability of the pair being *concordant*, minus the probability of the pair being *discordant*, is 0.27. A concordant pair of subjects agreed in their ranking of the two sentences. A discordant pair of subjects disagreed in their ranking.

When there are a lot of ties in the data (i.e., a given pair of subjects gave one or both sentences the same rating), as there are here, it is preferable to use a variant called *Goodman-Kruskal gamma*. The numerator for gamma is the same as for tau: the number of concordant pairs minus the number of discordant pairs. The denominator is smaller: the total number of pairs, not counting ties. So gamma will always be at least as large as tau; here it is 0.35.

If one variable is binary and the other is continuous, we describe association with the *point-biserial correlation coefficient*, r_{pb}, which can be calculated like an ordinary Pearson coefficient. So if we were wondering if there was an association between a subject's sex and their rating of the sentence about Mary drinking too much, there is probably none ($r_{pb} = -0.05$). Note that this example treats the rating as a continuous variable.

If both variables are binary, we report their association with the *phi coefficient*. Again, this can be calculated like a Pearson coefficient – covariance divided by the product of the standard deviations – though the coefficient will fall within a restricted range, not the full –1 to +1 range available for continuous variables.

We can illustrate the phi coefficient with data on the 2,201 people aboard the *Titanic*. Of 1,731 men, only 367 survived (21 percent). Of 470 women, 344 survived (73 percent). There was clearly a very different survival rate for men and women; the question is how to quantify it. Here the phi coefficient comes out as 0.46. The corresponding phi for survival vs age is only 0.10, indicating the lesser importance of age for survival. But these are only bivariate correlations; phi for survival vs sex does not take age (or class) into account. In order to cover all these bases at once, we would use multiple logistic regression (Chapter 16). This method gives a corrected number for the odds of survival for women vs men.

Table 14.2 *Cross-tabulations for survival vs sex and survival vs age*
on the Titanic

SURVIVED	SEX (phi = 0.46)		
	female	male	total
yes	344	367	711
no	126	1364	1490
total	470	1731	2201
SURVIVED	AGE (phi = 0.10)		
	adult	child	total
yes	654	57	711
no	1438	52	1490
total	2092	109	2201

Table 14.3 *Cross-tabulation of York quotative variants by*
grammatical person, observed

PERSON	VARIANT					
	be like	*go*	*say*	*think*	other	total
first	376	25	68	30	9	508
third	302	62	111	3	9	487
total	678	87	179	33	18	995

When one or both of our variables is nominal, we begin to assess their association using a *contingency table,* otherwise known as a *cross-tabulation* or *cross-tab*. Just as we make scatterplots to explore continuous data, a good first step with categorical data is to make a cross-tab. A cross-tab is simply a matrix using the categories of one variable for the columns and the categories of the other variable for the rows. Each cell is filled with the number of observations or cases for that combination of categories. So if one variable had three categories (red, blue, green) and the other had four (triangle, square, circle, star), we would have a 3×4 table, and each of the twelve cells would contain a number representing the quantity of that particular colored shape. Table 14.2 shows cross-tabs for the *Titanic* data discussed above.

We usually want to know if two variables are actually associated, and if they are, the strength of the association. The first question is answered using a significance test; indeed, all of the correlations discussed above have their corresponding significance tests (see Chapter 15.)

The second question can be answered with *Cramer's V*, which ranges from 0 (no association) to 1 (perfect association). Cramer's V is a useful metric that can be applied to nominal data regardless of the shape of the table. If the table is 2×2, Cramer's V equals the absolute value of phi; otherwise we derive it from chi-squared. To understand chi-squared, we return to the York quotative data.

Table 14.4 *Cross-tabulation of York quotative variants by grammatical person, expected (if no association)*

	VARIANT					
PERSON	*be like*	*go*	*say*	*think*	other	total
first	346.2	44.4	91.4	16.8	9.2	508
third	331.8	42.6	87.6	16.2	8.8	487
total	678	87	179	33	18	995

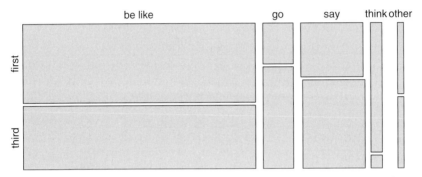

Figure 14.15. *Mosaic plot of York quotative variants by grammatical person*

We can use Table 14.3 – or the corresponding *mosaic plot* in Figure 14.15 – and see that the first-person context has slightly more *be like* and much more *think*, while the third-person context has more *go* and *say*. We suspect an association: knowing the grammatical person of a quotative sentence helps predict the quotative variant.

If there were no association between person and verb, but still the same overall proportions within the person and verb categories (these are called the *marginal frequencies*), the contingency table would look like Table 14.4.

To obtain chi-squared, we subtract each "expected" frequency E (in Table 14.4) from the corresponding "observed" frequency O (in Table 3), square the result, divide by the expected value E, and then take the overall sum, by adding each cell. This formula for chi-squared, which represents how dependent the two variables are, appears in (1). In this case, chi-squared is 55.8.

$$\chi^2 = \sum_{i=1}^{n} \frac{(O_i - E_i)^2}{E_i} \tag{1}$$

While we would certainly be interested in whether quotative use differs significantly between first- and third-person subjects, we leave the details of significance tests like these for Chapter 15.

To obtain Cramer's V – which measures the *strength* of an association (here, between quotative choice and grammatical person) – we divide chi-squared by

N (the total count) times k-1 (the number of categories of the variable with fewer categories minus one), and then take the square root, as summarized in (2). In the case of grammatical person and quotative choice, Cramer's $V = \sqrt{(55.8/(995 * (2 - 1)))} = 0.23$. This is not a very strong association, but it is larger than that between quotative choice and gender, where Cramer's $V = 0.12$. Gender is less associated with quotative choice than grammatical person is.

$$\phi_c = \sqrt{\frac{\chi^2}{N(k - 1)}} \tag{2}$$

Another approach to organizing categorical data in linguistics is *implicational scaling*; elsewhere, the same concept is often called *Guttman scaling.* It is a procedure employed with a number of binary variables or questions, if they can be placed in a consistent order, where the answer to one implies the answer to others. The original use of implicational scaling in linguistics was by De Camp (1971) in a study of Jamaican Creole. De Camp showed that if a speaker used, for example, the form *nyam* for "eat," then they definitely also used *nanny* for "granny" – but not necessarily the other way around. Similarly, using *nanny* implied using *pickni* for "child," but not vice versa.

If a set of linguistic variables is found to form an implicational scale, this means there is a strong type of association between them. The values of the variables do not co-occur freely, which would lead to 2^n combinations for n binary variables; instead, they are constrained by the scaling, allowing as few as n + 1 combinations. Implicational scaling typically scales linguistic variables relative to each other (in the horizontal dimension) as well as speakers relative to each other (in the vertical dimension). With implicational scales, varieties can be compared not only in terms of the ordering of linguistic features and speakers, but also in terms of the overall *scalability*, or goodness of fit, of the scaling model. Implicational scaling has been found to be particularly useful in relation to questions concerning individual variation, as opposed to statistical approaches that aggregate data for individuals into groups. For this reason, implicational scales continue to be used, especially in studies of creoles, bilingualism, and second language acquisition (see Rickford 2002).

9   Conclusion

If a dataset is "exploratory" – gathered based on an idea, but not a specific hypothesis – then descriptive statistics can suggest hypotheses to test. With "confirmatory" data, we will already have one or more hypotheses in mind. In testing them, we want to know how our sample relates to a larger population: inferential statistics (significance tests in Chapter 15; regression in Chapter 16).

When two subgroups of our data (males and females, first person and third person, treatment and control, etc.) differ on some descriptive statistic, we often want to know the probability that the two samples could actually derive from the same underlying population, despite the surface difference. In other words, we see what looks like an effect: a difference between groups. We want to estimate the size of the effect (descriptive statistics), but also decide whether it is a real, replicable, significant effect, or potentially a mere fluke (inferential statistics).

There are two situations when descriptive statistics can be enough, and inferential statistics are unnecessary or even inappropriate. The first, as mentioned above, is when the purpose of a piece of research is purely exploratory, designed to raise questions rather than answering them. The other situation is when the data are not a sample from a larger population. When a candidate wins an election, we do not ask about the statistical significance of the victory margin. Assuming there were no voting improprieties, the candidate with more votes – even one more vote – is the winner. And if we were studying the speech of a small village, with no plan to compare it to any other place – and if we interviewed every person in the village – we would not have to worry about any observed age or gender differences generalizing to a larger group of people. (However, we would still have to worry about analyzing a large enough sample of speech from each person to generalize about that individual's habits.)

Descriptive statistics are especially valuable when datasets are large, when it would be overwhelming to try to visualize or describe the patterns in the raw data. Descriptive statistics are a valuable set of simplifications that allow us to capture the essence of a dataset – and compare it to other datasets – using a few numbers, most of which have a simple derivation and interpretation.

References

ADTA (Average Daily Temperature Archive). 2011. Source data from National Climatic Data Center. Available at: http://academic.udayton.edu/kissock/http/Weather (accessed June 27, 2013).

DeCamp, D. 1971. Implicational scales and sociolinguistic linearity. *Linguistics* 9.73: 30–43.

Durham, M., B. Haddican, E. Zweig, D. E. Johnson, Z. Baker, D. Cockeram, E. Danks, and L. Tyler. 2012. Constant linguistic effects in the diffusion of *be like*. *Journal of English Linguistics* 40.4: 316–37.

Erceg-Hurn, D. M. and V. M. Mirosevich. 2008. Modern robust statistical methods: an easy way to maximize the accuracy and power of your research. *American Psychologist* 63.7: 591–601.

Francis, W. N. and H. Kucera. 1964. *A Standard Corpus of Present-Day Edited American English, for Use with Digital Computers*. Providence, RI: Brown University. Available at: www.archive.org/details/BrownCorpus (accessed June 27, 2013).

Noether, G. E. 1980. Why Kendall tau? *Teaching Statistics* 3.2: 41–3. Available at: www.rsscse-edu.org.uk/tsj/bts/noether/text.html (accessed June 27, 2013).

Pearson, K. 1895. Contributions to the mathematical theory of evolution. II. Skew variation in homogeneous material. *Philosophical Transactions of the Royal*

Society A 186: 343–414. Available at: http://visualiseur.bnf.fr/CadresFenetre? O=NUMM-55991&I=427&M=tdm (accessed June 27, 2013).

Peterson, G. E. and H. L. Barney. 1952. Control methods used in a study of the vowels. *Journal of the Acoustical Society of America* 24: 175–84.

Rickford, J. R. 2002. Implicational scales. In J. K. Chambers, P. Trudgill, and N. Schilling-Estes, eds. *The Handbook of Language Variation and Change*. Oxford: Blackwell, 142–67.

Statistics Canada. 2011. CANSIM. Table 202–0402. Distribution of total income of individuals, 2011 constant dollars, annual. www5.statcan.gc.ca/cansim/pick-choisir? lang=eng&id=2020402&pattern=2020402&searchTypeByValue=1 (accessed June 27, 2013).

Tukey, J. C. 1977. *Exploratory Data Analysis*. New York: Addison-Wesley.

US Census Bureau. 2011a. Current Population Survey. Annual Social and Economic Supplement. Table HINC-06. Income distribution to $250,000 or more for households: 2009. www.census.gov/hhes/www/cpstables/032010/hhinc/new06_000.htm (accessed June 27, 2013).

US Census Bureau. 2011b. Current Population Survey. Annual Social and Economic Supplement. Table PINC-11. Income distribution to $250,000 or more for males and females: 2009. www.census.gov/hhes/www/cpstables/032010/perinc/new11_000.htm (accessed June 27, 2013).

15   Basic significance testing

Stefan Th. Gries

1   Introduction

This chapter introduces the fundamentals of inferential statistics – that is, methods that help you make inferences or predictions based on your sample data. More specifically, in most empirical studies, researchers cannot study the complete *population* of a phenomenon of interest – that is, the complete set of objects or speakers of interest – but only a small *sample* of the phenomenon under investigation. For example, instead of investigating all relative clauses, you investigate a (hopefully carefully constructed) sample of relative clauses in a (part of a) corpus; instead of testing all non-native speakers of a language, you test a (hopefully randomly selected) sample of speakers, and so on. Obviously, you hope that whatever results – percentages, means, correlation coefficients – you obtain from a sample (which you studied) will generalize to the population (which you did not study). However, if researchers draw different samples from the same population and compute point estimates of percentages, means, correlation coefficients, they will just as obviously also get different point estimates; they will encounter variability. The most important application of inferential statistics is to assist researchers in quantifying and studying this variability to (i) arrive at better estimates of population parameters, and (ii) test hypotheses and separate random/accidental from systematic/meaningful variation.

Section 2 will introduce several basic concepts that underlie most inferential statistics. Section 3 presents a set of questions based on Chapter 14 and Section 2 of this chapter that are necessary to identify which statistical test is applicable in a particular research scenario. Sections 4.1 and 4.2 then discuss a small selection of statistical tests involving frequency data of discrete/categorical data and central tendencies (means and medians) respectively.

2   The logic of significance tests

To put the notion of statistical testing into perspective, an introduction to the framework of *null hypothesis significance testing* (NHST) is required. As the term NHST suggests, the notion of *hypothesis* plays a central role in this framework. A hypothesis is a statement that makes a prediction about the distribution of one variable (or about the relation between two or more variables) in a population and that has the implicit structure of a conditional sentence (*if* . . ., *then* . . . or *the more/less* . . ., *the more/less* . . .). Two different ways of characterizing hypotheses must be distinguished:

- *alternative hypotheses (H_1)* vs *null hypotheses (H_0)*: the former is a statement about an effect, a difference, a correlation regarding one or more variables; the latter is the logical counterpart of the former (i.e., a statement that predicts the absence of an effect, a difference, a correlation). Most of the time, the research hypothesis that is explored in an empirical study is an alternative hypothesis, predicting, say, a difference between percentages, a difference between group averages, a correlation between two or more variables, and so on.
- *text hypotheses* vs *statistical hypotheses*: each of the two above hypotheses comes in two forms. The former is a prediction in natural, "normal" language, such as in the H_1, in English ditransitives, recipients are shorter than patients. The latter is the former's translation into something that can be counted or measured – that is, its *operationalization*. This is an important step, not only because a proper operationalization is required to ensure the study's validity, but also because one text hypothesis can be translated into different statistical hypotheses. For instance, one statistical hypothesis for the above text hypothesis involves central tendencies such as means: in English ditransitives, the mean syllabic length of recipients is smaller than the mean syllabic length of patients. However, an operationalization based on counts/frequencies would also be possible: in English ditransitives, the number of recipients that are shorter than the average of all recipients and patients is larger than the number of patients shorter than that average. Needless to say, it is possible that the first statistical hypothesis is supported whereas the second is not, which is why a careful operationalization is essential and, obviously, will determine which statistical test you need to perform.

Significance tests are based on the following logic and steps: (i) you compute the effect you observe in your data (e.g., a frequency distribution, a difference in means, a correlation), (ii) you compute the so-called *probability of error p* to obtain the (summed/combined) probability of the observed effect and every other result that deviates from H_0 even more when H_0 is true, and (iii) you compare *p* to a significance level (usually 5 percent, i.e., 0.05) and, if *p* is smaller than the significance level, you reject H_0 (because it is not compatible enough with the data to stick to it) and accept H_1. Note that this does not mean you have *proven* H_1: after all, there is still a probability *p* that your observed effect/result arises under $H_0 - p$ is just too small (by convention) to stick to H_0 (see Cohen 1994 for a critical discussion of NHST).

The above immediately leads to the question of how that probability *p* is computed. One way is to write up all results possible and their probabilities

Table 15.1 *All possible results from asking three subjects to classify* walk *as a noun or a verb*

Subject 1	Subject 2	Subject 3	# noun	# verb	Probability
noun	noun	noun	3	0	0.125
noun	noun	verb	2	1	0.125
noun	verb	noun	2	1	0.125
noun	verb	verb	1	2	0.125
verb	noun	noun	2	1	0.125
verb	noun	verb	1	2	0.125
verb	verb	noun	1	2	0.125
verb	verb	verb	0	3	0.125

under H_0 and then check how likely the observed result and everything more extremely deviating from H_0 is. Imagine a linguist interested in conversion/zero-derivation in English. He presents the word *walk* independently to three subjects and asks them which word class it is: *noun* or *verb*. Imagine further that all three subjects responded *verb*. How likely is this result, assuming that, under H_0, *noun* and *verb* are equally likely? To answer this question, Table 15.1 summarizes the whole result space: the three left columns represent the subjects and their possible answers, columns four and five summarize the numbers of noun and verb responses for each possible outcome, and the rightmost column provides the probability for each of the eight results, which are equally likely under the H_0 and, thus, all $1/8$.

The linguist can now determine how probable the observed result – three times verb – and all other results deviating from H_0 even more – none, three times verb is the most extreme verb-favoring result you can get from three subjects – are. That probability is shown in the last row: $p=0.125$, which makes the observed result not significantly different from chance.

Obviously, the strategy of writing up every possible result, and so on, is not feasible with continuous data, or even with the binary data from above if the sample size becomes large. However, consider Figure 15.1 to see what happens as the number of trials increases. The top left panel shows the probability distribution for the data in Table 15.1: $p(0$ times verb$)=0.125$, $p(1$ times verb$)=0.375$, $p(2$ times verb$)=0.375$, and $p(3$ times verb$)=0.125$. If you perform six or twelve trials, you obtain the other distributions in the upper panel, and if you perform twenty-five, fifty, or one hundred trials, you obtain the distributions in the lower panel: clearly, as the number of trials increases, the discrete probability distribution looks more and more like a bell-shaped curve, whose distribution can therefore be modeled on the basis of the equation underlying a Gaussian normal distribution, as shown in (1).

$$Y = \frac{1}{\sigma\sqrt{2\pi}} e^{-(X-\mu)^2/2\sigma^2} \tag{1}$$

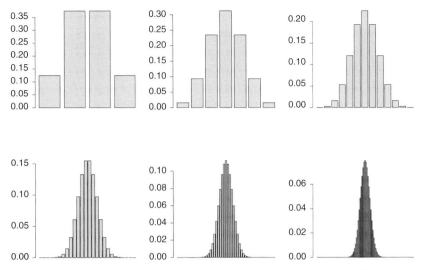

Figure 15.1. *Probability distributions for outcomes of equally likely binary trials (top row: 3, 6, and 12 trials; bottom row: 25, 50, and 100 trials)*

Thus, if the data under investigation are distributed in a way that is sufficiently similar to the normal distribution (or another one of several widely used probability density functions, such as the F-, t-, or χ^2-distribution), then one does not have to compute, and sum over, exact probabilities as in Table 15.1, but can approximate the p-value from parameters of equations underlying the above distributions (such as (1)); this is often called using *parametric tests*. Crucially, this approximation of a p-value on the basis of a function can be only as good as the data's distribution is similar to the corresponding function; the next section illustrates the relevance of this issue, as well as a few others, for selecting the right statistical test.

A second advantage of your data being distributed similarly to a known distribution is that this sometimes allows you to compute a so-called *confidence interval* on top of a descriptive statistic (such as a mean or a correlation). A 95 percent confidence interval helps you assess the precision of a statistic describing your sample; it

> identifies a range of values a researcher can be 95% confident contains the true value of a population parameter ... Stated in probabilistic terms, the researcher can state that there is a probability/likelihood of 0.95 that the confidence interval contains the true value of the population parameter.   (Sheskin 2007: 74)

Section 4 will provide two examples for confidence intervals.

3   Choosing significance tests

The decision for a particular statistical test is typically made on the basis of a set of questions that cover various aspects of the study you are conducting, the number and types of variables that are involved, and the size and distribution of the dataset(s) involved. The remainder of this section discusses these questions in (1) to (6), and their possible answers and implications.

1.   What kind of study is being conducted?

This question is usually easy to answer. At the risk of a slight simplification, studies are either *exploratory/hypothesis-generating* or *hypothesis-testing*. The former means that you are approaching a (typically large) dataset with the intentions of detecting structure(s) and developing hypotheses for future studies; your approach to the data is therefore data-driven, or bottom-up. The latter means you are approaching the dataset with a specific hypothesis in mind which you want to test. In this chapter, I will discuss only the latter type of study (see Chapter 14 for a discussion of the former type).

2.   How many and what kinds of variables are involved?

There are essentially four different possible answers. First, you may only have one dependent variable. In that case, you normally want to compute a *goodness-of-fit test* to test whether the results from your data correspond to other results (from a previous study) or correspond to a known distribution (such as a normal distribution). Examples include the following:

- Does the ratio of *no*-negations (e.g., *He is no stranger*) and *not*-negations (e.g., *He is not a stranger*) in your data correspond to a uniform distribution?
- Does the average acceptability judgment you receive for a sentence correspond to that of a previous study?

Second, you may have one dependent and one independent variable, in which case you want to compute a *monofactorial test for independence* to determine whether the values of the independent variable are correlated with those of the dependent variable. For example:

- Does the animacy of the referent of the direct object (a categorical independent variable) correlate with the choice of one of two post-verbal constituent orders (a categorical dependent variable)?
- Does the average acceptability judgment (a mean of a ratio/interval/ordinal dependent variable) vary as a function of whether the subjects providing the ratings are native or non-native speakers (a categorical independent variable)?

Third, you may have one dependent and two or more independent variables, in which case you want to compute a *multifactorial* analysis to determine whether the individual independent variables *and* their interactions correlate with the dependent variable. For example:

- Does the frequency of a negation type (a categorical dependent variable with the levels *no* vs *not*; see above) depend on the mode (a binary independent variable with the levels *spoken* vs *written*), the type of verb that is negated (a categorical independent variable with the levels *copula*, *have*, or *lexical*), and/or the interaction of these independent variables?
- Does the reaction time to a word w in a lexical decision task (a ratio/interval dependent variable) depend on the word class of w (a categorical independent variable), the frequency of w in a reference corpus (a ratio/interval independent variable), whether the subject has seen a word semantically related to w on the previous trial or not (a binary independent variable), whether the subject has seen a word phonologically similar to w on the previous trial or not (a binary independent variable), and/or the interactions of these independent variables?

Such multifactorial tests are discussed in Chapters 16 and 20.

Fourth, you have two or more dependent variables, in which case you want to perform a *multivariate* analysis, which can be exploratory (such as hierarchical cluster analysis, principal components analysis, factor analysis, multidimensional scaling) or hypothesis-testing in nature (MANOVA).

3.   Are data points in your data related such that you can associate data points to each other meaningfully and in a principled way?

This question is concerned with whether you have what are called independent or dependent samples. For example, your two samples (e.g., the numbers of mistakes made by ten male and ten female non-native speakers in a grammar test) are *independent* of each other if you cannot connect each male subject's value to that of one female subject on a meaningful and principled basis. This would be the case if you randomly sampled ten men and ten women and let them take the same test.

There are two ways in which samples can be *dependent*. One is if you test subjects more than once (e.g., before and after a treatment). In that case, you could meaningfully connect each value in the before-treatment sample to a value in the after-treatment sample, namely connect each subject's two values. The samples are dependent because, for instance, if subject #1 is very intelligent and good at the language tested, then these characteristics will make his results better than average in both tests, especially compared to a subject who is less intelligent and proficient in the language and who will perform worse in both tests. Recognizing that the samples are dependent this way will make the test of before-vs-after treatments more precise.

The second way in which samples can be dependent can be explained using the above example of ten men and ten women. If the ten men were the husbands of the ten women, then one would want to consider the samples dependent. Why? Because spouses are on average more similar to each other than randomly chosen people: they often have similar IQs, similar professions, they spend more time with each other than with randomly selected people, and so on. Thus, it would be useful to associate each husband with his wife, making this two dependent samples.

Independence of data points is often a very important criterion: many tests assume that data points are independent, and for many tests you must choose your test depending on what kind of samples you have. For instance, below I will discuss a *t*-test for independent samples and one for dependent samples.

4.   What is the statistic of the dependent variable in the statistical hypotheses?

There are essentially five different answers to this question. Your dependent variable may involve *frequencies/counts* (e.g., when you study which level(s) of a categorical variable are attested more/less often than others), *central tendencies* (e.g., when you explore whether the mean or median of a ratio/interval or ordinal variable is as high as you expected), *dispersions* (e.g., when you investigate whether the variability of a ratio/interval or ordinal variable around its mean or median is higher in one group than another), *correlations* (e.g., when you ask whether changing the values of one variable bring about changes in another), and *distributions* (e.g., whether samples of two ratio/interval variables are both normally distributed or not). Obviously, the nature of your dependent variable has important consequences for your statistical analysis; below, we will discuss examples involving frequencies and central tendencies.

5.   What does the distribution of the data look like? Normally or another way that can be described by a probability density function (or a way that can be transformed to correspond to a probability density function; see Section 5), or some other way?

6.   How big are the samples to be collected? $n<30$ or $n \geq 30$?

These final two questions are related to each other and to the above notion of parametric (vs non-parametric/distribution-free) tests. Parametric tests involve statistical approximations and rely on the sampled data being distributed in a particular way (for example, normally as represented in Figure 15.1 or the left panel of Figure 15.2). Sometimes, the data do not even have to be distributed normally as long as the sample size is large enough. However, the more the data violate distributional assumptions of the test you are considering (e.g., word lengths are often distributed as in the right panel of Figure 15.2), the safer it is to use a *non-parametric/distribution-free* alternative that does not rely on assumptions you know your data violate; see Section 4.2.2 for an example. See Chapter 3 for an example of a case where the distinction between parametric and non-parametric tests is important for analyzing grammaticality judgments.

Sometimes, tests have yet other requirements, such as particular minimal sample sizes or more complicated ones. In all cases, you must check your data for all of these to make an informed decision in favor of some test; ideally this involves a visual exploration of the data.

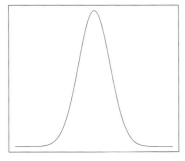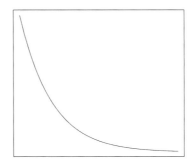

Figure 15.2. *A normal distribution (left panel); an exponential distribution (right panel)*

Once all the above questions have been answered and all other requirements have been checked, they usually point to one or two tests that address your question exactly. The following sections exemplify the choice of statistical tests and how they are then performed using some small examples. I am using the open-source language and programming environment R (www.r-project.org). Just as in many other scripting languages or spreadsheet applications, you perform (statistical) operations with *functions* (which tell R what to do, such as compute a log, a sum, or a mean), which take arguments (which tell R what to apply a function to and how). For example, sum(c(1, 2, 3, 4, 5)) applies the function sum to one argument (a vector containing the numbers from 1 to 5), mean(c(1, 2, 3, 4, 5)) computes the mean of the numbers from 1 to 5, and so on. The sections below will clarify this.

4   Performing significance tests and computing confidence intervals

This section exemplifies a small selection of frequently used tests; Section 4.1 exemplifies tests where the dependent variable is categorical; Section 4.2 exemplifies cases where central tendencies of ratio/interval and ordinal variables are tested.

4.1   Frequencies

This section introduces a goodness-of-fit test (Section 4.1.1), a test for independence (Section 4.1.2), and confidence intervals for percentages of categorical variables (Section 4.1.3).

4.1.1   The chi-square test for goodness of fit

This section discusses the test to use if you have answered the above questions as follows: you are conducting a study of one dependent categorical variable and you want to test whether the observed frequencies of the variable's levels – which are independent of each other – are distributed as expected from a particular probability distribution (e.g., the uniform distribution) or previous results. For example, you asked fifty subjects to indicate whether they think that *walk* is a noun or a verb (of course it can be both – you are interested in the subjects' first responses), and you obtained responses such that thirty subjects said *verb* and twenty said *noun*. If you want to test whether these two observed frequencies, thirty and twenty, differ significantly from the chance expectation that subjects would have responded *verb* and *noun* equally often, then you compute a chi-square test for goodness of fit. In addition to the above criteria, this test also requires that 80 percent of expected frequencies are greater than or equal to five.

First, you enter the frequencies into R in the form of a so-called *vector* (a sequence of elements such as numbers or strings) and give names to the frequencies, using <- as an arrow-like assignment operator and the function c (for "concatenate"); anything in a line after a pound sign is ignored and merely serves to provide commentary.

```
walk <- c(30, 20) # create a vector with the observed frequencies
names(walk) <- c("verb", "noun") # name the observed frequencies
```

Then you compute the test using the function chisq.test with two arguments: the vector walk you just created, and a vector p of the expected probabilities, and since your H_0 expects the two parts of speech to be equally frequent, this is two times 0.5. The result of this test you assign to a data structure you can call, say, walk.test:

```
walk.test <- chisq.test(walk, p=c(0.5, 0.5)) # compute the chi-square test
```

Nothing is returned, but walk.test now contains all relevant results:

```
walk.test # show the result
        Chi-squared test for given probabilities
data: walk
X-squared = 2, df = 1, p-value = 0.1573
```

The results shows that the distribution of verbs and nouns does not differ significantly from chance: $p>0.05$. However, you should also make sure that the assumptions of the test were met so you compute the expected frequencies (which in this case you do not really need R for). Obviously, both expected frequencies exceed five so the use of the chi-square test was legitimate.

```
walk.test$expected # show the expected frequencies
verb noun
  25 25
```

If the assumption regarding the expected frequencies is not met, exact alternatives for dependent variables with 2 or 3+ levels are the binomial test and the multinomial test respectively; the former is already implemented in the R function binom.test.

Table 15.2 *Fictitious data from a forced-choice part-of-speech selection task*

	College education = yes	College education = no	Totals
walk = noun	16	4	20
walk = verb	9	21	30
Totals	25	25	50

4.1.2   The chi-square test for independence

The following scenario arises more frequently: you are conducting a study involving independent observations of two categorical variables, one dependent and one independent, and you want to test whether the observed frequencies of the levels of the dependent variable vary across the levels of the independent variable. For example, if in the above example you not only registered how often subjects considered *walk* a verb or noun, but also whether each subject had a college education or not, then you may have obtained the following result:

To determine whether the frequencies with which *walk* was classified as a noun or a verb are correlated with the subjects' level of education, you compute a chi-square test for independence, which has the same assumption regarding the expected frequencies as the chi-square test for goodness of fit.

Again, you begin by entering the data. This time, because the data are tabular, you use the function matrix with two arguments: a vector of observed frequencies by column and the table's number of columns (ncol). It is again also useful to provide names to the data by adding row and column names in the form of vectors using the function list:

```
walk <- matrix(c(16, 9, 4, 21), ncol=2) # create a matrix with the observed
      frequencies
dimnames(walk) <- list(Walk=c("noun", "verb"), Education=c(">= college",
      "< college")) # name the dimensions of the matrix
walk # look at the matrix
      Education
Walk    >= college < college
  noun          16         4
  verb           9        21
```

You then use the function chisq.test with the matrix walk as its only argument and assign the results to walk.test again (overwriting the earlier results):

```
walk.test <- chisq.test(walk) # compute the chi-square test
walk.test # show the result
      Pearson's Chi-squared test with Yates' continuity correction
data:   walk
X-squared = 10.0833, df = 1, p-value = 0.001496
```

For 2×2 tables R automatically applies a continuity correction to the data (see Sheskin 2007: 628f.); if that is not desired, use correct=FALSE as another

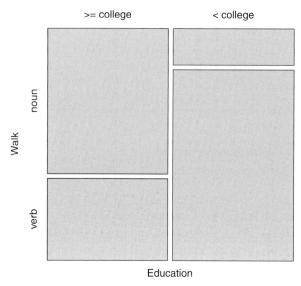

Figure 15.3. *Mosaic plot for the data in* walk

argument to chisq.test. The result shows there is a clear correlation between the part of speech assigned to *walk* and the education level of the subjects: *p*<0.05.

Before you explore what the correlation looks like, you should again test whether the expected-frequencies assumption is met, and it turns out it is:

```
walk.test$expected # show the expected frequencies
      Education
Walk    >= college < college
  noun          10        10
  verb          15        15
```

Finally, what kind of correlation do the data support? The quickest way to find out involves the so-called Pearson residuals, which correspond to the difference between each cell's observed minus its expected frequency, divided by the square root of the expected frequency. If a Pearson residual is positive/negative, then the corresponding observed frequency is greater/less than its expected frequency. Second, the more the Pearson residual deviates from 0, the stronger that effect. In R, this is easy to compute:

```
walk.test$residuals # show the Pearson residuals
      Education
Walk    >= college < college
  noun    1.897367 -1.897367
  verb   -1.549193  1.549193
```

The effect is that subjects with college education assigned the part of speech *noun* more often than expected, whereas subjects without a college degree assigned the part of speech *verb* more often than expected. This effect is also obvious from a graphical representation of the data (e.g., a so-called mosaic plot), in which the large areas for the ">=college:noun" and "<college:verb" combinations represent the effect you already inferred from the residuals:

```
mosaicplot(t(walk)) # create a mosaic plot
```

(The t() just transposes the table so its row–column organization corresponds to the above matrix.) If the assumption regarding the expected frequencies is not met, an exact alternative for 2×2 tables is the Fisher-Yates exact test; this test, as well as extensions to variables with more than two levels, is implemented in the R function fisher.test.

4.1.3   Confidence intervals for percentages

This section is concerned with how to compute a confidence interval for an observed percentage. For example, in a corpus sample of 815 instances of the verb *to run*, you may have found that 203 of these (24.91 percent) involve the prototypical sense "fast pedestrian motion." To better evaluate that percentage in the population, you now want to determine its 95 percent confidence interval. The required R function is called prop.test, and it needs three arguments: the number of relevant instances in the sample that make up the percentage (a.k.a. successes), the overall sample size, and the argument correct=FALSE, which means that you do not apply a continuity correction (for the sake of comparison with other software):

```
run.ci <- prop.test(203, 815, correct=FALSE) # compute the confidence
      interval
run.ci$conf.int # show the confidence interval
[1] 0.2206115 0.2799023
attr(,"conf.level")
[1] 0.95
```

That is, following Sheskin's logic from above, you can be 95 percent confident that the true percentage of this sense out of all instances of *to run* is between 22.06 and 27.99 percent. If you apply this approach to the *walk* data from Section 4.1.1, you obtain the result shown below. Importantly, the non-significant result from above is suggested by the fact that the confidence intervals overlap.

```
walk.verb <- prop.test(30, 50, correct=FALSE) # compute the confidence
      interval
walk.verb$conf.int # show the confidence interval
[1] 0.4618144 0.7239161
attr(,"conf. level")
[1] 0.95

walk.noun <- prop.test(20, 50, correct=FALSE) # compute the confidence
      interval
walk.noun$conf.int # show the confidence interval
[1] 0.2760839 0.5381856
attr(,"conf. level")
[1] 0.95
```

4.2   Central tendencies

This section introduces a test of means from independent samples (Section 4.2.1), the corresponding test for medians (Section 4.2.2), a test of means from dependent samples (Section 4.2.3), and the computation of confidence intervals for means (Section 4.2.4).

4.2.1   The *t*-test for independent samples

This section introduces one of the best-known tests for central tendencies, which you apply if you are studying data involving a normally distributed ratio/interval-scaled dependent variable and a binary independent variable (with independent data points), and you want to test whether the averages of the dependent variable in the two groups (i.e., the two means) defined by the independent variables differ significantly from each other. For example, you may be interested in two different subtractive word-formation processes, blending and complex clipping. The former typically involves the creation of a new word by joining the beginning of a source word with the end of another (*brunch, foolosopher*, and *motel* are cases in point), whereas the latter involves fusing the beginnings of two source words (*scifi* and *sysadmin* are examples). You are now comparing the two processes in terms of how similar the source words are to each other, where said similarity is operationalized on the basis of the Dice coefficient, essentially the percentage of shared letter bigrams out of all bigrams.

As usual, the first step is to get the data into R, but in cases like these, you usually load them from a tab-separated file that was created with a spreadsheet software and has the so-called case-by-variable format: the first row contains the column names, the first column contains the case numbers, and each row describes a single observation in terms of the variables defined by the columns. Table 15.3 exemplifies this format on the basis of an excerpt of data from Gries (2013: Section 4.3.2.1).

This is how you read such a .txt file like the above into a data frame word. form in R:

```
word.form <- read.delim(file.choose()) # load the data from a text file
```

Table 15.3 *Dice coefficients of source words for complex clippings and blends*

CASE	PROCESS	DICE
1	ComplClip	0.0678
2	ComplClip	0.0704
3	ComplClip	0.0483
. . .	. . .	. . .
79	Blend	0.1523
80	Blend	0.1507

The data from each column are now available by combining the name of the data frame (word.form) with a dollar sign ($) and the column name (e.g., PROCESS). It is usually advisable to briefly check the structure of the data frame to make sure that importing the data has been successful; the function str displays the structure of a data structure:

```
str(word.form) # inspect the structure of the data
'data.frame':      80 obs. of 3 variables:
 $ CASE    :  int 41  42 43 44  45 46 47  48  49 50 ...
 $ PROCESS: Factor w/ 2  levels "Blend","ComplClip": 2 2 2 22 2 2 ...
 $ DICE    :  num   0.0678 0.0704 0.0483 0.0871 0.0813 0.0532 0.0675 ...
```

Apart from the above criteria for the *t*-test, especially the assumption of normality, the *t*-test also requires that the variances of the data points in the two groups are homogeneous (i.e., not significantly different). Since the default test for variance homogeneity also requires the data points to be normally distributed, this criterion should be tested first. One R function that can be used is shapiro. test, which takes a vector of data points and tests whether these data points differ significantly from normality. However, since we have two groups of data points – one for blends, one for complex clippings – there is a better way, using the function tapply:

```
tapply(word.form$DICE, word.form$PROCESS, shapiro.test) # test for normality
```

This means: take the values of tapply's first argument (word.form$DICE), split them up into groups by tapply's second argument (word.form$PROCESS), and apply tapply's third argument (shapiro.test) to each group:

```
$Blend
        Shapiro-Wilk normality test
data:  X[[1L]]
W = 0.9727, p-value = 0.4363

$ComplClip
        Shapiro-Wilk normality test
data:  X[[2L]]
W = 0.9753,   p-value = 0.5186
```

Both *p*-values are not significant, indicating that the Dice coefficients in each group do not differ from normality. You can therefore proceed to test whether the variance of one group of Dice coefficients differs significantly from the other. The function var.test can take a formula as input, which consists of a dependent variable, a tilde, and (an) independent variable(s).[1] In this case, word.form $DICE is the dependent variable, and word.form$PROCESS is the independent variable:

---

[1] If you cannot test for homogeneity of variances with var.test because your data violate the normality assumption, you can use the function fligner.test, which requires the same kind of formula as var.test.

```
var.test(word.form$DICE ~ word.form$PROCESS) # test for variance homogeneity
        F test to compare two variances
data:   word.form$DICE by word.form$PROCESS
F = 0.6632, num df = 39, denom df = 39, p-value = 0.2042
alternative hypothesis: true ratio of variances is not equal to 1
95 percent confidence interval:
 0.3507687 1.2539344
sample estimates:
ratio of variances
         0.663205
```

Again, the *p*-value indicates a non-significant result: the variances do not differ from each other significantly and you can finally use the *t*-test for independent samples. The function is called t.test and it is usually used just like var.test (i.e., with a formula):

```
t.test(word.form$DICE ~ word.form$PROCESS) # compute a t-test
        Welch Two Sample t-test
data:   word.form$DICE by word.form$PROCESS
t = 16.4104, df = 74.928, p-value < 2.2e-16
alternative hypothesis: true difference in means is not equal to 0
95 percent confidence interval:
 0.05991431 0.07647069
sample estimates:
    mean in group Blend mean in group ComplClip
              0.1381300               0.0699375
```

Not only do you get the group means at the bottom, which show that the mean for blends is about twice as high as that for complex clippings, you also see that that result is highly significant: $p \lll 0.05$. A graphical representation that summarizes such data in a very clear and comprehensive way is the so-called box plot, which requires the function box plot, a formula, and usually the argument notch=TRUE:

```
box plot(word.form$DICE ~ word.form$PROCESS, notch=TRUE) # create a box plot
```

This plot provides a lot of information and should be used much more often than it is:

- the thick horizontal lines correspond to the medians;
- the upper and lower horizontal lines indicate the central 50 percent of the data around the median (approximately the first and third quartiles);
- the upper and lower end of the whiskers extend to the most extreme data point which is no more than 1.5 times the length of the box away from the box;
- values outside of the range of the whiskers are marked individually as small circles;
- the notches of the boxes provide an approximate 95 percent confidence interval for the difference of the medians: if they do not overlap, then the medians are probably significantly different (see Sheskin 2007: 40–4 for very comprehensive discussion).

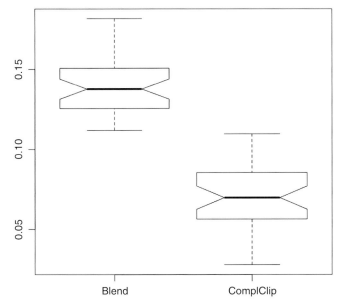

Figure 15.4. *Box plot of the Dice coefficients for the two subtractive word-formation processes*

If you cannot use the *t*-test because the data are not normally distributed, you can use the *U*-test instead, which is discussed in the following section. If you cannot use the *t*-test because the variances are not homogeneous, you can either use a version of the *t*-test which was designed to be less affected by unequal variances (the *t*-test by Welch, which is in fact R's default) or again the *U*-test.

4.2.2   The *U*-test

There are two main reasons to use a *U*-test. One is that you are studying data involving an ordinal-scaled dependent variable and a binary independent variable (with independent data points), and you want to test whether the averages of the dependent variable in the two groups (i.e., the two medians) defined by the independent variables differ significantly from each other. The other was mentioned at the end of the previous section: you have data that would usually be analyzed with a *t*-test for independent samples, but assumptions of the *t*-test are not met. The *U*-test also assumes that the data in the two groups are from populations that are distributed identically, but violations to this requirement affect the test results much less than those of the *t*-test (which is probably why this criterion is often not even mentioned in textbooks.)

Given the overall similarity of the two tests and in the interest of brevity, I will exemplify the *U*-test only on the basis of the same data as the *t*-test for independent samples. The name of the required function is wilcox.test and it requires the by now already familiar formula as input:

```
wilcox.test(word.form$DICE ~ word.form$PROCESS) # compute a U-test
    Wilcoxon rank sum test with continuity correction
data: word.form$DICE by word.form$PROCESS
W = 1600, p-value = 1.434e-14
alternative hypothesis: true location shift is not equal to 0
```

Given the large difference between the medians (recall Figure 15.4) and the highly significant result of the *t*-test, it is not surprising that the *U*-test also returns a highly significant result. (R also returns a warning not shown above because of the fact that there are three ties – i.e., three Dice values that are attested more than once. However, this is no need for concern since R automatically adjusts the way the *p*-value is computed accordingly.)

4.2.3   The *t*-test for dependent samples

The *t*-test discussed in Section 4.2.1 above involved a test of means from independent samples – in this section, I will discuss its counterpart for dependent samples. More specifically, you use the *t*-test for dependent samples if your data involve two groups of pairwise-associated data points on a ratio/interval scale and you want to test whether the means of the two groups are significantly different. The *t*-test for dependent samples also comes with the additional requirement that the pairwise differences between the samples' data points are normally distributed.[2]

As an example, consider a case where ten students take a grammar test and score a particular number of points. Then, they participate in an exercise session on the tested grammar topic and take a second grammar test; the question is whether their scores have changed. First, you enter the data of the ten subjects into two vectors before and after; crucially, the data points have to be in the same order for both before and after. That is, if the first data point of before belongs to subject 1, then so must the first data point of after, and so on.

```
before <- c(4 ,17, 8, 7, 13, 13, 3, 6, 12, 13) # create the 1st vector
after <- c(16, 16, 16, 17, 23, 22, 8, 20, 23, 11) # create the 2nd vector
```

To compute the pairwise differences between the two tests, you just subtract one vector from the other; R will perform a pairwise computation for you:

```
differences <- before-after # compute pairwise differences
differences # show the pairwise differences
[1]  -12    1  -8 -10 -10  -9  -5 -14 -11    2
```

---

[2] Reference works differ with regard to this criterion. Some cite the criterion mentioned above (that the pairwise differences must be normally distributed); others state that the data points in the two populations represented by the two samples must be normally distributed.

To test whether these differences are normally distributed, you can proceed as before:

```
shapiro.test(differences) # test for normality
      Shapiro-Wilk normality test
data:   differences
W = 0.874, p-value = 0.1112
```

Obviously, they are: $p>0.05$, which means you can perform a t-test for dependent samples. The function for this test is again t.test, but there are two small changes. First, to indicate that this time you need a t-test for dependent samples, you add the argument paired=TRUE. Second, when you did the t-test for independent samples and the U-test, you had one vector/factor per variable: the vector DICE for the dependent variable and the factor PROCESS for the independent variable, and then you used a formula. This time, you have one vector per level of the independent variable: one for the level "test before the treatment" (before) and one for the level "test after the treatment" (after). That means you cannot use the formula notation, but you just separate the two vectors with a comma:

```
t.test(before, after, paired=TRUE) # compute t-test for dependent samples
      Paired t-test
data: before and after
t = -4.4853, df = 9, p-value = 0.001521
alternative hypothesis: true difference in means is not equal to 0
95 percent confidence interval:
-11.433079 -3.766921
sample estimates:
mean of the differences
            -7.6
```

The result of the second test is on average 7.6 points better than the first, and that difference is very significant; $p<0.01$: it seems as if the treatment led to a substantial increase – in fact, to an increase of nearly 80 percent (since the means of before and after are 9.6 and 17.2 respectively). How can this result be represented graphically? One way would be to plot the vector differences in the form of a histogram. You use the function plot with the argument type="h" to plot the histogram, and the argument sort(differences) sorts the differences to be plotted in ascending order; the remaining arguments define the x- and y-axis labels to yield the left panel of Figure 15.5. It is plain to see that most differences are highly negative, which shows that the after values are larger.

```
plot(sort(differences), type="h", xlab="Subject", ylab="Difference: before –
      after") # plot a histogram of the differences
```

A second graphical representation is shown in the right panel: Each subject is represented by an arrow from that subject's score in the before-treatment test to the subject's score in the after-treatment test. The improvement is reflected in the fact that most arrows go upward, and the two numbers on the left indicate the speakers whose results did not improve.

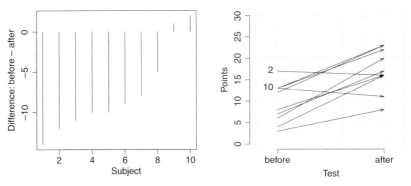

Figure 15.5. *Graphical representation of the differences between* before *and* after

If you cannot use a *t*-test for dependent samples, a non-parametric alternative is the Wilcoxon test. The function for this test is again wilcox.test, just add the argument paired=TRUE.

4.2.4   Confidence intervals for means

This section is concerned with how to compute a confidence interval for an observed mean. For example, you may have conducted a second experiment of the type in the previous section, with more subjects participating in a before- and an after-treatment test. You now want to know the mean of this second after-treatment test, as well as its 95 percent confidence interval. First, you enter the data:

```
after.2 <- c(10, 21, 8, 15, 23, 11, 12, 11, 13, 15, 21, 10, 9, 14, 9, 14, 12,
    4, 16, 13, 19, 19, 22, 18, 19) # enter the data
```

The function to compute confidence intervals for means is again t.test, and it requires the vector with the data points and conf.level with the desired confidence level. However, the computation of such a confidence interval requires that the data are distributed normally, which is why you need to run shapiro.test again.

```
shapiro.test(after.2) # test for normality
data: after.2
W = 0.9698, p-value = 0.6406
```

The data are distributed normally so you can proceed:

```
t.test(after.2, conf.level=0.95) # compute the confidence interval
data:   after.2
t = 14.5218, df = 24, p-value = 2.194e-13
alternative hypothesis: true mean is not equal to 0
95 percent confidence interval:
 12.28478 16.35522
sample estimates:
mean of x
    14.32
```

The mean number of points of this second group's after-treatment results after.2 is 14.32, with a 95 percent confidence interval of 12.28 (lower bound) and 16.36 (upper bound). If you compute the same kind of confidence interval for after, you will see that the confidence intervals of after and after.2 overlap, which suggests – but not demonstrates – that the means are not significantly difference (which is confirmed by a *t*-test).

5   Some final remarks

The above discussion could only discuss a small selection of tests and their assumptions and application. In this final section, I will briefly discuss four notions that are worth exploring: directional hypotheses, transformations, missing data, and multiple/post hoc tests.

First, given space constraints, all of the above discussed so-called *non-directional* alternative hypotheses and *two-tailed tests* – that is, tests of hypotheses that postulate a difference/an effect, but not the direction of said difference (e.g., *a* is not equal to *b*). However, if you not only expect some difference, but also the direction of that difference (*a* is larger than *b*), you can formulate a *directional hypothesis* and compute a *one-tailed test*. This is advantageous because, if you have a directional hypothesis, the effect you need to find in order to get a significant result is smaller; in other words, your prior knowledge will be rewarded. Thus, this should be among the first topics for further study.

Second, we have seen that parametric tests of ratio/interval data rely on distributional assumptions that need to be tested before, say, a *t*-test for independent samples can be computed. If those assumptions are not met, then one way to proceed is to use a test for ordinal data, as was discussed above at the end of Section 4.2.1. However, not only are tests that only utilize the ordinal information of data less powerful than their parametric counterparts, but for many more complex tests, non-parametric or exact alternatives are also not readily available. Therefore, an alternative to non-parametric tests is to apply a *transformation* to the original data, which, if the right transformation is applied correctly, can reduce the impact of outliers, normalize distributions, and homogenize variances. The most frequently used transformations of a vector x are the square-root transformation (sqrt(x)), the logarithmic transformation (log(x)), the reciprocal transformation (1/x), the arcsine transformation ($2*asin(sqrt(0.25))$ or $asin(sqrt(0.25))$), and the square transformation (x^2); if your data violate distributional assumptions, such transformation may be quite useful.

Third, observational and experimental data are often incomplete: particular types of corpus examples are not attested or cannot be annotated unambiguously; subjects do not respond to particular stimuli or do not show up for the after-treatment test. While a detailed treatment of the analysis of *missing data* is beyond the scope of this chapter, it is important to point out that missing data must not be ignored: they should be carefully recorded and investigated for patterns to determine whether they are in fact already a noteworthy and interpretable finding in and of themselves. For example, if a particular experimental stimulus exhibits a large number of non-responses, this may reveal something interesting about that stimulus or the studied hypothesis, or it may lead to you discarding the data from that stimulus from the statistical analysis. Thus, an analysis of missing data should be an indispensable analytical step.

Finally, a word on multiple/post hoc tests. Multiple testing arises when you perform several significance tests on the same dataset, and they are post hoc if you (decide to) perform these multiple tests only after you have performed a first test. An example of the first situation would be if you collected reaction times to words as well as, say, six predictors describing the words, and then ran all possible (six) pairwise correlations between the predictors and the reaction times as opposed to one multifactorial study. An example of the second situation would be if you tested the effect of one categorical independent variable with four levels a, b, c, and d on a ratio/interval dependent variable, obtained a significant result, and then ran all six pairwise comparisons of means: a vs b, a vs c, a vs d, b vs c, b vs d, and c vs d. The first situation is problematic because you might be accused of "fishing for results," but also for an additional statistical reason which also applies to the second situation: If you perform one significance test with a significance level of 95 percent, there is a probability of 0.05 that the decision to reject the null hypothesis is wrong. However, if you perform n independent significance tests each with a significance level of 95 percent, there is a probability of $1-0.95^n$ that at least one rejection of a null hypothesis is wrong; for $n=6$, this probability is already $1-0.95^6 \approx 0.265$. Thus, when you perform multiple tests, it is common practice to adjust your significance level from 95 percent for each test. For six post hoc tests, it would be necessary to adjust the significance level to 99.14876 percent, because $0.9914876^6=0.95$. However, even with such a so-called *correction for multiple testing*, testing all possible null hypotheses is to be discouraged. More discussion of these topics and all previous ones can be found in Crawley (2007); Baayen (2008); Johnson (2008); and Gries (2013).

References

Baayen, R. H. 2008. *Analyzing Linguistic Data: A Practical Introduction to Statistics using R*. Cambridge University Press.

Cohen, J. 1994. The earth is round (p<.05). *American Psychologist* 49.12: 997–1003.

Crawley, M. J. 2007. *The R Book*. Chichester: John Wiley and Sons.

Gries, S. Th. 2013. *Statistics for Linguistics Using R: A Practical Introduction*, 2nd edn. Berlin and New York: Mouton de Gruyter.

Johnson, K. 2008. *Quantitative Methods in Linguistics*. Oxford and Malden, MA: Blackwell.

Sheskin, D. J. 2007. *Handbook of Parametric and Nonparametric Statistical Procedures*, 4th edn. Boca Raton, FL: Chapman & Hall/CRC.

16 Multivariate statistics

R. Harald Baayen

1 Introduction

Multivariate analysis deals with observations made on many variables simultaneously. Datasets with such observations arise across many areas of linguistic inquiry. For instance, Jurafsky et al. (2001) provide an overview of the many factors that co-determine a word's acoustic duration (including its neighboring words, syntactic and lexical structure, and frequency). The importance of these factors is determined with the help of multiple regression modeling of data extracted from speech corpora. Koesling et al. (in press) used multivariate analysis to study the pitch contours of English tri-constituent compounds, with as predictors not only time and compound structure, but also speaker, word, a word's frequency of occurrence, and the speaker's sex. In morphology, the choice between two rival affixes can depend on a wide range of factors, as shown for various Russian affix pairs by Baayen et al. (in press). F. Jaeger (2010) showed that whether the complementizer *that* is present in an English sentence depends on more than fifteen different factors. Gries (2003) and Bresnan et al. (2007) clarified the many factors that join in determining the choice of particle placement and dative constructions, respectively. In psycholinguistics, multivariate methods are becoming increasingly important (see, e.g., Kuperman et al. 2009, for eye-tracking research), especially with the advent of so-called megastudies (Balota et al. 2004). Multivariate methods have a long history of use in sociolinguistics (Sankoff 1987), and play an important role in present-day dialectometry (Wieling 2013). What is common across all these studies is that they address linguistic phenomena for which monocausal explanations fail. Many phenomena can only be understood properly when a great many explananda are considered jointly. This is where multivariate statistics come into play.[1]

Table 16.1 presents a general description of a multivariate dataset with n cases or observational units, presented on the rows. Observations on k different random variables $X_1, X_2, \ldots, X_k$ (presented in the columns) describe the properties of a given case. These properties can be numerical (or continuous) (e.g., acoustic duration in ms, frequency of occurrence in a 100 million-word corpus, a response latency in a word naming experiment) or categorical (e.g., word category,

---

[1] This chapter assumes familiarity with all concepts discussed in Chapters 14 (Descriptive statistics) and 15 (Basic significance testing).

Table 16.1 *A multivariate dataset with* n *cases (rows) and* k *variables (columns)*

Cases	Variables			
	X_1	X_2	$\ldots$	X_k
1	x_{11}	x_{12}	$\ldots$	x_{1k}
2	x_{21}	x_{22}	$\ldots$	x_{2k}
3	x_{31}	x_{32}	$\ldots$	x_{3k}
$\vdots$	$\vdots$	$\vdots$	$\vdots$	$\vdots$
n	x_{n1}	x_{n2}	$\ldots$	x_{nk}

discourse type, the sex of a speaker, dialect). Predictors (or independent variables) that are categorical are referred to as *factors*. The values that a factor can assume are known as its *levels*. For instance, in a given dataset, a factor such as (major) Word Category may have as its levels *noun*, *verb*, *adjective*, and *adverb*.

The objective of multivariate analysis is to clarify how the variables pattern together and how they might distinguish the different cases on which the variables are observed. Most datasets are multivariate, and for a proper understanding of the structure of the data, it is often most informative to consider the different variables simultaneously.

Multivariate datasets fall into two main classes. On the one hand, we have datasets for which all variables are equally important. For such datasets, the primary interest will be in how the variables pattern together, and how they group or cluster the different cases, or on the causal relations between the variables (see, e.g., Section 7: Association, in Chapter 14). On the other hand, interest may focus on how a specific variable, henceforth the *response* (or dependent variable), is predicted from the other variables, henceforth the *predictors* (or independent variables). As discussed in Chapter 15, analyses that determine whether multiple predictors and their inter-actions significantly affect the outcome of a response variable are called multi-factorial analyses. The response in a multifactorial analysis can be numeric/continuous or categorical. In the latter case, the goal of the analysis can be described as classification – that is, the assignment of the different cases to the different classes defined by the levels of the response (see Section 3 below). However, not only the accuracy of the predictions, whether continuous or categorical, is of interest, but also how the variables pattern together to yield the predictions.

A great variety of multivariate techniques is available to the researcher (see Venables and Ripley 2002; Everitt 2005 for overviews), and it is impossible to do justice to the full richness of individual methods within the limits of a single chapter. This chapter provides an overview of some of the most important methods for analyzing data with a specific response variable, as well as examples illustrating what can be accomplished with each method. Specifically, the chapter focuses on multiple regression (Section 2, as well as Chapter 20) and classification models (Section 3). References are provided throughout to both book-length introductions and published studies using both types of methods. Although we discuss one method at a time, we emphasize that it will often be useful to study a given dataset with more than one technique, as the strengths of one may counter-balance the weaknesses of the other.

2   Multiple regression

2.1   Basic concepts

When the response variable is a measurement (e.g., acoustic duration in ms, response latency, pitch), and when there are no repeated measures, a multiple regression analysis models the response Y as a function of a weighted sum of the predictors and Gaussian (normally distributed) by-observation noise (ϵ).

$$(1) \qquad Y = \beta_0 + \beta_1 X_1 + \beta_2 X_2 + \dots + \beta_k X_k + \epsilon, \; \rightarrow \epsilon \sim \mathcal{N}(0, \sigma^2)$$

When all predictors X_i are numerical (or continuous variables), the analysis is described as a regression analysis. When all predictors X_i are factors (or catego-rical variables), the analysis is referred to as analysis of variance. When both factorial predictors and numerical predictors are combined, the analysis is an analysis of covariance.

The goal of regression modeling is to approximate the observed values of the response as precisely as possible by decomposing the response into a weighted sum of the predictors. Models as defined by (1) make several important simplify-ing assumptions that facilitate the estimation of the model's parameters (the coefficients $\beta_0, \beta_1, \dots, \beta_k$). First, the contribution of each predictor is assumed to be linear. When there is only one predictor, the fitted values are on part of a straight line (see Chapter 14 for a discussion of linearity). When there are two predictors, the fitted values are located on part of a flat surface. For more predictors, the fitted values are part of a flat hypersurface. Second, the errors (the difference between the observed and fitted values) are supposed to follow a normal distribution with mean zero and some unknown standard deviation (to be estimated from the data) (see Chapters 14 and 15 for discussions of normal distributions). Third, the errors are assumed to be independent (see Chapters 14 and 15 for discussions of [in]dependence), and all are supposed to follow the same normal distribution. This means that wherever one inspects the positioning of the observed data points with respect to the fitted line, plane, or hyperplane, one finds a cloud of points around the predicted values that is equally thick everywhere.

The regression model (1) specifies how the observed responses Y can be approximated given the values of the predictors X_i, $i = 1, \dots, k$. Analysis of variance is a special case of regression in which the fitted values are the group means defined by the levels of the factorial predictors. For instance, given two factors with two and three levels respectively, there are six group means. The

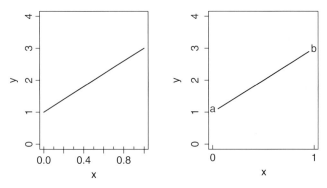

Figure 16.1. *A regression line (left) and a factorial contrast between a reference group mean* a *on the intercept and a group mean* b. *The difference between the two group means, the contrast, is equal to the slope of the line connecting* a *and* b: 2. *Both the regression line and the line connecting the two group means are described by the line* y = 1 + 2x.

regression equation for analysis of variance specifies how these group means can be constructed. There are many ways in which this can be achieved, all of which recode factor levels numerically using *dummy coding*. Here, we focus on *treatment coding*, which offers the advantage of clarity of interpretation for analysis of covariance. Analyses using treatment coding select one group mean as point of departure, and specify coefficients that quantify the differences between this group mean and the other group means. Figure 16.1 and Table 16.2 illustrate the basic principles.

First consider Figure 16.1. The left panel shows a standard regression line, for ten equally spaced values on the horizontal axis. The intercept β_0 of this line is at 1, and its slope β_1 equals 2. The right panel shows a similar line connecting two group means with values 1 for level *a* and 3 for level *b*. Since the group means of the two levels are exactly 1 unit apart on the horizontal axis, the difference between the two group means, 2, is equal to the slope of the line connecting the two group means. For both regression and analysis of variance, the same regression equation holds: $Y = 1 + 2X + \epsilon$. When a factor has more than two levels, say *m*, there are *m*–1 contrasts with the reference level, which are represented on *m*–1 orthogonal dimensions. Thus, a "univariate" one-way analysis of variance with a single factor with more than two levels is recoded under the hood as a multivariate regression model.

Table 16.2 illustrates dummy coding for a fictive dataset with six cases and two factorial predictors, one with three levels (i.e., a, b, c), and one with two levels (i.e., e, f). The reference group mean is represented by $A=a$ and $B=e$. Each of the other five group means is defined by a unique combination of the dummy predictors X_2, X_3, and X_4. The multiple regression equation (2), together with the dummy coding of Table 16.3, defines the group means listed in Table 16.3.

(2) $Y = \beta_0 X_1 + \beta_1 X_2 + \beta_2 X_3 + \beta_3 X_4 + \epsilon,$

Table 16.2 *An example of treatment dummy coding for two-way analysis of variance*

Cases	A	B	X_1	X_2	X_3	X_4
1	a	e	1	0	0	0
2	a	f	1	0	0	1
3	b	e	1	1	0	0
4	b	f	1	1	0	1
5	c	e	1	0	1	0
6	c	f	1	0	1	1

Table 16.3 *Predicted group means given the dummy coding in Table 16.2 and regression equation (2)*

Cases	A	B	predicted group mean
1	a	e	β_0
2	a	f	$\beta_0 + \beta_3$
3	b	e	$\beta_0 + \beta_1$
4	b	f	$\beta_0 + \beta_1 + \beta_3$
5	c	e	$\beta_0 + \beta_2$
6	c	f	$\beta_0 + \beta_2 + \beta_3$

The regression equations (1) and (2) define flat planes in two or more dimensions. In the case of regression, the fitted data points are on such planes, whereas in the case of analysis of variance, the predicted group means are located on these planes. However, the assumption that the regression surfaces are flat (hyper)planes is often too simplistic. The standard linear model allows the user to relax this assumption by introducing *multiplicative interactions*. For a regression model with predictors X_1 and X_2, the interaction is obtained by adding a third predictor which has as its values the product of the values of X_1 and X_2.

$$(3) \qquad Y = \beta_0 + \beta_1 X_1 + \beta_2 X_2 + \beta_3 X_1 X_2 + \epsilon.$$

The left and center panels of Figure 16.2 visualize the general regression surface defined by a multiplicative interaction. The left panel plots, for different values of X_2, the regression line for the response as a (still linear) function of X_1. For large negative values of X_2, the effect of X_1 has a negative slope. As the values of X_2 increase, this effect reverses and the slope becomes positive. The center panel uses a contour plot to present the joint effect of X_1 and X_2. Contour lines connect points with the same fitted value. Lighter shades of grey indicate higher values, darker shades of grey indicate lower values. The contour plot, which visualizes a hyperbolic plane, is easier to interpret, as it allows the analyst to compare the joint effect of X_1 and X_2 on the response for any pairs of (x_1, x_2) values. It should be kept in

Table 16.4 *Predicted group means for the data in Table 16.2 given the regression equation (4)*

Cases	A	B	Predicted group mean
1	a	e	β_0
2	a	f	$\beta_0 + \beta_3$
3	b	e	$\beta_0 + \beta_1$
4	b	f	$\beta_0 + \beta_1 + \beta_3 + \beta_4$
5	c	e	$\beta_0 + \beta_2$
6	c	f	$\beta_0 + \beta_2 + \beta_3 + \beta_5$

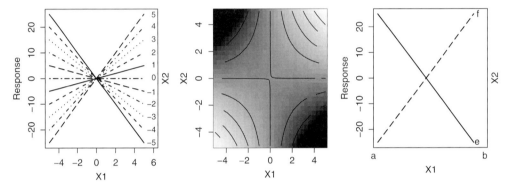

Figure 16.2. *Multiplicative interactions in the linear model*

mind that for a given dataset, only part of a hyperbolic plane is used – for instance, part of the upper left corner – just as when fitting data points to a straight line, only a line segment (i.e., only part of an infinitely long line) is used.

The third panel of Figure 16.2 illustrates the corresponding so-called *crossover interaction* for two factorial predictors, each with two levels. The effect of X_2 reverses for the levels of X_1. A model with an interaction for the 2×3 design described in Table 16.2 appears in (4).

$$(4) \qquad Y = \beta_0 X_1 + \beta_1 X_2 + \beta_2 X_3 + \beta_3 X_4 + \beta_4 X_2 X_4 + \beta_5 X_3 X_4 + \epsilon,$$

The expected group means are listed in Table 16.4. The weights β_4 and β_5 break the parallelism of the effect of factor B within each level of A. In Table 16.3, where there is no interaction, the contrast between the means for levels e and f is always the same, irrespective of the levels of A, and equal to β_3. With the interaction, as shown in Table 16.4, the effect is modified by β_4 for factor level b (of A) and by β_5 for factor level c (of A).

A linear model can comprise both numeric and factorial predictors. When the effect of a numeric covariate varies depending on the specific level of a given factor, we have an interaction of that covariate by the factor. An example is presented in Table 16.5 and Figure 16.3.

Table 16.5 *An example of treatment dummy coding for an analysis of covariance with an interaction*

Casey	A	X_1	X_2	X_3	X_2X_3
1	a	1	0	1	0
2	a	1	0	2	0
3	a	1	0	3	0
4	b	1	1	1	1
5	b	1	1	2	2
6	b	1	1	3	3

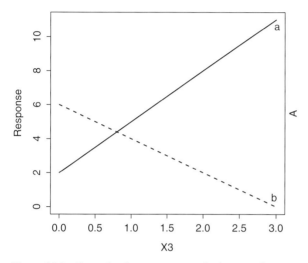

Figure 16.3. *Example of an interaction of a factor and a covariate in an analysis of covariance*

Figure 16.3 depicts a regression line with a positive slope for level *a* of factor *A*, but a negative slope for level *b*. Table 16.5 shows the dummy coding for this dataset, with a column of ones for the intercept, a contrast for level *b* of *A*, the values of the covariate (X_3), which repeat within the levels of *A*, and the multiplicative interaction (X_2X_3). The regression equation for this example is given in (5).

(5) $Y = \beta_0 X_1 + \beta_1 X_2 + \beta_2 X_3 + \beta_3 X_2 X_3 + \epsilon.$

The regression lines in Figure 16.3 are described by the equations $y = 2 + 3x$ for level *a* and $y = 6 - 2x$ for level *b*. The β weights for these data given the dummy coding in Table 16.5 and equation (5) are as follows. Given *a* as reference level, the intercept of the model will be the intercept of the regression line for level *a*, so $\beta_0 = 2$. The intercept for the second regression line is at 6, hence β_1, which quantifies the difference between the two group means when the covariate X_3 is 0 – that is, where the regression lines cross the y-axis – equals 4. The slope of the line for level a is $3 = \beta_2$. Finally, the slope for the regression line for level b is -2, a difference of -5 with the slope for level a. This difference is the contrast for the slopes of the two lines, hence $\beta_4 = -5$. Note that since the product $X_2 X_3$ is zero for factor level a, the coefficient for $X_2 X_3$ serves as a correction (i.e., a contrast) on the slope for the regression line for level a, but, as required, only within level b.

Given a regression equation for a given dataset, a first question that arises is how to estimate the parameters of the model. Fortunately, excellent algorithms are available for doing this, which have been implemented in many software packages. Although the mathematics for simple linear regression and analysis of variance are relatively straightforward, the more sophisticated algorithms underlying mixed-effects regression models and generalized additive models, which will be discussed below, require substantial training in mathematics. Fortunately, these models can be used responsibly without having to know the details of the underlying mathematical theory. In the case of analysis of (co)variance, dummy coding can be either hand-crafted by the analyst, or a specific dummy coding scheme can be specified, with the actual creation of dummy variables being left to the software.

When fitting a regression model to the data, the software will generally return several kinds of information to the user. First, information is provided about the estimated values of the coefficients for the intercept, the slopes, and the factor contrasts. For a given coefficient, a measure is provided about the uncertainty of the estimate in the form of a standard error. The ratio of the estimate and its standard error yields a statistic that follows a t-distribution. If the observed value of the t statistic is far out in one of the tails of the distribution, there is reason for surprise about the magnitude of the estimate, and a p-value based on the t-distribution will allow the researcher to evaluate whether a coefficient is surprisingly different from zero.

By way of example, consider a study of pitch (F0) in English tri-constituent compounds (Koesling et al. 2013). Three predictors are of interest here: *Time*, *Sex* (female versus male), and *Branching*. *Branching* is a factor that distinguishes between four kinds of compound stress patterns on the basis of branching direction (left or right) and location of the stress (first, second, or third noun), as exemplified in Table 16.6.

Table 16.6 *Four kinds of compound stress patterns in English tri-constituent compounds*

Code	Branching direction	Stress pattern	Example
LN1	left	[ŃN]N	[háy fever] treatment
LN2	left	[NŃ]N	[science fiction] book
RN2	right	N[ŃN]	business [crédit card]
RN3	right	N[NŃ]	family [Christmas dínner]

We expect pitch (in semitones) to decline over time. Pitch is also expected to be lower for men than for women. Of main interest is whether there are significant differences in pitch contours for the different types of compounds as distinguished by the factor *Branching*.

Table 16.6 presents the coefficients of a simple main effects model fitted to the data, described using the symbolic description language in (6). In this model formula, the intercept and the error term are not mentioned explicitly. Nevertheless, any software package will provide the analyst with estimates of both. In Table 16.6, the intercept (93.1331) represents the pitch predicted at word onset for female speakers for branching condition LN1. The negative slope for *Time* (−0.0327) indicates that pitch decreases over time, as expected. For male speakers, the intercept has to be lowered by 9.9297, again as expected. The three contrasts in the last part of Table 16.7 specify the difference in pitch between LN2 and LN1, between RN2 and LN1, and between RN3 and LN1. The small standard errors, the large *t*-values, and the small *p*-values suggest that all coefficients are significant.

(6)   Pitch ~ Time + Sex + Branching

Table 16.7 does not list all possible contrasts between the four branching conditions. Of the $\binom{4}{2} = 6$ possible contrasts, only three are listed. For instance, no information is provided as to whether there is a real difference between the RN2 and RN3 conditions. In addition, it would be useful to know which contrasts remain significant after being corrected for multiple comparisons. Figure 16.4 presents each of the six contrasts together with its 95 percent confidence interval, using Tukey's all-pairs comparison method (Hothorn, Bretz, and Westfall 2008). Of the four contrasts, only those between RN3 and LN2, and RN3 and RN2 do not reach significance, as their confidence intervals straddle zero.

The model considered thus far assumes that the slope of the effect is the same across all branching conditions, and the same across female and male speakers. This is a simplifying assumption, and we need to check whether it is justified by allowing interactions of *Time* by *Branching* and *Time* by *Sex* into the model. It turns out that both interactions improve the fit of the model to the data. In order to

Table 16.7 *Coefficients of an analysis of covariance model fitted to the pitch of English tri-constituent compounds*

	Estimate	Std error	*t* value	*p* value
Intercept	93.1331	0.0437	2,131.1298	0.0000
Time	−0.0327	0.0005	−59.6105	0.0000
Sex=male	−9.9297	0.0321	−309.4371	0.0000
Branching=LN2	0.3244	0.0447	7.2507	0.0000
Branching=RN2	0.4603	0.0447	10.3051	0.0000
Branching=RN3	0.4279	0.0447	9.5816	0.0000

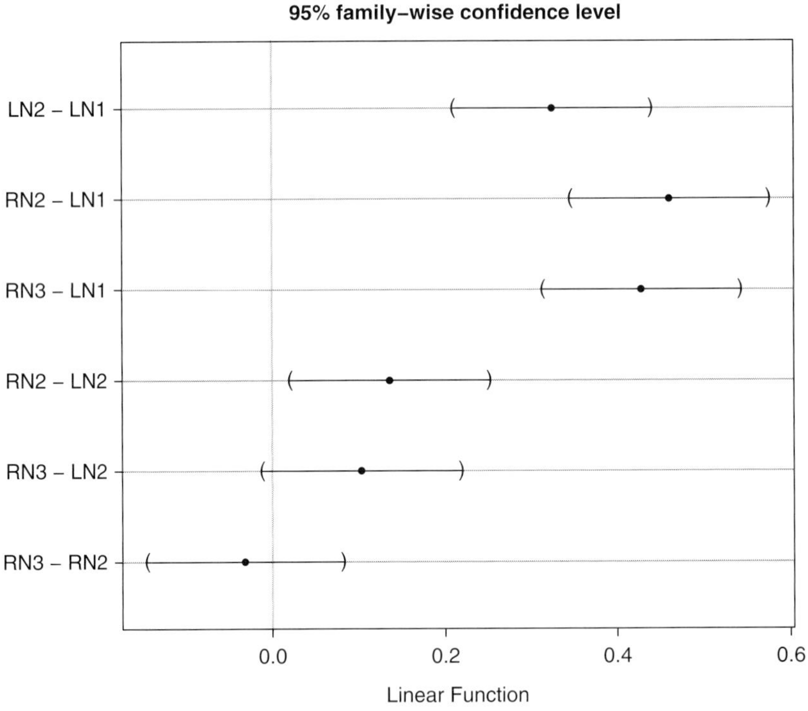

95% family–wise confidence level

Figure 16.4. *Tukey all-pairs confidence intervals for contrasts between mean pitch for different branching conditions across English tri-constituent compounds*

assess the importance of the various terms in the model, we compare a sequence of nested models, step by step increasing in complexity, as listed in (7). For the present data, the sequence of models (where we make explicit the presence of an intercept term by adding 1 to the model formula) is evaluated statistically by the sequential F-tests listed in Table 16.8, to which the reduction in AIC has been added as a measure of variable importance.

(7)   Pitch ~ 1
       Pitch ~ 1 + Time
       Pitch ~ 1 + Time + Sex
       Pitch ~ 1 + Time + Sex + Branching
       Pitch ~ 1 + Time + Sex + Branching + Time : Branching
       Pitch ~ 1 + Time + Sex + Branching + Time : Branching + Time : Sex

The column labeled "Res. Df" lists the residual degrees of freedom, which is equal to the number of observations in the data minus the number of parameters. The first model, which has an intercept only (which in this case represents the grand average) has only one parameter (the intercept), and hence 47,574−1=47,573 residual degrees of freedom. The second column, Df, lists the number of parameters required when adding one or more predictors. For *Time*, which requires a slope coefficient, one additional parameter is required. For *Branching*, which has four levels, three contrast coefficients are required when it is added in as a simple

Table 16.8 *Sequential model comparison for Pitch in English tri-constituent compounds (number of observations: 47,574)*

	Res. Df	Df	*F* value	*p* value	Reduction in AIC
intercept	47,573				
+time	47,572	1	3,549.746	0.000	1,159.878
+sex	47,571	1	95,840.330	0.000	52,383.491
+branching	47,568	3	44.433	0.000	127.023
+time*branching	47,565	3	11.822	0.000	29.456
+sex*branching	47,562	3	2.794	0.039	2.383

main effect. The column with *p*-values is obtained from the *F* statistics given "Df" and "Res. Df." The final column lists the change in AIC, Akaike's information criterion, which is defined in (8).

$$(8) \qquad AIC = 2k - 2 \ln(L)$$

L denotes the likelihood of the model, and *k* denotes the number of parameters. The AIC measure describes the tradeoff between a model's accuracy and its complexity. On the one hand, a model should be as accurate as possible. At the same time, the model should be as simple as possible. Simpler models have lower *k*, more accurate models have higher *L*. In other words, the AIC measure penalizes models for their complexity. Lower values of AIC indicate a better fit of the model. The greater the reduction in AIC obtained by adding a term to the model equation, the better the relative goodness of fit of the model. Furthermore, the greater the reduction in AIC is, the more important a term is.

For a set of *n* models with AIC values AIC_1, AIC_2, ..., AIC_n, we can select the model with the smallest AIC (model AIC_{min}), and calculate *evidence ratios* (ER), as defined in (9), that express the relative probability that the model with the minimum AIC is more likely to provide a more precise model of the data.

$$(9) \qquad ER = \exp\left(\frac{AIC_i - AIC_{min}}{2}\right)$$

From Table 16.8 it is therefore immediately clear that *Sex* is the most important predictor, followed by *Time* and, at a distance, by *Branching*. The interaction of *Sex* by *Branching* adds only a small improvement to the model's goodness of fit. Its evidence ratio, exp(2.383/2) = 3.32 nevertheless indicates that this model is approximately three times as likely to provide a description of the data that loses less information about the data than the model without the interaction.

A question with no definite answer is how to find the model that best describes the data. There are automatized search procedures that start with the simplest possible model and keep adding main effects and interactions until there is no significant improvement in goodness of fit. Instead of forward stepwise model selection, one can start with the most complex model and remove superfluous predictors until the simplest yet adequate model is obtained. Backward and forward selection heuristics can be combined. Some researchers prefer to use code that works through all possible models and then select the model with the best fit (e.g., Lumley and Miller 2009; Kuperman and Van Dyke 2011). Other researchers, such as Harrell (2001), argue that only one model should be fit to the data, as *p*-values become meaningless when large numbers of models are fitted and compared. The present author favors hypothesis-driven exploration of the data, with theoretically potentially relevant predictors being added successively to the model specification. Further motivation of this research strategy is deferred until after discussion of generalized additive mixed modeling. However, irrespective of how a final model for the data is obtained, replication studies will be crucial for consolidating the validity of the conclusions reached.

In the absence of new data, bootstrap validation is one way in which the stability of the model parameters can be evaluated. Bootstrap validation fits a given model to a large number of bootstrap samples. Each bootstrap sample is a sample with replacement from the original data points. Some observations will appear more than once in a given bootstrap sample, and other observations will not appear at all. These observations constitute unseen, new data points. The accuracy of the model fitted to the bootstrap sample can be gauged by comparing its predictions with the actual values of the response for the unseen data points. Averaging across all bootstrap samples yields information about the extent to which the model overfits the data, as well as about which predictors are significant across the bootstrap runs (e.g., Harrell 2001 for detailed examples of bootstrap validation).

Data points that are located outside the cloud of data points have the potential of seriously distorting a regression model. There are several measures that help protect against overly influential outliers. First, if a predictor has a highly skewed distribution, a square root transformation or a log transformation may result in a more symmetrical distribution (see Chapters 14 and 15). For instance, word frequency distributions have a long right tail, and without a logarithmic transform, a small minority of very high frequency words will adversely dominate the regression model. Second, if the distribution of the response is highly skewed, a transformation rendering it more normal may be necessary (Box and Cox 1964; Venables and Ripley 2002). Without an appropriate transformation of the response, the distribution of the residuals will be non-normal, violating the fundamental assumption of multiple regression that the errors should be identically distributed. Third, one can inspect the *leverage* of the data points to identify potentially harmful outliers. The leverage of a data point quantifies how much the parameters of the model would change if the data point were not included when fitting the model. The greater this change, the more likely the data point is an outlier (see Chatterjee, Hadi, and Price 2000 for a detailed discussion).

Finally, it is worth noting that regression modeling cannot tease apart the effect of predictors that are very strongly correlated (see discussion of Association in Chapter 14). Datasets with highly correlated predictors are described as *collinear*.

By way of example, a dataset with four frequency measures taken from different corpora of contemporary written English would be highly collinear. A consequence of collinearity is that the coefficients for collinear predictors may be significant, but with counterintuitive signs. For instance, frequency as a predictor for response latencies in various psycholinguistic tasks usually has a negative coefficient, indicating that as frequency increases, processing speed decreases. When two highly correlated frequency measures are entered into the regression equation, one will have the expected negative coefficient, but the other may have a significant positive coefficient. Jointly, the two highly correlated predictors provide a better fit, but from a cognitive perspective, the coefficients are no longer interpretable. The phenomena of *suppression* and *enhancement* in regression are well described in Friedman and Wall (2005). When the goal of modeling is to obtain accurate predictions, the adverse consequences of enhancement and suppression are not a concern. However, for the model coefficients to remain interpretable, the analyst has several choices. Centering and scaling (subtracting the mean, and dividing by the standard deviation) does not solve the problem, but only masks it (Belsley 1984; Dalal and Zickar 2012). The simplest option is to consider only one of a set of highly collinear predictors (e.g., select only one of the four frequency measures for inclusion in the model specification). Alternatively, a dimension reduction technique such as principal components analysis can be used to obtain a new frequency measure that combines the strengths of the four separate frequency variables.

2.2   Mixed-effects modeling

Datasets from experiments often have a repetitive structure that requires special attention. Consider an experiment in which twenty different speakers read aloud fifteen different words. Such a dataset will have the structure shown in Table 16.9, where for each Subject (speaker) there are n = 15 cases, one for each Item (word), and where for each Item (word) there are g = 20 cases, one for each Subject. Experimental designs with this kind of repetitive structure are known as *repeated measures* designs.

Factors such as Subject and Item typically have many levels, which distinguishes them from factors such as Word Category (noun, verb, adjective, adverb) or the speaker's sex (female, male). Furthermore, subjects and items are – ideally – sampled randomly from populations that have many more members than the subjects and items that happen to have been used in the experiment. By contrast, the levels "female" and "male" exhaust the levels of the speaker's sex, as there are no other levels in the population. Factors such as Subject and Item are referred to as *random effect factors*, and factors such as Sex as *fixed-effect factors*. In datasets with subjects and items, the other predictors can quantify properties of the subjects (e.g., age in years, sex, native speaker of English), properties of the items (e.g., a word's frequency, its word class, whether it is morphologically complex), or properties of the experiment (e.g., the number of trials a subject has progressed in the experiment

Table 16.9. *A repeated measures dataset with* gn *cases with observations on* k *variables collected for* n *items and* g *subjects*

Cases	Response			Predictors			
	Y	X_1	X_2	...	X_k	Subject	Item
1	Y_1	x_{111}	x_{121}	...	x_{1k1}	1	1
2	Y_2	x_{211}	x_{221}	...	x_{2k1}	1	2
3	Y_3	x_{311}	x_{321}	...	x_{3k1}	1	3
⋮	⋮	⋮	⋮	⋮	⋮	1	⋮
n	Y_n	x_{n11}	x_{n21}	...	x_{nk1}	1	n
n+1	Y_{n+1}	x_{112}	x_{122}	...	x_{1k2}	2	1
n+2	Y_{n+2}	x_{212}	x_{222}	...	x_{2k2}	2	2
n+3	Y_{n+3}	x_{312}	x_{322}	...	x_{3k2}	2	3
⋮	⋮	⋮	⋮	⋮	⋮	2	⋮
2n	Y_{2n}	x_{n12}	x_{n22}	...	x_{nk2}	2	n
⋮	⋮	⋮	⋮	⋮	⋮	⋮	⋮
(g−1)n+1	$Y_{(g-1)n+1}$	x_{11g}	x_{12g}	...	x_{1kg}	g	1
(g−1)n+2	$Y_{(g-1)n+2}$	x_{21g}	x_{22g}	...	x_{2kg}	g	2
(g−1)n+2	$Y_{(g-1)n+3}$	x_{31g}	x_{32g}	...	x_{3kg}	g	3
gn	Y_{gn}	x_{n1g}	x_{n2g}	...	x_{nkg}	g	n

when a given sentence is presented). For the example presented in Table 16.9, all the predictors X_i are bound to the items and represent properties of these items, as indicated by the indexation of the first subscript of the predictor values $x_{\ldots}$.

For repeated measures designs, the standard linear model is inappropriate. Although one could use dummy coding for subjects or items, this comes with several important disadvantages. First, the dummy coding will tune the model to the subjects and items in the experiment, but it will not allow inferences beyond exactly these subjects and items. The model does not generate predictions about unseen subjects and unseen items. Second, the standard linear model does not allow the user to gain insight into the correlational structure in the data with respect to subjects and items.

Mixed-effects models (Pinheiro and Bates 2000; West, Welch, and Galecki 2007) – that is, regression models that combine fixed-effect factors with random-effect factors such as subjects and items – treat random-effect factors as sources of random variation in the data. This random variation can manifest itself at various "sites" in a regression model. First, it can be tied to the intercept, in which case the intercept has to be adjusted upward or downward depending on which unit (level of a random-effect factor) was sampled for the experiment. For instance, if the response is the duration in ms of the vowel in a speech corpus, it is important to bring the speaker into the model as a random-effect factor, as speakers have different speech rates. Given an estimate of the average speech rate in the population, represented by the intercept (β_0) in the regression equation, the speech rate of a specific individual speaker can be obtained by taking the average speech rate β_0 and adjusting it upward (for slow speakers) or downward (for fast speakers) by an amount b_{0i} for speaker i. The mixed-effects regression model assumes that the b_{0i} adjustments follow a normal distribution with mean zero and unknown standard deviation that will be estimated from the data. In other words, the variation in speech rates is modeled as Gaussian noise around the population speech rate.

Such Gaussian noise need not be restricted to the intercept, it can extend to slopes and contrasts. For instance, the effect of frequency of occurrence can be stronger for some subjects, and weaker for others. This subject variation can be represented as Gaussian noise around the population slope for frequency. These considerations lead to the general mixed-effects regression equation in (10).

$$(10) \qquad Y = (\beta_0 + b_0) + (\beta_1 + b_1)X_1 + \ldots + (\beta_k + b_k)X_k + \epsilon,$$

$E, b_0, b_1, \ldots, b_k$ all are normally distributed with mean zero and unknown (and generally different) standard deviations. Table 16.10 charts the individual adjustments b_{ij} for coefficients $j = 0, 1, \ldots, k$ (columns) and subjects $i = 1, 2, \ldots, s$ (rows). Because the adjustments $b_{i.}$ are estimated for the same subject i, it is possible that any pair of (column) vectors of adjustments $\{b_{.n}, b_{.m}\}$ are correlated. As a consequence, the specification of a mixed-effects model is complete only with the matrix of pairwise correlations of the b (column) vectors. Which standard deviation and correlation parameters are actually required for a given dataset is an empirical issue. Generally, adjustments to the intercept (*random intercepts*) for subjects and items lead to substantially better models; less often, but regularly, adjustments to slopes (*random slopes*) are also well supported. In the literature, the adjustments are referred to as best linear unbiased predictors (BLUPS) or as posterior modes.

To illustrate mixed-effects modeling, consider again the study on pitch on English tri-constituent compounds. The AIC for the best model obtained above is 252,840.7. When we add random intercepts for *Subject* and for *Item*, the AIC of the model is 202,574, a decrease of no less than 50,266.7. A further improvement of the model is obtained by adding random slopes (contrasts) for *Sex*, which

Table 16.10 *Notation for adjustments to intercept and predictors*

Level number	Random intercepts	Random slopes			
	b_0	b_1	b_2	$\ldots$	b_k
1	b_{01}	b_{11}	b_{21}	$\ldots$	b_{k1}
2	b_{02}	b_{12}	b_{22}	$\ldots$	b_{k2}
$\vdots$	$\vdots$	$\vdots$	$\vdots$	$\vdots$	$\vdots$
S	b_{0s}	b_{1s}	b_{2s}	$\ldots$	b_{ks}

reduces the AIC by 539. The significance of the additional random effects structure (here, a standard deviation for the by-word adjustments for *Sex* and a correlation parameter for the by-word adjustments to the intercept and *Sex*) is assessed with a likelihood ratio test. The likelihood ratio statistic, defined as twice the difference of the log likelihoods of the more complex model (model 2) and the simpler model (model 1), as summarized in (11), follows a chi-squared distribution with, as degrees of freedom, the difference in the number of parameters. For the present data, the LRT statistic is 542.69, the number of additional parameters is 2, and the corresponding extremely small *p*-value indicates that the second model improves significantly on the goodness of fit.

(11) $2\ln(L2/L1) = 2[\log(L2) - \log(L1)]$

One consequence of including random intercepts and slopes is that the interaction of *Branching* by *Sex*, which was the weakest predictor (see Table 16.9), is no longer significant. With the individual speakers in the model, the factor *Sex*, which groups speakers into females and males, becomes less important. An important general methodological issue that is illustrated by this example is that analyses that fail to bring subject and item random intercepts and slopes into the model may be anti-conservative (i.e., they may produce *p*-values that are smaller than they should be), and therefore may mislead the analyst into believing that a non-significant effect is significant.

The estimates of the standard deviations and the correlation parameter are listed in Table 16.11. When reporting a mixed-effects model, it is essential to report these parameters, as they are an intrinsic part of the model and provide the reader with insight into the magnitude of the different sources of random variation in the data and their interrelations.

The large negative correlation for the by-word random intercepts and random contrasts for *Sex* invites further interpretation. Figure 16.5 presents a scatterplot of the words in the plane spanned by the two dimensions of word-related variability in pitch. The horizontal axis represents the by-word random intercepts, which are calibrated for the reference level of *Sex: female*. The vertical axis represents the additional by-word adjustment required for the male speakers. Recall that male

Table 16.11 *Standard deviations and correlation parameter for the random-effects structure of the mixed-effects model fitted to the pitch of English tri-constituent compounds*

Groups	Name	Std dev.	Correlation
Word	Intercept	0.58029	
	Sex=male	0.50815	−0.703
Speaker	Intercept	3.01529	
Residual		2.01422	

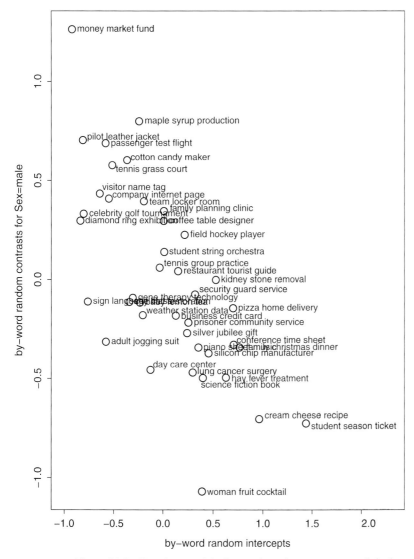

Figure 16.5. *Correlation of the by-word random intercepts and the by-word random slopes for Sex=male in the linear mixed-effects model fitted to the pitch of English tri-constituent compounds*

speakers have lower pitch, represented in the model by a downward shift of the population intercept for males. For some words, the shift for males is not down far enough; for others, it is too far down. The by-word random contrasts on the vertical axis show, for each word, how the intercept for the males has to be fine-tuned. In the lower right of the scatterplot, we find words such as *cream cheese recipe* and *student season ticket* for which females have a higher than average intercept (a large value on the horizontal axis), whereas in the upper left, one finds compounds such as *money market fund* and *pilot leather jacket* for which females have a lower than average intercept. Conversely, compared to the female baseline, the males have a higher than average pitch for the latter words, and a lower than average pitch for the former. What seems to be going on here is that pitch rises for words that speakers find more exciting and interesting. However, what is exciting and interesting differs between the sexes. Males show a clear disinterest in *woman fruit cocktail*, while the female disinterest in *money market fund* is absent for the males.

An example of more complex by-subject random-effects structure can be found in a large-scale self-paced reading study reported in Baayen and Milin (2010). Of interest here are two numerical predictors for the self-paced reading latencies: a word's frequency and its number of morphemes. The (log-transformed) frequency measure represents how practiced a word is, while the morpheme count is a measure of its morphological complexity. By-subject variation with respect to these predictors indicates that the experiment is picking up on by-subject varia-bility in using (remembering) the words, as well as by-subject variation in the ability to deal with morphological complexity.

Figure 16.6 presents the by-subject random effects structure characterizing this dataset. The top panels show the BLUPs, the bottom panels the subject-specific coefficients (the BLUPs incremented with the corresponding population mean

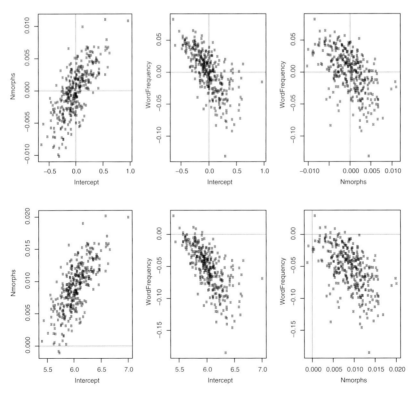

Figure 16.6. *Random effects structure for subject. Correlations of the BLUPs (upper panels); correlations of the by-subject coefficients (lower panels)*

values for the intercepts and slopes). In these scatterplots, dots represent subjects. All that changes between the upper and lower panels is position with respect to the vertical axis. The left panels indicate that fast responders (with a small BLUP, i.e., a small coefficient for the intercept) are least delayed by the number of morphemes in a word. Conversely, the slow responders are the ones who are delayed most by morphological complexity. The center panels show that fast responders (low values for the intercept) have little or no facilitation from word frequency. Slow responders, on the other hand, show healthy facilitation from word frequency. The right panels point to a trade-off between word frequency and morphological complexity, such that subjects who are least affected by morphological complexity are also the subjects with the weakest, if any, facilitation from word frequency. The importance of mixed-effects models for language studies is that they clarify not only the main trends in the population, but also the correlational structure tied to subjects and items. For the present example, the trade-off between storage and computation across the subject population is one of the most interesting findings of the study.

2.3   Generalized additive models

The preceding analyses assumed that the effects of predictors are linear, and can be described mathematically as straight lines, flat planes, or flat hyperplanes. For numeric predictors, the multiplicative interaction defines a curved surface, but when one predictor is held constant, the effect of the other predictor is still linear (see Figure 16.2). The linearity assumption may be plausible for some data, but it can be very implausible for other datasets. The pitch data discussed in the preceding sections are a case for which the linearity assumption does not make sense at all. Anyone who has ever inspected a pitch contour for English knows that pitch does not decrease linearly with time.

In order to model the functional dependency of pitch on time correctly, a flexible toolkit is required that allows the analyst to consider nonlinear functional relations in two dimensions (wiggly lines) or more than two dimensions (wiggly surfaces and hypersurfaces). Generalized additive models (GAMs; Hastie and Tibshirani 1990; Wood 2006) provide the user with exactly such a toolkit.

A GAM combines a standard linear model with regression coefficients β_0, $\beta_1, \ldots, \beta_k$

with smooth functions s() in one or more predictors.

$$(12)\qquad Y = \beta_0 + \beta_1 X_1 + \ldots + \beta_k X_k + s(X_i) + s(X_j, X_k) + \ldots + \epsilon, \quad \epsilon \sim \mathcal{N}(0, \sigma^2)$$

For smooths in one predictor, a good choice is using cubic regression splines. Cubic splines fit piecewise cubic polynomials (functions of the form $y = a + bx + cx2 + dx3$) to non-overlapping intervals of the predictor values, such that at the points where intervals meet, the so-called knots, the transitions are smooth (by forcing the first and second derivatives to be identical). The number of knots determines the smoothness of the curve. When too many knots are used, a curve is undersmoothed, when too few knots are postulated, the curve is oversmoothed. Recent advances in the mathematics of GAM modeling (see Wood 2006, 2011) have resulted in a range of algorithms (e.g., generalized cross-validation and relativized maximum likelihood estimation) that make the estimation of the proper number of knots part of the general parameter estimation process.

For smooths in higher dimensions with isotropic predictors (i.e., predictors expressed on the same scale, such as longitude and latitude in dialectometry), thin plate regression splines are available, which fit a wiggly regression surface as a weighted sum of geometrically regular surfaces. For both isotropic predictors and predictors that are measured on different scales, tensor products provide a flexible and generally faster alternative. Tensor products define wiggly surfaces given marginal basis functions, one for each dimension of the smooth. Typically, these basis functions are themselves cubic splines, and the greater the number of knots for the different basis functions, the more wiggly the fitted regression surface will be. Recently, it has become possible to combine splines and tensor products with random-effect factors, resulting in generalized additive mixed models (GAMMs).

Returning for a final time to the pitch data, the following sequence of models relax, step by step, the linearity assumptions with which we have worked thus far. Following the notational conventions of Wood (2006), with s() representing a cubic regression spline (when the basis function bs is set to cr) or a random effect (when the basis is set to re), we have the models in (13).

(13)   Pitch ~ 1 + Time + Sex + Branching + Time : Branching +
            s(Speaker, bs="re") + s(Word, bs="re") + s(Word, Sex, bs="re")
        Pitch ~ 1 + Time + Sex + Branching + Time : Branching +
            s(Speaker, bs="re") + s(Word, bs="re") + s(Word, Sex, bs="re") +
            s(Time, bs="cr")
        Pitch ~ 1 + Sex + Branching +
            s(Speaker, bs="re") + s(Word, bs="re") + s(Word, Sex, bs="re") +
            s(Time, bs="cr", by=Branching)
        Pitch ~ 1 + Sex + Branching +
            s(Speaker, bs="re") + s(Word, bs="re") + s(Word, Sex, bs="re") +
            s(Time, bs="cr", by=Branching) + s(Time, bs="cr", by=Sex)

The second model allows the pitch contour to be a nonlinear function of Time. The third model allows this nonlinear function to differ for the four *Branching* conditions. In other words, this model specification tests for an interaction of a smooth in *Time* by *Branching* condition. Separate linear terms for *Time* and its interaction

Table 16.12 *Model comparison for a series of models with increasing nonlinear structure fitted to the pitch dataset*

	Res. Df	Df	Deviance	F	*p* value	change AIC
linear	192,647					
+s(Time)	190,218	7.64	2,428.5	80.5	0.0000	588.2
+s(Time, by=Branching)	187,949	22.22	2,269.4	25.9	0.0000	526.6
+s(Time, by=Sex)	187,308	4.79	641.1	33.9	0.0000	153.0

with *Branching* are no longer necessary. The final model adds a further smooth to relax the assumption that the smooth in *Time* is the same for the two sexes. Table 16.12 indicates that these models provide increasingly good fits to the data.

Knowing that adding a smooth results in a significantly better fit does not inform us about the shape of the nonlinearity. As cubic splines and tensor products are black boxes to the end user, there are no parameters that might inform about the functional shape of the nonlinear prediction curves or surfaces. The only way to gain insight into these shapes is through visualization. The fitted smooths for *Pitch* as a function of *Time*, for each of the four branching conditions, is shown in Figure 16.7. For a discussion of the interpretation of these smooths, the reader is referred to Koesling et al. (2013).

The use of GAMs for modeling wiggly surfaces is illustrated for two datasets, one addressing auditory comprehension with EEG, the other addressing lexical diffusion in the dialectometry of Dutch.

Kryuchkova et al. (2012) studied the comprehension of isolated words, presented over headphones, using evoked response potentials measured at the scalp. They were specifically interested in the electrophysiological response to the danger of the words' referents, as gauged by independently collected danger ratings on a nine-point Likert scale. Here, we consider a generalized additive model, summarized in (14), fitted to the microvoltages elicited at channel FC2 with a spline in *Time* for the interval [100, 400] ms post-stimulus onset. See Chapter 8 for further details about this psycholinguistic methodology.

(14)   MicroVoltage ~ s(Time) + te(Time, Danger)

In this model equation, te denotes a tensor product. Figure 16.8 shows how the electrophysiological response of the brain varies with time as a function of a word's danger rating score. Darker shades of grey indicate lower (negative) voltages, whereas lighter shades of grey indicate higher (positive) voltages. Focusing on the 150–350 ms time window, the graph shows a negative inflection around 150–200 ms post-stimulus onset across all danger scores, followed by a positive inflection. For words with higher danger ratings, this positive inflection has a reduced amplitude. This reduced positivity in the 250–300 ms time interval fits well with research on emotion processing in other modalities (see Kryuchkova et al. 2012 for further details).

It is worth noting that although one could dichotomize Danger into a factor with levels "low" and "high," followed by an inspection of the time intervals at which the curves for the low and high conditions diverge, the result would be a model with an inferior goodness of fit, in line with the literature on the detrimental costs of dichotomization of numerical predictors (Cohen 1983; MacCallum et al. 2002; Baayen 2010). The beauty of GAMs is that they make it possible to let the data speak for themselves without having to impose prior – often arbitrary – categorizations.

A final example of modeling nonlinear regression surfaces is based on the study of Wieling, Nerbonne, and Baayen (2011), who investigated word pronunciation

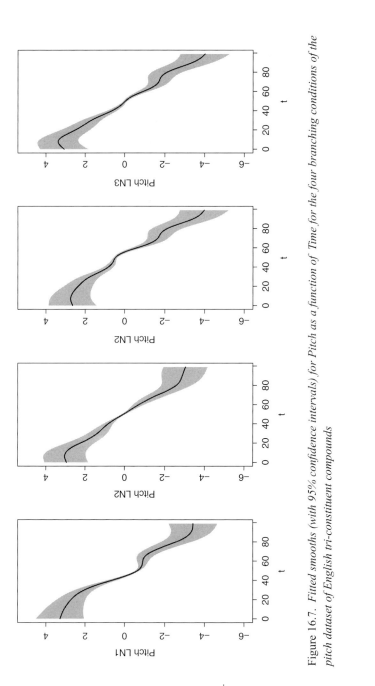

Figure 16.7. *Fitted smooths (with 95% confidence intervals) for Pitch as a function of Time for the four branching conditions of the pitch dataset of English tri-constituent compounds*

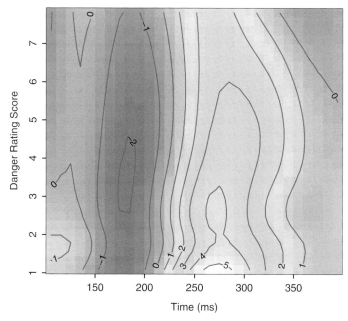

Figure 16.8. *Tensor product for the interaction of Time by Danger Rating Score at channel FC2*

distances from standard Dutch for 424 locations in the Netherlands. We focus here on an interaction of longitude, latitude, and word frequency, but note that other predictors representing socioeconomic variables related to the informants can be included as well, allowing the analyst to integrate sociolinguistics with dialectometry. The model equation, in (15), invokes a three-dimensional tensor that defines a complex hypersurface. This hypersurface can be represented graphically by means of a sequence of dialect maps for different frequencies, as shown in Figure 16.9 for four typical quantile frequencies.

(15)   DialectDistance ~ te(Longitude, Latitude, Frequency)

The contour plots in this figure present, from left to right, the dialect distance maps for word frequency at the 0.05, 0.33, 0.66, and 0.95 quantiles. The graphs indicate that dialect leveling, which has progressed furthest for the lower frequency words, is highly regionally cohesive. Figure 16.9 fits well with Wang's (1969) lexical diffusion model. The greater the geographical distance from the heartland of the Dutch standard (central west), and the greater a word's frequency, the less the standard language has penetrated a speaker's lexicon.

Generalized additive models offer the analyst a very powerful tool for understanding the structure of datasets in the language sciences. In the author's experience, models including nonlinear curves and surfaces often improve substantially over traditional models with linear effects and/or multiplicative interactions. Often, multiplicative interactions fail to detect the true but far more complex structure of

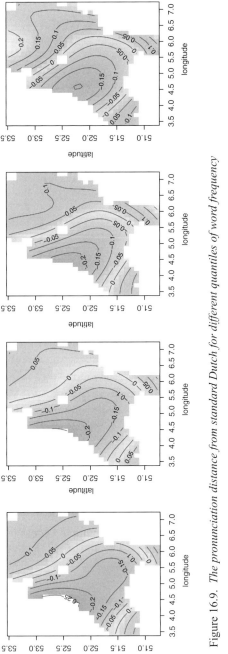

Figure 16.9. *The pronunciation distance from standard Dutch for different quantiles of word frequency*

the data. The results obtained with GAMs can be embarrassingly rich, in the sense that the results are far more complex than expected given current models. GAMs will often challenge the state of the art of current theories, and the author's intuition is that they may force the field to move more in the direction of dynamic systems approaches to language.

Model selection also becomes a more challenging process in the case of generalized additive modeling. Whereas for simple factorial designs it is still feasible to inspect the AIC for all possible models, this is no longer possible for GAMs. There are too many dimensions to explore, with too many options with respect to how many parameters should be invested in nonlinearities. Here, the only way to proceed is by hypothesis-driven model exploration. The three-way tensor for the Dutch dialects, for instance, was hypothesized on the basis of the theory of lexical diffusion. Higher-order inter-actions in theoretical hyperspace might be present (e.g., tensor products involving seven or eight predictors), but without theoretical insights to guide the analyst, the results, even if significant, would remain uninterpretable and hence not particularly helpful for the advancement of knowledge.

3   Classification

Thus far, we have considered numeric response variables. Response variables, however, can describe different classes of outcomes: alternative con-structions, alternative affixation patterns, correct versus incorrect responses, whether an informant is a dialect speaker, near-synonyms, and so on. For datasets with such response variables, the analyst may want to ascertain whether these classes are predictable from, and hence supported by, the other variables describ-ing the properties of the individual data points. As there are many different classification techniques available, only a small subset is reviewed here.

3.1   Logistic regression

For binary response variables – that is, variables that assume one of two values (success versus failures, correct versus incorrect responses, construction A versus construction B, and so on) – an extension of the multiple regression approach known as logistic regression is often a good choice (see, e.g., Jaeger 2008).

Binary response variables have the property that the variance depends on the mean. This property is easy to understand intuitively: when a success has a theoretical probability around 0.5, there will be enormous variability in the responses actually observed. But when the probability of a success is close to 0 or close to 1, the system will look like it is deterministic with only a little bit of leakage.

The property that the variance depends on the mean violates the fundamental assumption of the Gaussian framework of standard regression modeling, namely, that the errors are independent and identically distributed and follow a normal distribution. The solution offered by *logistic models* is to recast the dependent variable (that a novice to the field would want to cast as a proportion) in the form of a *logit*, the logarithm of the odds ratio, as summarized in (16).

(16)
$$\text{logit}(Y) = \log\left(\tfrac{\text{successes}}{\text{failures}}\right)$$
$$= \log\left(\tfrac{p}{1-p}\right),$$

In (16), *P* is the probability of success. This logit is modeled as a function of the other predictors, as in (17).

(17) $\text{logit}(Y) = \beta_0 + \beta_1 X_1 + \beta_2 X_2 + \ldots$

Now the whole machinery of multiple regression, including mixed-effects models and generalized additive modeling, is available to the analyst. Unlike for Gaussian models, however, there is no parameter for the error term, and errors (the difference between a predicted probability and the observed discrete outcome) are now referred to as deviances. Crucially, with logistic regression, it is the *probability* of a given class that is modeled.

Within linguistics, logistic models were pioneered by linguistics under the name of variable rule analysis, as discussed in Tagliamonte and Baayen (2012) and references cited there (see also Chapter 20). As a working example, their dataset on *was/were* variation is touched upon here.

The York data were collected to study the conditions under which *was* occurs in the spontaneous speech of inhabitants of York (UK) where the standard norm requires *were*, as in *There was still quite strong winds in these parts*. The response variable is *Form*, with levels *were* and *was*. Predictors are *Adjacency* (is the verb adjacent to its referent, with levels *adjacent* and *non-adjacent*), the informant's *Age*, and *Polarity* (*affirmative* versus *negative*).

(18)   `log(was/were) ~ Adjacency + Age*Polarity + s(Informant, bs="re")`

The logistic mixed-effects covariance model in (18) is visualized in Figure 16.10. (In the symbolic formula of the S language, Age*Polarity specifies main effects for *Age* and *Polarity* as well as an interaction between these two predictors.) Figure 16.10 indicates that the probability of *was* is somewhat greater under non-adjacency. As indicated by the right panel, there is a substantial effect of *Age* in interaction with *Polarity*. In negative sentences, the younger informants almost categorically prefer *was*, whereas the older informants prefer *were*. This effect is more muted in affirmative sentences. On the proportions scale, used in Figure 16.10, the effect of *Age* is nonlinear. This nonlinearity is due to the nonlinear nature of the transformation from logits to proportions. On the logit scale, the effect of *Age* is actually modeled (in this example) as linear.

Further examples of logistic modeling can be found in Bresnan et al. (2007), Jaeger (2010), and Baayen et al. (in press). The latter two papers discuss more complex logistic regression models. Janda, Nesset, and Baayen (2010) discuss in

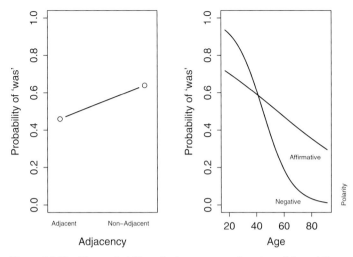

Figure 16.10. *The probability of using* was *as a function of Age, Adjacency and Polarity*

detail the consequences of treatment dummy coding for the correlational random-effects structure for logistic regression models.

3.2   Polytomous regression

Polytomous regression is a modeling option for datasets for which the response variable is discrete and has more than two levels. There are several strategies available for this kind of data. One option is to fit a series of binary logistic models contrasting one level with all the other levels, the *one versus rest* heuristic (Arppe 2008, 2012). (For including a random-effect factor as predictor, see Faraway 2006 and Arppe 2012.) Multinomial models (Venables and Ripley 2002; Højsgaard, Edwards, and Lauritzen 2012) estimate the effects for all response classes simultaneously. In practice, the one-versus-rest heuristic yields results that are very similar to those of more complex methods, whereas the results tend to be more transparently interpretable. Table 16.13 presents a summary of the coefficients (on the logit scale) for four Finnish near-synonyms for 'think,' predicted from properties of the Agent and properties of the Patient. For completeness, we note that Arppe (2008) considers many more predictors for this lexical choice. Given the present limited set of predictors, Table 16.13 indicates that for patients expressing an activity, *ajatella* is dispreferred (as indicated by a negative log odds) whereas *harkita* is strongly preferred (positive log odds).

3.3   Random forests

Regression models lose precision when, as is often the case for language data, the observations are distributed very unequally across the different

Table 16.13 *Log odds for four Finnish near-synonyms meaning 'think' (brackets mark non-significance)*

	ajatella	harkita	miettia	pohtia
Intercept	0.76	−2.7	−2	−1.9
Agent=Group	−1.4	(0.38)	(−0.33)	0.83
Agent=Individual	(−0.066)	(−0.13)	0.69	−0.59
Patient=Abstraction	−1.6	(0.28)	0.58	1.6
Patient=Activity	−2.1	2.4	(−0.12)	0.89
Patient=Communication	−2.5	1.1	1.3	1.2
Patient=DirectQuote	−4.6	(−15)	0.8	2.9
Patient=etta.CLAUSE	0.72	−1.1	−0.61	(−0.41)
Patient=IndirectQuestion	−3	(−0.029)	1.7	1.5
Patient=IndividualGroup	0.72	(0.076)	−0.75	(−0.99)
Patient=Infinitive	1.7	(0.21)	(−15)	(−1.4)
Patient=Participle	1.5	(0.13)	(−15)	(−0.92)

predictor values. Regression models may also work less well when the data are characterized by complex interactions. In the case of the York data, for instance, there are very few instances of negative adjacent sentences, and half of the informants show no variability at all in their use of *was* versus *were*. Such very unequal and complex data may challenge the regression modeling framework.

For this kind of data, but also for datasets with relatively few observations and a great many predictors, conditional inference trees and random forests (Breiman 2001; Strobl et al. 2008; Strobl, Malley, and Tutz 2009), building on earlier work on classification and regression trees (Breiman et al. 1984), are an excellent choice.

Conditional inference trees estimate a regression relationship by means of binary recursive partitioning. The ctree algorithm begins with testing the global null hypothesis of independence between any of the predictors and the response variable. The algorithm terminates if this hypothesis cannot be rejected. Otherwise, the predictor with the strongest association to the response is selected, where strength is measured by a p-value corresponding to a test for the partial null hypothesis of a single input variable and the response. A binary split in the selected input variable is carried out. These steps are recursively repeated until no further splits are supported.

Figure 16.11 presents a conditional inference tree for a Russian dataset (Sokolova, Janda, and Lyashevksaya 2012; Baayen et al. in press) that addresses the question of whether verb morphology (*Verb*, with the prefixes *po-*, *na-*, *za-*, and zero, i.e., no prefix, as levels) co-determines the choice between theme-object versus goal-object constructions. Further predictors are *Reduced* (is the construction reduced – levels *yes* versus *no*) and *Participle* (*yes*: passive participle, *no*: active form). The ovals in the recursive partitioning graph represent the choice points, and the *p*-value specifies the significance of the split. The branches are

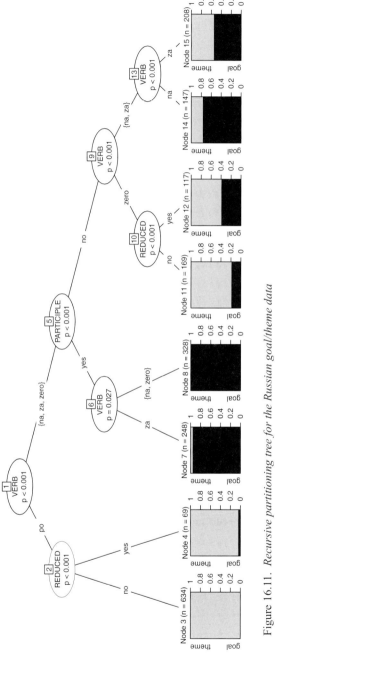

Figure 16.11. *Recursive partitioning tree for the Russian goal/theme data*

labeled with the class values governing the partitioned subsets. The thermometers at the leaf nodes present the proportion of goal constructions in black and the complementary proportions of the theme construction in light grey. The tree graph presents an easy-to-read summary of the structure of the data. The asymmetry of the tree, with different predictors appearing in the various branches, points to a complex interaction of *Verb* by *Reduced* by *Participle*.

The accuracy of recursive partitioning trees is often close to or comparable to that of regression models. However, a conditional inference tree locally optimizes the partitioning, which may have an adverse effect on its prediction accuracy. Random forests sidestep the limitations of a single locally optimal tree by constructing a large number of conditional inference trees, resulting in a (random) forest of conditional inference trees. Each tree in the forest is grown for a subset of the data generated by randomly sampling without replacement from observations and predictors. The predictions of the random forest are based on a voting scheme for the trees in the forest: Each tree in the forest provides a prediction about the most likely class membership, and the class receiving the majority of the votes is selected as the most probable outcome. Generally, the prediction accuracy of a random forest is greater than that of the locally optimal conditional inference tree, and highly competitive with the accuracy of logistic models.

Random forests also provide insight into the relative importance of the predictors by assessing the loss of prediction accuracy when the association between a predictor and the response variable is broken by randomly permuting the values of the predictor. The greater the decrease in accuracy, the more important a predictor is. For the Russian data, the variable importance scores are 0.003 for *Reduced*, 0.076 for *Participle*, and 0.335 for *Verb*, indicating that the verb morphology is the most important predictor of the construction.

Recursive partitioning is less effective for datasets with random-effect factors. In the languages sciences, subject variability is often the strongest predictor for such data, and often one finds that the tree graphs split almost exclusively on the subjects. Furthermore, unfortunately, with large numbers of subjects and items, recursive partitioning becomes computationally prohibitive. However, when information about subjects and items is withheld, recursive partitioning trees may still provide useful information about interactions in the data that help the formulation of mixed-effects regression models.

3.4   Memory-based learning

Memory-based learning (Daelemans and van den Bosch 2005; software available at http://ilk.uvt.nl/timbl), is a technique that assigns a class to an observation based on the class membership of its nearest neighbors. Unsurprisingly, the accuracy of a nearest neighbor classifier depends on the definition of what constitutes a nearest neighbor. The simplest similarity metric counts the number of features that two exemplars share. (If a predictor is numeric, it has to be binned into a small number of factor levels.)

Sets of neighbors can be at various distances. Some neighbors may differ in only one predictor value, others may differ with respect to two values, and so on. The set of neighbors taken into account can be restricted to the set of closest neighbors, but neighbor sets at larger distances can also be taken into account. Given a set of neighbors, an observation is assigned to the class that is best represented in this set of nearest neighbors.

The similarity metric for neighbors can be refined in many ways. For instance, predictors (or *features* in the terminology of memory-based learning) can be weighted for how informative they are about the response class across the dataset, and further adjusted for the number of different levels of a predictor. This often results in a highly effective classifier that is entirely competitive with the classifiers described in the preceding sections. Furthermore, memory-based learning scales up very well to large datasets and to datasets with predictors with many levels. From a theoretical perspective, memory-based learning is important because it is a computational implementation of exemplar theory, albeit only for discrete (or discretized) data.

Examples of linguistic studies making use of memory-based learning in computational linguistics are found in Daelemans and van den Bosch 2005. Krott, Baayen, and Schreuder (2001) made use of memory-based learning to predict interfixes in Dutch compounds; Plag, Kunter, and Lappe (2007) applied it to the analysis of stress patterns in English compounds; whereas Keuleers et al. (2007) used it to study Dutch plural inflection. Keuleers (2008) provides a detailed comparison of memory-based learning with the rule-induction approach of Albright and Hayes (2003), focusing on regular and irregular verbs in English.

3.5   Naive discrimination learning

Naive discrimination learning implements a classifier based on principles of human learning as formalized in the Rescorla-Wagner equations (Wagner and Rescorla 1972) and the equilibrium equations for the Rescorla-Wagner equations developed by Danks (2003).

Currently, there is only one implementation of the naive discrimination learning, the ndl package (Arppe et al. 2012) for R (R Core Team 2013). Several studies (Baayen 2011; Baayen et al. in press) suggest that its classificatory accuracy is comparable to that of other state-of-the-art classifiers. It is mentioned here as a model that offers a learning perspective on the probabilistic knowledge that speakers have of their language. For naive discrimination learning as a computational model of lexical processing, see Baayen et al. (2011).

Table 16.14 lists the weights from predictor-value pairs (rows) to the four Finnish 'think' verbs of Arppe (2008). Figure 16.12 shows the network layout, with darker shades of grey indicating stronger positive connections. Exactly mirroring the results with one-versus-rest polytomous regression (see

Table 16.14 *Naive discrimination learning weights for four Finnish near-synonyms for 'think'*

	ajatella	harkita	miettia	pohtia	Abbreviation
Agent=Group	0.23	0.13	0.07	0.37	AgnG
Agent=Individual	0.41	0.07	0.22	0.10	AgnI
Agent=None	0.42	0.08	0.11	0.18	AgnN
Patient=Abstraction	−0.12	0.01	0.11	0.22	PtntAb
Patient=Activity	−0.21	0.35	−0.00	0.07	PtntAc
Patient=Communication	−0.26	0.10	0.27	0.11	PtnC
Patient=DirectQuote	−0.39	−0.07	0.17	0.50	PtDQ
Patient=etta.CLAUSE	0.40	−0.05	−0.07	−0.06	P.CL
Patient=Event	0.28	−0.04	0.00	−0.03	PtnE
Patient=Indirect Question	−0.31	−0.01	0.37	0.17	PtIQ
Patient–IndividualGroup	0.39	−0.01	−0.08	−0.09	PtIG
Patient=Infinitive	0.51	0.00	−0.19	−0.10	PtnI
Patient=None	0.25	−0.01	0.01	−0.04	PtnN
Patient=Participle	0.49	−0.00	−0.18	−0.09	PtnP

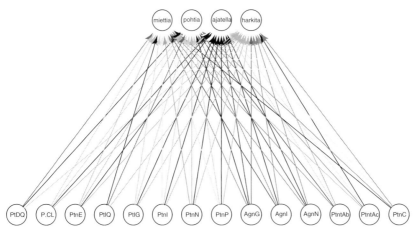

Figure 16.12. *The ndl network for the Finnish* think *verbs. Darker shades of grey indicate stronger positive connections, lighter shades of grey larger negative connections. For the abbreviations in the nodes, see Table 16.14.*

Table 16.13), for patients expressing an activity, *ajatella* is dispreferred with a large negative weight, whereas *harkita* is favored with a strong positive weight. The total support for a given verb is obtained by adding the weights from all relevant predictor-value pairs. For instance, a patient expressing an activity and an agent expressing an individual give rise to maximal support for *harkita* (summed weights 0.42) followed at a distance by *miettia* (0.21), *ajatella* (0.20), and *pohtia* (0.17).

4   Concluding remarks

This chapter has focused on multivariate regression and classification, both of which consider a response variable as functionally dependent on a set of predictors. A great many statistical methods have been developed for datasets for which there is no specific response variable, and for which the goal is to clarify how all variables pattern together (e.g., cluster, principal component, and discriminant analyses). Introductions to methods for dealing with such datasets can be found in, for instance, Everitt 2005, Baayen 2008, and Højsgaard et al. 2012.

Statistics is a field in which progress is rapid. As a consequence, many new techniques have become available in recent years (such as random forests and generalized additive mixed models) that considerably facilitate the analysis of language data. With the continued development of new statistical techniques that are increasingly well suited for the analysis of data from the complex dynamic systems that languages are, analysts will increasingly find themselves facing significant results that defy explanation within the conceptual framework within which a study was conceived. This, I believe, is good: Statistics will challenge linguistics to move beyond the boundaries of its current imagination.

References

Albright, A. and B. Hayes. 2003. Rules vs. analogy in English past tenses: a computational/experimental study. *Cognition* 90: 119–61.

Arppe, A. 2008. *Univariate, Bivariate and Multivariate Methods in Corpus-based Lexicography: A Study of Synonymy*. University of Helsinki.

2012. polytomous: Polytomous logistic regression for fixed and mixed effects [Computer software manual]. Available at: http://CRAN.R-project.org/package=polytomous (R package version 0.1.4; accessed June 28, 2013).

Arppe, A., P. Milin, P. Hendrix, and R. H. Baayen. 2012. ndl: Naive discriminative learning [Computer software manual]. Available at: http://CRAN.R-project.org/package=ndl (R package version 0.1.6; accessed June 28, 2013).

Baayen, R. H. 2008. *Analyzing Linguistic Data: A Practical Introduction to Statistics using R*. Cambridge University Press.

2010. A real experiment is a factorial experiment? *The Mental Lexicon* 5.1: 149–57.

2011. Corpus linguistics and naive discriminative learning. *Brazilian Journal of Applied Linguistics* 11: 295–328.

Baayen, R. H. and P. Milin. 2010. Analyzing reaction times. *International Journal of Psychological Research* 3: 12–28.

Baayen, R. H., P. Milin, D. Filipovic Durdjevic, P. Hendrix, and M. Marelli. 2011. An amorphous model for morphological processing in visual comprehension based on naive discriminative learning. *Psychological Review* 118.3: 438–81.

Baayen, R. H., L. A. Janda, T. Nesset, A. Endresen, and A. Makarova. In press. Making choices in slavic: pros and cons of statistical methods for rival forms. *Russian Linguistics*.

Balota, D., M. Cortese, S. Sergent-Marshall, D. Spieler, and M. Yap. 2004. Visual word recognition for single-syllable words. *Journal of Experimental Psychology: General* 133: 283–316.

Belsley, D. A. 1984. Demeaning conditioning diagnostics through centering. *The American Statistician* 38: 73–7.

Box, G. E. P. and D. R. Cox. 1964. An analysis of transformations (with discussion). *Journal of the Royal Statistical Society B* 26: 211–52.

Breiman, L. 2001. Random forests. *Machine Learning* 45: 5–32.

Breiman, L., J. H. Friedman, R. Olshen, and C. J. Stone. 1984. *Classification and Regression Trees*. Belmont, CA: Wadsworth International Group.

Bresnan, J., A. Cueni, T. Nikitina, and R. H. Baayen. 2007. Predicting the dative alternation. In G. Bouma, I. Kraemer, and J. Zwarts, eds. *Cognitive Foundations of Interpretation*. Amsterdam: Royal Netherlands Academy of Arts and Sciences, 69–94.

Chatterjee, S., A. Hadi, and B. Price. 2000. *Regression Analysis by Example*. New York: John Wiley and Sons.

Cohen, J. 1983. The cost of dichotomization. *Applied Psychological Measurement* 7: 249–54.

Daelemans, W. and A. van den Bosch. 2005. *Memory-based Language Processing*. Cambridge University Press.

Dalal, D. K. and M. J. Zickar. 2012. Some common myths about centering predictor variables in moderated multiple regression and polynomial regression. *Organizational Research Methods* 15: 339–62.

Danks, D. 2003. Equilibria of the Rescorla-Wagner model. *Journal of Mathematical Psychology* 47.2: 109–21.

Everitt, B. 2005. *An R and S-Plus Companion to Multivariate Analysis*. London: Springer.

Faraway, J. J. 2006. *Extending Linear Models with R: Generalized Linear, Mixed Effects and Non-parametric Regression Models*. Boca Raton, FL: Chapman and Hall/CRC.

Friedman, L. and M. Wall. 2005. Graphical views of suppression and multicollinearity in multiple regression. *The American Statistician* 59: 127–36.

Gries, S. T. 2003. *Multifactorial Analysis in Corpus Linguistics: A Study of Particle Placement*. London and New York: Continuum Press.

Harrell, F. 2001. *Regression Modeling Strategies*. Berlin: Springer.

Hastie, T. and R. Tibshirani. 1990. *Generalized Additive Models*. London: Chapman and Hall.

Højsgaard, S., D. Edwards, and S. Lauritzen. 2012. *Graphical models with R*. New York: Springer.

Hothorn, T., F. Bretz, and P. Westfall. 2008. Simultaneous inference in general parametric models. *Biometrical Journal* 50.3: 346–63.

Jaeger, F. 2010. Redundancy and reduction: speakers manage syntactic information density. *Cognitive Psychology* 61.1: 23–62.

Jaeger, T. 2008. Categorical data analysis: away from ANOVAs (transformation or not) and towards logit mixed models. *Journal of Memory and Language* 59.4: 434–46.

Janda, L. A., T. Nesset, and R. Baayen. 2010. Capturing correlational structure in Russian paradigms: a case study in logistic mixed-effects modeling. *Corpus Linguistics and Linguistic Theory* 6.1: 29–48.

Jurafsky, D., A. Bell, M. Gregory, and W. Raymond. 2001. Probabilistic relations between words: evidence from reduction in lexical production. In J. Bybee and P. Hopper, eds.

Frequency and the Emergence of Linguistic Structure. Amsterdam: John Benjamins, 229–54.

Keuleers, E. 2008. Memory-based learning of inflectional morphology. Unpublished Ph.D. dissertation, University of Antwerp.

Keuleers, E., D. Sandra, W. Daelemans, S. Gillis, G. Durieux, and E. Martens. 2007. Dutch plural inflection: the exception that proves the analogy. *Cognitive Psychology* 54: 283–318.

Koesling, K., G. Kunter, R. H. Baayen, and I. Plag. 2013. Prominence in triconstituent compounds: pitch contours and linguistic theory. *Language and Speech*, doi:10.1177/0023830913478914.

Krott, A., R. H. Baayen, and R. Schreuder. 2001. Analogy in morphology: modeling the choice of linking morphemes in Dutch. *Linguistics* 39.1: 51–93.

Kryuchkova, T., B. V. Tucker, L. Wurm, and R. H. Baayen. 2012. Danger and usefulness in auditory lexical processing: evidence from electroencephalography. *Brain and Language* 122: 81–91.

Kuperman, V. and J. Van Dyke. 2011. Effects of individual differences in verbal skills on eye-movement patterns during sentence reading. *Journal of Memory and Language* 65.1: 42–73.

Kuperman, V., R. Schreuder, R. Bertram, and R. H. Baayen. 2009. Reading of multi-morphemic Dutch compounds: towards a multiple route model of lexical processing. *Journal of Experimental Psychology: HPP* 35: 876–95.

Lumley, T. and A. Miller. 2009. leaps: regression subset selection [Computer software manual]. Available at: http://CRAN.R-project.org/package=leaps (R package version 2.9; accessed June 28, 2013).

MacCallum, R., S. Zhang, K. Preacher, and D. Rucker. 2002. On the practice of dichotomization of quantitative variables. *Psychological Methods* 7.1: 19–40.

Pinheiro, J. C., and D. M. Bates. 2000. *Mixed-effects Models in S and S-PLUS*. New York: Springer.

Plag, I., G. Kunter, and S. Lappe. 2007. Testing hypotheses about compound stress assignment in English: a corpus-based investigation. *Corpus Linguistics and Linguistic Theory* 3: 199–232.

R Core Team. 2013. *R: A language and environment for statistical computing. Vienna: R Foundation for Statistical Computing*. Available at: www.R-project.org (accessed July 5, 2013).

Sankoff, D. 1987. Variable rules. In U. Ammon, U. Dittmar, and K. J. Mattheier, eds. *Sociolinguistics: An International Handbook of the Science of Language and Society*, 3 vols. Berlin: Mouton de Gruyter, Volume I, 984–97.

Sokolova, S., L. A. Janda, and O. Lyashevksaya. 2012. The locative alternation and the Russian 'empty' prefixes: a case study of the verb gruzit' 'load'. In D. Divjak and S. T. Gries, eds. *Frequency Effects in Language Representation*. Berlin: Mouton de Gruyter, 51–86.

Strobl, C., J. Malley, and G. Tutz. 2009. An introduction to recursive partitioning: rationale, application, and characteristics of classification and regression trees, bagging, and random forests. *Psychological Methods* 14.4: 26.

Strobl, C., A.-L. Boulesteix, T. Kneib, T. Augustin, and A. Zeileis. 2008. Conditional variable importance for random forests. *Psychological Methods* 14.4: 323–48.

Tagliamonte, S., and R. H. Baayen. 2012. Models, forests and trees of York English: was/were variation as a case study for statistical practice. *Language Variation and Change* 24: 135–78.

Venables, W. N. and B. D. Ripley. 2002. *Modern Applied Statistics with S-Plus*. New York: Springer.

Wagner, A. and R. Rescorla. 1972. A theory of Pavlovian conditioning: variations in the effectiveness of reinforcement and nonreinforcement. In A. H. Black and W. F. Prokasy, eds. *Classical Conditioning*. New York: Appleton-Century-Crofts, Volume II, 64–99.

Wang, W. S.-Y. 1969. Competing changes as a cause of residue. *Language* 45: 9–25.

West, B., K. Welch, and A. Galecki. 2007. *Linear Mixed Models: A Practical Guide Using Statistical Software*. London: Chapman and Hall/CRC Press.

Wieling, M. 2013. Voices dialectometry at the University of Groningen. In C. Upton and B. Davies, eds. *Analysing 21st-century British English: Conceptual and Methodological Aspects of the 'Voices' Project*. London: Routledge.

Wieling, M., J. Nerbonne, and R. H. Baayen. 2011. *Quantitative social dialectology: explaining linguistic variation geographically and socially. PLOS ONE 6.9*. Available at: www.plosone.org/article/info%3Adoi%2F10.1371%2Fjournal.pone.0023613 (accessed July 5, 2013).

Wood, S. 2006. *Generalized Additive Models*. New York: Chapman and Hall/CRC.

    2011. Fast stable restricted maximum likelihood and marginal likelihood estimation of semiparametric generalized linear models. *Journal of the Royal Statistical Society B* 73: 3–36.

PART III

Foundations for Data Analysis

17   Acoustic analysis

Paul Boersma

1   Introduction

Acoustic analysis, once a method used primarily within the domain of phonetics, has become an increasingly necessary skill across the field of linguistics. To name just a few examples, phonologists sometimes appeal to acoustic data to substantiate theoretical arguments, sociolinguists tend to characterize vowel shifts and mergers in terms of their acoustic properties, and psycholinguists frequently draw on acoustic analysis techniques to construct stimuli for experiments.

The analysis of acoustic signals is mainly performed with the help of generally available software. Because of its capability of creating publication-quality graphics, the pictures in this chapter were made with Praat (Boersma and Weenink 1992–2012), a general set of tools for analyzing, synthesizing and manipulating speech and other sounds, bundled into a single integrated computer program. Praat is available free of charge for all current major computer platforms (nowadays MacOS, Windows, Linux) and is continually updated to accommodate new operating system developments and new analysis methods.

Graphical software allows us to perform acoustic analysis by inspecting visualized speech. The types of visualization addressed in the present chapter are the waveform, the pitch curve, the intensity curve, the spectrum, the spectrogram, and formant tracks. These types of visualization will be seen to help in measuring the following articulatory, acoustic, and auditory quantities: glottal period, resonance frequencies, pitch, duration, intensity, noisiness, and place of articulation. Examples of practical uses for each of these measures will appear throughout the chapter. (See Chapter 9 for a discussion of methodological considerations when making audio recordings.)

2   The waveform

The *waveform* is the direct visualization of sound as recorded by a microphone and represents air pressure as a function of time. In the waveform one can directly see when there is silence and how long the utterances are, but one can also infer many acoustic properties of speech, such as periodicity, intensity, and spectral qualities.

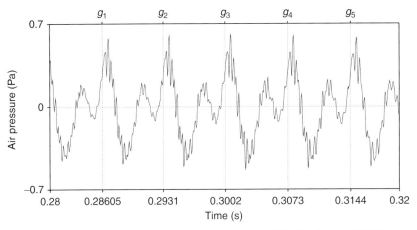

Figure 17.1. *Waveform of several periods of the Dutch vowel /i/, illustrating glottal fold vibration*

2.1   The waveform of a vowel

Figure 17.1 shows a part of the waveform of a recording of a token of the Dutch vowel /i/, as spoken by the present author in 1997. The horizontal axis represents the time as expressed in the number of seconds that have elapsed since the start of the recording. The vertical scale represents the air pressure recorded by the microphone. The vocal folds close approximately at the times g_1, g_2, g_3, g_4, and g_5. These are the times at which the folds hit one another, causing a loud clapping noise at the glottis, which leads to resonances in the vocal tract. Thus, the clap at g_2 causes strongly rising and falling air pressures just after g_2, and these resonances gradually die out, leading to smaller rising and falling air pressures as the time proceeds toward g_3. Just before g_3, the air pressure becomes strongly positive, which corresponds to the air being compressed in the glottis just before the vocal folds touch each other again.

The distance in time between consecutive vocal fold closures is the *vocal fold vibration period*, or T0; estimates of T0 are $g_2 - g_1 = 0.2931 - 0.28605 = 0.00705$ s and $g_3 - g_2 = 0.3002 - 0.2931 = 0.0071$ s. Therefore, approximately $1/0.0071 = 141$ of these periods fit in 1 second, so that the *vocal fold vibration frequency* must be about 141 Hz. This frequency is an important quantity in speech research, because humans tend to be able to hear it and languages therefore employ it in implementing tone and intonation. More specifically, the human auditory system has a periodicity detector, or *pitch detector*, which recognizes recurring wave-shapes: for the sound in the figure, humans tend to perceive a *pitch* of 141 Hz.

While pitch is the frequency with which the whole wave shape repeats itself, the waveform also contains other frequencies, namely those associated with the sine-like waves that represent resonances of the vocal tract. Figure 17.2 zooms in on Figure 17.1 and shows the period of a slow resonance: the duration of one vibration of the slow sine wave can be measured as the time between two

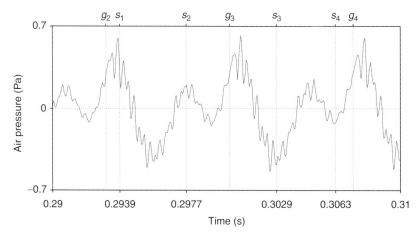

Figure 17.2. *Waveform of several periods of the Dutch vowel /i/, illustrating the first formant*

consecutive peaks – for example, $s_2 - s_1 = 0.2977 - 0.2939 = 0.0038$ s. It can also be measured as the time between two consecutive valleys – for example, $s_4 - s_3 = 0.3063 - 0.3029 = 0.0034$ s. Therefore, the period of the slow resonance is approximately 0.0036 seconds long. Approximately $1/0.0036 = 278$ of these periods fit in 1 second, so that the *slow resonance frequency* must be estimated as 278 Hz. Such values are typical for the Dutch high vowels /i/, /y/, and /u/. The slow resonance frequency is another important quantity in speech research, because humans can hear it and languages therefore employ it in implementing the phonological feature of vowel height. More specifically, the human auditory system has a *spectral analysis system* (namely the basilar membrane in the inner ear and the neural circuitry emanating from it), which dissects the incoming sound into its component sine waves: for the sound in the figure, humans tend to perceive a *first formant* of 278 Hz.

The third phenomenon that the waveform shows is a *rapid resonance frequency*. Figure 17.3 zooms in a bit more than Figure 17.2, and a rapidly vibrating resonance becomes clearly visible. Six periods of it lie between r_1 and r_7, which are $0.30270 - 0.30084 = 0.00184$ seconds apart. Each period therefore lasts $0.00184 / 6 = 0.000307$ s, so that $1 / 0.000307 = 3{,}200$ of these periods fit in 1 second. The rapid resonance frequency, which humans tend to perceive as the *second formant*, is therefore 3,200 Hz. This value is typical for the Dutch vowel /i/ (acoustically, this resonance corresponds to the third and fourth formants of the vocal tract; the true second formant may lie around 2,200 Hz, but it is weak and not visible in the figure).

The choice of the vowel /i/ as the example for the present section was informed by the large distance between the first and second formant. In vowels other than /i/, this distance tends to be much smaller. Figure 17.4 shows a part of the waveform of a token of Dutch /a/, with time markers every 0.001 seconds. Some consecutive

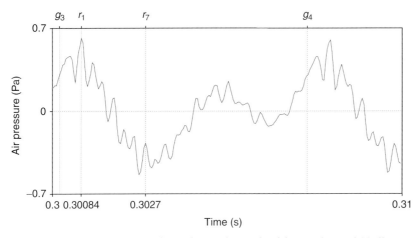

Figure 17.3. *Waveform of several periods of the Dutch vowel /i/, illustrating the second formant*

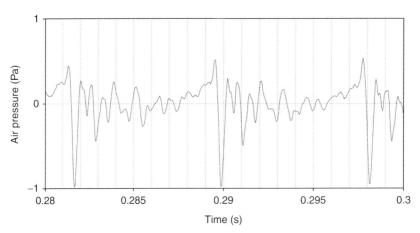

Figure 17.4. *Waveform of several periods of the Dutch vowel /a/, illustrating mangled formants*

major positive peaks and some consecutive major negative peaks are just over 0.001 seconds apart, and some consecutive peaks or valleys are a bit less than 0.001 seconds apart, but we cannot see any well-defined sine waves as we could with /i/. The waveform is made up of a slower and a faster resonance whose periods are a bit above and a bit below 0.001 seconds, respectively, but their periods are so close together that their sine waves visually interfere, so that the two resonances are hard to distinguish from each other visually. For reasons such as this, vowel formants are usually investigated not with the help of waveforms, but with the help of spectral techniques, as described in Sections 5 and 6.

A fourth type of property visible in the waveform is *duration*. Figure 17.5 shows the whole /i/ of Figures 17.1 through 17.3. The vowel starts at a time of

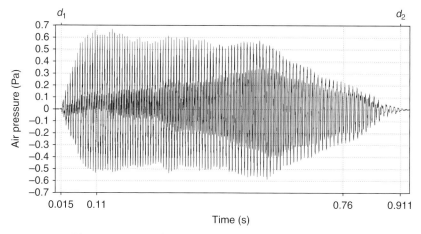

Figure 17.5. *Waveform of a whole Dutch /i/, illustrating duration and intensity*

$d_1 = 0.015$ seconds and ends at a time of $d_2 = 0.911$ seconds, from which we can conclude that its duration is $0.911 - 0.015 = 0.896$ seconds. Duration is an important quantity in speech research, because humans have a mechanism for measuring the duration over which a signal stays approximately stationary in terms of other percepts (such as the first and second formant here) and languages therefore employ duration as the major cue to the phonological length of vowels and consonants; moreover, duration is a cue to many other phonological elements (including stress, obstruent voicing, and vowel height) and to paralinguistic features of speech.

The fifth acoustic quantity visible in the waveform is *intensity*. In Figure 17.5, the top-to-top amplitude of the sound (peak minus valley) at a time of 0.11 seconds is more than 1.1 Pa, whereas at a time of 0.76 seconds it has fallen to approximately 0.5 Pa. Now, the *absolute amplitudes* of this sound at the time and place of recording are probably different from 1.1 and 0.5 Pa, because the gain of the recording was not calibrated (the fake numbers in Pa in the figure were computed from the sound file, where the minimum and maximum representable values were arbitrarily assigned the values of −1 and +1 Pa). However, the *relative amplitude* of the different parts of the sound (i.e., a fall by a factor of 2.2 between 0.11 and 0.76 seconds) is reliable, assuming that the speaker kept a constant distance to the microphone and nobody turned the gain control during the recording. Relative intensity is an important quantity in speech research, because it contributes to the perception of phonological phenomena such as stress, stridency, manner, voicing, and nasality.

2.2   Other waveforms

Figure 17.6 shows the waveform of the voiceless palatal plosive in [aca]. Between the two vowels, the figure indicates a silence with a duration of 140 ms, followed by a release burst with a duration of 24 ms. The voicing of the vowel

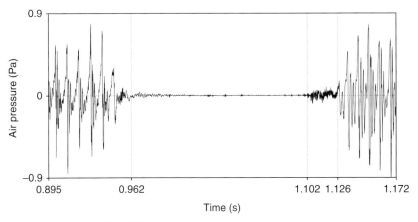

Figure 17.6. *Waveform of the voiceless palatal plosive in [aca], illustrating silence and release burst*

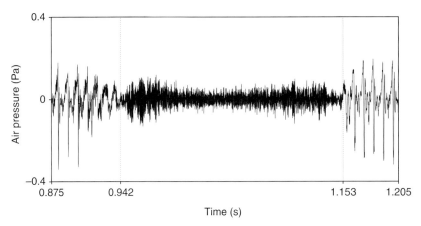

Figure 17.7. *Waveform of the voiceless palatal fricative in [aça], illustrating the many zero crossings*

starts right after the burst ends. This is a non-aspirated plosive, but the *voice onset time*, which is defined as the time at the start of voicing minus the time at the release, is rather positive, namely 24 ms. Of all the acoustic measurements discussed in this chapter, voice onset time is one of the few that can best be measured from the waveform.

Figure 17.7 shows the waveform of the voiceless palatal fricative in [aça]. The fricative noise lasts 211 ms and can be seen from the large number of times the waveform crosses the 0 Pa line every millisecond.

Finally, Figure 17.8 shows the waveform of the alveolar trill in [ara]. While the vocal folds continue to vibrate during the trill, four tongue tip closures cause the amplitude of the waveform to fall toward zero at the indicated four points in time.

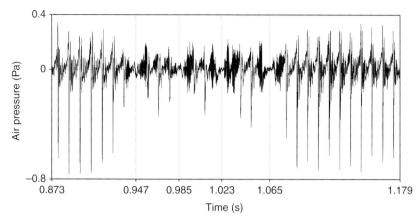

Figure 17.8. *Waveform of the alveolar trill in [ara], illustrating four passive tongue-tip closures*

Three periods of vibration fit into 1.065 – 0.947 = 0.118 seconds, so that there are approximately 3 / 0.118 = 25 tongue-tip vibrations per second.

2.3   Applications and limitations of waveform inspection

The usefulness of the waveform for acoustic research is that it is basic, shows whether there is speech or silence, and constitutes the main source of information on voice onset time. Most other acoustic phenomena are slightly or much easier to investigate with different types of visualization, such as pitch curves, spectra, and spectrograms, all of which are discussed in the following sections.

3   Periodicity analysis

In Figure 17.1, the glottal fold vibration frequency was determined by inspecting and measuring the waveform. If you want to determine the tonal pattern or intonation contour of a whole utterance, such a procedure is impractical. Fortunately, phonetic analysis software provides automated pitch measurement techniques.

3.1   Automated pitch measurement techniques

Most automated pitch measurement techniques are based on the self-similarity of the waveform. In Figure 17.1, for instance, the 7.1-ms part from 0.2931 to 0.3002 seconds is extremely similar to the adjacent 7.1-ms part from 0.3002 to 0.3073 seconds, whereas, for instance, the 5.0-ms part from 0.2952 to 0.3002 seconds is quite dissimilar from its adjacent 5.0-ms part from 0.3002 to 0.3052 seconds. Figure 17.9, which copies these and several other parts of Figure 17.1 just before and just after 0.3002 seconds, illustrates these similarity

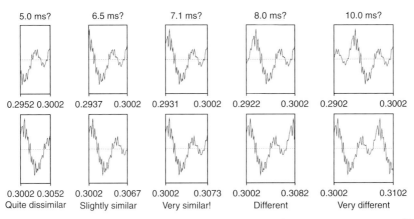

Figure 17.9. *Determining the pitch of the sound in Figure 17.1 at a time of 0.3002 seconds (cross-correlation method). The top row shows parts of the sound just before that time, and the bottom row shows equally long parts just after. The two parts look most similar if they are 7.1 ms long.*

verdicts. If we want to make a guess about the "true" glottal period at 0.3002 seconds, then 7.1 ms seems to be a much better candidate than 5.0 ms. In fact, 7.1 ms looks a much better candidate than 6.5 or 8.0 or 10.0 ms as well (in Figure 17.9), and if one does the computations, then 7.1 ms turns out to be a slightly better candidate than 7.0 or 7.2 ms. An automated pitch measurement technique based on *cross-correlation* (Talkin 1995) will now say that at 0.3002 seconds the glottal period is 7.1 ms and that therefore the pitch is $1/0.0071 = 141$ Hz. Analogous statements can be made about every time point in Figure 17.1: for every time point it is possible to look backward and forward in time and to determine how similar the immediate future is to the immediate past.

A general property of automated acoustic measurements is the use of an *analysis window.* In the example just mentioned, the F0 at 0.3002 seconds cannot be determined by looking at what happens at that time point; it can only be determined by looking some time into the past and some time into the future. If you want to detect any F0 between 100 Hz and 500 Hz, you will have to look into the past and future for at least 2.0 ms and at most 10.0 ms; so for the lowest F0 you want to detect (100 Hz), you will have to consider an analysis window of 20.0 ms (i.e., 10.0 ms in both directions).

A related technique is *autocorrelation.* In Figure 17.9, while cross-correlation works with windows whose lengths vary between 4.0 and 20.0 ms, the autocorrelation method works by looking at a time window with a constant length of 30.0 ms and computing the similarities of all amplitudes spaced apart within that window by times between 2.0 and 10.0 ms. Autocorrelation methods have a bad reputation in the literature, because early versions could produce much too high F0 estimates (typically, one octave higher than the true F0); however, this problem was solved by Boersma's (1993) *unbiased* autocorrelation method.

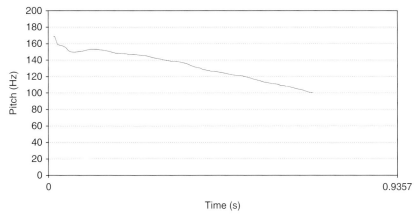

Figure 17.10. *Pitch curve for the [i] vowel of Figure 17.5*

3.2   What automated pitch measurements look like

In the [i] vowel of Figure 17.5 one can see that the glottal periods get longer toward the end of the vowel. Apparently, the glottal fold vibration frequency falls during the course of this vowel. The autocorrelation method tracks the development of this frequency in the way shown in Figure 17.10. The figure does not show pitch values from 0.8 seconds on; the automated pitch measurement method considers the signal insufficiently voiced or too quiet in that region.

Loosely, pitch measurement techniques can be said to measure either an articulatory phenomenon (i.e., the glottal fold vibration frequency), a mathematical phenomenon (i.e., [near-]periodicity), or an auditory phenomenon (i.e., the perceived pitch). What the autocorrelation method of Figure 17.10 measures is closest to the perceived pitch (without the niceties of experimental psychoacoustic results with non-periodic signals to which humans can nevertheless assign pitch), which is appropriate for intonation or tone research (Boersma 1993). The cross-correlation method has the disadvantage of making intonation or tone mistakes in the presence of noise, but comes closer to measuring the actual glottal pulses, and is therefore appropriate for measuring aspects of voice quality, such as jitter, shimmer, and harmonics-to-noise ratio (Boersma 1993, 2009).

3.3   Limitations of automated pitch measurements

In automated pitch measurements, several things can go wrong. In Figure 17.9, 7.1 ms is clearly the best candidate for the glottal period, but from Figures 17.2 and 17.3 we can see that the same sound contains sine waves that have peaks every 3.8 or 0.307 ms, so that 3.8 ms (the period of F1) and 0.307 ms (the period of F2) are pitch candidates that at least fall in the "fairly similar" rubric. These extraneous pitch candidates are normally overruled by the much better matching true glottal period of 7.1 ms, but in voiceless parts of the sound, where there is no true glottal period, these formants might become the best pitch candidates, especially if there is echo in the background. As a result, a pitch measurement procedure might misinterpret these formants as pitches, and in practice we see that pitch analysis tools will indeed show spurious pitches in voiceless stretches. To ameliorate this problem, pitch analysis tools often allow you to set a maximum pitch value above which the tool will ignore any pitch candidates. This "pitch ceiling" was 300 Hz for the male voice in Figure 17.10, and you can set it to 500 Hz for female voices. This works reasonably unless people are yelling, singing, or otherwise stretching their voice.

The situation is even worse at the lower side of the pitch range. In Figure 17.1 we can see that 142 ms is an almost equally viable candidate for a period as 71 ms – that is, the part from 0.2860 to 0.3002 seconds is very similar to the part from 0.3002 to 0.3144 seconds. This means that 1 / 142 ms = 70.5 Hz is almost an equally good pitch candidate as the true pitch of 141 Hz. In order to prevent the pitch analysis tool from making an "octave error" (i.e., proposing a pitch of 70.5 Hz instead of 141 Hz), the pitch analysis tool has to have a controlled small bias in favor of higher frequencies. In noisy situations, however, this bias might not suffice (i.e., the similarity over 142 ms might be greater than the similarity over 71 ms just by chance). To ameliorate this problem, pitch analysis tools often allow you to specify a minimum pitch value below which the tool will not look for pitch candidates. This "pitch floor" was 75 Hz for the male voice in Figure 17.10, and you can set it to 100 Hz for female voices. For creaky voices you should set the pitch floor much lower than 75 Hz (e.g., to 40 Hz).

The importance of a sufficiently high pitch floor in the presence of noise has been confirmed experimentally by Deliyski et al. (2005), who investigated the quality of several pitch measurement methods in ten situations: two speaker sexes (male, female) times five levels of background noise (fan, 60 Hz, white, talk, traffic). In seven of these ten situations, including all male conditions, the auto-correlation algorithm of Figure 17.10 outperformed another algorithm, but in the other three situations it performed worse, making many mistakes; all three situations were with female voices, and what probably contributed to the mistakes was the fact that the authors had set the pitch floor as low as 70 Hz. Speech researchers are therefore advised to take this setting seriously.

4   Intensity analysis

In the discussion of Figure 17.5 it was claimed that the course of the intensity could be seen from the waveform. However, this is just an approximation. If we take the height of the peaks in Figure 17.5 as a criterion, we have to conclude that the highest intensity lies around 0.15 seconds. But "intensity" refers to the period-averaged power in the signal, so it is also important to look at what happens between the peaks. Indeed we see in Figure 17.5 that around 0.6 seconds the signal is "thicker" – that is, the peaks may be lower, but the amplitudes between the peaks are greater than at 0.15 seconds. In order to measure exactly the course of the power in the signal, automated intensity measurements can help.

4.1   An automated intensity measurement technique

Figure 17.11 shows how the intensity curve of the sound in Figure 17.5 can be determined. We like the end result to be expressed at every moment in time as a number of dB above the human auditory intensity threshold.

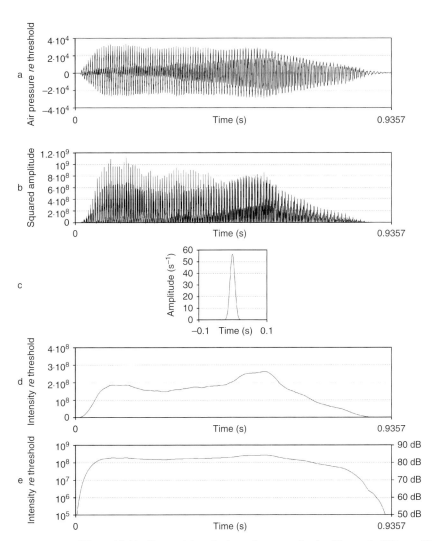

Figure 17.11. *Determining the intensity curve for the [i] vowel of Figure 17.5: (a) the original sound, as measured relative to the auditory threshold; (b) the square of this; (c) the Gaussian smoothing kernel, on the same time scale as the sound; (d) the intensity curve, computed as the convolution of the squared amplitude and the Gaussian; and (e) the intensity curve along a logarithmic scale*

As this threshold is defined as a pressure of 0.00002 Pa, we first divide the pressure curve of Figure 17.5 by this value of 0.00002 Pa. The result is in Figure 17.11a; the curve is identical to Figure 17.5 except for the vertical scaling. The next step comes from realizing that the power in a pressure signal is proportionate to the square of the pressure (physically, one can say that power equals air pressure times volume velocity, and if you increase the signal strength in such a way that the air pressure increases by a factor of ten, the air particles will also speed up by a factor of ten). Figure 17.11b therefore shows the square of Figure 17.11a; this cannot yet be called the intensity of the signal, because there are still within-period fluctuations. To smooth these away, we *convolve* the signal with the unit-area Gaussian kernel of Figure 17.11c, yielding the smoothed intensity curve of Figure 17.11d. The height of this curve is less than that of the peaks in Figure 17.11b, because in Figure 17.11d the original peaks have been averaged out with their surrounding valleys; the *area* under the curve in Figure 17.11d, however, is still the same as the area under the curve in Figure 17.11b. Finally, it is usual to draw the intensity curve along a logarithmic vertical axis, as in Figure 17.11e, where every factor of ten in intensity is awarded an equal part of the vertical space. These intensities, which are still taken relative to the auditory threshold (if the signal is calibrated), can be straightforwardly translated to values in dB, with, for example, a threshold-relative intensity of 10^8 corresponding to an intensity level of 80 dB, as illustrated in Figure 17.11e.

In the curves of Figures 17.11d and 17.11e, we see that the intensity peak around 0.6 seconds is indeed stronger than that around 0.15 seconds. Apparently, the "thickness" in the waveform of Figure 17.11a around 0.6 seconds outweighs the height of the peaks in the waveform around 0.15 seconds. Thus, automated intensity measurement techniques can provide precision that the human eye cannot.

5   Spectral analysis

The dissection of a sound into its component sine waves, which I illustrated with the waveforms of Figures 17.2 and 17.4, can be automated.

5.1   An automated spectral analysis technique

Figure 17.12 shows how the periodic [i]-like speech sound of Figure 17.2 can be approximated as the sum of six sine waves.

The top picture shows exactly two periods of this voiced sound. The sound marked "1+2" is a rough approximation of these two periods: one can see that it follows all slow movements of the original sound. This sound "1+2" is composed of two sine waves, namely the sound marked "1" and the sound marked "2" in the figure. The sound marked "1" is a sine wave with the same frequency as the glottal fold vibration (i.e., it has a frequency of F0 = 141.346 Hz). The sound marked "2"

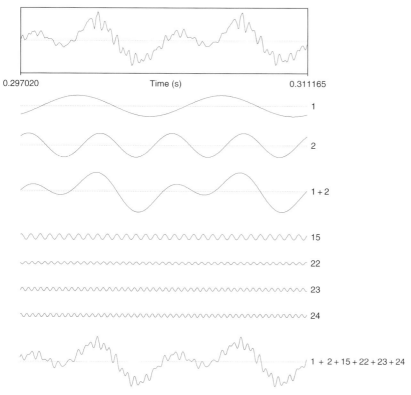

0.297020   Time (s)   0.311165

Figure 17.12. *Splitting up two periods of the [i] vowel of Figure 17.5 into six harmonics. At the top is the original sound. The rough features of the original sound are reconstructed by adding the first harmonic (1) and the second harmonic (2) to each other (1+2). When we add the 15th, 22nd, 23rd and 24th harmonics to this, the original waveshape is approximated even more closely (bottom).*

is a sine wave with exactly twice that frequency (i.e., it is the *second harmonic* of F0 and has a frequency of 2F0 = 282.692 Hz). In the figure it can be seen that this second harmonic has an amplitude slightly greater than that of the first harmonic (the sound marked "1"). When we add these two sounds to each other, we obtain the sound "1+2" – for instance, sound "1" starts with a negative value (at 0.297020 seconds), whereas sound "2" starts with a positive value, and in the sound "1+2" these negative and positive values add up to approximately zero, which is the value of "1+2" at its start. The summed curve "1+2" is computed in this way from the curves "1" and "2" at every time point.

When we include higher frequencies, the match between the summed sine waves and the original sound improves. When the 15th, 22nd, 23rd, and 24th harmonics, with amplitudes as shown in the figure, are added to the sound "1+2", we obtain the sound that is marked as "1+2+15+22+23+24" in the figure. This summed sound is very close to the original, both in its wave shape and in how it

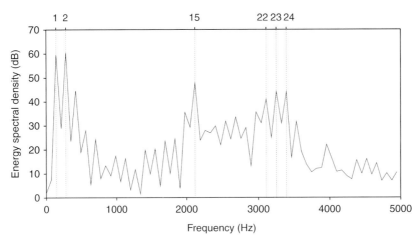

Figure 17.13. *The Fourier spectrum of the two-period [i]-like sound of Figure 17.12*

sounds to the human ear. Apparently, these two periods of the [i]-like sound of Figure 17.2 can be well approximated as the sum of six sine waves.

This method of approximating a periodic sound as a sum of sine waves was developed by Fourier (1822). I used Fourier's formulas to determine the amplitudes of the six waves in Figure 17.12, as well as to determine the *phase* (i.e., the horizontal time shift) of each sine wave in Figure 17.12. When this is done for every harmonic, not just for the six harmonics in Figure 17.12, we obtain Figure 17.13, which shows the strength of each frequency component up to 5,000 Hz. In spectral pictures like these, the horizontal axis represents frequency rather than time. We see that the 1st, 2nd, 15th, 22nd, 23rd, and 24th harmonics (marked along the top of the picture) are strong, but that most other harmonics also play a role; apparently, the match in Figure 17.12 would have been even better if we had added harmonics 3, 14, 21, 25, and so on. In between the harmonics, Figure 17.13 shows that the sound contains components of non-zero amplitude (a zero amplitude would have shown up as −∞ dB in the figure); this indicates that the sound is not perfectly periodic, as can be confirmed in the waveform of Figure 17.12 (top).

5.2   What automated spectral measurements look like

In the case of Figure 17.13 we had a longer sound from which we took exactly two periods, leading to a spectral shape with peaks at every harmonic, and valleys exactly in between the peaks. More usually, you will select a stationary part of a speech sound and ask your acoustic analysis program to provide an average spectrum over that selection.

The [i]-like sound of Figure 17.5 is stationary with respect to its formants (i.e., its formants do not change auditorily throughout the vowel); its F0, on the other hand, falls steadily. If we are interested in the formants rather than in the pitch, we

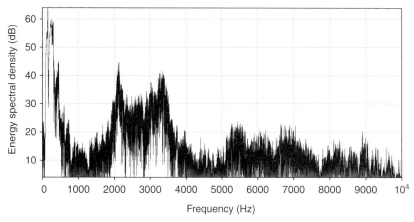

Figure 17.14. *Spectrum of the vowel [i]*

can do a spectral analysis on the whole sound. Figure 17.14 shows the spectrum of this longer sound. Pronouncing the sound with a moving pitch wipes out most of the harmonic structure of Figure 17.13 and allows us to see the formants quite well in the spectrum: Figure 17.14 shows a first formant at 300 Hz with a strength of 60 dB, an F2 at 2,150 Hz with a strength 15 dB lower than that, and an F3 and F4 at 3,000 and 3,400 Hz, respectively (these last two were not easy to distinguish in Figure 17.13).

Many more spectra of speech sounds, with explanations of how they come about articulatorily, can be found in Stevens (1998).

5.3   Applications and limitations of automated spectral measurements

Fourier's method of measuring the spectral content of speech sounds is especially appropriate for sounds with a stationary part, such as fricatives, vowels (monophthongs), and nasal consonants, but is less appropriate for speech sounds whose characteristics involve crucial dynamic changes, such as plosives, diphthongs, and trills. For those, the technique has to be extended to include change in time, as is done in the spectrogram.

6   The spectrogram

The spectrogram is the workhorse of speech visualization. It is employed with equal enthusiasm in textbooks (e.g., Ladefoged and Disner 2012) and handbooks (e.g., Ladefoged and Maddieson 1996). The spectrogram shows the frequency contents of a sound as a function of time, and thereby follows the capabilities of the basilar membrane in the inner ear, which also divides up the sound into its frequency components at every point in time.

6.1   How a spectrogram is computed

Spectrograms are computed in a way that combines elements from pitch analysis techniques (Section 3.1) with elements of spectral analysis techniques (Section 5.1).

As with pitch analysis (Section 3.1), there is the problem that a spectrum cannot be computed for a single moment in time. Instead, we have to suppose that the spectral characteristics of the sound stay constant for at least, say, 5 ms. We can then cut up the sound in 5-ms slices and determine the spectrum of each of these slices separately. This is what is done in the following sections.

6.2   What the spectrogram of a vowel looks like

Figure 17.15 shows a spectrogram of the vowels [a], [i], and [u]. Time runs from left to right and frequency runs from bottom to top. The vertical stripes that we see are not the slices of Section 6.1 (in good spectrographic visualizations, those are smoothed away), but the separate vocal fold vibrations. The dark horizontal bands are the formants; the harmonics of F0 cannot be seen, because 5 ms is so short that such spectral detail is smeared out (that is why a spectrogram with a short analysis window of 5 ms is called a *broadband spectrogram*).

For adult speakers, vowels can be inspected best if the visible frequency range of the spectrogram runs from 0 to 5,000 Hz, because that is where the main vowel-dependent formant frequencies are. In the spectrogram of Figure 17.15, the strongest frequencies are drawn in black, and the white parts of the figure depict frequencies whose strengths are 50 dB (a factor of 100,000 in power) or more below the strongest frequency in the figure; strengths in between these extremes are drawn as appropriate shades of grey. In spectrograms like these, higher frequencies are "emphasized" by 6 dB per octave with respect to lower frequencies, in order to replicate approximately how the basilar membrane integrates the

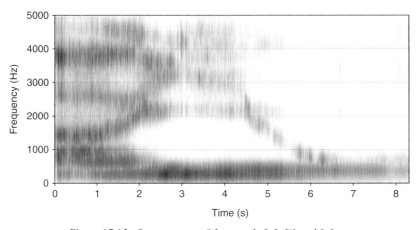

Figure 17.15. *Spectrogram of the vowels [a], [i] and [u]*

power in different frequency bands; without such a "pre-emphasis," more of the upper part of the figure would have been white.

Figure 17.15 shows steady vowels as well as the transitions between them. The steady state of the vowel [a] is visible between 0 and 1 seconds: its first formant (F1) is given by the dark band at 700 Hz, its second formant (F2) by the band at 1,400 Hz, its third formant (F3) by the band at 2,600 Hz, and its fourth formant (F4) by the band at 3,800 Hz. The steady state of [i] lies between 3 and 4 seconds; its F1 is seen as a strong band at 300 Hz, its F2 as a weaker band at 2,300 Hz, and its F3 and F4 together form a band at 3,100 Hz. How this state of affairs comes about is betrayed by the transition between 1 and 3 seconds: we see F2 rise and F3 fall, until they fall together at 2 seconds; after this, the original F2 (now by definition called F3) continues to rise above the original F3 (now by definition called F2), until it hits F4 just before 3 seconds. This crossing is repeated at the end of [i]: at 4 seconds F3 starts to fall, and it crosses F2 at 4.5 seconds (2,300 Hz), thereby becoming the new F2 by definition. F2 continues to fall until it reaches 700 Hz at 6.5 seconds, where the steady state of [u] starts. The resonance that falls from 3,100 to 700 Hz corresponds to the size of the cavity in front of the oral constriction: this cavity is small for [i], which has a pre-palatal constriction, and large for [u], which has a velar constriction. For details on how formant values relate to cavities, see Fant (1960) and Stevens (1998).

It can be seen by comparing Figure 17.15 with Figures 17.1 to 17.5 that the formants of vowels are much easier to read from the spectrogram than from the waveform, not only because in the waveform the formants tend to be mingled (Figure 17.4), but also because when zooming out to several seconds the formants continue to be visible in the spectrogram (Figure 17.15) but not in the waveform (Figure 17.5).

6.3   Other spectrograms

Figure 17.16 shows the spectrogram of the sound [ʂʃɕsʂsɕʃʂ] – that is, a dynamic sibilant whose spectral center of gravity rises from the lowest to the highest possible value and falls back again. The frequency range on the vertical axis is larger in Figure 17.16 than in Figure 17.15, since energy is concentrated at higher frequencies for fricatives than for vowels; a display depicting up to 5,000 Hz only would fail to show most of the spectral energy for [sʂs] at the center of Figure 17.16.

As in the case of the vowels, we see here not only the steady states, but especially the dynamic changes in the sound that result from the continuous movements of the articulators. The dynamic acoustics of the plosive of Figure 17.6 and the trill of Figure 17.8 are in Figures 17.17 and 17.18, respectively.

In Figure 17.17 we see that the first formant of the initial [a] moves down from its steady state of 700 Hz around 0.86 seconds to almost zero at 0.95 seconds. At the same time, F2 and F3 move up and F4 approaches F3 around 3,000 Hz. This closeness of F3 and F4, which is typical for palatals, can be seen even better at 1.12 seconds, where the opposite movements of all four formants can be seen.

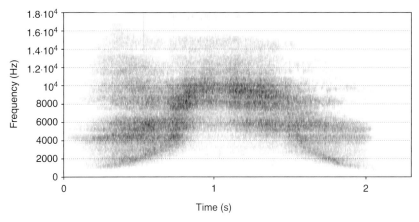

Figure 17.16. *Spectrogram of sibilants*

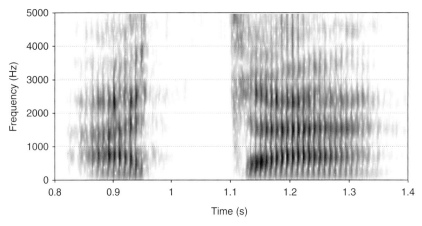

Figure 17.17. *Spectrogram of [aca], showing the four acoustic correlates of the plosive*

Formant transitions like these provide important cues about a consonant's place of articulation. Beside formant transitions, the plosive in Figure 17.17 is also characterized by the silence between 0.95 and 1.1 seconds. Such silences correspond to the closure of the active articulator (in this case, the tongue blade) against the passive articulator (the palate and upper teeth here). Plosives are also characterized by a release burst (around 1.11 seconds in Figure 17.17), which is caused by the sudden release (through a narrow slit) of the pressure that had built up behind the constriction during the closure.

In Figure 17.18 we see the same four tongue-tip closures that we saw in Figure 17.8, as lighter bands around 0.947, 0.985, 1.023, and 1.065 seconds. The closer vertical striping, with a period of about 0.01 seconds, is seen during the vowels before and after the trill and represents glottal fold vibration; this can also be seen in Figure 17.17.

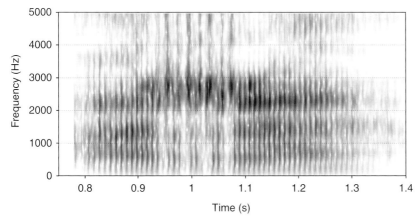

Figure 17.18. *Spectrogram of [ara]*

This section only discussed some basic aspects of the spectrograms of some speech sounds. For more of these, see the introductory textbook by Ladefoged and Disner (2012). For an in-depth treatment of the sounds of the world's languages, see the handbook by Ladefoged and Maddieson (1996). For an in-depth treatment of the causal relationships between articulation and acoustics, see Stevens (1998).

6.4   Limitations of the spectrogram

While the spectrogram visualizes the main acoustic landmarks as a function of time and frequency fairly well, it is not especially strong at visualizing the strengths of these landmarks. This is because these strengths are visualized as grey values, and the capability of the human eye to interpret more than a few different grey values at the same time is moderate. For more precise measurements one can collapse all the times of the spectrogram and obtain an average spectrum, as in Section 5.

7   Formant analysis

In Section 6.2, I discussed how formants, the acoustic landmarks that distinguish vowel quality, can be read from the black bands in the spectrogram. Under some conditions, computer software can help to automate these measurements.

7.1   Automated formant analysis techniques

Most automated formant analysis methods use a reverse all-pole filtering algorithm to extract formants (Burg 1968). This method regards speech production as consisting of a relatively independent *source* and *filter* (Fant 1960). The "source" here is the vocal fold vibration; the "filter" consists of the vocal tract resonances (i.e., the formants), each of which can be seen as a damped sine wave. Helped by a pre-emphasis technique, such as the one described in Section 6.2, to flatten the overall spectral slope, the algorithm manages to separate the source signal from the filter to some extent. The algorithm thereby manages to assign values to as many formants as you, the operator of the automated formant analysis, ask for.

7.2   Applications and limitations of the automated formant analysis

The automated analysis technique just described is notoriously brittle. It works correctly under a number of assumptions, but these assumptions can easily be violated in speech.

One assumption is that the vocal tract can be regarded acoustically as a cascade of resonating filters. This assumption is violated once there are side branches, such as those that appear in nasal consonants, lateral consonants, and nasalized vowels; such articulations cause *zeroes* in the spectrum, and these cannot be approximated well with an all-pole model. This is why automated formant analysis works best for oral vowels and glides, as in Figure 17.19, and is not advisable for nasal or lateral consonants. To be sure, a side branch that is present even in oral vowels is the trachea; for [i]-like vowels it can yield a visible dark band in the spectrogram around 1,500–2,000 Hz (Stevens 1998: 300), which an automated measurement can incorrectly regard as an F2.

Another assumption is that the speech signal can be decomposed into a glottal source signal and a filter signal that represents the influence of the supraglottal vocal tract. This is not necessarily true for small children, whose very light vocal folds may become synchronized to one of the resonances, usually F1. A related

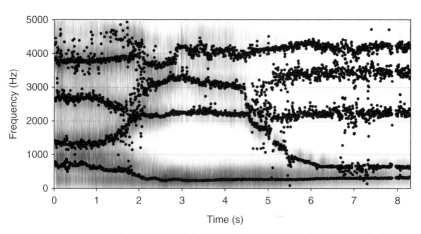

Figure 17.19. *Automated formant measurement in the vowels [a], [i] and [u], superimposed on the spectrogram of Figure 17.15*

requirement of the automated formant measurement method is that the spectral slope of the source is known, so that it can be compensated for; this is necessary because the reverse filtering algorithm can only be performed well on spectrally flat signals – that is, signals where high frequencies are approximately as strong as low frequencies. As vowels on average have a 6 dB/octave falling spectral slope (i.e., high frequencies are weaker than low frequencies), the automated formant measurement method typically applies a pre-emphasis filter before performing the reverse filtering algorithm. This filter emphasizes the high frequencies by applying a 6 dB/octave rising spectral slope from 0 or 50 Hz on, which compensates exactly for the 6 dB/octave falling spectral slope. The assumption of a 6 dB/octave falling spectral slope may work for modal phonation, but it is violated by creaky-voiced phonation and by breathy-voiced phonation.

Yet another assumption is that the length of the vocal tract is known. The reverse filtering algorithm has to be told how many formants it has to find below what maximum formant frequency. For female voices it is advisable to ask for five formants between 0 and 5,500 Hz, whereas for male voices the maximum formant frequency should be 5,000 Hz instead. These maximum frequencies depend on the length of the vocal tract, with 5,000 Hz assuming a vocal tract length of 340 meters per second (the speed of sound) divided by 5,000 Hz (the maximum frequency), multiplied by 5 (the number of formants to look for), divided by 2, which makes 17 cm. However, using a constant number of 5,500 Hz, for example, for all a person's vowels, assumes that the vocal tract length is the same for all vowels spoken by that person. This assumption is generally not met: Escudero et al. (2009) find that the maximum frequency for [i], a vowel that shortens the vocal tract, should be 700 Hz higher than the maximum frequency for [u], a vowel that lengthens the vocal tract.

Asking for five formants is necessary even if you are interested only in F1 and F2, because if you ask for only two formants the algorithm will distribute those two formants over the whole range, from 0 to 5,500 or 5,000 Hz. Asking for two formants between 0 and 2,200 or 2,000 Hz does not work either, because F2 tends to fluctuate heavily with articulation; that is why you want to measure F2 in the first place. As the fifth and higher formants do not depend on articulation too much (except for the vocal tract shortening and lengthening effects mentioned above), and formants above the 5th or 6th may be absent from the signal because of source or recording restrictions, it is usual to ask the automated measurement method for five formants.

If after reading these cautionary lines the reader can still trust automated formant analysis for his or her applications, then he or she is invited to go ahead with it. As automated formant measurement is by far the most commonly used method for acoustically analyzing vowel quality, the method can certainly make your vowel quality data comparable with data published by others. To enhance reliability, you are advised to take multiple measurements and then to take the median of the measured values, so that the influence of gross measurement errors is minimized.

8   Conclusion

This chapter has explained how you can measure acoustic properties of speech signals by hand. This is certainly a feasible line of approach if the number of sounds to be measured is limited. For larger datasets, acoustic analysis can be automated by annotating landmarks in the acoustic signal (e.g., the start and end points of a vowel) and using "scripts" in the analysis software to extract the needed acoustic measures (e.g., the first and second formant at the vowel midpoint). A discussion of such procedures lies beyond the scope of this chapter, but the internet provides many resources for this purpose, including tutorials on how to write scripts, as well as existing scripts that can be modified to obtain the measures needed for your specific project. Please consult the companion website for this volume for further details and links to such resources.

This short chapter has not been able to explain everything there is to know about acoustic measurements. For a very readable introduction, see Ladefoged and Disner (2012). For a handbook on the sounds of the world's languages, see Ladefoged and Maddieson (1996). For a technical overview, see Stevens (1998). There is also a wealth of literature on detailed acoustic correlates of many speech sounds and prosodic structures.

References

Boersma, P. 1993. Accurate short-term analysis of the fundamental frequency and the harmonics-to-noise ratio of a sampled sound. *Proceedings of the Institute of Phonetic Sciences (University of Amsterdam)* 17: 97–110.

2009. Should jitter be measured by peak picking or by waveform matching? *Folia Phoniatrica et Logopaedica* 61: 305–8.

Boersma, P. and D. Weenink. 1992–2012. Praat: doing phonetics by computer. Computer program available at: www.praat.org (accessed July 1, 2013).

Burg, J. P. 1968. A new analysis technique for time series data. In D. G. Childers, ed. *Modern Spectrum Analysis*. New York: IEEE Press, 42–8.

Deliyski, D. D., H. S. Shaw, and M. K. Evans. 2005. Adverse effects of environmental noise on acoustic voice quality measurements. *Journal of Voice* 19: 15–28.

Escudero, P., P. Boersma, A. S. Rauber, and R. A. H. Bion. 2009. A cross-dialect acoustic description of vowels: Brazilian and European Portuguese. *Journal of the Acoustical Society of America* 126: 1379–93.

Fant, G. 1960. *Acoustic Theory of Speech Production*. The Hague: Mouton de Gruyter.

Fourier, J. B. J. 1822. *Théorie analytique de la chaleur*. Paris: Chez Firmin Didot, père et fils.

Ladefoged, P. and I. Maddieson. 1996. *The Sounds of the World's Languages*. Malden, MA and Oxford: Blackwell.

Ladefoged, P. and S. Disner. 2012. *Vowels and Consonants*. 3rd edition. Malden, MA and Oxford: Blackwell.

Stevens, K. N. 1998. *Acoustic Phonetics*. Cambridge, MA and London: MIT Press.

Talkin, D. T. 1995. A robust algorithm for pitch tracking. In W. B. Kleijn and K. K. Paliwal, eds. *Speech Coding and Synthesis*. Amsterdam: Elsevier, 495–518.

18   Constructing and supporting a linguistic analysis

John Beavers and Peter Sells

1   Introduction

In this chapter, we discuss the notion and practice of "making an argument" in generative linguistics, taking examples from phonology, morphology, and syntax. Argumentation is central in linguistics, yet there are few explicit and thorough accounts of what it is to make an argument (though see Soames and Perlmutter 1979; Aarts 2001; Green and Morgan 2001; Kertész and Rákosi 2012 for argumentation in syntax). Our goal here is not to present a general philosophical discussion of argumentation, but rather to present the concept as it is typically practiced in linguistics. Through this, we will provide an overview of how to construct a linguistic analysis and support it. The chapter is structured as follows: we first outline how an argument is typically formulated, in abstract terms, based on the notion of supporting a hypothesis more generally. We then discuss various case studies of arguing for hypotheses of different degrees of abstraction, ranging from empirical arguments to theoretical arguments. We conclude with some discussion of writing style in argumentation.

2   Making an argument in linguistics

Making an argument is a creative exercise, to develop and motivate a hypothesis which provides some insight into some set of facts. There are a few linguists whose work has come to be associated with a strong emphasis on argumentation. David Perlmutter is one, and he writes in the introduction to Perlmutter 2010 (xx):

> I have tried to emphasize four things in my work in linguistics: explicit arguments for one hypothesis over others, extending the range of languages and phenomena for which linguistic theory is to be held accountable, making explicit the ways languages differ and the ways they are alike, and explanation in linguistics. All four were already present in my 1968 doctoral dissertation (Perlmutter 1971), especially in the chapter arguing for surface structure constraints on the order of clitic pronouns in Spanish and French (Perlmutter 1970b) [Perlmutter 1970].

This chapter has benefited from comments from Beth Levin, Scott Myers, Maria Polinsky, Devyani Sharma, and two anonymous reviewers.

> In writing that chapter, I was teaching myself how to do linguistics. I was learning how to construct alternative hypotheses and test their predictions against additional data. I discovered that the question of how such a surface structure constraint is to be formulated covered a range of issues, each statable as a separate hypothesis on which evidence could be brought to bear.

In this classic kind of argument discussed by Perlmutter, we are comparing two alternative hypotheses on empirical grounds. One – call it H – makes predictions which are supported by the data, and the other – call it H' – makes predictions which are not. From this, we conclude that H' is disconfirmed and in relative terms H is superior. It is not enough simply to show that H is compatible with the data; it must also be shown that an alternative H' is not. Thus at its heart an empirical linguistic argument in this style involves the four components listed below, where H and H' lead to different predictions relative to some data (see Larson 2010: 169ff.):

a.   A specific, clear statement of H that is to be argued for
b.   A description of the set of data that H is meant to account for
c.   A clear explanation of how H accounts for the patterns described in the data
d.   A comparison of H to some clearly articulated H', which shows H superior to H'.

H can be as simple as a surface-level generalization of basic linguistic categorization (e.g., some sequence is a constituent) or a more complex theoretical hypothesis (e.g., segments showing a voiced/voiceless alternation are underlyingly voiceless). The data description must be such that it outlines exactly the patterns within the data to be explained, while not deviating into unnecessary aspects of the data, so that a reader knows exactly what to pay attention to and what the scope of H is. Components (c) and (d) involve demonstrating clearly how H accounts for the data and, crucially, that the alternative H' does not. Indeed, the choice of H or H' may not be independent of one another – H may be developed specifically to respond to a prediction of some known H' or vice versa, or they may be developed in tandem to explore some specific difference in predictions. In the rest of this section, we dissect these components of an argument. This schema as such is not unique to linguistics – it is applicable to any empirical argument – but as we proceed we will focus on aspects of such arguments which are specific to linguistics, or at least commonly used in the field.

2.1   Using data as the basis of an argument and deriving predictions

In making an argument it is necessary first to establish what the pattern of fact is, and for that we must define what constitutes data. A piece of data in (generative) linguistics is a string – anything from a sound or sound sequence up to an entire discourse – whose validity in the language is shown either through (a) its existence in a corpus (by which it is assumed therefore to be acceptable to native speakers) or (b) an associated judgment provided by a native speaker regarding its acceptability or interpretation (or possibly other judgments, such as whether it is zeugmatic, stylistically appropriate, etc.). For example, it is linguistic data that English syllable structure allows the two-consonant sequences of voiceless stop plus liquid in (1a), where all are well formed except */tl/, and that, of those, only a subset may appear in three-consonant sequences, as shown in (1b).

(1)   a. pr, tr, kr, pl, *tl, kl
           b. spr, str, skr, spl, *stl, *skl

Syntax data might include sentences showing some word order pattern of a language. For example, (2) shows that an auxiliary verb such as *has* can occur either after the subject, as in (2a), or sentence-initially, as in (2b).

(2)   a. David has seen every movie about penguins.
           b. Has David seen every movie about penguins?

Crucial to much work in linguistics in the generative era is the fundamental insight in Chomsky's work that not just strings themselves but associated native speaker intuitions constitute data, and most particularly that *un*acceptable strings – those which native speakers regard as not conforming to their expectations about natural language use – also count as valid data. For instance, (2c) shows us something more about the distribution of auxiliaries, namely that they may not appear immediately after the main verb.

(2)   c. *David seen has every movie about penguins.

Acceptable data tell us what is possible in a language; unacceptable data tell us what is not (see Chapter 3 for a discussion of judgment data). A good hypothesis should have the potential to explain both kinds of facts.

The next component of the argument is the main hypothesis H, which should not only apply to the data, but also offer potential insight into the patterns in the data. In particular, the goal of H is to explain the judgment patterns for the data in terms of other features, typically by making appeal to its surface properties (e.g., which kinds of segments can be adjacent, where certain words can appear within phrases), as well as more abstract entities (e.g., phonemes, morphemes, constituents, null markers such as the plural of *sheep*) or principles (e.g., subject–verb agreement) that are hypothesized to reflect aspects of the language faculty even if not apparent on the surface. H itself can be at any level of abstraction – a relatively surface-level hypothesis about the distribution of basic linguistic elements, or a highly abstract hypothesis regarding a complex interaction of subtle principles.

But one key aspect of any good hypothesis is that H should be stated in some way that makes crystal clear why the patterns in the data should be the way they are, due to expectations H generates about possible and impossible data. These expectations should follow from the way H is stated, either because H is embedded within some given framework or references some more basic linguistic concepts that make those expectations clear. Even if independent of any framework, H should be stated in a way that makes some expectations clear. Those expectations constitute the predictions H makes, and unless they are clear, it will be impossible to determine (a) whether it actually says anything about the data at all and (b) whether H is superior to any alternative hypothesis. Furthermore, only if hypotheses make different predictions can they be compared empirically (see the second part of the quote from Perlmutter above). As Carlson (2003) notes, what linguists mean by the term "prediction" is precisely the test against additional data, with the hypothesis in mind; the data may in fact already be established and well known, but the key point is that the coverage of the hypothesis scales up from an initial set of facts to a wider set of facts.

Deriving a hypothesis and stating it clearly is something of an art, as we will try to illustrate with an example. Consider again (2a–b), and let us suppose that we have some antecedent definition or classification of the English auxiliary verbs. First, we observe that the auxiliary is not in initial position in (2a), and is in (2b) – that is, it has some property in (2b) which it lacks in (2a) (which instead has a different positional property of the auxiliary).[1] We can see further that this positional distinction corresponds to a semantic distinction: (2b) is a matrix polar interrogative clause (a "yes/no question"), while (2a) is a matrix declarative clause. Finally, importantly, there is not any other obviously differing property between the two examples (i.e., they are a minimal pair differing just in the feature under consideration). There are of course other interesting things about these data – the interpretation of the quantifier *every* or the irregular inflection on *see* – but for our purposes we have identified a correlation in need of explanation, and as long as these other observations are identical in both tokens of data, they are not germane to the central point.

> Hypothesis 1: If an English main clause is a polar interrogative, then the first word in that clause is an auxiliary verb.

This hypothesis is established in such a way as to be testable. First, it immediately – and correctly – predicts that (2b), which is an interrogative, has an initial auxiliary. The hypothesis embodies a generalization about a potentially large set of data, but it has been created based on a very small sample of data so far. To further validate hypothesis 1 we must look for more examples, specifically more interrogative clauses. We need to see how they are formed, paying particular attention to the first word (doing so will confirm or disconfirm the generalization which underlies the hypothesis). Conversely, we might consider various other auxiliaries, and look for examples where they are in initial position:

(3)   a. Will David speak to Kim?
        b. Can David sing "Goodnight Sweetheart Goodnight?"
        c. Did David forget his mother's birthday?

---

[1] This observation and the subsequent argument rest on the ancillary assumption that the category of auxiliary verb is independently identifiable, something that would ultimately need to be argued for.

These data are again interrogatives, and since they have initial auxiliaries, the hypothesis is again confirmed. Crucially, though, the prediction of (3) is *not* that all examples with initial auxiliaries are polar interrogatives, but rather that all polar interrogatives have initial auxiliaries. Thus some examples with initial auxiliaries may not be polar interrogatives. Further data shows this to be so (e.g., curses like *May all your hair fall out at an inopportune moment!*). It is thus important to consider carefully what *exact* predictions any given hypothesis makes – in this case, these additional factors follow from the shape of the hypothesis as a one-way implication (*if . . . then . . .*), a formulation that helps sharpen what predictions are made. Still further, from the way that hypothesis 1 is stated, we can also consider its contrapositive: if the first word in a clause is *not* an auxiliary verb, then the clause should *not* be a polar interrogative. This certainly holds for (2a), and we can look for other examples in which this obtains:

(4)   a. David will speak to Kim.
         b. David can sing "Goodnight Sweetheart Goodnight."
         c. David did forget his mother's birthday.

Here the interpretation is that these sentences are not interrogatives, again consistent with hypothesis 1.

So far, hypothesis 1 is stated in such a way as to make its empirical predictions clear, in particular because it is linked to surface-level properties of the data (illocutionary force, auxiliary position) relatively directly, in ways that make clear *exactly* what data to look for and why. An alternative would be to embed the hypothesis in a theoretical framework that would derive the same predictions. For example, in one version of Minimalist syntax terminology (Adger 2003), an auxiliary in the node T(Tense) will move to the position C (Complementizer) in polar interrogatives triggered by a featural interaction between the C position and the auxiliary verb in T, involving the interrogative feature Q (for "question"). In such a framework, hypothesis 1 could be stated as follows:

> Hypothesis 2:   English polar interrogative C has a Q feature which checks an uninterpretable, unvalued clause type feature [*u*clause-type:] on T.

In the absence of any context for what these notions mean, this hypothesis is not well formulated. But if the relevant framework is assumed – and its predictions are known or made clear – hypothesis 2 should amount to saying the same thing as hypothesis 1.

Nonetheless, a commonly made misstep at this point is simply to assert the correctness of hypothesis 1. Yet one part of the reasoning has not been completed: all we have shown so far is that hypothesis 1 is compatible with the given data. We have not yet *argued for* hypothesis 1, since it has not been compared to any alternative and shown to be superior. We turn to this next.

2.2   Completing the argument

Comparing the proposed hypothesis H to alternative hypotheses is crucial to a complete argument. It is not sufficient simply to show that H *can* serve as an analysis of some set of data; other hypotheses may be just as good as H. Rather, the goal is to show that H is a *preferable* analysis, which can only be done in comparison to other hypotheses. Regarding the development of alternative hypothesis H', suppose H itself is an initial hypothesis in the absence of any previous one. In this case H' might well be the null hypothesis (sometimes thus labeled H$_0$; see Chapter 15) – most generally that no particular hypothesis at all, or some default hypothesis, is to be entertained. In the teaching of many basic aspects of linguistic analysis, this style of argumentation is used. For instance, H might be the hypothesis that segments are organized into syllables or that words are organized into constituents. H' will be the hypothesis that these units of analysis do not exist.

Consider again the polar interrogative analysis above. Although hypothesis 1 certainly accounts for the data, to complete the argument we should at least make clear that had we assumed no hypothesis regarding the relationship of polar interrogatives to auxiliary position – the null hypothesis – the prediction would be that there is no correlation of auxiliary position and interpretation, with both interrogatives and declaratives found among sentences both with and without initial auxiliaries, contrary to fact.[2] Given that the null hypothesis fails, we now have an *argument* for the potential correctness of hypothesis 1.

In more advanced argumentation, we might adopt a more specific H' to compare H to. In this case, H' should be articulated at least to the same degree as H, but be formulated so as to make different predictions. We will then demonstrate that H covers the initial data while H' does not, or that they cover the same initial data, but there is additional data that H covers but not H'. In this case, H' is often determined by the context in which the argument is being made: H' might be a known prior analysis of the same initial facts, a hypothesis about related facts in another language, or just some novel alternative that seems "obvious" on the basis of the initial data, even if ultimately wrong.

For example, in some languages (such as modern Romance languages), a polar interrogative can be formed by placing not just an auxiliary but *any* inflected verb initially. Interestingly, on the basis of the above data, this hypothesis would work just as well for English:

> Hypothesis 3:   If an English main clause is a polar interrogative, then the first word in that clause is a verb.

In other words, we have not yet probed the role of the word "auxiliary" in hypothesis 1, as we have not yet considered examples with non-auxiliary verbs

---

[2] If this is not clear, consider the distribution of main verbs, which shows no correlation with the interpretation of the clause. Thus for any given position of the main verb (second, third, last), there is no expectation that the clause would be declarative or interrogative.

in them. So, if hypothesis 1 is correct and 3 is not, it will be the case that examples parallel to those in (3), but with a non-auxiliary verb in the initial position, will not be polar interrogatives. This is a testable prediction, for which we need examples such as those in (5).

(5)   a. *Spoke David to Kim.
        b. *Sings David "Goodnight Sweetheart Goodnight".
        c. *Forgot David his mother's birthday.

Such examples are not only not polar interrogatives, they are not possible senten-ces at all, disconfirming hypothesis 3 and supporting hypothesis 1.

We should add here a cautionary note. It is simple enough to disprove H' on the basis of incorrect predictions it makes, and to show that H makes correct pre-dictions. It is quite another matter to have "proved" that H is the right hypothesis. There may be other data out there somewhere that will invalidate H, or perhaps there will be a still better formulation of H which relates an additional set of data to the old data that had never previously been considered together. Thus the best that one can reasonably do in an argument – and thus the importance of comparison – is to show that H is the best hypothesis under consideration.

Furthermore, regarding data, it is often the case that the data may be naturally split into two (or more) subsets, for various reasons, although this is not strictly necessary. The first set may be considered the data under discussion – that is, the particular phenomenon that is specifically to be analyzed and for which H is primarily responsible for explaining. A second set of data that falls outside of this particular domain may be introduced as being relevant for "additional predictions" that H makes, thus providing further support for H – that is, the new data suggest that H is independently motivated, and is thus "on the right track." The way in which the data are split may depend on the specific hypotheses being compared, but some general heuristics are listed below:

a.   The initial dataset forms some unified domain – a class of words, a class of constructions, a set of examples illustrating an alternation of two or more forms, etc. The additional predictions constitute a differ-ent domain.

b.   The initial data reflect predictions that are more straightforward, super-ficial, or stronger, while the additional predictions are more subtle, weaker, or require more work to demonstrate, or perhaps are just inherently more complicated in some way.

c.   The initial data are known or largely known through prior literature, or show strong plausible similarities to known data, while the additional predictions are new facts which specifically support H (and not H').

For example, the data in (1) above partition naturally, simply because of the forms in question. And in comparing hypotheses 1 and 3 for English polar interrogative formation, the "additional predictions" in (5) conformed to (c) above, in that they were chosen on the basis of the formulation of H' so as to demonstrate that H' was not supported but H was. There are no hard-and-fast rules for how one presents the core data and how one decides what to call "additional" predictions, and it is always possible, of course, simply to lump all of the data together. However, it will often be that a division such as this can provide for a more streamlined overall argument, and even add a certain rhetorical flourish if the additional predictions are particularly impressive, subtle, or dramatic.

Finally, although we have focused on empirical arguments here, there are other, more conceptual arguments that can be made for hypothesis H over H'. It may be that both are empirically identical, but H is more intuitive, simpler, or more elegant, or involves fewer abstractions, or is otherwise preferred on conceptual grounds. Such arguments are also prized in some areas of linguistics, especially in the context of theoretical a prioris (see Sections 3.2. and 4.3). Yet the ultimate core of any linguistic hypothesis is its empirical coverage, and with the basic schema for an argument outlined here as background, we now consider several types of arguments that are in this mold. The main differences in our examples are, in each case, how abstract the hypothesis is, and thus what kinds of predictions are determined by the hypotheses and what sorts of data and alternatives are to be considered, although we will also discuss some more conceptual, non-empirical arguments as well.

3   Different types of simple hypotheses and their arguments

There are different kinds of hypotheses and associated arguments that linguists make. Some of the simplest – often needed to build more complex arguments – are those that establish the descriptive base of linguistics – that is, the "facts" of language. These arguments often involve basic linguistic categorization – that is, supporting the hypothesis that some string(s) belong to some category known to exhibit certain properties. The categories may be given by theoretical assumption, or may be more traditional categories like "phoneme" or "direct object." Such arguments typically rely on two major types of empirical evidence: contrast and distribution, though such arguments – and indeed almost all arguments – will likely also involve ancillary assumptions to frame the key issues, as with the arguments given above involving English auxiliary verbs. As arguments for basic categorization are among the simplest, we start with them, before turning to arguments based on naturalness and simplicity.

3.1   Argument based in contrast and distribution

Perhaps the most basic notion in linguistics is that of contrast, due to de Saussure (1959) (originally published in French in 1916), the principle by which we can discover the fundamental properties of linguistic systems, of linguistic structures, or of any other kind of linguistic expression. In many cases, the excitement and interest in linguistic study stems from the fact that it is not immediately clear which elements contrast, or how, and therefore this must be discovered. Stated in the most general terms, the way we make linguistic discoveries is quite abstract, but it is important to try to encapsulate what it is to reason with linguistic data. In order to make an argument that some string has a property P, we must be able to conceive of another string just like it but without P, or with a different property Q. Then, within the context of some analytic assumptions or a more specific theoretical system, we must hypothesize what kind of system could provide our expression with P, and a variation within the same system where it lacks P or has Q instead. All of our basic data above are interesting precisely because of such contrasts – for example, the segmental data in (1) are of linguistic interest because even within (1a), some logical combinations contrast in acceptability with others, and then compared to (1b), there is yet a different contrast.

3.1.1   Basic categorization

Basic linguistic categorization and the utility of contrast and distribution can be illustrated in terms of the English phonemic inventory, where two phones represent separate phonemes if and only if they contrast meaningfully in a language. The hypothesis that two phones are separate phonemes can be argued for by direct appeal to the definition of a phoneme, which provides an empirical "test": we must find a single context where the only differing factor is those phones (i.e., a minimal pair) and then evaluate whether a meaning contrast arises. If no such minimal pairs exist, the phones cannot be shown to contrast phonemically by this method, and are most likely allophones or variants of the same phoneme (i.e., different surface expressions of a single element in the sound system of the language; though see Section 3.1.2.).

For instance, an argument that /s/ and /z/ contrast phonemically can be based on one pair, as in (6).

(6)   a. sip
        b. zip

These data form a minimal pair, differing in one segment, and in fact differ in only one feature, [–voice] for *sip* and [+voice] for *zip* in their initial segments. This featural difference in turn corresponds to a semantic difference (a small drink vs a fast movement) – that is, it is a "difference which makes a difference" (Bateson 1972). On the basis of this simple argument, we can conclude that /s/ and /z/ contrast phonemically. The null hypothesis, that they do not, would be unable to explain the contrast in meaning.

On the same definition of a phoneme, the argument that two phones are allophones can be accomplished by one of two procedures. The first is to show that the two phones never form a minimal pair (that they are in complementary distribution, never appearing in the same environments, a distributional fact). The second is to show that if there is a minimal pair, they are not contrastive in meaning. Either argument would suffice, though making both would of course make the conclusion even more convincing. With some creativity, we can apply both tests to a pair of English sounds which are not separate phonemes. As it happens, neither is entirely straightforward, albeit in illustrative ways.

Consider the hypothesis that English [pʰ] and [p] are allophones, for which they are good candidates since they differ in just one feature. By the first test we need a range of data that show that the two phones never occur in the same contexts. Such data might consist of examples such as (7).

(7)   [pʰ]   [p]
        pit   spit
        pun   spun
        pill   spill
        . . .   . . .

From such data one can make a separate argument that to a first approximation, [pʰ] only occurs when initial in a (stressed) syllable and [p] elsewhere. Thus the two phones are in complementary distribution and therefore no minimal pair contrasting in only these phones can be found.[3] One can then argue that the two phones therefore do not contrast phonemically. This argument crucially involved two steps: first arguing for complementarity based on distribution, and then for allophony based on (the lack of) contrast. It is not uncommon that arguments must be "chained" in this way.

Complementarity would appear to render moot the second procedure (finding a non-contrastive minimal pair), thus suggesting that it is the "easier" argument. However, this is not necessarily the case, since the argument could be made based on constructed examples. Starting with the usual pronunciation of *pit* as [pʰɪt] and *spit* as [spɪt], we could create variants [pɪt] and [spʰɪt], with the two phones reversed. These would not be perceived of as semantically distinct from the typical pronunciations, even if somewhat odd to native speakers. Thus minimal pairs can be found, albeit in constructed examples, and there is no semantic contrast, supporting the hypothesis that the two phones are allophones. This argument requires the creative step of hypothesizing what would show the contrast, and then manipulating known data to test for it, another common procedure in linguistic argumentation (see Section 4.). Regardless of the argument(s) put forward, there is support for the hypothesis. The alternative hypothesis, that [p] and [pʰ] are *not* allophones, would incorrectly predict that these constructed contrasts should be meaningful, or that minimal pairs will be found naturally.

3.1.2   Making an informed argument

One aspect of making a linguistic argument that should be highlighted is that only "reasonable" hypotheses should be entertained or introduced. For example, in English, [h] and [ŋ] are in complementary distribution: [h] only

---

[3] See Davis and Cho (2003) for a precise discussion of where aspirated and non-aspirated voiceless stops appear in English.

appears as a syllable onset as in [hæt], and [ŋ] only appears as a syllable coda as in [sæŋ]. By the complementary distribution test outlined above, we appear to have support for a hypothesis that [h] and [ŋ] are allophones. However, while the application of the complementary distribution test is technically correct, the hypothesis itself violates the intuition underlying the concept of a phoneme, wherein non-contrasting forms are considered variants of the *same* sound. In this case [h] and [ŋ] do not share even one articulatory feature in common, unlike [s] and [z], which share all but one. Further, one cannot form a constructed contrast as with *spit* and *pit*: [ŋæt] and [sæh] are barely pronounceable in English, and would never be judged to have the same meanings as [hæt] and [sæŋ]. This again suggests the unreasonableness of the hypothesis.

3.1.3   Dealing with conflicting evidence

There is an important and instructive wrinkle to the argument that English /s/ and /z/ contrast phonemically: the contrast is sometimes neutralized. For instance, the notional plural -*s* for nouns has three surface forms, but these are entirely conditioned by the preceding context:

(8)   a. boot ~ boots [buts] (*[butz])
         b. hood ~ hoods [hʊdz] (*[hʊds])
         c. bus ~ buses [bʌsəz] (*[bʌsəs])

The three allomorphic variants are [s] if the preceding segment is voiceless, [z] if it is voiced, and [əz] if it is a sibilant (an alveolar or palatal fricative, regardless of voicing). Taken at face value, the fact that there is no semantic contrast between (8a) and (8b) in terms of the contribution of the plural morpheme might appear to undermine the argument that /s/ and /z/ contrast phonemically. However, the hypothesis can still be maintained with the caveat that the distinction is neutralized when preceded by an obstruent in the same syllable (due to voicing assimilation, see Section 3.2; note that in our *sip/zip* data the segments were word-initial). This shows that confounding data such as that in (8) may cause one to revise (or ultimately reject) a hypothesis supported by other data, as in (6). Thus while it is strictly true that the original hypothesis that /s/ and /z/ always contrast is "wrong," its essence can be maintained in a revised, more nuanced hypothesis.

More generally, let us think more about ways to deal with conflicting kinds of evidence when constructing an argument. In this and the preceding subsection we see that the apparent conflict can be resolved – that is, factored into different domains which do not directly impinge on each other – through some linguistic sensitivity. For [h] and [ŋ], distributional facts suggest one analysis, yet all phonetic properties suggest another. Here we would take the phonetic evidence to support the hypothesis that /h/ and /ŋ/ are different phonemes, as they cannot plausibly be related in a grammatical description, and seek other ways to account for their non-overlapping distribution. With regard to /s/ and /z/, we can make a different point. If we found any number of minimal pairs in which the two sounds contrast, as in (6), we would have to conclude that these two segments are separate phonemes. There would be no other way to account for the data. Given this, if we were then to find other data in which these two segments do *not* contrast, it *must* be the case that there is some other confounding factor that we have to take into account for a complete hypothesis. In this case, we would identify the preceding phonological context as the environment in which the phonemic contrast is neutralized. The analytic challenge lies in identifying the more general ("elsewhere," default, underspecified) set of properties or behaviors as against a more specialized or conditioned set.

3.1.4   Summary

What we have illustrated here and above are five points relating to contrast and distribution. First, in basic categorization the definitions will often give clues to what tests are needed to argue for the hypothesis that some expression has the given category. Second, sometimes making the argument will require side arguments leading up to it, or involve seeking out novel confirming data. Third, the hypothesis must be intuitively plausible. Fourth, the hypothesis may require sub-cases or caveats; these revisions do not necessarily invalidate the insight conveyed by the hypothesis so much as refine it. Fifth, the argument must be supported by at least one line of argumentation, but ideally more than one if they are available. That said, not every conceivable line of argumentation will be possible, and some tests may fail for independent (yet to be discovered) reasons. Especially in basic categorization, the evidence of an expression belonging to some linguistic category might be thought of as like showing the symptoms of a disease. A patient who goes to a doctor for a diagnosis might display one symptom of a particular disease, but the doctor would ideally want to see multiple symptoms before saying with confidence that the disease has been identified. However, the doctor would not necessarily expect the patient to manifest all possible symptoms – a confluence of at least some evidence is usually sufficient.

3.2   Argument based in parsimony and naturalness

The data in (8) raise yet another interesting issue regarding argumentation. In generative phonology, we consider the plural suffix to have a single phonemic form with three surface realizations. What is the 'underlying' form? Following English spelling, we might take it to be /s/. But we know that spelling is notoriously unreliable, especially in English. Looking at the surface forms in (8), we might alternatively hypothesize that the phonemic form is /z/. How can we compare these two hypotheses? Consider the rule systems that are needed in each case to generate the correct surface forms:

> Hypothesis 4:   The underlying form is /s/, but realize it in the following way:
>> i. after a sibilant, epenthesize ə and undergo voicing assimilation, else
>> ii. after a voiced segment, undergo voicing assimilation, else
>> iii. after a voiceless segment, no change.

Hypothesis 5:   The underlying form is /z/, but realize it in the following way:
i. after a sibilant, epenthesize ə, else
ii. after a voiceless segment, undergo voicing assimilation, else
iii. after a voiced segment, no change.

Either hypothesis can generate all the forms in (8), so it is unlikely that direct empirical evidence will decide between them. However, one can argue for the underlying /z/ hypothesis by looking more closely at the assumptions made. The phonological systems for each hypothesis are nearly the same: the same contexts are relevant and voicing assimilation occurs in each case (albeit in different contexts). However, the sibilant condition differs: underlying /s/ requires two operations (epenthesis followed by assimilation), while underlying /z/ requires just one (epenthesis). Occam's razor dictates that the underlying /z/ hypothesis is preferred, thus constituting an argument for hypothesis 5 over hypothesis 4.

There are other external considerations which might favor one hypothesis over another. For example, a [t]/[θ] alternation in some language may have analyses involving underlying /t/ or underlying /θ/, with both analyses being equally complex. However, the underlying /t/ analysis might be preferred on naturalness grounds, as the segment [t] is found in almost all languages, while [θ] is quite rare, so /t/ would constitute a more "normal" choice for the basis of the analysis (and therefore [θ] would only appear in special environments, as defined by a phonological rule). Although these are not empirical arguments per se (based on the body of data to be analyzed), they illustrate how consideration of elegance, simplicity, and naturalness can constitute an argument for one hypothesis H over its alternatives, when there is more than one empirically equivalent option.

4   More advanced arguments

Above we illustrated arguments of basic linguistic categorization made in terms of contrast and distribution, and also one more abstract argument about an underlying element. We can make arguments for still more abstract types of hypotheses, such as those supporting higher-order statements about basic primitives, those based on hypothesized principles and their interactions, or those that make crucial reference to differing sets of theoretical assumptions. The latter two types of arguments involve embedding the hypothesis within a larger framework of additional assumptions, a more complex procedure that often requires more subtle data or more careful thinking. For example, showing that sentences contain phrases and constituents does not necessarily distinguish between context-free phrase structure rules and X′-theory, both of which capture that fact. Rather, the choice of theoretical framework may make additional predictions that must be carefully deduced and tested for. In fact, the first step in constructing certain more complex arguments is often not showing that something is the case, but rather showing how one would show that something is the case – devising types of hypothetical data (e.g., "If we wanted to show that Japanese has subject–verb agreement, we would have to . . .") – and only then, as a second step, actually doing it, if even possible.[4] Still further, some generalizations may be difficult or even impossible to state unless one adopts a particular set of theoretical assumptions. We turn to specific examples of these sorts of more complex arguments next.

4.1   Argument based in abstract properties

We consider first an extended example that looks at generalizations that go beyond surface-level properties (albeit still rooted in basic linguistic categorization), and show how one can derive predictions from such hypotheses which are formulated so as to guide us into looking for appropriate data to argue for them, as well as reformulate them for accuracy as new data arises.

Another key innovation introduced by Chomsky (1957) was his demonstration that surface constituency and distributional properties alone do not capture the full range of language "facts." He argued that while the string in (9a) follows all the grammatical rules of English word and constituent order, it has two interpretations, shown in (9b, c).

(9)   a. The chicken is ready to eat.
         b. The chicken is ready for us to eat (it).
         c. The chicken is ready to start eating (its food).

In (9c), the chicken is understood as the eater, while in (9b) it is understood as the thing eaten. Moreover, as Chomsky showed, not all adjectives show this flexibility. Chomsky's (1964: 34) famous illustration is given in (10a) and (10b), illustrating different adjectives which each have only one interpretation, corresponding to (9b) and (9c) respectively.

(10)   a. John is easy to please.
         b. John is eager to please.

In (10a) John is the one pleased, but in (10b) he is the one pleasing, and neither example is ambiguous. Other adjectives behave the same (e.g., *apt*, *preparing*, and *likely* behave like *eager*; *tough*, *hard*, and *impossible* are like *easy*). As the only superficial difference in (10) is *easy* vs *eager*, we take it that the semantic difference is due to the difference in adjectives, but is somehow "below the surface," ultimately, in this case, connected to a syntactic distinction. When considering the empirical predictions of abstract syntactic hypotheses, there are two primary ways in which a minimal pair of superficially similar syntactic examples might differ:

a.   Both examples are grammatical, but they differ in the ways that their semantics are assigned (as in the examples above), as determined by their syntax.

b.   One example is grammatical and one is ungrammatical.

---

[4] In psychology, it is possible to construct an experiment in any kind of artificial condition to test an abstract idea. In linguistics, this is much harder, as one cannot rely on finding a language with the necessary properties.

Note that we have to control for each type of difference by looking at the other. For instance, (10a) has a variant (11), which is essentially synonymous.

(11)   It is easy to please John.

However, consider the corresponding variant of (10b):

(12)   It is eager to please John.

Think for a moment and you will notice that in this example the subject *it* has to be taken to signify an animal, or perhaps a robot – some specific thing that can be referred to by *it*. The meaning of the example is thus quite different from (10b), so that the difference between (11) and (12) is a difference of type (a). Conversely, we can also say that (12) cannot have the same sort of meaning as (11), and therefore *on that interpretation* it is unacceptable:

(13)   *It is eager to please John. (on the intended interpretation)

Controlling for the intended interpretation means that we actually have a contrast of type (b).[5] With that caveat, Chomsky's innovations allow us to consider arguments based on observations of type (a) to show different abstract properties about grammatical structure, and arguments based on observations of type (b) to show that one example falls within the grammatical system of the language in question and another falls outside.

   What grammatical principle could explain the data in (10)? In a sense, this is not different than basic categorization; the key is to develop a hypothesis that offers insight into the pattern and also generates further predictions that can be verified (i.e., one that "does some work"). The difference is just that the hypothesis may be more abstract. One way to analyze (10) is by appeal to the grammatical relationship between each adjective and the following infinitival verb. In (10a, b) *John* is the one pleased and the pleaser respectively, which correspond to the normal subject and object of *please*, a simple transitive verb (e.g., *John pleased Mary*). We can thus hypothesize that *John* is interpreted as the object of *please* in (10a), but as the subject of *please* in (10b):

> Hypothesis 6:   In a construction of the form NP *be* Adj *to* VP:
> a. Adj *easy* requires its subject NP to be understood as the object of the infinitival VP.
> b. Adj *eager* requires its subject NP to be understood as the subject of the infinitival VP.

Implicit in this is another property which we could just as well make explicit, namely that *easy* will never behave as in (b) and *eager* never as in (a):

---

[5] This is the same kind of observation that is made in even the most rudimentary arguments. For instance, when we categorize English as a fixed constituent order language, we might note that the examples *A dog bites a man* and *A man bites a dog* have different meanings. Strictly speaking, we are arguing that the grammar of English does not support a meaning of the second example in which a dog bites a man. That is, if we hold the meaning constant (to be that of the first example) the second example *is unacceptable on the intended interpretation*.

       c. The two adjectives differ in these properties: *easy* does not appear in the structure described by (b), and *eager* does not appear in the structure described by (a).

In hypothesis 6, we are appealing to notions that are not obvious on the surface: subject and object and the idea of one predicate "sharing" its subject or object with another. However, these notions are largely issues of basic linguistic categorization, and can be demonstrated by first demonstrating through contrast and distribution that the relevant noun phrases are subjects or objects. As long as we accept the assumption that the relevant noun phrases have these grammatical functions, we can begin to seek out evidence that the abstract hypothesis set out above is correct. The key will be in how we derive predictions from the hypothesis to test it out. We now look at three very simple such predictions.

     Prediction 1: The role of semantics   Although our original description of (10) appealed to semantic roles (e.g., "pleaser," "one pleased"), hypothesis 6 instead refers to grammatical functions (subject, object) associated with these roles. If we distinguish these – as we should – then technically we will have the prediction that actual semantic roles should not matter: swapping out VPs with other transitive verbs that assign different semantic roles to their subjects and objects should also yield grammatical sentences, even if the meanings differ. This is indeed the case:

(14)   a. John is easy to fight.
          b. John is eager to fight.

These data thus clarify that we indeed have a contrast of type (a), and had we tied the hypothesis to a different type of underlying category (e.g., thematic roles like "experiencer" and "stimulus") we might have made different predictions.

     Prediction 2: Monadic intransitive verbs   By associating the subject of *easy* with the object of the infinitival VP, hypothesis 7a predicts that the VP must allow an object in the first place. We can test for this by trying out verbs in the VP complement of *easy* that do not have objects. We would then predict that an example formed with *easy* would be ungrammatical, as it could not satisfy hypothesis 6, while the corresponding example with *eager* should be grammatical, as the VP would still have a subject for the subject of *eager* to be construed with. We demonstrate this by simply constructing the relevant examples:

(15)   a. *John is easy to run away.
          b. John is eager to run away.

Here we have a contrast of type (b), and, more importantly, it is predicted to exist on the basis of hypothesis 6. Thus the data support hypothesis 6, and hypothesis 6 offers an insight into *why* such a contrast exists.

Prediction 3: A different type of intransitive verb   The intransitive we considered above had only one argument, a subject. But hypothesis 6 also predicts that verbs lacking objects but taking PP complements should similarly not appear with *easy*. As it happens, this prediction is not borne out:

(16)   John is easy to talk to.

Given that hypothesis 7 has so far predicted several pieces of data, at this point we would not necessarily want to discard it entirely, but rather look for a revision that can capture the datum in (16) as well. Perhaps what (16) indicates is that while the subject of *eager* is understood as the subject of the infinitival VP, the subject of *easy* relates to a non-subject phrase within the VP:

> Hypothesis 7:   In a construction of the form NP *be* Adj *to* VP:
>   a.   Adj *easy* requires its subject NP to be understood as a non-subject of the infinitival VP.
>   b.   Adj *eager* requires its subject NP to be understood as the subject of the infinitival VP.

The two adjectives differ in these properties: *easy* does not appear in the structure described by (b), and *eager* does not appear in the structure described by (a). The revision in hypothesis 7 captures an insight similar to hypothesis 6 and captures all of the data hypothesis 6 did, but gives a better account for the new data. This again illustrates the comparative nature of argumentation – the old hypothesis was rejected in favor of a newer hypothesis that better captures some set of data beyond our initial data.

   Building on hypothesis 8, we now have a prediction that it should be possible to "rescue" (15a) from ungrammaticality by creating a variant which is grammatical due to an additional place within the VP with which the subject of *easy* can be construed. This prediction is borne out:

(17)   John is easy to run away from.

Given our hypothesis, this is expected and, crucially, we understand why (17) is grammatical: there is a syntactic position, namely the object of *from*, with which the subject *John* is construed. This is not the object of a verb, as in (10a) with *please*, but it is, crucially, not a subject.

4.2   Argument based in interactions of principles

   We now consider an example that argues for an abstract principle of grammar. The argument is based on how a set of abstract principles interact with one another. Perlmutter (1978) introduced the Unaccusative Hypothesis (UH), which is built on the idea that there are two kinds of intransitive verbs (see also Burzio 1986). "Unergative" verbs are intransitives whose single argument is agent-like and has the deep grammatical properties of the subject of a transitive verb, while "unaccusative" verbs are intransitives whose single argument is patient-like and has the deep grammatical properties of the object of a transitive verb.

> Hypothesis 8: The Unaccusative Hypothesis (initial) – There are two types of intransitives:
> a. Unergatives take an agent-like argument with the grammatical properties of a subject.
> b. Unaccusatives take a patient-like argument with the grammatical properties of an object.

The UH represents a fairly stable cross-linguistic classification, and differences between the two types of intransitives can be found in many languages. One example is how they interact with the formation of impersonal passives (i.e., passives of intransitive verbs), as found in Dutch. The impersonal passive of the putatively unergative example in (18a) is given in (18b); (18c) is an example with another unergative (from Perlmutter 1978: 168).

(18) a. De   jonge   lui   dansten   hier   veel.
          the   young   people   danced   here   a.lot
          'The young people danced here a lot.'

      b. Er wordt hier door de   jonge lui   veel   gedanst.
          it   is   here   by   the young people a.lot   danced
          'It is danced here a lot by the young people.'

      c. Er wordt in   deze   kamer vaak   geslapen.
          it   is   in   this   room   often   slept
          'It is often slept in this room.'

In the impersonal passive, the erstwhile subject of the unergative is expressed as a PP, and the subject position is filled with an expletive. However, the putatively unaccusative verbs in (19) do not allow impersonal passives, as shown in (20).

(19) a. Het   water   sijpelde/drippelde   uit   de   rots.
          the   water   seeped/dripped   out   of   rock
          'The water seeped/dripped out of the rock.'

      b. Zulke   dingen   zijn   hier   nooit   gebeurd.
          such   things   are   here   never   happened
          'Such things have never happened here.'

(20) a. * *Er* werd door het   water uit   de   rots   gesijpeld/gedrippeld.
              it   is   by   the   water out of   rock   seeped/dripped

      b. * *Hier* werd er   door zulke   dingen nooit   gebeurd.
               here   is   it   by   such   things   never   happened

What might explain this pattern? Perlmutter claimed it follows from the interaction of several independent principles. First, it is useful to outline the common analysis of a canonical personal passive, in which a notionally transitive verb occurs intransitively and its surface subject corresponds to the object of its transitive form, as illustrated in (21a) and (21b) for English.

(21)   a. The girl read the book.
         b. The book was read by the girl.

It is usually assumed that in personal passive formation the deep object is promoted to surface subject. As subject is taken to be a more prominent grammatical relation than object, passive involves promotion to a "higher rank" – from object to subject (there is also commensurate demotion of the original subject to a PP marked with *by* in English).

With this as background, Perlmutter set out to argue for a particular theoretical hypothesis:

> Hypothesis 9:   In all languages, all passive clauses involve promotion to subject (including impersonal passives).

The key prediction made by his proposal is the pattern in the Dutch data above, but to derive this prediction we have to look at how the UH interacts with other hypotheses. Perlmutter proposed first and foremost to assimilate the analysis of an unaccusative clause to that of passive. It is assumed across most syntactic frameworks that every clause must have a subject, as stated below, and if the underlying properties of the clause do not provide one, some other phrase must be promoted to be the subject.

> Subject Condition: Every clause must have a subject.[6]

If an unaccusative intransitive clause is base-generated with an object but no subject, and if every clause requires a subject, then this guarantees that promotion must take place. Hence, any *actual* clause containing an unaccusative verb will have a subject, albeit one promoted to that function in the course of the derivation of that clause. On the other hand, if the verb is unergative, the subject of the clause has not advanced, for it is already a subject from the initial step of the derivation. From this we can restate the UH as follows:

> Hypothesis 10:   Unaccusative Hypothesis (final) – There are two types of intransitives:
>   a. Unergatives take an agent-like deep subject.
>   b. Unaccusatives take a patient-like deep object.

The combination of the revised UH and the Subject Condition ensures that unaccusatives have single subject arguments that are in some sense also objects (i.e., together they derive hypothesis 8), explaining any independent evidence that unaccusative subjects have some object-like properties.

So far, nothing is explained about the contrast between (18) and (20). Perlmutter's argument for hypothesis 9 rests on a third, independently assumed principle:

---

[6] Examples include the Extended Projection Principle (EPP) of various Principles and Parameters approaches (Chomsky 1981), the Final-1 Law in Relational Grammar (Perlmutter and Postal 1983), the Subject Condition in Lexical-Functional Grammar (Lexical Mapping Theory; Bresnan and Kanerva 1989), and constraints in Head-driven Phrase Structure Grammar, which ensure that the first element of a verb's Argument Structure is the subject (Ginzburg and Sag 2000).

> 1 Advancement Exclusiveness Law (1AEX) No clause can involve more than one promotion to subject.

From this, Perlmutter's argument that all passives involve promotion can be completed. If a language allows impersonal passives at all, and assuming the UH and the 1AEX, if all passive clauses involve promotion to subject, it is predicted that passive will be possible with unergative verbs but not with unaccusatives. This is because according to the revised UH and the Subject Condition, clauses with unaccusative verbs have already had an object-to-subject promotion. By 1AEX, no further promotion should be possible, so if impersonal passives require promotion, they should not apply here. This is borne out in (20). Unergatives have no underlying promotion by the UH, so the 1AEX will not rule out impersonal passive formation if it involves promotion, correctly predicting (18).[7]

In contrast to the reasoning above, consider the null hypothesis: if impersonal passives do *not* involve promotion to subject, it is expected that any kind of intransitive predicate should yield a grammatical impersonal passive; the 1AEX would make no predictions in that case. However, the expectation is not borne out, as only some of the relevant examples are grammatical. Therefore the contrast between (18) and (20) supports the hypothesis that all passives involve promotion, due to the interaction of the UH, the Subject Condition, and the 1AEX.

4.3   Arguments involving theoretical constructs

The moral of the preceding subsection is that empirical data can be used to argue for the existence of theoretical principles, and that sometimes the relevant predictions arise not directly from the specific principle, but within the larger theoretical context as an interaction among various principles. Indeed, the fact that the interaction of different principles makes correct additional predictions also supports the correctness of each individual principle (see Chapter 19 for more on the need for independent verification). However, for the argument to go through, it is important that an appropriate theoretical system be adopted to provide these background assumptions. This raises a more general point: for advancing a particular hypothesis, only certain theoretical frameworks may allow the argument to be made. If the hypothesis is taken to be correct, this could in turn be used as an argument for such frameworks.

For example, hypothesis 10 makes crucial reference to the notion of "surface" and "deep" grammatical functions. Only some syntactic frameworks actually provide the appropriate theoretical machinery to distinguish such notions: in theoretical frameworks that admit multiple levels of syntactic representation for a given string, there is usually a "deep" and "surface" structure that can be

---

[7] In languages such as Dutch, the promotion part of the analysis is satisfied either by a preverbal PP or by the expletive *er*. In Perlmutter's proposal, the expletive is introduced as a deep object, then promoted to subject.

exploited to make such a distinction (Chomsky 1957, inter alios). Even in frameworks without multiple levels of syntactic representation this is possible – for example, in Lexical-Functional Grammar, arguments realized with the same grammatical function (in this case, subject) might have different featural analyses at the level of argument structure, making them more or less like canonical transitive subjects and objects (Bresnan and Zaenen 1990). Conversely, a simple phrase structure grammar typically lacks the expressive capability to make this distinction. Thus in terms of the degree to which the understanding of hypothesis 10 is taken as correct, an argument could be made for rejecting one kind of theory and continuing with a different kind.

However, care must be taken in making this kind of argument, on two grounds. First, it is often the case that, in practice, a particular theoretical framework is powerful enough that nearly anything can be stated in it, with some ingenuity on the part of the author. This means that care must be taken in presenting an argument that a given framework is truly incompatible with a given set of theoretical deductions. Second, it is often possible to find alternative ways of stating the hypothesis or of accounting for the data that can be done in terms of other equally plausible principles. Still, if a certain conclusion is sufficiently well supported and the predictions are clear, arguments for larger architectural differences are possible.

It is also possible to make "medium grain" arguments about the organization of different principles or mechanisms in different variants of the same framework. We do not illustrate the details here, but in frameworks which relate levels or stages of representation through explicit derivations, there have been many arguments made about the relative validity of constraints on the relevant derivations ("you are forbidden to do X") vs constraints on the relevant representations ("any structure with property P is disallowed") (e.g. Lasnik 2001; Rizzi 2001). Some such arguments are conceptual or based on notions of simplicity, but as with the Dutch impersonal passives, sometimes empirical data can be used to argue for the merits of each type of constraint.

5   Presenting your argument

The fundamental content of a good argument is this: the hypothesis is motivated because the data support it, especially over alternatives. This is what we have concentrated on above and what has scientific validity. In this final section we consider the fact that making a good argument in linguistics is almost as much about how one presents the argument as how one formulates it – an argument that is difficult to follow or poorly presented will be much less convincing, even if the substance underlying it happens to be sound. We thus sketch some important desiderata and a possible schema for outlining an argument, while noting that there may be many ways to present a valid argument in a convincing way, as long as they satisfy some of the basic desiderata.

A good argument will be structured so that one point leads directly into the next. Part of the author's job is to ensure that the reader can follow the steps in the argument, and as such it is often a good idea to create expectations on the part of the reader for what is to come. A simple way to do this is, first and foremost, to prime the reader in the introductory material by (a) summarizing the central problem in the domain under discussion, often with reference to prior knowledge/literature and what will additionally be shown, (b) stating the hypothesis clearly (at some level appropriate for an introduction) so the reader will know what to expect to see presented – a good argument does not need to be a mystery – and (c) outlining in advance the steps that will be taken to motivate the hypothesis (sometimes referred to informally as a "road map"). A good description of what will be shown and how it will be shown can make reading the argument easier, something that will facilitate the reader in ultimately accepting – or at least appreciating – the point being made.

Next, as each step of the argument is presented, a good style is to make clear which step the reader is currently in in terms of the stated outline, so the reader will know what is about to be shown and what will be coming next. At this point the relevant data appropriate for the given point can be presented and described concisely in a way that ties directly into the argument being made. If there is quite a lot of data to be presented, it should be separated into relevant chunks, each making a point, one step at a time in the developing argument. One effective way to introduce a set of data is to give a brief description of what aspect of the data the reader is to focus on *before* giving the actual examples, with a more in-depth description after the data are given, if necessary. When describing the data, it is important not to say more than is necessary and to keep the observations relevant to the point. There may be numerous things about any set of data that are worthy of attention, but in a given context only those that are relevant to the point at hand need be enumerated, for fear of distracting the reader. Furthermore, a good practice is also to make immediately clear after the data are presented and described how exactly they support the given hypothesis – essentially, recapping where in the argument the reader is so the reader can keep track. If appropriate, the author can also show how alternative hypotheses will or will not predict the same data; or this could come later in some more thorough comparison section. A rather poor style of argumentation and presentation is the "last man standing" gambit – a presentation which focuses largely on hypotheses to be rejected, an enumeration of alternative hypotheses which are presented as lacking in some desirable quality, which is then followed by the final and favored hypothesis as an inevitable conclusion, especially with little positive argumentation toward the hypothesis.

Although we said the description of the data should be made in a way that ties into the hypothesis being supported, care must be taken nonetheless to remain at least somewhat neutral to one's theory, for fear of assuming one's analysis in the description and thus "begging the question." A good style for clear and crisp data description is to describe the data as concisely as possible, often appealing to little more than surface-level features and basic, theory-neutral linguistic categorization, with an eye toward those properties that will ultimately tie into the hypothesis being made, even if that hypothesis is relatively theoretical or abstract. As we have stressed above, a good hypothesis will make clear its predictions about those facts, so the connection should ultimately be obvious. Finally, after the entire argument is presented, a summary that recaps what was shown, and possibly puts it into a larger perspective, can solidify the content of the argument in the mind of the reader.

Fundamentally, as discussed extensively above, the goal of an argument is not simply to show that the data fit the hypothesis. That would be to provide an analysis for some data, when in principle any one of a number of analyses would work just as well. Rather, the goal of an argument is to show either that (a) *if* one assumes the hypothesis under discussion *then* the data are exactly as predicted, or (b) *if* these are the data, *then* the hypothesis under discussion must be valid. Carefully worded prose makes clear the predictive quality of the relationship between the data and the hypothesis and thus makes for a stronger argument. Poorly worded prose will not make this clear. For example, language that implicitly presupposes the hypothesis being supported (e.g., "*because of* such and such principle the data are this way") or that simply (re)describes the data using the proposed analysis will not add up to an argument. To some degree, explicit comparison between the proposed hypothesis and an alternative – especially when they are developed together to contrast in specific ways, as in Section 2 – necessitates the use of appropriate language, provided the hypotheses are developed in equivalent detail and given equal consideration.

Equally as important as the structure of the argument and the prose which makes that structure clear is the use of prose that is appropriate for what is to be shown. In many ways, the question of appropriate wording could be considered to be rhetorical, but well-chosen wording can lead to a more forceful argument that will be more convincing. For example, as noted above, sometimes data beyond the core data are presented as "additional" predictions that further solidify the argument. There is no shame (well, not much) in employing some rhetorical flourish when presenting such predictions if they are especially subtle or demonstrate the point stunningly. Conversely, there is no gain in overselling or overstating an argument, framing it, for instance, as "proven," rather than "supported," "likely," or "reasonable," given certain evidence.

It is also important to establish the content of the hypotheses being compared, especially if one is from previous scholarship. For example, the hypothesis should not be introduced solely in terms of the person(s) who proposed it, but in terms of the key notions that it involves. With regard to hypothesis 2 above, it would be inappropriate to refer to it as "Adger's (2003) movement hypothesis"; a description such as "the hypothesis that T-to-C movement is triggered by an uninterpretable and unvalued feature on T (Adger 2003)" is more informative and shows that you have understood the theoretical content of the idea, and are not relying on the reader to make the connection between the author's name and the key components of the cited hypothesis.

These stylistic guidelines conform to accepted ways of presenting what should already be a developed argument, and like any commentary on writing, they have only heuristic value. Arguments can certainly be presented in other ways. For example, it is sometimes more expedient to save any hypothesis comparison until after the main hypothesis is motivated, perhaps because its predictions are subtle and must be explored in detail together, or perhaps because it is difficult to see why certain alternatives are less plausible until the full argument is made for the supported hypothesis. Alternatively, if the theoretical assumptions embodied or assumed in the hypothesis are sufficiently rich and complex, it might be that some space should be devoted to making clear how the framework and/or hypothesis conspire to derive certain predictions, after which confirmation within the data should be more straightforward, thus putting the hypothesis first and the data second.

References

Aarts, B. 2001. *English Syntax and Argumentation*, 2nd edn. Basingstoke: Palgrave Macmillan.

Adger, D. 2003. *Core Syntax*. Oxford University Press.

Bateson, G. 1972. *Steps to an Ecology of Mind: Collected Essays in Anthropology, Psychiatry, Evolution, and Epistemology*. University of Chicago Press.

Bresnan, J. and J. M. Kanerva. 1989. Locative inversion in Chicheŵa. *Linguistic Inquiry* 20: 1–50.

Bresnan, J. and A. Zaenen. 1990. Deep unaccusativity in LFG. In K. Dziwirek, P. M. Farrell, and E. Mejías-Bikandi, eds. *Grammatical Relations: A Cross-Theoretical Perspective*. Stanford: CSLI Publications, 45–57.

Burzio, L. 1986. *Italian Syntax*. Dordrecht: Reidel.

Carlson, G. 2003. On the notion 'showing something'. In J. Moore and M. Polinsky, eds. *The Nature of Explanation in Linguistic Theory*. Stanford: CSLI Publications, 69–82.

Chomsky, N. 1957. *Syntactic Structures*. The Hague: Mouton de Gruyter.

1964. *Current Issues in Linguistic Theory*. The Hague: Mouton de Gruyter.

1981. *Lectures on Government and Binding*. Dordrecht: Foris.

Davis, S. and M.-H. Cho. 2003. The distribution of aspirated stops and /h/ in American English and Korean: an alignment approach with typological implications. *Linguistics* 41: 607–52.

de Saussure, F. 1959. *Course in General Linguistics*. New York: Philosophical Library.

Ginzburg, J. and I. A. Sag. 2000. *Interrogative Investigations: The Form, Meaning, and Use of English Interrogatives*. Stanford: CSLI Publications.

Green, G. M. and J. L. Morgan. 2001. *Practical Guide to Syntactic Argumentation*, 2nd edn. Stanford: CSLI Publications.

Kertész, A. and C. Rákosi. 2012. *Data and Evidence in Linguistics: A Plausible Argumentation Model*. Cambridge University Press.

Larson, R. K. 2010. *Grammar as Science*. Cambridge, MA: MIT Press.

Lasnik, H. 2001. Derivation and representation in modern transformational syntax. In M. Baltin and C. Collins, eds. *Handbook of Contemporary Syntactic Theory*. Oxford: Blackwell, 62–88.

Perlmutter, D. M. 1970. Surface structure constraints in syntax. *Linguistic Inquiry* 1: 187–225.

 1971. *Deep and Surface Structure Constraints*. New York: Holt, Rinehart and Winston.

 1978. Impersonal passives and the unaccusative hypothesis. In *Proceedings of the 4th Annual Meeting of the Berkeley Linguistics Society* 4: 157–90.

 2010. My path in linguistics. In D. Gerdts, J. Moore, and M. Polinsky, eds. *Hypothesis A/Hypothesis B: Linguistic Explorations in Honor of David M. Perlmutter*. Cambridge, MA: MIT Press, xvii–xxxvii.

Perlmutter, D. M. and P. Postal. 1983. Some proposed laws of basic clause structure. In D. M. Perlmutter, ed. *Studies in Relational Grammar*, 3 vols. University of Chicago Press, Volume I, 81–128.

Rizzi, L. 2001. Relativized minimality effects. In M. Baltin and C. Collins, eds. *Handbook of Contemporary Syntactic Theory*. Oxford: Blackwell, 89–110.

Soames, S. and D. M. Perlmutter. 1979. *Syntactic Argumentation and the Structure of English*. Berkeley: University of California Press.

19   Modeling in the language sciences

Willem Zuidema and Bart de Boer

1   Introduction

Computers can be used for many different purposes in linguistic research. They can be used for data storage and search. They can be used as devices for speech analysis or synthesis. They can be used to present linguistic stimuli to subjects and record their responses. In all these applications, computers are used as sophisticated tools, and they are programmed according to purely practical criteria: as long as it gets the job done, the internal workings of the software are not the subject of the research.

However, computing can also become the focus of linguistic inquiry. Computers can be used to operationalize linguistic theories by implementing them as computer programs. This is done because linguistic theories may be so complex that their predictions can no longer be derived using verbal reasoning or pen-and-paper analysis. Moreover, turning a linguistic theory into a computer program forces the researcher to make her assumptions explicit. By running the program, and studying its behavior under a variety of circumstances, the researcher can test the theory against empirical findings and often discover unexpected consequences.

In this chapter, we discuss the use of computational models in the language sciences. Although formalization has had a central place since the 1950s in syntax, semantics, and phonetics in particular, the last two decades have seen an explosion of interest in mathematical and computational models in almost all linguistic subfields: from typology to language acquisition, from discourse to phonology, linguists are increasingly viewing formal modeling as an approach that ensures the internal consistency of theories (e.g., Steedman 2001; Wang and Minett 2005). However, although many proponents of modeling believe it makes their field more scientific and objective, it seems fair to say that the introduction of formal models has so far not led to a broad consensus among language researchers. On the contrary, models have often been at the heart of fundamental controversies (e.g., those about formalisms vs functionalism, nativism vs empiricism, single- vs dual-mechanism accounts of verb morphology; see, e.g., Pinker and Prince 1988).

An earlier version of this chapter was distributed among participants of the workshop "Models of language evolution: does the math add up?" at the *International Conference on the Evolution of Language*, April 2010, Utrecht.

One reason, we believe, that modeling has played more of a divisive than a unifying role is that there has been little attention to questions about modeling methodology: what kind of lessons can we expect to learn from a model? What makes a good or a bad model? How may different models of the same linguistic phenomenon relate to each other? How could models of different phenomena fit together? Thinking about such questions leads one to consider systematically the role of specific models in a given subfield: are they consistent with and complementary to each other? Are the assumptions that go into a particular model, if not (yet) supported by empirical findings, made plausible by results from other models?

The situation is not uniform across all linguistic subfields, of course, but we observe that in fields where one or two of these questions have received a lot of attention, the others tend to be ignored even more. For instance, in syntactic theory there has been an enormous amount of work (often of impressive mathematical sophistication) on comparing different syntactic frameworks and their ability to model native speaker intuitions about the grammaticality of carefully selected (but often highly contrived) sentences. However, in our view, this field has paid much too little attention to questions about whether that is really the most important criterion for evaluating models of language and about relations with cognitive and neural models. As we will emphasize in this chapter, the ability to reproduce a selected set of empirical phenomena is certainly not the only criterion for a good model.

Because it is impossible to cover all linguistic subfields, we will make our general points about methodology concrete using examples from two particular domains: the evolution of speech and the learnability of syntax. In both fields, computational modeling has played an important role, but in both we also believe progress has been hampered by lack of attention to modeling methodology and the questions one immediately asks about the relation between existing models when taking the view on modeling that we develop in this chapter.

For sustaining the success of modeling approaches in linguistic research, it is crucial that models start living up to their promise: modelers must make explicit how their models fit in with other modeling and empirical work, and how their modeling results affect judgments of plausibility of existing hypotheses in the field to which they wish to make a contribution. Moreover, they must do so based on careful consideration of other work, without overstating their results and misusing the prestige that comes with mathematical and computational approaches.

In Section 2, we will start with some considerations about the methodology of modeling in linguistics, and introduce the concepts of model sequencing and model parallelization (the latter is described in more detail in Section 4). In Sections 3 and 5 we will illustrate these concepts with two case studies on modeling in the evolution of speech and the learnability of syntax respectively. In Section 6 we will then draw some general lessons from these case studies, and sketch an agenda for future research in computational modeling of language.

2   Goals of modeling and the model circuitry

From the great many distinctions one can make between different model studies, there are three particularly useful ones that also allow us to establish some common terminology and formulate our view of the field. The first is a distinction based on function, between *predictive models* and *explanatory models* (Gilbert and Troitzsch 2005). Predictive models try to model a system as accurately as possible, and to make accurate predictions about the real system's behavior, as in weather forecasts, for example. Predictive models can also be used to reconstruct behavior in the past, and could be used, for example, in reconstructing the spread of language families or of particular instances of language change (e.g., Landsbergen 2009). Explanatory models, in contrast, aim to increase insight in a phenomenon. Explanatory models are generally much more abstract and further removed from reality than predictive models. The phenomenon under study is not modeled in all its detail; instead only its essentials are modeled. Crucially, what counts as "essential" very much depends on the research question, and simplifications that are appropriate for one question can be totally indefensible for another. Good explanatory models, moreover, explain the phenomenon of interest in terms of more fundamental phenomena which, at least in principle, can be independently motivated (models that simply reproduce the phenomenon of interest without providing such an explanation are sometimes called *phenomenological models*).

The second important distinction is one based on form, between *mathematical* and *computational models*. The distinction is not always strict, but mathematical models tend to be the most abstract and to strip down phenomena to their barest essentials. Typically (but not exclusively), mathematical modeling papers provide both a formalization of a phenomenon (e.g., using matrix algebra, logic, differential equations) and proofs about properties of the formal system. Such proofs are, by definition, universally valid and allow inferences about specific cases (deduction), although the simplifications necessary to arrive at a proof often greatly limit the applicability.

Computational models tend to be much more concrete and complex. Phenomena are formalized in a programming language, and the resulting programs studied experimentally. From different runs with different parameter settings, the modeler tries to infer general properties of the formal system (induction). The programs can be very complex, allowing for models with fewer abstractions, but often barring analytic proofs. In some cases, computational models are used to investigate versions of a mathematical model that are too complicated to study analytically (including *numerical models*, which are defined algebraically but studied using numerical methods on the computer).

A third major distinction concerns the validation of models: we distinguish between *internal validation* and *external validation* (also discussed in Chapter 7). Internal validation is about demonstrating that the phenomenon of interest indeed follows from the stated assumptions, and mathematical proof provides its most powerful form. This is much harder to achieve with computer models, although extensive testing and systematic exploration of the parameter space of a computational model can lead to a great degree of confidence. External validation is about checking whether the stated and unstated assumptions are supported by empirical evidence, or by the outcome of other, independent models, and whether the model's predictions are confirmed in the real world. As computational models are often formulated in more concrete terms, it tends to be easier to achieve external validation.

In the language sciences, we are mainly concerned with the external validation of explanatory models, which in all cases requires an interpretive step: explanatory models have, by definition, abstracted away many details of the phenomenon of interest, making it a matter of judgment whether abstractly formulated assumptions and predictions are supported by concrete evidence. In many fields, external validation is further complicated by the fact that there is little direct evidence about which assumptions and predictions are valid, since many of the causal events are unobservable because they happened in a distant past (as in historical and evolutionary linguistics), inside the brain or distributed over millions of language users. External validation is thus only achievable by *model sequencing*: assumptions and prediction of any particular model are validated mainly by results from other models, and only at various points in a string of models do empirical results come into play.

Moreover, because linguistics deals with complicated phenomena for which the appropriate simplifications have not necessarily been established, modeling research should employ *model parallelization*: for any particular phenomenon, researchers should develop multiple formalizations, compare results and relate observed differences to explicit and implicit assumptions embodied in these alternative models.

Modelers in language research must thus work out relations between different models, whether they stand in sequence or in parallel to each other. This terminology is, of course, based on the metaphor of electronic circuits; we will therefore refer to our perspective on modeling as the "model circuitry view." (See Chapter 18 for a discussion of the importance of independent verification in linguistic argumentation more generally.)

3   Model sequencing in practice: a case study on the evolution of speech

To make the ideas about different types of models, and in particular model sequencing, concrete, we will now discuss in some detail the use of models in one particular subfield of linguistics: the evolution of speech. This field is not only one that we have been active in ourselves, but it also offers a particularly good example of a field where modeling can make all the difference because of the paucity of empirical data, but where opportunities have perhaps been missed because of lack of attention to modeling methodology. We will start by briefly discussing some background to this field, and then survey the role of models in answering the key questions of the field.

In the research on how the speech abilities of humans evolved, the focus is usually on the differences between modern humans and the hypothetical latest common ancestor (henceforth, LCA) of humans, chimpanzees and bonobos. Modern humans, as every linguist knows, have a descended larynx, have voluntary control over speech (but much less so over emotional utterances), and have a large learned repertoire of linguistic utterances. Moreover, those utterances have a complex internal structure that is used productively, and there are regularities in the repertoires of speech sounds that humans use (phonological universals). The vocal abilities of the LCA are inferred from the abilities that humans, chimpanzees and other apes share or do not share. From such comparisons, it can be derived that the LCA had a repertoire of calls for communicative purposes, and therefore a limited ability to modulate the vocal tract. However, it most likely had a vocal anatomy more comparable to that of chimpanzees, and vocal folds comparable to those of chimpanzees and gorillas. The LCA did not, it seems, have modern human's descended larynx, it had less voluntary control over breathing (MacLarnon and Hewitt 1999), and probably did have supralaryngeal air sacs. Finally, it is generally assumed that the LCA, like all modern apes except humans, had only limited voluntary control over vocalizations, learned its vocalizations only to a very limited extent, and lacked internal (combinatorial) structure in its calls.

The challenge for research of the evolution of speech is to give an account of how the modern phenotype evolved from the LCA's phenotype – that is, how did the descended larynx, voluntary control, vocal learning, combinatorial phonology, and phonological universals evolve? A key issue here is to what extent the evolutionary changes should be considered adaptations for language, or to what extent they evolved for other reasons. Computer models (and to some extent mathematical models) have been used for a long time to investigate such issues, but in the existing literature (e.g., de Boer 2005; de Boer and Fitch 2010) there are some striking gaps in the range of topics considered, and some disturbing confusions about the role of various models. The most studied topics are the evolution of the vocal tract (Lieberman and Crelin 1971; Boë et al. 2002; de Boer 2009) and the emergence of phonological universals (de Boer 2000b; Oudeyer 2005; Zuidema and de Boer 2009). The evolution of voluntary control, vocal learning, and combinatoriality have received much less attention in the modeling literature, and the issue of how models of these different aspects fit together has been almost completely ignored.

The starting point for many models of how speech evolved is existing models of how speech perception and production work in human adults. Surveying the literature, we quickly find that many models that have been developed for the study of human speech are not necessarily directly usable in the study of the evolution of speech. Illustrative examples from modeling the acoustic production of speech are the three-parameter model of the vocal tract (Stevens and House 1955; Fant 1960), the coupled mass-spring model of the vocal folds (Dudgeon 1970; Ishizaka and Flanagan 1972), and the source-filter model of speech production (Fant 1960). These are simplified, explanatory models of the human vocal tract, the human vocal folds, and the (lack of) interaction between the human vocal folds and the vocal tract, respectively.

These models are well established in phonetics, and provide valuable insights in the process of speech production. However, some researchers in the evolution of speech – erroneously, in our view – reuse these models to represent properties of vocal tracts of our evolutionary ancestors or of other species (see the discussion about Riede et al. 2005 in Lieberman 2006). But this is based on a misunderstanding of the *explanatory nature* of the existing models, which involved simplifications that were very helpful for understanding speech production, but are specific to human adult vocal tracts. It is, in fact, unlikely that ape-like vocal tracts can make the deformations of the vocal tract that are assumed by the three-parameter model, and it is clear that the acoustic effects of supralaryngeal air sacs are not captured by it. It is further unknown whether chimpanzee-like vocal folds work in the same way as human vocal folds, and whether in chimpanzee-like vocalizations the vocal folds can really be considered acoustically independent of the vocal tract. Simplifications made in building these models must thus be re-evaluated in the light of what is known about ape and fossil vocal anatomy.

A second problem with existing models of the evolution of speech anatomy concerns its relation to models of the biological and cultural evolution of communication – that is, its external validation through model sequencing. Even if we could establish a sequence of vocal tracts, leading from ape-like to human-like shapes in gradual steps, that in itself, although an important step, would not provide an evolutionary explanation. As we and others have argued elsewhere (Parker and Maynard Smith 1990; Zuidema and de Boer 2003, 2009), evolutionary explanations must provide a "path of ever increasing fitness," where every new variant provides a fitness advantage in a population where the previous variant is still common. In the case of vocal tract evolution, it is unclear what the appropriate fitness function is. Existing models tend to assume that it is a simple function of the size of the acoustic space allowed by a particular vocal tract configuration. But fitness due to speech must be a function of how well an individual communicates with others in a population, which in turn depends on the communication system the population uses. However, the relation between the repertoire of speech sounds that emerges in a population and the anatomical and neurocognitive features of individuals is far from trivial.

Models that study the emergence of such repertoires have focused on vowel inventories, and on a role for self-organization in shaping them (Glotin 1995; Berrah and Laboissière 1999; de Boer 2000a; Oudeyer 2005), given constraints on the vowel space formalized by existing models of vowel perception and production. This group of models is a good example of model parallelization: different models making different simplifications modeling the same phenomenon. They are not a good example of model sequencing, however: although these models have yielded a beautiful connection between empirical data on vowel systems and biophysical constraints, it is clear that they only scratch the surface of the full set of phonological universals: they have, for instance, little to say about consonants, syllable structure or suprasegmental speech patterns.

Ultimately, the connection between phonology and anatomical and neurocognitive features needs to become clear to allow us to evaluate particular scenarios of the evolution of speech. However, despite the progress in modeling vocal tract evolution and vowel universals, we are still quite far from a model-based understanding of the evolution of speech. In the required sequence of explanatory models we still observe many gaps, for a variety of reasons.

One reason is that, when addressing these more complex issues, the limits of what is possible at present with computer models are reached quickly. It is then tempting to use high-level abstractions (such as distinctive features, constraints, and rule-based phonological explanations). However, making use of such abstractions, which, after all, have been derived for description of modern human language, and are in general not based on direct observation of neurocognitive mechanisms, incurs the risk of implicitly including the phenomena to be explained in the model – and thus resorting to phenomenological rather than explanatory modeling. For example, from typological studies it is known which consonants are unusual (e.g., uvular plosive [q]) and which are common (e.g., velar plosive [k]), but there is no language-independent biophysical and neurocognitive model that reliably predicts which articulations are more difficult to produce than others. Thus research into more complex aspects of speech is not only hampered by the computational complexity of such models, but also by our lack of knowledge about the underlying phenomena.

Likewise, we have no models of the evolution of the vocal folds. Although there are many models for human vocal folds (Dudgeon 1970; Ishizaka and Flanagan 1972; Titze 1973, 1974, 2008) and some models of the interaction between the vocal folds and the vocal tract (Flanagan and Meinhart 1964; Titze 2002, 2008), as far as we are aware, no models exist of either chimpanzee vocal folds or of hypothetical ancestral vocal folds. This undoubtedly has to do with the lack of anatomical data (although some has recently been presented by Demolin and Delvaux 2006), but also with the fact that vocal folds (and their interaction with the vocal tract) are much more difficult to model than the acoustics of the vocal tract itself.

Another reason is that in spite of much parallel modeling effort, in some domains no consensus is reached. There is, for example, strong controversy in the study of the articulatory abilities of Neanderthals and the role of modern human vocal anatomy (with its descended larynx). In this debate, Lieberman (Lieberman and Crelin 1971) and Carré, Lindblom, and MacNeilage (1995) propose that vocal anatomy has evolved for speech, while Boë et al. (2002)

propose that it has not evolved for speech, because (neural) control is more important. They reach opposite conclusions, even though they use very similar modeling techniques. The debate has led to a rather heated exchange (Boë et al. 2007; Lieberman 2007).

Finally, some topics seem to be simply overlooked. For instance, important innovations in the cognitive adaptations for using speech that occurred between the LCA and modern humans have not been addressed by modeling. These include the ability to use productively combinatorial structure of speech, and the (related) ability to learn large sets of complex utterances. Such models would be quite complex computationally, but their results might be transferable to other aspects of language, most notably syntax. After all, it has been proposed that the sequential processing and learning that are necessary for using syntax are based on adaptations for the sequential processing and learning mechanisms that are necessary for using combinatorial utterances (Carstairs-McCarthy 1999).

Given these gaps in our understanding of the evolution of speech, the possibilities for external validation are at present limited and we should guard against over-interpreting modeling results. A case in point is the reception of Nowak, Krakauer, and Dress (1999), who presented an information-theoretic model and a mathematical proof of the conditions for combinatorial coding to have a fitness advantage. This proof is an elegant example of internal validation. The model fits into a larger research program in which a number of proofs of mathematical models related to the evolution of language have been presented (Nowak and Krakauer 1999; Nowak, Komarova, and Niyogi 2001, 2002). These models have been interpreted by other researchers as having "demonstrated the evolvability of the most striking features of language" (Pinker 2000). However, this confuses internal validation (the models are internally consistent) with external validation (the models correspond to reality). The latter is unfortunately far from established, given the many simplifying assumptions in Nowak, Krakauer, and Dress's (1999) model, as we have pointed out elsewhere (Zuidema and de Boer 2009).

In conclusion, the evolution of speech offers us a good example of a field in which models have played a central role in making progress, but also of a field where it pays to step back a little and consider the relations between all the different models proposed. Such a "model circuitry" point of view quickly reveals a number of important gaps in the existing research, and helps both to set an agenda for future research and to put overly optimistic assessments of the state of the art into perspective.

4   Model parallelization

There are of course infinitely many ways in which models of the same phenomenon can differ. However, we are not talking about small differences between models that are best captured with different settings of one or several parameters. Rather, "model parallelization" is about studying models that differ *qualitatively* in the way they approximate reality (i.e., in the simplification that they make). We will discuss briefly two dimensions in which models may differ, one concerning the *ontological status* of language, the other the *linguistic representation* used.

With regard to the ontological status, the issue of what kind of "thing" a language is, we observe that many models of linguistic phenomena abstract away from individual linguistic cognition and individual differences, and treat a natural language as an independently existing entity. We therefore refer to this approach as "Platonic." For many questions in syntax, semantics, or phonology, the Platonic approach offers a reasonable abstraction. For instance, when providing a formal account of non-constituent coordination in English, as in *Mary wrote and Peter read the book* (Steedman 2001), it makes sense to ignore variation within the English language, differences between production and reception, performance constraints, or neural correlates of knowledge of language. It is still useful to develop alternative models for such a phenomenon, and evaluate the different predictions they make (e.g., those on information structure; Steedman 2001), but those alternative models will likely (and reasonably) share the simplifications from the Platonic approach.

For many important linguistic phenomena, however, the Platonic abstraction is not so obviously justified. In accounting for language universals, language change, language acquisition, and language evolution, it is crucial that models of several types are studied and compared. A possible conclusion of such a comparison, of course, might be that particular Platonic models do suffice, but the very fact that possible causal factors (such as heterogeneity in a population, or non-linguistic cognition) get abstracted out in the Platonic approach necessitates investigating these issues.

Fortunately, there are modeling traditions, such as "agent-based modeling" (e.g., Hogeweg 1988; Kirby 2002; Gilbert and Troitzsch 2005), that allow for language users and their interactions to be modeled directly. In such models, two or more agents are selected from the population to interact linguistically. Usually in such interactions, one agent is the speaker and another agent is the hearer, but it is also possible that both agents have the role of speaker and hearer during the interaction. Agents generally update their linguistic knowledge in reaction to an interaction. In this way, linguistic knowledge can be transferred from one agent to another and spread in a population. The exact nature of interactions and how the agents react to them depends completely on what the researcher wants to investigate and achieve with the model.

Many different schemes for selecting agents from the population are possible. It is possible that all agents have an equal probability to participate in each interaction (this is called a random mixing population), but it is also possible that certain subgroups of agents have a higher probability of interacting with each other than with other subgroups. This can be due to the modeled spatial location of agents, their social status, their age, or any other factor a researcher wishes to model. A scheme that is often used is that the population is divided into two subpopulations: one of teachers and one of learners. Teachers only interact with learners, and neither learners nor teachers interact among themselves. In addition, in such a scheme, often the learners are the only ones who update their linguistic knowledge. This is the simplest possible model of transfer of language from one generation to the next. Note that populations do not need to be static: agents can enter (this models immigration or birth) or leave the population (emigration or death), and the agents' behavior can change over time.

An approach different from both Platonic and agent-based models is where languages are described at the population level, without modeling details of individual behavior. One could model, for example, the proportion of the population that speaks a variant of the language as a number, and then model the way this changes over time using a dynamical system. A dynamical system is a system of mathematical equations that describe changes over time. This can be done with difference equations or with differential equations. Such equations can sometimes be solved analytically, but more often than not, they can only be investigated numerically, with a computer model. Such numerical simulations have been used, for example, to model language change (Wang and Minett 2005). The advantage of such models is that they make use of existing mathematical formalisms and may therefore be easier to read and interpret than computer models. A disadvantage is that it is not always easy to model mathematically what can be modeled straightforwardly with agent-based models.

The second key dimension in which models in linguistics tend to differ is in the linguistic representation used. In the brain of the individual language user, knowledge of language is represented in a complex network of neurons, connections, electrical currents, and chemical gradients. Models of language – thankfully – abstract out many of the complexities involved. Many models ignore the inherently continuous and stochastic aspects of the brain, and represent language with discrete, categorical variables and rules. Other models make other simplifications, though, and a true understanding of many phenomena in language again requires comparing these different models.

We identify four classes of representations of language: symbolic models, memory-based models, statistical models, and connectionist models; these are schematized in Figure 19.1. Symbolic models implement linguistic items as abstract, symbolic entities. Typically, no information is represented about how often a certain linguistic object occurs; nor is there a way of representing degrees of acceptability of different linguistic utterances. A linguistic utterance is either possible or not. This makes it relatively easy to analyze and understand the working of these models. Also, these models are usually usable for both production and perception (processing) of language. However, they may have difficulties learning: given that they have a hard time dealing with variation, they tend not to be very robust to noise (speech errors, linguistic variation).

Memory-based models do not generally represent higher-level abstractions than that which is observable. Also, they are fundamentally learning systems

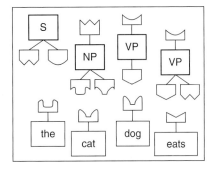

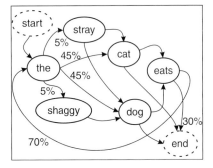
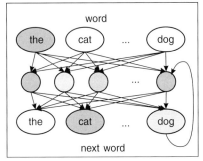

Figure 19.1. *Classes of representation of language*

that can deal with complex and noisy input. The most extreme memory-based system stores all information it observes. By defining a distance function on the items that are stored, the system can retrieve items that are close to a previously unobserved item. In a complete memory-based system, information about meaning, pronunciation, and other aspects of the utterance will be stored as well. This allows for generalizations about previously unobserved utterances: forms are expected to have meanings that are close to closely related forms, and meanings are expected to have corresponding forms that are close to closely related meanings.

Memory-based models can be highly successful in modeling human behavior that involves lots of rote learning, such as acquisition of large lexicons, of irregular stress assignment and of irregular verbs. They are robust to errors in the input, and to predictable variation, such as dialectal variation. With a good distance function they can even generalize well. It is often relatively easy to get an idea of what a memory-based model has learned. However, they have a hard time dealing with the combinatorial nature of human language, without some pre-programmed notion of what the basic elements that are being combined are. For example, it would be difficult for a purely memory-based system to figure out how to apply the different morphemes *-s* in *the cats bite the dog* vs *the cat bites the dog*. In order to do this, some notion of words, word classes, and morphemes is required.

A third class of models is statistical models. These do not store everything they observe, but store statistical information about how often linguistic items are observed. In one of the earliest (but still often used) instantiations (Shannon 1948), such models represent how likely words are to follow each other. Such models can be trained by counting the co-occurrence of words in large corpora of text (see Chapter 13). Many aspects of human language can be modeled to a reasonable extent by such non-hierarchical statistical models (known as Markov models). They can even deal to some extent with the combinatorial structure of human language. However, they have a hard time dealing with the long-distance dependencies that exist in human languages. This problem can be solved by augmenting it with components from symbolic models, such as representations of phrase structure (the result would be a *probabilistic grammar*, an approach that combines the strengths of the symbolic and statistical models we discussed).

The final class of models that we mention are connectionist models. These are also called neural networks, and are inspired by the way the brain is organized. They consist of nodes (modeling neurons) and connections (modeling axons). The nodes each have a level of activation. Connections go from one node to another node and have a weight associated with them. The activation of a node is a function of the sum over the products of the weight of each incoming connection multiplied by the activation of the node from which it originates. Input to the system consists of setting the right activations of the input nodes, and output of the system can be read from the activation of the output nodes. Nodes that are neither input nodes nor output nodes are called hidden nodes. It should be noted that there can be loops in the neural network: connections going "back" in a neural network are called recurrent connections.

Most connectionist models learn. This happens through adaptation of the connection weights based on the input (and possibly the output) that is presented to the network. In the example, the network would be presented with an input word and an output word and its weights would be adapted such that the node representing the output word has higher activation. Connectionist models are robust to noise and variation in the input. In addition, because knowledge is represented in a distributed way (it is distributed over the different connection weights and activations), the network is robust to loss of nodes and connections in a way very similar to the way real brains are robust to damage. This can be an advantage when using computer models to study models of brain damage and aphasia. The distributed representations are a disadvantage, however, when one wants to understand exactly what a connectionist model has learned and how it solves problems. It can be hard or impossible to reduce the distributed representation to a more abstract representation that provides insight about the problem.

On both dimensions – the ontological status and the linguistic representation – there is thus an enormous variation in existing and possible models in the language sciences, and there are often fierce debates about what the "correct" choices are. We argue that we need to move away from questions about the correct level or correct formalism: there is no single best choice that works for all research questions; rather, we need to compare parallel models and use simplifications that are appropriate for the particular issue we are studying.

5   Model parallelization in practice: a case study on the learnability of syntax

As a case study on the need for model parallelization, we will now briefly discuss several models relating to language learnability. This field provides a good example of a field where models have played a central role, but also of a field where modeling results have been widely misinterpreted. Careful attention to model parallelization could, we believe, have avoided these misunderstandings.

The seminal model study in this field is by Mark Gold (1967), who proved that several classes of formal languages are not learnable in a technical sense. Gold defined "learnability" as a property of a class of language, using the notion of "identification in the limit." The learning situation can be imagined as follows: a teacher selects a language L from a given class C of languages, and presents the grammatical sentences from L in an arbitrary order to a learner A. From the very start, the learner tries to guess which language the teacher has in mind. A class C is called *learnable* if there exists an algorithm A that is guaranteed to arrive (and stay) at the correct hypothesis in the limit of an infinite amount of examples. Gold went on to show that some popular classes of formal languages, including finite-state, context-free and context-sensitive languages, are not learnable in this sense. These results have been widely interpreted as providing support for a nativist view on language: if the type of grammars we need to describe natural language are not learnable, the argument goes, it is reasonable to conclude that they are not learned, but in essence innate.

Now, as is already clear from this informal description, Gold made a number of idealizations of the language learning situation, and it is thanks to these simplifying assumptions that his mathematical proofs were possible at all. One of these idealizations is that there is an infinite amount of data; in a sense, Gold is therefore even too lenient, given that actual language acquisition has to happen – and does happen – within a finite and even relatively short period of time. A number of alternative modeling frameworks, including PAC-learning (Valiant 1984), have been developed that are applicable to learning situations with time constraints, but these do not fundamentally change the analysis we present here and we will not discuss them.

In other idealizations, Gold appears too strict. In the original versions of his proofs, no reference is made to semantics, pragmatics, and phonological information, even though some (and perhaps many) cues from each of these domains are obviously available to the language-learning child. Moreover, Gold's best-known results are for situations where learners are presented only with positive evidence, but he obtained different learnability results when negative evidence is also available. These observations have led to quite heated debates, with researchers critical of nativism denouncing Gold's theorem (e.g., Elman et al. 1996), but others pointing out that the additional cues can also be modeled as strings and that negative evidence is almost absent from a learning child's linguistic input (Marcus 1993).

Many of the claims in these debates about Gold's results are factually incorrect, as reviewed extensively by Johnson (2004). Johnson also shows that the participants in the debate curiously overlooked a much more essential point: that Gold's definition of learnability as "identification in the limit" is fundamentally unpsychological, because it is a property of *predefined* classes, across all possible learning algorithms and all possible learning environments. In contrast, in real language learning there are strong biological constraints on the possible learning algorithms and environments, and the classes of language are not predefined, but rather a consequence of a learning cycle. Concretely, this means that Gold's proofs are perfectly consistent with a situation where a domain-general learning algorithm A is successful at learning many different languages $L_1, L_2, \ldots L_n$ from an unlearnable class C (Zuidema 2003). The fact that class C is *unlearnable* only implies that A cannot be (guaranteed to be) successful at learning all languages in C. Negative learnability results about classes, like the class of context-sensitive languages, are thus only relevant for people who would claim that all context-sensitive languages are possible targets for learning, which is an absurd claim, even for the staunchest *tabula rasa* empiricist.

Zuidema (2003) presented a simple computational model where a toy grammar induction algorithm is successful at learning some target context-free languages (i.e., a subclass of the context-free languages is learnable by the given algorithm). He showed that only languages from that subclass survive the process of cultural evolution where languages are transmitted from one generation to the next. Hence, subclasses of unlearnable superclasses might be perfectly learnable, and those subclasses will emerge in the cultural evolution of language, regardless of whether there are language-specific innate constraints. Together, these observations make clear that Gold's work simply has nothing to say about the nativism–empiricism controversy in linguistics. Moreover, all it took to demonstrate this fact is a simple agent-based model that avoided some of the common idealizations from the mathematical tradition of learnability research.

In short, Gold's theorem has played a crucial role in the debate about learnability and about innate specialization for language. Although many alternative models of learnability have been developed and used in the debate, typically they have adopted the conceptualization of the problem as provided by Gold, including notions of learnability as a property of predefined classes across all possible learners and learning environments. Careful comparison of Gold's model with models developed in a different paradigm (such as the learning paradigm of Solomonoff 1964) – as required by model parallelization – would have clarified the confusion about the relevance of Gold's theorem for cognitive science much sooner, and would have spared the field much unhelpful and bitter controversy.

6   Conclusions

We have presented a number of techniques that can be useful in linguistic modeling, but more importantly, we have tried to illustrate how we think models should fit together and how they should relate to empirical evidence. There are a number of lessons we would like to be drawn from our analysis. First, it seems that modelers should pay more attention to how their models relate to other models, and how they fit the bigger linguistic picture. Although most papers on linguistic modeling do a good job at internal validation and crediting other researchers' work, authors do not often make explicit how their models fit more broadly into linguistics outside the detailed issue they study, and in what way their model provides external validation for other models or how other models provide it for theirs.

Second, we note that there is no lack of models and no lack of data, but there is a rather uneven distribution of modeling effort over relevant questions. It is perhaps not surprising that (as in other fields of scientific inquiry) the majority of papers are concentrated around the easiest questions. Understandable as this is, we have now reached a stage where we should also attempt to tackle the more difficult questions, and consider carefully whether a collection of models together constitute a convincing explanation.

In order to make progress with computational models, a framework in which different models can be situated and compared with each other, and in which gaps in the modeling effort can be identified, would be useful. In the study of the cognitive processes underlying language, human behavior presents the point of reference. A problem is that non-modeling linguists have not yet reached consensus about how language works in the brain. However, there is at least a wealth of data that can be used for external validation of computer models. Increasingly, through studies of the workings and the genetics of the brain, data are available about the actual way the brain processes language.

Such data are not always available for the modeling of the history and evolutionary dynamics of language – these are historical processes and information is irretrievably lost. However, papers presenting complete scenarios "verbally" may be very useful in structuring a research program. Jackendoff (2002) is one of the few authors who provides a rather detailed scenario of evolution that may provide a useful framework if handled with care.

If these challenges are taken up by the field, in a few years we should have several models for each issue *in parallel*, as well as a set of models that *in sequence* really speak to the plausibility of a particular theory. Only then will we be approaching *external validation* of *explanatory models* of language, and the modeling approach will really prove its worth to the whole field of linguistics.

References

Berrah, A.-R. and R. Laboissière. 1999. Species: an evolutionary model for the emergence of phonetic structures in an artificial society of speech agents. In D. Floreano, J.-D. Nicoud, and F. Mondada, eds. *Advances in Artificial Life* (Lecture Notes in Artificial Intelligence 1674). Berlin: Springer, 674–8.

Boë, L.-J., J.-L. Heim, K. Honda, and S. Maeda. 2002. The potential Neandertal vowel space was as large as that of modern humans. *Journal of Phonetics* 30.3: 465–84.

Boë, L.-J., J.-L. Heim, K. Honda, S. Maeda, P. Badin, and C. Abry. 2007. The vocal tract of newborn humans and Neanderthals: acoustic capabilities and consequences for the debate on the origin of language. A reply to Lieberman (2007a). *Journal of Phonetics* 35.4: 564–81.

Carré, R., B. Lindblom, and P. F. MacNeilage. 1995. Rôle de l'acoustique dans l'évolution du conduit vocal humain. *Comptes Rendus de l'Académie des Sciences, Série II* 320 (série IIb): 471–6.

Carstairs-McCarthy, A. 1999. *The Origins of Complex Language: An Inquiry in the Evolutionary Beginnings of Sentences, Syllables, and Truth*. Oxford University Press.

de Boer, B. 2000a. Emergence of vowel systems through self-organisation. *AI Communications* 13: 27–39.

2000b. Self organization in vowel systems. *Journal of Phonetics* 28.4: 441–65.

2005. Evolution of speech and its acquisition. *Adaptive Behavior* 13.4: 281–92.

2009. Why women speak better than men (and its significance for evolution). In R. Botha and C. Knight, eds. *The Prehistory of Language*. Oxford University Press, 255–65.

de Boer, B. and W. T. Fitch. 2010. Computer models of vocal tract evolution: an overview and critique. *Adaptive Behavior* 18.1: 36–47.

Demolin, D. and V. Delvaux. 2006. A comparison of the articulatory parameters involved in the production of sounds of bonobos and modern humans. In A. Cangelosi, A. D. M. Smith, and K. Smith, eds. *The Evolution of Language: Proceedings of the 6th International Conference (evolang6)*. New Jersey: World Scientific, 67–74.

Dudgeon, D. E. 1970. Two-mass model of the vocal cords. *Journal of the Acoustical Society of America* 48.1A: 118.

Elman, J. L., E. A. Bates, M. H. Johnson, A. Karmiloff-Smith, D. Parisi, and K. Plunkett. 1996. *Rethinking Innateness. A Connectionist Perspective on Development*. Cambridge, MA: MIT Press.

Fant, G. 1960. *Acoustic Theory of Speech Production*. Gravenhage: Mouton de Gruyter.

Flanagan, J. L. and D. I. S. Meinhart. 1964. Source-system interaction in the vocal tract. *Journal of the Acoustical Society of America* 36.10: 2001–2.

Gilbert, N. and K. G. Troitzsch. 2005. *Simulation for the Social Scientist*, 2nd edn. Maidenhead: Open University Press.

Glotin, H. 1995. *La vie artificielle d'une société de robots parlants: Émergence et change-ment du code phonétique*. Grenoble: DEA sciences cognitives-Institut National Polytechnique de Grenoble.

Gold, E. M. 1967. Language identification in the limit. *Information and Control* (now Information and Computation) 10: 447–74.

Hogeweg, P. 1988. MIRROR beyond MIRROR, puddles of life. In C. Langton, ed. *Artificial Life: SFI Studies in the Sciences of Complexity*. Reading, MA: Addison Wesley, 297–315.

Ishizaka, K. and J. L. Flanagan. 1972. Synthesis of voiced sounds from a two-mass model of the vocal cords. *The Bell System Technical Journal* 51.6: 1233–68.

Jackendoff, R. 2002. *Foundations of Language*. Oxford University Press.

Johnson, K. 2004. Gold's theorem and cognitive science. *Philosophy of Science* 71: 571–92.

Kirby, S. 2002. Natural language from artificial life. *Artificial Life* 8.2: 185–215.

Landsbergen, F. 2009. *Cultural Evolutionary Modeling of Patterns in Language Change: Exercises in Evolutionary Linguistics*. Utrecht: LOT.

Lieberman, P. H. 2006. Limits on tongue deformation – Diana monkey formants and the impossible vocal tract shapes proposed by Riede et al. (2005). *Journal of Human Evolution* 50.2: 219–21.

2007. Current views on Neanderthal speech capabilities: a reply to Boë et al. (2002). *Journal of Phonetics* 35.4: 552–63.

Lieberman, P. H. and E. S. Crelin. 1971. On the speech of Neanderthal man. *Linguistic Inquiry* 2: 203–22.

MacLarnon, A. and G. P. Hewitt. 1999. The evolution of human speech: the role of enhanced breathing control. *American Journal of Physical Anthropology* 109.3: 341–3.

Marcus, G. F. 1993. Negative evidence in language acquisition. *Cognition* 46.1: 53–85.

Nowak, M. A. and D. Krakauer. 1999. The evolution of language. *Proceedings of the National Academy of Sciences* 96: 8028–33.

Nowak, M. A., D. Krakauer, and A. Dress. 1999. An error limit for the evolution of language. *Proceedings of the Royal Society of London* 266: 2131–6.

Nowak, M. A., N. L. Komarova, and P. Niyogi. 2001. Evolution of universal grammar. *Science* 291.5501: 114–18.

2002. Computational and evolutionary aspects of language. *Nature* 417.6889: 611–17.

Oudeyer, P.-Y. 2005. The self-organization of speech sounds. *Journal of Theoretical Biology* 233.3: 435–49.

Parker, G. A. and J. Maynard Smith. 1990. Optimality theory in evolutionary biology. *Nature* 348: 27–33.

Pinker, S. 2000. Survival of the clearest. *Nature* 404: 441–2.

Pinker, S. and A. Prince. 1988. On language and connectionism: analysis of a parallel distributed processing model of language acquisition. *Cognition* 28: 73–193.

Riede, T., E. Bronson, H. Hatzikirou, and K. Zuberbühler. 2005. Vocal production in a non-human primate: morphological data and a model. *Journal of Human Evolution* 48.1: 85–96.

Shannon, C. E. 1948. A mathematical theory of communication. *The Bell Systems Technical Journal* 27: 379–423, 623–56.

Solomonoff, R. J. 1964. A formal theory of inductive inference: parts 1 and 2. *Information and Control* 7.1,2: 1–22, 224–54.

Steedman, M. 2001. *The Syntactic Process*. Cambridge, MA: MIT Press.

Stevens, K. N. and A. S. House. 1955. Development of a quantitative description of vowel articulation. *Journal of the Acoustical Society of America* 27.3: 484–93.

Titze, I. R. 1973. The human vocal cords: a mathematical model part I. *Phonetica* 28.3: 129–70.

1974. The human vocal cords: a mathematical model part II. *Phonetica* 29.1: 1–21.

2002. Regulating glottal airflow in phonation: application of the maximum power transfer theorem to a low dimensional phonation model. *Journal of the Acoustical Society of America* 111.1 Pt 1: 367–76.

2008. Nonlinear source-filter coupling in phonation: theory. *Journal of the Acoustical Society of America* 123.5: 2733–49.

Valiant, L. G. 1984. A theory of the learnable. *Communications of the ACM* 27.11: 1134–42.

Wang, W. S.-Y. and J. W. Minett. 2005. The invasion of language: emergence, change and death. *Trends in Ecology & Evolution* 20.5: 263–9.

Zuidema, W. 2003. How the poverty of the stimulus solves the poverty of the stimulus. In S. Becker, S. Thrun, and K. Obermayer, eds. *Advances in Neural Information Processing Systems* 15 (Proceedings of NIPS 2002), Cambridge, MA: MIT Press, 51–8.

Zuidema, W. and B. de Boer. 2003. How did we get from there to here in the evolution of language? *Behavioral and Brain Sciences* 26.6: 694–5.

2009. The evolution of combinatorial phonology. *Journal of Phonetics* 37.2: 125–44.

20   Variation analysis

James A. Walker

1   Introduction

Variation analysis takes as its object of study differences in linguistic form with no apparent change in meaning or function. While other methods of linguistic analysis try to eliminate variation by finding structural or semantic contexts that disambiguate the choice of linguistic form, variation analysis seeks to understand variation by assessing which dimensions of the linguistic and/or social context correlate with the occurrence of a particular variant form. Linguistic variation is analyzed within different subfields of linguistics, such as sociolinguistics, historical linguistics, corpus linguistics, first and second language acquisition, and phonetics, each of which addresses slightly different research questions. The primary focus of this chapter is the analysis of linguistic variation within sociolinguistics, though the methods discussed here apply in principle to the other subfields. I begin by defining the central construct of variation analysis, the linguistic variable and its identification at the levels of phonetics/phonology and grammar, before proceeding through the steps of variation analysis: circumscribing the variable context, formulating and testing hypotheses through coding tokens for different independent variables, statistical testing, and interpreting results. I include some comments on the relationship between variation analysis and linguistic theory.

2   Identifying linguistic variables

The analysis of variation begins by noting that two or more linguistic forms are "different ways of saying the same thing," a phrase that will serve as a good provisional definition for the central construct of variation analysis, the *linguistic variable*. In this case, "the same thing" refers to a single underlying form (in phonology) or a single meaning or function (in morphosyntax), and the "different ways" refers to the variant forms (or *variants*). For example, some Spanish speakers sometimes produce a word like *avión* 'airplane' with a final alveolar [n] and sometimes with a final velar [ŋ]. Thus, in Spanish there is a linguistic variable (n) with two variants, [n] and [ŋ]. Similarly, when referring to the future, English speakers sometimes use a form of the present tense, as in (1a, b), sometimes a modal, as in (1c), and sometimes a periphrastic construction, as in (1d). These variant forms have an underlying discourse function in common, a reference to future time.

(1)   a. I *finish* on the twenty-seventh of June and I *start* the summer camp on the eighth of July. (Quebec City Speaker #9: 405)[1]
        b. In fact, I *'m leaving* on September the first for Belfast for a couple of weeks. (Montreal Speaker #19: 223)
        c. And he *'ll* probably live 'til a hundred. (Quebec City Speaker #29: 1480)
        d. My doctor tells me I *'m going to* live 'til a hundred. (Quebec City Speaker #29: 341)

The first step in variation analysis is identifying a linguistic variable of interest. What counts as a linguistic variable? Recall that we provisionally defined a linguistic variable as "different ways of saying the same thing." At the level of phonetics and phonology, it is uncontroversial that the same sound can be produced in a variety of different ways: consonants may be deleted or inserted, or may be altered in their voicing, place, or manner of articulation; and vowels may be deleted or inserted, raised or lowered, fronted or backed, diphthongized or monophthongized. In fact, phonological variation may simply be viewed as general phonological processes that have a non-categorical rate of occurrence (i.e., not 100 percent). Phonological variables occur relatively frequently in speech and are usually defined on the basis of a structural context, such as a phonological environment, a phonemic class, or a word or set of lexical items. For example, we can define the context of Spanish (n) as "word-final /n/."

Grammatical variation (i.e., variation at the level of morphology, syntax, or discourse) presents a set of challenges not encountered in studies of phonological variation. First, on a practical level, grammatical variables tend to occur less frequently in speech than do phonological variables, which raises the problem of collecting a sufficiently large sample for reliable quantitative analysis. Second, while phonological variables are defined on the basis of a structural context, grammatical variables are defined on the basis of a morphological, syntactic, semantic, or discourse context. For example, the English future variable in (1) is defined on the basis of reference to future time. Finally (and perhaps most crucially), since all such contexts involve considerations of meaning, the question of equivalence is less straightforward: are grammatical variants really different ways of saying "the same thing," or is each variant distinguished by semantic nuances (see Lavandera 1978)? For example, many prescriptive and descriptive studies of the English future assume that different forms of the future must have different meanings, and search for contexts to disambiguate them. Although this assumption of *form-meaning isomorphy* (i.e., one form for one meaning and one meaning for one form) is common in linguistics (see Bolinger 1977: x), many putative semantic differences are neutralized in spontaneous discourse (see Sankoff 1988). Since the different forms constitute the variants of the linguistic

---

[1] Examples are drawn from the Quebec English Corpus (Poplack, Walker, and Malcolmson 2006).

variable (i.e., the object of analysis), using difference in form to infer difference in meaning becomes circular. These considerations raise the question of how to distinguish true linguistic variables from forms that may convey subtly different meanings, which brings us to the first analytical step of variation analysis, circumscribing the variable context.

3   Circumscribing the variable context

If variables are "different ways of saying the same thing," a crucial methodological step in variation analysis is defining precisely what we mean by "the same thing," a step known as circumscribing the *variable context* (or the *envelope of variation*): where does the speaker have a choice between forms? Circumscribing the variable context is perhaps the most important analytical decision because it affects the extraction of tokens, the calculation of frequencies, and the interpretation of results.

The first important consideration in circumscribing the variable context is deciding what counts as variants of the linguistic variable. Crucially, any study of variation must take into consideration not only the occurrences of an interesting form (e.g., the deletion of word-final /t/ and /d/ in consonant clusters in English), but also all of the other contexts in which that form could have occurred, but did not (in the previous example, all non-deleted /t/ and /d/). This consideration, known as the *principle of accountability* (Labov 1972: 72), means that we cannot rely on simple numerical tallies of one form as a measure of frequency; rather, we must calculate rates of frequency relative to the other forms with which it covaries. For example, if we want to investigate potential gender differences in the use of *so* as an intensifier (e.g., *That's so cool!*), we cannot simply compare numbers of uses of *so* by men and women. If we collect ten tokens of *so* from men and twenty tokens from women, it does not necessarily mean that women use *so* more. We may find, once we also tally all contexts in which the form *so* could have been used (i.e., all intensified adjectives, regardless of which intensifier was used), that the relative frequency is identical (i.e., 10/20 [50 percent] for men and 20/40 [50 percent] for women).

The principle of accountability is harder to apply when the linguistic variable is a discourse form. For example, many people are interested in studying the English discourse marker *like* – examples are given in (2) – but it is not clear what *like* varies with (other discourse markers? nothing?), or where it can and cannot occur.

(2)   Just, a lot of different types of people, like, different- different races, different ages, lots of different people always in, like, every neighborhood that I lived in. (Toronto Speaker #24: 10–12)[2]

---

[2] Example taken from the Toronto English Corpus (Hoffman and Walker 2010).

Simply tabulating the number of occurrences of *like* in speech would tell us little about how frequently it occurs because we do not know how often the context in which it occurs is found in speech. Studies have attempted to operationalize the quantification of discourse markers by "normalizing" their rate of use (in terms of overall frequency per X words/clauses or per speaker), but acknowledge this as a compromise strategy (e.g., Levey 2006).

Approaches to defining the variable context can be broadly grouped in two:

- form-based: extract a set of forms that alternate with each other in a single (i.e., non-complementary) context or that are used for a single, identical meaning;
- function-based: define a linguistic function and extract all the forms that convey that function.

The form-based approach is common in studies of phonological variation, where the range of variants is relatively easy to circumscribe. It is also common in studies of morphological variation, where, again, a limited number of variants alternate in a strict context (e.g. verb suffixation for past tense marking, as in (3) below) with an easily identifiable, single meaning.

(3)   a. She *carried* me.   (Bequia Speaker #303: 225)[3]
           b. All the guys *carry* long ago.   (Bequia Speaker #301: 218)

However, in studies of grammatical and discourse variation, it may be difficult or even impossible to close off the set of variants with a form-based approach by identifying a single, identical meaning. As noted above, the question in grammatical variation is whether two forms can ever be said to mean *exactly* the same thing. The function-based approach sidesteps the requirement of strict semantic equivalence of variants by defining a common grammatical or discourse function (Dines 1980).[4] The variable context of many grammatical variables may be defined with either a form-based or a function-based approach: the decision of which approach to take depends largely on the goals of the analysis. For example, in a study of the future (examples given earlier in (1)), we might choose to include within the variable context only the most common forms, *will* and *going to* (form-based), or we might choose to include all of the forms that refer to future time (function-based): *will*, *going to*, simple present, present progressive, and so on. In these two cases, of course, the relative frequency of *will* and *going to* will differ.

---

[3] Examples taken from the Bequia Corpus (Walker and Meyerhoff 2006; Meyerhoff and Walker 2012).

[4] In a study of auxiliary verb variation in French, Sankoff and Thibault (1981) argue for "weak complementarity" – that is, grammatical variables exhibit a quantitatively inverse relationship across the speech community. In other words, if we correlate auxiliary variants with a social index (including social class, education, and access to the standard language), we see a gradual increase in one form and a decrease in the other. Sankoff and Thibault "normalize" their results by dividing the number of occurrences of each variant by the number of words in the text. Thus, while weak complementarity may obviate the requirement for semantic equivalence, it does not satisfy the principle of accountability.

In addition to determining where the variation *can* occur, defining the variable context involves determining where the variation *cannot* occur. Regardless of whether we take a form-based approach or a function-based approach, we want to exclude *categorical* contexts (in which there is no variation). Although they form an important part of any understanding of the linguistic variable and may inform our understanding of limits on variation or stages of change, their inclusion in an analysis of variation would severely skew the results in ways that would obscure the effect of factors on the genuinely variable portion of the data (Tagliamonte 2006: 86–7). For example, studies of (t/d)-deletion in English typically exclude tokens of *and*, because it rarely occurs with a final [d]. We also want to exclude *neutralization* contexts, in which we cannot reliably determine which of the variants occurred. For example, in a study of variable past-marking on regular verbs in English, seen earlier in (3), a following alveolar stop (e.g., *They walk[ed] to town*) neutralizes the distinction between the marked and unmarked variants.

We also want to take into account potential lexical effects, due to skewed distributions of individual lexical items, collocations, or classes. Studies of phonological variation commonly limit the number of tokens of a lexical item included per speaker so that frequent lexical items are not overrepresented in the data. In studies of grammatical variation, we typically exclude potential tokens that occur in fixed or "frozen" expressions. For example, a study of variable -*s*-marking in English verbs, as in (4), would exclude common discourse expressions such as *you know* and *I guess*, because their formulaic nature means that they never take -*s*.

(4)   a. If I go-Ø to a lake in- uh- in a car and a lake is handy, I get-s all nerved up.

(African Nova Scotian Speaker #16: 35–6)[5]

b. And you put-Ø that in there and give-Ø it to your child, they vomit-s.

(Samaná Speaker #2: 994–5)[6]

Once we have defined the variable context, we can then proceed to extract occurrences, or tokens, of the linguistic variable from the data and to code each of them for later analysis.

4   Formulating hypotheses

The goal of variation analysis is to explain linguistic variation through probabilistic statements about the distribution and conditioning of the variants.[7] For each variant, we want to know not only its relative frequency, but also whether

---

[5] Example taken from the African Nova Scotian English Corpus (Poplack and Tagliamonte 1991).

[6] Example taken from the Samaná English Corpus (Poplack and Sankoff 1987).

[7] Linguistic variation is sometimes explained through probabilistic statements expressed in the form of *variable rules*, which include a probability of application. The formulation of variable rules relies on linguistic and statistical reasoning, as well as on the relationship we assume exists between the variants, which not only corresponds to different linguistic processes, but may also yield different quantitative results. See Walker 2010a (Chapter 3: The analysis of linguistic variation) for a more detailed discussion of this issue.

contextual elements influence that frequency. If the variation is truly "free" or random, the frequency of each variant should remain roughly the same regardless of context: this prediction constitutes the *null hypothesis* (H_0) in variation analysis (see Chapters 15 and 18). What we refer to as the *linguistic variable* in variation analysis normally refers to the *dependent variable* in statistics. Disproving the null hypothesis requires testing alternative hypotheses and demonstrating that different contexts correlate meaningfully with differences in the relative frequency of a variant. *Independent variables* are the contextual elements whose effect on the dependent variable we are testing. These are often referred to in variation analysis as *factor groups*, which in turn consist of *factors* (e.g., "sex" is a factor group that consists of the factors "male" and "female").[8]

Each factor group that we test should represent a potentially meaningful explanation for observed variability. These explanations can be divided into two broad types: language-external and language-internal. Language-external explanations involve not only physiological explanations (factors relating to language production and processing), but also what we might call the *social-symbolic* functions of variation: the indication of membership in different social groups (e.g., social class, sex/gender, ethnicity) or the indication of participation in different discursive work in interaction (e.g., topic, style, persona). Typically, these factor groups are decided on at the beginning of the research project and directly influence the recruitment of speakers. For example, a study of gender-based differences should have robust representation of female and male speakers. For our study of ethnolinguistic variation in Toronto English, which focused on the impact of ethnicity on language variation, we not only included a factor group for the speaker's ethnic background, but also one that indicated their degree of orientation to their ethnic group, determined on the basis of responses to a questionnaire (Hoffman and Walker 2010; see below). (See Chapter 22 on the treatment of age and time in variation research; Chapter 7 on independent and extraneous variables; and Chapter 5 on sampling techniques.)

Language-internal explanations involve factors deriving from the linguistic system (i.e., phonetics/phonology, morphology, syntax, and discourse pragmatics). Phonetic explanations, potentially universal to all languages, stem from speech production, while phonological explanations arise from the organization of sounds within an individual language (though, in practice, the distinction between phonetic and phonological conditioning is not so neat). For example, adjacent segments may influence variation in phonetically predictable ways. However, there may be language-specific restrictions on the extent to which phonetically predictable processes can apply, in which case we would want to ascribe such effects to phonology. Grammatical explanations involve effects such as

---

[8] The terms "factor groups" and "factors" are often referred to as "factors" and "levels" in the social sciences and in statistics (see Chapter 16). This chapter uses the terminology currently used in sociolinguistics.

morphological class, syntactic status, the presence of other constituents in the sentence, tense-aspect, negation, and tracking of referents in discourse.

Since variation analysis is a research method rather than a theory of language, the hypotheses that we test through factor groups may be drawn from a number of sources. One source is previous studies: reviewing the literature on the linguistic variable being investigated and, as far as possible, replicating the factor groups tested in previous studies in order to permit comparisons across studies (see Chapter 7). For example, my study of variable zero copula in early African American English (AAE) (Walker 2000) replicated factor groups examined in most of the studies of this linguistic variable in other varieties of AAE: the preceding and following phonological context, the person and type of grammatical subject of the sentence, and the type of following grammatical category. Hypotheses may also be drawn from predictions made by linguistic theories, whether or not these theories were originally formulated within the study of language variation and change. For example, I adopted the theoretical framework of prosodic phonology to test whether the frequency of zero copula was conditioned by the prosodic structure of the phrase in which it occurred, even though this theory was not developed to test variable processes. Finally, the researcher's informal impressions before or during data collection or coding may serve as a source of hypotheses. My decision to use prosodic phonology in the study of zero copula stemmed from my sense while listening to the data of different "rhythms" of sentences with and without zero copula. As these examples demonstrate, hypotheses may be drawn from multiple empirical and/or theoretical sources simultaneously, each of which may guide the formulation of hypotheses.

The only restriction on formulating hypotheses is that they must lend themselves to empirical investigation and "operationalization" as factor groups. For studies that replicate the hypotheses of previous research, operationalizing factor groups should be relatively straightforward (assuming the operationalization has been clearly documented), although the researcher may wish to modify the factor groups in different ways or add to the factor groups investigated. For example, my study of zero copula in early AAE replicated the factor group of following grammatical category along the functional lines used in previous research: participles (5a), adjectives (5b), locatives (5c), and noun phrases (5d). However, in subsequent work on zero copula with Miriam Meyerhoff, we pursued a more syntactic division, splitting locatives into prepositionals (6a) and adverbials (6b), because we predicted that these two categories had different effects on zero copula (Walker and Meyerhoff 2006).

(5)   a. Tomorrow the tourist boat Ø coming. (Samaná Speaker #10: 767)
        b. Tansy's really good. (African Nova Scotian Speaker #14: 293)
        c. Through the field there where Doug Ø at.
                                    (African Nova Scotian Speaker # 32: 42)
        d. A hornet is a bad thing. (Nova Scotian Speaker #110, ctr 1A: 175)

(6)   a. That is in nature. (Bequia Speaker #104: 1241)
        b. Where you see that shop deh there. (Bequia Speaker #1: 738)

In some cases, hypotheses proposed in previous studies or in theoretical literature do not lend themselves easily to operationalization. For example, a common semantic hypothesis offered to explain the difference between futurate *will* and *going to* in English is that the former entails a higher degree of certainty by the speaker. Since we do not have direct access to speaker intent, we cannot test speaker certainty directly, though we may rely on indirect clues in the speaker's discourse. In our study of the English future, we operationalized speaker certainty indirectly by distinguishing between tokens modified by a specific adverbial, as in (7a), and those modified by a non-specific adverbial, as in (7b) (Torres Cacoullos and Walker 2009b). In fact, we found that *will* was more likely to be used with a *non*-specific adverbial than with a specific adverbial.

(7)   a. Well, *tomorrow* me and a couple friends **are going to** be going over to my
            friend's house. (Quebec Speaker #41: 1159)
        b. Well I- *someday* **I'll** be leaving. (Quebec Speaker #51: 726)

Since each factor group represents a hypothesis, it must make a clear prediction about observed effects. For example, the factor group of following grammatical category is included in studies of zero copula because of putative differences in the way that English and creoles treat different predicate types. If the factor group is statistically significant and shows an effect in the predicted direction, we have evidence to support our hypothesis. If the factor group is not significant, we have evidence to refute our hypothesis. If the factor group is significant, but the effect is not in the predicted direction (as in the example of adverbials and the English future discussed above), we need to examine our hypothesis and consider alternative accounts.

5   Coding data

Once hypotheses have been operationalized as factor groups, every token must be *coded* as one of the factors in each of the factor groups. The factors constituting each factor group must be *exhaustive* and *mutually exclusive* – that is, each token must be codeable as one and only one of the factors in the factor group. When setting up factors, it is generally a good idea to code more finely to begin with, since factors can later be collapsed; whereas coding fewer distinctions means that if a finer coding is required, the researcher would have to return to the tokens to recode them. For example, coding a factor group such as "preceding phonological context" for specific segments as factors (e.g., [p], [t], [k] . . .) allows you to collapse these factors into larger classes (e.g., "consonants" vs "vowels") during the analysis, whereas if you begin by coding as larger classes, you cannot subdivide the classes later on without recoding.

Although coding tokens is very time-consuming, since it involves making decisions for each factor group about hundreds or thousands of tokens, it is nevertheless vital that these decisions be consistent. Before starting to code, it is a good idea to draw up a set of *coding instructions* or protocols containing a complete list of all the factor groups and their factors. Since many of the applications used in variation analysis require a single-character code for each factor, coding instructions should also include these codes, along with example tokens and notes about decisions made while coding: Figure 20.1 shows an example page from the coding instructions for

CODING INSTRUCTIONS:FUTURE		
Factor Group #1	**Morphosyntactic Expression (Variants)**	
	FORMS OF *WILL*	
W	*will* + simple infinitive (full form)	*Uh, someone else **will** get that, it's alright. (QEP.QC/067: 1.516).*
L	*'ll* + simple infinitive (contracted form)	*I think there**'ll** be more and more people speaking English. (QEP.QC/060: 1.1780)*
O	*won't*	*So I **won't** be seeing them until about October I guess. (QEP.QC/007: 1.421)*
d	Back shifted *will* (future in the past other than future perfect (=*would have*) or progressive (=*would be – -ing*))	*She was taking all the children that **would be** sixteen years old. (AN/015/22) I decided I'D COME in- in to Sillery to- to- to uh- to continue my schooling (QEP.QC/002)*
	FORMS OF *GOING TO*	
G	*be going to* + simple infinitive (full form)	*So that's what I fear **is going to** happen. (QEP.QC/004: 1.1240)*
g	*gonna (gon/gonna/goin'* etc.) + simple infinitive (any type of contracted GOING TO)	*It's not as if we**'re gonna go** to Spain or something and sing the person a song. (QEP.QC/041: 420)*
J	Backshifted *going to*	*I thought she **was gonna make** me sweep the yard. (AN/048/290)*
	FORMS OF THE PRESENT TENSE	
P	Simple present tense	*they uh- they said, "From now on, that's what you ARE."(QEP.QC/002)*
p	Present progressive	*He said, "We**'re getting** a divorce tomorrow."(QEP.QC/006: 1.2455)*
f	Backshifted present progressive (future past progressive)	*They said they **was coming** back, they ain't come back. (SE/020/363)*

Figure 20.1. *Excerpt from coding instructions for the English future*

our study of English future reference. Coding instructions are useful not only for coding by multiple researchers (to ensure consistency among coders), but also as a record of coding decisions that we can consult later and use when writing up the methodology of the study. Since coding is a dynamic, iterative process, we can revise the instructions during coding, as unanticipated tokens or factors arise, provided that previously coded tokens are recoded in line with the new instructions. For purposes of transparency and replicability, coding protocols must also document all principled exclusions, as mentioned briefly in relation to example (4).

Tokens may be extracted and coded directly into a data file in the statistical application. This practice has the advantage of allowing a quick analysis at any time during coding. Many researchers code into a word-processing document (such as Word) or a spreadsheet program (such as Excel) so that they can include more detail, use the data across different software, or sort tokens in different ways. Data can then be imported in an appropriate format into statistical applications. Since each token must be coded for a number of factor groups, and switching between factor groups is likely to increase coding errors, some researchers code by factor group rather than by token. Researcher preferences vary, but the common goal is to minimize error while optimizing the time involved. Figure 20.2 shows an example of part of a completed coding sheet for the future and part of its equivalent token file in GoldVarb (regression analysis software used in sociolinguistics).

Once all tokens have been coded, we can examine the distribution of variants across factors to test the predictions made by our hypotheses.

6   Analyzing variation

In essence, variation analysis consists of quantitative comparison, most commonly among the overall frequencies of each variant as a proportion of the variable context and the relative frequencies of each variant (or one variant of interest) across different factors within the same factor group. Although we can determine whether any differences are meaningful by using tests of statistical significance (see Chapter 15, 'Basic Significance Testing'), we normally want to consider multiple hypotheses about contextual effects: for example, we typically hypothesize that (ing) is affected not only by the following phonological context and grammatical status of the word, but also by the sex/gender of the speaker, and so on. Increasing the number of hypotheses complicates the statistical models required for variation analysis and calls for techniques that take into account the effects of multiple hypotheses simultaneously. In the following subsections, I briefly discuss a few of the more common statistical techniques (see Chapters 15 and 16 for more details).

6.1   Multiple regression

Since the early 1970s, variation analysis has made use of *multiple regression*, a statistical tool that determines the significance of each factor group

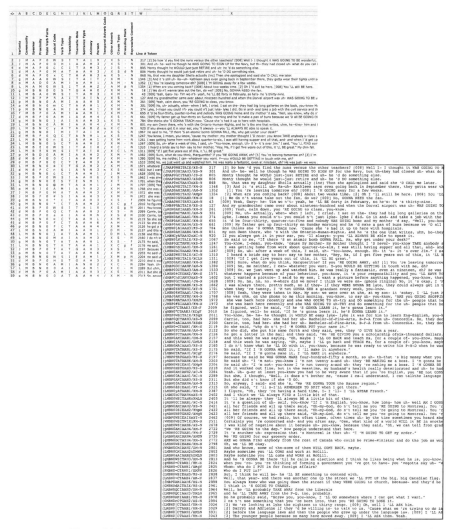

Figure 20.2. *Fragment of an Excel coding sheet and GoldVarb token file for the coding of the English future*

and estimates the relative contribution made by each factor in every factor group (independent variable) to the occurrence of a particular variant (a value of the dependent variable) when all factor groups are considered together. This estimate may be expressed as a *factor weight*, a *coefficient*, or a *logodds* value (see Chapter 16 for details): the value of the estimate indicates the strength of effect. Factor weights (e.g., generated by GoldVarb) and coefficients range between values of 0 and 1, and factor weights may be centered on 0.5, with values above 0.5 favoring the occurrence of the variant and those below 0.5 disfavoring. Logodds values (e.g., generated by Rbrul; Johnson 2010) range between positive infinity (∞) and negative infinity ($-\infty$) and are centered on 0, with positive values favoring the variant and negative values disfavoring. Summary statistics provided by multiple regression include a numerical measurement of the overall likelihood that the variant will occur (the *input* or *corrected mean*) and how much variation is accounted for by the statistical model (the *coefficient of determination* or R^2).

To determine which factor groups exert a statistically significant effect, many multiple regression applications perform a step-up/step-down procedure, which looks for the configuration of factors that provides the best fit to the observed distribution of variants.[9] The step-up procedure adds each factor group to the input in turn and determines whether this significantly improves the prediction of the model; the step-down procedure begins by forcing all of the factor groups and the input into one analysis and then takes away each factor group in turn to determine whether this produces a statistically significant change in fit. The best step-up and the best step-down should contain the same factor groups. Table 20.1 shows the results of a stepwise multiple regression for several social and linguistic factor groups selected as significant for the (ing) variable (*singing ~ singin'*) in Toronto English. For each factor, its contribution to the occurrence of the alveolar variant *-in'* is expressed as a percentage (relative frequency), a centered factor weight, and a logodds value.

In sociolinguistics, the interpretation of multiple regression relies on the notion of a *constraint hierarchy*, the idea that factors are ranged within each factor group according to their relative favorability to the occurrence of a particular variant. To some extent, given a significant effect, the numerical values within this range matter less than the relative ranking of factors. In Table 20.1, each factor group shows a hierarchy of conditioning. For example, *-in'* is more likely to occur in verbal and monomorphemic forms of (ing) (e.g., *going* and *something*, respectively) than with nominal/gerundive forms (e.g., *the turning*). Since the constraint hierarchy represents the variable grammar, it can be compared across speakers and groups: speakers or groups who share a constraint hierarchy are judged to share the same linguistic system. An additional point of comparison across analyses is the relative strength of each factor group within the multiple regression analysis, indicated either by the order with which factor groups are selected as significant (as shown in the "best model" below the table), by the change in the coefficient of determination when each factor group is included, or by the range of each factor group in the analysis (the difference between the highest and lowest factor weight within the factor group). As shown in Table 20.1, the factor group with the greatest effect on (ing) is the ethnicity of the speaker, followed by the following and preceding phonological contexts, and then grammatical status.

Although multiple regression does not require tokens to be distributed evenly across all combinations of factors, the procedure does assume that the effects of each factor group operate independently of each other. For this reason, it is important to consider whether there is any interdependence between factor groups. One type of lack of independence is *multicollinearity*, whereby two or more independent variables are highly correlated and therefore not in fact independent (e.g., housing and income; see Chapter 16 for a discussion). Another type

---

[9] Johnson (2010) expresses some of the statistical concerns around stepwise multiple regression.

Table 20.1 *Factors contributing to the occurrence of the alveolar variant -in'* *in Toronto English*

	Total N:	2,701		
	Input:	0.13		
	Nagelkerke R^2:	0.216		

	logodds	N	%	Factor weight	
Ethnicity					
Italian	0.798	1,303	30	.69	
Portuguese	0.629	611	28	.65	
British/Irish	0.284	452	21	.57	
Chinese	−1.711	335	4	.15	
Range:					54
Following phonological context					
Coronal	0.635	822	32	.65	
Labial	0.210	310	28	.55	
Vowel	0.023	1,142	24	.51	
Pause	−0.868	427	10	.30	
Range:					35
Preceding phonological context					
Velar	0.758	436	44	.68	
Vowel	0.100	642	32	.53	
Labial	−0.225	291	23	.44	
Coronal	−0.633	1,332	15	.35	
Range:					33
Grammatical status					
Verbal	0.410	1,749	31	.60	
Monomorphemic	0.115	511	15	.53	
Nominal	−0.526	441	10	.37	
Range:					23

All factor groups selected as significant. Best model: Ethnicity (1.13×10^{-28}) + preceding phonological context (1.33×10^{-21}) + following phonological context (2.01×10^{-17}) + grammatical status (9.39×10^{-8})

is *interaction*, where some sub-part of a variable interacts with another (e.g., an interaction of age and gender, such that younger men significantly favor use of some phonetic feature, in contrast to other age/gender combinations). While multicollinearity is generally treated as a data problem to be resolved before analysis, interactions can be of interest and form part of an analysis.

We can check for interdependence of certain types by cross-tabulating each factor group against every other factor group and looking for gaps or interactions in the distribution of data. Common issues that arise may be dealt with in the following ways. First, if small numbers of tokens are found in some cells, factors within a factor group may be combined into a smaller number of divisions, increasing the proportion of data in each factor. For example, in our study of the future, we initially made a fine distinction of adverbials according to their temporal-aspectual properties, but since so few of each type of adverbial actually occurs in discourse, we combined them into the related, larger-scale division of "specific" and "non-specific." Second, if two or more factor groups with a high degree of dependence are found, these may be combined into a single "interaction group." For example, studies of verbal -s are normally interested in the effects of the type of subject (pronoun or Noun Phrase) and the grammatical person (first, second or third). However, since the distinction between pronoun and NP subjects only exists in third person, it is common to combine these two factor groups into one (first person pronoun, second person pronoun, third person pronoun, third person NP). Similarly, it is common to combine social factors to test for inter-actions, evaluating complex categories such as "middle-class women" or "younger men," alongside age, class, or gender as independent variables. Finally, separate multivariate analyses can be performed on the data, excluding each of the interacting factor groups in turn; comparing the variance between the analyses will determine which analysis provides the best fit to the data and therefore which factor group is more likely to be responsible for the observed patterns. For example, in our study of variable omission of English complemen-tizer *that* (Torres Cacoullos and Walker 2009a), because we could not run the lexical type, semantic class, and frequency of the matrix-clause verb in the same analysis, we ran three multivariate analyses, keeping the other factor groups constant, but including one of the three factor groups above. Comparing the goodness-of-fit of each model to the data, we found that the lexical type of the verb provided a better account for the observed variation than did semantic class and frequency.

6.2   Mixed-effects models

Most factor groups examined in variation analysis are assumed to represent *fixed effects* – that is, we assume that the factors analyzed for a given factor group include all possible levels found in a given population. For example, coding for speakers' social class assumes that the factor levels included (e.g., working class, lower middle class, upper middle class, upper class) exhaust the primary levels found in the population of interest, so results will generalize to all speakers in that speech community. Similarly, an internal factor group such as following phonological context usually exhausts, rather than samples, all the following contexts of interest to the study. By contrast, our sampling of speakers and contexts (e.g., words) is typically random (i.e., we cannot sample every speaker or every word), so the results may not be representative of the entire sampling population. For example, individual speakers and contexts may contrib-ute different numbers of tokens or may show different overall frequencies of particular variants. This consideration leads us to the possibility that some factor groups may represent *random effects*. Increasingly, variation analysis makes use of *mixed-effect models* (see Pinheiro and Bates 2000; Johnson 2010; see also Chapter 16), which designate factor groups in the multiple regression model as either fixed effects or random effects. Once random effects have been taken into consideration in the statistical model, we can be reasonably confident that any remaining fixed effects are genuine, which increases the likelihood that the results of our statistical models can be generalized to the sampling population. For example, my studies of (t/d)-deletion and the use of singular agreement in existentials with plural reference in Toronto English show that ethnicity is significant for both variables when only fixed effects are included in the analysis (Hoffman and Walker 2010; Walker 2010b). Once a mixed-effects model is used, with speaker included as a random effect, the significance of ethnicity holds for (t/d)-deletion, but not for singular agreement. This difference in results suggests that much of the apparent effect of ethnicity in the grammatical variable has to do with individual speaker differences and that, at least in this speech community, phonological variation has a social meaning that is lacking in grammatical variation.

6.3   Correlation and factor analysis

We have so far been discussing variation analysis as a tool for testing hypotheses, asking whether certain factor groups (independent variables) exert statistically significant effects on a linguistic variable (the dependent variable). However, we may want to ask other types of questions that require variation analysis in which multiple regression is inappropriate.

One question that is often asked in variation analysis is whether all of the different measures actually represent different effects. We might wonder, for example, whether all of the independent variables are indeed independent of each other, or whether there is a smaller set of effects that these factor groups are testing. The goal of this may be either to reduce multicollinearity before performing a regression analysis, or simply to reduce noise and clarify the contribution of distinct factors. Another question we might ask is whether speakers' use of one linguistic variable is comparable to their use of other variables: rather than grouping speakers according to various social characteristics (sex, social class, ethnicity) and testing the effects of those factor groups on a linguistic variable, we could group individual speakers on the basis of multiple linguistic variables and look for sociolinguistic characteristics that speakers in each group have in common. These types of questions can be addressed using analytic approaches other than, or combined with, multiple regression.

If we are comparing two (independent or linguistic) variables, we can use a simple two-dimensional measurement of correlation, such as Spearman's rank correlation coefficient (ρ) or Pearson's product-moment correlation coefficient (r) (see Chapter 15 for details). For example, in a study of the effects of frequency on (t/d)-deletion (Walker 2012), I compared four measurements of lexical frequency: the number of tokens of each lexical item in the token file, in the corpus from which they were drawn, and from two publicly available corpora of English.

Plotting each pair of measurements of frequency on a two-dimensional scatter-gram allowed me to draw trend lines (or regression lines) to determine the strength and significance of correlation between each pair. However, since we typically want to compare more than two variables, we need to make use of techniques that allow for multidimensional correlation.

The most common statistical techniques for measuring underlying relationships between multiple variables are factor analysis (FA) and principal components analysis (PCA). Although there are some mathematical and theoretical differences between these techniques and what they are used for (see, e.g., Chapter 5 in Baayen 2008), their basic purpose is to reduce a larger set of variables (dependent, independent, or linguistic) to a smaller set of underlying factors or components by identifying correlations among variables and isolating the components (or factors) associated with those correlations.

Because it has been more commonly used in variation analysis (e.g., Horvath and Sankoff 1987; Van de Velde, van Hout, and Gerritsen 1997; Hoffman and Walker 2010), I will focus on PCA. To my knowledge, the earliest use of PCA in sociolinguistics is Horvath and Sankoff's (1987) study of English in Sydney, Australia, which grouped speakers according to their use of several linguistic variables. Using the number of tokens uttered by each speaker in their sample of each variant for four vowel variables, PCA reduced these variables to four component factors that were then used to group speakers: native-speaker status (which accounted for 32 percent of the variance among speakers); sex and social class (15 percent); age and ethnicity (9 percent); and degree of interaction with the core speech community (8 percent). More recently, our study of ethnolinguistic variation in Toronto English (Hoffman and Walker 2010) grouped speakers according to several (independent) social variables. Using the quantified responses to thirty-six questions related to ethnic orientation given by each speaker, PCA reduced these variables to four component factors: the ethnic composition of the speaker's social network and their use of the heritage language (which accounted for 35 percent of the variance among speakers); the degree of interaction the speaker had with their grandparents (15 percent); the speaker's perceptions of discrimination in work (10 percent); and housing (9 percent). We subsequently used the individual speaker scores on the first factor to group speakers according to their degree of "ethnic orientation."

7   Variation and linguistic theory

In linguistic theory, variation has tended to be viewed as a problem to be avoided or solved, no doubt because of the view in theoretical linguistics that the proper object of study is competence (the knowledge of language contained in the individual speaker's brain), rather than performance (language in use), which is assumed to be unsystematic. However, variation analysis shows that there is a great deal of systematicity in performance data, which we would not expect if performance is entirely unrelated to competence. How do we accommodate the fact of variation in linguistic theory?

One approach is to argue that variation is simply a form of code-switching, an alternation between linguistic systems that are internally invariant. While this remains a possibility, it lacks empirical verifiability, since it has not been demonstrated that variation obeys the same constraints as code-switching between recognizably distinct languages. Other research has begun to address the role of variation in grammars more directly, leading to the introduction of new methodologies into theoretical research.

Some linguists resist allowing variation within linguistic theory because they assume that there cannot be optionality in the computational system of language. If this assumption is true, the mechanism that generates variation must lie outside the linguistic system. For example, under the Minimalist Program (Chomsky 1995), once lexical or functional elements are merged in syntactic representation, only one syntactic output is possible, and variation can only occur pre- or post-syntactically, when words or features are selected from the lexicon or when features are spelled out in phonology and morphology. Within this approach, Adger (2006) derives variation in subject–verb agreement in non-standard English using a set of features ([±singular], [±participant], [±author]) and a spell-out rule for each form. Since each form may be spelled out from a different number of combinations of features, and the speaker has some optionality in lexical selection, Adger's approach makes predictions about the relative frequency of each form. In an approach based on Distributed Morphology (Halle and Marantz 1993), Nevins and Parrott (2009) similarly argue for the use of features and spell-out rules, though they posit an additional "impoverishment rule" that (variably) removes person and number features from the representation, giving rise to variation in the output.

There have been a number of attempts to model variation by working within another theoretical framework, Optimality Theory (OT; Prince and Smolensky 1993). In OT, the linguistic system generates multiple candidates that are evaluated by a hierarchy of ranked constraints, each of which can be violated to satisfy a higher-ranked constraint. For example, Nagy and Reynolds (1997) model variable word-final deletion in Faetar (a Francoprovençal dialect spoken in Italy) by allowing the crucial constraints to "float" through the hierarchy, yielding multiple rankings and producing different output frequencies. Anttila (1997) similarly proposes to derive variation from probabilities generated by freely ranked constraints, though restricted to different "strata" within the hierarchy. More recent approaches to variation within OT have adopted "Stochastic OT" (Boersma 1997; Boersma and Hayes 2001), in which constraints are ranked not only with respect to each other, but also along a continuous, numerical scale. In this approach, learners derive numerical rankings for each constraint through the Gradual Learning Algorithm (GLA), which models repeated exposure to output forms. Variation arises when the ranges of constraints on the scale overlap, to produce multiple rankings and outputs. Testing this model on artificial and natural linguistic data, Boersma and Hayes (2001) find that the GLA produces grammars that can generate relative frequencies that match that of the input fairly closely. Bresnan, Deo, and Sharma (2007) have similarly applied the GLA to grammatical variation.

Some of the approaches described above model probabilities generated by the grammar, while others model probabilities generated by exposure to input. These different responses to the question of how variation relates to language competence involve the introduction of diverse new methodologies to theoretical linguistics, including the measurement of variation in linguistic judgments (Chapter 3), in natural speech (this chapter), in corpora (Chapter 13), and in computational modeling (Chapter 19).

Although the interface of linguistic theory and variation analysis is promising, there are a number of issues that remain to be addressed. Without agreement on criteria for distinguishing code-switching from system-internal variation, we are obliged to consider seriously the possibility of optionality within the linguistic system; this, in turn, requires the use of appropriate methods. As we have seen in this chapter, variation analysis requires the use of multivariate statistics, but many theoretical approaches still often rely on a single factor or constraint to derive the variation. Theoretical approaches wishing to incorporate variation may need to begin to avail themselves of the methodological and statistical tools of variation analysis.

8   Conclusion

Although variation analysis may differ from other methodological approaches within linguistics, it is still essentially about doing (socio)linguistic analysis, and many of the questions that we face in variation analysis are the same as those that we encounter in other approaches. Careful data collection, coding, and statistical analysis simply provide us with additional tools for attempting to answer these questions: the key is knowing when and how to use these tools. The important questions we want to ask in any research project is:

- What is the research question?
- How can the research question be operationalized as an empirically verifiable hypothesis?
- What are the most appropriate tools to use in adducing evidence to answer the research question? Which statistical technique is most appropriate?
- What do the quantitative results say about the research question?

These questions should not be viewed as a step-by-step recipe for conducting research. As we have seen, the research process is dynamic and iterative, in that the research question may change as the analysis proceeds, or additional questions may be encountered, and we may have to return to earlier questions again and again before achieving a satisfactory interpretation. Rarely does the first set of results constitute the final analysis: for every table that gets published, there are a dozen earlier tables that do not.

As I noted in the introduction, the methods of variation analysis are common to a number of subfields of linguistics, but they are most commonly associated with the subfield of "sociolinguistics." Although the term "*socio*linguistics" may imply that variation analysis is suitable for answering questions that are posed in only one subfield of linguistics, the methods are flexible enough that it should be able to provide results that can lead to socially *and* linguistically meaningful explanations for linguistic behavior.

References

Adger, D. 2006. Combinatorial variability. *Journal of Linguistics* 42: 503–30.

Anttila, A. 1997. Deriving variation from grammar. In F. Hinskens, R. van Hout, and W. L. Wetzels, eds. *Variation, Change and Phonological Theory.* Amsterdam: John Benjamins, 35–68.

Baayen, H. 2008. *Analyzing Linguistic Data: A Practical Introduction to Statistics using R.* Cambridge University Press.

Boersma, P. 1997. How we learn variation, optionality, and probability. *Proceedings of the Institute of Phonetic Sciences of the University of Amsterdam* 21: 43–58.

Boersma, P. and B. Hayes. 2001. Empirical tests of the Gradual Learning Algorithm. *Linguistic Inquiry* 32: 45–86.

Bolinger, D. 1977. *Meaning and Form.* London: Longman.

Bresnan, J., A. Deo, and D. Sharma. 2007. Typology in variation: a probabilistic approach to be and n't in the Survey of English Dialects. *English Language and Linguistics* 11: 301–46.

Chomsky, N. 1995. The *Minimalist Program.* Cambridge, MA: MIT Press.

Dines, E. R. 1980. Variation in discourse – 'and stuff like that'. *Language in Society* 9: 13–31.

Halle, M. and A. Marantz. 1993. Distributed Morphology and the pieces of inflection. In K. Hale and S. J. Keyser, eds. *The View from Building 20.* Cambridge, MA: MIT Press, 111–76.

Hoffman, M. F. and J. A. Walker. 2010. Ethnolects and the city: ethnic orientation and linguistic variation in Toronto English. *Language Variation and Change* 22: 37–67.

Horvath, B. and D. Sankoff. 1987. Delimiting the Sydney speech community. *Language in Society* 16: 179–204.

Johnson, D. E. 2010. Why stepwise isn't so wise. Paper presented at *New Ways of Analyzing Variation* 39. San Antonio, TX, November 4–6.

Labov, W. 1972. *Sociolinguistic Patterns.* Philadelphia: University of Pennsylvania Press.

Lavandera, B. 1978. Where does the sociolinguistic variable stop? *Working Papers in Sociolinguistics* 40: 6–19.

Levey, S. 2006. The sociolinguistic distribution of discourse marker like in preadolescent speech. *Multilingua* 25: 413–41.

Meyerhoff, M. and J. A. Walker. 2012. Grammatical variation in Bequia (St Vincent and the Grenadines). *Journal of Pidgin and Creole Languages* 27: 209–34.

Nagy, N. and W. Reynolds. 1997. Optimality Theory and word-final deletion in Faetar. *Language Variation and Change* 9: 37–55.

Nevins, A. and J. Parrott. 2009. Variable rules meets impoverishment theory: patterns of agreement levelling in English varieties. *Lingua* 120: 1135–59.

Pinheiro, J. C. and D. M. Bates. 2000. *Mixed Effects Models in S and S-PLUS*. New York: Springer.

Poplack, S. and D. Sankoff. 1987. The Philadelphia story in the Spanish Caribbean. *American Speech* 64: 291–314.

Poplack, S. and S. Tagliamonte. 1991. African American English in the diaspora: the case of old-line Nova Scotians. *Language Variation and Change* 3: 301–39.

Poplack, S., J. A. Walker, and R. Malcolmson. 2006. An English 'like no other'? Language contact and change in Quebec. *Canadian Journal of Linguistics* 51: 185–213.

Prince, A. and P. Smolensky. 1993. *Optimality Theory: Constraint Interaction in Generative Grammar*. New Brunswick, NJ: Rutgers University.

Sankoff, D. 1988. Sociolinguistics and syntactic variation. In F. J. Newmeyer, ed. *Linguistics: The Cambridge Survey. Volume IV: Language: The Socio-cultural Context*, 4 vols. Cambridge University Press, 140–61.

Sankoff, D. and P. Thibault. 1981. Weak complementarity: tense and aspect in Montreal French. In B. B. Johns and D. R. Strong, eds. *Syntactic Change: Natural Language Studies*. Ann Arbor: Department of Linguistics, University of Michigan, 205–16.

Tagliamonte, S. 2006. *Analysing Linguistic Variation*. Oxford and Malden, MA: Blackwell.

Torres Cacoullos, R. and J. A. Walker. 2009a. On the persistence of grammar in discourse formulas: a variationist study of that. *Linguistics* 47: 1–43.

2009b. The present of the English future: grammatical variation and collocations in discourse. *Language* 85: 321–54.

Van de Velde, H., R. van Hout, and M. Gerritsen. 1997. Watching Dutch change: a real time study of variation and change in standard Dutch pronunciation. *Journal of Sociolinguistics* 1: 361–91.

Walker, J. A. 2000. Present accounted for: prosody and aspect in early African American English. Unpublished Ph.D. dissertation, University of Ottawa.

2010a. *Variation in Linguistic Systems*. London and New York: Routledge.

2010b. Grammatical variation and the sociolinguistic monitor: plural existentials in Toronto English. Paper presented at *New Ways of Analyzing Variation* 39. San Antonio, TX, November 4–6.

2012. Form, function, and frequency in phonological variation. *Language Variation and Change* 24: 397–414.

Walker, J. A. and M. Meyerhoff. 2006. Zero copula in the eastern Caribbean: evidence from Bequia. *American Speech* 91: 146–63.

21 Discourse analysis

Susan Ehrlich and Tanya Romaniuk

1   Introduction

The term "discourse" has a variety of meanings both within linguistics and outside of it and, correspondingly, discourse analysis refers to a wide range of analytic methods. In this chapter, we will focus on methods of discourse analysis that are associated with sociocultural linguistics, "a broad interdisciplinary field ... encompassing the subfields of sociolinguistics and linguistic anthropology, among others" (Bucholtz and Hall 2005: 586). Given our emphasis on socially oriented approaches to discourse analysis, following Schiffrin (1994: 415) we define discourse as language embedded in social interaction – that is, unlike approaches to discourse that conceptualize it as a linguistic unit commensurate with (but larger than) a sentence or a morpheme, we regard discourse as fundamentally different from these other kinds of linguistic units. Under a formalist definition of discourse, for example, the organization of words into sentences is regarded as equivalent to the organization of sentences into discourse (see Kamp and Reyle 1993 and Lambrecht 1994 for more on the treatment of discourse from a formal perspective). Yet, as both Schiffrin (1994) and Cameron (2001) have pointed out, the process of determining whether a string of words constitutes a grammatical sentence or not relies upon linguistic knowledge, in contrast to the process of imposing coherence on a string of sentences (i.e., interpreting them as a discourse), which involves, for the most part, the mobilization of non-linguistic and contextual knowledge. Put another way, "discourse is not amenable to a 'pure' formalist analysis" (Cameron 2001: 13) in the way that other kinds of linguistic units are.

Outside of linguistics, scholars in the humanities and social sciences, influenced by the work of Foucault, have also been interested in "discourse," to the extent that discourse constructs and constitutes social realities. For Foucault, power is exercised through discourses of knowledge (e.g., the discourses of the social sciences, of the medical sciences), which function to define and categorize, and, in turn, to regulate and control the objects of their expertise – that is, social identities and social practices are "brought into being" as a result of socially and historically

We thank the two editors of this volume and an anonymous reviewer for insightful comments on a previous draft of this chapter. In particular, we are grateful to Rob Podesva, who helped us enormously in making the revisions to our chapter.

contingent domains of knowledge, what Foucault calls "discourses." While Foucault's work has stimulated an enormous interest in "discourse analysis" among scholars in the humanities and social sciences, Foucauldian discourse analysis does not generally involve the close analysis of texts (Fairclough and Wodak 1997; Bucholtz 2003) and, in fact, does not necessarily involve the analysis of language. A distinction can be drawn, then, between sociocultural linguists, who engage in the detailed analysis of discourse, and scholars in the humanities and social sciences, for whom the notion of discourse is much more abstract. However, this is not to say that linguistically oriented discourse analysts are uninterested in discourse in a Foucauldian sense. On the contrary, discourse analysts from a variety of traditions (e.g., critical discourse analysis) attempt to show how the nitty-gritty details of socially situated linguistic interactions can be constitutive of social identities and social practices.

In the remainder of this chapter, we describe and exemplify, with sample analyses, three approaches to discourse analysis: *conversation analysis, interactional sociolinguistics*, and *critical discourse analysis*.[1] We chose these three approaches because they capture the breadth of the field, ranging from the details of talk (a focus of conversation analysis) to the ideologies that underlie them (a focus of critical discourse analysis).[2] In organizing our discussion according to analytic method, we may inadvertently give the impression that practitioners of discourse analysis always employ a single, internally consistent method, and, moreover, that our own analyses adhere strictly to the method being exemplified. Neither of these propositions is completely accurate. There are many examples in the literature of discourse analysts adopting an eclectic approach to their data – that is, using a variety of methods in order to best answer their research questions.[3] As Bucholtz (2011: 37–8) remarks, for at least some discourse analysts, the choice of analytic method(s) is driven more by the analysts' research questions and less by their commitment to a particular kind of analysis.

2   Description of the data

In illustrating some of the similarities and differences among the discourse analytic methods we have chosen to exemplify, our sample analyses

---

[1] As will become evident, we do not view the distinctions among these approaches as always clear-cut – for example, from our perspective, "critical" analyses can be conducted using a wide range of methods, including those from conversation analysis and interactional sociolinguistics.

[2] There are, of course, other approaches to discourse analysis that we could have described in this chapter, such as ethnography of communication (e.g., Hymes 1962; Saville-Troike 1982) or discursive psychology (e.g., Davies and Harré 1990; Edwards and Potter 1992; Potter 2012), but space constraints do not permit us to provide a comprehensive overview of all approaches to discourse analysis.

[3] The work of conversation analysts may generally be considered an exception to this claim about eclecticism, although many discourse analysts use the tools that conversation analysis provides (e.g., the analysis of sequence organization, of turns-at-talk, etc.) in their analyses.

draw on data from a single institutional setting, a courtroom trial.[4] While other exemplifications of discourse analytic methods (e.g., Stubbe et al. 2003; Benwell and Stokoe 2006) have generally analyzed a *single* piece of data from the different perspectives, we have adopted a slightly different strategy – that is, we examine *different kinds of data* within a *single* setting, under the assumption that each approach to discourse analysis has somewhat different goals, which, in turn, may necessitate different objects of analysis (i.e., different kinds of data). By focusing on different kinds of data within a single setting, then, we believe that we can better compare and contrast both the analytic tools employed by the different approaches and the more general principles that influence the kinds of research questions asked and the kinds of contextual information deemed relevant to an analysis.

The data for this chapter come from an American rape trial, *Maouloud Baby* v. *the State of Maryland*, which took place in the state of Maryland in 2004. The testimonies analyzed here are necessarily explicit, given the subject matter. They also provide an ideal case for demonstrating what different discourse analytic approaches add to our understanding of a highly charged communicative event with extreme consequences for participants. While interactions in which there is seemingly little at stake (e.g., conversations between friends, family talk, service encounters) comprise a significant number of discourse analytic studies, one of the theoretical approaches we illustrate – critical discourse analysis – is a political enterprise concerned with bringing power relations, specifically inequality, to light. What we show is that highly consequential talk, of the kind discussed here, lends itself to a critical discourse analytic approach and, at the same time, is compatible with the approaches of conversation analysis and interactional sociolinguistics.

At the trial, the accused, Maouloud Baby, was convicted of first-degree rape and some other sexually related offenses and sentenced to 15 years in jail. Maouloud appealed this decision and, upon appeal, the Maryland Court of Special Appeals (the second highest court in Maryland) reversed Maouloud's convictions in September 2006 and ordered a new trial. In April 2008, after Maouloud and the State cross-appealed to the Maryland Court of Appeals (the highest court in Maryland), the Court of Appeals also reversed Maouloud's convictions and ordered a new trial. This new trial has not taken place and, according to the prosecuting attorney in the case (pers. comm.), will probably not occur because the complainant is reluctant to testify again.

In order to provide some contextualization for the sample analyses that follow, we briefly describe the events under investigation in this trial. The complainant, Jewel Lankford, and the accused, Maouloud Baby, met at a McDonald's restaurant on the night of the events in question – December 13, 2003. Jewel was with her

---

[4] Sample analysis #1 is based on some of our collaborative work (Romaniuk and Ehrlich 2013), while sample analyses #2 and #3 are based on work by Susan Ehrlich (Ehrlich 2011, 2012, 2013).

best friend, Lacey Simmons. Upon leaving the McDonald's, Maouloud asked whether he and his friend, Michael (Mike) Wilson, could get a ride to a party in Jewel's car. The young women agreed; however, upon discovering there was no party they instead drove to another location where they spent a brief amount of time together. The four then drove back to the McDonald's and Lacey left the group to be with her boyfriend. Jewel then agreed to drive Mike and Maouloud to a residential neighborhood where she parked her car and agreed to sit in the back seat of the car with the two young men. It was at this point that the accounts of Jewel and Maouloud began to diverge.[5] According to the prosecution, Mike and Maouloud then sexually assaulted Jewel in a variety of ways. Mike then asked Maouloud to leave the car and continued to sexually assault Jewel.[6] After some time, Mike got out of the car and Maouloud re-entered, and again, against her will, pushed his penis into Jewel's vagina. Eventually he stopped, after which Mike got back into the car, and drove Jewel's car to a neighborhood across the street from the McDonald's, where the three parted ways. The prosecution argued that all of the sexual acts of aggression were non-consensual, while the defense argued that they were consensual.

Our discussion is based on audio recordings of the trial. While audio recordings are the primary medium for linguistically oriented discourse analysis, it is not uncommon to draw on textual or video data, as well. Video data enable the analyst to consider the embodied nature of communication and to examine the diverse semiotic resources (e.g., gesture, gaze) therein (e.g., Goodwin 2007). For a discussion of methodological considerations for video-recording interaction, see Chapter 10 and Kissmann 2009.

3   Conversation analysis

As a method of analyzing talk and interaction, conversation analysis (CA) emerged in the 1960s and 1970s in the work of sociologist Harvey Sacks, and his collaborators, Emanuel Schegloff and Gail Jefferson. Many of the ideas developed in Sacks' (1992) lectures (1964–72), which constitute much of the basis for CA, were heavily influenced by the work of Harold Garfinkel and Erving Goffman (see Heritage 1984 and Drew and Wootton 1988, respectively). From Garfinkel's ethnomethodological approach, Sacks developed a concern with the "common sense resources, practices and procedures through which members of a society produce and recognize mutually intelligible objects, events and courses of action" (Liddicoat 2007: 2). At the same time, Sacks shared a strong interest in Goffman's concept of "the interaction order," which emphasized the study of

---

[5] We note that the Court of Special Appeals remarked in its opinion that the accused's testimony "was surprisingly consistent" with the complainant's (*Maouloud Baby* v. *State of Maryland*, Court of Special Appeals of Maryland, 2005).

[6] Michael Wilson did not have a trial, as he pled guilty to his charges.

actual instances of social interaction by asserting that ordinary activities of daily life were an important subject for study. Drawing on these ideas, Sacks sought "to develop an alternative to mainstream sociology: specifically, an observational science of society and social action" (Speer and Stokoe 2011: 9), grounded in the "details of actual events" (Sacks 1984: 26). Working with such "details" means that there are some key differences between CA and other social scientific approaches, such as sociology. For example, CA provides detailed descriptions of naturally occurring data rather than "experimental" or "research-provoked" data; embodies a perspective on talk-in-interaction that is "organizational and procedural"; and views talk-in-interaction as a "situated achievement" (ten Have 2007). Ten Have (2007: 9) aptly summarizes the analytic focus of CA as "not explaining *why* people act as they do, but rather explicating *how* they do it." These differences reflect one of the fundamental assumptions of CA: that conversation is not random or unstructured, but is in fact orderly, and participants construct their talk in orderly ways (Sacks 1984). Accordingly, an analyst's principal task is to discover the orderly practices, devices and patterns through which participants produce and understand their own behavior and that of others in social interaction.

In illustrating similarities and differences between a CA approach and other forms of discourse analysis using an institutional setting, we arrive at an important distinction between the kinds of data analysts may use. Within CA, some have made the distinction between "pure" (e.g., ten Have 2007) or "basic" (Heritage 2005) CA and "applied" CA. "Basic" CA views conversation as an institution in and of itself – the fundamental or primordial scene of social life (Schegloff 1996b: 4) – and is concerned with discovering what Sacks (1984: 26) calls "the machinery of conversation" (i.e., the orderly practices participants co-construct in interaction). "Applied" CA, on the other hand, is connected to the goal of identifying institutional talk as distinct from ordinary conversation. Whereas "ordinary conversation" is understood as encompassing forms of interaction that are not restricted to specialized settings, in institutional talk, participants have institution-specific goals to accomplish, and the kinds of interactional contributions that can be made are more limited (Drew and Heritage 1992a). Heritage (2005: 106) suggests that research on institutional talk builds on the findings of "basic" CA by drawing on the many available findings concerning fundamental orders of conversational organization (e.g., sequence organization, turn taking, repair) and the practices through which they are accomplished. Our first sample analysis, then, is a form of "applied" CA in the sense that it builds on what we know about one of these organizational systems, repair, from the findings of "basic" CA, and examines it in an institutional context.[7]

---

[7] It is important to keep in mind, however, that "not everything said in some context . . . is relevantly oriented to that context" (Schegloff 1991: 62), so conversation analysts do not assume that everything found in talk in an institutional setting is a feature of that setting. Instead, a CA approach sees "institutionality" as an emergent property of talk-in-interaction, whereas more critical approaches view the way people interact in social institutions as a reflection of existing macrolevel social forces.

4   Sample analysis #1: CA

The data that we analyze in this chapter were transcribed from audio-taped recordings of the trial. Our transcriptions are based on the unique method developed by Gail Jefferson (e.g., 2004), which seeks to capture *how* people say what they say. (See Appendix 21.1 for transcription conventions.) As a result, the transcripts are more detailed in their representation of the linguistic and interactional features of the talk than those often used by other kinds of discourse analysts. And this is because a CA transcript embodies, both in its format and in the phenomena it tries to capture, the analytic concerns conversation analysts bring to the data (e.g., the dynamics of turn taking are captured by identifying precisely overlaps, silence, and the onset of participants' speech) (Hutchby and Wooffitt 2008). See Chapter 12 for a detailed discussion of transcription across the subfields of linguistics.

As in any form of qualitative analysis, there is not one (best) way to begin. Starting from a pre-given question (perhaps inspired by the literature, some theoretical consideration, or practical interests), however, has generally been looked upon with suspicion in CA. Early on in his lectures, Sacks (1992: Lecture 5 [1967]) proposed the practice of "unmotivated looking." The term is meant to imply that the analyst be open to discovering what is going on in the data rather than searching for a particular pre-identified or pre-theorized phenomenon. For conversation analysts, careful and repeated listening to (and viewing of) recorded interaction in transcribing data and producing a transcript constitutes an important initial step in the process of data analysis. Indeed, because producing a transcript requires the analyst to attend to very subtle details of the interaction not necessarily obvious at first hearing/viewing, transcription operates as an important "noticing device" (see Chapter 12).

But what should one "notice?" As Schegloff (1996a: 172) describes, "analyses may begin with a noticing of the action being done and be pursued by what about the talk or other conduct – in its context – serves as the practice for accomplishing that action. Or it may begin . . . with the noticing of some feature of the talk and be pursued by asking what – if anything – such a practice of talking has as its outcome." In order to ground such "noticings" and further observations in the talk, analysts attend to a number of different features of its organization, including, for example, the design and coordination of turns-at-talk (where turns are composed of turn constructional units, or TCUs; e.g., Sacks, Schegloff, and Jefferson 1974); the organization of turns into sequences of action, such as adjacency pair-based sequences (e.g., Schegloff 2007); the coordination of vocal and nonvocal conduct (e.g., Goodwin 1981); and resources for repairing problems of speaking, hearing, or understanding (e.g., Hayashi, Raymond, and Sidnell 2013). We do not have the space to discuss these in detail here; however, our analysis – indeed, *any* CA analysis – is informed by these organized features of interaction and, like conversation analysts, we draw upon them, where necessary, as analytic resources in what follows.[8]

Turning to our data, the practice we describe was first observed in the process of transcribing the defendant's (MB) testimony from the trial. Early on in the direct examination, the defense lawyer (DE) asks MB about his relationship to the complainant, Jewel Lankford, before and after the incident in question. In (1), MB displays an apparent difficulty in answering a question about how he feels about her "now" (line 6).

```
(1)         Baby-Direct 8:22:10–8:22:30 (#1)
            01  DE:  You heard Jewel Lankford testify.
            02  MB:  Yes.
            03  DE:  Did you know her before that night,
            04  MB:  No I didn't.
            05       (0.4)
            06  DE:  How do you feel about her now as you testify.
            07  MB:  ->Uh:::m=hh (1.8) I'm sorry for having to put her-
            08       ->goin- uh havin- (.) put her- goin' through this
            09       ->(0.2) really.
            10  DE:  How do you feel about your family.
            11  MB:  ->Sorry for putting my family through it too.
```

Our initial observation about this instance was that a speaker's utterance-in-progress is halted in some way (here, by MB's cut-off intonation on "her," "goin," "havin," and "her" in lines 7–8) and subsequently adjusted (via self-repair) to convey something different from what was originally under way. Based on this observation, our next step was to develop an account of the interactional motivation(s) for this repaired utterance. The question is: what possible understandings of the talk by the recipients (i.e., the lawyers, judge, and jury) does this speaker show an orientation to by repairing the utterance-in-progress and modifying the previously articulated composition of the turn? For example, is the repair being implemented in the service of error correction (e.g., to correct apparent problems in speaking or to correct factual inaccuracies; see Schegloff, Jefferson, and Sacks 1977) or are there other interactional contingencies being addressed? In order to answer this question, we provide an analytic gloss of what is going on in this instance.

At line 7, MB first exhibits some hesitation ("Uh::m=hh") and degree of thought (evident in the 1.8-second pause) in formulating a response, but then MB begins to express regret "for having to put her-." However, as we noted, this construction is never brought to completion. Instead, the candidate replacement initially offered ("goin'") is temporarily suspended and he exhibits further difficulty in responding, vacillating between two ways of formulating his response

---

[8] As with any approach, there are different possibilities for developing an analysis in CA (for helpful discussions of a range of analytic tools and strategies, see, for example, Hutchby and Wooffitt 2008; Sidnell 2010). Accordingly, the one we offer is necessarily selective, due in part to limitations of space and to our analytic focus.

("havin put her [through this]" and "her goin [through this]"[9]). Ultimately, MB opts for the one that removes himself as the agent responsible for the difficulties that Jewel has endured. Since the defendant has been charged with rape, it is not in his interest to admit that he is the agent responsible for the complainant's suffering. Indeed, the altered version of his response – "I'm sorry for … her goin' through this really" – removes him as the cause of her difficulties and, thus, represents a version of events that is more consistent with consensual sex than with rape. It is also revealing to note how Maouloud's answer to the following question regarding how he feels about his family ("sorry for putting my family through it too"; line 12) suggests that he was likely on his way to saying "I'm sorry for having to put her through this" (indeed, the "too" actually locates this formulation as the same as the previous one).[10] In this example, then, we see self-repair, and the operation of grammatical reformulation (see Schegloff 2013), being mobilized to replace one version of events with a version that is more in keeping with the defendant's claim of consensual sex – that is, the defendant removes himself as the subject and agent of the complainant's suffering. As Schegloff (1988: 16) asserts, "it is this joining of a description of what some talk is doing with an account of how it is doing it – the method or device by which that practice is a practice for achieving that outcome – which makes the description an analysis."

The point of developing a description (albeit brief) of what is going on in this example, then, is that it provided us with "something to look for" (i.e., composition) and "a place to look for it" (i.e., position), and these two things constitute major components of an array of practices and phenomena in talk-in-interaction (Schegloff 2003: 246). The "something to look for," at a very general level, concerns the organization of repair, the organized practices that address systematic problems in speaking, hearing, and understanding talk. Although previous research on self-repair in English has tended to focus on its formal properties – for example, its "technology" (e.g., Wilkinson and Weatherall 2011; Kitzinger 2013), or its relation to syntax (e.g., Fox, Hayashi, and Jasperson 1996; Fox, Maschler, and Uhmann 2009), following Jefferson's (1974) pioneering work on the interactional import of self-repair, we instead proceeded by focusing on the possible *actions* that repair can accomplish. So, our "something to look for," more specifically, was *a speaker halts his/her own emerging utterance in some way which is then aborted, recast or redone in ways that address other contingencies than correcting an error or correcting factual inaccuracies*, and our "place to look for it" was *within a speaker's turn constructional unit (i.e., same-turn)*. As a result, our next step involved locating similar "specimens" based on this description – what is often referred to in CA as "building a collection" – something that can only

---

[9] The square brackets indicate talk that is not in fact articulated but is a plausibly projectable continuation.

[10] Although describing a somewhat different phenomenon, this is akin to what Jefferson (1996: 8, inter alios) called a "suppression-release," whereby "you're being very careful not to say something, and you succeed in not saying it, and it sneaks out in the next utterance."

be done once a practice has been identified. Building a collection enriches analyses of single cases by specifying the scope of the phenomenon (based on comparing similar and different instances) and testing the robustness of a description of it (Liddicoat 2007).[11] Once we collected all instances of self-repair by the four principal participants in the trial (i.e., the defendant, the complainant, and the defense and prosecuting attorneys), we could proceed case-by-case to develop an account of the actions accomplished via self-repair and the import of each instance.

Our analysis revealed that these participants deployed self-repair during the trial to adjust the construction of a turn in its course so as to modify or fine-tune it in ways that serve various kinds of interactional contingencies. Recurrent contingencies we identified include: (1) presenting a preferred version of events; (2) restricting the epistemic status of claims; and (3) conforming to constraints on asking questions. Excerpt (1) serves as an illustration of the first of these, but space considerations prevent us from exemplifying the other two.

Once we categorized each instance according to the actions accomplished, we were in a position to ask whether there was something distinctive about these self-repairs (i.e., something that sets them apart from what may occur in ordinary conversation). Drew and Heritage (1992a: 23) assert that interactional practices in institutional settings "may be shaped by reference to constraints that are goal-oriented or functional in character." What our analysis shows is how the practice of self-repair has been "shaped by" some of the goal-oriented constraints that the courtroom imposes on witnesses and lawyers in the context of an adversarial legal system. In this context, self repairs are used by (1) witnesses and lawyers to alter their utterances such that their side's version of events is supported; (2) both the defendant and the complainant to modify their utterances in ways that enhance their credibility as careful and reliable observers; and (3) the lawyer to reformat the form of his question in a way that conforms to a constraint on leading questions in direct examination.

Overall, then, rather than stop at a description of self-repairs in the environment, we suggested that in the same way, for example, that turn-taking systems can be adapted to the exigencies of institutional contexts, our examination of the interactional import of another organizational practice, self-repair, shows that it may also be adapted in accordance with institutionally specific tasks and constraints. And, while turn-taking systems may be constrained in terms of the allocation of turn-types, with respect to the practice of self-repair we also suggested that the constraints seem to manifest themselves in terms of the *directionality* of the repair.

---

[11] In terms of actually building a collection of candidate instances, the general rule of thumb is to "cast a wide net" (Clayman and Gill 2004), which means that analysts should include boundary cases as well as negative or "deviant" ones. Deviant cases in CA are not *exceptions*, but rather indications of orderliness not yet accounted for by the description. We simply do not have the space to illustrate this type of analysis here, but see Schegloff (1968) for an exemplar. That said, not all work that is produced from a CA perspective will necessarily include a discussion of deviant cases. Indeed, it will depend on the kind of claims the analyst makes.

In other words, in ordinary conversation, where Heritage (2005: 109) notes that interactional practices may be deployed "in pursuit of every imaginable social goal," speakers may repair utterances in a range of ways – for example, so that they conform to a version of events that serves their own self-interests, *or* so that they conform to a version of events that serves the interests of others. In the courtroom, however, where lawyers and witnesses must persuade a judge and/or jury that *their* version of events is the most credible, we do not find participants repairing their utterances in ways that support the opposing side's version of events. Thus, we claimed that the directionality of self-repair in the courtroom is shaped by the kinds of actions lawyers and witnesses perform in orienting to setting-specific tasks and constraints. Of course, none of the actions we have outlined above are accomplished solely through the use of self-repair. Indeed, there are many other dimensions of the organization of talk through which participants evoke and orient to the institutional context of their talk (see, for example, Drew and Heritage 1992b). For the purposes of exemplifying CA as a method of analysis, we have identified another feature of organization, namely, self-repair, through which participants situate themselves in relation to the tasks and constraints of institutions and, in this particular case, the courtroom.

5   Interactional sociolinguistics

Interactional sociolinguistics (IS) developed primarily out of the work of John Gumperz and his colleagues (e.g., Gumperz 1982a, 1982b), specifically, their investigations of language use between members of diverse linguistic and cultural groups located in large, heterogeneous, urban centers. Of interest to Gumperz and his associates were the misunderstandings or communication breakdowns that occurred between members of these different linguistic and cultural groups, and the fact that such problems did not seem to be due to differences in grammatical knowledge, but rather to differences in contextualization conventions. According to Gumperz (1992b: 42), the situating of utterances in their contexts "is cued by empirically detectable signs" – what he calls "contextualization cues" (Gumperz 2001: 221–2):

> I use the term contextualization cue to refer to any verbal sign which, when processed with symbolic grammatical and lexical signs, serves to construct the contextual ground for situated interpretation and thereby affects how constituent messages are understood ... As metapragmatic signs (Lucy 1993), contextualization cues represent speakers' ways of signaling and providing information to interlocutors and audiences about how language is being used at any one point in the ongoing exchange ... Moreover, contextualization strategies signal meaning largely by cueing indirect inferences. In conversation, we could not possibly express all the information that interlocutors must have to plan their own contributions and attune their talk to that of their interlocutors, so it is easy to see a reason for this indirectness.

We see from this passage that the term "contextualization cue" "refer[s] to any verbal sign" that helps to trigger interlocutors' inferences about the appropriate contextualizing frame for a particular utterance.[12] Contextualization cues are thus formal linguistic devices that can operate at different levels of the linguistic system, including "intonation, rhythm, lexical selection, organization of information in an utterance or in a stretch of discourse, or language or dialect selection" (Duranti 2001: 19). They can be said to frame utterances in the sense that they convey information about the kinds of speech activities that interlocutors are engaged in (e.g., whether they are joking or being serious). Indeed, for Tannen (1993: 4), contextualization cues are intimately connected to frame analysis (Goffman 1974), as they constitute the structural means by which frames are "cued" in interaction. The significant role that these formal devices play in the activation of contextualizing frames is particularly evident in the work that Gumperz and his colleagues have conducted on cross-cultural and inter-ethnic communication. Such work demonstrates the culturally specific nature of these cues and the misreadings and misunderstandings that can arise when different meanings are attached to them.

One of the features of an IS analysis that makes it distinct from a CA approach to discourse analysis is its concern with *implicit* meanings – that is, an IS approach to discourse goes beyond analyzing what is overtly stated in discourse, focusing also on the implied meanings that are triggered by contextualization cues. So, at the same time that an IS analysis will investigate surface linguistic features of a text and their role in cueing contextualizing frames, it will also investigate the nature of the sociocultural context that is potentially signaled by these contextualization cues. And this has significant implications for the kinds of methods that IS employs: given that the contextualizing frames indexed by surface linguistic features are not overtly expressed, IS analysts must have ways of accessing information about the context in which such features occur. As Schiffrin (1994: 106) says, incorporating contextual knowledge into an analysis is "necessary to interactional sociolinguistics." Thus, in doing IS, analysts combine the close analysis of naturally occurring interactions with their knowledge about participants' understandings of the broader sociocultural context in which such data occur (see also Stubbe et al. 2003). This latter type of "data" – information about the broader sociocultural context – is typically collected from ethnographic research. While bringing in the broader context and ethnographic information is an integral part of an IS analysis, this information is usually excluded in CA work.

6   Sample analysis #2: IS

In what follows we provide a sample analysis of data from the trial – a monolingual setting – where it is assumed that contextualization conventions are shared. For Gumperz (2001: 223), an IS analysis begins with ethnographic

---

[12] In other work, Gumperz (1992a) says that contextualization cues do not only refer to verbal signs, but also to non-verbal signs.

research that attempts to discover "recurrent encounter types" that pose problems for interactants, and to determine, through observation and/or interviews, how participants in such encounters handle the problems and what their assumptions are about their causes. The results of this kind of ethnographic research then form the basis for selecting "representative sets of interactions for recording" that will contain "empirical evidence to confirm or disconfirm ... analysts' interpretations." So, unlike the "unmotivated looking" of CA, the IS strategy is to be guided by ethnographic fieldwork in choosing one's data and in developing interpretations or hypotheses about the data (see Chapter 10). Once the relevant data are recorded, they are transcribed; what is important about IS transcripts is that they contain enough detail such that features of talk "likely to serve as contextualization cues" are captured (Schiffrin 1994: 106). In Gumperz's (2001: 223) words:

> Once isolated, events are transcribed and *interactional texts* ... are prepared by setting down on paper all those perceptual cues: verbal and nonverbal, segmental and nonsegmental, prosodic, paralinguistic, and others that, as past and ongoing research shows, speakers and listeners demonstrably rely on as part of the inferential process.   [emphasis in original]

Thus, like CA transcripts, IS transcripts are quite detailed and fine-grained due to the various linguistic levels at which contextualization cues can operate.

In producing the analysis that follows, ethnographic research did not determine the choice of data, as is recommended by Gumperz's (2001) procedures. It did, however, influence the *way* of looking at the data (perhaps we could call this a case of "motivated looking") – that is, it influenced the kinds of unstated contextual meanings that Ehrlich believed could be cued by contextualization devices. One of the things learned in Ehrlich's interview with the state (prosecuting) lawyer about the trial was that both the defendant and the complainant were African American. While this was something that Ehrlich (and others who heard the audiotapes) had suspected due to their use of African American Vernacular English, it was surprising that there were no explicit references to race at any point during the trial (other than to a *Hispanic* young man, who was also a passenger in Jewel's car at some point during the evening in question). Given that one of the goals of trial lawyers is to undermine the credibility of opposing witnesses, it seemed that lawyers might attempt to achieve such a goal by invoking discriminatory racial stereotypes about African Americans that could potentially resonate with the racist beliefs of jury members.[13] Put somewhat differently, the ethnographic data provided information about the sociocultural context of the trial, which, in turn, gave Ehrlich ideas about the kinds of implicit meanings that might be indexed by contextualization cues.[14]

---

[13] These ideas are based, to some extent, on Ehrlich's previous research on trial discourse (e.g., Ehrlich 2001), which showed trial lawyers invoking certain kinds of gendered stereotypes and ideologies as a way of undermining the credibility of witnesses.

[14] Gill (2000: 180) points out that discourse analysts must be attentive not only to what is said in a text, but also "to what is not said – to silences." In focusing on the absence of explicit references to

The excerpts presented below come from the cross-examination of the accused, Maouloud Baby, in particular, a segment of the cross-examination where the state lawyer refers to, and quotes from, a transcript of the accused's police interrogation.[15] These kinds of intertextual practices are very common in the courtroom: lawyers will quote, indirectly report, reframe, and/or summarize written documents, verbal statements and/or audio or video recordings from previous contexts (e.g., depositions, affidavits, and interviews), often for strategic purposes. In the Baby trial, almost half of the cross-examination of the accused involved the state lawyer's use of the police interrogation; as such, the police interrogation became a strategic and significant tool in the lawyer's attempts to undermine the credibility of the accused. Soon after the cross-examination began, the state lawyer made reference to the fact that Maouloud admitted in his direct examination that he had lied to the police. However, rather than having Maouloud confirm *once* that he had lied to the police, the lawyer instead moved through the transcript of the police interrogation line by line, page by page, asking questions of Maouloud in which he quoted from and even re-enacted lines from the transcript. Ehrlich collected all the instances of these questions in order to determine how these quotations and re-enactments on the part of the cross-examining lawyer were being contextualized. For example, we know from previous research on footing (Goffman 1981) that "taking on other's voices" (e.g., Schiffrin 1994; Tannen 2007 [1989]) can be affiliative or disaffiliative, depending on the context. That is, when speakers move from producing their own speech to animating the speech of others (in Goffman's [1981] terms, when a footing shift occurs), they will inevitably convey their own stance on that reported (i.e., animated) speech. In this particular context, given what Ehrlich knew (from ethnographic data) about cross-examination in trial settings, she expected, as trial participants would also expect, the lawyer to take up a negative stance vis-à-vis the witness – that is, she did not expect his quotations and re-enactments of the accused's words to be a sign of solidarity with the accused. As Schiffrin (1994: 113) says about IS's method of determining meaning, one moves from an utterance to the "contexts in which that utterance is embedded" because "what are provided by context ... are situated inferences about the meaning of an interactional move."

With the expectation that the cross-examining lawyer's quotations and animations might be meant to depict the accused in an unflattering way, Ehrlich then thought about what kinds of contextualization cues might be signaling these meanings and, moreover, what other kinds of contextualizing frames might be triggered by these contextualization cues. In thinking about the particular *kinds* of speech events that were quoted or re-enacted by the lawyer, namely, *lies*, already

race, one could say that the research question developed, to some extent, out of "silences" in the discourse.

[15] Since much of Ehrlich's previous research on trial discourse has focused on these kinds of intertextual practices, she was originally interested in this particular segment of the cross-examination because it exemplified such practices, not because she necessarily thought that the sociocultural frame of race would emerge.

Ehrlich was able to discern something about his stance toward the accused. But, since she was interested in contextualization cues, Ehrlich also looked to some of the formal linguistic properties used in representing the lies for evidence of this kind of stance-taking. For example, Ehrlich observed that often a lie that was presumably told once by Maouloud during the police interrogation was repeated numerous times by the cross-examining lawyer in the trial. Excerpt (2) is just one such example of this kind of repetition.

```
(2)        Baby-Cross: Touch: 12:32:00
     01 SE:  °Okay° (.) now: I wanna focus your attention (7.5)
     02       to:: the bottom of nineteen (1.1) and detective
     03       Hayle basically is saying (0.6) "The girl ↑to:ld
     04       us (.) you had sex with her right?" (0.6) And
     05       your answer on the top of page twenty is (.)
     06       "I dunno:, I didn't ↑touch the girl."
     07       (1.2)
     08 MB:  hh Can you tell me what li:ne that's on=
     09 SE:  =That's the top-=first line one. page twe:nty.
     10       (0.6) you sa:id (.) "I didn't ↑touch the girl."
     11       (0.5)
     12 MB:  Oh on page twenty. ( )
     13 SE:  Yes:. (0.3) "I didn't touch the girl." (.) Is-
     14       those are your words right,
     15       (5.4)
     16 MB:  Yea:h.
     17       (0.2)
     18 SE:  Okay. (1.0) and now: we can't possibly have any
     19       confusion over (.) the- the different (.)
     20       definition of sEX versus sexual activity .h
     21       because now you're saying you didn't (.) even
     22       (0.5) touch her.
     23 SE:  That's a comple:te lie.
     24 MB:  Mhmm
     25       (2.5)
     26 JU:  .h You need to say y[es or no]
     27 MB:                      [Ye:s. ye]s. sorry.
     28 SE:  And then when detective Hayle follows up (.) on
     29       (.) line four: (.) "you didn't ↑touch that girl:."
     30       (.) Your answer was "un uh" kinda like what you
     31       just did (.) when you meant (.) no.
     32 MB:  Yeah.
     33 SE:  And then (3.8) I ain't touc- you said (.) in
     34       li:ne one=I didn't touch the girl. (.) line two
     35       I ain't touch her. (.) line (.) line three.
     36       line four you didn't touch that girl un huh.
     37       In other words you lied three times in the span
     38       of about (.) five seconds. (.) I didn't touch
     39       the girl, I ain't touch her, you didn't touch her,
     40       un huh. Three times (.) one two three (.) ma:jor
```

```
41      lies.
42  MB:  Yes.
43  SE:  'Cause you di:d touch her.
44  MB:  Yes I did touch her.
```

In excerpt (2), the lawyer, SE, is questioning Maouloud about three lies that he told in the police interrogation (lies that appeared on pages 19–20 of the transcription): "I didn't touch the girl"; "I ain't touch her"; and "un uh" in response to the police detective's question, "You didn't touch that girl." Notice that these lies are either quoted or re-enacted a number of times in this excerpt: in each of lines 6, 10, and 13, the lie, "I didn't touch the girl" is animated by the lawyer; in lines 31–39, all three of the lies are quoted twice, with one aborted occurrence of "I ain't touch her" in line 31.

Following Matoesian (2001: 80), we can say that the expanse of discourse (in terms of space and time) that Maouloud's lies occupied in his cross-examination is larger/longer than the expanse of discourse that they presumably occupied in the police interrogation. As Matoesian points out, this kind of discourse expansion represents one technique by which lawyers "stretch" and thus emphasize a piece of evidence for juries.[16] In this sense, the repetition in excerpts like (2) can be viewed as a kind of contextualization cue: on an interactional level, the repetition foregrounds or makes salient certain propositional content (i.e., Maouloud's lies); on a more macro-level, the way that Maouloud's utterances are "contextualized" (i.e., as salient information that the jury should pay particular attention to) functions to construct Maouloud's identity as a unreliable witness. Indeed, Ehrlich argued that the expansion of the discourse denoting Maouloud's lies (relative to what presumably occurred in the police interrogation) had the effect of depicting the accused as someone who lied often and repeatedly, and who was probably also lying within the context of the trial (Ehrlich 2011).

This foregrounding or highlighting of Maouloud's lies was not only achieved via repetition, but also via another kind of contextualization cue – prosody. Excerpt (3) is illustrative of the way that the cross-examining lawyer used marked shifts in prosody or voice quality to re-enact many of Maouloud's lies. Put in Goffman's (1981) terms, while Maouloud is the author of these lies (i.e., Maouloud originally composed and produced them), the lawyer in this context is the voice box or the animator of Maouloud's speech.

(3)   Baby-Cross: Counting: 12:10:31
```
01  SE:  Now: on th- the next pa:ge, page seven. [(0.6)]=
02  MB:  [hhhhh]
03  SE:  =uh:m: detec- on the bottom of page twen- line
04       twenty two: (0.5) detective Ri:ley says he's
05       tryin tuh figure out what happened and he says
06       (0.4) "uh you guys asked if you all wanted to
```

---

[16] See Tannen (2007 [1989]: 76) for similar comments about the function of repetition in ordinary conversation.

```
07        hang out." (.) right. (0.4) And your response
08        on line twenty four: sir (.) is "<I AIN't A:Sked
09        her NO:thing.>"
10 MB:    Yes.
11 SE:    But you ha:d talked to her. You ha:d asked her
12        things right,
13 MB:    Yes but like I told you I did lie to the pohlice.
14 SE:    Well th- >we're gonna<- that's what we're going
15        through [ right now.    ]=
16 MB:           [Oh a(l)right.]
17 SE:    =I'm simply counting up how many [there is alright,
18 MB:                                     [Ahright
19 SE:    So that- you admit you did lie there.=
20 MB:    =Yeah I lied.
21 SE:    Okay.
```

In this excerpt, the lawyer is questioning Maouloud about his response to one of the detective's questions on page 7 of the transcript. In lines 8–9, the lawyer animates Maouloud's response to this question, "I ain't asked her nothing," and in so doing, he increases his volume, slows down his speech, and draws out the words, prosodically marking off the utterance from the surrounding talk.[17] As revealed later in the excerpt, this response is in fact another of Maouloud's lies, confirmed by Maouloud in line 20. Both repetition and prosody, then, seemed to be functioning as contextualization cues in the cross-examining lawyer's talk, foregrounding and highlighting the lies produced by Maouloud in the police interrogation. However, Ehrlich (2011) argued that the foregrounding and highlighting of Maouloud's lies did something more than just characterize him as a dishonest witness. Notice that one of the lies repeated in excerpt (2), "I ain't touch her," and the lie prosodically marked off in excerpt (3), "I ain't asked her nothing," both contain non-standard features of American English (i.e., the negative marker "ain't" and double negatives, the former of which is a distinctively African American Vernacular English feature when used in the past tense [Wolfram 2004]). While sociolinguistic studies of linguistic variation in the courtroom have shown that individuals who speak non-standard varieties are likely to be evaluated negatively by judges and juries (e.g., O'Barr 1982), Ehrlich's ethnographic data suggested a further motivation for the repeated highlighting of the non-standard features of Maouloud's speech. Given that it revealed that both the accused and the complainant were African American, Ehrlich speculated that the non-standard features of Maouloud's speech made salient by the cross-examining lawyer were meant to be emblematic of African American

---

[17] Couper-Kuhlen (1996) suggests that the absolute, as opposed to the relative, use of pitch register can contextualize verbal repetition as mimicry rather than quotation. Without more sophisticated ways of measuring pitch register, however, up to this point Couper-Kuhlen's insights have not been applied to these data. In other words, in pursuing some of these research questions, the analysis could be greatly enhanced by collaborating with a socio-phonetician (see Chapter 17 for foundations of acoustic analysis).

Vernacular English (AAVE) and, by extension, were meant to indirectly invoke the racial category of the accused. Put somewhat differently, Maouloud's non-standard variety of English (highlighted by the lawyer in his animations of Maouloud's lies) functioned as a contextualization cue in this context, indexing or "pointing to" his racialized identity as an African American man.

Previous research on "crossing" into AAVE has suggested that the social meanings indexed by this variety are associated not only with race, but also with gender (Bucholtz 1999; Cutler 1999). More specifically, AAVE has been said to index a certain version of African American masculinity, one that is associated with traits such as toughness, hyperphysicality, physical violence, and urban street smarts.[18] Indeed, excerpt (4) offers one piece of evidence from the interactional data indicating that the non-standard features of Maouloud's speech are meant to draw attention to these kinds of social meanings.

```
(4)        Baby-Cross: Street-smart: 12:00
           01  SE:  You're a smart-(.) you're a smart man. (0.4)
           02        Aren't you, (.) You consider yourself smart?
           03        (1.0)
           04  MB:  I'm not dumb. I'm abou-I'm a:verage.
           05        (1.1)
           06  SE:  You're intelligent. Wouldn't you say you're
           07        intelligent,
           08        (0.9)
           09  MB:  (m)hhhh
           10        (1.1)
           11  SE:  Ye(s) no,=
           12  MB:  =I mean there's-there's like hhhm intelligent means:
           13        really sma:rt I don't know what ki[nd of intellig-]
           14  SE:                                     [I me:an        ]=
           15        =s:treet smart.
           16        (0.2)
           17  MB:  O[h yes.] (.) m(hh)m
           18  SE:   [Sir, ]
           19        You're re:al street smart aren't you.
           20        (0.3)
           21  MB:  Ya I got street smarts.
```

In this sequence, the lawyer is attempting to establish whether Maouloud considers himself to be smart in lines 1–2 and lines 6–7. Maouloud seems to have some difficulty answering these questions, not knowing exactly what label to attach to his kind of intelligence. In lines 14–15, the lawyer offers the label "street smart" as a good characterization of Maouloud's intelligence, and Maouloud confirms that he has "street smarts" (lines 17 and 21). Ultimately, this characterization of the

---

[18] Ehrlich (2011) suggested that because AAVE indexes a particular version of African American *masculinity*, as opposed to a generalized African American identity, the lawyer was not likely to implicate the complainant in the (negative) racialized meanings triggered by the use of AAVE.

accused bolstered the claim about the implicit meanings signaled by Maouloud's non-standard linguistic features – that is, in highlighting such features, the lawyer attempted to further undermine the credibility of the accused by indirectly index-ing a certain version of African American masculinity – one associated with a variety of negatively stereotyped social meanings within the context of the US, including urban *street smarts*. The invoking of racialized meanings in public discourse is a delicate matter and, thus, it is perhaps not surprising that, as suggested, the lawyer cues such meanings *indirectly*, relying on his recipients to draw inferences based on their cultural background knowledge. An IS method, then, because it focuses on implicit meanings triggered by contextualization cues, seems to offer a particularly good way of getting at "culturally sensitive" topics such as race – topics that are often only presupposed or indirectly stated in discourse.

7   Critical discourse analysis

In spite of diverse methods and theories, critical approaches to dis-course analysis generally hold the view that dominant social structures and social practices have a discursive dimension and, by extension, that discourse is impli-cated in social and political inequalities. As Fairclough (2001: 230) says, the way that "language figures within social relations of power" or "works ideologically" is often opaque; through analysis, however, critical discourse analysts believe that the demystification and denaturalizing of such opaque aspects of language is made possible. This is at least one of the ways in which critical discourse analysis (CDA) is "critical": it promotes an awareness of the "naturalized" dimensions of discourse (i.e., those aspects of discourse that seem commonsensical and inevi-table), with the view that such awareness may, in turn, have the effect of "subvert [ing] the practices [CDA] analyses" (Chouliaraki and Fairclough 1999: 33).

Fairclough (2001: 232–3) and van Dijk (1993: 251) both cite a number of social theories and theorists as influencing the development of CDA, including Marxism, particularly the work of Gramsci and Althusser, the Frankfurt School, Foucault, Pecheux, and Bakhtin, among others. From these diverse origins come the following, very general, principles/perspectives that inform much work in CDA:[19]

1.   There is a dialectical relationship between discourse and "the social": "discourse is socially *constitutive* as well as socially shaped" (Fairclough and Wodak 1997: 258; emphasis in original).
2.   Discourse contributes to the production and reproduction of social inequalities, given its role in constituting social relations and social identities.

---

[19] This list of common principles and perspectives is adapted from Baxter (2010: 127–8).

3.   Analysis can make visible the ideological effects of discourse.

4.   CDA scholarship has an emancipatory agenda (van Dijk 2001) – that is, "it is committed to progressive social change" (Fairclough 2001: 230).

5.   Scholarly research is never neutral, and analysts in general, and the CDA analyst in particular, should make explicit his/her politically engaged stance, acknowledging in a reflexive way the a priori assumptions brought to bear on analyses.

While these general principles elucidate a fundamental assumption of CDA – that linguistic and discursive analysis can make a valuable contribution to critiques of the social world (Blommaert 2005) – they do not provide much information about the analytic methods for doing so. Indeed, despite the fact that Hallidayan systemic-functional linguistics informed much early work in CDA (e.g., Fowler et al. 1979; Kress and Hodge 1979), a striking feature of contemporary work is its methodological pluralism (for discussion, see Blommaert 2005; Wooffitt 2005; Benwell and Stokoe 2006; Baxter 2010). In fact, even among CDA's most renowned practitioners today – Norman Fairclough, Teun van Dijk, and Ruth Wodak – there are significant theoretical and methodological differences in the way that the discursive dimensions of social inequality and ideology are approached.[20] Wooffitt (2005: 137–8), for example, remarks that "unlike conversation analytic research, which adheres to a distinctive set of methodological principles," "there is no one way of doing CDA." More significantly, perhaps, van Dijk (2001: 96), himself a leading scholar in the area, views CDA not so much as a particular method of analysis, but rather as a "critical" perspective on doing scholarship – one that focuses on social issues and the discursive manifestations of power and ideology. Further support for this view of CDA as a *perspective*, as opposed to a *method*, comes from Stubbe et al. (2003: 368) in their comparison of five approaches to discourse analysis. They say that the analytic techniques used by scholars who approach discourse from a critical perspective are wide-ranging and variable: "some focus on macrolevel discourse strategies, examining rhetorical patterns, for example, while others adopt a conversation analytic or interactionally oriented approach; still others take a more grammatical approach, exploring relevant details of syntactic and semantic organization." Like Stubbe et al., we view critical approaches to discourse analysis as unified by a set of general theoretical principles, such as those outlined above, rather than by an adherence to a certain set of analytic techniques.[21]

---

[20] For example, van Dijk (e.g., 2008) adopts a "socio-cognitive" approach to CDA, exploring the mediating influence of personal and social cognition in the relationship between discourse structures and social structures. Wodak, by contrast, uses a "discourse-historical" approach to CDA (e.g., Wodak 2001; Reisigl and Wodak 2001), an approach which uses ethnography "to integrate systematically all available background information in the analysis and interpretation of the many layers of a written or spoken text" (Fairclough and Wodak 1997: 266).

[21] Accordingly, we view sample analysis #2 of this chapter as a "critical" analysis in the sense that it involves a social issue/problem and attempts to understand how discourse is implicated in this issue/problem.

8   Sample analysis #3: CDA

Given CDA's commitment to social critique, it is perhaps not surprising that most analyses begin with a social problem, as opposed to an interactional or discursive one. As Fairclough (2001: 236) says, the first step of a CDA analysis is to "focus upon a social problem that has a semiotic aspect." The analysis of the "social problem" that follows (based on Ehrlich 2012) emerged out of Ehrlich's ongoing research on the discursive aspects of rape cases. Ehrlich became interested in a type of rape case that has appeared relatively recently in courts in the United States – what has been termed a post-penetration rape case. She read the appellate decisions of many of these cases, including the Baby case, before acquiring the audio-taped recordings of the Baby trial. In listening to the trial, Ehrlich discovered that, even though the case had been framed as a post-penetration rape case in its appellate decisions, it was not framed in these terms within the context of the trial, neither by the prosecution nor by the defense. This discovery prompted many questions. For example, based on her own research and the research of feminist legal scholars, Ehrlich knew that, despite widespread reform to rape statutes in Canada and the United States, the adjudication of rape cases continues to be informed by "traditional cultural mythologies about rape" (Comack 1999: 234). Thus, it seems probable that the disjunction between the version of events put forward in the Baby case (in the trial as opposed to in the appellate decisions) could be a specific instance of a more general trend in rape cases – one in which the interpretations of adjudicating bodies are affected by rape mythologies/ideologies. This, then, became the social problem to investigate, using the Baby case as the data.

In delineating the process of arriving at this research question, our aim is to "draw out" some of the differences among our sample analyses. Unlike a CA analyst, Ehrlich approached her data with certain expectations about what she might find, given the setting in which her research was conducted – a legal case concerning the crime of rape. In the same way that an IS analyst will be influenced by ethnographic fieldwork when attempting to determine what aspects of context are being cued by contextualization devices, so Ehrlich was influenced by previous research on rape cases (particularly, the idea that discriminatory gendered ideologies circulate in these contexts) in attempting to develop a hypothesis about why the appellate decisions framed the Baby case in the way they did.

As the preceding discussion indicates, a salient feature of communication processes in institutions is the shifting of texts across contexts, what Blommaert has characterized as "text trajectories" (Blommaert 2005: 62). A text will shift in the legal system, for example, when a portion of trial testimony is represented in the closing argument of a lawyer, when it is then discussed by a jury, and when it is ultimately excerpted in the appellate decisions of judges. Given the relevance of these kinds of text movements to the differing interpretations of the Baby case, Ehrlich's analysis was conducted within a framework for the critical analysis of discourse developed in Blommaert (2005), using what he characterizes as a "forgotten context" in more orthodox CDA studies (e.g., Fairclough 1995) – this notion of text trajectories. Such an approach draws on ideas from linguistic anthropology, specifically, the work of Bauman and Briggs (1990) and Silverstein and Urban (1996), and investigates how discourse gets "entextualized" – that is, turned into texts, which can then be moved from one context to another. For Blommaert (following Bauman and Briggs 1990), what is significant about these kinds of movements or "text trajectories" for CDA are the transformations in meaning that can occur when texts are transplanted into new contexts. More specifically, in institutions, where lay participants may not have access to/control over all contextualizing spaces, Blommaert argues that these transformations in meaning can be deeply implicated in larger patterns of social inequality.

One of the features, then, that distinguishes this analysis from our previous two sample analyses is the fact that it does not focus exclusively on the trial data; instead, following Blommaert (2005), it examines the way that aspects of the trial data were turned into texts, and recontextualized in other settings within the legal system. As Bucholtz (2003: 61) notes about this type of approach to discourse analysis (what she calls a "natural histories of discourse" approach):

> If some approaches to discourse analysis emphasize oral discourse, and others focus on written texts, then natural histories of discourse call attention to the interplay between the oral and the written and between earlier and later versions of the "same" oral or written discourse.

Indeed, it was the "interplay" between "earlier and later versions of the 'same' . . . discourse" that first struck Ehrlich as significant about the Baby case, and it was this "interplay" that then became the object of her investigation.

As noted above, the Baby case became known as a post-penetration rape case in its appellate decisions, even though it was not initially framed in this way. Post-penetration rape is defined as a situation in which both parties initially consent to sexual intercourse, but at some time during the act of intercourse, one party, typically the woman, withdraws her consent; after this withdrawal of consent, the other party, typically the man, forces the woman to continue intercourse against her will (Davis 2005: 732–3).[22] Thus, while the prosecution argued that Jewel never consented to the sexual acts of aggression initiated by Maouloud, the appellate court's post-penetration framing of the case, by contrast, was predicated on the assumption that Jewel *did* consent to sex with Maouloud and only withdrew

---

[22] The question that has arisen in these cases is whether a rape can legally occur if a victim initially consents to intercourse but then withdraws her consent "post-penetration." Some courts have found post-penetration rape to be a legal impossibility – that is, if a woman consents to sexual intercourse, that initial consent prevents the sexual act from ever legally becoming a rape. Other courts have held that a withdrawal of consent post-penetration negates any earlier consent and thereby subjects the defendant to rape charges if he continues what has become non-consensual sexual intercourse. The appeals in the Baby case revolved around this precise issue.

her consent after she was penetrated.[23] (And note that this was the case even though the jury found Maouloud guilty of rape.)

Ehrlich's first step, then, was to determine what aspect of Jewel's behavior became construed as consent under the post-penetration rape framing of the case. Jewel's testimony in re-direct examination (following cross-examination), which describes the events that transpired once she agreed to sit in the back seat of the car with Maouloud and Mike, reveals that after enduring much non-consensual sex (lines 34–37, 46–49, 61–64, 66–68), Jewel agrees to have intercourse with Maouloud as long as he stops when she tells him to stop (lines 71–83). (As this part of the analysis focuses primarily on the content of the talk and not on its linguistic form, the excerpt is provided in Appendix 21.2 rather than in the body of the chapter.) And it was this agreement that came to be understood as Jewel consenting to sexual intercourse with Maouloud, once the case became framed as a post-penetration rape case.[24] So, while it is true that, by her own admission, Jewel allows Maouloud "to take his turn," it is also significant that she reports saying "it hurts" (lines 45–50, 55–56) and "no" multiple times (lines 5–11, 40–42) in response to Maouloud's and Mike's previous sexual advances – that is, Jewel's agreement to have sexual intercourse with Maouloud occurs after she has experienced much unwanted sexual aggression from the two men. How, then, do we understand and interpret agreement that occurs in such a context?

In considering this question, Ehrlich turned to the definition of consent provided by the judge in her instructions to the jury. Like many rape statutes in the United States, the Maryland rape statute has undergone statutory reform over the last few decades and requires that consent be "voluntary" and "freely-given." Based on the Maryland rape statute, the judge defined consent for the jurors as "actually agreeing to the act of intercourse," as opposed to "merely submitting as a result of force or threat of force" (cited in *State of Maryland* v. *Maouloud Baby, Court of Appeals of Maryland, 2007*). Based on this definition of consent, it seemed reasonable to conclude that Jewel's "agreement" to allow Maouloud to take his turn (the agreement that we see represented in lines 71–83) was not "actually agreeing to the act of intercourse," but rather was "submitting as a result of force or the fear of force." Clearly, the jury drew the same conclusion, since they found Maouloud guilty of rape and some other sexually related charges.[25]

---

[23] Interestingly, the defense argued that Maouloud never *penetrated* Jewel. Thus, the post-penetration framing of the case was also at odds with the defense's argument within the trial.

[24] The issue for the courts *then* became whether this initial "consent" protected the sexual intercourse from legally becoming a rape or not.

[25] While the jury ultimately convicted Maouloud, it was the jury's questions to the judge and the judge's refusal to answer their questions that led to the defense's appeal and the eventual overturning of Maouloud's convictions. Because this appeal concerned the issue of post-penetration rape, the Baby case essentially *became* a post-penetration rape case. Appellate courts can only address issues in their opinions that have been invoked during appeals. Thus, while the two appellate courts in Maryland (the Court of Special Appeals and the Court of Appeals) disagreed about whether post-penetration rape was a legal possibility, because of this procedural constraint, they both treated post-penetration rape as the central issue in the case.

Returning to the "interplay" of these various texts in the trajectory of the trial and the possible differences "between earlier and later versions of the 'same' … discourse," the next step in the analysis was to determine how the appellate courts represented Jewel's "agreement." Excerpt (5) from the Court of Special Appeals opinion represents the "facts" of the case from Jewel's perspective.

(5)   Court of Special Appeals of Maryland: Maouloud Baby v. State of Maryland, 2005

Upon their arrival at McDonald's, Lacey left the group to join a friend, after which the complainant agreed to drive appellant and Mike to a residential neighbourhood where she parked her car. The complainant complied with the request of appellant and Mike to sit between them on the back seat of her car. Mike put her hand down in his pants and asked her "to lick it." Appellant then asked her to expose her breasts; when she did not comply, he fondled her breast with his hand.

After Jewel acquiesced to the boys' insistence that they stay ten more minutes, she found herself on her back with appellant removing her jeans and Mike sitting on her chest, attempting to place his penis in her mouth. After she told them to stop, the pair moved her around so that her body was up in appellant's lap as he held her arms and Mike tried to insert his penis in her, but briefly inserted it into her rectum by mistake. After Mike again tried to insert his penis in the complainant's vagina, appellant inserted his fingers in her vagina. After appellant exited the car, Mike inserted his finger, then his penis into her vagina.

Mike then got out of the car and appellant got in. Appellant told Jewel that it was his turn and, according to the complainant, the following transpired:

Q. [ASSISTANT STATE'S ATTORNEY]: And what else did he say?
A. He, after that we sat there for a couple seconds and he was like so are you going to let me hit it and I didn't really say anything and he was like I don't want to rape you.
* * *
Q. So when Maouloud said I don't want to rape you, did you respond?
A. Yes. I said that as long as he stops when I tell him to, then-
Q. Now, that he could?
A. Yes.
* * *
Q. Did you feel like you had a choice?
A. Not really. I don't know. Something just clicked off and I just did whatever they said.
* * *
Q. Now when you told [appellant] if I say stop, something like that, you have to stop. What did he do after you spoke those words?
A. Well he got on top of me and he tried to put it in and it hurt. So I said stop and that's when he kept pushing it in and I was pushing his knees to get off me.
Q. You were on your back and he was on top of you?
A. Yes.

Q. Did he stop pushing his penis into your vagina?
A. Not right away.
Q. About how long did he continue to put his penis into your
    vagina?
A. About five or so seconds.
Q. And then what happened?
A. And that's when he just got off me and that's when Mike got in
    the car...

What we see in this excerpt is a difference in the way that various parts of Jewel's testimony are represented: when the opinion represents the events following Maouloud's re-entry into the car (i.e., Jewel's so-called agreement), it directly quotes Jewel's trial testimony (and this is the only instance of direct quotes in the entire opinion); when the opinion represents the events preceding Maouloud's re-entry (i.e., the series of non-consensual activities that Jewel reports preceded her "agreement" for Maouloud to take his turn), it represents her trial testimony indirectly. Previous research on the use of reported speech in legal contexts (e.g., Philips 1986; Rumsey 1990; Trinch 2010) has pointed to the greater authority and reliability that direct speech (i.e., direct quotes) is understood to convey relative to indirect speech, given its (supposed) exactitude in the reporting of speech. Philips (1986: 154), for example, argues that "quoting is reserved for information being presented as evidence directly related to proof of the elements of a criminal charge, to foreground this information, and to give it more fixedness and credibility as 'exact words' than other forms of reported speech are given." Ehrlich argued that the differential use of reported speech in the excerpt above, then, functions to highlight the importance of the events related to Jewel's so-called agreement, while downgrading the significance of the events leading up to this so-called agreement. However, Ehrlich also suggested that these back-grounded events provide contextualizing information that is *crucial* to understanding what Jewel is actually doing when she allows Maouloud to "take his turn." Rather than creating a sense of this contextualizing relationship, the textual foregrounding and backgrounding that we see in excerpt (5) has the effect of decontextualizing Jewel's agreement by creating a distinction or separation between the two sets of events. Ultimately, then, Ehrlich argued that the appellate courts' representation of the "facts" of the Baby case supported an interpretation of Jewel's agreement as consent, rather than "submi[ssion] as a result of force or threat of force," which, in turn, supported an understanding of this case as a post-penetration rape case.

Space constraints do not permit elaboration upon the combination of linguistic ideologies, gendered ideologies, and legal conventions that functioned to reframe this case as a post-penetration rape case in the appellate decisions. Very briefly, Ehrlich suggested that such an understanding of the case, in accordance with the "referentialist" or "textualist" linguistic ideology, relied on a decontextualized "reading" of Jewel's qualified agreement to have sex with Maouloud, erasing the series of non-consensual sexual acts that preceded the "agreement." In turn, a context-free reading of Jewel's so-called agreement made difficult its interpretation as submission or compliance – an interpretation that seems consistent with the Maryland rape statute and with the decision of the jury. From a methodological point of view, it is important to notice that the problematic interpretation of consent seen in the appellate courts' representation of the trial "facts" would not have been evident if the trial *or* the appellate decisions had been the exclusive object of analysis – that is, it was only by looking at the "interplay" of texts in the case's text trajectory that the meaning of the transformations became apparent and, by extension, their grounding in ideology.

9   Narrative analysis

Although we have not framed any of our three sample analyses in terms of the notion of "narrative," we certainly could have. Indeed, many scholars of language and the law have pointed out that the courtroom, and legal cases more generally, involve a multiplicity of, often conflicting and competing, narratives, told by a multiplicity of tellers (e.g., Harris 2001). In the Baby trial, for example, at least two different narratives emerged in the courtroom (i.e., a narrative of consensual sex vs one of sexual assault), yet the official story of the case (i.e., that of post-penetration rape) was one that conformed to neither of these. Scholarly work on the analysis of narratives has been conducted in a variety of disciplines and from a variety of perspectives; within the discipline of linguistics alone, there is a range of methods used to analyze narratives, including the three approaches to discourse analysis reviewed here. Arguably, the most influential model for analyzing narrative within linguistics was developed by Labov and Waletzky (1967) and Labov (1972), based on data collected in sociolinguistic interviews (see Chapter 6). While this work was extremely significant in demonstrating that units of discourse display structure and systematicity in the way that other linguistic units do, it has in recent years been the subject of much controversy. (But see Johnstone 2001 for a discussion of some of the confusions surrounding this model.) As many critiques of Labov's model have suggested, the fact that it was based on narratives elicited in response to a researcher's questions meant that the narratives were "largely monologic" and "well-organized with a beginning, middle and an end" (Georgakopoulou 2011: 397). More recent work within CA and IS has investigated narratives or stories as they are embedded in naturally occurring interactional contexts. Such work has demonstrated the highly collaborative nature of narratives and their context sensitivity in terms of the forms they take and the actions or functions they perform. For further work on narrative along these lines, see Sacks (1974); Jefferson (1978); Goodwin (1984); Johnstone (1990); Schiffrin (1996, 2006); Bamberg (1997); Ochs and Capps (2001); Norrick (2010); Mandelbaum (2012); De Fina and Georgakopoulou (2012).

10   Conclusion

The approaches to discourse analysis exemplified in this chapter all involve the close analysis of texts in relation to aspects of their social and cultural context.[26] While our sample analyses have presumably illustrated this shared perspective, they have also, perhaps more obviously, pointed to areas of divergence. For example, the analytic status of extra-discursive features of context (e.g., whether and to what extent such features are utilized) has been much debated in the field, and our sample analyses elucidate some of the contentious issues in these debates.[27] In our first sample analysis, we demonstrated that conversation analysts ground their analyses of orderly practices of talk by showing how they are accomplishments of the participants themselves (rather than being based on the assumptions of the analyst). Accordingly, analysis is principally concerned with the turn-by-turn unfolding of interaction, without appealing to contextual factors exogenous to the interaction itself. Our following two sample analyses proceeded in a somewhat different way, under the assumption that contextual information relevant to an analysis may not always be overtly apparent or oriented to by the participants within an interaction itself. So, for example, while our IS analysis was also focused on participants' perspectives, it attempted, through ethnographic research, to retrieve some of the implicit meanings signaled by participants' use of surface textual features (i.e., contextualization cues). Our CDA analysis also appealed to information from outside of the immediate interaction in attempting to ground its claims – more specifically, the idea that rape trials are cultural sites where linguistic and gendered ideologies are known to circulate and, by extension, to shape discourse.

As we noted in the introduction, while previous exemplifications of discourse analytic approaches have often used a single piece of data for purposes of comparison and contrast (e.g., Stubbe et al. 2003), we have used different kinds of data within a single interactional setting. Each approach to discourse analysis inevitably asks different kinds of research questions and, in turn, these questions will necessitate different objects of analysis. By offering sample analyses of different dimensions of one institutional speech event, we hope to have provided a methodological description that does justice to the principal issues and concerns of each approach: CA, IS, and CDA.

---

[26] While the approaches described in this chapter necessitate examining data in a qualitative light, some discourse analysts have found it fruitful to additionally examine quantitative patterns. Schiffrin (1981), for example, draws on quantitative patterns to show that the structure of narratives constrains where the historical present can be used. In a study on tag questions, Moore and Podesva (2009) used quantitative methods to show that the grammatical and phonological form of tag questions varied from one group of adolescent girls to the next; qualitative methods were then used to uncover the functions that distinct forms served in interaction. As in other domains of linguistic inquiry, qualitative and quantitative methods can be combined in mutually beneficial ways.

[27] Indeed, a particularly well-known example is an article by Schegloff (1997), which provoked a series of rebuttals, counter-rebuttals, and other articles debating the relative merits of CDA and CA (e.g., Schegloff 1998; Wetherell 1998; Billig 1999a, b; Schegloff 1999; van Dijk 1999; Weatherall 2000; Stokoe and Weatherall 2002).

Appendix 21.1

Transcription conventions

1. Temporal and sequential relationships

[	A left bracket indicates the onset of overlapping speech
]	A right bracket indicates the point at which overlapping utterances end
=	An equals sign indicates contiguous speech
(0.5)	Silences are indicated as pauses in tenths of a second
(.)	A period in parentheses indicates a micro-pause (less than two-tenths of a second)

2. Aspects of speech delivery

.	A period indicates falling intonation contour
,	A comma indicates continuing intonation
?	A question mark indicates rising intonation contour
¿	An inverted question mark indicates a rise stronger than the comma but weaker than the question mark
_	An underscore indicates flat intonation contour
:	Colons indicate lengthening of preceding sound (the more colons, the longer the lengthening)
-	A hyphen indicates an abrupt cutoff sound
yes	Underlining indicates emphatic stress
YES	Upper case indicates noticeably increased amplitude or pitch reset
°yes°	The degree sign indicates noticeably decreased amplitude in speech
>yes<	Indicates talk that is noticeably faster than surrounding talk
<yes>	Indicates talk that is noticeably slower than surrounding talk
hh	The letter "h" indicates audible aspirations (the more hs the longer the breath)
.hh	A period preceding the letter "h" indicates audible inhalations (the more hs the longer the breath)
y(h)es	h within parentheses within a word indicates aspiration, possibly laughter

3. Other notational devices

(guess)	words within single parentheses indicate likely hearing of that word
((coughs))	information in double parentheses indicates additional details
( )	empty parentheses indicate hearable yet indecipherable talk

Appendix 21.2

Baby: Jewel's re-direct[28]

```
01      L:      Okay. Now, about the- when you said- when- when they started to
02              do these things and you said, "No, I'm not that kind of person."
```

---

[28] As will be evident, this transcription is much less detailed than those in our other sample analyses. In general, the particular phenomena of interest to discourse analysts will influence how detailed their transcriptions need to be and what types of details are represented. Because this analysis does not depend on information about aspects of speech delivery (e.g., loudness, speed), for example, these features are not included in the transcription.

03		Jewel, how many times did you say "No," when you were in the
04		backseat.
05	J:	I don't know how many times. Every time I said, "No," or "I have
06		to go," or "My ten minutes are up," then they'd add uh- add
07		time or be like, "As soon as you get done with this, you can
08		leave."
09	L:	Well, was it- do you think it was- was it more than once that
10		you said [no.]
11	J:	[Yes.]
12	L:	And I have to go?=
13	J:	=Yes.
14	L:	More than five times?
15	J:	Yes.
16	L:	More than ten times? (1.0) Too many to count? You're nodding,
17		is that yes?
18	J:	Yes.
19	L:	Okay. Now uhm, uh- in those times when you were saying "No," and
20		"Stop," where was Maouloud. (1.0) Was he in the car?
21	J:	Yes.
22	L:	(5.0) And when, uhm, M-Mike first tried to put his penis in you
23		and he said- "If I can't- "he wasn't able to do that, is tha
24		what you said?
25	J:	Yes.
26	L:	And he said, "If I can't fit, you can't fit," who was he talking
27		to, Jewel.
28	J:	M-talking to Maouloud.
29	L:	And Maouloud was still in the car at the [time] that happened?
30	J:	[Yes.]
31	L:	What was Maouloud doing at the time Mike was trying to put his
32		penis in you.
33	J:	Uhm, he was sitting like, I mean he was kind of hunched over
34		like in- on the- like, in the back of Mike. And that's when he
35		opened my legs and stuck his fingers.
36	L:	When who opened his legs [and stuck his] fingers.
37	J:	[Maouloud.]
38	L:	And this is after Mike said, "If I can't fit, you can't fit?"
49	J:	Yes.
40	L:	((clears throat)) (4.0) Now you said that you said "No," and
41		"Stop" too many times to count.
42	J:	Yes.
43	L:	Did you ever say, "It hurts?"
44	J:	Yes.
45	L:	How many times did you say, "It hurts," Jewel.
46	J:	Uhm, I know I kind of yelled a little bit when they put- when he
47		put his fingers in. [And then-]
48	L:	[when-] when who put his fingers in.
49	J:	Maouloud. And uhm, I know I also said it hurt- when he tried to
50		put it in, I told him to stop.
51	L:	When Maouloud put it in?
52	J:	Yes.

53	L:	And when Mike put his penis in your rectum?
54	J:	Yes.
55	L:	You said, "It hurts?"
56	J:	Yes.
		((18 lines omitted from transcript))
57	L:	Okay, and by the time Mike got out of the car and Maouloud got
58		in the car, you had been, correct me if I'm wrong, uhm, Mike had
59		put his fingers in your-in your vagina.
60	J:	Yes. Uh- and Maouloud.
61	L:	And Maouloud. And Mike had tried to put his penis in your mouth.
62	J:	Yes.
63	L:	And Maouloud had uhm, grabbed your- your shirt and touched you
64		on the breast.
65	J:	Yes.
66	L:	And Mike had put his penis in your rectum.
67	J:	Yes.
68	L:	And Mike had put his penis in your vagina.
69	L:	And that was all before Maouloud got out of the car.
70	J:	Yes.
71	L:	And so by the time Maouloud got back in the car, and you said
72		and- and he said to you, "Are you gonna let me have my turn."
73		(2.0) Did you think that if you allowed that to happen, then you
74		would be able to leave and go home?
75	D:	Objection, your honour. Leading.
76	J:	Sustained as leading.
77	L:	What did you think, Jewel, would happen if you let him do it at
78		that point.
79	J:	I just wanted to go home.
80	L:	(1.0) You just wanted to go home. (2.0) And you said, did you
81		you said that you told him, "Okay, if I tell you to stop, will
82		you stop?" Did he say anything when you said that to him?=
83	J:	=He said, "Okay."
84	L:	And then he tried to put his penis in you. And what did you say,
85		Jewel?
86	J:	I said, "Ow, it hurts." And I was pushing his knees.
87		((sniffles)) But he kept pushing. ((sniffles))
88	L:	Did you tell him to stop?
89	J:	Yes.
90	L:	Did he stop?
91	J:	No, after uh- he stopped after like, ten seconds or so.
92		((sniffles))

References

Bamberg, M. 1997. Oral versions of personal experience: three decades of narrative analysis. *Journal of Narrative and Life History* 7: 1–4.

Bauman, R. and C. L. Briggs. 1990. Poetics and performance as critical perspectives on language and social life. *Annual Review of Anthropology* 19: 59–88.

Baxter, J. 2010. Discourse-analytic approaches to text and talk. In L. Litosseliti, ed. *Research Methods in Linguistics*. London: Continuum, 117–37.

Benwell, B. and E. Stokoe. 2006. *Discourse and Identity*. Edinburgh University Press.

Billig, M. 1999a. Whose terms? Whose ordinariness? Rhetoric and ideology in conversation analysis. *Discourse & Society* 10.4: 543–58.

  1999b. Conversation analysis and the claims of naivety. *Discourse & Society* 10.4: 572–6.

Blommaert, J. 2005. *Discourse: A Critical Introduction*. Cambridge University Press.

Bucholtz, M. 1999. "You da man": narrating the racial other in the productions of white masculinity. *Journal of Sociolinguistics* 3: 443–60.

  2003. Theories of discourse as theories of gender: discourse analysis in language and gender studies. In J. Holmes and M. Meyerhoff, eds. *The Handbook of Language and Gender*. Malden, MA: Blackwell, 43–68.

  2011. *White Kids: Language, Race, and Styles of Youth Identity*. Cambridge University Press.

Bucholtz, M. and K. Hall. 2005. Identity and interaction: a sociocultural linguistic approach. *Discourse Studies* 7.4–5: 585–614.

Cameron, D. 2001. *Working with Spoken Discourse*. London: Sage.

Chouliaraki, L. and N. Fairclough. 1999. *Discourse in Late Modernity: Rethinking Critical Discourse Analysis*. Edinburgh University Press.

Clayman, S. E. and V. Gill. 2004. Conversation analysis. In A. Bryman and M. A. Hardy, eds. *Handbook of Data Analysis*. London: Sage, 589–606.

Comack, E. 1999. *Locating Law: Race/Class/Gender Connections*. Halifax, Nova Scotia: Fernwood Publishing.

Couper-Kuhlen, E. 1996. The prosody of repetition: on quoting and mimicry. In E. Couper-Kuhlen and M. Selting, eds. *Prosody in Conversation: Interactional Studies*. Cambridge University Press, 366–405.

Cutler, C. 1999. Yorkville Crossing: white teens, hip hop and African American English. *Journal of Sociolinguistics* 4: 428–42.

Davies, B. and R. Harré. 1990. Positioning: conversation and the production of selves. *Journal for the Theory of Social Behavior* 20: 43–63.

Davis, A. 2005. Clarifying the issue of consent: the evolution of post-penetration rape law. *Stetson Law Review* 34: 729–66.

De Fina, A. and A. Georgakopoulou. 2012. *Analyzing Narrative: Discourse and Sociolinguistic Approaches*. Cambridge University Press.

Drew, P. and A. J. Wootton, eds. 1988. *Erving Goffman: Exploring the Interaction Order*. Cambridge: Polity Press.

Drew, P. and J. Heritage. 1992a. Analyzing talk at work: an introduction. In Drew and Heritage 1992b, 1–65.

  1992b. *Talk at Work: Interaction in Institutional Settings*. Cambridge University Press.

Duranti, A. 2001. Linguistic anthropology: history, ideas, and issues. In A. Duranti, ed. *Linguistic Anthropology: A Reader*. Malden, MA: Blackwell, 1–41.

Edwards, D. and J. Potter. 1992. *Discursive Psychology*. London: Sage.

Ehrlich, S. 2001. *Representing Rape: Language and Sexual Consent*. London: Routledge.

  2011. Animating police interrogations in the courtroom. Paper presented at the 12th International Pragmatics Conference, Manchester, UK, July 3–8.

2012. Text trajectories, legal discourse and gendered inequalities. *Applied Linguistics Review* 3.1: 47–73.

2013. Post-penetration rape and the decontextualization of witness testimony. In J. Conley, C. Heffer, and F. Rock, eds. *Legal-Lay Communication: Textual Travels in the Legal System*. Oxford University Press, 189–205.

Fairclough, N. 1995. *Critical Discourse Analysis: The Critical Study of Language*. London: Longman.

2001. The discourse of new labor: critical discourse analysis. In M. Wetherell, S. Taylor, and S. Yates, eds. *Discourse as Data: A Guide for Analysis*. London: Sage, 229–66.

Fairclough, N. and R. Wodak. 1997. Critical discourse analysis. In T. van Dijk, ed. *Discourse Studies: A Multidisciplinary Introduction*, 2 vols. London: Sage, Volume II, 258–84.

Fowler, R., G. Kress, R. Hodge, and T. Trew. 1979. *Language and Control*. London: Routledge and Kegan Paul.

Fox, B. A., M. Hayashi, and R. Jasperson. 1996. Resources and repair: a cross-linguistic study of syntax and repair. In E. Ochs, E. A. Schegloff, and S. A. Thompson, eds. *Interaction and Grammar*. Cambridge University Press, 185–237.

Fox, B., Y. Maschler, and S. Uhmann. 2009. Morpho-syntactic resources for the organization of same-turn self-repair: cross-linguistic variation in English, German and Hebrew. *Gesprächsforschung* 10: 245–91.

Georgakopoulou, A. 2011. Narrative analysis. In R. Wodak, B. Johnstone, and P. Kerswill, eds. *The Sage Handbook of Sociolinguistics*. London: Sage, 396–411.

Gill, R. 2000. Discourse analysis. In M. Bauer and G. Gaskell, eds. *Qualitative Researching with Text, Image and Sound*. London: Sage, 172–90.

Goffman, E. 1974. *Frame Analysis*. New York: Harper and Row.

1981. Footing. In E. Goffman, ed. *Forms of Talk*. Oxford: Blackwell, 124–59.

Goodwin, C. 1981. *Conversational Organization: Interaction Between Speakers and Hearers*. New York: Academic Press.

1984. Notes on story structure and the organization of participation. In J. M. Atkinson and J. Heritage, eds. *Structures of Social Action: Studies in Conversation Analysis*. Cambridge University Press, 225–46.

2007. Participation, stance and affect in the organization of activities. *Discourse and Society* 18: 53–73.

Gumperz, J. J. 1982a. *Discourse Strategies*. Cambridge University Press.

ed. 1982b. *Language and Social Identity*. Cambridge University Press.

1992a. Contextualization and understanding. In A. Duranti and C. Goodwin, eds. *Rethinking Context: Language as an Interactive Phenomenon*. Cambridge University Press, 229–52.

1992b. Contextualization revisited. In P. Auer and A. Di Luzio, eds. *The Contextualization of Language*. Amsterdam: John Benjamins, 39–53.

2001. Interactional sociolinguistics: a personal perspective. In D. Schiffrin, D. Tannen, and H. Hamilton, eds. *The Handbook of Discourse Analysis*. Oxford: Blackwell, 213–28.

Harris, S. 2001. Fragmented narratives and multiple tellers: witness and defendant accounts in trials. *Discourse Studies* 3: 53–74.

Hayashi, M., G. Raymond, and J. Sidnell, eds. 2013. *Conversational Repair and Human Understanding*. Cambridge University Press.

Heritage, J. 1984. *Garfinkel and Ethnomethodology*. Cambridge: Polity Press.

2005. Conversation analysis and institutional talk. In K. L. Fitch and R. E. Sanders, eds. *Handbook of Language and Social Interaction*. Mahwah, NJ: Lawrence Erlbaum, 103–47.

Hutchby, I. and R. Wooffitt. 2008. *Conversation Analysis: Principles, Practices, and Applications*, 2nd edn. Cambridge: Polity Press.

Hymes, D. 1962. The ethnography of speaking. In T. Gladwin and W. C. Sturtevant, eds. *Anthropology and Human Behaviour*. Washington, DC: Anthropology Society of Washington.

Jefferson, G. 1974. Error correction as an interactional resource. *Language in Society* 3.2: 181–99.

1978. Sequential aspects of storytelling in conversation. In J. Schenkein, ed. *Studies in the Organization of Conversational Interaction*. New York: Academic Press, 219–48.

1996. On the poetics of ordinary talk. *Text and Performance Quarterly* 16.1: 1–61.

2004. Glossary of transcript symbols with an introduction. In G. H. Lerner, ed. *Conversation Analysis: Studies from the First Generation*. Amsterdam: John Benjamins, 13–31.

Johnstone, B. 1990. *Stories, Community, and Place: Narratives from Middle America*. Bloomington: Indiana University Press.

2001. Discourse analysis and narrative. In D. Schiffrin, D. Tannen, and H. E. Hamilton, eds. *Handbook of Discourse Analysis*. Oxford: Blackwell, 635–49.

Kamp, H. and U. Reyle. 1993. *From Discourse to Logic*. Kluwer: Dordrecht.

Kissmann, U., ed. 2009. *Video Interaction Analysis: Methods and Methodology*. Frankfurt: Peter Lang Verlag.

Kitzinger, C. 2013. Repair. In J. Sidnell and T. Stivers, eds. *The Handbook of Conversation Analysis*. Oxford: Wiley-Blackwell, 229–56.

Kress, G. and R. Hodge. 1979. *Language as Ideology*. London: Routledge and Kegan Paul.

Labov, W. 1972. The transformation of experience in narrative syntax. *Language in the Inner City*. Philadelphia: University of Pennsylvania Press, 354–96.

Labov, W. and J. Waletzky. 1967. Narrative analysis: oral versions of personal experience. In J. Helms, ed. *Essays on the Verbal and Visual Arts*. Seattle: University of Washington Press, 12–44.

Lambrecht, K. 1994. *Information Structure and Sentence Form*. Cambridge University Press.

Liddicoat, A. 2007. *An Introduction to Conversation Analysis*. London: Continuum.

Mandlebaum, J. 2012. Storytelling in interaction. In J. Sidnell and T. Stivers, eds. *The Handbook of Conversation Analysis*. Oxford: Wiley-Blackwell, 492–508.

Matoesian, G. 2001. *Law and the Language of Identity: Discourse in the William Kennedy Smith Rape Trial*. New York: Oxford University Press.

Moore, E. and R. Podesva. 2009. Style, indexicality, and the social meaning of tag questions. *Language in Society* 38: 447–85.

Norrick, N. 2010. *Conversational Narrative: Storytelling in Everyday Talk*. Amsterdam: John Benjamins.

Ochs, E. and L. Capps. 2001. *Living Narrative: Creating Lives in Everyday Storytelling*. Cambridge, MA: Harvard University Press.

O'Barr, W. M. 1982. *Linguistic Evidence: Language, Power, and Strategy in the Courtroom*. New York: Academic Press.

Philips, S. 1986. Reported speech as evidence in an American trial. In D. Tannen and J. Alatis, eds. *Georgetown University Roundtable 85 Languages and Linguistics: The Interdependence of Theory, Data and Application*. Washington: Georgetown University Press, 154–70.

Potter, J. 2012. Discourse analysis and discursive psychology. In H. Cooper, ed. *American Psychological Association Handbook of Research Methods in Psychology: Quantitative, Qualitative, Neuropsychological, and Biological*. Washington: American Psychological Association Press, 111–30.

Reisigl, M. and R. Wodak. 2001. *Discourse and Discrimination*. London: Routledge.

Romaniuk, T. and S. Ehrlich. 2013. On the interactional import of self-repair in the courtroom. In J. Sidnell, M. Hayashi, and G. Raymond, eds. *Conversational Repair and Human Understanding*. Cambridge University Press, 273–313.

Rumsey, A. 1990. Wording, meaning, and linguistic ideology. *American Anthropologist* 92.2: 346–61.

Sacks, H. 1974. Some consideration of a story told in ordinary conversations. *Poetics* 15: 127–38.

  1984. Notes on methodology. In J. M. Atkinson and J. Heritage, eds. *Structures of Social Action: Studies in Conversation Analysis*. Cambridge University Press, 21–7.

  1992. *Lectures on Conversation*, 2 vols. Oxford: Blackwell.

Sacks, H., E. A. Schegloff, and G. Jefferson. 1974. A simplest systematics for the organization of turn-taking for conversation. *Language* 50.4: 696–735.

Saville-Troike, M. 1982. *The Ethnography of Communication: An Introduction*. Oxford: Basil Blackwell.

Schegloff, E. A. 1968. Sequencing in conversational openings. *American Anthropologist* 70: 1075–95.

  1988. Description in the social sciences I: talk-in-interaction. *IPRA Papers in Pragmatics* 2.1: 1–24.

  1991. Reflections on talk and social structure. In D. Boden and D. H. Zimmerman, eds. *Talk and Social Structure*. Berkeley: University of California Press, 44–70.

  1996a. Confirming allusions: toward an empirical account of action. *American Journal of Sociology* 102.1: 161–216.

  1996b. Issues of relevance for discourse analysis: contingency in action, interaction and co-participant context. In E. H. Hovy and D. R. Scott, eds. *Computational and Conversational Discourse: Burning Issues – An Interdisciplinary Account*. Berlin: Springer, 3–35.

  1997. Whose text? Whose context? *Discourse and Society* 8.2: 165–87.

  1998. Reply to Wetherell. *Discourse and Society* 9.3: 413–16.

  1999. 'Schegloff's texts' as 'Billig's data': a critical reply. *Discourse and Society* 10.4: 558–72.

  2003. The surfacing of the suppressed. In P. Glenn, C. LeBaron, and J. Mandelbaum, eds. *Studies in Language and Social Interaction: A Festschrift in Honor of Robert Hopper*. Mahwah, NJ: Lawrence Erlbaum, 241–62.

  2007. *Sequence Organization in Interaction: A Primer in Conversation Analysis*. Cambridge University Press, 41–70.

  2013. Ten operations in self-initiated, same-turn repair. In J. Sidnell, M. Hayashi, and G. Raymond, eds. *Conversational Repair and Human Understanding*. Cambridge University Press.

Schegloff, E. A., G. Jefferson, and H. Sacks. 1977. The preference for self-correction in organization of repair in conversation. *Language* 53.2: 361–82.

Schiffrin, D. 1981. Tense variation in narrative. *Language* 57: 45–62.

1994. *Approaches to Discourse*. Oxford: Blackwell.

1996. Language as self-portrait: sociolinguistic constructions of identity. *Language in Society* 25: 167–203.

2006. *In Other Words: Variation in Reference and Narrative*. Cambridge University Press.

Sidnell, J. 2010. *Conversation Analysis: An Introduction*. Oxford: Wiley-Blackwell.

Silverstein, M. and G. Urban. 1996. *Natural Histories of Discourse*. University of Chicago Press.

Speer, S. A. and E. Stokoe. 2011. An introduction to conversation and gender. In S. A. Speer and E. Stokoe, eds. *Conversation and Gender*. Cambridge University Press, 1–27.

Stokoe, E. H. and A. Weatherall. 2002. Gender, language, conversation analysis and feminism. *Discourse and Society* 13.6: 707–13.

Stubbe, M., C. Lane, J. Hilder, E. Vine, B. Vine, M. Marra, J. Holmes, and A. Weatherall. 2003. Multiple discourse analyses of a workplace interaction. *Discourse Studies* 5.3: 351–88.

Tannen, D. 1993. Introduction. In D. Tannen, ed. *Framing in Discourse*. Oxford University Press, 3–13.

2007 [1989]. *Talking Voices: Repetition, Dialogue, and Imagery in Conversational Discourse*. Cambridge University Press.

ten Have, P. 2007. *Doing Discourse Analysis: A Practical Guide*, 2nd edn. London: Sage Publications.

Trinch, S. 2010. Disappearing discourse: performative texts and identity in legal contexts. *Critical Inquiry in Language Studies* 7: 207–29.

van Dijk, T. 1993. Principles of critical discourse analysis. *Discourse and Society* 4: 249–83.

1999. Critical discourse analysis and conversation analysis. *Discourse and Society* 10.4: 459–60.

2001. Multidisciplinary CDA: a plea for diversity. In R. Wodak and M. Meyer, eds. *Methods of Critical Discourse Analysis*. London: Sage, 95–120.

2008. *Discourse and Context: A Sociocognitive Approach*. Cambridge University Press.

Weatherall, A. 2000. Gender relevance in talk-in-interaction and discourse. *Discourse and Society* 11.2: 286–8.

Wetherell, M. 1998. Positioning and interpretative repertoires: conversation analysis and post-structuralism in dialogue. *Discourse and Society* 9.3: 387–412.

Wilkinson, S. and A. Weatherall. 2011. Insertion repair. *Research on Language and Social Interaction* 44.1: 65–91.

Wodak, R. 2001. The discourse-historical approach. In R. Wodak and M. Meyer, eds. *Methods of Critical Discourse Analysis*. London: Sage, 63–94.

Wolfram, W. 2004. The grammar of urban African American Vernacular English. In B. Kortmann and E. Schneider, eds. *Handbook of Varieties of English*. Berlin: Mouton de Gruyter, 111–32.

Wooffitt, R. 2005. *Conversation Analysis and Discourse Analysis: A Comparative and Critical Introduction*. London: Sage.

22   Studying language over time

Hélène Blondeau

1   Introduction

As linguists, how do we capture the passage of time in our empirical research? Long relegated to the periphery of core linguistics due to the legacy of de Saussure (1984 [1916]), the relationship between language and time has traditionally been associated with the research domain of historical linguistics. However, a number of domains of linguistic research have challenged the Saussurean dichotomy between diachrony and synchrony, and developed methodological approaches to take into account the relationship between language and time.

Various approaches have been adopted to analyze the passage of time and its effect on linguistic structure and processes. Linguists have assessed stability or instability in language through the observation of speech events, the linguistic behavior of individuals over their life span, successive generations of a given speech community, the history of a language over a longer span, or, at the broadest level, the evolution of language. Depending on their research questions, linguists have focused on the individual, the community, a specific language or dialect, or the language faculty as a whole. The various fields of linguistics have problematized the time dimension differently. First language (L1) acquisition studies examine the question of time alongside cognitive developmental stages in early childhood. While the focus of second language acquisition (SLA) is also on the individual, this field observes the development of interlanguage stages within a time span that can encompass a longer portion of the individual's life span. Historical linguistics apprehends the time dimension through a much larger time scale, trying to understand, for example, how modern Romance languages, such as French, Spanish, Catalan, and Portuguese, emerged over centuries from spoken Latin, or how a specific linguistic phenomenon has evolved or grammaticalized over time. Sociolinguistics fits somewhere in between on this continuum, with one of its central research questions relating to linguistic change in progress at the community level, but also with an interest in the development of sociolinguistic competence at the individual level. These various objects of inquiry have directly impacted research design and methodological choices within the discipline.

As is commonly noted, the choice of methodological approach depends on the nature of the research problem at hand. In other words, decisions related to the design of a scientific study, such as deciding what kind of information a study

494

should collect (type of data, number of participants, length of data collection, etc.) and what analytical tools are necessary (qualitative or quantitative methodologies), first require one to consider carefully the larger research problem and assess what data are needed to respond to specific research questions.

Across the social sciences, several types of methodologies allow an analysis of conditions and events that influence a particular social phenomenon or evaluation of social change or stability over time. In all cases, comparison is a key component of the research design. A methodological distinction prevalent across the social sciences differentiates the types of comparison possible: a *cross-sectional* study, by definition synchronic, allows comparison at a specific moment in time among groups representing different positions relative to time (age, generation, etc.); a *longitudinal* study, by definition diachronic, involves comparisons among distinct time periods. A cross-sectional study is considered an *indirect approach* to the time dimension, while a longitudinal study constitutes a *direct approach*. The uses of these methodologies in linguistics are reviewed in this chapter, with particular attention to research domains that share a common interest in analyzing the effect of time on language behavior. Given space limitations, this chapter focuses mainly on the two domains of sociolinguistics and second language acquisition (SLA), with some incursions into L1 acquisition and historical linguistics when needed. (See Chapter 11 for more on methods used in historical linguistics; and Chapter 19 for a discussion of methods used in the analysis of the evolution of language.)

In sociolinguistics, a central interest in the relationship between variation and language change has resulted in the development of insightful methodological approaches to take into account the passage of time, often with a focus on group behavior. In the study of language acquisition, since the notion of acquisition corresponds by definition to a process that develops over time during the course of an individual's life, research paradigms have also developed methodological approaches to tackle the time dimension, though often with a focus on the individual. In addition to highlighting parallel methodologies across the two subfields, I identify points of divergence in methodological practice as well, to facilitate potential sharing of methodological expertise across research traditions. The chapter starts by reviewing the distinction between indirect and direct approaches to the study of time in linguistics, and then discusses in detail the advantages and challenges of synchronic and diachronic methods for the analysis of variation and change over time in each of the two sample research domains.

2 Indirect and direct approaches to time in linguistics

In linguistics, the time dimension has been approached from both a direct and an indirect perspective, as is the case in many social sciences. As noted, direct studies correspond to a longitudinal approach, involving collection of data relating to a given linguistic phenomenon at different points in time. In such an approach, data must be collected from the same speakers or the same groups of

Table 22.1 *Indirect and direct approaches to time*

	Indirect approach	Direct approach
Sociolinguistics	Apparent time	Real time
L1/L2 acquisition research	Cross-sectional	Longitudinal

speakers at various points in time, with a periodic design over weeks, months, or even years (Ruspini 2000). The goal is to observe directly how the linguistic behavior of individual speakers or groups changes or evolves over a certain time period. Indirect studies, or a cross-sectional approach, involve the examination of data at a single point in time. In this approach, data only need to be collected once, with the researchers indirectly inferring the impact of the passage of time on patterns or relationships in the data. For example, linguists might look at how beginners, intermediate, and advanced learners master a specific linguistic structure. Since the goal of indirect methods is to investigate how observable differences at one point in time can indicate the impact of time, the grouping of individuals must relate to time, relying on categories such as length of exposure, proficiency level, age, or life stage.

Although the conceptual distinction between cross-sectional and longitudinal perspectives has been present in many linguistic domains, this contrast has not always been described using consistent terminology. As illustrated in Table 22.1, both sociolinguistic and acquisition research have built on this fruitful methodological contrast, but have used different labels.

In the research paradigm of language acquisition, more specifically in second language acquisition, the use of both cross-sectional and longitudinal methodologies has been long established. However, the cross-sectional approach is more commonly used, with differences between developmental groups (e.g., two or more age groups in the case of L1 acquisition, or beginner versus intermediate learner groups in the case of SLA) often being interpreted as a *pseudo-longitudinal* effect. The direct approach, examining the language behavior of learners over a period of time, is less common, but has been growing since the 1970s (Ellis 1985).

In the field of variationist sociolinguistics, a similar methodological distinction has been employed. Here again the indirect approach is more common, mainly for reasons of feasibility. Since the first sociolinguistics studies of Martha's Vineyard (Labov 1965) and New York City (Labov 1966, 2006), sociolinguists have used the *apparent time* approach, a cross-sectional design through which the linguistic behavior of different generations of speakers is compared synchronically in order to infer the effect of time (i.e., to infer a pseudo-longitudinal effect). The apparent time model has been viewed as a useful indirect method to open a window on language change in the absence of real-time evidence. The logical follow-up to an inquiry into change in progress in a community is to return to the community at a later time to verify if the inferred hypotheses developed using the apparent time model are confirmed in real time. In other words, by employing the synchronic methodology a second time, the investigators gain access to direct evidence – in other words, actual diachrony. More recently, a new wave of studies has further developed a *real-time* approach, which directly documents the effect of time on language practices longitudinally. This research is relatively recent in sociolinguistics and can be dated to the end of the 1990s (Sankoff 2006).

An area that uses both methodological approaches and connects the fields of acquisition and sociolinguistics is the recent interest in the development of sociolinguistic competence, with an emphasis on how individual speakers develop variability in their L1 or L2. In L1 acquisition, the focus is on children (Khattab 2002; Foulkes et al. 2010; Khattab and Roberts 2010), while in second language acquisition, the emphasis has been on the sociolinguistic behavior of young adults in instructed (Bayley and Regan 2004; Dewaele 2004; Regan et al. 2009; Mougeon, Nadasdi, and Rehner 2010) or naturalistic (Sankoff et al. 1997; Blondeau et al. 2002) contexts. The interdisciplinary nature of the research questions in this work has led to the development of more sophisticated combinations of direct and indirect observation of language variation.

In sum, linguists make creative use of synchronic data collection to indirectly measure the passage of time using pseudo-longitudinal designs. Research domains have also developed methodological approaches to directly take into account the passage of time using longitudinal studies where feasible. As in most linguistics research, research practices in these fields have favored synchronic approaches, with diachronic approaches being relatively limited, for reasons reviewed later. The next sections first review the advantages and challenges of indirect methods, and then discuss direct methods.

3 Indirect methods

The most common research practice in linguistics is to adopt an indirect, or synchronic, approach to the time dimension. This can be described as a "snapshot" approach as it relies on various techniques to infer facts about change over time from taking a single, carefully designed "snapshot" at the present time. Over the years, an imposing body of research involving the indirect approach has developed in linguistics. The subsections that follow illustrate standard designs for synchronic "snapshot" or cross-sectional studies.

3.1 Cross-sectional studies in language acquisition research

The main focus in the fields of first or second language acquisition is to understand how language competence develops over time. Although the scope of inquiry is broad and has led to the development of an array of theoretical paradigms, the time dimension has taken a central place in empirical research design since the inception of both research domains.

Table 22.2 *The pseudo-longitudinal effect in SLA*

Synchronic:	Group 1 – Briefest exposure to L2	→	Group 2 – Medium-exposure to L2	→	Group 3 – Longest exposure to L2
Diachronic:	Individual at Time 1		Individual at Time 2		Individual at Time 3

In the early 1960s, many research ideas, concepts, and methodological techniques in SLA were borrowed from research on L1 acquisition, and it is in this context that the field of SLA inherited the notion of a developmental sequence (Ellis 1985; Cook 2010). At that time, more than a decade before the development of the interlanguage hypothesis (Selinker 1972), the notion of a critical period (Lennenberg 1957), as well as the comparison between L1 and L2 development, emerged as central research questions for the new field of SLA. In particular, the relationship between age and acquisition was considered vital to understanding the differences between L2 and L1 acquisition. Since then, scholars in SLA have used cross-sectional research designs extensively, a method commonly used in other scientific areas to capture the dimension of time faster than direct observation over time.

Cross-sectional research in SLA aims to infer how an L2 develops by collecting a body of data at a single point in time. This is a *one-wave* (as opposed to *multi-wave*) design: observations collected in a single "wave" of sampling are used to make inferences about language development by comparing subgroups of speakers from the population under study. Typically, different subgroups that have been exposed to the target language for different lengths of time are taken to represent indirectly stages of acquisition. By slicing the population into categories related to time, cross-sectional studies provide a snapshot of language development. Note that this model assumes that comparing the language skills of those exposed to the target language for shorter and longer lengths of time simulates tracking the development of those skills in a single learner over the course of real time. Table 22.2 illustrates how a pseudo-longitudinal effect can be inferred from the synchronic comparison of different groups of learners, each positioned at different points related to the time dimension, and their correspondence to a potential learner positioned on a diachronic developmental continuum.

Experimental cross-sectional studies manipulate a time-related independent variable (length of exposure to the L2 in the case of Table 22.2), in order to understand effect of time on a specific linguistic phenomenon, the dependent variable. One area of research that has generated many cross-sectional studies is research into the order of development of various linguistic features. For example, Padilla and Lindholm's (1976) study of the development of interrogatives, negatives, and possessives by nineteen Spanish-English bilingual children between the ages of 2 and 6.5 is a cross-sectional study in which biological age was used to determine if bilingual children simultaneously acquire both languages or transfer the knowledge of their first language to the other. Krashen's (1981) formulation of the Natural Order hypothesis was also based on a cross-sectional research design, looking at groups of L2 speakers at different points in their learning career. While age was the time-related factor in the Padilla and Lindholm study (1976), Krashen divided his population according to the stage of their learner career.

These two cross-sectional examples highlight the fact that although both studies use a time-related factor, the grouping criteria are not always the same. SLA design protocols reveal an array of time-related factors, such as length of exposure, stage of the learner career, biological age, biological age at time of the onset, and generation. Levels of proficiency[1] have frequently been employed in instructed settings, whereas in naturalistic settings, factors such as age of onset or length of stay (which may often be a proxy for social network factors) have proven to be useful. The fact that SLA research done in instructed contexts is more prevalent than in naturalistic contexts certainly explains in part why the level of proficiency grouping criteria is the most common.

The cross-sectional experimental method requires many decisions regarding sampling procedures. The sample (i.e., the group of subjects analyzed) should represent the population under study (i.e., the larger group of people about whom one aims to draw conclusions). A careful design of the sample is crucial, and various sampling options exist. Researchers conducting cross-sectional studies in SLA have generally preferred a stratified random sample or a judgment sample strategy over a purely random sample (see Chapter 5). In such studies, participants are generally stratified according to independent variables relevant to the population under study. Although sampling criteria related to time, such as age and duration of exposure, are used to detect a pseudo-longitudinal effect, other independent variables, such as gender or place of origin, can also be taken into account or controlled for (see Chapter 7). The sample design affects the scope of analysis possible in a given study: time-sensitive effects might be particular to an individual, an L1, an L2, or may derive from universal properties, and not all sample designs will be sufficiently robust to distinguish among these explanations.

For many years the cross-sectional approach has contributed to answering various research questions associated with the time dimension in language acquisition, such as the comparison of the developmental sequence of an L1 or an L2, the question of a critical or sensitive period for language acquisition, the difference between adult and child leaners' ultimate attainment, and the development of sociolinguistic competence.

One of the advantages of cross-sectional studies is that they are relatively easy to administer, since they require only one wave and no repeated measurements. As such, they can provide an immediate picture without the delay associated with the

---

[1] Some circularity can arise when defining proficiency by language use and then determining language differences according to proficiency level. Ideally, a generalized proficiency test that looks at features other than the one being studied should be used to establish the level of proficiency.

longitudinal approach. However, authors routinely acknowledge the need for longitudinal data collection in real time to confirm hypotheses drawn from synchronic data. In particular, alternative explanations are possible for "snapshot" data; this has been more clearly articulated in sociolinguistics, discussed next. Longitudinal analysis is thus generally considered the logical next step in further investigating hypotheses developed from synchronic results or to corroborate such results. Before examining longitudinal research designs, I review the use of indirect methods in sociolinguistics.

3.2   Apparent time studies in sociolinguistics

Sociolinguistics as a research domain emerged in the mid 1960s with the development of quantitative studies of speech communities in various social settings, exemplified by the seminal work of William Labov in Martha's Vineyard (1965) and New York City (1966). During the first wave of sociolinguistic studies, investigators anchored their analyses at the community level and developed a quantitative approach to analyze the contribution of various linguistic and social factors to linguistic variation at one point in time. Largely motivated by the question of linguistic change, which by definition implies variation (Weinreich, Labov, and Herzog 1968), researchers developed an analytical model that could capture changes in progress at the community level.

The focus on language change in this first trend of sociolinguistic research is shared by both historical linguistics and sociolinguistics. While the former has generally examined long periods of time in studying language change, the latter has focused on change in progress in a given community at a given point in time. The historical record was the main data source for historical linguistics, but sociolinguists developed new data collection procedures anchored in a quantitative approach, with some reliance on more traditional methods of historical linguistics as a point of comparison. Despite their differences in focus and methodology, the intersection between the two domains has generated a lot of attention.[2] One of the differences between the two fields lies in the source and quality of the data, which was captured by Labov's (1994: 11) famous observation that "Historical linguistics is the art of making the best use of bad data." Thus, despite the strength of historical linguistics in tracing linguistic changes over long periods of time, the data are limited as they have survived mainly by chance, certainly not by design, leading to inherent limitations in findings and interpretations (see Chapter 11 for a discussion of these challenges). In contrast, data collected in variationist sociolinguistics, explicitly designed to take into account the passage of time in a synchronic perspective, is able to access contemporary

---

[2] This common ground is evident in the fact that one of the seminal articles establishing the theoretical model of variationist sociolinguistics (Weinreich, Labov, and Herzog 1968) was published in a book entitled *Directions for Historical Linguistics* (Lehmann and Malkiel 1968); it is also clear in the number of contemporary sociolinguists who have contributed chapters in the more recent *Handbook of Historical Linguistics* (Joseph and Janda 2003).

communities to offer a fine-grained description of the variation potentially leading to changes in progress at the community level.[3]

Among the various social factors explored in sociolinguistics, age played a central role in the development of this early model, specifically because of its potential for providing indirect information about language change. In the absence of data or information on previous stages of a language, variation according to age was considered a point of access to change at the community level and has continued to be used indirectly to infer change in progress, leading to the development of what Labov has called the apparent time construct (Labov 1963, 1966; Bailey et al. 1991; Eckert 1997; Bailey 2002), an approach that has dominated the field of sociolinguistics since its inception.

The apparent time approach was first applied in the sociolinguistic study of Martha's Vineyard, the first study of its kind, more than fifty years ago (Labov 1965). Labov, who was interested in understanding the island's vowel system, decided to interview a sample of sixty-nine speakers from different age groups, occupations, and ethnicities, to look at variation in their way of speaking. It was clear to him that the pattern observed according to age, combined with the effect of other social factors, was an indication that change was taking place at a community level, which led to the formulation of a hypothesis of change in progress.

One of the premises of the apparent time construct is that after the critical period, which delimits the formative period of language acquisition, individual speakers' linguistic behavior changes minimally over the course of the life span, and individual vernaculars remain essentially stable. Labov based his interpretations of the Martha's Vineyard case on this assumption: If we accept the premise that individual vernaculars are stable after the critical period, differences in the linguistic behavior of successive generations of adult speakers in a given community can reflect language change in its historical sense. According to this hypothesis, the differentiation according to age in Martha's Vineyard was interpreted as a reflection of a change in progress. However, in order to anchor his interpretation on more solid grounds, Labov also compared his findings with data from earlier dialect surveys, which provided another temporal benchmark. Even if the data were not collected in the exact same way, such points of comparison in time had the advantage of offering a glimpse of real-time change.

To further test the apparent time construct, Labov (1966) undertook a large investigation in New York City, a precedent followed by many others studies in urban settings around the world (for a review of the 1966–2006 period, see Labov 2006: Chapter 15). Labov collected data from a representative sample of the New York City community. By comparing the speech of successive generations, he was able to assess stability or change in progress at the community level and identified a *generational change-in-progress* at the community level for linguistic variables.

---

[3] In a sense, the two fields could be viewed as complementary, as the newly developed research trend in historical sociolinguistics illustrates (Tagliamonte 2002; Hernández-Campoy and Conde-Silvestre 2012).

Several years later, a team of sociolinguists in Montreal used a similar methodology (Sankoff and Sankoff 1973) to discover that the pronunciation of /r/ in Montreal French was also involved in a rapid change in progress at the community level (Clermont and Cedergren 1979). Using the apparent time construct, they suggested that the apical /r/, a variant mainly used by older speakers, was in decline, pointing to the emergence of the posterior variant as the new community norm.

Sampling procedures for apparent-time studies in sociolinguistics are also designed with the notion of representativity in mind, and options include random, stratified or judgment, and network samples (see Chapter 5), the latter two types being typically used. Sociolinguistic samples generally exclude very young speakers[4] (prior to the end of the critical period) or the very old, to avoid combining effects related to individual acquisition or aging-related language loss with the core focus on historical change at the community level.

Even with such exclusions, sociolinguists have to be careful in interpreting their data because differences across age groups could also be explained as *age grading* phenomena (Hockett 1950). Age-graded language use refers to individual modification of linguistic behavior according to socio-symbolic norms associated with various stages of an individual's life (Eckert 1997; Chambers 2003). In such a case, apparent differences observed across age groups do not necessarily indicate change occurring in the community over time, but rather age-specific norms for language use, which can remain stable over many generations and not lead to any significant change at the community level. This is illustrated in Macaulay's (1977) study of glottal replacement of the /t/ phoneme in certain linguistic environments in Glasgow English. The high level of use of the nonstandard variant among adolescent boys, as compared with the sharp decline in use by adult men, especially those holding white-collar jobs, is best interpreted not as a change under way among younger speakers, but as a withdrawal from the vernacular variant on the part of middle-class speakers as they enter the labor force (Sankoff 2004). In comparison, women in the higher social classes showed a steady decrease in the use of the stigmatized variant as they aged. In this case, a fine-grained analysis of age, social class, and gender favored an age-grading interpretation over a generational change interpretation (Chambers 2003; Sankoff 2004). Furthermore, Eckert (1997) warns against assuming that universal divisions according to chronological age divisions are always appropriate in any apparent time study: distinct communities may associate specific values (and linguistic practices) with specific ages or life stages for culturally specific reasons, and research that fails to fully understand these locally salient categories runs the risk of obscuring important dimensions of language variation by imposing categories that do not align with those that are culturally meaningful in the research site. (See Chapter 5 and Chapter 10 for more discussion of the need for understanding emic social structures in sociolinguistic research design.)

---

[4] Some studies of sociolinguistic competence have looked at the development of variability in children's production and constitute an important exception.

In deciding between age-grading and change-in-progress as available interpretations, linguists should ideally calibrate their hypotheses against other types of historical evidence, such as data extracted from earlier dialect atlas surveys or other details from the historical record, and thereby show that any claimed apparent time pattern confirms a more long-standing trajectory of change in the community. In the Martha's Vineyard study, the New York study, and the Montreal study, the proposed interpretation was supported by data from dialectologists (e.g., Kurath et al. 1941; Vinay 1950). Data from the historical record or linguistic data collected at another point in time is crucial to establish temporal benchmarks for the purpose of distinguishing between the phenomena of age grading and generational change.

Most variationist sociolinguistic studies have relied on the apparent time construct (Sankoff 2006). However, in order to confirm previous hypotheses, many scholars in the fields have also employed a direct diachronic approach. The use of direct real-time evidence helps to disentangle age differences based on generational change from those deriving from age grading; it can also test the validity of the apparent time construct and reveal more complex patterns of individual and group change over time. Notably, all three seminal communities discussed above–Martha's Vineyard, New York, and Montreal – have been restudied using the direct approach, discussed next.

4   Direct methods

Diachronic approaches involve the direct tracking of a linguistic phenomenon over more than one point in time. In the next two subsections I examine how SLA and sociolinguistics have approached this task in relation to their object of study. While we can trace longitudinal research in the area of acquisition back to the mid 1970s, this trend is relatively more recent in sociolinguistics, where a systematic discussion of such methods only emerged at the beginning of the 1990s. Again, the two fields share many similarities in their use of direct methods, but due to differences in terminology and research focus they are discussed in separate subsections below.

4.1   Longitudinal analysis in SLA

Despite the fact that textbooks often stress that longitudinal studies are less common than cross-sectional studies in SLA, with less systematic methodologies (Ellis 1985; Larsen-Freeman and Long 1991; Doughty and Long 2003; Long 2007; Myles 2008; Philp 2009), there has in fact been research interest in this area for nearly 40 years and, in some areas, a much steadier trend since the beginning of the 2000s (Ortega and Iberri-Shea 2005; Ortega and Byrnes 2008; Duff 2010). Ellis (1985) associates the emergence of longitudinal research in SLA with the aim of mapping L2 acquisition routes in real time and comparing them with what we know about L1 acquisition routes; he points to the work of Hatch (1978) as pioneering this perspective in the field.

Ortega and Iberri-Shea (2005) emphasize that the one defining criterion of longitudinal research is the *multi-wave* data collection model (i.e., collection of data at more than one point in time), which contrasts directly with cross-sectional studies. At least two phases of data collection are necessary to produce direct evidence of the speakers' L2 development, and in practice SLA studies often involve more than two waves.

Ortega and Iberri-Shea (2005) also argue for a definition of longitudinal studies that includes not only multi-wave data collection, but also a conceptual focus on capturing change and a focus on antecedent-consequent relationships. This suggests that a longitudinal conceptualization must be included in the study design long before the first wave of data collection takes place. The data collection procedure should ideally specify in advance the length of the study and justify the number of waves required, and the interpretation must address antecedent-consequent relationships inherent to understanding the development of a second language. This is in contrast to a post hoc addition of a second wave to a study that originally consisted of a one-wave design, a practice that can lead to suboptimal reliability, validity, and replicability of a study (see Chapter 7 for details of these research design desiderata).

Although multi-wave studies have to be executed via repeated data collection, the length of the study, the exact number of waves, and the spacing of the measurements can vary depending on the focus of the research. In research on L1 acquisition, the span is often measured in terms of weeks, months, or years; in SLA, the span is often measured in terms of months, with a much longer time span, often years, used for investigating questions such as fossilization or ultimate attainment. The details of these decisions are typically made in relation to biological or institutional time scales (Ortega and Iberri-Shea 2005: 37).

Evidence in real time has proven useful not only to contrast L1 and L2 development narrowly, but also to answer other types of research questions – for example, in the area of advanced capacities (Ortega and Byrnes 2008) or differences in ultimate achievement between children and adults. Longitudinal studies have been conducted of children (Sato 1990; Watson-Gegeo 1992) and adult learners (Liceras et al. 1997; Iwashita 2001) in both naturalistic and formally instructed contexts. Other researchers in SLA have made a plea for case studies and longitudinal research to understand the role of interaction in acquisition over time (Duff 2010).

Most longitudinal studies in SLA have concentrated on fewer participants than is typical for cross-sectional studies. A case study perspective can offer a more holistic or ethnographic description of the process of acquisition (Gass and Selinker 2008 [1994]). Any loss in representativity in longitudinal studies (due to the reduced number of participants) is generally justified by the compensation in terms of fine-grained analysis of actual language development over several intervals of time. Longitudinal studies in SLA can even be limited to the speech of only one speaker, as in the seminal case study of Patty, a Chinese adult learner of

English, who was followed for over a decade (Lardiere 2006, 2007). This tendency is why longitudinal analysis is often associated with the qualitative paradigm (Larsen-Freeman and Long 1991: 12, Duff 2010: 52).

Research designs are diverse and flexible, but longitudinal case studies in SLA often collect data in a naturalistic setting, whereas cross-sectional studies are more often conducted in instructed contexts. However, in recent years, Ortega and Iberri-Shea (2005) have noted an increase in longitudinal study designs that adopt a quantitative and/or experimental paradigm. In addition, the use of longitudinal studies has extended to numerous areas, such as L2 program outcomes, instructional effectiveness (Lyster 2004), and research in the context of study abroad programs (Kinginger and Blattner 2008). In the domain of L1 acquisition, an increase in longitudinal studies has also been noted (Myles 2008; Sekali 2012) in relation to the increased availability of electronic corpora (see Chapters 11 and 13). The development of digital humanities is changing the landscape of the research in many areas of linguistics by providing access to a large body of data, opening the door to larger longitudinal studies.

Before turning to sociolinguistics, it is worth mentioning the recent development of longitudinal studies that investigate sociolinguistics competence, a research area that connects the fields of acquisition and sociolinguistics. In L1 acquisition, researchers have tracked the development of variability in children's speech (Roberts 1997; Khattab 2002, 2011; Foulkes and Docherty 2006). For example, Foulkes and Docherty (2006) built their analysis by combining both cross-sectional and longitudinal experiments that looked at children's language production. While the cross-sectional segment of their study focused on forty children divided into four discrete groups, ranging from 2 to 4 years, the longitudinal segment followed thirteen children, all part of the same 2-year-old age range. Other researchers have looked at the development of sociolinguistic competence in a second language, among young adults (Bayley and Regan 2004; Dewaele 2004). While some in this area have used cross-sectional designs in instructed settings (Mougeon, Nadasdi, and Rehner 2010), others have opted for a longitudinal design, as Regan, Howard, and Lemée (2009) did in their study on second language acquisition in a study abroad context.

4.2   Real-time analysis in sociolinguistics

In sociolinguistics, studies that examine language use over time using a multi-wave approach are usually referred to as real-time studies. As noted earlier, one of the main reasons for the development of real-time study was the desire to provide direct evidence of language change, and to distinguish between two potential interpretations offered by synchronic comparison: age grading and generational change (Labov 1994).

According to Sankoff (2005), three of the pioneers of real-time study are Hermann (1929) and Brink and Lund (1979). Hermann's effort to capture the trajectory of change in Charmer, Switzerland, was made possible by the replication of an earlier study conducted by Gauchat. Brink and Lund's large-scale real-time investigation of Copenhagen speech further developed real-time methodology in sociolinguistics. Since then, and particularly toward the end of the twentieth century, many trained sociolinguists who first explored a situation through the lens of apparent time have returned to their original speech community to collect data again at a later time point (Cedergren 1988; Trudgill 1988; Bailey et al. 1991; Ashby 2001; Mougeon, Nadasdi, and Rehner 2009).

Many of these studies opted for a replication of their original cross-sectional study; in the social sciences, this re-sampling of different individuals from the same population at different points in time is referred to as a *trend study*. Other studies have chosen to follow up with the same individual speakers or cohort of speakers on multiple occasions; in the social sciences, this re-sampling of the same individuals at different points in time is referred to as a *panel study*. Some sociolinguists have opted for a hybrid method, combining trend and panel approaches for a multidimensional understanding of change at both the individual and the group level.[5]

Sociolinguists have selected trend or panel designs based on the objectives and focus of the research, as well as the availability of resources. Trend studies allow systematic comparison of community behavior over time; panel studies allow researchers to trace the path of the change at the individual level, as well as providing insight regarding the mutability of individual linguistic systems over time, particularly after the end of the critical period. Each design is described in more detail next.

4.2.1   Trend studies in sociolinguistics

The large majority of real-time studies in sociolinguistics belong to the trend study category, which is becoming increasingly popular, with an upsurge in the past decade (José 2010). (This is in contrast to longitudinal research in SLA studies, which has tended to favor a panel design due to the nature of the research questions involved.) The general objective of a trend study is to establish generalizations about the *community* with regard to language variation over time, either language change or stable variation. Cross-sectional follow-up investigations generally go back to the community a generation or two later,[6] with the objective of verifying or falsifying in real time the initial hypotheses developed according to

---

[5] The use of the standard terms "trend" and "panel" are increasingly common in sociolinguistics. By contrast, it is still the case that relatively few sociolinguists use the terms "cross-sectional" and "longitudinal," terms widely used in the social sciences. With few exceptions (e.g., Sankoff 2005; José 2010; Van Hofwegen and Wolfram 2010), sociolinguists have focused on the distinction between apparent time and real time without making clear connections with parallel methodologies in other fields of linguistics and the social sciences.

[6] Although Wagner (2008) exploited a shorter real-time depth of a couple of years, generally real-time studies opt for a longer time depth of at least half a generation or a decade (Labov 1981; Bailey et al. 1991). Studies on public discourse can explore longer periods of decades or centuries and are therefore relevant for historical sociolinguistics (Arnaud 1998; Poplack and St-Amand 2007; Poplack and Dion 2009; Nevalainen, Raumolin-Brunberg, and Mannila 2011).

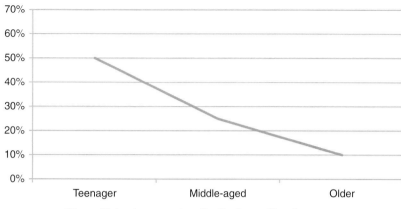

Figure 22.1. *Apparent-time distribution at Time 1*

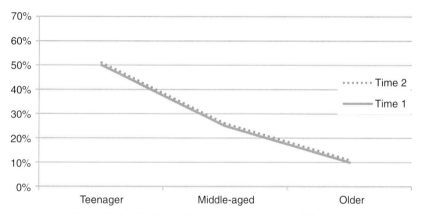

Figure 22.2. *Real-time distribution at Time 1 and Time 2: age-grading interpretation*

the apparent-time construct during the first visit. By replicating the synchronic methodology a second time (wave 2), or even more (wave n), investigators gain access to direct evidence of language change or stability. However, such studies are challenging since they need an exact replication of the methodological procedure in terms of sampling and data collection.

Figures 22.1–3 illustrate potential interpretations of results based on a first and a second wave of data collection. Figure 22.1 compares three populations differentiated according to age (teenagers, middle-aged speakers, and older speakers), each of which displays a different percentage of usage of a specific variant at a single point in time, Time 1. In the absence of any additional evidence, it is difficult to distinguish between age-grading and change-in-progress interpretations of the apparent time data in Figure 22.1. Figures 22.2 and 22.3 illustrate possible findings of a real-time study and display the usage for the same three groups for both Time 1 and Time 2, the latter being a second wave of data

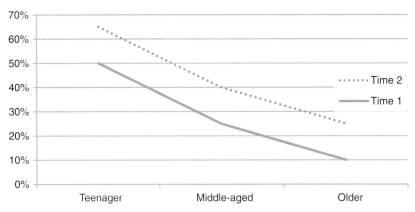

Figure 22.3. *Real-time distribution at Time 1 and Time 2: community change interpretation*

collection. In Figure 22.2, the three groups at Time 2 display an identical distribution (i.e., teenagers who are now middle-aged have the same usage that the earlier middle-aged group had); the interpretation strongly supported here is age-grading. In Figure 22.3, by contrast, all rates have shifted over, such that teenagers who are now middle-aged more or less retain their original usage levels, and new teenagers have even higher rates of use; this points to a possible change in progress at the community level. This comparison shows the importance of real-time data for distinguishing among potential explanations.

With this objective in mind, original investigators, as well as new scholars, have decided to replicate entirely or partially previous studies conducted during the early wave of sociolinguistic studies in the 1960s and 1970s. Some scholars have returned to their field site and replicated their original study with a new representative sample of the community, as Cedergren (1988) did for Spanish in Panama, Trudgill (1988) for English in Norwich, Bailey et al. (1991) for English in Texas, Ashby (2001) for Hexagonal French in Tours, and Mougeon, Nadasdi, and Rehner (2009) for Ontario French. In other cases, new scholars who were not involved in the original study have decided to replicate seminal studies, such as the Martha's Vineyard study (Blake and Josey 2003; Pope, Meyerhoff, and Ladd 2007), the Montreal French study (Thibault and Vincent 1990), the Verrat study in Finland (Nahkola and Saanilahti 2004), and the Denmark study (Gregersen 2007). Another option has been to design a totally new study with a real-time design in mind from the beginning (José 2010).[7]

Results have revealed that there is a much more complex relationship between the phenomena of age-grading and generational change than was previously recognized, and that the two phenomena are not necessarily totally independent (Labov 1994). These tests of the apparent-time construct require the inspection not

---

[7] An ideal study would require having the real-time design in mind at T1 to resolve potential methodological problems and ensure replicability.

only of variables potentially involved in change (Sankoff and Wagner 2006; Sankoff et al. 2006; Mackenzie and Sankoff 2010), but also of stable variables, which have not so far received as much attention (Sankoff 2005; Wagner 2008; José 2010).

Since real-time analyses using the trend study techniques have shown a complex portrait of the relationship between community change and individual variation (Labov 1994), a closer look at individual behavior over the life span is needed to better understand the situation. This can be achieved through panel studies.

4.2.2   Panel studies in sociolinguistics

A panel study monitors longitudinally the linguistic behavior of an individual or a cohort of individuals over time (Blondeau 2006a). The panel model has been employed less frequently than the trend model in sociolinguistics, mostly for reasons of feasibility. However, panel studies are crucial to questions relating to the stability of individual vernaculars after the end of the critical or sensitive period, and to exploring the role of individual trajectories in the context of changes in progress at the community level.

When documenting the linguistic behavior of individual speakers or cohorts of individuals over time, one of the objectives is to explore how language change in its historical sense is reflected at the individual level. In particular, it is necessary to establish whether language change takes the form of discrete differences between generations, with relative stability within individuals' life spans after their initial acquisition, or more continuous change occurring throughout the life span of individuals. Panel studies' objectives are four-pronged: they shed light on the mutability of the linguistic system over the life span, which could here be connected to the question of a critical or sensitive period in acquisition; they distinguish between age-grading, community change, and life-span change; they measure the contribution of an individual to linguistic change at the community level by distinguishing between active participants and conservators at the individual level (Blondeau 2006b; Nevalainen, Raumolin-Brunberg, and Mannila 2011; Wagner and Sankoff 2011); and they test the validity of the apparent-time construct and therefore have potential theoretical implications for sociolinguistics as a whole (Sankoff and Blondeau 2007; Blondeau et al. 2002; Sankoff and Wagner 2006; Mackenzie and Sankoff 2010).

As illustrated in the sample graphs in Figures 22.4 and 22.5, individual behavior can show diverse trajectories at different points in time. In Figure 22.4, two individuals (A = older, B = younger) are compared at three points in time on the x-axis. Speaker A has a lower use of an incoming variant than speaker B for all three time points, and neither A nor B shows change in rate of use over time. In such a case, we would interpret the two speakers as remaining stable across their life span, with a generational change occurring at the community level. In Figure 22.5, however, speaker A has a consistently lower use of an incoming variant than speaker B for all three time points, but also both A and B increase their

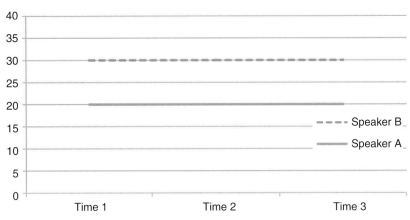

Figure 22.4. *Stability over time for two speakers*

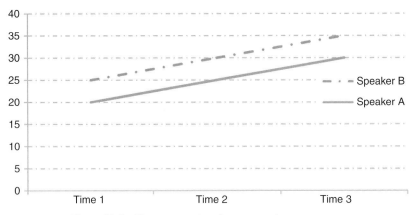

Figure 22.5. *Change over time for two speakers*

use of the form from T1 to T2 to T3. In such a case, the comparison would suggest that an individual speaker can change over the course of their life span (either with or without a change-in-progress at the community level).

Panel studies have been performed on various languages (for English: Baugh 1996; Cukor-Avila 2002; Bowie 2005; Harrington 2006; Van Hofwegen and Wolfram 2010; for French: Thibault and Daveluy 1989; Yaeger-Dror 1994; Blondeau 2001; 2011; Sankoff, Blondeau, and Charity 2001; Wagner and Sankoff 2011; for Swedish: Sundgren 2002; 2009). Some panel studies in socio-linguistics focus on case studies, while others use larger groups of speakers. A seminal case study is the longitudinal analysis of the recorded broadcasts of Queen Elizabeth II's Christmas radio addresses, from the 1950s to the present day, which showed that the Queen's production of vowels and diphthongs has changed over time to sound closer to, though not quite attaining, Standard Southern British norms (Harrington, Palethorpe, and Watson 2000, 2005; Harrington 2006). Other examples of the case study approach include Sankoff's (2004) analysis of two speakers from age 7 to age 35, based on data taken from the *Seven Up* series, as well as Baugh (1996), who looked at the transition between adolescence and adulthood for four African Americans over a period of eleven years. Other panel studies have investigated relatively larger groups (Sundgren 2002, 2009; Sankoff and Wagner 2006; Sankoff and Blondeau 2007; MacKenzie and Sankoff 2010; Van Hofwegen and Wolfram 2010). However, the second-wave cohort of a panel study is generally smaller than the first-wave cohort. This is due to the fact that success rate in recruitment decreases over time. This problem is even more complicated when the longitudinal aspect of the research was not part of the initial study design. For the second wave of the Montreal panel study, 50 percent of the original speakers were re-interviewed, which is considered a successful rate in such a situation (Thibault and Vincent 1990).

In terms of results, panel studies have provided evidence that speakers can modify the way they speak to different degrees as they age (Sankoff and Blondeau 2007), and can therefore individually participate in language change in progress at the community level. Based on the results of recent panel studies, Sankoff (2005) has proposed to add a new category, life span change, under a typology of types of language change. So far, depending on the variable under study, considerable heterogeneity in the relationship between individual and group change has been found. For some variables, individuals are taking part in a change-in-progress, but remain behind the leaders of the change (Sankoff and Blondeau 2007). However, for other variables, the same individuals can display different behavior remaining stable or even becoming more conservative (Blondeau, Sankoff, and Charity 2002; Blondeau 2006a, b, 2012; Wagner and Sankoff 2011), and in a specific cohort, some speakers may be more conservative than others (Nevalainen, Raumolin-Brunberg, and Mannila 2011). Individuals who participate in change in certain variables therefore do not necessarily participate in all ongoing changes in a community (Blondeau, Sankoff, and Charity 2002; Blondeau 2006b; Wagner and Sankoff 2011). However, too few studies have been performed so far to be able to make firm statements and generalizations. What is clear is that the introduction of the panel study methodology has raised questions about funda-mental assumptions made in sociolinguistics, and that sociolinguists need to develop more panel studies on variables at different levels of linguistic structure, as well as above and below the level of consciousness (Blondeau et al. 2002).

Some scholars have combined panel and trend components in their studies (Thibault and Daveluy 1989; Thibault and Vincent 1990; Arnaud 1998; Sundgren 2002, 2009; Zilles 2005; Sankoff and Wagner 2006; Sankoff and Blondeau 2007; Mackenzie and Sankoff 2010). Such hybrid approaches combine the two real-time methods in a single study in order to provide a fine-grained picture of the trajectories of specific variables with regard to language change in its historical sense, but also to enhance our understanding of community trends, individual trajectories, and the connection between the apparent time construct and dia-chrony. Although a hybrid approach can address the relationship between change at the individual and at the community level, results coming from these two angles are not necessarily easy to reconcile (Sankoff and Wagner 2006; Sankoff and Blondeau 2007).

5   Conclusions

Across linguistics, a similar methodological contrast between indirect and direct approaches to the study of language over time exists. This chapter has reviewed the main characteristics of these cross-sectional and longitudinal perspectives, with a focus on SLA and sociolinguistics, two linguistic domains where the time dimension occupies a central position. Both domains share a reliance on cross-sectional designs, which provide an indication of diachronic changes, but not necessarily a faithful representation of real-time processes. Such studies in any field often call for follow-up studies in real time to counterbalance the inherent limitations and uncertainties associated with a synchronic perspective.

Some of the inherent limitations of indirect approaches have indeed been addressed with longitudinal methods in both fields recently. While there are many points in common in the use of cross-sectional methodology, the two sample research domains discussed in this chapter have made slightly different use of longitudinal methodology. In sociolinguistics, the follow-up enterprise has taken two routes, both helpful for clarifying earlier hypotheses made in synchrony. The trend design is essentially a comparison of two cross-sectional studies over time to measure the progress or the stability of specific linguistic features over time, and the panel design has focused on a better understanding of individual vernaculars over time, and is therefore closer to the longitudinal approach in SLA. In variationist sociolinguistics, both trend and panel studies maintain the quantitative paradigm. By contrast, in SLA there has traditionally been a greater distance between cross-sectional research, which is experimental and quantitative, and longitudinal research, which has often been more qualitative; this was especially the case in early work, when researchers used case studies to focus on a very small number of participants with repeated waves of data collection. This approach contributed to a better understanding of developmental processes, and disentangled certain research problems unresolved under the cross-sectional quantitative paradigm. More recently, longitudinal research designs adopting a quantitative perspective have become more common in SLA as well. The difference between cross-sectional and longitudinal approaches no longer corresponds to a distinction between quantitative and qualitative linguistics (Larsen-Freeman and Long 1991), and new research questions – for example, the development of sociolinguistic competence – have fostered creative uses of both indirect and direct methods. The use of a quantitative or qualitative study design (and a direct or an indirect method) to examine language change over time is a decision ultimately linked to the research questions at hand and the researcher's general orientation in the discipline.

References

Arnaud, R. 1998. The development of the progressive in nineteenth century English: a quantitative survey. *Language Variation and Change* 10: 123–52.

Ashby, W. 2001. Un nouveau regard sur la chute du ne en français parlé tourangeau: s'agit-il d'un changement en cours? *Journal of French Language Studies* 11: 1–22.

Bailey, G. 2002. Real and apparent time. In J. K. Chambers, P. Trudgill, and N. Schilling-Estes, eds. *The Handbook of Language Variation and Change*. Malden, MA: Blackwell, 312–32.

Bailey, G., T. Wikle, J. Tillery, and J. Sand. 1991. The apparent time construct. *Language Variation and Change* 3: 241–64.

Baugh, J. 1996. Dimensions of a theory of econolinguistics. In G. Guy, D. Feagin, D. Schiffrin, and J. Baugh, eds. *Towards a Social Science of Language. Papers in Honor of William Labov*, 2 vols. Amsterdam: Benjamins, Volume I, 397–419.

Bayley, R. and V. Regan. 2004. Introduction: the acquisition of sociolinguistic competence. *Journal of Sociolinguistics* 8.3: 323–38.

Blake, R. and M. Josey. 2003. The /ay/ diphthong in a Martha's Vineyard community: what can we say 40 years later after Labov? *Language in Society* 32: 451–85.

Blondeau, H. 2001. Real time changes in the paradigm of personal pronouns in Montreal French. *Journal of Sociolinguistics* 5: 453–74.

2006a. Panel studies and language variation. In K. Brown, ed. *Encyclopedia of Languages and Linguistics*, 2nd edn, 14 vols. Oxford: Elsevier, Volume IX, 150–4.

2006b. La trajectoire de l'emploi du futur chez une cohorte de Montréalais francophones entre 1971 et 1995. *Revue Canadienne de Linguistique Appliquée/Canadian Journal of Applied Linguistics* 9.2: 73–98.

2011. *Cet «autres» qui nous distingue. Tendances communautaires et parcours individuels dans le système des pronoms du français québécois*. Quebec: Presses de l'Université Laval.

2012. Hors de LA norme point de salut? La piste montréalaise des hypothétiques en si. *Revue française de linguistique appliquée* 27.1: 55–66.

Blondeau, H., G. Sankoff, and A. Charity. 2002. Parcours individuels dans deux changements linguistiques en cours en français montréalais. *Revue Québécoise de Linguistique* 31.1: 13–38.

Blondeau, H., N. Nagy, G. Sankoff, and P. Thibault. 2002. La couleur locale des Anglo-Montréalais. *Acquisition et Interaction en Langue Etrangère* 17: 73–100.

Bowie, D. 2005. Language change over the lifespan: a test of the apparent time construct. In S. Evans Wagner, ed. *University of Pennsylvania Working Papers in Linguistics* 11.2: 45–58.

Brink, L. and J. Lund. 1979. *Social Factors in the Sound Changes of Modern Danish. Proceedings of the Ninth International Congress of Phonetic Sciences*, 2 vols. University of Copenhagen. Volume II, 196–203.

Cedergren, H. 1988. The spread of language change: verifying inferences of linguistic diffusion. In P. H. Lowenberg, ed. *Language Spread and Language Policy: Issues, Implications, and Case Studies* (Georgetown University Round Table on Language and Linguistics 1987). Washington, DC: Georgetown University Press, 45–60.

Chambers J. 2003. *Sociolinguistic Theory*. Oxford: Blackwell.

Clermont J. and H. Cedergren. 1979. Les R de ma mère sont perdus dans l'air. In P. Thibault, ed. *Le français parlé. Études sociolinguistiques*. Edmonton, Alberta: Linguistic Research, 13–28.

Cook, V. 2010. The relationship between first and second language acquisition revisited. In E. Macaro, ed. *The Continuum Companion to Second Language Acquisition*. London: Continuum, 137–57.

Cukor-Avila, P. 2002. She say, she go, she be like: verbs of quotation over time in African American Vernacular English. *American Speech* 77: 3–31.

de Saussure, F. 1984 [1916]. *Cours de linguistique générale*. Paris: Payot.

Dewaele, J.-M. 2004. The acquisition of sociolinguistic competence in French as a foreign language: an overview. *Journal of French Language Studies* 14: 301–19.

Doughty, D. J. and M. Long. 2003. The scope of inquiry and goals of SLA. In C. J. Doughty and M. H. Long, eds. *Handbook of Second Language Acquisition*. Oxford: Blackwell.

Duff, P. 2010. Research approaches in applied linguistics. In R. Kaplan, ed. *Handbook of Applied Linguistics*, 2nd edn. Oxford University Press, 45–59.

Eckert, P. 1997. Age as a sociolinguistic variable. In F. Coulmas, ed. *The Handbook of Sociolinguistics*. Malden MA: Blackwell, 151–67.

Ellis, R. 1985. *Understanding Second Language Acquisition*. Oxford University Press.

Foulkes, P. and G. J. Docherty. 2006. The social life of phonetics and phonology. *Journal of Phonetics* 34: 409–38.

Foulkes, P., G. J. Docherty, G. Khattab, and M. Yaeger-Dror. 2010. Sound judgments: perception of indexical features in children's speech. In D. Preston and N. Niedzielski, eds. *A Reader in Sociophonetics*. Berlin: Mouton de Gruyter, 327–56.

Gass, S. and L. Selinker. 2008 [1994]. *Second Language Acquisition: An Introductory Course*, 3rd edn. New York and London: Routledge.

Gregersen, F. 2007. The LANCHAT Corpus of spoken Danish: report from a corpus in progress. In H. Toivanen and P. J. Henrichsen, eds. *Current Trends in Research on Spoken Language in the Nordic Countries*, 2 vols. Finland: Oulu University Press, Volume II, 130–43.

Harrington, J. 2006. Evidence for a relationship between synchronic variability and diachronic change in the Queen's annual Christmas broadcasts. In J. Cole and J. Hualde, eds. *Laboratory Phonology*, 10 vols. Berlin: Mouton de Gruyter, Volume IX, 125–44.

Harrington, J., S. Palethorpe, and C. I. Watson. 2000. Does the Queen speak the Queen's English? *Nature* 408: 927–8.

2005. Deepening or lessening the divide between diphthongs? An analysis of the Queen's annual Christmas Broadcasts. In W. J. Hardcastle and J. M. Beck, eds. *A Figure of Speech: A Festschrift for John Laver*. Mahwah, NJ: Lawrence Erlbaum, 227–62.

Hatch, E. M. 1978. Discourse analysis and second language acquisition. In E. M. Hatch, ed. *Second Language Acquisition: A Book of Readings*. Rowley, MA: Newbury House, 401–35.

Hermann, M. E. 1929. Lautvanderungen in des Individualsprache einer Mundart. Nachrichten der Gesellschaft der Wissenschaften zu Gottingen. *Philosophisch-historische Klasse* 11: 195–214.

Hernández-Campoy, J. M. and J. C. Conde-Silvestre. 2012. *Handbook of Historical Sociolinguistics*. Malden, MA: Wiley.

Hockett, D. F. 1950. Age grading and linguistic continuity. *Language* 26.4: 449–57.

Iwashita, N. 2001. The role of task-based conversation in the acquisition of Japanese grammar and vocabulary. Unpublished Ph.D. dissertation. Department of Linguistics and Applied Linguistics, University of Melbourne.

José, B. 2010. The apparent-time construct and stable variation: final /z/ devoicing in northwestern Indiana. *Journal of Sociolinguistics* 14.1: 34–59.

Joseph, B. and R. Janda. 2003. On language, change, and language change – or, of history, linguistics, and historical linguistics. In B. Joseph and R. Janda, eds. *The Handbook of Historical Linguistics*. Oxford: Blackwell, 3–180.

Khattab, G. 2002. /l/ production in English-Arabic bilingual speakers. *International Journal of Bilingualism* 6.3: 335–53.

2011. Acquisition of Lebanese Arabic and Yorkshire English /l/ by bilingual and monolingual children: a comparative spectrographic study. In Z. M. Hassan and B. Heselwood, eds. *Instrumental Studies in Arabic Phonetics*. Amsterdam and Philadelphia: John Benjamins, 325–54.

Khattab, G. and J. Roberts. 2010. Working with children. In M. Di Paolo and M. Yaeger-Dror, eds. *Sociophonetics: A Student's Guide*. London and New York: Routledge, 163–78.

Kinginger, C. and G. Blattner. 2008. Histories of engagement and sociolinguistic awareness in study abroad: colloquial French. In L. Ortega and H. Byrnes, eds. *The Longitudinal Study of Advanced L2 Capacities*. New York and London: Routledge, 223–46.

Krashen, S. D. 1981. *Second Language Acquisition and Second Language Learning*. Oxford: Pergamon Press.

Kurath, H., M. L. Hanley, B. Bloch, G. S. Lowman, Jr., and M. L. Hansen. 1941. *Linguistic Atlas of New England*, 3 vols. Providence, RI: American Council of Learned Societies.

Labov, W. 1963. *The social motivation of a sound change.* Word 19: 273–309. (Revised as Chapter 1 of W. Labov. 1972. *Sociolinguistic Patterns*. Philadelphia: University of Pennsylvania Press, 2–42.)

1965. *On the mechanism of linguistic change.* Word 19: 273–309.

1966. *The Social Stratification of English in New York City.* Washington, DC: Center for Applied Linguistics.

1981. What can be learned about change in progress from synchronic descriptions? In D. Sankoff and H. Cedergren, eds. *Variation Omnibus*. Edmonton, Alberta: Linguistic Research, 177–99.

1994. *Principles of Linguistic Change. Volume I: Internal Factors*, 3 vols. Oxford: Basil Blackwell.

2006. *The Social Stratification of English in New York City*, 2nd edn. Cambridge University Press.

Lardiere, D. 2006. Attainment and acquirability in second language acquisition. *Second Language Research* 22.3: 239–42.

2007. *Ultimate Attainment in Second Language Acquisition: A Case Study*. New York: Routledge.

Larsen-Freeman, D. and M. H. Long. 1991. *Introduction to Second Language Acquisition Research*. London and New York: Longman.

Lehmann, W. and Y. Malkiel, eds. 1968. *Directions for Historical Linguistics*. Austin: University of Texas Press, 97–195.

Lenneberg, E. 1957. *Biological Foundations of Language*. New York: Wiley.

Liceras, J., D. Maxwell, B. Laguardia, Z. Fernandez, R. Fernandez, and L. Diaz. 1997. A longitudinal study of Spanish non-native grammars: beyond parameters. In. A. T. Pérez-Leroux and W. Glass, eds. *Contemporary Perspectives on the Acquisition of Spanish*, 2 vols. Somerville, MA: Cascadilla Press, Volume I, 99–132.

Long, M. H. 2007. *Problems in SLA*. Mahwah, NJ: Lawrence Erlbaum.

Lyster, R. 2004. Research on form-focused instruction in immersion classrooms: implications for theory and practice. *Journal of French Language Studies* 14: 321–41.

Macaulay, R. K. 1977. *Language, Social Class and Education: A Glasgow Study*. Edinburgh University Press.

Mackenzie, L. and G. Sankoff. 2010. A quantitative analysis of diphthongization in Montreal French. *University of Pennsylvania Working Papers in Linguistics* 15.2 (Selected Papers from NWAV 37): 1–10.

Mougeon, R., T. Nadasdi, and K. Rehner. 2009. Evolution de l'alternance je vas/ je vais/ m'as dans le parler d'adolescents franco-ontariens. In L. Baronian and F. Martineau, eds. *Le français d'un continent à l'autre: Mélanges offerts à Yves-Charles Morin*. Quebec: Les Presses de l'Université Laval, 327–74.

2010. *The Sociolinguistic Competence of Immersion Students*. Bristol: Multilingual Matters.

Myles, F. 2008. Investigating learner language development with electronic longitudinal corora: theoretical and methodological issues. In L. Ortega and H. Byrnes, eds. *The Longitudinal Study of Advanced L2 Capacities*. New York and London: Routledge, 58–72.

Nahkola, K. and M. Saanilahti. 2004. Mapping language changes in real time: a panel study on Finnish. *Language Variation and Change* 16: 75–92.

Nevalainen, T., H. Raumolin-Brunberg, and H. Mannila. 2011. The diffusion of language change in real time: progressive and conservative individuals and the time depth of change. *Language Variation and Change* 23: 1–43.

Ortega, L. and G. Iberri-Shea. 2005. Longitudinal research in SLA: recent trends and future directions. *Annual Review of Applied Linguistics* 25: 26–45.

Ortega, L. and H. Byrnes. 2008. The longitudinal study of advanced L2 capacities: an introduction. In L. Ortega and H. Byrnes, eds. *The Longitudinal Study of Advanced L2 Capacities*. New York and London: Routledge, 3–20.

Padilla, A. M. and K. Lindholm. 1976. Acquisition of bilingualism: an analysis of linguistic structures of Spanish/English speaking children. In G. D. Keller, T. Teschner, and S. Viera, eds. *Bilingualism in the Bicentennial and Beyond*. New York: Bilingual Press, 97–142.

Philp, J. 2009. Epilogue: exploring the intricacies of interaction and language development In A. Mackey and C. Polio, eds. *Multiple Perspectives on Interaction. Second Language Research in Honor of Susan M. Gass*. New York and London: Routledge, 254–73.

Pope, J., M. Meyerhoff, and R. Ladd. 2007. Forty years of language change on Martha's Vineyard. *Language* 83.3: 615–27.

Poplack, S. and A. St-Amand. 2007. A real-time window on nineteenth century vernacular French: the Récits du français québécois d'autrefois. *Language in Society* 36.5: 707–34.

Poplack, S. and N. Dion. 2009. Prescription vs praxis: the evolution of future temporal reference in French. *Language* 85: 557–87.

Regan, V., M. Howard, and I. Lemée. 2009. *The Acquisition of Sociolinguistic Competence in a Study Abroad Context*. Bristol: Multilingual Matters.

Roberts, J. 1997. Acquisition of variable rules: a study of (-t, d) deletion in preschool children. *Journal of Child Language* 24: 351–72.

2000. Longitudinal studies in the social sciences. *Social Research Update* 20. Available at: http://sru.soc.surrey.ac.uk/SRU28.html (accessed July 3, 2013).

Sankoff, D. and G. Sankoff. 1973. Sample survey methods and computer-assisted analysis in the study of grammatical variation. In R. Darnell, ed. *Canadian Languages in their Social Context*. Edmonton, Alberta: Linguistic Research, 7–64.

Sankoff, G. 2004. Adolescents, young adults and the critical period: two case studies from 'Seven Up'. In C. Fought, ed. *Sociolinguistic Variation*. Oxford University Press, 121–39.

2005. Cross-sectional and longitudinal studies in sociolinguistics. In U. Ammon, N. Dittmar, K. J. Mattheier, and P. Trudgill, eds. *An International Handbook of the Science of Language and Society*, 2 vols. Berlin: Mouton de Gruyter, Volume II, 1003–13.

2006. Apparent time and real time. In K. Brown, ed. *Encyclopedia of Language and Linguistics*, 2nd edn, 14 vols. Oxford: Elsevier, Volume I, 110–16.

Sankoff, G. and S. Wagner. 2006. Ager grading in retrograde movement: the inflected future in Montréal French. *University of Pennsylvania Working Papers in Linguistics* 12.2 (Selected Papers from NWAV 34): 203–16.

Sankoff, G. and H. Blondeau. 2007. Language change across the lifespan: /r/ in Montreal French. *Language* 83.3: 560–88.

Sankoff, G., H. Blondeau, and A. Charity. 2001. Individual roles in a real-time change: Montréal (r>R) 1947–1995. In H. van de Velde and R. van Hout, eds. 'r-atics: Sociolinguistic, phonetic and phonological characteristics of /r/. *Etudes & Travaux* 4: 141–58.

Sankoff, G., P. Thibault, N. Nagy, H. Blondeau, M. O. Fonollosa, and L. Gagnon. 1997. Variation and the use of discourse markers in a language contact situation. *Language Variation and Change* 9: 191–218.

Sankoff, G., H. Blondeau, M. Friesner, and D. Hall. Le facteur temps et le changement phonétique dans le français montréalais. Les français d'ici. Queen's University, Kingston, Ontario, June.

Sato, C. 1990. *The Syntax of Conversation in Interlanguage Development*. Tubingen: Gunter Narr.

Sekali, M. 2012. First language acquisition of French grammar (from 4 months to 4 years old): introduction. *Journal of French Language Studies* 22.1: 1–6.

Selinker, L. 1972. Interlanguage. *International Review of Applied Linguistics* 10.3: 209–31.

Sundgren, E. 2002. Aterbesok I eskiluna. en undersokning av morfologisk variation och forandering I nutida talsprak. Unpublished Ph.D. dissertation, Uppsala University.

2009. The varying influence of social and linguistic factors on language stability and change: the case of Eskilstuna. *Language Variation and Change* 21.1: 97–133.

Tagliamonte, S. 2002.Comparative sociolinguistics. In J. K. Chambers, P. Trudgill, and N. Schilling-Estes, eds. *The Handbook of Language Variation and Change*. Malden, MA: Blackwell, 729–63.

Thibault, P. and M. Daveluy. 1989. Quelques traces du passage du temps dans le parler des Montréalais. *Language Variation and Change* 1.1: 19–45.

Thibault, P. and D. Vincent. 1990. *Un Corpus de français parlé*. Montreal: Recherches Sociolinguistiques.

Trudgill, P. 1988. Norwich revisited: recent linguistic changes in an English urban dialect. *English World Wide* 9: 3–49.

Van Hofwegen, J. and W. Wolfram. 2010. Coming of age in African American English: a longitudinal study. *Journal of Sociolinguistics* 14: 27–52.

Vinay, J. P. 1950. Bout de langue ou fond de gorge? *French Review* 23.6: 489–98.

Wagner, S. 2008. Linguistic change and stabilization in the transition from adolescence to adulthood. Unpublished Ph.D. dissertation, University of Pennsylvania.

Wagner, S. and G. Sankoff. 2011. Age grading in the Montréal French inflected future. *Language Variation and Change* 22.3: 275–313.

Watson-Gegeo, K. A. 1992. Thick explanation in the ethnographic study of child socialization: a longitudinal study of the problem of schooling for Kwara'ae (Salomon Islands) children. *New Directions for Child and Adolescent Development* 58: 51–66.

Weinreich, U., W. Labov, and M. Herzog. 1968. Empirical foundations for a theory of language change. In W. Lehmann and Y. Malkiel, eds. *Directions for Historical Linguistics*. Austin: University of Texas Press, 97–195.

Zilles, A. M. 2005. The development of a new pronoun: the linguistic and social embedding of a gente in Brazilian Portuguese. *Language, Variation and Change* 17: 19–53.

Index